Research Anthology on Implementing Sentiment Analysis Across Multiple Disciplines

Information Resources Management Association
USA

Volume I

Published in the United States of America by
IGI Global
Engineering Science Reference (an imprint of IGI Global)
701 E. Chocolate Avenue
Hershey PA, USA 17033
Tel: 717-533-8845
Fax: 717-533-8661
E-mail: cust@igi-global.com
Web site: http://www.igi-global.com

Library of Congress Cataloging-in-Publication Data

Names: Information Resources Management Association, editor.
Title: Research anthology on implementing sentiment analysis across multiple disciplines / Information Resources Management Association, editor.
Description: Hershey PA : Engineering Science Reference, [2022] | Includes bibliographical references and index. | Summary: "This reference book of contributed chapters discusses the tools, methodologies, applications, and implementation of sentiment analysis across various disciplines and industries such as the pharmaceutical industry, government, and the tourism industry and presents emerging technologies and developments within the field of sentiment analysis and opinion mining"-- Provided by publisher.
Identifiers: LCCN 2022016823 (print) | LCCN 2022016824 (ebook) | ISBN 9781668463031 (h/c) | ISBN 9781668463048 (ebook)
Subjects: LCSH: Sentiment analysis.
Classification: LCC QA76.9.S57 R47 2022 (print) | LCC QA76.9.S57 (ebook) | DDC 005.1/4--dc23/eng/20220622
LC record available at https://lccn.loc.gov/2022016823
LC ebook record available at https://lccn.loc.gov/2022016824

British Cataloguing in Publication Data
A Cataloguing in Publication record for this book is available from the British Library.

List of Contributors

Table of Contents

Volume II

Volume IV

Preface

Sentiment analysis is a field that is gaining traction as more organizations and fields discover the myriad benefits and opportunities it offers. Regardless of industry, it is always useful to know what consumers think, whether that be about a product, a service, or a company in general. With sentiment analysis technology, it has never been easier to understand what audiences want and need. Organizations must embrace this technology and integrate it into their business strategies and tactics in order to successfully reach and communicate with their audience.

Staying informed of the most up-to-date research trends and findings is of the utmost importance. That is why IGI Global is pleased to offer this four-volume reference collection of reprinted IGI Global book chapters and journal articles that have been handpicked by senior editorial staff. This collection will shed light on critical issues related to the trends, techniques, and uses of various applications by providing both broad and detailed perspectives on cutting-edge theories and developments. This collection is designed to act as a single reference source on conceptual, methodological, technical, and managerial issues, as well as to provide insight into emerging trends and future opportunities within the field.

The *Research Anthology on Implementing Sentiment Analysis Across Multiple Disciplines* is organized into six distinct sections that provide comprehensive coverage of important topics. The sections are:

1. Fundamental Concepts and Theories;
2. Development and Design Methodologies;
3. Tools and Technologies;
4. Utilization and Applications;
5. Organizational and Social Implications; and
6. Critical Issues and Challenges.

The following paragraphs provide a summary of what to expect from this invaluable reference tool.

Section 1, "Fundamental Concepts and Theories," serves as a foundation for this extensive reference tool by addressing crucial theories essential to understanding the concepts and uses of sentiment analysis in multidisciplinary settings. Opening this reference book is the chapter "Fundamentals of Opinion Mining" by Profs. Ashish Seth and Kirti Seth from INHA University, India, which focuses on explaining the fundamentals of opinion mining along with sentiment analysis and covers the brief evolution in mining techniques in the last decade. This first section ends with the chapter "Sentiment Analysis in Crisis Situations for Better Connected Government: Case of Mexico Earthquake in 2017" by Profs. Rodrigo Sandoval-Almazán, Asdrúbal López Chau, and David Valle-Cruz from the Universidad Autónoma del Estado de México, Mexico, which adapts the methodology of sentiment analysis of social media posts to an expanded version for crisis situations.

Section 2, "Development and Design Methodologies," presents in-depth coverage of the design and development of sentiment analysis for its use in different applications. This section starts with "Integrating Semantic Acquaintance for Sentiment Analysis" by Profs. Rashmi Agrawal and Neha Gupta from Manav Rachna International Institute of Research and Studies, India, which focuses on semantic guidance-based sentiment analysis approaches and provides a semantically enhanced technique for annotation of sentiment polarity. This section closes with "An Extensive Text Mining Study for the Turkish Language: Author Recognition, Sentiment Analysis, and Text Classification" by Profs. Durmuş Özkan Şahin and Erdal Kılıç from Ondokuz Mayıs University, Turkey, which provides theoretical and experimental information about text mining and discusses three different text mining problems such as news classification, sentiment analysis, and author recognition.

Section 3, "Tools and Technologies," explores the various tools and technologies used for the implementation of sentiment analysis for various uses. This section begins with "Tools of Opinion Mining" by Profs. Neha Gupta and Siddharth Verma from Manav Rachna International Institute of Research and Studies, India, which examines how opinion mining is moving to the sentimental reviews of Twitter data, comments used on Facebook, videos, or Facebook statuses. This section closes with the chapter "Opinion Mining for Instructor Evaluations at the Autonomous University of Ciudad Juarez" by Profs. Abraham López, Alejandra Mendoza Carreón, Rafael Jiménez, Vicente García, and Alan Ponce from the Universidad Autónoma de Ciudad Juárez, Mexico, which considers how opinion mining can be useful for labeling student comments as positive and negative and, for this purpose, creates a database using real opinions obtained from five professors over the last four years, covering a total of 20 subjects.

Section 4, "Utilization and Applications," describes how sentiment analysis is used and applied in diverse industries for various applications. The opening chapter in this section, "A Survey on Implementation Methods and Applications of Sentiment Analysis," by Profs. Sudheer Karnam, Valarmathi B., and Tulasi Prasad Sariki from VIT University, India, compares different methods of solving sentiment analysis problems, algorithms, merits and demerits, and applications and also investigates different research problems in sentiment analysis. The closing chapter in this section, "Communicating Natural Calamity: The Sentiment Analysis of Post Rigopiano's Accident," by Profs. Nicola Capolupo and Gabriella Piscopo from the University of Salerno, Italy, aims at understanding the dynamics that led to the exchange and value co-creation/co-production in the interaction between P.A. and citizens during natural calamities and proposes a horizontal communication model in which both actors cooperate to respond to a crisis.

Section 5, "Organizational and Social Implications," includes chapters discussing the impact of sentiment analysis on society and shows the ways in which it can be used in different industries and how this impacts business. The chapter "Open Issues in Opinion Mining" by Profs. V. Uma and Vishal Vyas from Pondicherry University, India, explains the various research issues and challenges present in each stage of opinion mining. The closing chapter, "eWOW of Guests Regarding Their Hotel Experience: Sentiment Analysis of TripAdvisor Reviews," by Profs. Zelia Breda and Rui Costa from GOVCOPP, University of Aveiro, Portugal; Prof. Gorete Dinis from GOVCOPP, Polytechnic Institute of Portalegre, Portugal; and Prof. Amandine Angie Martins of the University of Aveiro, Portugal, focuses on sentiment analysis of comments made on TripAdvisor regarding one resort located in the Algarve region in Portugal.

Section 6, "Critical Issues and Challenges," presents coverage of academic and research perspectives on the challenges of using sentiment analysis in varied industries. Opening this final section is the chapter "Multimodal Sentiment Analysis: A Survey and Comparison" by Profs. Ramandeep Kaur and Sandeep Kautish from Guru Kashi University, India, which provides a full image of the multimodal sentiment analysis opportunities and difficulties and considers the recent trends of research in the field. The closing chapter, "A Sentiment Analysis of the 2014-15 Ebola Outbreak in the Media and Social Media," by Prof. Nilmini Wickramasinghe from Swinburne University of Technology, Australia & Epworth Health-Care, Australia; Prof. Blooma John of the University of Canberra, Australia; and Dr. Bob Baulch from the International Food Policy Research Institute, Malawi, analyzes news articles on the Ebola outbreak from two leading news outlets, together with comments on the articles from a well-known social media platform, from March 2014 to July 2015.

Although the primary organization of the contents in this multi-volume work is based on its six sections, offering a progression of coverage of the important concepts, methodologies, technologies, applications, social issues, and emerging trends, the reader can also identify specific contents by utilizing the extensive indexing system listed at the end of each volume. As a comprehensive collection of research on the latest findings related to sentiment analysis, the *Research Anthology on Implementing Sentiment Analysis Across Multiple Disciplines* provides social media analysts, computer scientists, IT professionals, AI scientists, business leaders and managers, marketers, advertising agencies, public administrators, government officials, university administrators, libraries, instructors, researchers, academicians, and students with a complete understanding of the applications and impacts of sentiment analysis across fields and disciplines. Given the vast number of issues concerning usage, failure, success, strategies, and applications of sentiment analysis, the *Research Anthology on Implementing Sentiment Analysis Across Multiple Disciplines* encompasses the most pertinent research on the applications, impacts, uses, and development of sentiment analysis.

Section 1

Fundamental Concepts and Theories

Chapter 1
Fundamentals of Opinion Mining

Ashish Seth
INHA University, Tashkent, India

Kirti Seth
INHA University, Tashkent, India

ABSTRACT

Mining techniques in computer science have been evolving for the last two decades. Opinion mining is the latest buzzword in this evolution and goes to a deeper level to understand the drive behind people's behavior. Due to the richness of social media opinions, emotions, and sentiments, opinion mining examines that how people feel about a given situation, be it positive or negative. This chapter primarily focuses on explaining the fundamentals of opinion mining along with sentiment analysis. It covers the brief evolution in mining techniques in the last decade. The chapter elaborates on the significance of opinion mining in today's scenario and its features. It also includes a section to discuss the applications, challenges and research scope in opinion mining.

INTRODUCTION

The research in the field of sentiments and opinions has been going since a long back, but the term sentiment analysis and opinion mining were first introduced by Nasukawa and Dave in the year 2003. But after the year 2000, the research in the field of opinion mining has grown rapidly. The major reason behind this explosive growth is the expansion of World Wide Web. In addition to this, following factors also contributes to make it more demanding

- Recent innovations of machine learning techniques in information retrieval and language processing.
- Due to the expansion of World Wide Web and drastic growth of social network, trained datasets for machine learning algorithms are easily available (Mukherjee & Liu, 2012).

DOI: 10.4018/978-1-6684-6303-1.ch001

With the recent developments in technology, communication among the people is becoming convenient day by day, the major percentage of this communication is happening through internet via various channels such as email, Facebook, Twitter, LinkedIn, Telegram, WhatsApp, etc. This huge data generated over internet communications will be a potential gold mine for discovering the hidden information into them.

In computer science both the terms "opinion mining" and "sentiment analysis" are often used interchangeably. Let us first look at the English definition of two key terms "opinion" and "sentiment".

What Is Opinion?

Opinions play very important role in making decisions. To make any decisions, these opinions are key factors to conclude our decision. Opinion in general is a subjective statement not an objective statement. Subjective statement describes what a person thinks or believes about something. Opinion is defined as "a belief or judgment that fall short of absolute conviction, certainty, or positive knowledge; it is a conclusion that certain facts, ideas etc. are probably true or likely to provide so". Alternatively, "it is an estimation of the quality or worth of someone or something" (Pang & Lee, 2008).

What Is Sentiment?

Sentiments are central to almost all human activities and act as key influencers of our behaviors. An individual makes any opinion based on the sentiments he had with the object in context. Sentiment is defined as "an attitude toward something; refined or tender emotion; manifestation of the higher or more refined feelings". It is a thought influenced by a proceeding from feeling or emotion. Sentiments are generally be classified in two ways i.e. Supervised Learning and Unsupervised learning

- ***Classification Using Supervised Learning*:** It is implemented by building a classifier; two sets of documents are required in this set which are known as training set and test set. This approach is popularly known as Machine Learning based technique. Frequently used algorithms based in these techniques are support vector machines (SVM), Naive Bayes classifier and Maximum entropy. The basic task for this classification is choosing the appropriate set of features for classification. The most commonly used features include presence of term and their frequency, phrases, parts of speech, negations and opinion words.
- ***Classification Using Unsupervised Learning*:** In this approach, text is classified by comparing it against the word lexicons or sentiment lexicons. The value of these sentiment lexicons is determined prior to the sentiment analysis. Sentiment lexicons are defined by the expressions and collection of words that are used to express views, opinions and people's feelings. The words in text are identified as positive or negative word lexicon. The document is scanned for the presence of these positive and negative word lexicons. Based on the presence of each type of word lexicons in the document it is considered as positive or negative document.

Opinion Mining or sentiment analysis is the computational study of opinions, sentiments and emotions expressed in text. It deals with rational models of emotions, rumors and trends within user communities and with the word-of-mouth inside specific domains. Opinion Mining is attracting an increasing interest from last few years.

Though the data present on the social media is huge and reflect people's opinion, it is highly unstructured, unclean and filtering the meaningful information out of them is tedious task. Typically, each site contains a large volume of opinion data which is not always easily deciphered in long blogs and forum postings. The average human reader will have difficulty identifying relevant sites and extracting and summarizing the opinions in them. Automated sentiment analysis systems are therefore needed.

The technique of transforming the noisy data by a series of sentiment analysis termed as opinion mining. Alternatively, the challenge of analyzing the huge data has created a new scope in computer science which is referred as opinion mining. In the broadest terms, opinion mining is the science of using text analysis to understand the drivers behind public sentiment.

Task of Opinion Mining

An ocean of unstructured data is flowing across the internet; this unstructured, noisy data can be a source of useful information if mined in a scientific way to predict the behavior or mood of public in general. Such data is growing exponentially with time; it keeps on adding when people talk about their likes and dislikes on internet or any social media on the web. Being free to express views people do share their experience in an honest and unsolicited manner, without fear of being an answerable, they mostly share our true feelings towards a politician, a product, brand, or a global event.

Opinion mining aims to deduce some useful information out of this unstructured data by identifying and categorizing the entire text into various elements which are commonly known as opinion representative (see Figure 1)

Figure 1. Task of opinion mining

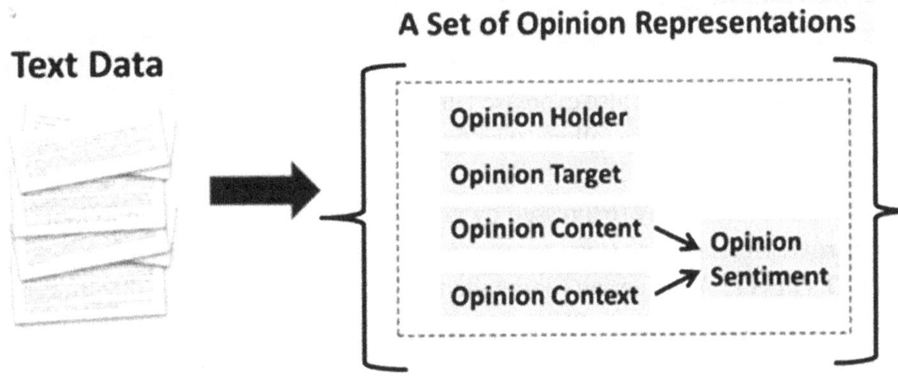

Representation of Opinion

Opinions are expressed through two representations, basic and detailed representation.

- **Basic Representation:** This help us to make a basic conclusion out of the statement under consideration. It consists of three main components (see figure 2).

   - **Opinion Holder:** Person who expresses his view, this can be a person or organization which holds a particular opinion about something (e.g. person, place, product, event, organization).
   - **Opinion Target:** Object (thing or person) on which opinion is expressed.
   - **Opinion Content:** Statement of expression.
- **Detailed Representation:** This helps us to give a better or detailed conclusion out of the statement under consideration. It consists of two main components.
   - **Opinion Context:** Under what situation was the opinion expressed (e.g. place, duration)?
   - **Opinion Sentiment:** What does the opinion tell us about the opinion holder feelings (i.e. favoring or opposing the person, positive or negative comments, satisfaction or dissatisfaction etc.).

Figure 2. Components of opinion representation

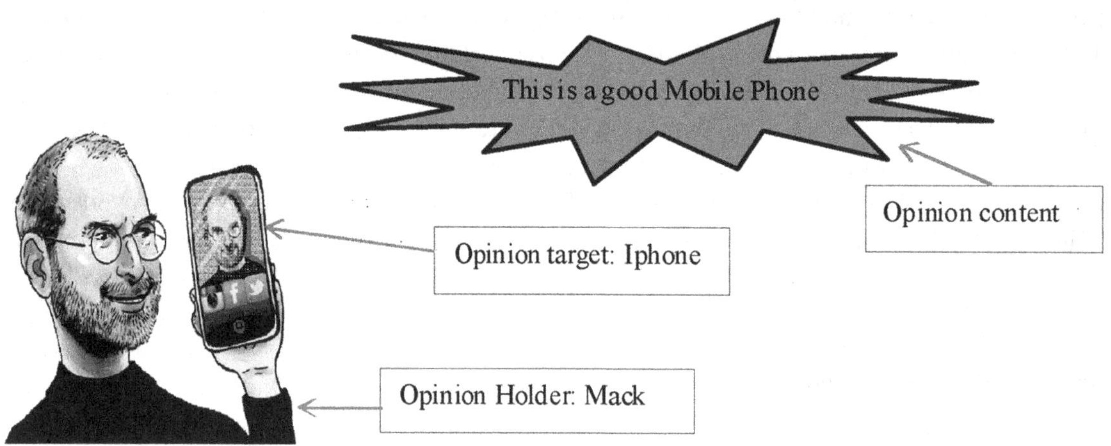

These components of opinion are also expressed in different perspective. In context of above example, components can also be expressed as follows (see figure 3)

- **Opinion Holder:** INC society (expressed by group of people rather than individual)
- **Opinion Target:** Hotel service (may represent one entity, group of entity, etc.).
- **Opinion CONTENT:** A paragraph (or detailed article on the object).
- **Opinion Context:** Year 1938, Tashkent (reflect the place as well as year, may also include more attribute).
- **Opinion Sentiment:** May reflect positive, happy, negative or favorable sentiments.

Figure 3. Representation of opinion components in a text

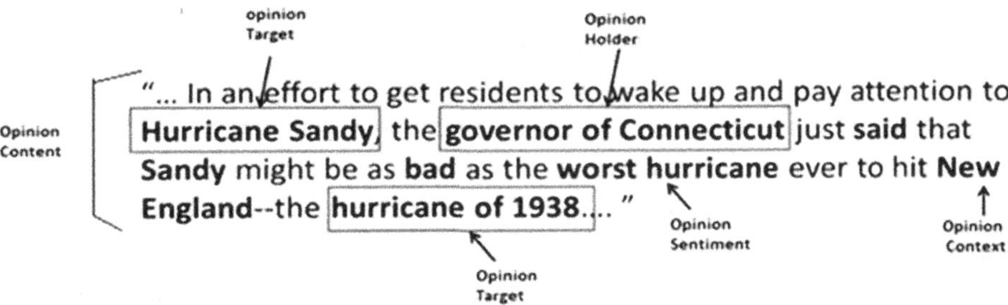

IMPORTANCE OF OPINION MINING

Human by nature always make opinion about their experience about a particular object or thing or any incident they come across in their life. This is because of the presence of very special feature he own called 'intelligence' which makes him different from all other live existences in nature.

Individual opinions are often reflective of a broader reality. A single customer who takes issue with a new product's design on social media likely speaks for many others. The same goes for a member of the public who takes to a political campaigner's web page to praise or criticize the policies proposed. By careful observation one can identify the driving sources of the sentiment, it can then be used to expose critical areas of strength and weakness by using opinion mining.

Public opinions may help the company to make effective plan to hit the target, strategies needed to reinvigorate profitability or reclaim slipping market share. Within the public sector this same data can be used to build strategies and campaigns that resonate with the electorate and react to voters' changing needs. By analyzing conversations for both sentiment and the topics driving that sentiment, a retail bank might discover that of customers' criticisms, queue length and waiting times. A fast food chain might be interested to know that relative to their closest competitor, many consider their portion size too small, though their friendly customer service is a plus. This information of customer service could be further broken down into the sub-categories of turnaround time, order correctness and delivery time.

Opinion mining is not new, in the past, when an individual needed opinion, he/she asked friends and family, currently it fetches more interest to larger organizations and businesses due to technological innovations and moving the people toward more social networks (Bollen et al., 2011).

APPLICATIONS

With the explosive growth of social media and the advancement in technology, organizations are increasingly using the social media contents for decision making. With the presence of social media in many forms such as forum discussions, blogs, micro blogs, twitter, comments, and postings a person is no longer restricted to opinions of one's friends and family but can refer social media on the web to get reviews about the product.

Acquiring public and consumer opinions has long been a huge business itself for marketing, public relations, and political campaign companies. Underlying the importance of opinion to sales of product, organizations or a business, earlier commercials bodies are regularly conducts surveys, opinion polls, and focus groups. With the increasing presence of social media on the web, for an organization, it may no longer be necessary to conduct surveys, opinion polls, and focus groups in order to gather public opinions because there is an abundance of such information publicly available.

In recent years, companies start focusing on data available on web. Sentiment analysis applications have been widely used in every possible domain, from consumer products, services, healthcare, and financial services to social events and political elections. Many big corporations like Microsoft, Google, Hewlett-Packard, SAP, and SAS have built their own in-house sentiment analytics center to mine these public opinion data available on the web.

Practical applications and industrial interests have provided strong motivations for research in sentiment analysis. Below are some of the application areas which show as application of opinion mining.

- ***Shopping (E-Commerce):*** Online Shopping is emerging day to day and widely used nowadays. In today's hectic and busy schedule these options provide convenience shopping at home itself. Generally, to get an overall idea of the product, customers frequently visit the feedback page of the concerned product. This page provides number of feedbacks mentioned by existing users of the product. These feedbacks reflect the existing user opinion about the product and help the current customer to make his buying decision. Popular shopping sites like Flipkart, Amazon etc. have provision to compare products with all desired description and feedback of customers, it also displays the opinion result to the user in a "Graphical formats" for quick and easy understanding about the quality/features and services of product. An opinion mining and sentiment analysis tool helps users to select the product to purchase.
- ***Entertainment:*** Beforehand review of any kind of popular event, program or current release of any movie can be helpful in providing more information about the event. These reviews are based on people feedback. Internet movie database can help the online users to view feedback for movies and other programs. These online reviews provide great help to the customers to decide when there are lots of options available to choose from. Opinion mining can be used for movie or show or TV programs to promote or conclude the users' response to analyse it.
- ***Business:*** Businesses and large organizations in the real world always spend considerable amount of budget to understand people opinions about their products and services. At the same time consumers or customers also look for the opinions of other users of a product to look for their queries related to a particular product. People opinion for a product proves a great help to make their decision of purchasing it or continuing their search. As people are more and more connected with the social media, companies want to utilize this to analysis their own performance in terms of the services provided and customer satisfaction about the released product. For this companies ask their customer to provide feedback on their portals. This approach makes saving on a marketing budget. Customer feedback on a company's portal helps them to raise their issue in case of dissatisfaction or appreciate if they found the product justified to its worth. This way companies can be able to analysis the customer mood or sentiment through the feedback and can incorporate the suggestions to enhance the product sale.
- ***R&D (Research and Development):*** Online customer feedback plays an important role to understand public opinion about the product. Feedbacks at any online shopping portal are increasingly used by industry to improve the quality of the products. Online sites can even invite customers to not only comment on existing product but can describe their expectation and ask the customers to provide their own design views in order to customize new product as per customer requirements.

For example, customer not only comment about the battery life but can add more information like time required to charge, its weight etc. these inputs from customer help the industry to improve in the design of the product.

- ***Politics:*** Nowadays twitter is proved to be an excellent medium to know the political view of public in general. Political parties can extract these views to predict their win or loss in an election, they can also use them to declare a candidate based on his or her popularity in public. These data on internet help these political parties to have an overall knowledge about public opinion which helps them to focus on weakness and strength. In a political election, opinions about political candidates not only help individuals to cast their vote but one can get feedback of popularity of candidates, as these opinions help to generate candidate impression to normal public.
- ***Academics:*** The demand of Massive online interactive courses (MOOC) are continuously increasing, student opinion plays most important role to ensure about the effectiveness of such programs. In MOOC courses, student's sentiments can be used to design the program. Student's feedback may help to understand and analysis the requirements to make it better for future student's Opinion Mining will help organizations running online courses to be aware of their problems (weakness) and best(strength) within them through student opinion given in the form of feedback and comments.
- ***Health:*** Online health care will be going to dominate in the near future. The patient report can be shared and consulted by several doctors sitting at home. Users or patients can share prescriptions or treatment, which may help to cure them while they suffer from any illness like headache, fever, digestion, high blood pressure, and diabetes. People are sharing online about their gym experience which suggest which particular exercise is good for a particular part of body, it also contains their opinions to control blood pressure, back pain, migraine etc. which helps all to get rid of problems in their life. Based on these huge data of views and suggestion, users also share their feedback and comment. These comments can be mined in a systematic way to conclude which of the particular remedies are working while others who didn't succeed.
- ***Travel & Transportation:*** With the evolution of technology and dominance of social media increasing on internet, touring business has been improved in recent years. Users prefer to make their touring plans through online. It has been observed that a person before going to any place for touring or business purpose would collect opinion of other people about the place, people, food, weather, etc. on internet. Transportation like tour and travel, logistic, cab service which is very helpful to people to choose best services mentioned in the feedback and comments from past experience shared by the users. For trading, transportation has been very crucial and important factor; transportation can be any movable items from one place to another as per the requirement. There are many transport modes for example road, air, rail, etc. People share their transport experience on the internet about their business which can be carefully mined and analyzed to budget the expenses incurred for transport

Apart from real-life applications, many application-oriented research papers have also been published. Table 1 summarizes some of the important work done on opinion mining.

Table 1. Literature review on opinion mining

S. no	Year	Researchers	Work Done
1	2012	Kamal et al.	implemented a rule-based system to mine product features, opinions and their reliability scores.
2	2011	Bollen et al.	used the twitter moods to predict the stock markets.
3	2011	Miller et al.	sentiment flow in social media was investigated
4	2011	Mohammad and Yang	mail sentiments were used to determine how genders differed on emotional axes
5	2011	Mohammad	emotions in novels and fairy tales were tracked
6	2011	Bollen et al.	twitter moods were used to predict the stock market
7	2011	In Bar-Haim et al. (2011) and Feldman et al. (2011)	expert investors in microblogs were identified to perform sentiment analysis of stocks.
8	2011	Groh and Hauffa	sentiment analysis was used to characterize social relations.
9	2010	Zhang and Skiena	blog and news sentiment was used to predict trading strategies
10	2010	McGlohon et al.	based on reviews various products and merchants were ranked
11	2010	Hong and Skiena	relationships between the NFL betting line and public opinions in blogs and twitter were identified
12	2010	O'Connor et al.	twitter sentiment was linked with public opinion polls
13	2010	Tumasjan et al.	twitter sentiment used to predict election results
14	2010	Chen et al.	the authors studied political standpoints
15	2010	Yano and Smith	method proposed for predicting comment volumes of political blogs
16	2009, 2010	Asur and Huberman (2010), Joshi et al. (2010) Sadikov et al. (2009)	Twitter data, movie reviews, and blogs were used to predict box-office revenues for movies
17	2010	Ding and Liu	used the supervised learning approach to present the problem of object and attribute co-reference.
18	2010	Paul et al.	suggested a comparative LexRank approach to summarize contrastive viewpoints in opinionated text.
19	2010	Tumasjan et al.	used twitter sentiments to predict election results.
20			
21	2009	Sakunkoo and Sakunkoo	social influences in online book reviews.
22	2008	Chen and Xie	define online customer views as a new element in the marketing communication mix. They studied the role of customer reviews in marketing.
23	2008	Ding et al.	proposed a holistic approach to infer the semantic orientation of an opinion word based on review context and combine multiple opinions words in same sentence.
24	2008	Murthy and Bing Liu	proposed a method which study sentiments in comparative sentences and also deals with context-based sentiments by exploiting external information available on the web
25	2007	Liu et al.	model was proposed to predict sales performance.
26	2007	Ghose et al.	uses econometrics to identify the economic value of text showing that user feedback affects the pricing power of merchants.
27	2007	Park et al.	examines the involvement of the online customer reviews in affecting the purchasing intentions.
28	2007	Archak et al.	uses product demand as the objective function and derive a context aware interpretation of opinions showing how the opinions affects the user's choice.

continues on following page

Table 1. Continued

S. no	Year	Researchers	Work Done
29	2004	Hu and Liu	worked on feature level opinion mining and determined the polarity of the object features without considering the strength of the opinions
30	2003	Dave et al.	trained a classifier using reviews from major websites.
31	2003	Turney and Littman	find out the semantic orientation of a text by calculating its statistical association with a set of positive and negative words
32	2002	Pang et al.	perform document level sentiment classification using standard machine learning techniques
33	2002	Morinaga et al.	presented a framework for mining product reputation on internet.
34	2000	Tatemura	Perform collaborative exploration of movie reviews from various viewpoints based on browsing of virtual reviewers
35	1997	Hatzivassiloglou and McKeown	to find the semantic orientation of the adjectives and predicted whether two conjoined adjectives are of same polarity
36	1997	Terveen et al.	proposed PHOAKS (people helping one another know stuff), to help users locate information on the web. The system uses a collaborative filtering approach to recognize and reuse recommendations
37	1994	Wiebe	study the naturally occurring narratives and regularities in the writings of authors and presents an algorithm that tracks the point of view on the basis of these regularities.

Challenges of Opinion Mining

To classifying a text written in a natural language into a positive or negative feeling is sometimes a very complicated task that even different human annotators disagree on the classification to be assigned to a given text. Interpretation of the text by an individual may be different from others; this is because of difference in cultural factors and each person's experience. Secondly, shorter the text, and worse written, the more difficult the task becomes, as in the case of messages on social networks like Twitter or Facebook. It is a hard challenge for language technologies to parse such kind of data to interpret some useful information from it (Bolanle et al., 2012).

In recent years, postings in social media have helped reshape businesses, and sway public sentiments and emotions. Since opinion mining is a relatively new filed, thus there are several challenges to be faced. Basic challenges that always threats to the correctness of results originated from public opinion is related to the authenticity of the extracted data and the methods used in it.

Challenges of opinion mining are as follows:

Existence of Multilanguage

Globally, there exist many languages and a particular product is used globally by different language speaking people. There feedback or comment on the product can be in different languages which make it complex task to drive a public opinion from the feedback. Moreover, customer are free to express their experience about the product in their own way, this further add more complexity to the mining process as the feedback data will tend towards unstructured shape which is always hard to analyze (Turney, 2002). Even if we assume that all the feedback should be provided in any structured format, still feedback given in different languages will be a challenge.

For example, if the same feedback is provided in five different languages will be treated as five different set of statement by any miner application.

- **In English:** The product is very light weight
- **In French:** Le produit est très léger
- **In Hindi:** उत्पाद बहुत हल्का वजन है
- **In German:** Das Produkt ist sehr leicht
- **In Russian:** Продукт очень легкий

Therefore, even they are saying the same thing in the uniform format, it is still a challenge to understand each language and deduce the same meaning out of it.

Grammar

Noun words are also be said as featured words but verbs and adjective can also be used as feature words which are challenging to judge.

Consider some user feedback on earphone are as follows:

Arohi gave a feedback: "I like the sound quality "
and Ketan's feedback is: "The sound is awesome"
Similarly Raj feebback is: "The sound is superb"

Here Arohi, Ketan and Raj are speaking about the same quality of the product but in different manner. The words which are similar/opposite in their meaning are also difficult task to group together

For Example: "Camera size of mobile phone is small".

Here adjective "small" used in positive manner but if user makes the statement like:

"The battery time is also small"

here the word "small" represent negative meaning for the phone battery. To identify such adjective words which define different meaning in same situation is a difficult to handle it.

Use of Short Words

Users are allowed to feedback in any format, they are free to write in any manner. Users can use symbols, abbreviation, capital letter or small letter, shortcut and regional language in their feedbacks (Figure 4)

Ex.

camera as cam,
pictures as pix,
fine as fi9,

goods as guds
great as gr8
etc.

Figure 4. Use of short words in comment, feedback and communications

It is difficult to handle such kind of data, requires careful mining to conclude users point of view. Many users have different point of view using same kind words in their feedback which is challenging to sort out the positive, negative or neutral meaning out of the text.

Presence of Spam and Fake Reviews

The contents on the web can be both authentic as well as spam. For an effective sentiment analysis, this spam content should be detected and removed before processing. This can be achieved by detecting outliers, identifying duplicates, and by considering reviewer reputation.

Limitation of Filtering

Classification filtering has certain limitation while determining concept or most popular thought, this limitation should be reduced to improve sentiment classification results. These limitations may rise to the risk of creating irrelevant opinion sets and it results false summarization of sentiment.

Limited Availability of Opinion Mining Tools

The tools required for opinion mining is not freely available. They are very expensive and currently affordable only to large organizations and government bodies. It is not available to common people for their research and data analysis. This restricted availability is also a challenge to analyses to data in an effective way. Mining software should be accessible to all people to make task of opinion mining simple.

Integration of Opinion Words With Implicit and Behavior Data

For an effective sentiment analysis, the implicit data and opinion words should be integrated; it will help to determine the actual behavior of sentiment words within the implicit data.

Domain-Independence

Domain dependent nature of sentiment words is one big challenge for opinion mining and sentiment analysis. One features set may give very good performance in one domain, at the same time it perform very poor in some other domain (Dmitry et al., 2010).

Overheads in Natural Language Processing

The natural language overhead like ambiguity, co-reference, Implicitness, inference etc. create hindrance in sentiment analysis.

Research Areas

The major scope in this area is as follows:

1. Identification of Spam data and handling.
2. Mining short sentences like abbreviations.
3. Improving sentiment word identification algorithm.
4. Designing automatic analyzing tool.
5. Effective Analysis of policy opinionated content.
6. Treating and handling bi polar sentiments.
7. Generation of highly content lexicon database.

TOOLS AND SOURCES

Here are some tools or sources used for performing opinion mining **WordNet** (source: https://wordnet.princeton.edu/)

WordNet is a huge database of English words that are connected together by their semantic relationships. It is a collection of words (lexical database) that has been frequently used by major search engines and IR research projects. The database can be accessed through Princeton University's website (https://wordnet.princeton.edu/) and can be downloaded for non-commercial use for use on Linux/Unix/Mac systems. Alternatively, it is considered as a supercharged dictionary or thesaurus with a defined structure.

The Wordnet Hierarchy

Nouns, verbs, adjectives and adverbs are grouped into sets of cognitive synonyms (synsets), each expressing a distinct concept (Morinaga et al., 2002). Synsets are interlinked by means of conceptual-semantic and lexical relations.

A synset, therefore, corresponds to an abstract concept. It forms relations with other synsets to form a hierarchy of concepts. For a given synset, some basic terminology used are as follows:

- **Hypernyms:** Are the synsets that are more general.
- **Hyponyms:** Are the synsets that are more specific.

Hyponyms have an "is-a" relationship to their hypernyms. Along with "is-a" relationships, we can explore "is-made-of" and "comprises" relationships. For a given synset, we can therefore see the following relationships:

- **Holonyms:** Are things that the item is contained in.
- **Meronyms:** Are components or substances that make up the item.

These different forms can be understood in the following example (see Figure 5)

Figure 5. Representation of word phrase in various forms

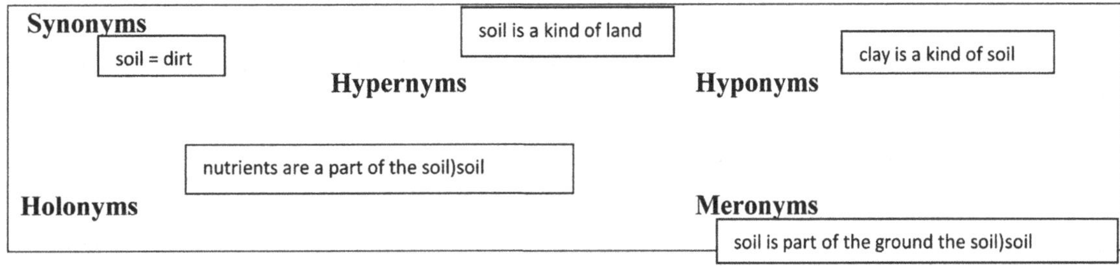

TreeTagger

(source: http://www.ims.unistuttgart.de/forschung/ressourcen/werkzeuge/treetagger.en.html)

The TreeTagger is a tool for annotating text with part-of-speech and lemma information. It was developed by Helmut Schmid in the TC project at the Institute for Computational Linguistics of the University of Stuttgart. This software is freely available for research, education and evaluation.

REFERENCES

Bollen, J., Mao, H., & Zeng, X.-J. (2011). Twitter mood predicts the stock market. *Journal of Computational Science*, *2*(1), 1–8. doi:10.1016/j.jocs.2010.12.007

Davidov, D., Tsur, O., & Rappoport, A. (2010). Semi-supervised recognition of sarcastic sentences in twitter and amazon. In *Proceedings of the fourteenth conference on Computational Natural Language Learning*, Uppsala, Sweden (pp. 107-116).

Morinaga, S., Yamanishi, K., Tateishi, K., & Fukushima, T. (2002). Mining product reputations on the web. In Proceedings of the eighth ACM SIGKDD international conference on Knowledge discovery and data mining, Edmonton, Canada (pp. 341-349). ACM.

Mukherjee, A., & Liu, B. (2012, August). Mining contentions from discussions and debates. In *Proceedings of the 18th ACM SIGKDD international conference on Knowledge discovery and data mining* (pp. 841-849). ACM.

Ojokoh, B. A., & Kayode, O. (2012). A feature-opinion extraction approach to opinion mining. *Journal of Web Engineering*, *11*(1), 51–63.

Pang, B., & Lee, L. (2008). Opinion mining and sentiment analysis. *Foundations and Trends in Information Retrieval*, *2*(1-2), 1–135. doi:10.1561/1500000011

Turney, P. D. (2002). Thumbs up or thumbs down? Semantic orientation applied to unsupervised classification of reviews. In *Proceedings of the Association for Computational Linguistics (ACL)* (pp. 417–424).

ADDITIONAL READING

Brandseye. (2017). What is opinion mining? Retrieved from https://www.brandseye.com/news/what-is-opinion-mining-next-level-sentiment-analytics/

Brandseye. (2017). What is really driving sentiment. Retrieved from https://www.brandseye.com/news/what-drives-sentiment-topic-analysis/

Chen, Y., & Xie, J. (2008). Online Consumer Review: Word-of-Mouth as a New Element of Marketing Communication Mix. *Management Science*, *54*(3), 477–491.

Coursera. (n.d.). 5.5 Opinion Mining and Sentiment Analysis: Motivation [video tutorial]. Retrieved from https://ru.coursera.org/learn/text-mining/lecture/o93Yl/5-5-opinion-mining-and-sentiment-analysis-motivation

Das, S., & Chen, M. (2001). Yahoo! for Amazon: Extracting market sentiment from stock message boards. In *Proceedings of the Asia Pacific finance association annual conference (APFA)* (Vol. 35, p. 43).

Dellarocas, C., Zhang, X. M., & Awad, N. F. (2007). Exploring the value of online product reviews in forecasting sales: The case of motion pictures. *Journal of Interactive Marketing*, *21*(4), 23–45. doi:10.1002/dir.20087

Dictionary. (n.d.). Opinion. Retrieved from http://www.dictionary.com/browse/opinion

Ding, X., & Liu, B. (2010). Resolving object and attribute coreference in opinion mining. In *Proceedings of 23rd international conference on computational linguistics (Coling 2010)* (pp. 268-276).

Ding, X., Liu, B., & Yu, P. S. (2008, February). A holistic lexicon-based approach to opinion mining. In *Proceedings of the 2008 international conference on web search and data mining* (pp. 231-240). ACM.

Do-Hyung, P., Lee, J., & Han, I. (2007). The effect of on-line consumer reviews on consumer purchasing intention: The moderating role of involvement. *International Journal of Electronic Commerce, 11*(4), 125–148. doi:10.2753/JEC1086-4415110405

Encyclopedia Britannica. (n.d.). Public opinion. Retrieved from https://www.britannica.com/topic/public-opinion

Ganapathibhotla, M., & Liu, B. (2008, August). Mining opinions in comparative sentences. In *Proceedings of the 22nd International Conference on Computational Linguistics* (Vol. 1, pp. 241-248). Association for Computational Linguistics.

Hatzivassiloglou, V., & McKeown, K. R. (1997). Predicting the semantic orientation of adjectives. *Proceedings of Annual Meeting of the Association for Computational Linguistics* (ACL-1997).

Hearst, M. (1992). Direction-based text interpretation as an information access refinement in Text-Based Intelligent Systems. In *Text-based intelligent systems: Current research and practice in information extraction and retrieval* (pp. 257–274). Hillsdale, NJ: L. Erlbaum Associates Inc.

Hu, N., Pavlou, P. A., & Zhang, J. (2006, June). Can online reviews reveal a product's true quality?: empirical findings and analytical modeling of Online word-of-mouth communication. In *Proceedings of the 7th ACM conference on Electronic commerce* (pp. 324-330). ACM.

Jotheeswaran, J., & Koteeswaran, S. (n.d.). Sentiment analysis: A survey of current research and techniques. Research & Reviews. Retrieved from http://www.rroij.com/open-access/sentiment-analysis-a-survey-of-current-researchand-techniques.php?aid=56063

Kim, W. Y., Ryu, J. S., Kim, K. I., & Kim, U. M. (2009, November). A method for opinion mining of product reviews using association rules. In *Proceedings of the 2nd International Conference on Interaction Sciences: Information Technology, Culture and Human* (pp. 270-274). ACM.

Liu, Y., Huang, X., An, A., & Yu, X. (2007). ARSA: A sentiment - aware model for predicting sales performance using blogs. In *Proceedings of ACM SIGIR Conf. on Research and Development in Information Retrieval (SIGIR-2007).* 10.1145/1277741.1277845

Medhat, W., Hassan, A., & Korashy, H. (2014). Sentiment analysis algorithms and applications: A survey. *Ain Shams Engineering Journal, 5*(4), 1093-1113. Retrieved from https://www.sciencedirect.com/science/article/pii/S2090447914000550

Michael, J. Paul, ChengXiang Zhai and Roxana Girju (2010). Summarizing contrastive viewpoints in opinionated text. In *Proceedings of the 2010 conference on the empirical methods in natural language processing*, MIT Massachusetts (pp. 66-76).

Peter, D. (2003). Turney and Michael L Littman. (2003). Measuring Praise and criticism: inference of semantic orientation from association. *ACM Transactions on Information Systems, TOIS, 21*(4), 315–346.

Princeton University. (n.d.). Retrieved from https://wordnet.princeton.edu/

Roberto, G. Ibanez, Smaranda Muresan and Nina Wacholder.(2011). Identifying Sarcasm in Twitter: A Closer Look. In *Proceedings of the 49th Annual Meeting of the Association for Computational Linguistics*, Portland, OR, June 19-24 (pp. 581-586).

Sentiment analysis symposium. (n.d.). Pre-symposium tutorial, May 7. Retrieved from http://2012.sentimentsymposium.com/tutorial.html

Tumasjan, A., Sprenger, T. O., Sandner, P. G., & Welpe, I. M. (2010). Predicting elections with twitter: What 140 characters reveal about political sentiment. In *Proceedings of the International Conference on Weblogs and Social Media* (ICWSM-2010).

Wikipedia. (n.d.). Sentiment analysis. Retrieved from https://en.wikipedia.org/wiki/Sentiment_analysis

Wikivisually. (n.d.). Sentiment analysis. Retrieved from https://wikivisually.com/wiki/Sentiment_analysis

This research was previously published in Extracting Knowledge From Opinion Mining; pages 1-19, copyright year 2019 by Engineering Science Reference (an imprint of IGI Global).

Chapter 2
Real Time Sentiment Analysis

Sandip Palit
https://orcid.org/0000-0002-8517-6966
Academy of Technology, Kolkata, India

Soumadip Ghosh
https://orcid.org/0000-0003-4817-5363
Academy of Technology, Kolkata, India

ABSTRACT

Data is the most valuable resource. We have a lot of unstructured data generated by the social media giants Twitter, Facebook, and Google. Unfortunately, analytics on unstructured data cannot be performed. As the availability of the internet became easier, people started using social media platforms as the primary medium for sharing their opinions. Every day, millions of opinions from different parts of the world are posted on Twitter. The primary goal of Twitter is to let people share their opinion with a big audience. So, if the authors can effectively analyse the tweets, valuable information can be gained. Storing these opinions in a structured manner and then using that to analyse people's reactions and perceptions about buying a product or a service is a very vital step for any corporate firm. Sentiment analysis aims to analyse and discover the sentiments behind opinions of various people on different subjects like commercial products, politics, and daily societal issues. This research has developed a model to determine the polarity of a keyword in real time.

1. INTRODUCTION

Sentiment analysis is the process of analysing people's way of thinking, and feelings towards a particular product or service. Before taking any decision, we try to gather other's opinion on that topic (Shayaa et al., 2018). Previously we used to ask people, for their personal opinion. But with the advent of Web 2.0, social media became the primary platform for sharing our opinions. So, analysing the posts and tweets became the better option than personally collecting the feedbacks. The main steps of sentiment analysis are (Guevara et al., 2018): Data acquisition, Text processing, Feature extraction, Sentiment classification, Evaluation and Results. There are various approaches for sentiment analysis, like the

DOI: 10.4018/978-1-6684-6303-1.ch002

Machine learning approach and the lexicon-based approach. In the machine learning based approach, the model was trained using a labelled dataset. The lexicon-based approach depends on the dictionary or a bag of words containing pre-tagged lexicons. Tools for sentiment analysis include python NLTK, GATE, Opinion finder, LingPipe and LIWC (Alessia et al., 2018). Brand monitoring, customer service, market research and analysis are some of the applications of sentiment analysis. Brandwatch reported that every second, six thousand tweets are posted on Twitter (van Dijck J., 2011). So, it is the best source for analysing opinions. Twitter API allows us to extract the tweets within a rate limit. TextBlob is a python library for Natural Language Processing tasks, like translation and language detection, sentiment analysis, tokenization and part-of-speech tagging. Natural Language Toolkit (NLTK) provides the stop words, which is important for feature extraction.

2. LITERATURE REVIEW

Web 2.0 (Murugesan S., 2007) is an enhanced version of the Web 1.0. It forms the foundation for social media platforms. It is strongly characterised by the change from static to dynamic or user-generated content. Some of its advantages are: better media support, dynamic and real-time discussion. It enables the user to add their opinions in the form of posts or tweets. Web 2.0 tools (Thackeray et al., 2008) allows the user to create and modify content on many social platforms, like Twitter, Facebook and Youtube. This promotes interactive content, which results in a better user experience. A major part of this data is unstructured texts, such as tweets, reviews and blogs.

Although the first academic studies for analysing public opinion was during World War 2, the evolution of modern sentiment analysis took place in the mid-2000s, whose main purpose was to understand people's opinion on various online products (Kumar & Vadlamani, 2015). In recent years, researchers started applying sentiment analysis on social media platforms like Twitter and Facebook. This also works well on various other topics like the stock market, disasters, medicines, election and software engineering (Mäntylä et al., 2018).

'Opinion mining and sentiment analysis' by Pang and Lee (2008) was the top-cited paper on sentiment analysis. It focuses mainly on the fundamentals and basic application of Sentiment analysis. It also developed some free resources like lexicons and datasets.

One of the pioneer works on Reviews analysis done by Pang, Lee and Vaithyanathan (2002), tried to classify the overall statement, instead of classifying by topics. Using standard machine learning techniques like Naïve Bayes, Support Vector Machine and Maximum Entropy Classification, they classified the movie reviews as positive or negative.

Turney's works (2002) on document level semantic classification was also a widely cited work from 2002. He developed a simple unsupervised learning algorithm to classify reviews as thumbs up (recommended) or thumbs down (not recommended), based on the semantic orientation of the phrases present in the review. They achieved an average accuracy of 74%.

Mamta and Ela Kumar (2019) developed a lexicon-based framework to perform real-time sentiment analysis on Twitter. In the data pre-processing stage, they removed the special characters from the tweets, indirectly removing the emojis. Emojis are important in understanding the positive or negative tone of the statement (Walther & D'addario, 2001). In our approach, we manually decoded these emojis. Nowadays, we use lots of acronyms. Usage of acronyms can decrease the accuracy of our model (Palmquist R.D., 2008), so we expanded those acronyms using the python regex module.

3. APPROACHES FOR SENTIMENT ANALYSIS

Sentiment analysis techniques can be classified mainly into three main categories: the Lexicon based approach, the Machine learning approach and the Hybrid approach (Dorothy & Rajini, 2016).

3.1. Machine Learning Based Approach

Machine learning approaches can be classified into supervised, unsupervised and semi-supervised learning techniques. In sentiment analysis, mainly the supervised learning technique is followed. It requires a large number of labelled training documents. The model is trained based on the previous dataset, and then that model is used to classify an unseen text. The accuracy of this technique is greatly influenced by the dataset.

Some prominent classifiers: support vector machine (Mullen et al., 2004), neural network (Kim Y., 2014), Naïve Bayes (Troussas et al., 2013) and maximum entropy (Roa et al., 2016). B. Pang, L. Lee, and S. Vaithyanathan (2002) reported that the support vector machine got the highest accuracy (82.9) on IMDB dataset.

3.2. Lexicon Based Approach

Lexicon based approach relies on a dictionary consisting of the pre-tagged lexicons. Firstly, the input text is broken down into tokens by a tokenizer. Then the stop words are removed, to enhance the accuracy. The remaining tokens are matched with the dictionary and the scores are added. The final classification of the text depends on the total score. A score greater than threshold means a positive impact and a score lesser than threshold means a negative impact.

Lexicon based approach can be further sub-divided into dictionary-based techniques and corpus-based techniques. The dictionary-based approach (Park et al., 2016), starts with a small set of opinion words and then gradually expanding it by adding antonyms and synonyms from the WordNet dictionary. The corpus-based approach (Rice et al., 2013) looks for syntactic patterns in the corpora. It has a large dataset of labelled training data. The corpus-based approach gives better accuracy than the dictionary-based approach.

3.3. Hybrid Approach

The hybrid approach of sentiment analysis attains the best of both worlds: the accuracy of machine learning approach and the speed of lexicon-based approach. Nurulhuda Zainuddin, Ali Selamat and Roliana Ibrahim (2018) proposed a new hybrid classification for twitter by embedding a feature selection method. They also compared the classification accuracy of principal component analysis, random projection and latent semantic analysis.

4. METHODOLOGY

We have performed various researches on the real-time extraction and polarity determination of tweets. The focus of our research was to extract the recent tweets with that particular keyword, and then finding its opinion polarity. Figure 1 shows the flowchart diagram of our proposed methodology.

Figure 1. Flowchart diagram of the proposed methodology

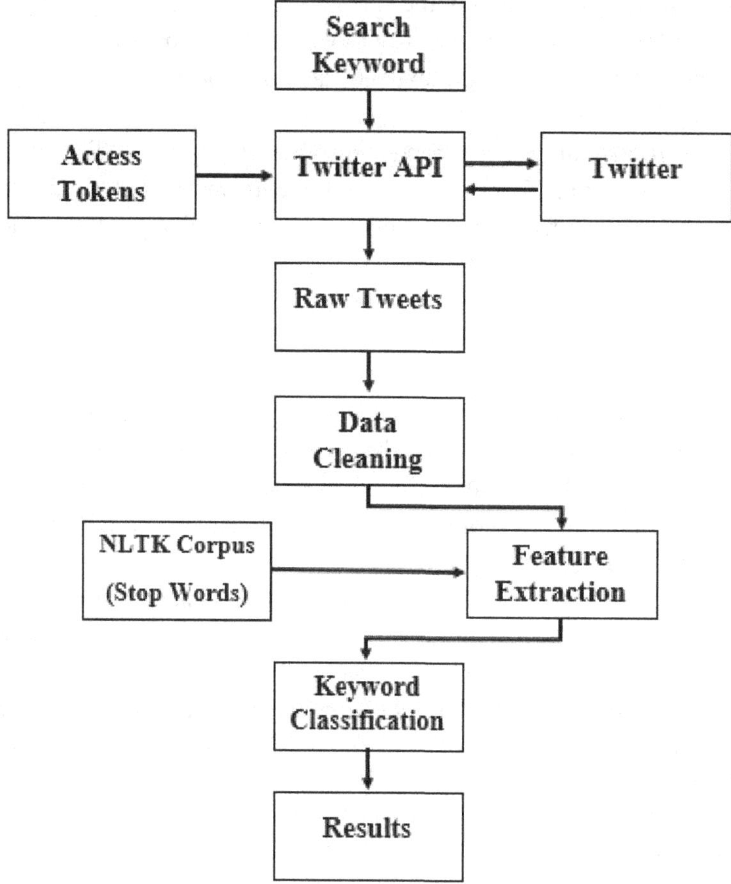

Firstly, the model takes the Keyword and the access tokens from the user. The recent tweets with that keyword are extracted from twitter through the Twitter API (Bucher T., 2013). Then we performed data cleaning on the raw tweets, like decoding emojis, expanding the acronyms, removing URL, links and twitter handle. We removed the stop words and performed the feature extraction. Then we identified the positive and negative impact of the words (Rajan et al., 2014). The final keyword classification was performed based on the overall polarity score. The output was displayed in the form of general report, detailed report and a Pie chart.

4.1. Data Collection

Based on the given keyword, tweets are extracted from twitter using the tweepy twitter API. Twitter emerged as the best microblogging site (Java et al., 2007). Every day, millions of tweets on different topics are posted on twitter. So, twitter is the ideal source for sentiment analysis (Pak & Paroubek, 2010).

Firstly, we created an app with the twitter developer account, to get the access tokens like the consumer API key, consumer API secret key, access token and access token secret. Tweepy uses open authorization protocol to authenticate the incoming requests (Roesslein J., 2009). GET requests are rate limited to 180 calls every 15 minutes. After authenticating using the consumer API key and consumer API secret key, we set the access tokens like the access token and access token secret. Now we can directly access the tweets from twitter. Using the Cursor, we searched for the recent occurrences of the given keyword. Then we extracted the raw tweets and stored in a csv file.

4.2. Data Cleaning

To enhance accuracy, we must perform some pre-processing on the raw tweets (Krouska et al., 2016). At first, we replaced the acronyms with their English expansion. Table 1 contains some of the acronyms with their expansions that we used in our model.

Table 1. Acronyms and their English expansions

Acronym	English Expansion	Acronym	English Expansion
LOL	Laughing Out Loud	FYI	For Your Information
ASAP	As Soon As Possible	AKA	Also Known As
TBA	To Be Announced	RIP	Rest in Peace
DIY	Do It Yourself	IDK	I Don't Know
OMG	Oh My God	EOD	End of Day

In our daily communication, we use lots of acronyms to save time. Sometimes, we use those acronyms in our tweets also. The classifier won't automatically recognise the acronyms. It will treat the acronyms and their meaning or expansions as different, which will decrease the accuracy of the classifier. So, we manually replaced the acronyms with their expansions, by using the regular expression library.

Another important aspect is the use of Emojis in tweets. Use of proper emojis can change the tone of the statement. Table 2 shows some of the emojis that we replaced with their expression, to have a better understanding of the statement.

Let us consider two statements: "We are the runners-up:-)" and "We are the runners-up:-(". The first statement implies that the author is happy that they are the runners-up. So, overall polarity is positive. The second statement implies that the author expected to be the winner, and they are sad about being the runners-up. So, overall polarity is negative. This is how an emoji can change the polarity of the statement (Felbo et al.,2017).

Table 2. Emojis with the expression

Emojis	Expression	Polarity (as per TextBlob)
:D :-D	Very Happy	1.0
:) :-)	Happy	0.8
:I :-I	Neutral	0.0
:(:-(	Sad	- 0.5
:'(:'-(	Very Sad	-0.65

Then we removed all the URLs, links, HTML tags and the unwanted special characters from the tweets. We did this because we are concerned with the information, without caring about the sources of that information. Finally, we trimmed the sentence to remove the extra spaces at the beginning and at the end.

4.3. Feature Extraction

Feature extraction was performed to select only useful information. After cleaning each tweet, we split it into words or tokens to remove the stop words. Stop words are the commonly used word (such as and, are, by, for) that do not impact the overall polarity of the statement (Silva & Ribeiro, 2003). We imported the stop words from the nltk corpus and we removed all the words that matched with those stop words, to increase the efficiency and decrease the storage usage. We joined the remaining words, and then performed spelling correction using the correct() method of TextBlob.

4.4. Keyword Classification

The sentiment is closely related to emotions, and polarity measures the orientation of those emotions. Polarity can be Positive, Negative or Neutral (Wilson et al., 2005). The polarity value ranges from -1 (extremely negative) to +1 (extremely positive). In our model, we iterated through each processed tweet and identified its polarity with the help of the TextBlob library. As per the lexicon-based approach, TextBlob searched each word of the tweet, in the TextBlob dictionary to find out the individual polarity. If that word was present in the positive sentiment word list, then it gave a positive polarity, and if that word was present in the negative sentiment word list, then it gave a negative polarity. If that word was not found, then it gave a neutral polarity. The polarity of the statements depends on the overall score of the individual polarities.

Based on the polarity value, we classified them into seven classes: strongly positive, positive, weakly positive, neutral, weakly negative, negative and strongly negative. We initialised counters for each class and incremented it based on the range of polarity values. Polarity values within the range -1 to -0.6 means 'strongly negative", -0.6 to -0.3 means 'negative', -0.3 to 0 means 'weakly negative', exactly 0 means 'neutral', 0 to 0.3 means 'weakly positive', 0.3 to 0.6 means 'positive' and 0.6 to 1 means 'strongly positive'. Finally, we calculated the percentage of all these classes.

The report is divided into three sections. The general report shows the overall sentiment orientation of that keyword. The detailed report shows the percentage of each class. Lastly, the Pie chart gives a better visualisation of the classification.

5. RESULTS AND DISCUSSION

Before starting our analysis, we should specify the consumer API key, consumer API secret key, access token and access token secret. Initially, this model takes the Keyword or Hashtag as input and the Number of tweets that the user wants to analyse. As there is a rate limit on twitter API, so it is better to avoid analysing on a very large number of tweets. The model extracts the tweets and performs pre-processing. Then classification is done and we get the report shown in Figure 2.

Figure 2. Experiment report

```
How people are reacting on World by analyzing 1000 tweets.
General Report:
Weakly Positive

Detailed Report:
5.30% people thought it was strongly positive
14.50% people thought it was positive
24.80% people thought it was weakly positive 34.00%
people thought it was neutral
16.10% people thought it was weakly negative
3.70% people thought it was negative
1.20% people thought it was strongly negative
```

How people are reacting on World by analyzing 1000 Tweets.

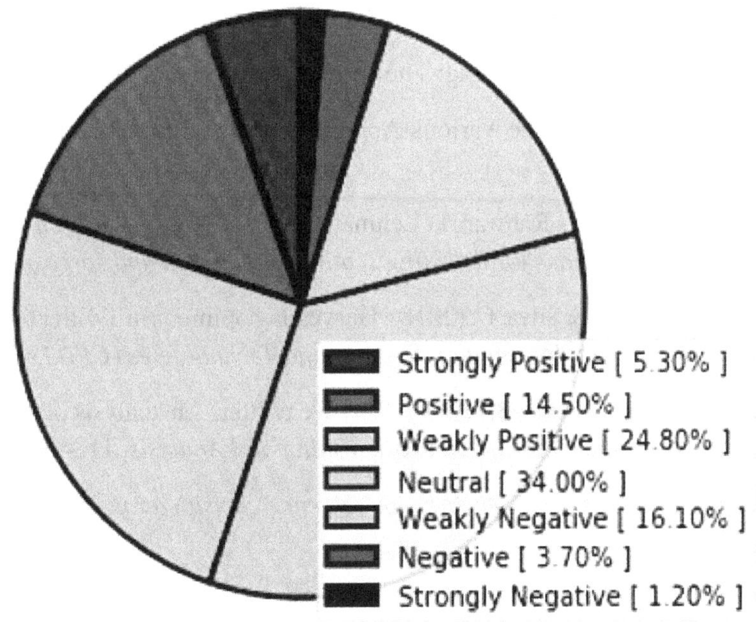

We performed our experiment with the 'World' keyword, on 1000 tweets. We chose this keyword, as this is very general and people can have different types of opinion. Figure 2 shows the Sentiment Analysis report. The first section identified that the overall orientation is weakly positive. The next section gave a detailed report of the sentiment analysis. Considering the top 3 classes we have found that 34% tweets on World are Neutral, 24.8% tweets are Weakly Positive and 16.1% tweets are Weakly Negative. The Pie chart gave a better visualisation of the same. On comparing the positive negative and neutral part, we found that it has a positive orientation favoured by 44.8% tweets.

6. CONCLUSION AND FUTURE WORKS

In our research, we proposed an enhanced data cleaning methodology. This will surely increase the accuracy of lexicon-based sentiment analysis. We used the recent version (0.15.2) of TextBlob library to perform the analysis part. For stop words, we used the NLTK corpus. We focussed on the importance of Acronyms expansion in our methodology. We manually expanded the most commonly used acronyms, but expanding every acronym was impossible. So, in future, if we get a dataset containing the acronyms with their expansions, then we can further increase the accuracy. There are some acronyms datasets available, but those are for a specific domain. We also focused on the usage of emojis in our tweets. We explained the impact of emojis and how we can analyse them. In this way, we should try to analyse the other emojis also. Emojis are very important in sentiment analysis of tweets. We must take care of the different versions of emojis, and different representations of emojis in various social media platforms. Then we can try analysing the emoticons and GIFs.

REFERENCES

Alessia, D., Ferri, F., Grifoni, P., & Guzzo, T. (2015). Approaches, tools and applications for sentiment analysis implementation. *International Journal of Computers and Applications*, *125*(3).

Bucher, T. (2013). Objects of intense feeling: The case of the Twitter API. *Computational Culture, 3*.

Dorothy, M., & Rajini, S. (2016). The Various Approaches for Sentiment Analysis. *Survey (London, England)*.

Felbo, B., Mislove, A., Sogaard, A., Rahwan, I., Lehmann, S. (2017). *Using millions of emoji occurrences to learn any-domain representations for detecting sentiment, emotion and sarcasm*. Academic Press.

Guevara, J., Costa, J., Arroba, J., & Silva, C. (2018). Harvesting opinions in Twitter for sentiment analysis. *2018 13th Iberian Conference on Information Systems and Technologies (CISTI),* 1-7.

Java, A., Song, X., Finin, T., & Tseng, B. (2007). Why we twitter: An analysis of a microblogging community. *International Workshop on Social Network Mining and Analysis*, 118-138.

Kim, Y. (2014*). Convolutional neural networks for sentence classification*. Academic Press.

Krouska, A., Troussas, C., & Virvou, M. (2016). The effect of preprocessing techniques on Twitter sentiment analysis. *2016 7th International Conference on Information, Intelligence, Systems \& Applications (IISA)*, 1-5.

Mamta, E. K. (2019). *A Real-Time Twitter Sentiment Analysis and Visualization System: TwiSent*. Academic Press.

Mäntylä, M. V., Graziotin, D., & Kuutila, M. (2018). The evolution of sentiment analysis—A review of research topics, venues, and top cited papers. *Computer Science Review*, *27*, 16–32. doi:10.1016/j.cosrev.2017.10.002

Mullen, T., & Collier, N. (2004). Sentiment analysis using support vector machines with diverse information sources. *Proceedings of the 2004 conference on empirical methods in natural language processing*, 412-418.

Murugesan, S. (2007). Understanding Web 2.0. *IT Professional, 9*(4), 34-41.

Pak, A., & Paroubek, P. (2010). Twitter as a corpus for sentiment analysis and opinion mining. *LREc*, *10*, 1320–1326.

Palmquist, R. D. (2008). *Translation techniques for acronyms and ambiguities*. US Patent 7,359,849.

Pang, B., & Lee, L. (2008). Opinion mining and sentiment analysis. *Foundations and Trends in Information Retrieval*, *2*(1-2), 1–135. doi:10.1561/1500000011

Pang, B., Lee, L., & Vaithyanathan, S. (2002). Thumbs up? Sentiment classification using machine learning techniques. *Proceedings of the ACL-02 Conference on Empirical Methods in Natural Language Processing*, *10*, 79-86. 10.3115/1118693.1118704

Park, S., & Kim, Y. (2016). Building thesaurus lexicon using dictionary-based approach for sentiment classification. *2016 IEEE 14th International Conference on Software Engineering Research, Management and Applications (SERA)*, 39-44.

Rajan, A. P., & Victor, S. P. (2014). Web sentiment analysis for scoring positive or negative words using Tweeter data. *International Journal of Computer Applications, 96*(6).

Rao, Y., Xie, H., Li, J., Jin, F., Wang, F. L., & Li, Q. (2016). Social emotion classification of short text via topic-level maximum entropy model. *Information & Management*, *53*(8), 978–986. doi:10.1016/j.im.2016.04.005

Ravi, K., & Ravi, V. (2015). A survey on opinion mining and sentiment analysis: Tasks, approaches and applications. *Knowledge-Based Systems*, *89*, 14–46. doi:10.1016/j.knosys.2015.06.015

Rice, D. R., & Zorn, C. (2013). Corpus-based dictionaries for sentiment analysis of specialized vocabularies. *Political Science Research and Methods*, 1-16.

Roesslein, J. (2009). *Tweepy Documentation*. Academic Press.

Shayaa, S., Jaafar, N. I., Bahri, S., Sulaiman, A., Wai, P. S., Chung, Y. W., . . . Al-Garadi, M. A. (2018). Sentiment Analysis of Big Data: Methods, Applications, and Open Challenges. Academic Press.

Silva, C., & Ribeiro, B. (2003). The importance of stop word removal on recall values in text categorization. *Proceedings of International Joint Conference on Neural Networks*, *3*, 1661–1666.

Thackeray, R., Neiger, B. L., Hanson, C. L., & McKenzie, J. F. (2008). Enhancing promotional strategies within social marketing programs: Use of Web 2.0 social media. *Health Promotion Practice*, *9*(4), 338–343. doi:10.1177/1524839908325335 PMID:18936268

Troussas, C., Virvou, M., Espinosa, K. J., Llaguno, K., & Caro, J. (2013). Sentiment analysis of Facebook statuses using Naive Bayes classifier for language learning. *IISA*, *2013*, 1–6.

Turney, P. D. (2002). Thumbs up or thumbs down? Semantic orientation applied to unsupervised classification of reviews. *Proceedings of the 40th Annual Meeting on Association for Computational Linguistics*, 417-424.

van Dijck, J. (2011). Tracing Twitter: The rise of a microblogging platform. *International Journal of Media & Cultural Politics*, *7*(3), 333–348. doi:10.1386/macp.7.3.333_1

Walther, J. B., & D'addario, K. P. (2001). The impacts of emoticons on message interpretation in computer-mediated communication. *Social Science Computer Review, 19*(3), 324-347.

Wilson, T., Wiebe, J., & Hoffmann, P. (2005). Recognizing contextual polarity in phrase-level sentiment analysis. *Proceedings of human language technology conference and conference on empirical methods in natural language processing*, 347-354. 10.3115/1220575.1220619

Zainuddin, N., Selamat, A., & Ibrahim, R. (2018). Hybrid sentiment classification on twitter aspect-based sentiment analysis. *Applied Intelligence*, *48*(5), 1218–1232.

This research was previously published in the International Journal of Synthetic Emotions (IJSE), 11(1); pages 27-35, copyright year 2020 by IGI Publishing (an imprint of IGI Global).

Chapter 3
Deep Learning for Sentiment Analysis: An Overview and Perspectives

Vincent Karas
University of Augsburg, Germany

Björn W. Schuller
University of Augsburg, Germany

ABSTRACT

Sentiment analysis is an important area of natural language processing that can help inform business decisions by extracting sentiment information from documents. The purpose of this chapter is to introduce the reader to selected concepts and methods of deep learning and show how deep models can be used to increase performance in sentiment analysis. It discusses the latest advances in the field and covers topics including traditional sentiment analysis approaches, the fundamentals of sentence modelling, popular neural network architectures, autoencoders, attention modelling, transformers, data augmentation methods, the benefits of transfer learning, the potential of adversarial networks, and perspectives on explainable AI. The authors' intent is that through this chapter, the reader can gain an understanding of recent developments in this area as well as current trends and potentials for future research.

INTRODUCTION

In recent years, the amount of information available on the Internet has grown rapidly. At the beginning of 2019, Twitter had 326 million monthly active users, and 500 million tweets were sent per day Cooper (2019). Facebook, the largest social media platform, reported 2.41 billion monthly active users for the second quarter of 2019 Facebook (2019). Every minute, 4.5 million YouTube videos and 1 million Twitch videos are viewed, and the Google search engine processes 3.8 million queries (Desjardins, 2019). This trove of online content constitutes a valuable resource for business applications, e.g. for providing the users with personalised search recommendations and tailored advertisements. If the data is harnessed

DOI: 10.4018/978-1-6684-6303-1.ch003

properly, it may deliver new insights that can help improve existing products and services and inspire future business models. Among the available content, text, in particular, is rich in information, as it can contain nuanced emotions, multiple layers of meaning and ambiguities. However, this complexity also results in it being challenging to analyse. Natural Language Processing (NLP), which addresses this challenge, has become a popular field of research.

Sentiment Analysis (SA), which is often also referred to as opinion mining or comment mining in the literature, is a discipline of NLP-based text analysis whose goal is to determine the writer's feelings about a particular topic. Emotions have been shown to play an essential role in human decision making (Bechara, Damasio, & Damasio, 2000) and behaviour in general. Consequentially, SA has many conceivable applications in business and academia. Examples include companies looking to improve their services by automatically assessing customer reviews (Hu & Liu, 2004), (Zvarevashe & Olugbara, 2018), comparing products online, or analysing newspaper headlines (Rameshbhai & Paulose, 2019).

Sentiment also plays an important role in the financial market. Ranjit, Shrestha, Subedi, and Shakya (2018) used SA to predict the exchange rates of foreign currencies. Shah, Isah, and Zulkernine (2018) predicted stock prices in the pharmaceutical industry based on the sentiment in news coverage. C. Du, Tsai, and Wang (2019) classified financial reports in terms of expected financial risk using SA.

In addition, there are medical applications for SA. Müller and Salathé (2019) introduced an open platform for tracking health trends on social media. Luo, Zimet, and Shah (2019) created an NLP framework to investigate sentiment fluctuation on the subject of HPV vaccination, expressed by Twitter users between 2008 and 2017.

Furthermore, political analysts and campaigns can benefit from mining the opinions and emotions expressed towards candidates, issues and parties on social media. Jose and Chooralil (2016) used an ensemble classifier approach to predict results of the 2015 election in Delhi. Joyce and Deng (2017) applied SA to tweets collected in the run-up to the 2016 US presidential election and compared them to polling data. They found that automatic labelling of tweets outperformed manual labelling.

Many tools used in sentiment analysis are designed for a specific application, which negatively impacts their diffusion. Joshi and Simon (2018) introduced a cloud-based open-source tool which provides various APIs in order to perform SA on data from arbitrary sources.

While SA has attracted considerable attention, the field still faces challenges. These include domain dependence, negations, handling fake reviews (Hussein, Doaa Mohey El-Din Mohamed, 2018), as well as incorporating context, dealing with data imbalance and ensuring high-quality annotations (Boaz Shmueli & Lun-Wei Ku, 2019).

This chapter introduces the reader to selected methods used for sentiment analysis, with a focus on techniques based on deep learning. Its contribution consists of a discussion of the latest advances in the state of the art, as well as an outlook concerning ongoing trends in the field and recommendations on future research directions.

The rest of the chapter is structured as follows. In the next section, the fundamentals of SA and select machine learning concepts are presented. Topics covered include a categorisation of analysis approaches by level of granularity, how to measure sentiment, traditional sentiment analysis methods employing lexica and machine learning, as well as tools for word embedding and sentence modelling such as autoencoders, GloVe, fastText and Word2vec. The chapter will then continue with its main section, focusing on current developments in deep learning-based SA. Topics include popular neural network architectures and their combination into hybrid models, capturing contextual information by adding attention, Transformer networks and the challenges and benefits of transfer learning. In the following section, solutions and recommendations for readers seeking to apply state-of-the-art models to SA are presented. The subsequent section involves an overview of promising research opportunities in the field. Recent data augmentation techniques, zero-shot learning and the potential of generative adversarial networks are covered. In addition, the need for developing explainable AI systems is discussed as well as improving generalisation across topics and languages and defending against adversarial attacks. Finally, a conclusion sums up this chapter.

BACKGROUND

This section presents a taxonomy of sentiment analysis and key methods and frameworks used for sentence modelling and generating word embeddings.

Levels of Sentiment Analysis

A text can be analysed for its sentiment content at different levels. These are document, sentence and phrase levels (P. Balaji, O. Nagaraju, & D. Haritha, 2017). Sentiment analysis at phrase level is also commonly referred to as aspect level analysis, a name that will be adopted for this chapter. The level of analysis informs the choice of deep learning models.

As a motivational example, consider an automotive company wanting to classify product reviews of their cars. A review might read as follows:

"This is a great car. It handles well in corners and has superb acceleration. Like its predecessor, it has a V6 engine. However, I do not like what they did with the new voice-controlled infotainment system. It gets confused too easily to be useful."

The following subsections illustrate the application of SA at different levels based on the example review:

Document Level SA

The task at this level is to classify the entire document as having a positive or negative sentiment (Pang, Lee, & Vaithyanathan, 2002). Such an analysis can serve to determine a general verdict, e.g. to find out whether a reviewer likes or dislikes a product. Therefore, this approach can work only if the document describes a single issue.

For the example review, it appears that the customer has an overall positive opinion. However, there is also criticism. In order to understand the positive and negative feelings expressed by the customer, the document needs to be examined in greater detail.

Sentence Level SA

At this level, individual sentences are examined for their sentiment content. This approach requires splitting the document into objective sentences, which contain factual information, and subjective sentences that reflect opinions and feelings. The classification of subjectivity was investigated by Wiebe, Bruce, and O'Hara (1999). Subjective sentences are then subjected to SA and rated accordingly. Performing

SA at sentence level makes a similar assumption to document level SA in that individual sentences are referring to only one entity, which will often not be true (Christy Daniel & Shyamala, 2019).

Considering our sample review at the sentence level, a more detailed picture emerges: The customer expresses positive sentiment in the first two sentences. The third sentence is a factual statement. The last two sentences show negative sentiment.

Aspect Level SA

Aspect-level analysis examines individual entities within sentences, making it more fine-grained than the previous approaches. It can discover in detail which elements of a topic are liked or disliked, which is useful since the author's opinion on a subject will rarely be entirely positive or negative. Thus, the objective of an aspect-level analysis is to discover the slant of the text (P. Balaji et al., 2017). Multiple sub-tasks can be defined at this level:

1. **Target extraction:** This identifies the entities that sentiments refer to.
2. **Sentiment classification:** The rating of the sentiment.
3. **Temporal opinion mining:** This task is concerned with discovering the temporal relationships in the text and how those affect the evolution of sentiment.
4. **Opinion holder identification:** A text may reference different persons, each having individual opinions.

For the example review, a targeted aspect-level analysis can reveal that the customer approves of the car's driving characteristics, as they commend the acceleration and handling in corners. At the same time, the customer disapproves of a new feature in the infotainment system. For the manufacturer, this is valuable information for identifying the strengths and weaknesses of the product. Opinion holder identification is also quite useful for this task. The example review features a single customer who emphasises a good driving experience, but there could also be references to, e.g. family members having different priorities.

Now that the basic approaches for extracting sentiment from documents have been identified, the next subsection will address the question of how sentiment can be quantified.

Measuring Sentiment

Just as the analysis of a document may be performed at different levels, the discovered sentiment may also be measured at different levels of granularity. One possibility is a binary approach based on polarity, i.e. the text is positive or negative. A neutral state may be added as a third class. Alternatively, categorical emotions may be used. Ekman (1999) identified six basic emotions, namely, happiness, anger, sadness, disgust, surprise and fear. A more fine-grained description is provided by continuous affect dimensions such as valence, arousal, dominance, or novelty. Plutchik (1980) introduced a model which combines elements of the categorical and continuous approaches. It encompasses eight types of emotions, namely joy, anticipation, trust, surprise, fear, anger, disgust and sadness. The emotions are arranged as opposing pairs in a wheel. In addition, each emotion can appear at different levels of intensity, e.g. trust ranges from acceptance to admiration.

Consider the sentences "This car is all right." and "This car is great." Both express a positive sentiment, but it is much stronger in the second sentence, which should result in a higher level of valence being detected.

Having introduced levels of granularity and ways to measure sentiment, the next section will explore algorithms traditionally used in SA:

Traditional Approaches for Sentiment Analysis

The methods used for SA can be placed into two broad categories: lexica-based approaches and machine learning approaches. This chapter considers deep learning-based algorithms separately in the following section; therefore, they are not discussed among the machine learning algorithms in this section.

Lexicon-Based Approach

The lexicon-based approach aggregates the polarity and strength of individual words in the document to calculate the overall sentiment. (Turney, 2002). It requires a dictionary of words with associated semantic orientation. The research into lexica-based SA has largely focused on adjectives, cf. Hatzivassiloglou and McKeown (1997), Hu and Liu (2004), Wiebe (2000) and Taboada, Anthony, and Voll (2006).

The dictionary or lexicon can be compiled manually (Taboada, Brooke, Tofiloski, Voll, & Stede, 2011) or automatically starting from a seed list of opinion words. Automatic lexicon compilation is accomplished with thesaurus-based and corpus-based methods. Thesaurus-based methods expand the seed list by parsing existing dictionaries for synonyms or antonyms, while corpus-based methods exploit statistical co-occurrence of words with similar polarity in a corpus, or calculate similarity measures between words (Kaur, Mangat, & Nidhi, 2017).

Machine Learning-Based Approach

Machine learning algorithms perform sentiment classification or regression according to features contained in the text. They can – among many possible discriminations – be divided into linear classifiers and probabilistic classifiers.

Support Vector Machine (SVM) is an example of an (in principle) linear classifier, i.e. it attempts to predict a label y (+1 or -1) from features x based on the function:

$$y = f(x) = w^T x + b \quad (1)$$

It was developed within the statistical learning theory (Vapnik, 2000). The algorithm searches a hypothesis space of functions in order to find a hyperplane that separates classes. In the simple case, considered up to now, of a linear SVM, the hyperplane lies in the input space. In the generalised form of SVM, a dot product called a kernel is used to define a Reproducing Kernel Hilbert Space as the feature space (Evgeniou & Pontil, 2001). SVM attempts to maximise the distance between the named hyperplane and the instances of each of the two classes (extensions for more than two classes exist, such as one vs one, or one vs all).

Naïve Bayes (NB) is an example of a probabilistic classifier, which predicts a conditional probability $p(y|x)$. Naïve Bayes uses Bayes' rule to determine the probability of a class c belonging to a vector of BoW features x:

$$p(c|x) = \frac{p(c)p(x|c)}{p(x)} \tag{2}$$

This simple algorithm assumes that the features are conditionally independent, which allows it to decompose the numerator (Pang et al., 2002). The classifier then takes the form:

$$p_{NB}(c|x_1,\cdots,x_n) = \frac{p(c)\prod_{i=1}^{n} p(x_i|c)}{p(x)} \tag{3}$$

Maximum Entropy (ME) is another probabilistic algorithm. It has been used for SA of tweets (Neethu & Rajasree, 2013), (Gautam & Yadav, 2014). The intuitive assumption of this classifier is that the underlying probability distribution should have maximum entropy, i.e. be as uniform as possible within the constraints imposed by the training data (Nigam, Lafferty, & Mccallum, 1999). Those constraints apply to the feature functions $f_i(d, c)$, whose expected value within the model and the training data are demanded to be equal. The probability distribution takes an exponential form (Della Pietra, Della Pietra, & Lafferty, 1997):

$$p_{ME}(c|d) = \frac{1}{Z_d} e^{\sum_{i=1}^{n} \lambda_i f_i(d,c)} \tag{4}$$

Here Z_d is a normalisation factor, and λ_i is a parameter to be estimated. Unlike NB, ME does not assume independence of features, and therefore, it can outperform NB on tasks where that assumption does not hold (Pang et al., 2002).

Sentence Modelling and Word Embeddings

In order to perform SA on a document, the text first has to be converted into a form that the SA algorithm can process. This is done by assigning a vector to each word in the document. A simple solution would be to use an approach known as Bag-of-Words (BoW). The number of occurrences of each unique word within the corpus is determined and used to sort the words in descending order. Then, a one-hot encoding can be applied to that list of words. The same approach can be used with n-grams (word sequences of length n).

A naïve BoW, as described above, is easy to implement but has several disadvantages. First, it can result in very high-dimensional representations, up to the number of entries in the vocabulary. Second, such an encoding does not capture the linguistic relationships between words. However, the goal of sentence modelling should be to obtain feature representations which guarantee that the similarity between two vectors reflects the semantic and syntactic relationship between the corresponding words.

The following subsections introduce a selection of established methods and tools that can be used to discover useful representations for NLP tasks, including but not limited to SA.

Autoencoders

A useful representation should capture the relevant information contained in the raw data, allow for clustering into categories, and reduce the number of features sufficiently to avoid the curse of dimensionality. An example of a deep architecture designed to learn such representations in an unsupervised manner is the autoencoder.

An autoencoder (AE) consists of two networks connected in sequence: The encoder processes the input data and generates a feature vector at its output layer. That vector is usually of lower dimensionality than the input; however, a variant called sparse autoencoder may increase the dimensionality of the encoder output but regularise it to produce sparse activations. The features generated by the encoder are used as the input to the decoder, which produces an output of the same shape as the input data. The autoencoder is trained by setting the target of the decoder to be the same as the input data. Since the layer in the middle of the network has fewer parameters, it acts as a bottleneck, forcing the network to learn how to compress the input into a compact representation. This process can be called self-supervised, as the autoencoder learns by optimising the reconstructing error of the data without a need for labels. Figure 1 illustrates the basic structure of an autoencoder.

Figure 1. Autoencoder architecture. Input is compressed by the encoder, then reconstructed by the decoder. This forces the network to learn an efficient representation of the data.

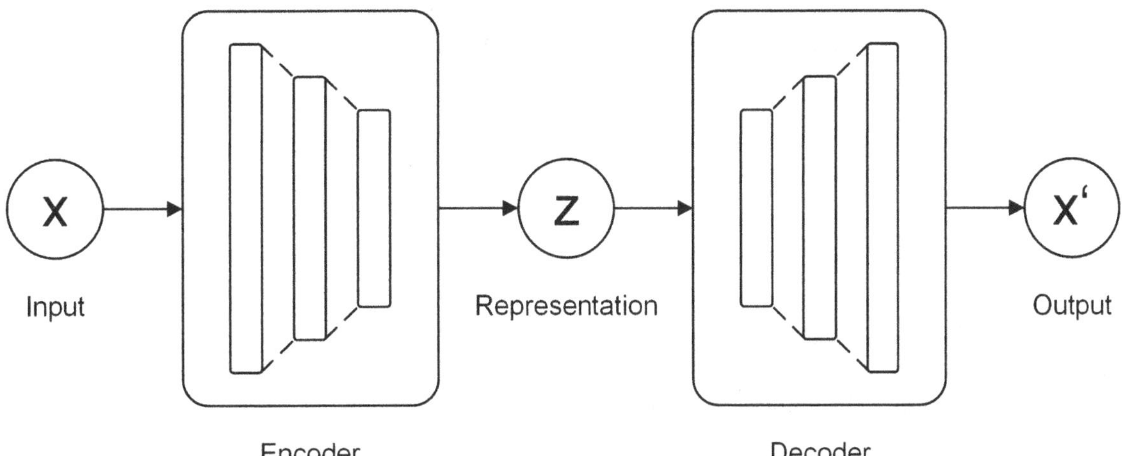

AEs and their variants are popular tools for sentiment analysis. They are frequently employed in semi-supervised strategies when only part of the data is labelled. The variational autoencoder (VAE) learns latent representations in a probabilistic manner (Kingma & Welling, 2013). Examples from the literature that utilise VAEs for SA include aspect-level classification of user reviews (Fu et al., 2019), multi-task learning for improved generalisation (Lu, Zhao, Yin, Yang, & Li, 2018) and a semi-supervised variant that makes use of the labels in the decoder to boost accuracy (W. Xu, Sun, Deng, & Tan, 2017). Winner-take-all autoencoders (Makhzani & Frey, 2015) enforce sparsity by having the neurons in the embedding layer compete for contributing to the output. Maitra and Sarkhel (2018) used a shallow winner-take-all autoencoder to classify social media texts in multiple languages as overtly, covertly or non-aggressive.

Denoising autoencoders (DA) make the representation more robust by corrupting the input with noise and learning to reconstruct a clean version. A stacked denoising autoencoder (SDA) combines multiple denoising autoencoders, with the latent representation of one AE acting as input to the next one (Vincent, Larochelle, Bengio, & Manzagol, 2008). This allows for learning potent representations while keeping the number of parameters small, saving computational resources and reducing the amount of training data needed to prevent overfitting. During training, the layers are tuned one by one. (Sagha, Cummins, & Schuller, 2017).

Conventional autoencoders have recently become less relevant for generating word embeddings, as NLP researchers increasingly favour the new Transformer networks, which are discussed separately in this chapter's main section on deep learning. The following subsections present several popular open-source frameworks that provide pre-trained word embeddings. For tasks that involve small datasets, pre-trained embeddings learned on large corpora can help mitigate the problem of encountering unseen words at test time (Hsu & Ku, 2018).

Word2vec

Word2vec[1] was introduced by Mikolov, Chen, Corrado, and Dean (2013). It is an extension of the continuous Skip-gram model developed by Mikolov, Sutskever, Chen, Corrado, and Dean (2013). Skip-gram is a log-linear model; the choice of linearity is motivated by training efficiency being valued over additional complexity in the representations. It analyses a sequence of training words T and for each word w, attempts to predict both previous and subsequent words within a context c. The objective that Skip-Gram attempts to maximise is an average log probability given by:

$$\frac{1}{T}\sum_{t=1}^{T}\sum_{-c\leq j\leq c, j\neq 0}\log p\left(w_{t+j} \mid w_t\right) \tag{5}$$

The conditional probability is formulated as a softmax function, which makes the computation of the gradient inefficient for large vocabularies. Word2vec extends Skip-gram by optimising the algorithm, which allows training on larger corpora. This is done by simplifying the softmax function, as well as discarding frequently occurring words that carry little information, e.g. function and conjunction words such as “the” and “and”. The authors of Word2vec also demonstrated that phrases can be encoded by the model and that the linear properties of the learned word vectors allow reasoning based on simple arithmetic. For example, the representation of the word “queen” could be found by the following expression:

$$v_{queen} = v_{king} - v_{man} + v_{woman} \tag{6}$$

GloVe

GloVe[2] (Global Vectors) was derived by Pennington, Socher, and Manning (2014). The name reflects that global statistics of a corpus are captured. It is a log-bilinear model with a weighted least-squares objective function for unsupervised learning of word representations. The objective function that GloVe attempts to minimise is given by:

$$J = \sum_{i,j=1}^{V} f\left(X_{ij}\right)\left(w_i^T \tilde{w}_j + b_i + b_j - \log X_{ij}\right) \tag{7}$$

GloVe operates on word co-occurrence counts, i.e. on a matrix X whose entries show how many times a word appears in the context of other words. The set of all words together forms the vocabulary V. The word learning of GloVe is based on the ratios of word co-occurrence probabilities, which compared to the raw probabilities are better at distinguishing relevant words (Pennington et al., 2014).

fastText

fastText[3] is an open-source library for text representation learning and text classifier learning provided by Facebook AI Research. It is based on the works of Bojanowski, Grave, Joulin, and Mikolov (2017) and Joulin, Grave, Bojanowski, and Mikolov (2017). In fastText, instead of assigning a fixed vector to each word, words are modelled as bags of character n-grams. For text classification, simple linear models are used, whose performance on SA tasks has been shown to be comparable with deep architectures while being lightweight and faster to train.

THE CURRENT STATE OF DEEP LEARNING-BASED SA

In this section, a number of key concepts and methods for deep learning are presented.

Advantages and Applications of Deep Learning

Deep learning is a popular form of machine learning that has allowed researchers to achieve breakthroughs in many fields, including computer vision (Krizhevsky, Sutskever, & Hinton, 2012) and speech recognition (Hinton et al., 2012). This part of the chapter will introduce key concepts of deep learning.

Deep learning is based on deep neural networks, i.e. models which contain hidden layers. This multi-layered architecture allows deep models to overcome a shortcoming of conventional machine learning algorithms such as SVM, which is the requirement of feature engineering. Those algorithms needed a suitable feature extractor to turn raw data into representations they could learn from, which required considerable expertise and effort from the researcher (LeCun, Bengio, & Hinton, 2015).

On the other hand, deep models can adjust their internal states to find appropriate representations without the need for extensive preprocessing of the data. They are capable of learning advanced concepts through a stack of modules connected by nonlinear functions. Each module processes the features extracted by the previous ones, which leads to the development of increasingly complex representations. Bengio,

Courville, and Vincent (2013) provide an in-depth discussion of desirable properties of representations and how various deep learning methods can be leveraged for representation learning.

Common Network Architectures

Models based on deep learning have the capability of detecting intricate patterns in data and continue to produce state of the art results in many fields. The following subsections introduce important architectures and techniques and examples of their application to sentiment analysis.

Recurrent Neural Network (RNN)

Recurrent Neural Networks are capable of processing sequential inputs, which makes them attractive for handling data of varying length, e.g. speech or text. An RNN makes use of its hidden units to maintain a state vector, which stores information on the previous elements in the input sequence (LeCun et al., 2015). Thus, the RNN can remember the inputs it has seen. The network can be unfolded along the temporal dimension, effectively making it a deep feedforward architecture, with each unit processing one element in the input sequence and generating an output and a state, which feeds into the next unit. The equations for an RNN are as follows:

$$h_t = \sigma\left(U^h x_t + W^h h_{t-1} + b^h\right), \tag{8}$$

$$o_t = softmax(W^0 h_t + b^0) \tag{9}$$

With h, x, o being the hidden state, input and output respectively and subscripts denoting the time step. U and W are parameter matrices, and b are bias vectors. An illustration of an unfolded RNN can be seen in Figure 2.

Figure 2. Unfolded RNN architecture. Data is processed sequentially, with the hidden state being propagated through time.

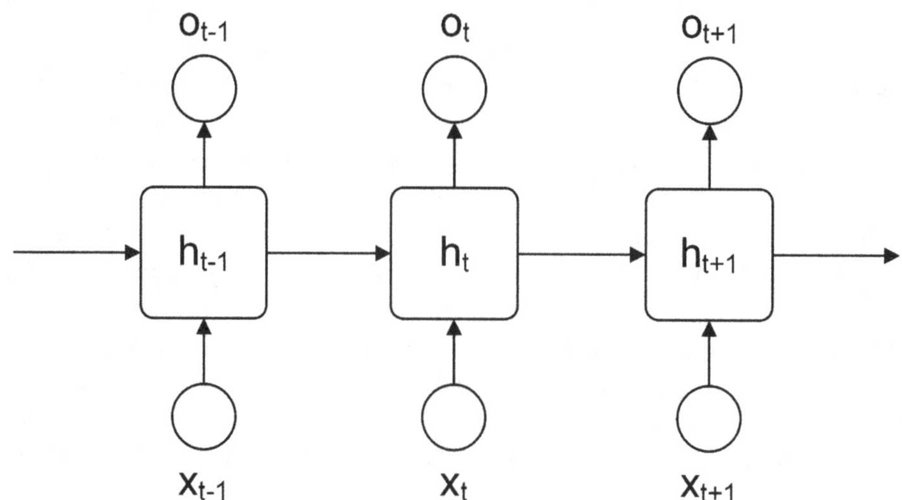

In some cases, it can be desirable to use both past and future information contained in a sequence. Bidirectional RNNs achieve this by combining two RNNs, with each net reading the sequence in a different direction. They have been extensively used in NLP, including in sentiment analysis (Tian, Rong, Shi, Liu, & Xiong, 2018).

Plain RNNs suffer from a common problem in training deep architectures with backpropagation, which is that gradients either tend to zero or become very large across many layers. These effects are known as the vanishing gradient problem and exploding gradient problem, respectively. They make it difficult to learn relationships across large time intervals.

To address this problem, Hochreiter and Schmidhuber (1997) proposed an RNN variant called Long Short-Term Memory (LSTM). In this architecture, the standard recurrent cells in the hidden layers are replaced with memory blocks designed to maintain information (Graves, 2012). The original LSTM is built around a self-recurrent internal structure called a constant error carousel (CEC), which prevents the error from vanishing. Furthermore, it uses two multiplicative gates to regulate its connections: the input gate restricts information entering the cell, and the output gate controls information leaving the cell. Gers, Schmidhuber, and Cummins (2000) improved the LSTM by adding a third gate, named forget gate, in place of the fixed CEC connection. This allows the network to reset its previously learned state, which solves the problem of internal states growing too large over long sequences. The LSTM cell can now be described by the following equations:

$$i_t = \sigma\left(W^i x_t + U^i h_{t-1} + b^i\right), \tag{10}$$

$$f_t = \sigma\left(W^f x_t + U^f h_{t-1} + b^f\right), \tag{11}$$

$$o_t = \sigma\left(W^o x_t + U^o h_{t-1} + b^o\right), \tag{12}$$

$$g_t = \tanh\left(W^g x_t + U^g h_{t-1} + b^g\right), \tag{13}$$

$$c_t = f_t \cdot c_{t-1} + i_t \cdot g_t, \tag{14}$$

$$h_t = o_t \bullet \tanh(c_t) \tag{15}$$

Here c_t is the cell state at time t.

Cho, van Merriënboer, Bahdanau, and Bengio (2014) introduced the Gated Recurrent Network (GRU), which simplifies the LSTM cells. The hidden cells contain two gates: a reset gate which makes the cell forget its hidden state and replace it with the current input, and an update gate which controls the contribution of the previous hidden state to the next time step.

An example of the application of RNNs to sentiment analysis is the work of D. Tang, Qin, and Liu (2015). They performed document-level SA on four large datasets containing IMDB and Yelp reviews, using two gated RNN models with adaptive sentence modelling.

Convolutional Neural Network (CNN)

Convolutional Neural Networks process data in the form of arrays (e.g. videos, images, audio spectrograms and word embeddings) through multiple layers that extract hierarchical features. This is achieved by a combination of convolutional layers and pooling layers.

A convolutional layer makes use of arrays of weights called filter banks. A filter slides across the input data, computing a weighted sum at each position. This results in a new array called a feature map, whose size can be adjusted by zero-padding the input data or changing the filter dimensions and stride. A convolutional layer can construct multiple feature maps by applying different filters. The results are passed through a nonlinear activation, e.g. a (potentially "leaky") rectified linear unit (ReLU). The idea behind the use of these filters is to detect certain features in the input data by matching it to the pattern specified by the filter. For a visual recognition system, those features could be simple lines or edges in the first layers, which are then combined to form objects of increasing complexity. The name convolutional layer is due to the fact that the sliding filter effectively performs a discrete convolution of the input.

Pooling layers merge the information contained in neighbouring cells of a feature map. Implementations of CNNs commonly use max-pooling layers, which will retain only the maximum value of the features in a patch, resulting in a smaller map. Pooling has the advantage of reducing the dimension of the internal representations, as well as introducing an invariance to small shifts and distortions (LeCun et al., 2015).

In addition to sequences of convolutional layers, nonlinearities and pooling for feature extraction, CNNs also incorporate fully connected layers to combine the features for classification. The complete network can be trained through backpropagation. Figure 3 illustrates an example of a CNN architecture.

Figure 3. CNN architecture. A stack of convolutional and pooling layers is used to extract features, which are combined by fully connected layers for classification.

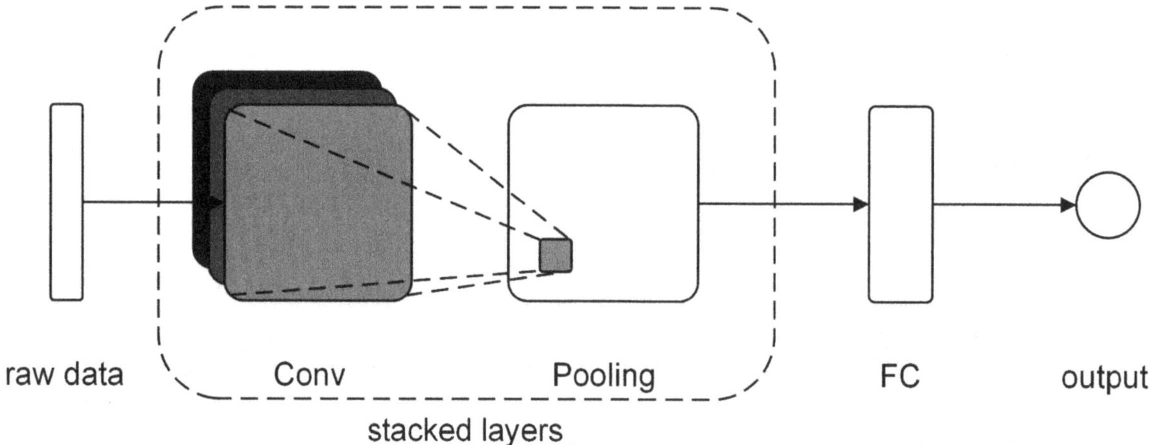

The breakthrough of CNNs came in the field of computer vision in 2012, when a model by Krizhevsky et al. (2012) won the ImageNet Large Scale Visual Recognition Challenge (ILSVRC) with a top-5 test error rate of 15.3%, which was more than 10% ahead of the second-best entry. CNNs can also be applied to sentiment analysis of text. Kim (2014) showed that a simple CNN which processed embeddings generated by word2vec could perform very well in sentence classification, even improving upon the state of the art at the time.

Hybrid Network

A hybrid network includes components from multiple basic neural network architectures. An example of this is combinations of convolutional and recurrent nets (C-RNNs). As shown previously, CNNs are useful for feature extraction in a hierarchical manner, while RNNs are well suited for processing sequential data and capturing important aspects in memory. A C-RNN allows for the combination of these advantages by processing word embeddings through convolutions and feeding the resulting features to a recurrent network.

Hybrid models are a widely used technique in SA. X. Wang, Jiang, and Luo (2016) performed SA on short texts using combinations of word2vec and randomly initialised word vectors and CNN-GRU/CNN-LSTM models, finding that the joint architecture outperformed CNN and RNN alone. More recently, Hassan and Mahmood (2018) proposed a C-RNN architecture that uses recurrent layers instead of pooling layers in order to overcome the problem of CNNs extracting features locally at each stage and thus needing to be very deep to capture long-term dependencies.

The previously discussed methods can be enhanced through a concept called attention, which will be introduced next.

Capturing Context Through Attention

When sentiment analysis is performed on a text, some words will matter more than others. To determine the sentiment towards a certain target requires knowing the context, i.e., relevant words in the rest of the sequence. When an encoder attempts to model those relationships implicitly, as, e.g., RNNs do when compressing the entire input sequence into a fixed-length representation vector, this can lead to problems with long-term dependencies in very long texts. What is needed is a way for the network to learn how to focus on specific elements of the input, as a human reader would do. This is achieved through the attention mechanism.

Attention was first proposed by Bahdanau, Cho, and Bengio (2014), who used it for the purpose of neural machine translation. A common approach to that task is to use an encoder-decoder structure, with the encoder creating a high-level representation of the input sentence and the decoder turning it into an output sentence in a different language. This model was expanded by an attention component which taught it how to align certain words in the input and output sequences, leading to improved performance in English-French translation.

A general way of describing attention is as a function that takes a query Q and a set of key-value pairs (K_i, V_i) and computes a weighted sum of the values based on a comparison between the query and the keys (Vaswani et al., 2017). Thus, assuming an input sequence of hidden states $(h_1,\ldots,h_T)$ as the keys, a context vector c_i is computed by:

$$\alpha_{ij} = \frac{\exp\left(e_{ij}\right)}{\sum_{k=1}^{T} \exp\left(e_{ik}\right)}, \tag{16}$$

$$c_i = \sum_{j=1}^{T} \alpha_{ij} h_i \tag{17}$$

Here, e_{ij} is an alignment model that functions as a measure of similarity between the query and a key. It is used to compute the weight α_{ij} of each value through a softmax function, and the context vector is the sum of those contributions (Bahdanau et al., 2014). Figure 4 illustrates the concept of attention.

Figure 4. Dot product attention. The dot product is used as a similarity measure between query and keys. A softmax function computes the attention weights of the values, which are then summed into the output.

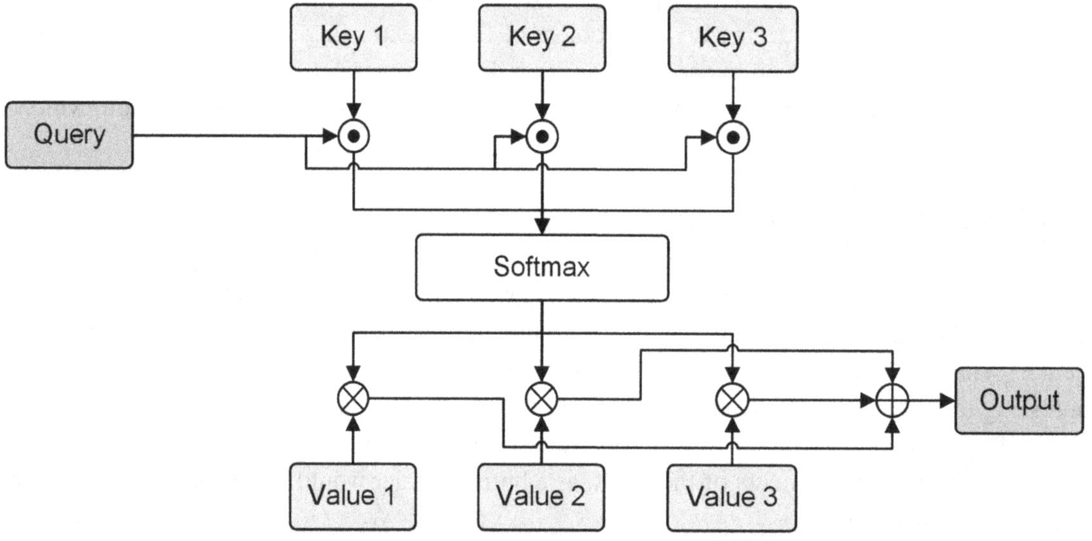

Attention has become a popular method in sentiment analysis. Works that use attention for aspect-level SA include Q. Liu, Zhang, Zeng, Huang, and Wu (2018), Chen, Sun, Bing, and Yang (2017), and D. Tang, Qin, and Liu (2016). It has been combined with RNNs (Ran, 2019), (G. Liu & Guo, 2019), CNNs (J. Du, Gui, Xu, & He, 2018), (Wu, Cai, Li, Xu, & Leung, 2018) and employed in hybrid networks (Zhu, Gao, Zhang, Liu, & Zhang, 2018). Deng, Jing, Yu, and Sun (2019) used an LSTM with sparse self-attention to construct a sentiment lexicon.

Zichao Yang et al. (2016) proposed a hierarchical attention network (HAN) for document classification that applied attention at word and sentence level. Z. Liu et al. (2019) used HAN for sentence representation learning. N. Xu (2017) combined a text HAN with an image HAN for public sentiment classification. Another work by Niu and Hou (2017) used hierarchical attention with bidirectional LSTM for text modelling. Stappen et al. (2019) employed HAN for detecting sentiment change in transcripts of interviews.

A significant development in the fields of SA and NLP in general that has been enabled by attention was the invention and subsequent popularisation of Transformer networks.

Transformer Networks

Vaswani et al. (2017) introduced a novel type of networks known as Transformers, which do not require recurrent or convolutional layers. Instead, those networks rely on self-attention, i.e. computing attention between all the elements in the input sequence, and make use of multiple structures called attention heads for fine-grained analysis (G. Tang, Müller, Rios, & Sennrich, 2018). The architecture of a Transformer is illustrated in Figure 5, based on Vaswani et al. (2017). The Transformer consists of an encoder and a decoder block, followed by a linear layer and a softmax layer. The encoder and decoder are composed of N blocks, with each block containing multi-head attention and a feedforward network, as well as residual connections and layer normalisation. Positional encoding is added to the input and output embeddings to allow the model to understand word order.

Figure 5. Transformer architecture

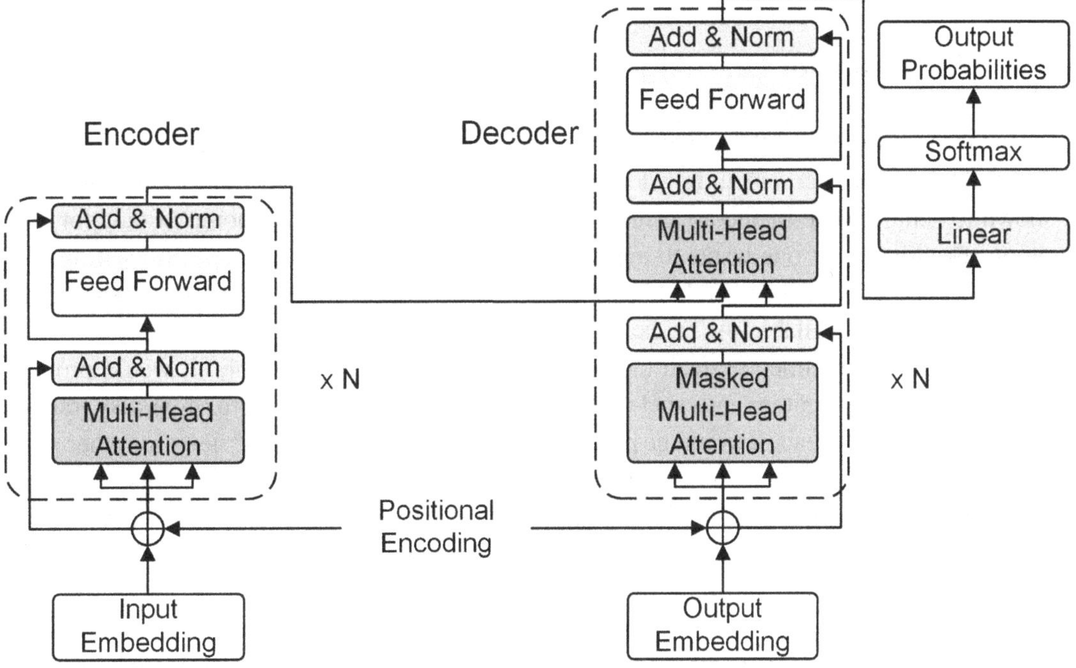

Recently, the work by Devlin, Chang, Lee, and Toutanova (2018) on transformers has led to a major breakthrough in NLP. They introduced a framework named Bidirectional Encoder Representations from Transformers (BERT). BERT involves two steps:

1. **Pre-training:** BERT is pre-trained on a document-level corpus using unsupervised learning on two tasks: A Masked Language Model (MLM) randomly masks input tokens in order to teach BERT to predict words based on their context. In addition, Next Sentence Prediction (NSP) is used to learn the relationships between sentences.
2. **Fine-tuning**: The pre-training is used to initialise models for the downstream tasks that BERT should solve. Each model is then fine-tuned separately through end-to-end learning with task-specific data.

The main contribution of BERT is its improvement upon previous unsupervised representation learning methods by using a bidirectional architecture to generate more powerful representations. Models created with BERT showed excellent performance, surpassing the state of the art in eleven NLP tasks by wide margins, including a 7.7% improvement on the GLUE, a benchmark task for natural language understanding (A. Wang et al., 2018). This has led to great popularity of this type of models in the NLP research community.

Among many other applications, Transformers have also been used for sentiment analysis. Q. Zhang, Lu, Wang, Zhu, and Liu (2019) introduced interactive multi-head attention (IMAN) pre-trained on BERT to achieve new state of the art results in aspect-level SA. Jiang, Wu, Shi, and Zhang (2019) proposed a Transformer-based memory network (TF-MN) for sentiment-based Q&A. Cheng et al. (2019) introduced a VAE framework which uses Transformers as encoder and decoder. Gao, Feng, Song, and Wu (2019) used BERT for targeted sentiment classification.

Adapting With Transfer Learning

As shown in the introduction to this chapter, sentiment analysis has many academic and business applications, but still faces challenges, including domain dependence. While deep learning-based methods have been shown to achieve state-of-the-art results, they require a considerable amount of data for training. A common scenario is that one wants to apply a deep learning approach to a specific setting, but it is not feasible to collect and label enough data to train a model. However, there is a large, labelled dataset from a different setting available. As an example of this problem consider the classification of product reviews depending on sentiment. Given the wide variety of products available, it would probably be prohibitively expensive to gather and label a sufficiently large amount of data to separately train a classifier for each product. Instead, it would be preferable to make use of existing reviews for other products. Simply applying a model trained on that data to the new problem will likely yield worse performance, since the same words may have different meaning or polarity depending on the subject of the text (Save & Shekokar, 2017). Because of these issues, a new research field has emerged that combines SA methods with transfer learning (R. Liu, Shi, Ji, & Jia, 2019).

Definitions of Transfer Learning

In their survey paper, Pan and Yang (2010) present a useful categorisation of transfer learning and its relation to other fields. They define machine learning problems in terms of domains D and tasks T. A domain D consists of a feature space spanning all possible features X and a marginal probability distribution $P(X)$. A task T encompasses a label space Y and a function $f(\bullet)$:

$$D = \{X, P(X)\} \tag{18}$$

$$T = \{Y, f(\bullet)\} \tag{19}$$

In transfer learning, as opposed to traditional machine learning, the domains and/or tasks of the source and target settings are different. The survey paper distinguishes the following variants: Inductive transfer learning (the domains are identical, and the tasks are different), Transductive transfer learning (the domains are different, and the tasks are identical) and Unsupervised transfer learning (domains and tasks may be different and labels are not available in each case). In addition, four categories are presented based on what is being transferred: instances, feature representations, model parameters and relational knowledge. Weiss, Khoshgoftaar, and Wang (2016) follow this categorisation in their survey on recent transfer learning methods, while also distinguishing between homogeneous (same feature space in source and target) and heterogeneous (different feature spaces) transfer learning approaches.

For the purpose of this chapter, the focus is placed on transductive transfer learning. This problem is closely related to domain adaptation, and the terms transfer learning and domain adaptation are used somewhat interchangeably in NLP (Pan & Yang, 2010). Within the context of sentiment analysis, the term cross-domain sentiment classification is also commonly used in the literature. Its definition is equivalent to that of transductive transfer learning. A recent survey on the topic of cross-domain transfer learning can be found in R. Liu et al. (2019). Next, several transfer methods are presented along with examples of their applications to SA.

Methods of Transfer

Structural Correspondence Learning (SCL) was introduced by Blitzer, McDonald, and Pereira (2006). It is a feature transfer algorithm that relies on domain-independent features called pivots to learn correspondences between features in the source and target domains. Those pivots are then used to map source and target features into a common latent space, making SCL an example of a symmetric feature transfer algorithm (Weiss et al., 2016). SCL only considers one-to-one mappings between features. N. Li, Zhai, Zhang, and Liu (2017) extended SCL to include one-to-many mappings and used it for cross-lingual SA, with English as the source and Chinese as the target. Spectral Feature Alignment (SFA) was proposed by Pan, Ni, Sun, Yang, and Chen (2010). This algorithm creates clusters of source and target features in a common latent space. It constructs a bipartite graph, using domain-independent features as a bridge to bring corresponding domain-specific features closer together. The pivots are selected by computing the mutual information between features and domains. SFA does not require labelled data in the target domain. Recently, Hao et al. (2019) introduced CrossWord, which makes use of stochastic word embedding to learn an alignment between domains.

Autoencoders have been successfully applied to transfer learning as well. Glorot, Bordes, and Bengio (2011) extracted a high-level shared representation across multiple domains (Amazon product reviews) in an unsupervised manner with SDAs. The benefit of this approach is that is scales well with larger amounts of data. Zhou, Zhu, He, and Hu (2016) used SDAs to learn language-independent features and perform cross-lingual SA from English to Chinese. Long, Wang, Cao, Sun, and Yu (2016) proposed a framework combining unsupervised pre-training with denoising autoencoders and supervised fine-tuning with deep neural nets to improve transferability.

Ganin et al. (2016) introduced Domain-Adversarial Neural Network (DANN) to improve upon existing autoencoder-based methods. DANN is an augmentation technique for feedforward networks, allowing them to learn features that are both discriminative and invariant to domain shift while being trainable with backpropagation.

Yu and Jiang (2016) apply the pivot prediction concept of SCL to neural networks. They introduce two auxiliary binary tasks to detect the presence of positive and negative domain-independent words in a sentence. The network is then jointly trained to learn both the feature embedding and the classifier at the same time, outperforming several state-of-the-art methods.

Attention models can also be applied to cross-domain SA. Z. Li, Zhang, Wei, Wu, and Yang (2017) introduced the Adversarial Memory Network (AMN) as an improvement over previous deep learning-based methods in terms of interpretability of the pivots. Z. Li, Wei, Zhang, and Yang (2018) developed the Hierarchical Attention Transfer Network (HATN). HATN consists of two subsets named P-Net and NP-Net. The P-Net discovers pivots, and the NP-Net performs feature alignment using the pivots as a bridge. The advantage of this method over algorithms like SCL and SFA is that the pivots are selected automatically. CCHAN (Manshu & Xuemin, 2019) is another combined attention model, consisting of a cloze task network (CTN) performing the word embedding task and a convolutional HAN (CHAN) for sentiment classification. The two networks are jointly trained in an end-to-end fashion. The Hierarchical Attention Network with Prior knowledge information (HANP) was further recently proposed by Manshu and Bing (2019). It adds prior knowledge of the contextual meaning of sentiment words via a sentiment dictionary match (SDM) layer to identify domain-dependent and domain-independent features simultaneously.

Yin, Liu, Zhu, Li, and Wang (2019) introduced Capsule Net with Identifying Transferable Knowledge (CITK). This method includes domain-invariant knowledge extracted with a lexicon-based method in the network to help with pivot identification and generalisation.

Transformers have also shown promising results for cross-domain applications due to their capability of learning high-level feature representations. A recent example is the work by Myagmar, Li, and Kimura (2019), applying transformers to Amazon product reviews.

SOLUTIONS AND RECOMMENDATIONS

This section presents solutions and makes recommendations for readers interesting in applying state-of-the-art models to SA problems. First, a number of popular datasets and challenges are described.

Datasets and Tasks

IMDB Dataset

The IMDB dataset[4] (Maas et al., 2011) contains 50000 movie reviews that are annotated as positive or negative. The reviews are highly polarised, and the data is split evenly between positive and negative reviews.

Yelp Dataset

The Yelp review dataset[5] (X. Zhang, Zhao, & LeCun, 2015) was created from the ongoing Yelp Dataset Challenge. It encompasses two tasks: predicting the review polarity and predicting the number of stars given by the user. The dataset is evenly split between classes, with 280000 training and 19000 test samples for each polarity and 130000 training and 10000 test samples for each star rating.

Stanford Sentiment Treebank

The Stanford Sentiment Treebank (SST) dataset[6] (Socher et al., 2013) contains 215154 phrases parsed from 11855 sentences that were extracted from movie reviews. It provides both coarse-grained (binary) and fine-grained (five points) annotations.

SemEval-2017 Task 4

Task 4 of the International Workshop on Semantic Evaluation (Rosenthal, Farra, & Nakov, 2017) is concerned with SA on Twitter. The task was held yearly since 2013 and continuously expanded. The 2017 task added Arabic as a second language to English. There were five subtasks: polarity classification of single tweets, targeted polarity classification of single tweets in two and five classes, estimating the distribution of a set of tweets across two and five classes.

Applying State of the Art Models

The current state of the art in SA, as well as NLP in general, is based on Transformer networks. This means that pre-trained word embeddings generated by GloVe, Word2vec and fastText are no longer recommended. In 2018, all competitors in the SocialNLP EmotionX Challenge (Hsu & Ku, 2018) used one of those toolkits. By 2019, all the best contributions were utilizing pre-trained embeddings generated with BERT.

As discussed in the previous section, BERT provides powerful text representations through pre-training on a large document corpus. Versions of BERT trained for various languages and of different sizes (named BERT-Base and BERT-Large) have been made publicly available[7]. Thus, the recommended workflow for readers interested in using BERT for SA is to obtain a suitable pre-trained model, e.g. BERT-Large in English, and then further adapt it to their specific task.

An instructive example of how this tuning can be achieved is given in the work of C. Sun, Qiu, Xu, and Huang (2019). They outline three steps for improving the performance of BERT-Base and BERT-Large:

1. **Further Pre-training:** BERT is pre-trained on a large collection of documents. In a subsequent step, additional pre-training on within-task or in-domain data is performed.
2. **Multi-Task Learning:** The model is trained on multiple tasks simultaneously, with the tasks sharing layers except for the final classification layer. This allows knowledge from different tasks to be shared.
3. **Fine-Tuning on the target task:** The model is further trained to adapt it to a specific task.

Following this approach and testing a number of fine-tuning strategies, including the layer-wise optimisation approach from Howard and Ruder (2018), (C. Sun et al.) developed BERT_large+ITPT, which achieved new state-of-the-art results on a number of text processing tasks, including SA. Specifically, the model obtained test error rates of 4,21% on the IMDB dataset and 1.81% and 28.62% on the coarse-grained and fine-grained tasks of the Yelp dataset, respectively.

Transformer-based methods are continuing to evolve. Many researchers develop variants of BERT, such as RoBERTa (Y. Liu et al., 2019), which further optimises the training process. Recently, Zhilin Yang et al. (2019) introduced XLNet, which replaces the autoencoding paradigm of BERT with generalised autoregression. XLNet incorporates ideas from the Transformer-XL (Dai et al., 2019), an autoregressive model which improves upon the standard Transformer by better handling long-term dependencies. The advantages of XLNet over BERT are that it predicts permutations of a sequence, allowing it to learn bidirectional context more effectively and that it does not rely on masking, which solves several inherent problems of BERT, such as the assumption that masked tokens are independent.

XLNet further improved upon the state of the art in a number of language understanding tasks including SA, yielding test error rates of 3.20% on IMDB, 1.37% on coarse-grained Yelp and 27.05% on fine-grained Yelp, as well as 3.2% on SST.

To conclude this section, readers are recommended to use the latest developments in Transformer models for SA. While XLNet has outperformed BERT in a number of popular SA tasks and may become the new standard due to its powerful permutation-based language modelling, BERT variants like RoBERTa could still be useful depending on the problem to be solved. Thus, the readers are encouraged to experiment with these models while observing further developments in the field.

FUTURE RESEARCH DIRECTIONS

NLP in general and sentiment analysis in particular are already being used in many business applications, as discussed in the introduction to this chapter. The amount and diversity of available data continue to grow, which motivates the use of deep learning techniques due to their potent feature extraction capabilities. This section outlines a number of trends and promising research opportunities.

Data Augmentation

One open issue is the need for compensating class imbalance, i.e. the number of instances of each class not being evenly distributed in a labelled dataset. Class imbalance affects many datasets collected in realistic settings, and often a minority class will be of great interest. This is problematic since many classifiers, including deep learning methods, will exhibit a bias towards the majority class (Johnson & Khoshgoftaar, 2019).

Data augmentation is a data-based solution to this problem. It enriches the dataset with additional examples of minority instances. While such augmentation can be easily applied to image data, e.g. by adding noise, rotating or mirroring, it is less straightforward for NLP, as the resulting text sample still needs to make sense. Consequentially, this technique has received comparatively little attention in textual SA. Recently, however, a promising approach for applying data augmentation to SA has been presented by Rizos, Hemker, and Schuller (2019), who use it for improving online hate speech classification. The strategies employed in the paper include: replacing words with synonyms which are discovered through similarities of their embeddings, shifting the positions of words within the sentence, and generating new text through sequential prediction with RNNs or transformers.

Zero-Shot Learning

Aside from improving training through data augmentation, an interesting strategy for dealing with missing data is to apply zero-shot learning techniques. The goal of zero-shot learning, also referred to as zero-data learning, is to recognise classes at test time that were not seen during training (Larochelle, Erhan, & Bengio, 2008), i.e. there were no instances of those classes for the model to learn from. In the related case where only a few instances are present in the training data, methods are commonly referred to as one-shot or few-shot learning.

Zero-shot learning is increasingly used for large-scale classification problems where annotating all classes extensively is not possible. For the field of visual object detection, there already exist numerous benchmark datasets such as Animals with Attributes (AWA) (Lampert, Nickisch, & Harmeling, 2014). Recently, Xian, Lampert, Schiele, and Akata (2019) published an overview of the state of the art in zero-shot learning, finding a proliferation of approaches but a lack of comparability and flaws of methodology, and introduced a novel dataset called Animals with Attributes 2 (AWA2), along with proposing a standardised evaluation procedure.

Zero-shot learning techniques frequently rely on knowledge in a semantic embedding space (Norouzi et al., 2014), (Z. Zhang & Saligrama, 2015). Applying such techniques to NLP and SA tasks in particular is a promising research direction.

Adversarial Learning

The concept of adversarial networks was introduced by Goodfellow et al. (2014). In a generative adversarial network (GAN), two networks, named generator and discriminator, compete with each other, with the generator attempting to produce samples resembling that of a target distribution and the discriminator attempting to differentiate between real and artificial samples. A basic GAN architecture is depicted in Figure 6.

The concept of adversarial training has been applied to many disciplines, including sentiment analysis. Numerous works make use of adversarial networks for cross-domain sentiment classification (Y. Zhang, Barzilay, & Jaakkola, 2017), (Duan, Zhou, Jing, Zhang, & Chen, 2018), (W. Liu & Fu, 2018). In addition, adversarial networks can be used in a generative way to change the style of sentences, outperforming previous approaches based on encoder-decoder architectures (Choi, Choi, Park, & Lee, 2019), (John, Mou, Bahuleyan, & Vechtomova, 2019). While these results are promising, adversarial networks applied to text and speech have yet to reach the same levels of performance as in image generation (Han, Zhang, Cummins, & Schuller, 2019).

Transfer Learning

An emerging trend that is certain to play a major role in the future is the proliferation and improvement of transfer learning methods. This will allow businesses to leverage existing knowledge in the form of models and datasets for new applications, which could significantly speed up time to market and reduce development costs. In terms of research opportunities, cross-lingual transfer is attractive, since most studies on sentiment analysis focus on English documents.

Figure 6. GAN architecture. The generator creates a fake sample mimicking the training data. The discriminator attempts to tell real from fake samples. Both networks are trained against each other until an equilibrium is reached.

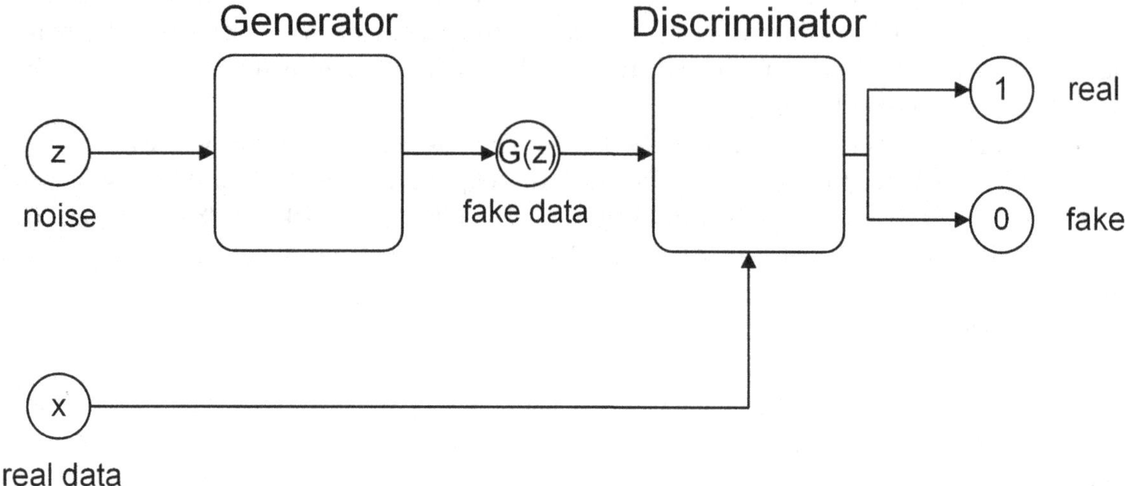

Explainable AI

While deep learning-based models have achieved impressive results, they are frequently applied in a black-box manner, i.e., no information is given about how those systems reach a conclusion. This is a consequence of the massive datasets processed and the highly complex features derived from them by the deep learning algorithms, which may be difficult or impossible for humans to understand. This lack of transparency limits the effectiveness of such systems and is the motivation for the development of explainable AI (XAI). XAI aims to create models that can maintain high levels of performance while allowing humans to understand and trust their decisions (Mathews, 2019).

XAI strategies can be classified into two broad categories: model-based (intrinsic) and post-hoc explainability (Murdoch, Singh, Kumbier, Abbasi-Asl, & Yu, 2019). Intrinsic approaches aim to make the model itself more explainable, e.g. by reducing its complexity. Post-hoc methods are designed to analyse an existing model. An example of a popular post-hoc framework is LIME (Marco Tulio Ribeiro, Singh, & Guestrin, 2016). Murdoch et al. (2019) formulate three criteria for grading an interpretation: predictive accuracy, descriptive accuracy, and relevancy.

A possible solution for interpretability is the use of attention. (Letarte, Paradis, Giguère, & Laviolette, 2018) introduced a self-attention network based on the Transformer. They found that visualising the relationships between words found by attention helped explain differences in the model's behaviour between topic classification and sentiment analysis. (Peters, Niculae, & Martins, 2018) demonstrated how regularised attention can be used to create sparse, ordered structures in the layers of deep neural networks, which benefits interpretability.

As automated solutions spread and become increasingly complex, explainable AI will continue to become more relevant, both as a means for building trust with the customers employing a system and as a way for the business offering that system to improve performance.

Defending Against Adversarial Attacks

On a related note, an important area of research that is starting to be explored is the robustness of NLP algorithms. Complex classifiers, while being powerful pattern detectors, are also prone to changing their predictions based on small perturbations in the input data. This weakness has been shown to be exploitable through so-called adversarial attacks. The attacker designs manipulated instances of input data (adversarial samples), which are misclassified by the targeted model. Recently, M. T. Ribeiro, Singh, and Guestrin (2018) demonstrated how to apply this concept to NLP, using semantically equivalent adversarial rules (SEARs) to construct adversarial examples from text while maintaining the semantic content. Given these vulnerabilities, further investigation into adversarial attacks in order to improve models and make them safer to use is a promising line of research.

Multimodal Sentiment Analysis

Another interesting research direction is to perform SA based on multiple modalities, e.g. text, audio and visual data from videos. This will allow for a more robust sentiment detection, as the model can combine information across modalities for decision making. A recent work on cross-domain sentiment analysis that makes use of Bag-of-Words features derived from text, speech and facial expressions is (Cummins et al., 2018).

CONCLUSION

This chapter has introduced sentiment analysis as an important topic in natural language processing. It has highlighted numerous business and academic applications, including customer analytics, financial market predictions and estimating public sentiment from social media posts, and provided a categorisation of sentiment analysis approaches. Deep learning was presented as a useful collection of methods to extract information from increasingly large amounts of unstructured data. The basic architectures of CNNs and RNNs were introduced, as well as their combination into hybrid networks. Current trends and state-of-the-art methods were explored, covering attention, transfer learning and Transformer networks. The challenges of explainable AI, data augmentation, zero-shot learning, adversarial learning. the threat of adversarial attacks and the potential of multimodal analysis were explained and highlighted as opportunities for future research.

ACKNOWLEDGMENT

This research was supported by the BMW Group.

REFERENCES

Bahdanau, D., Cho, K., & Bengio, Y. (2014, September 1). *Neural Machine Translation by Jointly Learning to Align and Translate*. Retrieved from https://arxiv.org/pdf/1409.0473v7

Balaji, P., Nagaraju, O., & Haritha, D. (2017). Levels of sentiment analysis and its challenges: A literature review. In *Proceedings of the 2017 International Conference on Big Data Analytics and Computational Intelligence (ICBDAC)* (pp. 436–439). IEEE. 10.1109/ICBDACI.2017.8070879

Bechara, A., Damasio, H., & Damasio, A. R. (2000). Emotion, decision making and the orbitofrontal cortex. *Cerebral Cortex (New York, N.Y.)*, *10*(3), 295–307. doi:10.1093/cercor/10.3.295 PMID:10731224

Bengio, Y., Courville, A., & Vincent, P. (2013). Representation Learning: A Review and New Perspectives. *IEEE Transactions on Pattern Analysis and Machine Intelligence*, *35*(8), 1798–1828. doi:10.1109/TPAMI.2013.50 PMID:23787338

Blitzer, J., McDonald, R., & Pereira, F. (2006). Domain Adaptation with Structural Correspondence Learning. In *EMNLP '06, Proceedings of the 2006 Conference on Empirical Methods in Natural Language Processing* (pp. 120–128). Association for Computational Linguistics. doi:10.3115/1610075.1610094

Bojanowski, P., Grave, E., Joulin, A., & Mikolov, T. (2017). Enriching Word Vectors with Subword Information. *Transactions of the Association for Computational Linguistics*, *5*, 135–146. doi:10.1162/tacl_a_00051

Chen, P., Sun, Z., Bing, L., & Yang, W. (2017). Recurrent Attention Network on Memory for Aspect Sentiment Analysis. In *Proceedings of the 2017 Conference on Empirical Methods in Natural Language Processing* (pp. 452–461). Copenhagen, Denmark: Association for Computational Linguistics. 10.18653/v1/D17-1047

Cheng, X., Xu, W., & Wang, T., Chu, W., Huang, W., Chen, K., & Hu, J. (2019). Variational Semi-Supervised Aspect-Term Sentiment Analysis via Transformer. In *Proceedings of the 23rd Conference on Computational Natural Language Learning (CoNLL)* (pp. 961–969). Hong Kong, China: Association for Computational Linguistics. 10.18653/v1/K19-1090

Cho, K., van Merriënboer, B., Bahdanau, D., & Bengio, Y. (2014). On the Properties of Neural Machine Translation: Encoder-Decoder Approaches. In *Proceedings of SSST-8, Eighth Workshop on Syntax, Semantics and Structure in Statistical Translation* (pp. 103–111). Doha, Qatar: Association for Computational Linguistics. 10.3115/v1/W14-4012

Choi, W., Choi, S. J., Park, S., & Lee, S. (2019). Adversarial Style Transfer for Long Sentences. *2019 International Conference on Electronics, Information, and Communication (ICEIC)*. 10.23919/ELINFOCOM.2019.8706482

Christy Daniel, D., & Shyamala, L. (2019). An insight on sentiment analysis research from text using deep learning methods. *International Journal of Innovative Technology and Exploring Engineering*, *8*(10), 2033–2048. doi:10.35940/ijitee.J9316.0881019

Cooper, P. (2019). *28 Twitter Statistics All Marketers Need to Know in 2019*. Retrieved from https://blog.hootsuite.com/twitter-statistics/

Cummins, N., Amiriparian, S., Ottl, S., Gerczuk, M., Schmitt, M., & Schuller, B. (2018). Multimodal Bag-of-Words for Cross Domains Sentiment Analysis. In *ICASSP-2018, Proceedings of the 2018 IEEE International Conference on Acoustics, Speech and Signal Processing (ICASSP)* (pp. 4954–4958). IEEE. 10.1109/ICASSP.2018.8462660

Dai, Z., & Yang, Z., Yang, Y., Carbonell, J., Le, Q., & Salakhutdinov, R. (2019). Transformer-XL: Attentive Language Models beyond a Fixed-Length Context. In *Proceedings of the 57th Annual Meeting of the Association for Computational Linguistics* (pp. 2978–2988). Florence, Italy: Association for Computational Linguistics. 10.18653/v1/P19-1285

Della Pietra, S., Della Pietra, V., & Lafferty, J. (1997). Inducing features of random fields. *IEEE Transactions on Pattern Analysis and Machine Intelligence*, *19*(4), 380–393. doi:10.1109/34.588021

Deng, D., Jing, L., Yu, J., & Sun, S. (2019). Sparse Self-Attention LSTM for Sentiment Lexicon Construction. *IEEE/ACM Transactions on Audio, Speech, and Language Processing*, *27*(11), 1777–1790. doi:10.1109/TASLP.2019.2933326

Desjardins, J. (2019). *What Happens in an Internet Minute in 2019?* Retrieved from https://www.visualcapitalist.com/what-happens-in-an-internet-minute-in-2019/

Devlin, J., Chang, M.-W., Lee, K., & Toutanova, K. (2018). *BERT: Pre-training of Deep Bidirectional Transformers for Language Understanding.* CoRR, abs/1810.04805

Du, C., Tsai, M., & Wang, C. (2019). Beyond Word-level to Sentence-level Sentiment Analysis for Financial Reports. *Proceedings of the 2019 IEEE International Conference on Acoustics, Speech and Signal Processing (ICASSP).* 10.1109/ICASSP.2019.8683085

Du, J., Gui, L., Xu, R., & He, Y. (2018). A Convolutional Attention Model for Text Classification. In X. Huang, J. Jiang, D. Zhao, Y. Feng, & Y. Hong (Eds.), Lecture Notes in Computer Science: Vol. 10619. *Natural Language Processing and Chinese Computing* (pp. 183–195). Springer International Publishing. doi:10.1007/978-3-319-73618-1_16

Duan, X., Zhou, Y., Jing, C., Zhang, L., & Chen, R. (2018). Cross-domain Sentiment Classification Based on Transfer Learning and Adversarial Network. In *Proceedings of the 2018 IEEE 4th International Conference on Computer and Communications (ICCC)* (pp. 2302–2306). IEEE. 10.1109/CompComm.2018.8780771

Ekman, P. (1999). Basic emotions. Handbook of Cognition and Emotion, 98(45-60), 16.

Evgeniou, T., & Pontil, M. (2001). *Support Vector Machines: Theory and Applications* (Vol. 2049). Springer. doi:10.1007/3-540-44673-7_12

Facebook. (2019). *Facebook Reports Second Quarter 2019 Results*. Retrieved from https://investor.fb.com/investor-news/press-release-details/2019/Facebook-Reports-Second-Quarter-2019-Results/default.aspx

Fu, X., Wei, Y., Xu, F., Wang, T., Lu, Y., Li, J., & Huang, J. Z. (2019). Semi-supervised Aspect-level Sentiment Classification Model based on Variational Autoencoder. *Knowledge-Based Systems*, *171*, 81–92. doi:10.1016/j.knosys.2019.02.008

Ganin, Y., Ustinova, E., Ajakan, H., Germain, P., Larochelle, H., Laviolette, F., . . . Lempitsky, V. S. (2016). Domain-Adversarial Training of Neural Networks. *J. Mach. Learn. Res., 17*, 59:1-59:35. Retrieved from http://jmlr.org/papers/v17/15-239.html

Gao, Z., Feng, A., Song, X., & Wu, X. (2019). Target-Dependent Sentiment Classification With BERT. *IEEE Access: Practical Innovations, Open Solutions, 7*, 154290–154299. doi:10.1109/ACCESS.2019.2946594

Gautam, G., & Yadav, D. (2014). Sentiment analysis of twitter data using machine learning approaches and semantic analysis. In M. Parashar (Ed.), *Proceedings of the 2014 Seventh International Conference on Contemporary Computing (IC3): 7 - 9 Aug. 2014, Noida, India* (pp. 437–442). Piscataway, NJ: IEEE. 10.1109/IC3.2014.6897213

Gers, F. A., Schmidhuber, J., & Cummins, F. (2000). Learning to forget: Continual prediction with LSTM. *Neural Computation, 12*(10), 2451–2471. doi:10.1162/089976600300015015 PMID:11032042

Glorot, X., Bordes, A., & Bengio, Y. (2011). Domain Adaptation for Large-scale Sentiment Classification: A Deep Learning Approach. In *ICML'11, Proceedings of the 28th International Conference on International Conference on Machine Learning* (pp. 513–520). Omnipress. Retrieved from https://dl.acm.org/citation.cfm?id=3104482.3104547

Goodfellow, I. J., Pouget-Abadie, J., Mirza, M., Xu, B., Warde-Farley, D., Ozair, S., & Bengio, Y. (2014). Generative Adversarial Nets. In *NIPS'14, Proceedings of the 27th International Conference on Neural Information Processing Systems* (Vol. 2, pp. 2672–2680). MIT Press. Retrieved from https://dl.acm.org/citation.cfm?id=2969033.2969125

Graves, A. (2012). Supervised Sequence Labelling with Recurrent Neural Networks (2nd ed.). In Studies in Computational Intelligence: Vol. 385. Berlin: Springer Berlin Heidelberg. doi:10.1007/978-3-642-24797-2

Han, J., Zhang, Z., Cummins, N., & Schuller, B. (2019). Adversarial Training in Affective Computing and Sentiment Analysis: Recent Advances and Perspectives [Review Article]. *IEEE Computational Intelligence Magazine, 14*(2), 68–81. doi:10.1109/MCI.2019.2901088

Hao, Y., Mu, T., Hong, R., Wang, M., Liu, X., & Goulermas, J. Y. (2019). Cross-domain Sentiment Encoding through Stochastic Word Embedding. *IEEE Transactions on Knowledge and Data Engineering, 1*, 1. Advance online publication. doi:10.1109/TKDE.2019.2913379

Hassan, A., & Mahmood, A. (2018). Convolutional Recurrent Deep Learning Model for Sentence Classification. *IEEE Access: Practical Innovations, Open Solutions, 6*, 13949–13957. doi:10.1109/ACCESS.2018.2814818

Hatzivassiloglou, V., & McKeown, K. (1997). Predicting the Semantic Orientation of Adjectives. In *Proceedings of the 35th Annual Meeting of the Association for Computational Linguistics and 8th Conference of the European Chapter of the Association for Computational Linguistics* (pp. 174–181). Madrid, Spain: Association for Computational Linguistics. 10.3115/976909.979640

Hinton, G., Deng, L., Yu, D., Dahl, G., Mohamed, A., Jaitly, N., Senior, A., Vanhoucke, V., Nguyen, P., Sainath, T., & Kingsbury, B. (2012). Deep Neural Networks for Acoustic Modeling in Speech Recognition: The Shared Views of Four Research Groups. *IEEE Signal Processing Magazine*, *29*(6), 82–97. doi:10.1109/MSP.2012.2205597

Hochreiter, S., & Schmidhuber, J. (1997). Long short-term memory. *Neural Computation*, *9*(8), 1735–1780. doi:10.1162/neco.1997.9.8.1735 PMID:9377276

Howard, J., & Ruder, S. (2018). Universal language model fine-tuning for text classification. In *Proceedings of the 56th Annual Meeting of the Association for Computational Linguistics (*Volume 1*: Long Papers).* Melbourne, Australia: Association for Computational Linguistics. 10.18653/v1/P18-1031

Hsu, C.-C., & Ku, L.-W. (2018). SocialNLP 2018 EmotionX Challenge Overview: Recognizing Emotions in Dialogues. In *Proceedings of the Sixth International Workshop on Natural Language Processing for Social Media* (pp. 27–31). Melbourne, Australia: Association for Computational Linguistics. 10.18653/v1/W18-3505

Hu, M., & Liu, B. (2004). Mining and Summarizing Customer Reviews. In *KDD '04, Proceedings of the Tenth ACM SIGKDD International Conference on Knowledge Discovery and Data Mining* (pp. 168–177). New York, NY: ACM. 10.1145/1014052.1014073

Hussein, D. M. E.-D. M. (2018). A survey on sentiment analysis challenges. *Journal of King Saud University -. Engineering and Science*, *30*(4), 330–338. doi:10.1016/j.jksues.2016.04.002

Jiang, M., Wu, J., Shi, X., & Zhang, M. (2019). Transformer Based Memory Network for Sentiment Analysis of Web Comments. *IEEE Access: Practical Innovations, Open Solutions*, *1*, 179942–179953. Advance online publication. doi:10.1109/ACCESS.2019.2957192

John, V., Mou, L., Bahuleyan, H., & Vechtomova, O. (2019). Disentangled Representation Learning for Non-Parallel Text Style Transfer. In *Proceedings of the 57th Annual Meeting of the Association for Computational Linguistics* (pp. 424–434). Florence, Italy: Association for Computational Linguistics. 10.18653/v1/P19-1041

Johnson, J. M., & Khoshgoftaar, T. M. (2019). Survey on deep learning with class imbalance. *Journal of Big Data*, *6*(1), 27. doi:10.118640537-019-0192-5

Jose, R., & Chooralil, V. S. (2016). Prediction of election result by enhanced sentiment analysis on twitter data using classifier ensemble Approach. In *Proceedings of the 2016 International Conference on Data Mining and Advanced Computing (SAPIENCE)* (pp. 64–67). IEEE. 10.1109/SAPIENCE.2016.7684133

Joshi, O. S., & Simon, G. (2018). Sentiment Analysis Tool on Cloud: Software as a Service Model. In *Proceedings of the 2018 International Conference On Advances in Communication and Computing Technology (ICACCT)* (pp. 459–462). Sangamner, India: Springer. 10.1109/ICACCT.2018.8529649

Joulin, A., Grave, E., Bojanowski, P., & Mikolov, T. (2017). Bag of Tricks for Efficient Text Classification. In *Proceedings of the 15th Conference of the European Chapter of the Association for Computational Linguistics: Volume 2, Short Papers* (pp. 427–431). Valencia, Spain: Association for Computational Linguistics. Retrieved from https://www.aclweb.org/anthology/E17-2068

Joyce, B., & Deng, J. (2017). Sentiment analysis of tweets for the 2016 US presidential election. In *Proceedings of the 2017 IEEE MIT Undergraduate Research Technology Conference (URTC)* (pp. 1–4). IEEE. 10.1109/URTC.2017.8284176

Kaur, H., & Mangat, V., & Nidhi (2017). A survey of sentiment analysis techniques. *2017 International Conference on I-SMAC (IoT in Social, Mobile, Analytics and Cloud) (I-SMAC)*. 10.1109/I-SMAC.2017.8058315

Kim, Y. (2014). Convolutional Neural Networks for Sentence Classification. In *Proceedings of the 2014 Conference on Empirical Methods in Natural Language Processing (EMNLP)* (pp. 1746–1751). Doha, Qatar: Association for Computational Linguistics. 10.3115/v1/D14-1181

Kingma, D. P., & Welling, M. (2013, December 20). *Auto-Encoding Variational Bayes*. Retrieved from https://arxiv.org/pdf/1312.6114v10

Krizhevsky, A., Sutskever, I., & Hinton, G. E. (2012). ImageNet Classification with Deep Convolutional Neural Networks. In *NIPS'12, Proceedings of the 25th International Conference on Neural Information Processing Systems* - Volume 1 (pp. 1097–1105). Curran Associates Inc.

Lampert, C. H., Nickisch, H., & Harmeling, S. (2014). Attribute-Based Classification for Zero-Shot Visual Object Categorization. *IEEE Transactions on Pattern Analysis and Machine Intelligence*, *36*(3), 453–465. doi:10.1109/TPAMI.2013.140 PMID:24457503

Larochelle, H., Erhan, D., & Bengio, Y. (2008). Zero-data Learning of New Tasks. In *AAAI'08, Proceedings of the 23rd National Conference on Artificial Intelligence* (Vol. 2, pp. 646–651). AAAI Press. Retrieved from https://dl.acm.org/citation.cfm?id=1620163.1620172

LeCun, Y., Bengio, Y., & Hinton, G. (2015). Deep learning. *Nature*, *521*(7553), 436–444. doi:10.1038/nature14539 PMID:26017442

Letarte, G., Paradis, F., Giguère, P., & Laviolette, F. (2018). Importance of Self-Attention for Sentiment Analysis. In *Proceedings of the 2018 EMNLP Workshop BlackboxNLP: Analyzing and Interpreting Neural Networks for NLP* (pp. 267–275). Brussels, Belgium: Association for Computational Linguistics. 10.18653/v1/W18-5429

Li, N., Zhai, S., & Zhang, Z., & Liu, B. (2017). Structural Correspondence Learning for Cross-lingual Sentiment Classification with One-to-many Mappings. In *AAAI'17, Proceedings of the Thirty-First AAAI Conference on Artificial Intelligence* (pp. 3490–3496). AAAI Press. Retrieved from https://dl.acm.org/citation.cfm?id=3298023.3298075

Li, Z., & Wei, Y., Zhang, Y., & Yang, Q. (2018). Hierarchical Attention Transfer Network for Cross-Domain Sentiment Classification. *AAAI Conference on Artificial Intelligence; Thirty-Second AAAI Conference on Artificial Intelligence*. Retrieved from https://aaai.org/ocs/index.php/AAAI/AAAI18/paper/view/16873

Li, Z., & Zhang, Y., Wei, Y., Wu, Y., & Yang, Q. (2017). End-to-end Adversarial Memory Network for Cross-domain Sentiment Classification. In C. Sierra (Ed.), *IJCAI'17, Proceedings of the 26th International Joint Conference on Artificial Intelligence* (pp. 2237–2243). AAAI Press. Retrieved from https://dl.acm.org/citation.cfm?id=3172077.3172199

Liu, G., & Guo, J. (2019). Bidirectional LSTM with attention mechanism and convolutional layer for text classification. *Neurocomputing*, *337*, 325–338. doi:10.1016/j.neucom.2019.01.078

Liu, Q., Zhang, H., Zeng, Y., Huang, Z., & Wu, Z. (2018). Content Attention Model for Aspect Based Sentiment Analysis. In *WWW '18, Proceedings of the 2018 World Wide Web Conference* (pp. 1023–1032). Geneva, Switzerland: International World Wide Web Conferences Steering Committee. 10.1145/3178876.3186001

Liu, R., Shi, Y., Ji, C., & Jia, M. (2019). A Survey of Sentiment Analysis Based on Transfer Learning. *IEEE Access: Practical Innovations, Open Solutions*, *7*, 85401–85412. doi:10.1109/ACCESS.2019.2925059

Liu, W., & Fu, X. (2018). Introduce More Characteristics of Samples into Cross-domain Sentiment Classification. In *ICPR 2018, Proceedings of the 2018 24th International Conference on Pattern Recognition (ICPR)* (pp. 25–30). IEEE. 10.1109/ICPR.2018.8545331

Liu, Y., Ott, M., Goyal, N., Du Jingfei, Joshi, M., Chen, D., . . . Stoyanov, V. (2019, July 26). *RoBERTa: A Robustly Optimized BERT Pretraining Approach*. Retrieved from https://arxiv.org/pdf/1907.11692v1

Liu, Z., Bai, X., Cai, T., Chen, C., Zhang, W., & Jiang, L. (2019). Improving Sentence Representations with Local and Global Attention for Classification. In *IJCNN 2019, Proceedings of the 2019 International Joint Conference on Neural Networks (IJCNN)* (pp. 1–7). Curran Associates, Inc. 10.1109/IJCNN.2019.8852436

Long, M., Wang, J., Cao, Y., Sun, J., & Yu, P. S. (2016). Deep Learning of Transferable Representation for Scalable Domain Adaptation. *IEEE Transactions on Knowledge and Data Engineering*, *28*(8), 2027–2040. doi:10.1109/TKDE.2016.2554549

Lu, G., Zhao, X., Yin, J., & Yang, W., & Li, B. (2018). Multi-task learning using variational auto-encoder for sentiment classification. *Pattern Recognition Letters*. Advance online publication. doi:10.1016/j.patrec.2018.06.027

Luo, X., Zimet, G., & Shah, S. (2019). A natural language processing framework to analyse the opinions on HPV vaccination reflected in twitter over 10 years (2008 - 2017). *Human Vaccines & Immunotherapeutics*, *15*(7-8), 1496–1504. doi:10.1080/21645515.2019.1627821 PMID:31194609

Maas, A. L., Daly, R. E., Pham, P. T., Huang, D., Ng, A. Y., & Potts, C. (2011). Learning Word Vectors for Sentiment Analysis. In *Proceedings of the 49th Annual Meeting of the Association for Computational Linguistics: Human Language Technologies* (pp. 142–150). Association for Computational Linguistics. Retrieved from https://www.aclweb.org/anthology/P11-1015

Maitra, P., & Sarkhel, R. (2018). A K-Competitive Autoencoder for Aggression Detection in Social Media Text. In *Proceedings of the First Workshop on Trolling, Aggression and Cyberbullying (TRAC-2018)* (pp. 80–89). Association for Computational Linguistics. Retrieved from https://www.aclweb.org/anthology/W18-4410

Makhzani, A., & Frey, B. (2015). *Winner-take-all autoencoders*. MIT Press.

Manshu, T., & Bing, W. (2019). Adding Prior Knowledge in Hierarchical Attention Neural Network for Cross Domain Sentiment Classification. *IEEE Access: Practical Innovations, Open Solutions, 7*, 32578–32588. doi:10.1109/ACCESS.2019.2901929

Manshu, T., & Xuemin, Z. (2019). CCHAN: An End to End Model for Cross Domain Sentiment Classification. *IEEE Access: Practical Innovations, Open Solutions, 7*, 50232–50239. doi:10.1109/ACCESS.2019.2910300

Mathews, S. M. (2019). Explainable Artificial Intelligence Applications in NLP, Biomedical, and Malware Classification: A Literature Review. *Advances in Intelligent Systems and Computing, 998*, 1269–1292. doi:10.1007/978-3-030-22868-2_90

Mikolov, T., Chen, K., Corrado, G. S., & Dean, J. (2013). *Efficient Estimation of Word Representations in Vector Space*. Retrieved from https://arxiv.org/pdf/1301.3781.pdf

Mikolov, T., Sutskever, I., & Chen, K., Corrado, G., & Dean, J. (2013). Distributed Representations of Words and Phrases and Their Compositionality. In *NIPS'13, Proceedings of the 26th International Conference on Neural Information Processing Systems - Volume 2* (pp. 3111–3119). Curran Associates Inc. Retrieved from https://dl.acm.org/citation.cfm?id=2999792.2999959

Müller, M. M., & Salathé, M. (2019). Crowdbreaks: Tracking health trends using public social media data and crowdsourcing. *Frontiers in Public Health, 7*(APR), 81. Advance online publication. doi:10.3389/fpubh.2019.00081 PMID:31037238

Murdoch, W. J., Singh, C., Kumbier, K., Abbasi-Asl, R., & Yu, B. (2019). Definitions, methods, and applications in interpretable machine learning. *Proceedings of the National Academy of Sciences of the United States of America, 116*(44), 22071–22080. doi:10.1073/pnas.1900654116 PMID:31619572

Myagmar, B., Li, J., & Kimura, S. (2019). Cross-Domain Sentiment Classification With Bidirectional Contextualized Transformer Language Models. *IEEE Access: Practical Innovations, Open Solutions, 7*, 163219–163230. doi:10.1109/ACCESS.2019.2952360

Neethu, M. S., & Rajasree, R. (2013). Sentiment analysis in twitter using machine learning techniques. In *2013 Fourth International Conference on Computing, Communications and Networking Technologies (ICCCNT)* (pp. 1–5). IEEE. 10.1109/ICCCNT.2013.6726818

Nigam, K., & Lafferty, J., & Mccallum, A. (1999). Using maximum entropy for text classification. In *IJCAI-99, Proceedings of the IJCAI-99 Workshop on Machine Learning for Information Filtering* (pp. 61–67). AAAI Press.

Niu, X., & Hou, Y. (2017). Hierarchical Attention BLSTM for Modeling Sentences and Documents. Lecture Notes in Computer Science, 10635, 167–177. doi:10.1007/978-3-319-70096-0_18

Norouzi, M., Mikolov, T., Bengio, S., Singer, Y., Shlens, J., Frome, A., . . . Dean, J. (2014). Zero-Shot Learning by Convex Combination of Semantic Embeddings. In *2nd International Conference on Learning Representations, ICLR 2014*. Conference Track Proceedings.

Pan, S. J., Ni, X., Sun, J.-T., Yang, Q., & Chen, Z. (2010). Cross-domain Sentiment Classification via Spectral Feature Alignment. In *WWW '10, Proceedings of the 19th International Conference on World Wide Web* (pp. 751–760). New York, NY: ACM. 10.1145/1772690.1772767

Pan, S. J., & Yang, Q. (2010). A Survey on Transfer Learning. *IEEE Transactions on Knowledge and Data Engineering*, *22*(10), 1345–1359. doi:10.1109/TKDE.2009.191

Pang, B., Lee, L., & Vaithyanathan, S. (2002). *Thumbs up? Sentiment classification using machine learning techniques*. Association for Computational Linguistics. Retrieved from https://dl.acm.org/ft_gateway.cfm?id=1118704&type=pdf

Pennington, J., Socher, R., & Manning, C. D. (2014). Glove: Global Vectors for Word Representation. *Proceedings of the 2014 Conference on Empirical Methods in Natural Language Processing (EMNLP)*. Retrieved from https://www.aclweb.org/anthology/D14-1162.pdf

Peters, B., Niculae, V., & Martins, A. F. T. (2018). Interpretable Structure Induction via Sparse Attention. In *Proceedings of the 2018 EMNLP Workshop BlackboxNLP: Analyzing and Interpreting Neural Networks for NLP* (pp. 365–367). Brussels, Belgium: Association for Computational Linguistics. 10.18653/v1/W18-5450

Plutchik, R. (1980). A general psychoevolutionary theory of emotion. In R. Plutchik & H. Kellerman (Eds.), *Theories of Emotion* (pp. 3–33). Academic Press. doi:10.1016/B978-0-12-558701-3.50007-7

Rameshbhai, C. J., & Paulose, J. (2019). Opinion mining on newspaper headlines using SVM and NLP. *Iranian Journal of Electrical and Computer Engineering*, *9*(3), 2152–2163. doi:10.11591/ijece.v9i3.pp2152-2163

Ran, J. (2019). A Self-attention Based LSTM Network for Text Classification. *Journal of Physics: Conference Series*, *1207*, 12008. doi:10.1088/1742-6596/1207/1/012008

Ranjit, S., Shrestha, S., Subedi, S., & Shakya, S. (2018). Foreign Rate Exchange Prediction Using Neural Network and Sentiment Analysis. *2018 International Conference on Advances in Computing, Communication Control and Networking (ICACCCN)*. 10.1109/ICACCCN.2018.8748819

Ribeiro, M. T., Singh, S., & Guestrin, C. (2016). Why Should I Trust You?": Explaining the Predictions of Any Classifier. In *KDD '16, Proceedings of the 22Nd ACM SIGKDD International Conference on Knowledge Discovery and Data Mining* (pp. 1135–1144). New York, NY: ACM. 10.1145/2939672.2939778

Ribeiro, M. T., Singh, S., & Guestrin, C. (Eds.). (2018). *Semantically equivalent adversarial rules for debugging NLP models*. Retrieved from https://www2.scopus.com/inward/record.uri?eid=2-s2.0-85061785761&partnerID=40&md5=be8d9d4a9111c0f0f6ba388f3dcc16bb

Rizos, G., Hemker, K., & Schuller, B. (2019). Augment to Prevent: Short-Text Data Augmentation in Deep Learning for Hate-Speech Classification. In *CIKM '19, Proceedings of the 28th ACM International Conference on Information and Knowledge Management* (pp. 991–1000). New York, NY: ACM. 10.1145/3357384.3358040

Rosenthal, S., Farra, N., & Nakov, P. (2017). SemEval-2017 Task 4: Sentiment Analysis in Twitter. In *Proceedings of the 11th International Workshop on Semantic Evaluation (SemEval-2017)* (pp. 502–518). Vancouver, Canada: Association for Computational Linguistics. 10.18653/v1/S17-2088

Sagha, H., Cummins, N., & Schuller, B. (2017). Stacked denoising autoencoders for sentiment analysis: A review. *Wiley Interdisciplinary Reviews. Data Mining and Knowledge Discovery*, *7*(5), e1212. doi:10.1002/widm.1212

Save, A., & Shekokar, N. (2017). Analysis of cross domain sentiment techniques. *2017 International Conference on Electrical, Electronics, Communication, Computer, and Optimization Techniques (ICEEC-COT)*. 10.1109/ICEECCOT.2017.8284637

Shah, D., Isah, H., & Zulkernine, F. (2018). Predicting the Effects of News Sentiments on the Stock Market. *2018 IEEE International Conference on Big Data (Big Data)*. 10.1109/BigData.2018.8621884

Shmueli, B., & Ku, L.-W. (2019). *SocialNLP EmotionX 2019 Challenge Overview: Predicting Emotions in Spoken Dialogues and Chats*. Retrieved from https://arxiv.org/abs/1909.07734

Socher, R., Perelygin, A., Wu, J., Chuang, J., Manning, C. D., Ng, A., & Potts, C. (2013). Recursive Deep Models for Semantic Compositionality Over a Sentiment Treebank. In *Proceedings of the 2013 Conference on Empirical Methods in Natural Language Processing* (pp. 1631–1642). Seattle, WA: Association for Computational Linguistics. Retrieved from https://www.aclweb.org/anthology/D13-1170

Stappen, L., Cummins, N., Meßner, E.-M., Baumeister, H., Dineley, J., & Schuller, B. W. (2019). Context Modelling Using Hierarchical Attention Networks for Sentiment and Self-assessed Emotion Detection in Spoken Narratives. In *Proceedings of the 2019 IEEE International Conference on Acoustics, Speech and Signal Processing (ICASSP)* (pp. 6680–6684). Brighton: IEEE. 10.1109/ICASSP.2019.8683801

Sun, C., Qiu, X., Xu, Y., & Huang, X. (2019). How to Fine-Tune BERT for Text Classification? In M. Sun, X. Huang, H. Ji, Z. Liu, & Y. Liu (Eds.), *LNCS sublibrary. SL 7, Artificial intelligence:* v. 11856. *Chinese Computational Linguistics: 18th China National Conference, CCL 2019, Kunming, China, October 18-20, 2019, Proceedings* (pp. 194–206). Cham: Springer. 10.1007/978-3-030-32381-3_16

Taboada, M., Anthony, C., & Voll, K. (2006). Methods for Creating Semantic Orientation Databases. *Proceeding of LREC-06, the 5th International Conference on Language Resources and Evaluation*. Retrieved from https://www.microsoft.com/en-us/research/publication/methods-for-creating-semantic-orientation-databases/

Taboada, M., Brooke, J., Tofiloski, M., Voll, K., & Stede, M. (2011). Lexicon-based methods for sentiment analysis. *Computational Linguistics*, *37*(2), 267–307. doi:10.1162/COLI_a_00049

Tang, D., Qin, B., & Liu, T. (2015). Document Modeling with Gated Recurrent Neural Network for Sentiment Classification. In *Proceedings of the 2015 Conference on Empirical Methods in Natural Language Processing* (pp. 1422–1432). Lisbon, Portugal: Association for Computational Linguistics. 10.18653/v1/D15-1167

Tang, D., Qin, B., & Liu, T. (2016). Aspect Level Sentiment Classification with Deep Memory Network. In *Proceedings of the 2016 Conference on Empirical Methods in Natural Language Processing* (pp. 214–224). Austin, TX: Association for Computational Linguistics. 10.18653/v1/D16-1021

Tang, G., Müller, M., Rios, A., & Sennrich, R. (2018). Why Self-Attention? A Targeted Evaluation of Neural Machine Translation Architectures. In *Proceedings of the 2018 Conference on Empirical Methods in Natural Language Processing* (pp. 4263–4272). Brussels, Belgium: Association for Computational Linguistics. 10.18653/v1/D18-1458

Tian, Z., Rong, W., Shi, L., Liu, J., & Xiong, Z. (2018). Attention Aware Bidirectional Gated Recurrent Unit Based Framework for Sentiment Analysis. In W. Liu, F. Giunchiglia, & B. Yang (Eds.), *Knowledge Science, Engineering and Management* (pp. 67–78). Springer International Publishing. doi:10.1007/978-3-319-99365-2_6

Turney, P. D. (2002). *Thumbs up or thumbs down?: semantic orientation applied to unsupervised classification of reviews*: Association for Computational Linguistics. Retrieved from https://dl.acm.org/ft_gateway.cfm?id=1073153&type=pdf

Vapnik, V. N. (2000). *The Nature of Statistical Learning Theory*. Springer New York., doi:10.1007/978-1-4757-3264-1

Vaswani, A., Shazeer, N., Parmar, N., Uszkoreit, J., Jones, L., Gomez, A. N., & Polosukhin, I. (2017). Attention is All you Need. In I. Guyon, U. V. Luxburg, S. Bengio, H. Wallach, R. Fergus, S. Vishwanathan, & R. Garnett (Eds.), Advances in Neural Information Processing Systems (Vol. 30, pp. 5998–6008). Curran Associates, Inc. Retrieved from http://papers.nips.cc/paper/7181-attention-is-all-you-need.pdf

Vincent, P., Larochelle, H., Bengio, Y., & Manzagol, P.-A. (2008). Extracting and Composing Robust Features with Denoising Autoencoders. In *ICML '08, Proceedings of the 25th International Conference on Machine Learning* (pp. 1096–1103). New York, NY: ACM. 10.1145/1390156.1390294

Wang, A., Singh, A., Michael, J., Hill, F., Levy, O., & Bowman, S. (2018). GLUE: A Multi-Task Benchmark and Analysis Platform for Natural Language Understanding. In *Proceedings of the 2018 EMNLP Workshop BlackboxNLP: Analyzing and Interpreting Neural Networks for NLP* (pp. 353–355). Brussels, Belgium: Association for Computational Linguistics. 10.18653/v1/W18-5446

Wang, X., Jiang, W., & Luo, Z. (2016). Combination of Convolutional and Recurrent Neural Network for Sentiment Analysis of Short Texts. *Proceedings of COLING 2016, the 26th International Conference on Computational Linguistics: Technical Papers*. Retrieved from https://www.aclweb.org/anthology/C16-1229.pdf

Weiss, K., Khoshgoftaar, T. M., & Wang, D. (2016). A survey of transfer learning. *Journal of Big Data*, *3*(1), 1817. doi:10.118640537-016-0043-6

Wiebe, J. (2000). Learning Subjective Adjectives from Corpora. In *Proceedings of the Seventeenth National Conference on Artificial Intelligence and Twelfth Conference on Innovative Applications of Artificial Intelligence* (pp. 735–740). AAAI Press. Retrieved from https://dl.acm.org/citation.cfm?id=647288.721121

Wiebe, J., Bruce, R., & O'Hara, T. P. (1999). Development and Use of a Gold-Standard Data Set for Subjectivity Classifications. *Proceedings of the 37th Annual Meeting of the Association for Computational Linguistics*. Retrieved from https://www.aclweb.org/anthology/P99-1032.pdf

Wu, X., Cai, Y., Li, Q., Xu, J., & Leung, H.-F. (2018). Combining Contextual Information by Self-attention Mechanism in Convolutional Neural Networks for Text Classification. Lecture Notes in Computer Science, 11233, 453–467. doi:10.1007/978-3-030-02922-7_31

Xian, Y., Lampert, C. H., Schiele, B., & Akata, Z. (2019). Zero-Shot Learning—A Comprehensive Evaluation of the Good, the Bad and the Ugly. *IEEE Transactions on Pattern Analysis and Machine Intelligence*, *41*(9), 2251–2265. doi:10.1109/TPAMI.2018.2857768 PMID:30028691

Xu, N. (2017). Analyzing multimodal public sentiment based on hierarchical semantic attentional network. In *Proceedings of the 2017 IEEE International Conference on Intelligence and Security Informatics (ISI)* (pp. 152–154). IEEE. 10.1109/ISI.2017.8004895

Xu, W., Sun, H., Deng, C., & Tan, Y. (2017). Variational Autoencoder for Semi-Supervised Text Classification. In *AAAI'17: Proceedings of the Thirty-First AAAI Conference on Artificial Intelligence* (Vol. 4, pp. 3358–3364). San Francisco, CA: AAAI Press.

Yang, Z., Yang, D., Dyer, C., He, X., Smola, A., & Hovy, E. (2016). Hierarchical Attention Networks for Document Classification. In *Proceedings of the 2016 Conference of the North American Chapter of the Association for Computational Linguistics: Human Language Technologies* (pp. 1480–1489). San Diego, CA: Association for Computational Linguistics. 10.18653/v1/N16-1174

Yang, Z., Dai, Z., Yang, Y., Carbonell, J., Salakhutdinov, R. R., & Le, Q. V. (2019). XLNet: Generalized Autoregressive Pretraining for Language Understanding. In *Advances in Neural Information Processing Systems 32* (pp. 5754–5764). Curran Associates, Inc. Retrieved from http://papers.nips.cc/paper/8812-xlnet-generalized-autoregressive-pretraining-for-language-understanding.pdf

Yin, H., Liu, P., Zhu, Z., Li, W., & Wang, Q. (2019). Capsule Network With Identifying Transferable Knowledge for Cross-Domain Sentiment Classification. *IEEE Access: Practical Innovations, Open Solutions*, *7*, 153171–153182. doi:10.1109/ACCESS.2019.2948628

Yu, J., & Jiang, J. (2016). Learning Sentence Embeddings with Auxiliary Tasks for Cross-Domain Sentiment Classification. In *Proceedings of the 2016 Conference on Empirical Methods in Natural Language Processing* (pp. 236–246). Austin, TX: Association for Computational Linguistics. 10.18653/v1/D16-1023

Zhang, Q., Lu, R., Wang, Q., Zhu, Z., & Liu, P. (2019). Interactive Multi-Head Attention Networks for Aspect-Level Sentiment Classification. *IEEE Access: Practical Innovations, Open Solutions*, *7*, 160017–160028. doi:10.1109/ACCESS.2019.2951283

Zhang, X., Zhao, J., & LeCun, Y. (2015). Character-Level Convolutional Networks for Text Classification. In *NIPS'15, Proceedings of the 28th International Conference on Neural Information Processing Systems* - Volume 1 (pp. 649–657). Cambridge, MA: MIT Press.

Zhang, Y., Barzilay, R., & Jaakkola, T. (2017). Aspect-augmented Adversarial Networks for Domain Adaptation. *Transactions of the Association for Computational Linguistics*, *5*(1), 515–528. doi:10.1162/tacl_a_00077

Zhang, Z., & Saligrama, V. (2015). Zero-Shot Learning via Semantic Similarity Embedding. In *ICCV'15, Proceedings of the 2015 IEEE International Conference on Computer Vision (ICCV)* (pp. 4166–4174). ACM. 10.1109/ICCV.2015.474

Zhou, G., Zhu, Z., He, T., & Hu, X. T. (2016). Cross-lingual sentiment classification with stacked autoencoders. *Knowledge and Information Systems, 47*(1), 27–44. doi:10.100710115-015-0849-0

Zhu, Y., Gao, X., Zhang, W., Liu, S., & Zhang, Y. (2018). A bi-directional LSTM-CNN model with attention for Aspect-level text classification. *Future Internet.* Advance online publication. doi:10.3390/fi10120116

Zvarevashe, K., & Olugbara, O. O. (2018). A framework for sentiment analysis with opinion mining of hotel reviews. *Proceedings of the 2018 Conference on Information Communications Technology and Society (ICTAS).* 10.1109/ICTAS.2018.8368746

ADDITIONAL READING

Manning, C., Surdeanu, M., Bauer, J., Finkel, J., Bethard, S., & McClosky, D. (2014). The Stanford CoreNLP Natural Language Processing Toolkit. In *Proceedings of 52nd Annual Meeting of the Association for Computational Linguistics: System Demonstrations* (pp. 55–60). Baltimore, Maryland: Association for Computational Linguistics. 10.3115/v1/P14-5010

Peters, M., Neumann, M., Iyyer, M., Gardner, M., Clark, C., Lee, K., & Zettlemoyer, L. (2018). Deep Contextualized Word Representations. *In Proceedings of the 2018 Conference of the North American Chapter of the Association for Computational Linguistics: Human Language Technologies*, Volume 1 *(Long Papers)* (pp. 2227–2237). New Orleans, Louisiana: Association for Computational Linguistics. 10.18653/v1/N18-1202

Poria, S., Cambria, E., Bajpai, R., & Hussain, A. (2017). A review of affective computing: From unimodal analysis to multimodal fusion. *Information Fusion, 37*, 98–125. doi:10.1016/j.inffus.2017.02.003

Thongtan, T., & Phienthrakul, T. (2019). Sentiment Classification Using Document Embeddings Trained with Cosine Similarity. In *Proceedings of the 57th Annual Meeting of the Association for Computational Linguistics: Student Research Workshop* (pp. 407–414). Florence, Italy: Association for Computational Linguistics. 10.18653/v1/P19-2057

Zimbra, D., Abbasi, A., Zeng, D., & Chen, H. (2018). The State-of-the-Art in Twitter Sentiment Analysis: A Review and Benchmark Evaluation. *ACM Trans. Manage. Inf. Syst.*, 9(2), 5:1-5:29. doi:10.1145/3185045

KEY TERMS AND DEFINITIONS

Adversarial Learning: A learning paradigm based on two models attempting to achieve opposing goals.

Attention: A mechanism which allows a model to place additional emphasis on specific features.

Autoencoder: A network composed of an encoder and a decoder that can learn compact representations of its input data in a self-supervised manner.

Data Augmentation: A technique for improving the performance of a model by enriching the training data, e.g. by generating additional instances of minority classes.

Deep Learning: A form of machine learning which uses multi-layered architectures to automatically learn complex representations of the input data. Deep models deliver state-of-the-art results across many fields, e.g. computer vision and NLP.

Explainable AI: An emerging area of research whose goal is to make the decision-making processes of deep models understandable for humans.

Sentence Modelling: The task of converting a text into a representation that can be processed by a machine learning algorithm.

Sentiment Analysis: The task of discovering the underlying feelings expressed in a text. Methods are commonly classified by their scope, i.e. whether they consider aspects, sentences, or the entire document.

Transfer Learning: A collective term for machine learning techniques concerned with adapting a model across different domains and/or tasks.

Transformer: A type of deep model with an encoder-decoder structure that combines self-attention with feedforward networks.

ENDNOTES

1. The code for Word2vec has been made publicly available at https://code.google.com/archive/p/word2vec/.
2. The code for GloVe, along with pre-trained word vectors, is publicly available at https://github.com/stanfordnlp/GloVe.
3. The code for fastText is publicly available at https://github.com/facebookresearch/fastText.
4. The IMDB dataset is available at http://ai.stanford.edu/~amaas/data/sentiment/. It is also included in Tensorflow https://www.tensorflow.org/datasets/catalog/imdb_reviews.
5. The Yelp dataset is available at https://github.com/zzhang83/Yelp_Sentiment_Analysis or in Tensorflow https://www.tensorflow.org/datasets/catalog/yelp_polarity_reviews.
6. The SST dataset is publicly available at http://nlp.stanford.edu/~socherr/stanfordSentimentTreebank.zip.
7. Implementations of both BERT-Base and BERT-Large are publicly available at https://github.com/google-research/bert.

This research was previously published in Natural Language Processing for Global and Local Business; pages 97-132, copyright year 2021 by Business Science Reference (an imprint of IGI Global).

Chapter 4
Sentiment Analysis Techniques, Tools, Applications, and Challenge

Chitra A. Dhawale
P. R. Pote College of Engineering and Management, India

Vandana V. Chaudhari
Smt. G. G. Khadse College, India

ABSTRACT

Sentiment (opinion) refers to the feelings of a human being, which are generally reflected through speech and writing in a particular natural language. The analysis of these sentiments are therefore carried with the help of natural language processing, text analysis, and computational linguistics to identify and extract subjective information in source materials. Generally speaking, sentiment analysis aims to determine the attitude of a speaker or a writer with respect to some topic or the overall contextual polarity of a document. Sentiment analysis is widely applied to reviews and social media for a variety of applications, ranging from marketing research, political reviews, policy making, decision making, customer service, etc. In this chapter the authors include the introduction to sentiment analysis, various approaches for classification of sentiment analysis, various tools used, the application areas, challenges, and future research direction in this most demanding area.

INTRODUCTION

It is a general human tendency that whenever we want to take important decision, we seek the opinion from our friends or relatives and after thinking or analyzing the feedback or opinion of other people, we can reach the conclusion for taking final decision. Before the invention of Internet i.e World Wide Web, many of us asked our friends for which vehicle to purchase, whom they were planning to vote in elections, which washing machine to go for, which tourist place to visit, which doctor to concern, which bank to deposit money, which shopping place the best one, where to stay in city and which hotel to prefer

DOI: 10.4018/978-1-6684-6303-1.ch004

etc etc……But the limitation was ; we could have to take decision based on limited number of people's opinion/feedback but the invention of World Wide Web made it possible to collect the feedback from large number of people and not limited to our friends or relatives, As a stranger we can get nonbiased and authenticate feedback.

The people can give the opinion or feedback on websites or blogs, given opinion or review may be in terms of text and it's possible for us to filter or mine the text data. Here the opinion mining comes in role. Sentiment analysis or opinion mining is the study of people's opinion, attitude or emotion towards anything. It is the process of finding users opinion about a particular topic or product. The topic can be anything like, news, event, movie, etc. There is a slightly different perception between sentiment analysis and opinion mining. Sentiment analysis identifies the sentiment expressed in a text form and then analyzes it whereas opinion mining extracts and analyzes people's opinion about an entity. But at most many researchers uses opinion mining and sentiment analysis interchangeably. Here also we use opinion mining and sentiment analysis interchangeably.

During vacations, many people plans for holidays. While planning the holidays they have to think lots of things related to destination to make their holiday more enjoyable which includes whether it's a peak season or off season over there?, what kind food they can get there?, availability of accommodation according to budget?, the local transport facility, how is the locality over there?, is there medical facility available if require?, etc. And here is a requirement of a good tool which answers all these questions.

For planning enjoyable holidays the planner needs to get all this information easily. The one choice for him to get all this information is that, he has to talk in person with different peoples already visited over there. But of course this is very tedious and hectic way. The better choice is to make use of Internet. As we know vast information is available over the Internet which includes many reviews and opinions of many different peoples regarding the different things. Many different applications related to tourism information are also available on the Internet which provides a huge amount of personal reviews for traveling related information. These reviews can appear in different forms like blogs, Wiki or forum websites, social networking website etc. The information in these reviews is useful to both tourist and traveling manager for understanding and planning the trip. But as we see there is lots of reviews are available related to particular place and it is not possible for the person to go through all, because the given reviews are not in specific format, they depend on the writer. So there must be some tool which filters the useful reviews according to the people's expectation and provide good results.

BASICS OF SENTIMENT ANALYSIS

Sentiment analysis is the study of computing sentiments, opinions and emotions from the text. The primary goal of sentiment analysis is to detect the subjective information from text and define the mind set of author about point

Data Source

The data is obtained from following sources-

Blogs

It's easy to create the blogs that's why people create the blog and uses this blog to share their opinion regarding any topics. We get a huge volume of data from the blogs.

Review Sites

Before purchasing any product firstly the user take the review of that product and a large number of reviews are available on Internet because the people share their opinion about any product that they used.

Dataset

The multi-domain sentiment dataset is available. Most of the work and analysis is done on movie reviews; that movie reviews dataset is used for classification.

Micro-Blogging

It is very popular communication tool on Internet. Daily millions of messages appear for micro-blogging such as Twitter, Facebook, and Tumbler etc. These messages sometimes used for classifying sentiment.

CLASSIFICATION OF SENTIMENT ANALYSIS

As sentiment analysis and opinion mining are latest area of research and much research work is done in this area, the existing work can be classified form different point of views: like which technique is used, the level of detail of text analysis, rating level, view of text etc.

The classification diagram is shown in Figure 1:

Techniques of Sentiment Analysis

The following three techniques are used for classification.

1. Machine learning
2. Lexicon-based
3. Statistical and rule-based approaches.

Machine Learning

This is one of the most useful techniques available in sentiment analysis to categorized sentence or document into positive, negative or neutral categories. This technique classified into two basic approaches as follows:

Supervised Machine Learning Approach

Supervised machine learning techniques are used for classified document or sentences into a finite set of class i.e. into positive, negative and neutral. The training data set is available for all kinds of classes (Jalaj et al, 2013). Some of the machine learning techniques like Naive Bayes (NB), Maximum Entropy (ME), for text categorization Support Vector Machines (SVM) is a more useful technique. Here we give some machine learning methods in the natural language processing area are K-Nearest neighborhood, ID3, C5, centroid classifier, winnow classifier, and the N-gram model.

Supervised learning can be further classified into Probabilistic classifier, Linear classifier, Decision tree classifier and Rule based classifier

Probabilistic Classifier

The Following methods are used in Probabilistic Classifier.

1. Naïve Bayes Classifier(NBC)

The Naive Bayes classifier is one of the simplest and, most commonly used classifier.

In many real world problems like Sentiment analysis, email Spam Detection, email Auto Grouping, email sorting by priority, Document Categorization and Sexually explicit content detection Naïve Bayes Classifier is used. The major advantage of Naïve Bayes is it requires low processing memory and less time for execution. A naive Bayes classifier is a simple probabilistic classifier based on Bayes' theorem and is particularly suited when the dimensionality of the inputs are high (Amit et al, 2014).

For Calculating the posterior probability P(c|x) from P(c), P(x) and P(x|c) Following equation used as

$$P(c/x)=(P(x/c)P(c))/P(x)$$

Where,

P(c|x) is the posterior probability of *class* (c, *target*) given *predictor* (x, *attributes*).
P(c) is the prior probability of *class*.
P(x|c) is the likelihood which is the probability of *predictor* given *class*.
P(x) is the prior probability of *predictor*.

2. Bayesian Network(BN)

Assumption about the NB classifier is that it is independence of the features. The other extreme assumption is to assume that all the features are fully dependent. This leads to the Bayesian Network model which is a directed acyclic graph whose nodes represent random variables, and edges represent conditional dependencies. BN is considered a complete model for the variables and their relationships. It is not used frequently in Text mining, because the computation complexity of BN is very expensive (Vidisha et al, 2016).

Figure 1. Sentiment analysis classification

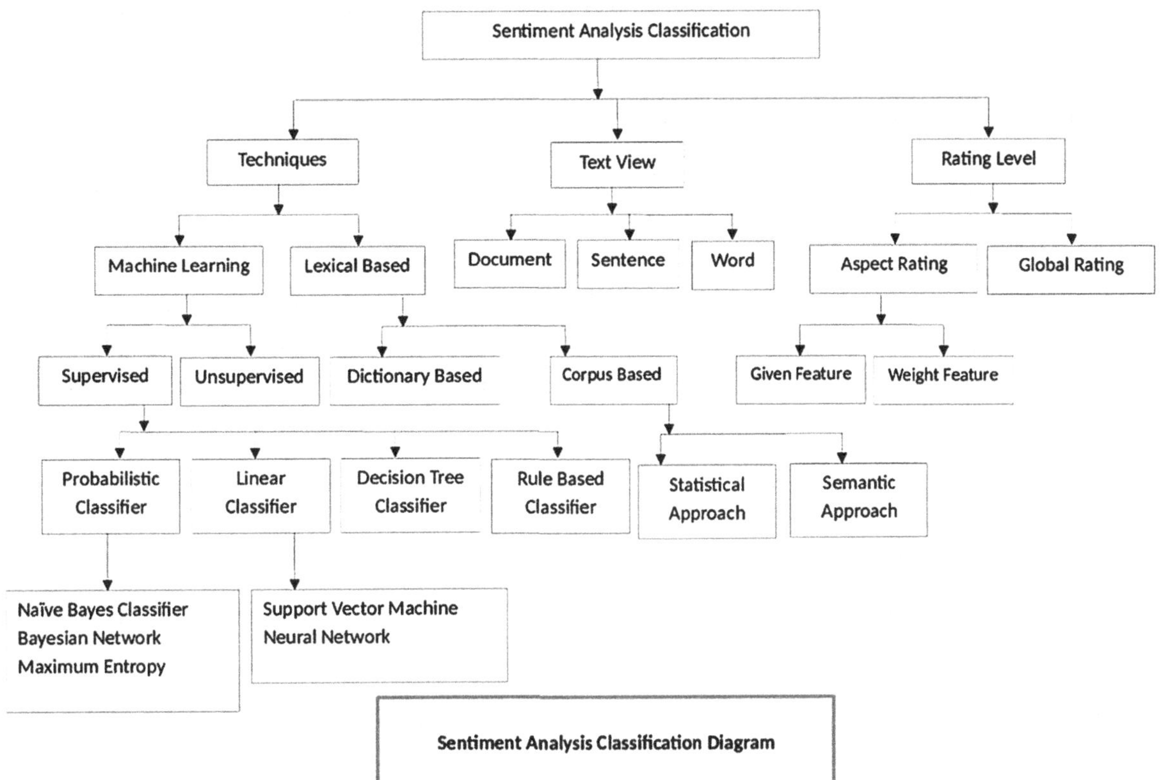

3. Maximum Entropy Classifier(ME)

In most of the natural language processing applications Maximum Entropy (ME) classifier proved effective in use. Unlike Naïve Bayes Classifier the Max Entropy does not assume that the features are conditionally independent of each other. Max Entropy classifier can be used for sentiment analysis and also to solve a large variety of text classification problems such as language detection, topic classification etc. In this classifier more time is needed to train as compare to Naïve Bayes.

Advantages of using MaxEntropy are specified as follows:

- Accuracy
- Consistency
- Performance / Efficiency
- Flexibility

Linear Classifier

There are following methods in Linear Classifier

1. Support Vector Machine

Support vector machine can be used for classification and regression purpose.

Generally in text categorization SVM machine learning classifier is used. It has been shown that Support Vector Machines (SVMs) to be highly effective at traditional text categorization. SVM have large-margin, rather than probabilistic classifiers. Main principle of SVM is to determine linear separators in search space which can best separate the different classes. The tweets to be classified are converted into word vectors. SVM seeks a decision surface to separate training data point into two classes and make decision based on support vectors (Yakashi et al, 2015).

2. Neural Network

It consists of many neurons where the neuron is its basic unit. The inputs to the neurons are denoted by the vector over line Xi which is the word frequencies in the ith document. There are a set of weights A which are associated with each neuron used in order to compute a function of its inputs. Based on inputs and weights output is generated (Vidisha et al, 2016).

Decision Tree Classifier

Decision tree builds regression or classification models in the form of a tree structure means that the Decision tree classifier provides a hierarchical decomposition of the training data space in which a condition on the attribute value is used to divide the data.

It breaks down a dataset into smaller and smaller subsets while at the same time an associated decision tree is incrementally developed. The division of the data space is done recursively until the leaf nodes contain certain minimum numbers of records which are used for the purpose of classification (Vidisha et al, 2016). And finally we get a tree with decision modes and leaf nodes.

Rule Based Classifier

Rule based classifier is very simple. The only rule applied here is concerned with the emotions in text. This method returns the positive and negative emotions matched in text. Like positive emoticons are concerned with positiveness in text while negative emotions are concerned with negativeness (Yakshi et al, 2015).

In rule based classifiers, the data space is modeled with a set of rules. The left hand side represents a condition on the feature set expressed in disjunctive normal form while the right hand side is the class label. The conditions are on the term presence. Term absence is rarely used because it is not informative in sparse data (Vidisha et al, 2016).

Unsupervised Machine Learning Approach

To classify the document in categories text classification is useful. In text classification, it is easy to collect unlabeled documents but sometimes it is difficult to create labeled documents, this difficulty can be avoided by using the unsupervised method. It divides the document into sentence and categorize, each sentence using keyword list of each category's (Yakshi et al, 2015). As sentiment words and phrases maybe used for sentiment classification in an unsupervised manner so it is not hard to imagine that. Unsupervised machine learning techniques don't use training data set for classification. Means to classify data into categories Clustering algorithms like K-means clustering, Hierarchical clustering are used. The other unsupervised method Semantic Orientation also use to generate accurate result for classification.

The Lexicon-Based Approach

To calculate the sentiment polarity for a review; using the semantic orientation of words or sentences in the review; the lexicon-based approach is used. The subjectivity and opinion in text is measure in semantic orientation. It depends on finding the opinion lexicon which is used to analyze the text.

There are two methods in this approach.

Dictionary Based Approach

This approach depends on finding opinion seed words, and then searches the dictionary of their synonyms and antonyms.

Corpus Based Approach

Begins with a seed list of opinion words, and then finds other opinion words in a large corpus to help in finding opinion words with context specific orientations.

1. Statistical approach
2. Semantic approach

Text View

Sentiment analysis has been investigated mainly at three levels- document level, sentence level, feature level.

Document Level Sentiment Analysis

At this level of sentiment classification, a single review about a single topic is considered. Document level analysis is not desirable in forums and blogs. The important thing in this type of analysis is subjectivity or objectivity classification. The document level sentiment classification has its own advantages and disadvantages. We get an overall polarity of opinion text about a particular entity from a document is the advantage. The Disadvantage is that the different emotions about different features of an entity could not be extracted separately (Mohammed et al, 2014). In document level classification both supervised and unsupervised learning methods can be used. Any supervised learning algorithm like Naive Bayesian, support Vector Machine, can be used to train the system. For training and testing data, the reviewer rating (in the form of 1-5 stars), can be used. The features that can be used for the machine learning are term frequency, adjectives from part of speech tagging, opinion words and phrases, negations, dependencies, etc. The unsupervised learning can be done by extracting the opinion words inside a document. The point-wise mutual information can be made use of to find the semantics of the extracted words.

Sentence Level Sentiment Analysis

In sentence level classification the same document level classification methods can be applied to the problem. The polarity of each sentence is calculated in the sentence level sentiment analysis. We have to find objective and subjective sentences. The subjective sentences contain opinion words which help in determining the sentiment about the entity. After which the polarity classification is done into positive and negative classes. In case of simple sentences, a single sentence bears a single opinion about an entity. Sentence level sentiment classification is not desirable in complex sentences. Knowing that a sentence is positive or negative is of lesser use than knowing the polarity of a particular feature of a product. The advantage of sentence level analysis lies in the subjectivity/objectivity classification. The traditional algorithms can be used for the training processes (Mohammed et al, 2014).

Feature Level Sentiment Analysis

This approach is the most important approach to opinion mining. The phrase level classification is done by finding out the phrases that contain opinion words. This analysis has advantage and disadvantage also. In some cases, the exact opinion about an entity can be correctly extracted. But in some other cases, where contextual polarity also matters, the result may not be fully accurate. Negation of words can occur locally. In such cases, this level of sentiment analysis suffices. But if there are sentences with negating words which are far apart from the opinion words, phrase level analysis is not desirable. Also long range dependencies are not considered here. The words that appear very near to each other are considered to be in a phrase (Mohammed et al, 2014).

Applications of Sentiment Analysis

- **Review-Related Websites**

Sentient analysis helps in developing review-related websites. The capabilities that a review-oriented search engine would serve very well as the basis for the creation and automated upkeep of review and opinion aggregation websites. These sites are used as an alternative to sites that solicit feedback and reviews; one could imagine these sites to proactively gather such information.

Topics need not be restricted to product reviews, but could include opinions about candidates running for office, political issues, and so forth (Amit et al, 2014)

- **In Business**

Sentiment analysis is used to predict the mood of people about any product, by comparing their product with their competitor products, also to check the opinion about the quality of their product.

Sentiment analysis helps in business to get customer real time opinion, and this real time opinion helps them for designing new marketing strategies to improve product feature and sell. In stock market also to detect whether the stock price is getting lower or higher and to help the investor for taking the decision related to buying or selling the stock; the sentiment analysis is used.

- **Government Intelligence**

Sentiment analysis would also help to predict the mood of public about political parties, politiciansas well as to analyze the opinion of peoples about government regulations proposals and pending policies.

Means the sentiment analysis plays useful role for helping political parties to understand the issues that are close to voter's heart.

- **Different Domains**

As the negative opinion from customers or any other party can damage your reputation,in the brand reputation management the main focus is on product, company and not on customer.So to determine how company's brand and service is being apparent by community; online sentiment analysis is used.

- **Recommender System**

Recommender system is useful for extracting the rating text from user review. The sentiment analysis is used in recommender systems by recommending the product which has positive feedback only and not recommending the negative feedback product to the user.

- **Summarization**

There are large number of reviews are posted in web for one product and its difficult for customer to check which are the positive point of that product and which are the negative point.It's not possible to read all the reviews.Also it is hard for product manufacturer to analyze the review.By considering this fact the sentiment analysis and opinion mining use to provide the summary of product depending on their feature and key field, so it's easy to take decision for customer and product manufacturer.

- **Online Commerce**

The sentiment analysis is generally used in ecommerce. The user has facility to share the experience about their shopping or the product quality and also they provide the summary of product by giving rating scores. Not only about the product but user can give feedback on hotels and travel destination also which is useful for other customer to select the good quality hotel and destination point.

Tools

See Table 1.

Table 1. Tool and Uses

Sr. No.	Tool Name	Uses
1	Stanford's Core NLP Suite (Jayashri et al, 2013)	part of speech tagging, grammar parsing (identifying things like verb phrases and noun), tokenization (splitting of text into words),named entity recognition,co-reference resolution system, bootstrapped pattern learning
2	Natural Language Toolkit (Jayashri et al, 2013)	tokenizing, parsing, and identifying named entities,classification, stemming, tagging, semantic reasoning, provides lexical resources such as WordNet
3	Apache OpenNLP (Jayashri et al, 2013)	tokenization, parsing, chunking, co-reference resolution, named entity recognition, part of speech tagging, and segmentation
4	GATE	tokenizer, POS tagging, co-reference tagger, gazetteer, sentence splitter, named entities transducer
5	WEKA (Wilson et al, 2005)	Machine learning algorithm for Data Mining, Data pre-processing, Classification, Regression, Clustering, Association rules, Visualization.
6	LingPipe (Jeonghee et al, 2003)	Entity extraction, Clustering, POS tagging, Classification.
7	Pattern (Si Li et al, 2010)	Data mining, POS tagging, Machine learning, Network analysis, Visualization, N-gram search, WordNet, Sentiment analysis,
8	Robust Accurate Statistical Parsing (Xiaohui et al, 2012)	Statistical Parser, Tokenization, Tagging, Lemmatization and Par
9	Review Seer tool (Modha et al, 2013)	The Naïve Bayes classifier approach is used in this to collect positive and negative opinion to assign the score for the extracted feature terms. Also it used for automate the work done by aggregation sites.
10	Web Fountain (Modha et al, 2013)	It uses the beginning definite Base NounPhrase (bBNP) heuristic approach for extracting the product features. It is possible to develop a simple web interface.
11	Red Opal (Modha et al, 2013)	This tool is used to determine the opinion depending upon the feature of the product.The score is assigned to each product base feature for the review of customer and the result shown with the web (Amit et al, 2014)
12	Opinion observer[(Modha et al, 2013)	This is an opinion mining system for analyzing and comparing opinions (Yakshi et al, 2015) on the Internet using user generated contents. This system shows theresults in a graph format showing opinion of the productfeature by feature. It uses WordNet Exploring method toassign prior polarity.
13	Earshot	It give the real time sentiment data filtered by location
14	Radian6	It uses sentiment analysis to streamline social media workflows.
15	VendAsta	This shows about how sentiment trends have shifted over time.
16	Yext	It generates the notification when sentiment start to fall
17	ListenLogic	Used for cleaning up your sentiment data
18	People Browser	To find all the reference of your brand, competitor and industry and analyze the sentiment.
19	Tweetstats	To generate the graph of your tweet statement this tool is used. You have to enter your Twitter handle.
20	Hootsuite	This tool allows you to manage as well as measure your social networks.
21	Marketing Grader	If you are regularly blog posting then it use over 35 metrics to calculate your grade.
22	EMOTICONS	In gives the emoticons contained in the text
23	LIWC	It uses for the dictionary and sentiment classified categories
24	SentiStrengh	It contains the LIEC dictionary with new features to weak and strength sentiments.
25	SentiWordNet	It has the lexical dictionary and gives the scores by using the semi machine learning approaches

continues on following page

Table 1. Continued

Sr. No.	Tool Name	Uses
26	SenticNet	For concluding the polarity at semantic level and uses Natural language Processing approach
27	Happiness Index	Affective Norms for English Words(ANEW) and scores for evaluating happiness in the text
28	AFINN	ANEW but it more focus on the language of microblogging platforms
29	Sentiment140	It is the API for allows to classify the tweets to polarity positive, negative and neutral
30	NRC	It has a set of human provided words with their emotional tags.
31	FRN	The feature relation network considering syntactic n-gram relations.

CHALLENGES OF SENTIMENT ANALYSIS

Domain Specific Sentiment

Sentiment is written according to the domain and the meaning of word is get change when the context changes. The accuracy of classification can be subjective according to the domain in which it applied because there are many words whose meaning change when the domain is change. E.g. if we consider the statement "go read the book" indicate positive sentiment while considering the book domain but it indicate the negative when concerning about the movie domain.

Unavailability of Opinion Mining Software

As the opinion mining software is very expensive so it is afforded by big company or government only the common citizen's not get the benefit of that software.

Spam and Fake Reviews Detection

The web data contains both necessary and unnecessary data, and to give accuracy in work the unnecessary data should eliminated before processing.

Combined Sentence and Multiple Opinions in a Sentence

The word appear in sentence is positive in one situation and negative in other situation also. The multiple opinions is given in single statement which goes positive in some part and negative in other; it's difficult to analyze such type of statement. E.g. the picture quality of camera is amazing, but it's too heavy to carry.

Different Ways to Express the Opinion

People give their opinion according as they think and they vary from person to person and they write their opinion in their language.

Use of Abbreviations, Orthographics and Shortform Words

Though people use social media more and use that for chatting, so they use shortforms for expressing their views that's why it's difficult to analyze the sentence. Also people use orthographic words for expressing their excitement e.g. Sooo Cute....

Multilingual Sentiment Analysis

There is lot of research in sentiment analysis for English language so most researchers give their focus on analyzing English language data because of the availability of resources like corpora and lexicons. There are less number of Internet user speak English so there is growing need to construct the lexicon and corpus for other languages.

Selection of Keyword

In topic based classification it uses a set of keywords to classify texts in different classes. In sentiment analysis we have to classify the review into positive and negative which are different from each other and to build up the right set of keyword is not a little task.

Co-Reference Determination

The problem occur in sentiment analysis is to determine the co-reference means which was a noun and which was pronoun. e.g. "I read that book and went to dinner; it was awful." Itrefers to what? The accuracy of sentiment analysis is improve by determining the co-reference determination.

SUMMARY

It has been seen that sentiment analysis and opinion mining is very large and interesting area of research. The chapter tell that there are different data sources are available to gather review data like blogs, review sites, dataset and micro blogging. The sentiment analysis can be classified depending upon the different factor like techniques, text view and level of rating. Some methods are there for classify like Naïve Bayes, Support Vector, Max Entropy etc. and each method used for specific purpose in classification. There are many tools are available on Internet for doing work on sentiment analysis. This chapter suggests many tools which are useful to perform different task. Also there are many challenges to perform sentiment analysis task like domain specific sentiment, spam and fake reviews detection, combined sentence and multiple opinions in a sentence, different ways to express the opinion, use of abbreviations, orthographics and shortform words, multilingual sentiment analysis, selection of keyword, co-reference determination and there is need to do research to solve these challenges efficiently.

REFERENCES

Bo Pang & Lee. (2002). Thumbs up? Sentiment classification using machine learning techniques. *Proceedings of the Conference on Empirical Methods in Natural Language Processing (EMNLP),* 79–86.

Bollegala. (2012). *Cross-domain sentiment classification using a sentiment sensitive thesaurus*. IEEE.

D'Andrea, Ferri, Grifoni, & Guzzo. (2015). Approaches, Tools and Applications for Sentiment Analysis Implementation. *International Journal of Computer Applications, 125*(3).

Dhokrat, Khillare, & Mahender. (2015). Review on Techniques and Tools used for Opinion Mining. *International Journal of Computer Applications Technology and Research, 4*(6), 419 - 424.

Gang Li, F. L. (2010). *A clustering-based approach on sentiment analysis*. IEEE. doi:10.1109/ISKE.2010.5680859

Gupte, Joshi, Gadgul, & Kadam. (2014). Comparative Study of Classification Algorithms used in Sentiment Analysis. *International Journal of Computer Science and Information Technologies, 5*(5), 6261–6264.

Haiping Zhang, M. X. Y. S., & Yu, Z. (2011). *Feature level sentiment analysis for Chinese product reviews*. IEEE.

Hang Cui, M. D. (2006). *Comparative experiments on sentimentclassication for online product reviews*. American Association for Artificial Intelligence.

Hasan. (2011). *Proximity-based sentiment analysis*. IEEE.

Hu, M., & Liu, B. (2004). *Mining and summarizing customer review*. ACM.

Jalaj, Modha, Pandi, & Modha. (2013). Automatic Sentiment Analysis for Unstructured Data. *International Journal of Advanced Research in Computer Science and Software Engineering Research, 3*(12).

Jeonghee Yi, R. B. W. N., & Nasukawa, T. (2003). *Sentiment analyzer: Extracting sentiments about a given topic using natural language processing techniques*. IEEE.

Kala & Sindhu. (2012). Opinion Mining And Sentiment Classification: A Survey. *ICTACT Journal on Soft Computing, 3*(1).

Khairnar & Kinikar. (2013). Machine Learning Algorithms for Opinion Mining and Sentiment Classification. *International Journal of Scientific and Research Publications, 3*(6). Retrieved from www.ijsrp.org

Khairullah Khan, B. B. (2010). *Sentence based sentiment classification from online customer reviews*. ACM.

Kumar, A., & Sebastian, T. M. (2012). Sentiment Analysis: A Perspective on its Past, Present and Future. *I.J. Intelligent Systems and Applications, 10*, 1-14. Retrieved from http://www.mecs-press.org/

Mohammed, J. (2014). Data Mining And Analysis Fundamental Concepts and Algorithms. Academic Press.

Mullen, T., & Collier, N. (2004). Sentiment analysis using support vector machines with diverse information sources. *EMNLP, 4*, 412–418.

Nasukawa, T., & Yi, J. (2003). Sentiment analysis: Capturing favorability using natural language processing. *Proceedings of the 2nd International Conference on Knowledge Capture*, 70–77. 10.1145/945645.945658

Pang, B., & Lee, L. (2004). A sentimental education:Sentiment analysis using subjectivity summarization based on minimum cuts. *Proceedings of the 42nd Annual Meetingon Association for Computational Linguistics*.

Pradhan & Vala. (2016). A Survey on Sentiment Analysis Algorithms for Opinion Mining. *International Journal of Computer Applications, 133*(9).

Sharma, Mangat, & Kaur. (2015). Sentiment Analysis And Opinion Mining. *Proceedings of 21st IRF International Conference*.

Si Li, W. X. G. C., Zhang, H., & Guo, J. (2010). Exploiting combined multi-level model for document sentiment analysis. *International Conference on Pattern Recognition IEEE*.

Sing, T. K. M. J. K. (2012). *Development of a novel algorithm for sentiment analysis based on adverb-adjective-noun combinations*. IEEE.

Theresa Wilson, P. H. (2005). *Proceedings of human language technology conference and conference on empirical methods in natural language processing*. Association for Computational Linguistics.

Vijyalaxm, Chopra, Oswal, & Chaturvedi. (n.d.). The How, When and Why of Sentiment Analysis. *International Journal Computer Technology and Application, 4*(4), 660–665.

Wiebe, J., & Riloff, E. (2005). *Creating subjective and objective sentence classifiers from unannotated texts. In Computational Linguistics and Intelligent Text Processing* (pp. 486–497). Springer.

Xiaohui Yu, J. X. H. A. A., & Liu, Y. (2012). *Mining online reviews for predicting sales performance: A case study in the movie domain. IEEE Transactions on Knowledge and Data Engineering, 24*.

Yang & Wong. (2009). Classifying web review opinions for consumer product analysis. ACM.

This research was previously published in Exploring the Power of Electronic Word-of-Mouth in the Services Industry; pages 35-48, copyright year 2020 by Business Science Reference (an imprint of IGI Global).

Chapter 5
Tasks, Approaches, and Avenues of Opinion Mining, Sentiment Analysis, and Emotion Analysis:
Opinion Mining and Extents

Amira M. Idrees
https://orcid.org/0000-0001-6387-642X
Faculty of Computers and Information Technology, Future University in Egypt, Egypt

Fatma Gamal Eldin
Faculty of Computers and Information Technology, Future University in Egypt, Egypt

Amr Mansour Mohsen
Faculty of Computers and Information Technology, Future University in Egypt, Egypt

Hesham Ahmed Hassan
Faculty of Computers and Artificial Intelligence, Cairo University, Egypt

ABSTRACT

Every successful business aims to know how customers feel about its brands, services, and products. People freely express their views, ideas, sentiments, and opinions on social media for their day-to-day activities, for product reviews, for surveys, and even for their public opinions. This process provides a fortune of valuable resources about the market for any type of business. Unfortunately, it's impossible to manually analyze this massive quantity of information. Sentiment analysis (SA) and opinion mining (OM), as new fields of natural language processing, have the potential benefit of analyzing such a huge amount of data. SA or OM is the computational treatment of opinions, sentiments, and subjectivity of text. This chapter introduces the reader to a survey of different text SA and OM proposed techniques and approaches. The authors discuss in detail various approaches to perform a computational treatment for sentiments and opinions with their strengths and drawbacks.

DOI: 10.4018/978-1-6684-6303-1.ch005

INTRODUCTION

Opinion as stated by (Najjar & Al-augby, 2021) is an individual belief or verdict about a specific issue or entity. Opinion mining is a kind of performance analyses for a document arguing an object or an artefact and its features (Radi & Shokouhyar, 2021). It aims to defining a set of factors and then spotting the sentiment of the author concerning the defined object. Item classification has different successful approaches (Khedr, Idrees, and Elseddawy, 2016), in this research, we will focus on the text classification approaches.

The fields of sentimental analysis, opinion mining (Hassan, 2019) and emotion analysis (Peeyusha, 2020) precipitously gained outstanding reputation due to the opinionated nature of Internet data (Ahuja, 2017). Sharing views, thoughts, ideas, and sentiments opinions for products, services, movies, restaurants, hotels and even political opinions, is a typical Social Media activity (NehaGupta & Agrawal, 2020). Various disciplines, like educational (Idrees and Hassan, 2018) (Khedr, Kholeif, and Hessen, April 2015) (Khedr and Idrees, 2017A) (Khedr and Idrees, 2017B), agricultural (Hassan, Dahab,, Bahnassy, Idrees, & Gamal, 2015) (Hassan, Dahab, Bahnasy, Idrees, & Gamal, 2014), health (Hazman & Idrees, 2015), and business intelligence, can benefit a great deal from extracting valuable information (Badawy, Abd El-Aziz, Idress, Hefny, & Hossam, 2016) (Helmy, Khedr, Kolief, & Haggag, 2019) (Idrees, 2015) (Khedr, Abdel-Fattah, and Nagm-Aldeen, 2015). Processing such unstructured, informal style of data requires complicated analysis methods and techniques, which makes opinion mining problem a more advanced and more complicated problem in comparison to other text processing fields (Basiri & Kabiri, 2020).

Sentiment analysis is a category of data mining that measures the inclination of people's opinions through natural language processing (NLP) techniques to extract and analyze subjective data from the internet - mostly social media and similar sources (Păvăloaia, Ionut, & Fotache, 2020). The analyzed data quantifies the general public's sentiments or reactions toward certain products, people or ideas and reveal the contextual polarity of the information (Al-Yazidi, Berri, Al-Qurishi, & Alrubaian, 2020). It involves different NLP techniques for collecting and examining different data shared on social media. The process of information extraction is a very critical and challenging mission (Lee and Lau, 2020). The sentiment extraction techniques include machine learning (supervised and unsupervised), lexical-based approaches, text processing, classification, tokenization, stemming, tagging, parsing, semantic reasoning, wrappers, POS tagger, hierarchical word clusters, a dependency parser for tweets, annotated corpora and web-based annotation tools. By utilizing the techniques of NLP (Rajput, 2020) it is possible to analyze the web huge structured and unstructured data repository and to obtain feelings expressed in various comments, questions or requests (Samad, Khounviengxay, & Witherow, 2020). On the other hand, Opinion mining has a significant difference from Sentiment analysis. Opinion mining has various and diverse levels from those of sentimental analysis. Sentiment analysis value can be either positive or negative, opinion mining, on the contrary has a deeper level since it represents the authors opinion. The author opinion may be sad, happy, angry.... etc.

Challenges Facing Sentimental Analysis, Opinion Mining and Emotional Analysis

Traditionally, the communication was simply monologue or, at most a restricted two-way communication (Alison Attrill-Smith, 2020). Mostly, the communication was done without using any interactive means, mainly through e-mail. With the progression of time from mid to late 90s, slowly the conventional and traditional media started getting replaced by the social media (Elinor, 2020). Social media can be defined as the set of web-based broadcast technologies that enable the democratization of content, giving people the ability to emerge from consumers of content to publishers. With the ability to achieve massive scalability in real time, the social media technologies allow people to connect with each other to produce or re- produce value through online conversation and collaboration. Social media was earlier restricted to essential tools and websites which were used by professors and computer experts (Geelan, 2020). Social media changed into a channel through which people connect and converse with companies, managements, media, and even with each other (Anna, 2020).

Various forms of social media like Internet forums, personal websites, advanced bulletin board systems and online chat ensured that the individual's voice reached to the mass audience (Helmy, Emam, Khedr, & Bahloul, 2020) (Jizdny, 2020). Nowadays, social media has quickly revolved to be the primary method of how people communicate with each other (Poongodi, 2020). The social media has altered the way people and organizations communicate (Elinor, 2020). The contribution of multimedia on social media – by easily uploading audios, videos, text and images – added a new dimension for social media (Al-Yazidi, Berri, Al-Qurishi, & Alrubaian, 2020). Social media tiled a new approach for every individual to become a publisher of his ideas and views. The social media not only brought advantages, but also brought an equal number of threats along with some key issues and new challenges concerning social media SA analysis (Zhan, 2020).

One of the most challenging aspects is the spam or fake opinions. According to recently published researches, scams cost individuals, organizations and governments trillions of dollars each year in estimated losses (Smith & Franks, 2020). Another challenging issue facing social analysis and opinion mining is the language related aspect (Taboada, 2020). Using slangs, jargons or special characters like smileys, are widely adopted on social media sites (Izazi, Mahadi, & Tengku-Sepora, 2020).The subjectivity and tone of text are essentially vulnerable to ambiguity; text can convey distinctive meaning to distinctive people (Jackson, 2020). Sarcasm and irony are considered even a tougher challenge, sometimes people say the opposite of what's true, which makes opinion mining and emotion analysis a difficult task (Kamath, Guhekar, Makwana, & Dhage, 2020). One of the examples is stated as: "What a great Samsung! It stopped working in two days". The skill of detecting both levels in different types of analysis (document, sentence, or word) is a very complicated challenge (Ahmed, 2021). Moreover, the capability of providing a description for the extracted opinion or emotion and the capability of providing a representative weight for the influence of the extracted opinion over the context according to the holder's knowledge is an even more challenging task (Liu, Teng, & Gong, 2021). The capability to apply multilingual method for opinion mining and emotion analysis is also a very complicated challenge that would need more sophisticated natural language techniques (Nakayama, 2021).

On the other hand, other challenges could be that the sentence can comprehend sentimental words, these words may not direct any sentiment (Loukachevitch, 2021) for instance, the phrase, "Please tell me which vehicles is good for hill climb racing?", likewise, many sentences free of sentiment phrases may suggest ideas, views or thoughts, for instance, the phrase, "vehicles with down force like the Dragster consume a lot of electricity " this sentence in fact represent a negative view with no integration of any phrase (Mostafa, Helmy, Khedr, & Idrees, 2020). Emotion Causality in Text is also an important challenge for emotion detection. Osorio et al. stated that if the emotion and its cause are known, then, the prediction of any of future reactions will be easy (Osorio-Arjona, 2021). This will be of a significant impact on the emotional analysis, in the analysis of reviews about a product for example, if a sad emotion is detected and the cause of this sad emotion is defined, it would be easy to specify the complaint or the part of the product that the customers are seeking enhancement in.

There are two types of emotion causality, explicit and implicit causal relations (Afify, Sharaf Eldin, Khedr, & Alsheref, 2019). Explicit relations (stated), transition words and phrases will be used. If the relationship within the sentence in implicit (unstated), the reader must infer the relationship. For example, "I am happy because I'm the first on my class". The word 'because' is a word that implies an explicit relation, which means that the proceeding sentence will indicate the cause. The work applied in the explicit causality depends on finding the pattern of the relation. These patterns as are as follows:

Pattern 1: pattern consists of [verb relator word then statement]
Pattern 2: [Noun statement, verb, Noun statement]
Other words like cause of, due to, since

Li et al. (Zhaoning Li, 2020) formulated causality extraction as a sequence labeling problem based on a novel causality tagging scheme. On this basis, they proposed a neural causality extractor with the BiLSTM-CRF model as the backbone, named SCITE (Self-attentive BiLSTM-CRF wIth Transferred Embeddings), which can directly extract cause and effect without extracting candidate causal pairs and identifying their relations separately. To address the problem of data insufficiency, they transferred contextual string embedding's, also known as Flair embedding's, which are trained on a large corpus in their task. In addition, to improve the performance of causality extraction, they introduced a multi-head self-attention mechanism into SCITE to learn the dependencies between causal words (Sayed, Salem, and Khedr, 2019). They evaluated their method on a public dataset, and experimental results demonstrated that their method achieved significant and consistent improvement compared to baselines. Their test got score of 92% accuracy for causal sentences and 98% for non-causal. Moreover, the research in (Moghimifar, 2020) identified explicit causal relationships in text using Bayesian networks. They proposed a method for automatic inference of causal relationships from human written language at conceptual level. To this end, they leveraged the characteristics of hierarchy of concepts and linguistic variables created from text and represented the extracted causal relationships in the form of a Causal Bayesian Network. Their experiments demonstrated superiority of their approach over the existing approaches in inferring complex causal reasoning from the text. They applied the experiment and got 94.44% precision and 61.82% recall.

Levels of Sentiment Analysis, Opinion Mining, and Emotion Analysis

Sentimental analysis, opinion mining and emotion analysis involve three major levels – word level, sentence level, and document level. The level of the analysis determines the task required for the process (Tiun, 2020). Document-level aims to classify a whole document as conveying a positive or a negative opinion or emotion. It deliberates the entire document an elementary information item (Medhat, 2014). Sentence-level SA targets sentences, the first step is to identify whether the sentence is subjective or objective (Mostafa, Khedr, & Abdo, 2017). If the sentence is subjective, Sentence-level SA will determine whether the sentence expresses positive or negative opinions (Jabreel, 2021)

The word level is the most complicated one due to the struggle in the analysis phase, however the analysis phase is more straight forward at the sentence and document levels (Taboada, 2020). Semantic-based analysis and machine learning are the two main techniques used for the review of sentimental analysis (Rajput A., 2020). There have been various studies that have used machine-learning technique (Peeyusha, 2020). A lot of progress has been made over the last years in the area of opinion mining and emotion analysis (Jabreel, 2021). This chapter will give a general perspective to the current state of research and the technologies that have been used in recent studies.

Document Level Analysis

The main process of performing a document level analyze, is done through parsing the text automatically to determine its meaning (Najjar & Al-augby, 2021). It can be conceptualized as a multi-class text classification problem (Jabreel, 2021), in which the goal is to determine whether the overall opinion expressed in a given text is positive, negative or even neutral. There are many variants of this task. One is to classify a text according to a rating scale, e.g., 1 = “worst” to 5 = “best”. It is also possible to formulate the problem as a regression problem. The goal, in this case, is to predict the intensity of the sentiment that represents better the mental state of the author (Mohammad, Bravo-Marquez, Salameh, & Kiritchenko, 2018). The intensity is a real value in the range from 0 (negative) to 1 (positive). Since it is a text classification problem, we can apply any existing supervised learning method, e.g., naive Bayes or Support Vector Machines (Zhang, Yoshida, & Tang, 2008).

Sentence Level Analysis

In sentence level SA, OM and EA, every sentence is processed and analyzed to determine its polarity. Each sentence is given a positive, negative, or neutral opinion (Mohsen, Hassan, and Idrees, 2016). The whole process is closely associated with subjectivity classification. The process is a twofold treatment; firstly, identify whether the sentence expresses an opinion or not, then assess the polarity of the opinion. The main difficulty of the sentence level SA comes from the fact that, even the objective sentences can be carrying an opinion (Mohsen, Hassan, and Idrees, 2016).

Word Level Analysis

This level performs a finer analysis. In this level, opinion is characterized by a polarity and a target of opinion. In this case, treatments are twofold: first identify the entity and aspects of the entity in question, and then assess the opinion on each aspect.

Opinion Mining (OM) Process

According to the research in (Liu, 2014) Looking to opinion mining as a process, it is composed of the following steps:

1. Entity extraction and Entity categorization.
2. Aspect extraction.
3. Opinion holder extraction and standardization
4. 4.Time extraction and standardization.
5. Aspect sentiment classification.
6. Opinion quintuple generation.

Each of these steps are going to be discussed in more details in the following subsections.

Entity Extraction and Entity Categorization

An entity e is a product, service, or topic. It is associated with a pair, e: (T, W), where T is a set of sub-components, W is a set of attributes of e. Each component or sub-component has its peculiar set of attributes. for example: A Benz car is an entity. It has a set of components, (e.g., battery, doors, engine, trunk .... Etc.) as well as a set of attributes, (e.g., speed, size, weight .... Etc). The battery component also has its own set of attributes, e.g., battery life, and battery size. Entity can be represented as a tree and the root of the tree is the name of the entity. Each non-root node is a component or sub-component of the entity. Each link is a part-of relation while Each node is associated with a set of attributes. finally, An opinion can be expressed on any node and any attribute of the node. On the other hand, one can express an opinion about the car itself (the root node), e.g., "I do not like Benz car", or on any one of its attributes, e.g., "The speed of Benz car is slow".

Aspect Extraction

The aspects of an entity e are the components and attributes of e. An aspect expression is a word or phrase that appeared in text specifying an aspect. For example: In the Benz car domain, an aspect could be the engine quality. Aspect expressions are usually noun terms and noun phrases, but can also be verbs, verb phrases, adjectives, and adverbs.

Opinion Holder Extraction and Standardization

The holder of an opinion is the person who expresses the opinion. Opinion holders are also called opinion sources. Some studies identify opinion holders from opinion documents. For product reviews and blogs, opinion holders are usually the authors of the postings. Opinion holders are more important in news articles as they often explicitly state the person or organization that holds an opinion.

Time Extraction and Standardization

It deals with time extraction and standardization. The time extracted is the time when the opinion was given. The time when the opinion is given is expressed by t.

Aspect Sentiment Classification

where it is determined whether an opinion on an aspect is positive, negative or neutral, and a numeric sentiment rating to the aspect is assigned.

Opinion Quintuple Generation

An opinion (or regular opinion) is a quintuple, (e_i, a_{ij}, oo_{ijkl}, h_k, t_l), Where ei is the name of an entity, a_{ij} is an aspect of e_i, oo_{ijkl} is the orientation of the opinion about aspect a_{ij} of entity e_i, h_k is the opinion holder,

t_l is the time when the opinion is expressed by h_k. The opinion orientation oo_{ijkl} can be positive, negative or neutral, or it can be expressed with different strength/intensity levels.

An entity ei is represented as a finite set of aspects,

$$Ai = \{a_{i1}, a_{i2}, \ldots, a_{in}\}.$$

The entity itself is expressed with a final set of entity expressions

$$OEi = \{oe_{i1}, oe_{i2}, \ldots, oe_{is}\}$$

Each aspect aij ∈ Ai of the entity can be expressed by any one of a finite set of aspect expressions.

$$AEij = \{ae_{ij1}, ae_{ij2}, \ldots, ae_{ijm}\}$$

Opinionated document d contains opinions on a set of entities $\{e_1, e_2, \ldots, e_r\}$ from a set of opinion holders $\{h_1, h_2, \ldots, h_p\}$. The opinions on each entity e_i are expressed on the entity itself and a subset of its aspects.

Emotion Analysis

Conventionally, emotions are defined as the perception of a neurological impulse that pledges behavior (AED, 2020). Society has been scrutinizing emotions for centuries (Goldenberg, 2020). Given the heavy focus on feelings, it's not surprising that emotions can be simply described as a subjective feeling, view or judgment (Shixia & Huamin, 2010) mostly reached by a direct experience although it could be acquired indirectly. While emotions are associated with bodily reactions that are activated through neurotransmitters and hormones released by the brain, feelings are the conscious experience of emotional reactions (Joseph Ledoux, 2018). Many different types of emotions have a very powerful impact on how people sentient and cooperate with their day-to-day life (Goldenberg, 2020). People are mainly ruled by their emotions, these emotions control their choices and the actions they take. Everyone's perceptions are influenced by the emotions he experiences at any given moment.

Psychologists have also tried to identify the different types of emotions that people experience. A few different theories have emerged to categorize and explain the emotions that people feel (Ledoux, 2018). During the 1970s, psychologist Paul Eckman identified six basic emotions that he suggested, were universally experienced in all human culture (Delbrouck & Dupont, 2020). The emotions he identified were happiness, sadness, disgust, fear, surprise, and anger. He later expanded his list of basic emotions to include such things as pride, shame, embarrassment, and excitement. People respond to emotions using physiological responses (Chaudhuri, 2006) numerous types of physiological reactions have different meanings. Some very common physiological reactions are heart rate changes, blood pressure, sweating, and so on, which directly affect human actions and facial expressions (Liu, 2011). The following subsections are going to discuss the emotion mining changeable directions, the emotional mining using information retrieval (IR) techniques, emotion mining on Lexicon based techniques.

Information Retrieval Techniques for Emotional Analysis

Information retrieval refers to the retrieval of a specific definite information from a group of unstructured text documents (Pandey, 2021) (Dahab, Idrees, Hassan, & Rafea, 2010). Information retrieval techniques in both opinion mining and emotion mining, target the retrieval of the tokens that will represent emotions (Sujon, 2021). As reported by (Pandey, 2021), Information retrieval can be classified to two models, "Boolean models" and "vector space models". Figure 1 reveals the categorization of these models. This classification will be further discussed in the following subsections. Table 1 represents a comparison between various models according to the determined criteria and the accuracy level for each emotion retrieval model.

Figure 1. Techniques and sub techniques for information retrieval techniques

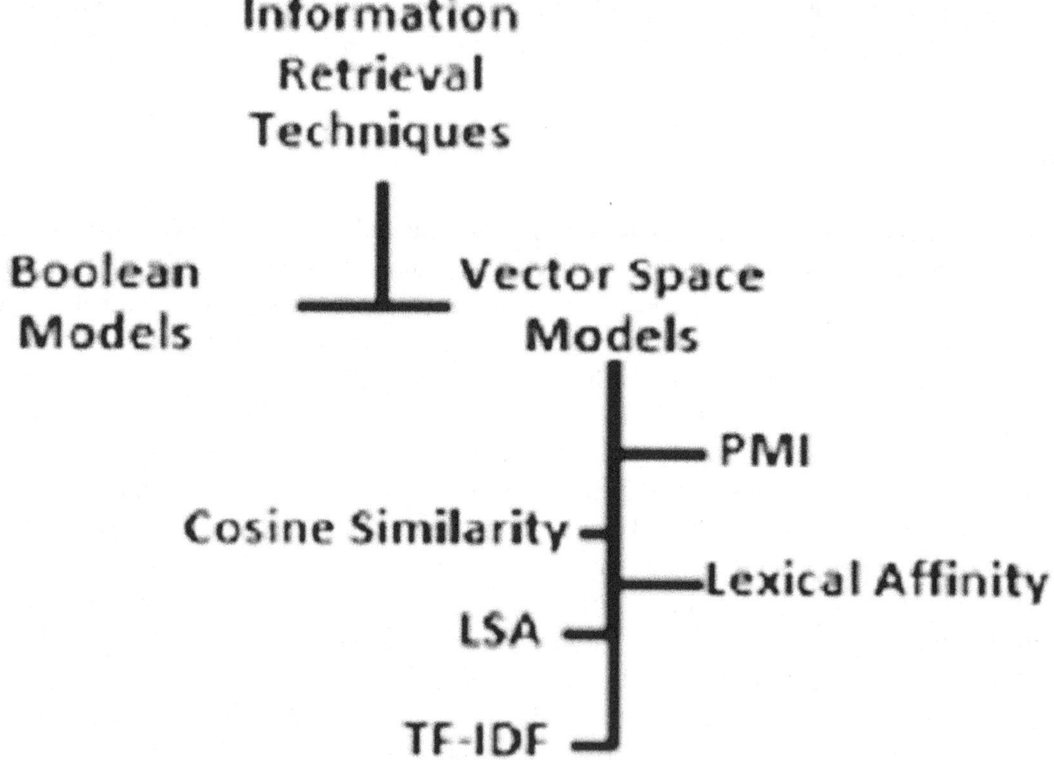

Boolean Models in Information Retrieval Techniques for Emotional Analysis

The main purpose of using Boolean models search approaches in emotion analysis, is to find the required tokens in a specified text document (Sabharwal, 2021). If a customer is inquiring about "cars and bicycles". His query can be simply responded by retrieving the documents having these the word

Table 1. Information retrieval techniques

Model	Paper, year	Dataset	Accuracy	Domain	Emotions used
Cosine Similarity	(Gohary, Sultan, Hana, & Dosoky, 2013)	Children Stories	65%	General	Joy, fear, sadness, anger, disgust, surprise
	(Martinazzo, Dosciatti, & Paraiso, 2012)	Tweets news	70%	Portuguese language	Joy, fear, sadness, anger, disgust, surprise
	(Agrawal & An, 2012)	Tweets	86%	General	Happy, sadness, anger, fear, surprise, disgust
PMI	(Agrawal & An, 2012)	Wikipedia, eBooks	58%, 50%	General	Happy, Sad, Anger, Fear, Surprise, Disgust, Neutral
	(Polisetty, Polisetty, & .Rao, 2014)	Movie reviews	Unknown	General	anger, disgust, fear, joy, sadness, surprise, Emoticons
LSA	(Wang & Zheng, 2013)	ISEAR	Avg. 39.4%	General	Anger, disgust, fear, guilt, joy, sadness, shame
TF-IDF	(Patil & Patil, 2013)	ISEAR	71.64%	General	Anger, Disgust, fear, joy, sad

"car" and the word "bicycle". Boolean models depend on three operands "and", "or" and "not". The AND operator restricts your search results between only two or more keywords. Note that, the absence of an operator among words is interpreted as an AND operator. The OR operator expands your search. An OR operator will return any posts that contain at least one of the search terms. Moreover, a NOT operator ignores posts containing the keyword. Using the NOT operator will exclude any posts containing the keyword following the operator. Moreover, in Boolean search, parentheses and quotation marks are very helpful. Quotation marks indicates that the words to be searched for should appear as a phrase and in their exact same order. The terms in parentheses are and operations that occur inside them to be searched first. Sometimes called nesting, parentheses add a level of organization for your Boolean search, allowing you to formulate complex search strings.

Vector Space Models in Information Retrieval Techniques for Emotional Analysis

Vector space model (VSM) uses algebraic approach by applying different models, each with its own perspective (Wilhelm, 2021). VSM represents documents and queries as vectors of weights. Each weight is a measure of the rank of a term in a document or a query. The term weights are calculated according to the frequency of the term in the document or the query.

The main steps can be briefly stated as follows:

- Build the Opinion quintuple generation vector for all extracted emotion terms.
- Apply a weighting technique
- Apply a similarity measure which parameters is the user query and the extracted terms with respect to the term weight

Cosine Similarity (CS)

According to (Ansorena, 2021) CS is calculated as shown in equation (1)

$$Similarity(A,B) = \frac{A \times B}{|A| \times |B|} = \frac{\sum_{i=1}^{n} A_i \times B_i}{\sqrt{\sum_{i=1}^{n} A_i^2} \times \sqrt{\sum_{i=1}^{n} B_i^2}} \tag{1}$$

where A, B are considered document vectors.

The research in (Gohary, Sultan, Hana, & Dosoky, 2013) followed the (CS) model for obtaining the Arabic text emotions. The research applied their model on Arabic kids' fairy tales. The study's main goal was to build an emotional lexicon using that same dataset. The dataset was split to two portions, the purpose of the first portion is to manual build the lexicon emotion, while the purpose of the second portion was to apply the purported methodology for the emotion mining and to prove its relevance. The study concentrated on six emotions {Joy, fear, sadness, anger, disgust, and surprise}. The methodology focusses on annotating every sentence within the document with the determined emotion, then the emotion for the entire document is determined through weighting technique for the detected sentences' emotions. The research attained an accuracy of 65% average. Earlier, a study carried out in (Martinazzo, Dosciatti, & Paraiso, 2012) which reached an accuracy of 70%. The study was conducted on Brazilian text and the required pre-processing steps were done with respect to the Brazilian language nature and built a lexicon emotional manual. This manual included all the token and their associated emotions, finally, the document matrix was built, and the cosine similarity measure was applied. The research was quit promising, however, the accuracy level was also average, more work was done during the same year by others. (Agrawal & An, 2012) reached an F-measure of 86%. The research was able to reach this accuracy level by the help of WordNet. The WordNet was considered the lexical database source and a corpus for the statements with their associated emotions.

Point-Wise Mutual Information (PMI) Similarity Measure

PMI measures the impact of one token to the other which formulates the whole sentence meaning (Jing, 2021). (Khedr and El Seddawy, 2015) explains this process as follows:

Consider x, y to be two distinct words, accordingly we can find:

- P(x, y) is the probability that x and y can be found in the same sentence
- P(x) is the probability that x is found individually in the sentence.
- P(y) is the probability that y is found individually in the sentence.

The distribution of x and y in a dataset or a document is measured as shown in equation 2.

$$I(x,y) = \log_2 \frac{p(x,y)}{p(x)p(y)} \tag{2}$$

The research in (Agrawal & An, 2012) proposed a methodology for using unsupervised context-based learning to detect sentence emotions level. PMI similarity is utilized in every phase by calculating the correlation between the words of the document, e.g. (looks, beautiful). The findings were 52.5% accurate for the un-stemmed WIKIPEDIA dataset text and 58.08% for the stemmed WIKIPEDIA dataset text. An Alternative study used the GUTENBERG dataset. Using the GUTENBERG dataset research reached an accuracy of 54.76% for un-stemmed text and 55.34% for stemmed text. moreover, in (Polisetty, Polisetty, & .Rao, 2014), proposed an approach for Emoticons analysis for movie reviews. Emoticons are the emotions that are represented by faces' reaction. The sentences in the movies' dataset were classified to six basic emotions (anger, disgust, fear, joy, sadness and surprise). The research followed the same approach by using a lexicon of words, however, this lexicon had an additional feature by providing a relation between the six categories of emotions with emoticons using these words. PMI was applied after the exhaustive preprocessing phase that included all required tasks.

Latent Semantic Analysis (LSA)

The main purpose of LSA according to (Yang, 2021) is to analyze all the relations among the document and to extract the most important terms that represent the documents perspective. The model consists of a matrix for the terms in the document. The matrix includes a column for each term and a row for each document. The term frequency in each document is calculated and assigned to the term/document cell. Later, the singular value decomposition (SVD) method is applied on the model constructed matrix, finally, the similarity is measured for all documents. Wang and Zheng applied and improved LSA model in (Wang & Zheng, 2013) by using LSA for emotions classification using VSM model targeting to increase the accuracy level. Thc research succeeded to reach a raise of 4% than the normal accuracy level as illustrated in figure 2.

Figure 2. Comparison between the results of LSA and improved LSA

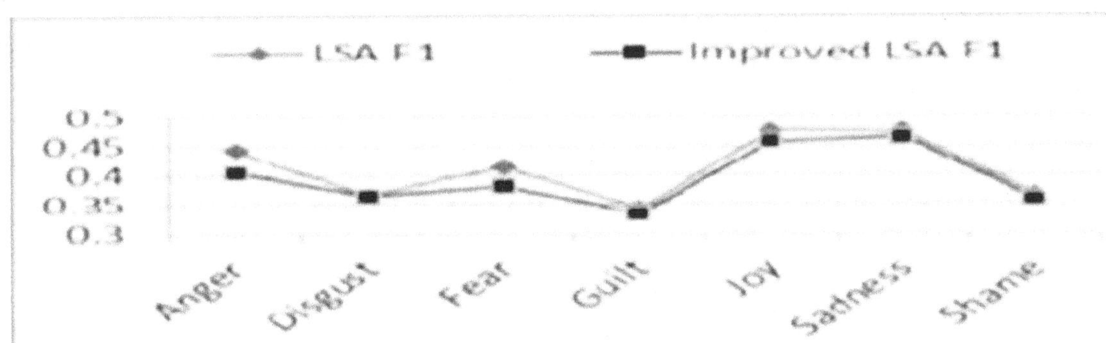

Probabilistic Tf-idf

Tf-idf (Hassan and Idrees, 2010), (Khedr and El Seddawy, 2015) is a weighting scheme used to indicate the relative frequency of tokens in a specific corpus document (tf) when compared to the inverse term frequency in the whole corpus (idf). The tf equation is presented in equation (3), the idf equation is shown in equation (4). The TF/IDF is computed by multiplying TF with IDF as exemplified in equation (5) (Mohsen, Idrees, & Hassan, 2019).

$$tf\left(t,d\right)=0.5+\frac{0.5*f\left(t,d\right)}{\max\left\{f\left(w,d\right):w\ d\right\}} \tag{3}$$

$$idf(t,D) = \log_2 \frac{N}{|\{d\ D : t\ d\}|} \tag{4}$$

$$Tf - idf(t, d, D) = tf(t, d) \times idf(t, D) \tag{5}$$

The research in (Patil & Patil, 2013) introduced a novel method to classify emotions of a headline news dataset. The first - and most obvious phase, is the preprocessing phase. In the preprocessing phase, the preprocessing phase comprised filtering, tokenization, stemming and pruning. The training set was then determined and the Tf-Idf (El Azab, Idrees, Mahmoud, & Hefny, 2016) was computed. After the Tf-idf was calculated for the documents' terms, the SVM is utilized to categorize the words that represent the emotions and their emotion classification. The classification method was then employed to conduct the testing. Patil method proved to achieve an accuracy level of 71.64%.

Lexicon Based Techniques

Lexicon based technique aims to build a lexicon for various types of emotions, this lexicon is then used for classifying the text according to the word level to know in which category of emotion is the word. Figure 3 shows the techniques used for building the lexicon which consists of Concept Net, Dictionary based, and Lexicon based.

Figure 3. Lexicon based techniques

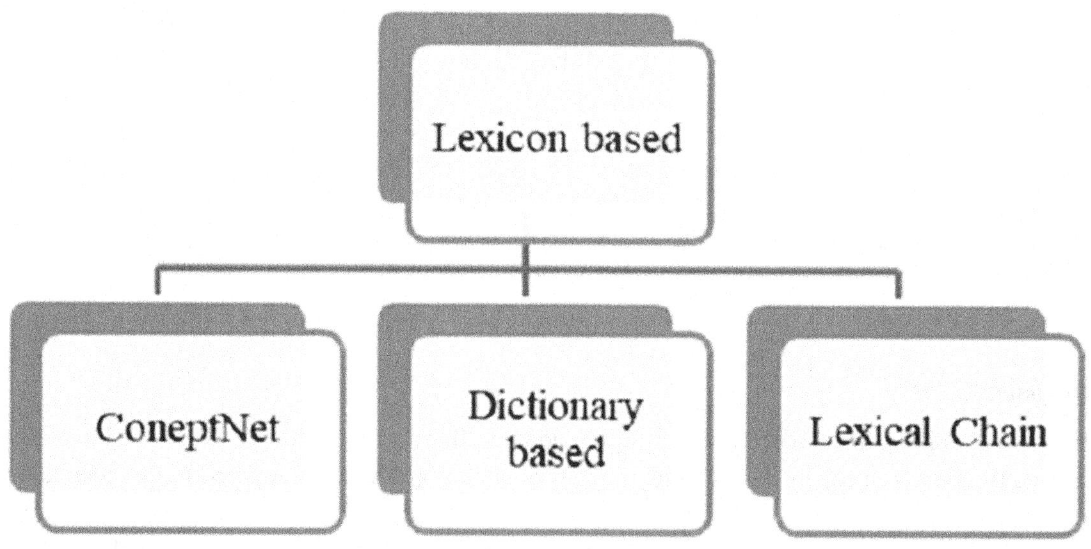

Concept Net, using this technique, the text is analyzed targeting to extract the main concept from it. Concept net is expressed as a direct cyclic graph where the ovals are the concepts that represent specific knowledge, and the edges represent the relations between concepts. These edges are also related to ontology that represent specific topic or knowledge as in figure 4. In (R.Ezhilarasi & Minu, 2012), they built an emotion ontology network for classifying text according to emotion classes by taking that expected to be emotions and check them using WordNet (Miller, 1995), they then built the ontology using these words. When a sentence is parsed to the system, it passes through natural language processing steps such as linguistic analysis, and then to classify a determined word, a search for this word is performed in the ontology net.

Figure 4. Example on concept net

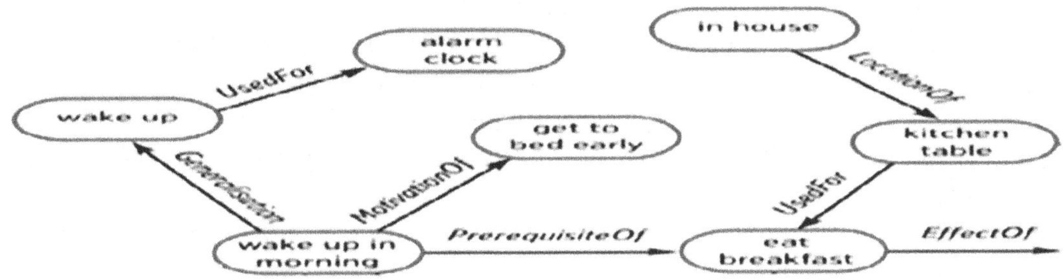

Lexical chain (TURNEY & LITTMAN, 2003) is a technique based on natural language processing; it treats sentences that contain same concepts as nouns of same meaning. So, we can get sequence of words that are related to each other and produces a linguistic ontology. The lexical chain gets scores through 1) Length of chain: The number of occurrences of members of the Chain., 2) homogeneity index: The number of members being occurred in the chain, the score at last is calculated by multiplying homogeneity index by length of the chain. Kumar and Suresh (Kumar & R.Suresh, Emotion Detection using Lexical Chains, 2012) used six basic emotions (happiness, sadness, anger, fear, disgust and surprise) with support of lexical chain lexicon based for each emotion keyword, the lexical chain is constructed by putting words related to each other for each emotion through semantic relationships. Each lexical chain is scored through the length of chain and the homogeneity index. The selected chains are those with high scores to identify the emotion of document. The accuracy is 86%.

Dictionary based technique aims to classify the emotion of a word based on using the definition of this word in dictionaries like WordNet (Miller, 1995) and their hierarchies. The research in (Tokuhisa, Inui, and Matsumoto, 2008) classified the emotions of the input to their system by proposing a data-oriented method for knowing the emotion of a sentence in dialog chatting system from the semantic content of the words, then connect the emotion classification in the context of human computer dialog, and assign massive examples of emotion-provoking events that can be extracted from the Web by accuracy, and those examples can be used to build a semantic content-based model for fine-grained emotion classification. The model also considers the quantity and accuracy of emotion-provoking examples to be collected and Emotion-provoking corpus to get data from it. Then build the corpus using many sentences that are assumed to be take place under ten categories of emotions by using similarity algorithms. They got accuracy of 84.6%. Moreover, in (Boa, et al., 2012) a high quality moderate sized emotion lexicon is manually created using Mechanical Turk and WordNet Affect (Strapparava & Mihalcea, 2007) ; the lexicon is built based on questioners distributed to the subscribers of Mechanical Turk.

In (Lei, Raob, Li, Quan, & Wenyin, 2013), a lexicon is presented based system which target to classify the documents based on their emotions; the idea is based on building a lexicon of words that represent the emotions. The lexicon is built manually by extracting the main words representing each emotion by the user from a set of documents. The set of included emotions is (Touching, empathy, boredom, anger, amusement, sadness, surprise, warmness). They got accuracy of 59.11%. moreover, in (Gohary, Sultan, Hana, & Dosoky, 2013), this research is concerned with the automatic detection of emotions in Arabic text based on a moderate sized Arabic lexicon used to annotate Arabic children stories. The research used a corpus that consists of 100 documents, containing 2,514 sentences. The detection of the emotion was based on the sentence level. the sentence classification was measured by kappa value as if the value is one it will be totally agreement and 0 not agreed. The average value of Kappa (Cohen, 1968) in this research is 0.46 which means that moderate agreement. After annotating, the Lexicon was built for the six emotion categories (Joy, fear, sadness, anger, disgust, surprise) from annotated sentences and directly from English emotions lexicon. Then he got 65% f-measure for the six emotions.

In Table 2, different related works discussed above presented in using Lexicon based techniques in emotion classification. The table compared to the accuracy results, the emotions used and the technique that has been applied.

More recently, in 2021 the research in (Jan, 2020) implemented a dictionary-based method where two lexicons, namely, the lexicon for peace and the lexicon for protest, are used and expanded using Word2Vec to determine community sentimental opinion during 2016 Kashmir Unrest. The proposed approach achieved the accuracy of 71.795%. VADER is a lexicon as well as rule-based SA framework implemented by Anton and Martin. VADER performed better when compared to existing SA lexicons (Daniel, 2021). It combined VADER with (SVM) to categorize the sentiments of customer response. Anton and Martin method was quite efficient with mean AUC of 0.896 and F1 score of 0.834.

Table 2. Emotion classification related work using lexicon based techniques

Technique	Paper, year	Dataset	Accuracy	Domain	Emotions used
LB	(R.Ezhilarasi & Minu, 2012), 2012	WordNet	Unknown	General	–
	(Kumar and R.Suresh, 2012),2012	Wiki news articles	80%	General	happiness, sadness, anger, fear, disgust and surprise
	(Lei, Raob, Li, Quan, & Wenyin, 2013), 2013	BBC News	63.57%	General	Touching, empathy, boredom, anger, amusement, sadness, surprise,
	(Gohary, Sultan, Hana, & Dosoky, 2013),2013	Children Stories	61.68%	General	Joy, fear, sadness, anger, disgust, surprise
	(Tokuhisa, Inui, and Matsumoto, 2008), 2008	EP corpus	Unknown	Dialogue systems	happiness, pleasantness, relief, fear, sadness, disappointment, unpleasantness,
	(Patil & Patil, 2013), 2013	ISEAR dataset	71.64%	General	Anger, Disgust, fear, joy, sad

SA BASIC STEPS

The SA process is performed through determining the text from documents, then parsing the text automatically by applying determined steps to find their meaning. Basic sentiment analysis of text documents follows a straightforward process steps which will be debated in more details in the following subsections (Jabreel, 2021).

Step 1: Preprocessing;
Step 2: Identify the sentiment-bearing expression and component.
Step 3: Give a sentiment rating for every phrase and component (-1 to +1).
Step 4: Optional: Combine scores for multi-layered sentiment analysis.

Step 1: Preprocessing

The text preprocessing stage is the initial stage of SA. This stage includes all routines and processes to prepare the data to be used later on in the proceeding steps. The purpose of preprocessing is to produce a term set that can represent the document. The process performed in text preprocessing among others are tokenization, filtration, lemmatization, stemming and POS tagging. Each of these steps are going to be discussed in more details in the following subsections.

1. Tokenization

There are two forms of tokenization, namely sentence tokenization and word tokenization (Gerard, 2021). Sentence tokenization, also known as sentence segmentation, is the procedure of dividing a string into its component sentences later on, splitting each sentence into a series of tokens (Ö., 2021). One way of performing this task is through stripping away any punctuations or white spaces. The final production of this phase is a set of tokens.

2. Filtration

Filtration is reducing the noise of textual data by removing stop words. Stop words are the words that occur most in any language (Rasheed, 2021). Stop words do not affect the meaning of the text. The removal of stop words can be done by using pre-compiled stop-word lists or by using a more sophisticated method for dynamic stop-word identification (cornford, deinet, & de palma, 2021).

3. Lemmatization

Lemmatization is a process that is very similar to stemming. It aims to clutch all the words - with different forms - into their root form so that they can be analyzed as a single word (Mohan & Vedantham, 2021). In lemmatization, the term "lemma" means to group together different forms of a word. In the extraction of each word's suitable lemma, Morphological analysis plays the main role. Morphological analysis intends to explore the minimal unit of meaning (Goodwin, 2021). Since lemmatization have the capacity to work on parts of speech, using the lemmatization process, the root words will be related to a verbal speech. For example, a lemmatizer should map "gone", "going" and "went" into "go". Lemmatization can be used for grouping the user sentimental opinion into similar forms which can be suitable for further usage (Mohan & Vedantham, 2021).

4. Stemming

Stemming usually refers to a basic heuristic process of reducing words to their stem, base or root form (Mohan & Vedantham, 2021). To achieve this goal correctly the derivational affixes must be removed. E.g. "interesting" to "interest".

5. Part of Speech

Part-of-speech (POS) tagging is one of the basic preprocessing building blocks for any language processing (Mohan & Vedantham, 2021). "POS" tagging is the process of labeling up each word in a text with its type, e.g. a verb, noun, adverb, adjective.... etc (M.V.L. & Pakary, 2021). Tables from Table 3 to Table 7 shows the most popular POS tags.

Table 3. Noun POS

NN	Common noun
NNS	Plural common noun
NNP	Proper noun
NNPS	Plural proper noun
PRP$	Possessive pronoun (his, her my)
PRP	Personal pronoun (I, he, she, him, her)
WP	Wh- pronoun (what, which, who, whom)
WP$	Wh- possessive pronoun (whose)

Table 4. Verb POS

MD	Modal verb (can, could, may, must)
VB	Base verb (take)
VBC	Future tense, conditional
VBD	Past tense (took)
VBF	Future tense
VBG	Gerund, present participle (taking)
VBN	Past participle (taken)
VBP	Present tense (take)
VBZ	Present 3rd person singular (takes)

Table 5. Adjective / Adverb POS

JJ	Adjective
JJR	Comparative adjective
JJS	Superlative adjective
RB	Adverb
RBR	Comparative adverb
RBS	Superlative adverb
WRB	Wh- Adverb (how, where, why)

Table 6. Determiner POS

DT	Determiner (a, the, an...)
PDT	Predeterminer (all, both...)
WDT	Wh- determiner (which)

Table 7. Symbol POS

SYM	Symbol
POS	Possessive Marker (', 's)
LRB	Open parenthesis
RRB	Close parenthesis
,	Comma
-	Hyphen / dash
:	Colon
;	Semi-Colon
.	Terminating punctuation (!, ., ?)
``	Open quote
"	Close quote
$	Currency symbol

POS delivers data about how each word in a sentence is being used within the scope of a phrase. Assigning part of speech is sometimes complicated, as a specific word may suggest various implications depending on the sentence where the word is being utilized (M.V.L. & Pakary, 2021). Many machine learning methods, systems and approaches have been applied to the problem of POS tagging (Nunsanga., 2021). The mechanisms of POS tagging initiated in the 1960s (Màrquez, 2020). Since then, different researchers have come up with various techniques and methods to improve the process of POS tagging for different languages in terms of precision and effectiveness (Rasheed, 2021). Most of the earlier tagging systems were based on the rule-based method or stochastic methods (M.V.L. & Pakary, 2021). POS is very beneficial for SA; for example, nouns and pronouns are likely to denote a named entity, while adjectives and adverbs frequently designate those entities in an emotional term. By identifying adjective-noun combinations, such as "awful diving" and "average drumming,".

A sentiment analysis system achieves its first indication that it's looking at a sentiment-bearing phrase. Of course, not every sentiment-bearing phrase takes an adjective-noun form. "Cost us", is a noun-pronoun combination but bears some negative sentiment. Accurate part of speech tagging is critical for reliable sentiment analysis, so it's important that a rules-based system account for these variations (Catlin & Mohler, 2021). In most SAs, in order to find the orientation of subjective sentences, only Adjective, Adverb, Verb and their suitable combination are considered. These combinations refer to as "linguistic patterns". In literature four types of words i.e., adjectives, adverbs, verbs and nouns or their combination, are used for SA because only these four types of words show the sentiment. Nouns are usually used for product features extraction and only some subjective sentences use nouns to express the sentiment (Khan, 2016).

Step 2: Identify Each Sentiment-Bearing Phrase and Component

There can be many methods and algorithms to implement SA systems. Nowadays, however, there is a deeper step taken by many researchers. SA can be divided as shown in Figure 5 to Machine learning approaches and lexicon-based approaches. Machine learning approaches can be divided to supervised and unsupervised learning. Supervised learning can be divided into linear classifiers, decision tree classifiers, rule-based classifier, probabilistic. linear classifiers can be divided to support vector machine (SVM) and neural networks (NN). Probabilistic can be divided to Naïve Bayes Network (NB), Bayesian network, and Maximum entropy. Lexicon-based approaches can be divided into dictionary-based approaches and corpus-based approaches. corpus-based approaches can be divided into statistical and semantic. The following subsections are going to discuss each of these approaches in details.

Machine Learning Approaches

Machine learning (ML) is a branch of artificial intelligence (AI) that converges on constructing applications that are capable of learning from data and can improve their accuracy through time without being programmed to do so. (Sayed, Salem, and Khder, 2019). The main focal point of ML is to develop a computer program that is capable of self-learning. Different machine learning algorithms are applied in data mining, pattern recognition and some computational theories. It is divided into 3 main categories (Supervised, Unsupervised and Semi-Supervised). Table 8 shows the different scientific studies for each classification.

Figure 5. Methods and algorithms to implement SA systems

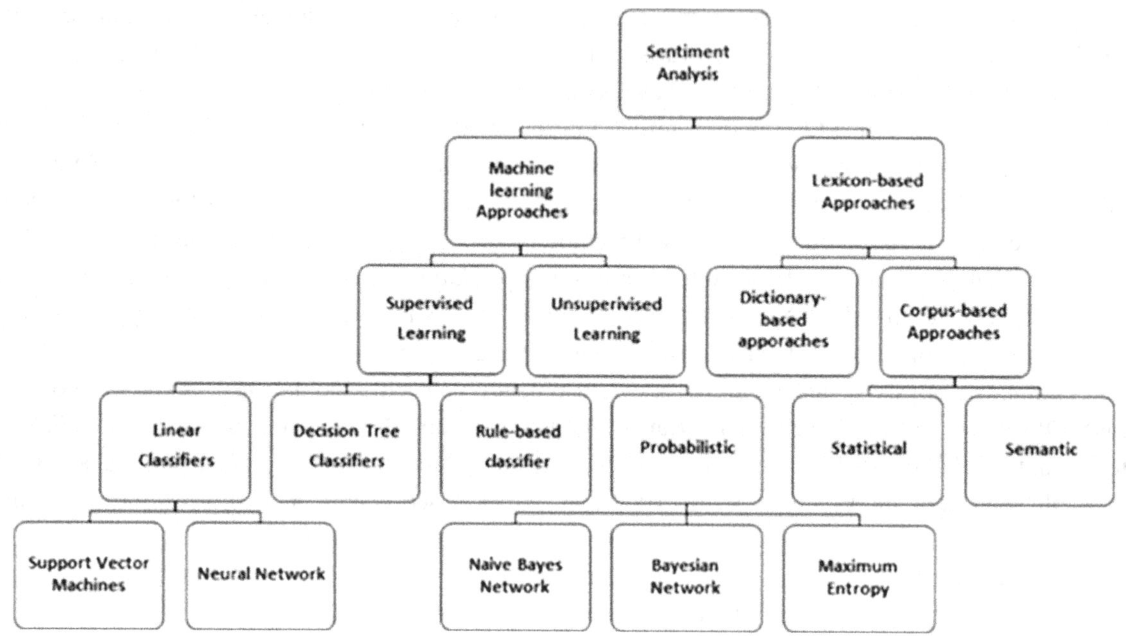

Table 8. Machine learning techniques

Technique	Sub technique	Paper, year	Dataset	Accuracy	Domain	Emotions used
Supervised	Support vector machine	(Inkpen, keshtkar, & Ghazi, 2009)	Newspapers headlines	48%,	General	Happiness, sadness, anger, disgust, surprise, fear, no emotion
			annotated blog corpus	65.45%		
		(Binal, Wu, & Potdar, 2009)	Student reviews	NO	E-learning	negative(Sad, confused, frustrated), positive(happy, engaged, excited), neutral
		(Haji, Chen, & Vidyasagar, 2010)	Blogs	96.4%.	General	sadness, happiness, anger, fear, disgust and surprise
		(Patil & Patil, 2013)	ISEAR dataset	71.64%	General	Anger, Disgust, fear, joy, sad
	Naïve BAYES	(Boa, et al., 2012)	online news collection	53.67%	General	Touched, Empathy, Boredom, Anger, Amusement, sadness, surprise, warmness
		(Donglei, Zhikai, Yulan, & Deyu, 2019)	News dataset	43.072%	General	Touching, Anger, Amusement, Sadness, Shock and Curiosity
	Deep Learning	(Ankush, et al., 2019)	News dataset	71.43%	General	Anger, Happy and sad
Unsupervised	Graph based	(Sugandh, Mulye, & Wadhai, 2011)	–	–	General	anger, fear, happiness, sadness

Supervised Learning

Supervised learning is a ML task in which we have input variables (x) and output variable (Y) then an algorithm is applied to map the input to the output. The target is to use the mapping function on new input data (x) to predict the output variables (Y) for that data. It is termed supervised learning since the progression of the learning algorithm is through the trained dataset. Supervised learning can be thought of as a teacher supervising the learning process (Idrees & Hassan, A Proposed Framework Targeting the Enhancement of Students' Performance in Fayoum University, 2018). Some of supervised learning approaches are discussed in the following subsections.

- *Linear Classification*

Linear classification is a classification algorithm based on a linear predictor function. It combines a set of weights with the feature vector (Karimuzzaman, 2021). The research in (Dey, 2021) demonstrated sign character recognition of standard data set. The author evaluated the linear classification method by which achieved accuracy nears about 100%. The research suggested the real-time (HMM) positioned organization to analyze sign language adaptation, tracking data, and the resulting architecture. The research in (Karimuzzaman, 2021) recommends that one may choose LR among the linear classification model if there is a high correlation, multicollinearity, multivariate normality, and high dimensionality among predictors. Moreover, the research in (Albayati, 2020) tackles ASA by using a Deep Learning approach. In his work, one of word embedding methods, such as a first hidden layer for features extracting from the input dataset and Long Short-Term Memory (LSTM) as a deep neural network, has been used for training. The model combined with Softmax layer is applied to turn numeric outputs from LSTM layer into probabilities to classify the outputs to positive or negative. There are two datasets that are used for training the model separately with each one. The first one is ASTD dataset as a dialectal Arabic type about different tweets from internet, the results with this dataset are compared with another academic work that used the same one. The results from this work outperforms through accuracy about 14.95% and F-score about 15.14% more than what performed in the previous work. The second one is HTL dataset as a modern standard Arabic type about opinions of reviewers on different hotels from several countries. This dataset is bigger in size than the first one to show the size effect on the results of this model. So, the accuracy increased about 11% and F-score about 10.8% more than what performed with the first dataset.

- *Support Vector Machine (SVM)*

SVM is a discriminative classifier that aims at separating the training examples by a determined separator such as spaces, then it constructs a hyper plane or a set of hyper planes in a high- or infinite-dimensional space which then can be used for classification, regression, or other tasks. In (Inkpen, keshtkar, & Ghazi, 2009), a Text Affect dataset was used (Strapparava & Mihalcea, 2007) and SVM was applied over a segment equal 1250 headlines from the dataset which produced an accuracy of 48%. Another annotated corpus was also used in which SVM is applied on 2090 sentences and produced an accuracy of 65.45%. Moreover, in (Binal, Wu, & Potdar, 2009), targeted to detect the emotions during E-learning as it affects the learning experience. They proposed a conceptual framework that can extract, analyze, and predict the emotion of learners to assist the lecturer for decision support by applying the natural language steps using GATE tool (tokenization, sentence, splitter, POS tagger). These steps allowed the proposed framework to detect the students' emotions towards the subject. The student could experience either positive (happy, engaged, excited), negative (sad, confused, frustrated) or neutral emotional experience. Another research in (Haji, Chen, & Vidyasagar, 2010) have used the GATE tool, with detecting and annotating emotions' terms in the corpus. The resulted words are considered as input features to the support vector machine for training. The system proved the success by an accuracy of 96.4%. Moreover, in (Patil & Patil, 2013) a proposed approach which joined SVM with tf-idf for emotions' classification and reached an accuracy of 71.64%. Moreover, in (Balabantaray, Mohammad, & Sharma, 2012) support vector machines are also applied and reached an accuracy of 73.24%. Other research applied SVM in different fields such as in (Khedr, Kholeif, & Saad, 2017). Finally, recent research such as (Nida, Kirmani, Mohd, Muttoo, & Mohd, 2019) proposed a method that applied support vector machine approach with the support of an emotions' terms' dictionary. The emotions were Joy, fear, sadness, anger, disgust, surprise. The research used different datasets that were collected from news headlines and were classified among 3 corpuses. An accuracy of 59.71% was achieved for corpus 1, 63.24% for corpus 2 and 67.86% for corpus 3.

- *Neural Network*

Neural networks are also known as artificial neural networks (Ehsan Haghighat, 2021). Neural networks are a set of machines learning algorithms that stimulate the human brain. They are designed to recognize certain patterns, by translating data through machine observation. The patterns recognized by them are in numerical format. A specialized neural network contains many extremely connected processing elements called nodes. These nodes operate in parallel to resolve a particular dilemma. A node is responsible for conducting the computations that are coordinated freely on a neuron, this is triggered when the threshold stimuli is meet. A node combines input from the data together with the weights that either increases or decreases that input, thus modifying inputs in accordance with the mission that the algorithm is attempting to discover. The product of "input * weight" is summed up and passed through a node's function. If the signals are passed through, the neuron is 'activated'.

Deep learning is a branch of neural network that comprises many concealed levels and mirrors the process of neurons within the human brain in the process of providing a precise result. The research in (Avudaiappan.T, 2020) used Neural networks to increase the accuracy of sentiments of the tweets (Budhi, 2021). They proposed a system that uses tweets from Twitter for sentimental analysis. The data set is downloaded from Twitter API. To clean the words preprocessing steps are performed which includes stemming, removal of numbers, punctuations, stop words, white spaces and converting all the tweets into same case letters. Then the sentence is tokenized. The data set consists of 2000 training data set and 2000 testing data set in both Korean and English languages. Then FNN is applied on the data set. This system also uses Tensor Flow platform for creating neural network. Accuracy is used as the evaluation measure. This inputs 100 neurons for processing. This neural network uses three hidden layers for sentiment prediction. Multilayer perceptron produces accuracy of 52.60% as a result.

Moreover, the research in (Gowrij, Vimalia, & Senduru, 2021) proposed a system where the data can be mined utilizing the Twitter exploration function, which helped them in data cleaning. To analyze the data, they used a deep learning algorithm. To enhance the data analyzing accuracy, long short-term memory (LSTM) and recurrent neural networks (RNN) are used. Another research in (Santos, 2014) proposed a new deep convolutional neural network that exploits from character- to sentence-level information to perform sentiment analysis of short texts. They applied their approach for two corpora of two different domains: the Stanford Sentiment Treebank (SSTb), which contains sentences from movie reviews; and the Stanford Twitter Sentiment corpus (STS), which contains Twitter messages. For the SSTb corpus, their approach achieved a state-of-the-art result for single sentence sentiment prediction in both binary positive/negative classification, with 85.7%accuracy, and fine-grained classification, with 48.3% accuracy. For the STS corpus, their approach achieved a sentiment prediction accuracy of 86.4%.

- *Decision Tree Classifier*

Decision Trees are flexible Machine Learning algorithm that can perform both classification and regression tasks. They are extremely powerful algorithms, with the ability of matching complicated datasets. Apart from That, decision trees are the essential component of random forests, which are amongst the most powerful Machine Learning algorithms that are currently available. The structure of a decision tree can be considered as a Directed Acyclic Graph (DAG). DAG is a sequence of nodes in which each edge is produced from prior to later. The graph streams in a single direction, no object can be a child of itself. DAG starts with a root node, the attributes become interior nodes. The internal nodes perform a decision according to this decision the sample space is partitioned into two subtrees. The leaf nodes denote a classification, when the leaf node is reached, the algorithm will designate the label of the matching leaf. This process is called sample space recursive partitioning. Decision trees use complicated yet effective functions to pick the best path split. It is important to discover the best attribute/feature that achieves the finest classifying of the training data. This procedure is repeated until a leaf node is attained. This repeated procedure is called the recursive binary splitting. The selecting approach is said to be a greedy approach, as it evaluates all splits and pick the one returning the lowest cost. Decision tree algorithm have low bias and high variance since it repetitively partitions the data into smaller subsets, which makes the final subsets (leaf nodes) entails few or only one data points.

The research in (Zharmagambetov & Pak, 2016) represented a modern approach to the task of sentiment analysis of movie reviews by using deep learning recurrent neural networks and decision trees. These methods are based on statistical models, which are in a nutshell of machine learning algorithms. Another research in (Alshamsi, 2020) represented a research paper that aims to obtain a dataset of tweets and apply different machine learning algorithms to analyze and classify text. They explored text classification accuracy using different classifiers for classifying balanced and unbalanced datasets. They found that the performance of different classifiers varied depending on the size of the dataset. The results also revealed that the Naive Byes and ID3 gave a better accuracy level than other classifiers, and the performance was better with the balanced datasets. The different classifiers (K-NN, Decision Tree, Random Forest, and Random Tree) gave a better performance with the unbalanced datasets. Moreover, in (Chen, 2021), a study is proposed to explore whether customer voices from social media reviews are different during the COVID-19 outbreak. They proposed a new method to reduce interpersonal contact when collecting data. A text mining scheme which includes least absolute shrinkage and selection operator (LASSO), and decision trees (DT) are presented to discover the essential factors for customers to increase their satisfaction from unstructured online customer reviews. Finally, three real world review sets were employed to validate the effectiveness of the presented text mining scheme. Experimental results can help companies to properly adapt to similar epidemic situations in the future and facilitate their sustainable development.

- *Rule Based Classifier.*

The expression rule-based classification is used to signify any classification method that utilize IF-THEN rules in class prediction. Great thing about rule-based in sentiment analysis is that it entails a very little preprocessing, so it will need no to minimal Stemming, tokenization, Lemmatization, Normalization…. etc., In rule-based Sentiment Analysis, the algorithm computes the sentiment score from a set of a manually generated rules (Hobson, 2019). For instance, the algorithm can count the number of times the writer used the term "great" in his review and increases its estimated sentiment. It sounds very straight forward, but this is exactly what really happens, only on a much larger scale.

At the essence, some Corpus collects sentiment lexicon features (words, expressions, emojis…. etc.). These lexicons are ranked on a certain scale from extremely negative to extremely positive. Then an average of those ratings is computed, all the neutral terms are omitted. In addition to lexicons, there are typically some fascinating twists. For instance, the word "extremely" has no underlying negative or positive sentiment, it merely just increases the strength of the term it is affixed to. Furthermore, there are words that decrease the strength, moreover, punctuations have significances. For instance, negations like "not" in "not very good" inverses the original sentiment, etc. Positive and negative adjustments like "extremely" or "hardly" are allocated in two groups, and they increase or decreases the strength with the same factor, which indicates that "quite" and "extremely" are the same. There are some problems concerning selecting negative, positive and neutral scoring. Let's see an example to clarify. Which of these sentences are considered more negative "The food has nothing tasty" or "The food tastes horrible"? the second sentence is rated negative, while the first sentence's score is neutral, while it is expected to have an even higher score. Look at this sentence, "my disappointment was getting greater everyday" the term "greater" will for sure get a higher score when it is meant to be an increase in negativity.

In (Ke, Sheng, Li, Silamu, & Guo, 2021) a natural language explanation framework is proposed for sentiment analysis that provides sufficient domain knowledge for generating additional labelled data for each new labelling decision. A rule-based semantic parser transforms these explanations into programmatic labelling functions that generate noisy labels for an arbitrary amount of unlabeled sentiment information to train a sentiment analysis classifier. Experiments on two sentiment analysis datasets demonstrate the superiority it achieves over baseline methods by leveraging explanations as external knowledge to joint training a sentiment analysis model rather than only labels. An ablation study is conducted to clarify the relative contribution of natural language explanations. another research in (Chikersal, 2015) described a Twitter sentiment analysis system developed by combining a rule-based classifier with supervised learning. They submitted their results for the message-level subtask in SemEval 2015 Task 10 and achieved a F1-score of 57.06%. The rule-based classifier is based on rules that are dependent on the occurrences of emoticons and opinion words in tweets. Whereas the Support Vector Machine (SVM) is trained on semantic, dependency, and sentiment lexicon-based features. The tweets are classified as positive, negative or unknown by the rule-based classifier, and as positive, negative or neutral by the SVM. The results we obtained show that rules can help refine the SVM's predictions.

Moreover, a research in (Saeed, 2021) proposed a supervised learning approach for Arabic reviews sentiment classification. This approach utilizes optimized compact features that depend on a well representative feature set coupled with feature reduction techniques, which manages to guarantee high accuracy and time/space savings simultaneously. The employed feature set includes a triple combination of N-gram features and positive/negative N-grams counts features obtained after considering negation handling. The proposed approach examines two different linear transformation methods; principal component analysis (PCA) as an unsupervised transformation method and latent Dirichlet allocation (LDA) as a supervised transformation method. A spam detection process is executed prior to the learning for the purpose of increasing the classifier robustness using rule-based classifier. In the spam detection module, the reviews' dataset is handled for spam detection before proceeding into the core sentiment classification framework. The purpose of this module is to filter out the negatively influencing data (spam reviews). The idea behind the spam detection involved is a stacking ensemble based on integrating a rule-based classifier and a machine learning technique. A set of content-based features is used, such as words count, unique words percentages, and review rating deviation that relies on a triple combination of negation handled N-gram features. The proposed approach has been experimented with five Arabic opinion text datasets of different domains and varying sizes (1.6 up to 94 K reviews). Experiments have been conducted for two-class (positive/negative sentiments) and three-class (positive/negative/neutral sentiments) classification problems. Accuracy values have been recorded in the range of 95.5–99.8% for the two-class classification problem and 92–97.3% for the three-class classification problem. The LDA feature reduction outperformed PCA by an average of 4.34% and 3.52% in accuracy and F1 Score measures, respectively. The overall approach outperformed the existing related works in literature by far of 23% and 34% for accuracy and F1 Score, respectively. The experimental studies and the obtained results show the efficiency of the proposed solution, which employs optimized features that rely on integrating a feature reduction module, together with a well representative feature set based on negation handled triple combination of N-gram features and positive/negative N-grams counts features. The overall results demonstrate great improvement with 24% increase in accuracy, 93% savings in the feature space, and 97% decrease in the classification execution time.

- *Probabilistic*

Probabilistic classifiers use mixture models for classification. The mixture model assumes that each class is a component of the mixture. Each mixture component is a generative model that provides the probability of sampling a particular term for that component. These kinds of classifiers are also called generative classifiers (Kiprono, 2016). Probabilistic models can be challenging to design. Most often, the problem lies in the lack of data regarding the domain necessary to completely indicate the conditional dependency between arbitrary variables. If available, estimating the complete conditional probability for an event may be unfeasible (Brownlee, 2019). A traditional approach in dealing with this challenge is to by using simplifying assumptions, such as assuming that all random variables in the model are conditionally independent. This is a drastic assumption, although it proves useful in practice, providing the basis for the Naive Bayes classification algorithm. An alternative approach is to develop a probabilistic model of a problem with some conditional independence assumptions. This provides an intermediate approach between a fully conditional model and a fully conditionally independent model. Bayesian belief networks are one example of a probabilistic model where some variables are conditionally independent. Thus, Bayesian belief networks provide an intermediate approach that is less constraining than the global assumption of conditional independence made by the naive Bayes classifier, but more tractable than avoiding conditional independence assumptions altogether (Brownlee, 2019).

- *Naïve Bayes (NB)*

Naïve Bayes (Khedr, El Seddawy, and Idrees, 2014) is a statistical probabilistic classifier trained effectively in a supervised learning setting. Many work has been done in sentimental analysis using NB. In this section we are going to discuss some of the most remarkable ones. In 2012 A method based on NB was proposed by (Boa, et al., 2012). Boa's method consisted of two modules targeting to obtain the emotions from a social network. The first module was the emotion terms module. This module used naïve Bayes to determine the emotions within documents and words. The second module was an LDA topic module that utilized LDA to classify the topic from documents (Othman, Hassan, Moawad, and Idrees, 2018) (Othman, Hassan, Moawad, and Idrees, 2016). The two modules work coherently to classify documents according to their associated emotions with regard to the topic and its relation to these documents. This system had an accuracy of 53.6%. More recently, in 2015, (Yann, Yoshua, & Geoffrey, 2015) applied a computational model for data representation learning with respect to the extraction level by applying a set of multiple processing layers, Yann and Geoffrey model was able to reach a level of adequate accuracy of 52%. Another very remarkable method was proposed in (Donglei, Zhikai, Yulan, & Deyu, 2019) which constructed a model that utilized NB networks to detect hidden topics about emotions. The research assumed that terms within the same sentence carry similar emotions. The proposed model reached an accuracy of 43.072%. Another research conducted in 2019 (Ankush, et al., 2019) proposed an approach to detect emotions from text using deep learning. The proposed approach focused on only three emotions, angry, sad and happy. Ankush reached the highest accuracy level. The average f-measure was 59.68% for the happy emotion, 80.79% for the sad emotion, and 73.55% for the angry emotion.

- *Bayesian Network*

Bayesian Networks provide a useful tool to visualize the probabilistic model for a domain, review all the relationships between the random variables, and reason about causal probabilities for scenarios given available evidence. Bayesian networks are a type of probabilistic graphical model comprised of nodes and directed edges. Bayesian network models capture both conditionally dependent and conditionally independent relationships between random variables. The models can be prepared by experts or learned from data, then used for inference to estimate the probabilities for causal or subsequent events. The research in (Weng, 2021) proposed a comprehensive seismic risk analysis that enables a better understanding of seismic disaster chains and rescue scenarios. The approach is based on a Bayesian network constructed using scenario-based methods. The final network structure is achieved by learning parameters. To determine the critical secondary disasters and the key emergency-response measures, probability adaptation and updating using the Bayesian model was performed. The practical application of the model is illustrated using the Wenchuan earthquake and the Jiuzhaigou earthquake in China. The two examples show that the model can be used to predict the potential effects of secondary disasters and the final seismic losses. The results of the model can help decisionmakers gain a comprehensive understanding of seismic risk and implement practical emergency-rescue measures to reduce risk and losses.

The research in (Luis Guti´errez, 2019) has used Bayesian networks precisely as a sentiment classifier, achieving reasonable outcomes and in some situations better, when compared with different approaches. Moreover, in (Luis Guti´errez, 2019), a parallel algorithm was developed for Bayesian networks structure learning from significant-size datasets. The algorithm is implemented using a MapReduce cluster and is employed to obtain dependencies between words. The method allows the process of extracting sentiments. The analysis of the results gained from a blogs dataset shows that the approach can extract features with fewer predictor variables associated to the entire data set, ensuing better predictions than usual methods. The research in (Gonzalo A.Ruzab, 2020) consider Bayesian network classifiers to implement sentiment analysis on two datasets in Spanish, namely: "2010 Chilean earthquake" and "2017 Catalan independence referendum". To automatically manage the number of edges supported by the training examples in the Bayesian network classifier, they implemented a Bayes factor approach for this goal, generating additional realistic networks. The outcome indicates the effectiveness of applying the Bayes factor measure compared to (SVM) and random forests. The network allows the identification of the relations among words and proposes remarkable information to historically and socially features of the event dynamics.

- *Maximum Entropy*

The maximum entropy principle (MEP)is a method of picking up the best distribution from several different probability distributions. These distributions should express a certain state of knowledge, and the selected distribution should represent the best maximum entropy choice. Maximum entropy is usually used in systems with a high degree of uncertainty, maximum entropy ensures the avoidants of adding any extra biases or uncalled for assumptions into the analysis. Utilizing the maximum entropy principle to a problem involves algebraically solving a series of equations for several unknowns. According to (B.Y. Duan, 1999), MEP has been applied in most information systems. engineering analysis, optimum design. The research applied MEP in a synthetic problem of pretensioned steel net; other researches utilized MEP to solve structural optimum design; distribution and assignment of traffic; analysis and optimum design of underground water net in a city as well as finite element with some interesting results.

In SA, Maximum Entropy classification can be used to estimate the polarity of given comments. These comments can be classified into two classes, positive or negative. The research in (B. Pang, 2002) was the first to use supervised sentiment approach. They compared NB, Maximum Entropy classification, and SVM tactics, and found that the usage of unigrams as capabilities yielded precise effects. Various classifiers have been compared in (R. Xia, 2011), the accuracy of SVM classifier was 86.4%, Maximum entropy classifier was 85.4%, and accuracy of Naive Bayes was 85.8%. (Soni, 2017) used Naïve Bayes, Maximum entropy classifier, they compared Naïve Bayes and maximum entropy classifier and they found that Max entropy classifier with Google translator provide better accuracy, i.e., 74.04%, while (Mishra, 2020) used SVM, ME and NB, to arrange human conclusions. Moreover, (Renault, 2020) provided an empirical evidence that the preprocessing method and the size of the dataset have a strong impact on the correlation between investor sentiment and stock returns. Since investor sentiment and stock returns are highly correlated, they found that investor sentiment derived from messages sent on social media helps in predicting large capitalization stocks return at a daily frequency. Tiwari compared maximum entropy, support vector machine, random forest and multilayer perceptron to their benchmark Naive Bayes model. They performed a grid search for hyperparameter optimization and found that the best performance is achieved by a Maximum Entropy classifier, closely followed by a Support Vector Machine classifier. More complex and time-consuming algorithms do not improve the accuracy of classification. This result suggests that machine learning algorithms may be more decisive in complex context or linguistic structure, but that for short texts published on social media, the text preprocessing method plays a bigger role. Tiwari found that more complex algorithms (Random Forest and Multilayer Perceptron) do not improve the precision of the classification compared to more simple methods such as

Maximum Entropy or Support Vector Machine. Given the cost associated with the optimization of the hyperparameters (time, complexity, lack of transparency and computing power costs), simple classifier such as Naive Bayes, support vector machine, or maximum entropy), will often do the trick for social media sentiment analysis.

Unsupervised Learning

Unsupervised Learning (UL) is a machine learning technique in which the users do not need to supervise the model (E., 2021). UL permits the model to operate on its own to find patterns and information that were previously unobserved. It mainly deals with the unlabeled data. UL Algorithms permit users to operate more complex processing tasks compared to supervised learning. Even Though, unsupervised learning is more unpredictable compared with other learning methods. Unsupervised learning algorithms comprise clustering, anomaly detection, neural networks, etc.

Unsupervised learning (Sas & Guptaj, 2021) is a type of learning in which the machine is trained with un-labelled information. Classification is achieved by associating the features of a given text with sentiment lexicons whose sentiment values are determined prior to their use. Clustering methods such as k-means, mean shift clustering and so forth are used. According to the model in (E., 2021), there are many applications for unsupervised machine learning, for example, clustering automatically splits the dataset into groups base on their similarities. Anomaly detection can discover unusual data points in your dataset. It is useful for finding fraudulent transactions. On the other hand, association mining identifies sets of items which often occur together in your dataset while Latent variable models are widely used for data preprocessing. Like reducing the number of features in a dataset or decomposing the dataset into multiple components.

In SA, unsupervised learning is used to classify sentiments with no already labeled output. This makes it hard to evaluate these opinions because there are no pre-prepared answers, which makes it hard to decide what tool or model to use in analyzing the sentiment of these unlabeled text data. The core point here is to compare the performance of these tools using labeled data—i.e., using an unsupervised learning tool/model to analyze texts that have been correctly classified already. Unsupervised learning methods are used to determine the more precise sentence-level sentiments with the help of contextual dependencies (Patel, 2021), they are more suitable for the aspect-based sentiment analysis as they are found to be more adaptable to different contexts and domains with the change in information rather than changing the entire model structure. GloVe stands for Global Vectors for word representation. It is an unsupervised learning algorithm which finds its prime application in generating word embeddings based on the co-occurrence information of words present in the corpus (Shivani Malhotra, 2021). The process of building the word embeddings in GloVe is carried out by training the collection of global word to word co-occurrence statistics from the corpus. The resulting embeddings exhibit intriguing one-dimensional substructure of vector space.

In 2016, Facebook's AI research team released a library for learning word embeddings and performing sentiment classification known as fastText. According to (Shivani Malhotra, 2021), this library helped to build an unsupervised and supervised learning algorithm to obtain word vectors using a deep learning model. The results presented major improvement of fastText when compared to other embeddings such as word2vec, GloVe, etc. This improvement refers to dividing the word into sub-words known as n-grams (where n is total number of sub-words). The building blocks for sentiment classification in this case are sub-words or n-grams and not words or sentences. The research in (Yi Han, 2021) developed a rule-based methodology for extracting and analyzing the sentiment expressions of users on a large scale, from myriad reviews available on social media and e-commerce platforms. The methodology further advances current unsupervised attribute-level sentiment analysis approaches by enabling efficient identification and mapping of sentiment expressions of individual users onto their respective attributes. Experiments on a large dataset scraped from a major e-commerce retail store for apparel and indicate 74.3%–93.8% precision in extracting attribute-level sentiment expressions of users and demonstrate the feasibility and potentials of the developed methodology for large-scale need finding from user reviews. Another research in (Shivani Malhotra, 2021) proposed an valuable transfer learning-based model. This model is inspired by ULMFit, the results were represented on challenging sentiment analysis tasks such as contextualization and regularization. They empirically justified the effectiveness of the proposed model by utilizing it to three conventional datasets for sentiment classification task. their model accomplished the state-of-the-art outcomes remarkably when compared to acknowledged baselines in terms of classification accuracy.

Lexicon Based Techniques

Although some of the previous discussed researches have used a lexicon, however, they were a supportive component to the main approach to build the emotions' corpus in addition to the manual process to build these lexicons. Lexicon based techniques mainly aims at supporting emotion mining field by building an emotions' lexicon for various types of emotions, this lexicon is then used for emotion mining in the targeted documents. Different techniques are proposed for building the emotions' lexicon, they are Concept net, Lexical Chain, Corpus Based, and Dictionary Based. Table 9 presents a brief comparison among these techniques while the following subsections discuss each technique.

Table 9. Lexicon based techniques

Technique	Paper, year	Dataset	Accuracy	Domain	Emotions used
Concept Net	(R.Ezhilarasi & Minu, 2012)	WordNet	unknown	General	–
Lexical chain	(Kumar and R.Suresh, 2014)	Wiki news articles	86%	General	happiness, sadness, anger, fear, disgust and surprise
Corpus based	(Lei, Raob, Li, Quan, & Wenyin, 2013)	BBC News	63.57%	General	Touching, empathy, boredom, anger, amusement, sadness, surprise, warmness
	(Gohary, Sultan, Hana, & Dosoky, 2013)	Children Stories	65%	General	Joy, fear, sadness, anger, disgust, surprise
Dictionary based	(Tokuhisa, Inui, & Matsumoto, 2008)	EP corpus	Unknown	Dialouge systems	happiness, pleasantness, relief, fear, sadness, disappointment, unpleasantness, loneliness, anxiety, and anger

Concept Net

Using this technique, the text is analyzed for extracting the main domain concepts targeting to build the concept net. Concept net represents the concepts with their relationships with highlighting the relationship between the concepts and the related topic. The research in (R.Ezhilarasi & Minu, 2012), built an emotion ontology network for classifying the text documents according to emotion classes. The main idea can be summarized as identifying the tokens which is expected to represent the emotions and confirm these expectations using WordNet (Miller, 1995). Confirmed emotions' terms are then used for building the ontology net for further documents'' classifications.

Lexical Chain

Lexical chain technique (Turney & Litiman, 2003) is based on natural language processing paradigm. Lexical chain builds a linguistic ontology net by detecting the relation between sentences in the corpus according to the terms' similarity which exist in these sentences. Lexical chain considers a number of criteria including the length of the sentence namely the chain length, the number of the term occurrence in the chain. The classification is then determined by determining the product of the homogeneity index and the chain length. The research in (Kumar and R.Suresh, 2014), considered detecting six basic emotions (happiness, sadness, anger, fear, disgust and surprise) in their research, their proposed approach reached an accuracy of 86%. In this research, the lexical chains are constructed in a terms' semantic relations basis and the chains score is calculated, and finally, high scores chains are highlighted to represent the emotions of the document.

Corpus Based

Corpus based techniques aims at building an emotion corpus which can be used later for emotion mining tasks. Lei and his colleagues presented a lexicon-based system in (Lei, Raob, Li, Quan, & Wenyin, 2013) which targeted to classify the documents based on their emotions and reached an accuracy of 59.11%. The main idea of the research was based on extracting the main words representing each emotion by the user from a set of documents and build a lexicon of words representing the emotions. The emotions set included (Touching, empathy, boredom, anger, amusement, sadness, surprise, warmness). Another research in (Gohary, Sultan, Hana, & Dosoky, 2013), focused on the automatic detection of emotions in Arabic text based on the sentence level which reached an f-measure score equal 65%. The proposed approach was based on a moderate sized Arabic lexicon which was used to annotate Arabic children stories dataset terms. The corpus consisted of 100 documents with 2,514 sentences. The sentence classification was measured according to the kappa statistics value, a value equal 1 represents a total agreement while a value equal 0 represents a total disagreement. The average value of Kappa in this research was 0.46 which represented that moderate agreement. The Lexicon was built for the six emotion categories (Joy, fear, sadness, anger, disgust, surprise) from annotated sentences and directly from English emotions lexicon.

Dictionary Based

Dictionary based technique aims to classify the emotion represented in a token based on the definition of this word in dictionaries such as WordNet (Miller, 1995) and their hierarchies. Tokuhisa, Inui and Matsumoto presented a research in (Tokuhisa, Inui, & Matsumoto, 2008) which reached an accuracy of 84.6%. The research aimed at documents' classification according to the emotions of these documents following their sematic meaning. The proposed research targeted the dialog chatting system for extracting emotions' terms, then this step was then followed by connecting this results with the context of human computer dialog and assign massive examples of emotion-provoking events that can be extracted from the Web by determining their accuracy level with determining the accuracy threshold. These examples are then used to build a semantic content-based model for fine-grained emotion classification. The model also considered the quantity and accuracy of emotion-provoking examples to be collected and Emotion-provoking corpus for extracting data. Moreover, in (Boa, et al., 2012), a high quality moderate sized emotion lexicon is manually created using Mechanical Turk and WordNet Affect the lexicon is built based on questioners distributed to the subscribers of Mechanical Turk.

Phrase Rating

The explored sentiments are then rated according to defined criteria to generate the final sentimental status of the data. The rating process could be applied by either simple methods as direct mathematical form or by more accurate directions as terms weighting. The selection is left to the developers' perspective.

CONCLUSION

This chapter provided an overview on the field of sentimental analysis, opinion mining and emotion mining. The chapter included discussing the business as well as the technical perspectives of the field. The basic definitions are identified, the process steps are also introduced in detail, and the different applied techniques are discussed. The paper also discussed the main steps of the mining process included all phases. Moreover, a review of the techniques for emotion mining in text have been presented and their relationship with opinion mining. Finally, a comparison among different techniques has been discussed through some criteria such as datasets and error rates.

REFERENCES

Abdulhakeem, Q., & Albayati, A. S.-A. (2020). A Method of Deep Learning Tackles Sentiment. *Iraq Journal of Computing*, *20*(4). Advance online publication. doi:10.33103/uot.ijccce.20.4.2

AED. (2020, January 21). An atlas of personality, emotion and behaviour. journal.pone, 15. doi:10.1371/journal.pone.0227877

Afify, E., Sharaf Eldin, A., Khedr, A. E., & Alsheref, F. K. (2019). User-Generated Content (UGC) Credibility on Social Media Using Sentiment Classification. *FCI-H Informatics Bulletin*, *1*(1), 1–19.

Agrawal, A., & An, A. (2012). Unsupervised Emotion Detection from Text using Semantic and Syntactic Relations. *The 2012 IEEE/WIC/ACM International Joint Conferences on Web Intelligence and Intelligent Agent Technology*.

Ahmed, A. Y. M. (2021). *Sentiment Analysis on Bangla Text Using Long Short-Term Memory (LSTM) Recurrent Neural Network. In Trends in Computational and Cognitive Engineering. 1309*. Springer. doi:10.1007/978-981-33-4673-4_16

Ahuja, S. (2017). *Using the Flipped Classroom to Improve Knowledge Creation of Master's-Level Students in Engineering*. IGI Global. doi:10.4018/978-1-5225-2399-4.ch028

Al-Yazidi, S. A., Berri, J., Al-Qurishi, M., & Alrubaian, M. (2020, June). Measuring Reputation and Influence in Online Social Networks: A Systematic Literature Review. *International Journal of Artificial Intelligence Tools, 99*, 105824–105851. Advance online publication. doi:10.1109/ACCESS.2020.2999033

Alison Attrill-Smith, C. F. (2020). *The Oxford Handbook of Cyberpsychology* (C. F. Alison Attrill-Smith, Ed.). Oxford University Press.

Alshamsi, A. B. (2020). Sentiment Analysis in English Texts. *Advances in Science, Technology and Engineering Systems Journal, 5*(6).

Amit Goldenberg, D. G. (2020, February 24). Collective Emotions. *Current Directions in Psychological Science, 1*(2), 154–160. Advance online publication. doi:10.1177/0963721420901574

Anand Joseph Daniel, J. M. (2021, Feb 9). *A Novel Sentiment Analysis for Amazon Data with TSA based Feature Selection*. doi:10.12694/scpe.v22i1.1839

Ankush, C., Umang, G., Manoj, K. C., Radhakrishnan, S., Michel, G., & Puneet, A. (2019). Understanding Emotions in Text Using Deep Learning and Big Data. *Computers in Human Behavior*, 309–317.

Anna Mauranen, S. V. (2020). *ELF, language change and social networks: evidence from real-time social media data* (S. V. Anna Mauranen, Ed.). Cambridge University Press.

Ansorena, I. L. (2021, January 5). On the benchmarking of port performance. A cosine similarity approach. *International Journal of Process Management and Benchmarking, 11*(1), 1. doi:10.1504/IJPMB.2021.112258

Avudaiappan.T, J. S. (2020). Twitter Sentimental Analysis Using Neural Network. *International Journal of Scientific & Technology Research, 9*(2).

Badawy, M., Abd El-Aziz, A., Idress, A. M., Hefny, H., & Hossam, S. (2016). A survey on exploring key performance indicators. *Future Computing and Informatics Journal, 1*(1-2), 47–52. doi:10.1016/j.fcij.2016.04.001

Balabantaray, R. C., Mohammad, M., & Sharma, N. (2012). Multi-Class Twitter Emotion Classification: A New Approach. *International Journal of Applied Information Systems, 4*(1).

Basiri, M. E., & Kabiri, A. (2020). *HOMPer: A new hybrid system for opinion mining in the Persian language*. doi:10.1177/0165551519827886

Binal, H., Wu, C., & Potdar, V. (2009). A New Significant Area: Emotion Detection in E-learning Using Opinion Mining Techniques. *The 3rd IEEE International Conference on Digital Ecosystems and Technologies.*

Boa, S., Xu, S., Zhang, L., Yan, R., Su, Z., Han, D., & Yu, Y. (2012). Mining Social Emotions from Affective Text. *IEEE Transactions on Knowledge and Data Engineering, 24*(9), 1658–1669. doi:10.1109/TKDE.2011.188

Brownlee, J. (2019, October 11). *A Gentle Introduction to Bayesian Belief Networks*. Retrieved from https://machinelearningmastery.com/introduction-to-bayesian-belief-networks/

Budhi, G. S., Chiong, R., Pranata, I., & Hu, Z. (2021, January 08). Using Machine Learning to Predict the Sentiment of Online Reviews: A New Framework for Comparative Analysis. *Archives of Computational Methods in Engineering*, 1–24. doi:10.100711831-020-09464-8

CatlinJ.MohlerT. (2021, January 01). Retrieved from https://www.lexalytics.com/

Chaudhuri, A. (2006). *Emotion and Reason in Consumer Behavior*. Taylor & Francis. doi:10.4324/9780080461762

Chen, W.-K. D. R.-S. (2021). Using a Text Mining Approach to Hear Voices of Customers from Social Media toward the Fast-Food Restaurant Industry. *MDPI*. doi:10.3390/su13010268

Chikersal, P. P. (2015). SeNTU: Sentiment Analysis of Tweets by Combining a Rule-based Classifier. In *Proceedings of the 9th International Workshop on Semantic Evaluation* (pp. 647–651). SemEval.

Cohen, J. (1968). Weighted kappa: Nominal scale agreement provision for scaled disagreement or partial credit. *Psychological Bulletin*, *70*(4), 213–220. doi:10.1037/h0026256 PMID:19673146

Cornford, R., Deinet, S., & De Palma, A. (2021, January). Fast, scalable, and automated identification of articles for biodiversity and macroecological datasets. *Global Ecology and Biogeography, 30*(1), 339-347. doi:10.1111/geb.13219

Dahab, M. Y., Idrees, A., Hassan, H. A., & Rafea, A. (2010). Pattern Based Concept Extraction for Arabic Documents. *International Journal of Intelligent Computing and Information Sciences, 10*(2).

Delbrouck, J.-B., & Dupont, N. T. (2020). Modulated Fusion using Transformer for Linguistic-Acoustic Emotion. *Anthology*.

Dey, V. S. (2021). *Advances in Intelligent Systems and Computing* (Vol. 1187). Singapore: Springerlink. doi:10.1007/978-981-15-6014-9

Donglei, T., Zhikai, Z., Yulan, C., & Deyu, Z. (2019). Hidden topic–emotion transition model for multi-level social emotion detection. *Knowledge-Based Systems*, 426–435.

Duan, B. Y. Y. Z. (1999). Maximum entropy principle and topological optimization of truss structures. Computational Mechanics in Structural Engineering, 179-192. doi:10.1016/B978-008043008-9/50052-1

E., K. A. (2021). *Unsupervised Machine Learning*. Retrieved from https://www.guru99.com/unsupervised-machine-learning.html#:~:text=Unsupervised%20Learning%20is%20a%20machine,deals%20with%20the%20unlabelled%20data

Ehsan Haghighat, R. J. (2021, January). A Keras/TensorFlow wrapper for scientific computations and physics-informed deep learning using artificial neural networks. *Computer Methods in Applied Mechanics and Engineering*, *373*(1), 1.

El Azab, A., Idrees, A. M., Mahmoud, M. A., & Hefny, H. (2016). Fake Account Detection in Twitter Based on Minimum Weighted Feature set. *International Journal of Computer, Electrical, Automation, Control and Information Engineering*, *10*(1), 13–18.

Elinor, C. (2020). *Media Distortions: Understanding the Power Behind Spam, Noise and Other Deviant Media.* The University of Liverpool Repository. Retrieved from https://www.peterlang.com/view/title/70160

Ezhilarasi, R., & Minu, R. (2012). *Automatic Emotion Recognition and Classification.* International Conference on Modelling Optimization and Computing.

Falak Jan, A. A. (2020). Opinion Mining through Enhanced Lexicon Approach. *Journal of Web Engineering & Technology, 7*(3).

Farhad Moghimifar, A. R. (2020, November 26). *Learning Causal Bayesian Networks from Text.* Academic Press.

Geelan, T. &. (2020, Nov 26). The Trials and Tribulations of Social Media and Transnational Labour Solidarity. *Protest Technologies and Media Revolutions.*

Gerard, C. (2021). *ext classification and sentiment analysis. In: Practical Machine Learning in JavaScript.* Apress. doi:10.1007/978-1-4842-6418-8_4

Gohary, A. F., Sultan, T. I., Hana, M. A., & Dosoky, M. M. (2013, May-June). A Computational Approach for Analyzing and Detecting Emotions in Arabic Text. *International Journal of Engineering Research and Applications, 3*(3), 100–107. http://www.ijera.com/papers/Vol3_issue3/S33100107.pdf

Goldenberg, A. G. (2020, April 24). Collective Emotions. *Current Directions in Psychological Science, 29*(2), 154–160.

Gonzalo, A., & Ruzab, P. A. (2020, May). Sentiment analysis of Twitter data during critical events through Bayesian networks classifiers. *Future Generation Computer Systems, 106*, 92–104.

Goodwin, A. P. (2021). Multidimensional morphological assessment for middle school students. *Journal of Research in Reading.*

Gowrij, S., Vimalia, S., & Senduru, S. (2021, January 09). Sentiment Analysis of Twitter Data Using Techniques in Deep Learning. *Data Intelligence and Cognitive Informatics*, 613-623.

Gupta, N., & Agrawal, R. (2020). *Hybrid Computational Intelligence.* Academic Press. doi:10.1016/B978-0-12-818699-2.00001-9

Haji, B., Chen, W., & Vidyasagar, P. (2010). Computational Approaches for Emotion Detection in Text. IEEE international conference on digital ecosystems, and technologies (DEST 2010).

Han, Y. M. M. (2021, June). Analysis of sentiment expressions for user-centered design. *Expert Systems with Applications, 171*(1). doi:10.1016/j.eswa.2021.114604

Hassan, A. M. (2019). Emotion Analysis for Opinion Mining From Text: A Comparative Study. *International Journal of e-Collaboration, 15*(1), 38–58.

Hassan, H., Dahab,, M., Bahnassy, K., Idrees, A., & Gamal, F. (2015). Arabic Documents classification method a Step towards Efficient Documents Summarization. *International Journal on Recent and Innovation Trends in Computing and Communication*, 351-359.

Hassan, H. A., Dahab, M. Y., Bahnasy, K., Idrees, A. M., & Gamal, F. (2014). Query answering approach based on document summarization. *International Open Access Journal of Modern Engineering Research, 4*(12).

Hassan, H. A., & Idrees, A. M. (2010). Sampling Technique Selection Framework for Knowledge Discovery. In *INFOS2010 - 2010 7th International Conference on Informatics and Systems* (pp. 1-8). IEEE.

Hazman, M., & Idrees, A. M. (2015). *A healthy nutrition expert system for. In E-Health and Bioengineering Conference (EHB)*. IEEE.

Helmy, Y., Emam, O., Khedr, A., & Bahloul, M. (2020). A Survey on Effect of KPIs in Higher Education based on Text Mining Techniques. *International Journal of Scientific and Engineering Research, 11*(3).

Helmy, Y., Khedr, A. E., Kolief, S., & Haggag, E. (2019). An Enhanced Business Intelligence Approach for Increasing Customer Satisfaction Using Mining Techniques. *International Journal of Computer Science and Information Security, 17*(4).

Hobson, L. (2019). *Natural Language Processing in Action: Understanding, Analyzing, and Generating Text with Python*. Manning Publications.

https://www.mturk.com/mturk. (n.d.). Retrieved from https://www.mturk.com/mturk

Idrees, A. M. (2015). Towards an Automated Evaluation Approach for E-Procurement. In *2015 13th International Conference on ICT and Knowledge Engineering (ICT & Knowledge Engineering 2015)* (pp. 67-71). IEEE.

Idrees, A. M., & Hassan, M. (2018). A Proposed Framework Targeting the Enhancement of Students' Performance in Fayoum University. *International Journal of Scientific and Engineering Research, 9*(11).

Inkpen, D., Keshtkar, F., & Ghazi, D. (2009). Analysis and generation of emotion in texts. *International Conference on Knowledge Engineering Principles and Techniques.*

Izazi, Z. Z., Mahadi, T., & Tengku-Sepora. (2020). Slangs on Social Media: Variations among Malay Language. *Pertanika, 28*(1), 17 - 34. Retrieved from http://www.pertanika.upm.edu.my/

Jabreel, M. M. (2021). Introducing Sentiment Analysis of Textual Reviews in a Multi-Criteria Decision Aid System. *Applied Sciences (Basel, Switzerland), 11*(1), 216.

Jackson, P. (2020). Understanding understanding and ambiguity in natural language. *Procedia Computer Science, 169*, 209–225.

Jing, Y. W. (2021). Relation Representation Learning Via Signed Graph Mutual Information Maximization for Trust Prediction. *Symmetry, 13*(1), 115.

Jizdny, J. (2020). *The Role of Marketing Communication in Social Media on Conversion of Customers in FMCG e-Commerce*. ProQuest.

Joseph Ledoux, S. G. (2018, February). The subjective experience of emotion: A fearful view. *Current Opinion in Behavioral Sciences, 19*, 67–72. doi:10.1016/j.cobeha.2017.09.011

Kamath, A., Guhekar, R., Makwana, M., & Dhage, S. N. (2020). Sarcasm Detection Approaches Survey. *Advances in Intelligent Systems and Computing, 1158*, 593-609. doi:10.1007/978-981-15-4409-5_54

Karimuzzaman, M. I. (2021). Predicting Stock Market Price of Bangladesh: A Comparative Study of Linear Classification Models. *Annals of Data Science*. doi:10.1007/s40745-020-00318-5

Ke, Z., Sheng, J., Li, Z., Silamu, W., & Guo, Q. (2021). Knowledge-Guided Sentiment Analysis Via Learning From Natural Language Explanations. *IEEE, 9*, 3570-3578. doi: . doi:10.1109/ACCESS.2020.3048088

Khan, J. &. (2016). Sentiment Analysis at Sentence Level for Heterogeneous Datasets. *Proceedings of the Sixth International Conference on Emerging Databases*. doi: 10.1145/3007818.3007848

Khedr, A., Kholeif, S., & Hessen, S. (2015, April). Enhanced Cloud Computing Framework to Improve the Educational Process in Higher Education: A case study of Helwan University in Egypt. *International Journal of Computers and Technology*, *14*(6), 5814–5823.

Khedr, A., Kholeif, S., & Saad, F. (2017). An Integrated Business Intelligence Framework for Healthcare Analytics. *International Journal of Advanced Research in Computer Science and Software Engineering*, *7*(5), 263–270.

Khedr, A. E., Abdel-Fattah, M. A., & Nagm-Aldeen, Y. (2015). A Literature Review of Business Process Modeling Techniques. *International Journal of Advanced Research in Computer Science and Software Engineering*, *5*(3), 43–47.

Khedr, A. E., & El Seddawy, A. I. (2015). A Proposed Data Mining Framework for Higher Education System. *International Journal of Computers and Applications*, *113*(7), 24–31.

Khedr, A. E., El Seddawy, A. I., & Idrees, A. M. (2014). Performance Tuning of K-Mean Clustering Algorithm a Step towards Efficient DSS. *International Journal of Innovative Research in Computer Science & Technology*, *2*(6), 111–118.

Khedr, A. E., & Idrees, A. M. (2017). Adapting Load Balancing Techniques for Improving the Performance of e-Learning Educational Process. *Journal of Computers*, *12*(3), 250–257.

Khedr, A. E., & Idrees, A. M. (2017). Enhanced e-Learning System for e-Courses Based on Cloud Computing. *Journal of Computers*, *12*(1).

Khedr, A. E., Idrees, A. M., & Elseddawy, A. (2016). Enhancing Iterative Dichotomiser 3 algorithm for classificat decision tree. *WIREs Data Mining and Knowledge Discovery, 6*.

Kiplagat Wilfred Kiprono, E. O. (2016, July). Comparative Twitter Sentiment Analysis Based on Linear and Probabilistic Models. *International Journal on Data Science and Technology*, *2*(4), 41–45. doi:10.11648/j.ijdst.20160204.11

Kumar, M., & Suresh, R. (2012). Emotion Detection using Lexical Chains. *International Journal of Computers and Applications*, *57*(4).

Lee, S. Y., & Lau, H. Y. (2020). An Event-comment Social Media Corpus for Implicit Emotion Analysis. *Proceedings of the 12th Conference on Language Resources and Evaluation (LREC 2020)* (pp. 1633–1642). Marseille: European Language Resources Association (ELRA).

Lei, J., Raob, Y., Li, Q., Quan, X., & Wenyin, L. (2013). Towards building a social emotion detection system for online news. *Journal of Future Generation Computer Systems*, *37*, 438–448.

Zhaoning Li, Q. L. (2020, Nov 8). Causality Extraction Based on Self-Attentive. BiLSTM-CRF with Transferred Embeddings. *arxiv*, 1-39.

Liu, L. Z. (2014). Aspect and Entity Extraction for Opinion (Vol. 1). Springer. https://doi.org/10.1007/978-3-642-40837-3_1

Liu, S., Teng, J., & Gong, Y. (2021). Extraction Method and Integration Framework for Perception Features of Public Opinion in Transportation. *Sustainability*, *13*(1), 254.

Loukachevitch, N. (2021). Automatic Sentiment Analysis of Texts: The Case of Russian. The Palgrave Handbook of Digital Russia Studies, 501-516.

Luis Guti'errez, J. B.-C. (2019). A Review on Bayesian Networks for Sentiment Analysis. In *Proceedings of the 7th International Conference on Software Process Improvement (CIMPS 2018)* (pp. 111-120). CIMPS. DOI: 10.1007/978-3-030-01171-0_10

Màrquez, L. (2020). A Machine Learning Approach to POS Tagging. *Machine Learning*, *39*(1), 59–91. doi:10.1023/A:1007673816718

Martinazzo, B., Dosciatti, M. M., & Paraiso, E. C. (2012). Identifying Emotions in Short Texts for Brazilian Brazilian Portuguese. In *Brazilian conference on intelligent systems.* Redes Neurais.

Miller, G. A. (1995). WordNet: A lexical database for English. *Communications of the ACM*, *38*(11), 39–41. doi:10.1145/219717.219748

Mishra, B. K. (2020). *Implementation of n-gram Methodology for Rotten Tomatoes Review Dataset Sentiment Analysis.* IGI Global. Doi:10.4018/978-1-7998-2460-2.ch036

Mohammad, S., Bravo-Marquez, F., Salameh, M., & Kiritchenko, S. S. (2018). Affect in tweets. *12th International Workshop on Semantic Evaluation*, 1–17.

Mohan, S., & Vedantham, H. (2021). Product Recommendation Systems Based on Customer Reviews Using Machine Learning Techniques. In I. J. Jacob (Ed.), Data Intelligence and Cognitive Informatics. Algorithms for Intelligent Systems (p. 941). Springer. https://doi.org/10.1007/978-981-15-8530-2_21

Mohsen, A., Hassan, H., & Idrees, A. (2016). A Proposed Approach for Emotion Lexicon Enrichement. *International Journal of Computer Electrical Automation Control and Information Engineering*, *10*(1).

Mohsen, A., Hassan, H., & Idrees, A. (2016). Documents Emotions Classification Model Based on TF-IDF Weighting. *International Journal of Computer Electrical Automation Control and Information Engineering*, *10*(1), 252–258.

Mohsen, A. M., Idrees, A. M., & Hassan, H. A. (2019). Emotion Analysis for Opinion Mining From Text: A Comparative Study. *International Journal of e-Collaboration*, *15*(1).

Mostafa, A., Khedr, A. E., & Abdo, A. (2017). Advising Approach to Enhance Students' Performance Level in Higher Education Environments. *Journal of Computational Science*, *13*(5), 130–139.

Mostafa, A. M., Helmy, Y. M., Khedr, A. E., & Idrees, A. M. (2020). A proposed architectural framework for generating personalized users' query response. *Journal of Southwest Jiaotong University, 55*(5).

M.V.L., N., & Pakary, P. (2021). *Part-of-Speech Tagging in Mizo Language: A Preliminary Study.* Singapore: Springer. doi:10.1007/978-981-15-8530-2_49

Najjar, E., & Al-augby, S. (2021, January 5). *Sentiment Analysis Combination in Terrorist Detection on Twitter: A Brief Survey of Approaches and Techniques.* Springer Nature.

Nakayama, M. (2021, January 7). Textual analysis of online reviews as a lens for cross-cultural assessment. *International Journal of Culture, Tourism and Hospitality Research.*

Nida, H., Kirmani, M., Mohd, M., Muttoo, A., & Mohd, M. (2019). Automatic Emotion Classifier. *Progress in Advanced Computing and Intelligent Engineering*, 565-572.

Nunsanga, M. V. L. P. P. (2021, January 9). Part-of-Speech Tagging in Mizo Language: A Preliminary Study. *Data Intelligence and Cognitive Informatics*, 625-635. doi:10.1007/978-981-15-8530-2_49

Ö. S. (2021). Introduction to Apple ML Tools. In *Develop Intelligent iOS Apps with Swift.* Berkeley, CA: Apress. doi:10.1007/978-1-4842-6421-8_2

Osorio-Arjona, J. H.-R. (2021). Social media semantic perceptions on Madrid Metro system: Using Twitter data to link complaints to space. *Sustainable Cities and Society.*

Othman, M., Hassan, H., Moawad, R., & Idrees, A. M. (2016). Using NLP Approach for Opinion Types Classifier. *Journal of Computers, 11*(5), 40–410.

Othman, M., Hassan, H., Moawad, R., & Idrees, A. M. (2018). A Linguistic Approach for Opinionated Documents Summary. *Future Computing and Informatics Journal, 3*(2), 152–158.

Pandey, S. M. (2021). Hybrid Model with Word2vector in Information Retrieval Ranking. *Data Analytics and Management*, 761-773.

Pang, B., L. L. (2002). Sentiment classification using machine learning techniques. *Conference on Empirical Methods in Natural Language Processing*, 10, 79–86. 10.3115/1118693.1118704

Patel, H. J. (2021). Unsupervised Learning-Based Sentiment Analysis with Reviewer's Emotion. *Evolving Technologies for Computing, Communication and Smart World, 694.* doi:10.1007/978-981-15-7804-5_6

Patil, C. G., & Patil, S. S. (2013). Use of Porter Stemming Algorithm and SVM for Emotion Extraction from News Headlines. *International Journal of Electronics, Communication & Soft Computing in Science & Engineering, 2*(7), 9–13.

Păvăloaia, V.-D., Ionut, D. A., & Fotache, D. (2020, November 25). Social Media and E-mail Marketing Campaigns. *Symmetry.*

Peeyusha, K. S. P. G. (2020). *A Comparative Study on Different Techniques of Sentimental Analysis* (Vol. 1154). Springer. doi:10.1007/978-981-15-4032-5_81

Polisetty, S. P., Polisetty, M., & Rao, T. (2014). An Approach for Emotion Identification from Weblog Corpora. *Int.J. Computer Technology and Application*, *5*(1), 1–7.

Poongodi, T. S. (2020). Blockchain in social networking. *Cryptocurrencies and Blockchain Technology Applications*, 55-76.

Radi, S., & Shokouhyar, S. (2021). Toward consumer perception of cellphones sustainability: A social media analytics. *Science Direct, 25*, 217-233. doi:10.1016/j.spc.2020.08.012

Rajput, A. (2020). *Natural Language Processing, Sentiment Analysis and Clinical*. Cornell University.

Rasheed, I. B. (2021). A hybrid feature selection approach based on LSI for classification of Urdu text. *Machine Learning Algorithms for Industrial Applications*, *907*, 3–18.

Rasheed, I. B. H. (2021). *A Hybrid Feature Selection Approach Based on LSI for Classification of Urdu Text* (Vol. 907). Springer. doi:10.1007/978-3-030-50641-4_1

Renault, T. (2020). *Sentiment analysis and machine learning in finance: a comparison of methods and models on one million messages*. Digital Finance.

Sabharwal, N. &. (2021). BERT Model Applications: Question Answering System. *Hands-on Question Answering Systems with BERT*, 97-137.

Saeed, R. R. (2021, January 3). Optimizing Sentiment Classification for Arabic Opinion Texts. *Cognitive Computation*, *13*, 164–178.

Samad, M., Khounviengxay, N. D., & Witherow, M. A. (2020, July 28). Effect of Text Processing Steps on Twitter Sentiment Classification using Word Embedding. *arXiv, 1*.

Santos, C. N. (2014). *Deep Convolutional Neural Networks for Sentiment Analysis of Short Texts. Proceedings of COLING the 25th International Conference on Computational Linguistics*. Dublin City University and Association for Computational Linguistics. Retrieved from https://www.aclweb.org/anthology/C14-1008

Sas, S., & Guptaj, R. (2021). *Subjectivity Detection for Sentiment Analysis on Twitter Data* (Vol. 130). Singapore: Springer. doi:10.1007/978-981-15-5329-5_43

Sayed, M., Salem, R. K., & Khder, A. E. (2019). A Survey of Arabic Text Classification Approaches. *International Journal of Computer Applications in Technology*, *95*(3), 236–251.

Shivani Malhotra, V. K. (2021, January 2). Bidirectional transfer learning model for sentiment analysis of natural language. *J Ambient Intell Human Comput*. doi:10.1007/s12652-020-02800-7

Shixia, Y., & Huamin, N. (2010). OpinionSeer: Interactive Visualization of Hotel Customer Feedback. *IEEE Transactions on Visualization and Computer Graphics, 16*, 9-11.

Smith, R. G., & Franks, C. (2020). *Counting the costs of identity crime and misuse in Australia, 2018–19.* AIC Reports Statistical Report.

Soni, A. (2017). Multi-lingual sentiment analysis of twitter data by using classification algorithms. *Second International Conference on Electrical, Computer and Communication Technologies (ICECCT)*, 1–5.

Strapparava, C., & Mihalcea, R. (2007). SemEval-2007 Task 14: Affective Text. *The 4th International Workshop on Semantic Evaluations.*

Sugandh, R., Mulye, A., & Wadhai, V. (2011). A Framework for Extensible Emotion Analysis System. *IACSIT International Journal of Engineering and Technology*, *3*, 540–546.

Sujon, M. (2021). Social Media Mining for Understanding Traffic Safety Culture in Washington State Using Twitter Data. *Journal of Computing in Civil Engineering*, *35*(1).

Taboada, M. (2020, February). Sentiment Analysis: An Overview from Linguistics. *Annual Review of Linguistics*. Advance online publication. doi:10.1146/annurev-linguistics-011415-040518

Tiun, S. M.-G. (2020). Various Pre-processing Strategies for Domain-Based Sentiment Analysis of Unbalanced Large-Scale Reviews. *International Conference on Advanced Intelligent Systems and Informatics*, *1261*, 204-214.

Tokuhisa, R., Inui, K., & Matsumoto, Y. (2008). Emotion Classification Using Massive Examples Extracted from the Web. *The 22nd International Conference on Computational Linguistics.*

Tokuhisa, R., Inui, K., & Matsumoto, Y. (2008). Emotion Classification Using Massive Examples Extracted from the Web. *The 22nd International Conference on Computational Linguistics.*

Turney, P. D., & Littman, M. L. (2003). Measuring Praise and Criticism: Inference of Semantic Orientation from Association. *ACM Transactions on Information Systems*, *21*, 315–346.

Turney, P. D., & Litiman, M. L. (2003). Measuring Praise and Criticism: Inference of Semantic Orientation from Association. *ACM Transactions on Information Systems*, *21*, 315–346.

Walaa Medhat, A. H. (2014, December). Sentiment analysis algorithms and applications: A survey. *Ain Shams Engineering Journal*, *5*(4), 1101.

Wang, X., & Zheng, Q. (2013). Text Emotion Classification Research Based on Improved Latent Semantic Analysis Algorithm. *Proceedings of the 2nd International Conference on Computer Science and Electronics Engineering (ICCSEE 2013).*

Weng, Y. Z. (2021, January 21). *A Bayesian Network Model for Seismic Risk Analysis.* Wiley Journals. doi:10.1111/risa.13690

Wilhelm, S. J. (2021). A New Explicit Algebraic Wall Model for LES of Turbulent Flows Under Adverse Pressure Gradient. *Flow Turbulence Combust*, 1–35. doi:10.1007/s10494-020-00181-7

Xia, C. Z. (2011). Ensemble of feature sets and classification algorithms for sentiment classification. *Inf. Sci.*, *181*, 1138–1152.

Yang, J. L. (2021). Measuring the short text similarity based on semantic and syntactic information. *Future Generation Computer Systems*, *114*, 169–180.

Yann, L., Yoshua, B., & Geoffrey, H. (2015). Deep learning. *Nature.*

Zhan, Y. (2020). *A social media analytic framework for improving operations and service management: A study of the retail pharmacy industry*. doi:10.1016/j.techfore.2020.120504

Zhang, W., Yoshida, T., & Tang, X. (2008). Text classification based on multi-word with support vector machine. *Knowledge-Based Systems*, *21*, 879–886.

Zharmagambetov, A. S., & Pak, A. A. (2016). Sentiment analysis of a document using deep learning approach and decision trees. In *Twelve International Conference on Electronics Computer and Computation (ICECCO)* (pp. 1-4). IEEE. doi: 10.1109/ICECCO.2015.7416902

This research was previously published in E-Collaboration Technologies and Strategies for Competitive Advantage Amid Challenging Times; pages 171-209, copyright year 2021 by Information Science Reference (an imprint of IGI Global).

Chapter 6
Sentiment Analysis in Crisis Situations for Better Connected Government:
Case of Mexico Earthquake in 2017

Asdrúbal López Chau
https://orcid.org/0000-0001-5254-0939
Universidad Autónoma del Estado de México, Mexico

David Valle-Cruz
Universidad Autónoma del Estado de México, Mexico

Rodrigo Sandoval-Almazán
https://orcid.org/0000-0002-7864-6464
Universidad Autónoma del Estado de México, Mexico

ABSTRACT

One of the pillars of connected government is citizen centricity: an approach in which citizen participation is essential. In Mexico, social networks are currently one of the most important means by which citizens express their needs and provide opinions to the government. The goal of this chapter is to contribute to citizen centricity by adapting the methodology of sentiment analysis of social media posts to an expanded version for crisis situations. The main difference in this approach from the normally accepted one is that instead of using pre-defined classes (positive and negative) for sentiments, the authors first determined the different data categories and then applied them to the classic process of sentiment analysis. This approach was tested using posts on Mexico's earthquake in 2017. They found that needs, demands, and claims made in the posts reflect sentiments in a better way, and this can help to improve the government-citizen connection.

DOI: 10.4018/978-1-6684-6303-1.ch006

INTRODUCTION

The connected government strategy is based on six fundamental pillars: citizen centricity, common standardized infrastructure, back-office reorganization, governance, new organizational model, and social inclusion (Kaczorowski, 2004). To further strengthen these pillars, in recent years, governments have turned their attention to Internet-based technology. This has resulted in an increase of public services, reduction of costs, and improvement in the government's relationship with the electorate. Governments have also been able to exploit their considerable investments in information and communication technologies to strengthen their international competitive advantage (Kaczorowski, 2004: p. 3).

As a consequence of the adoption of new technologies, affordable channels for connecting citizens with government have become possible (Mahmood, 2014). Social Media networks are a clear example of these channels. They have become very important in modern society and a powerful means of expression where people can freely share opinions, including those concerning their needs, aspirations and claims on government topics. Therefore, social networks represent one of the most common tools used by citizens and governments. These platforms have worked as a mechanism for the improvement of government-to-citizen interactions and communications, as well as for the improvement of interaction between citizens, and streamlining citizen participation actions.

An important social networking tool is micro-blogging. Twitter is the most commonly used platform of this type, worldwide. Data extracted from micro-blogging platforms have been used in many studies to identify the polarity of sentiments in posts. This information has been useful for decision making in organizations. In most of these studies, only two categories (positive and negative) have been considered. In other cases, sentiments have been categorized into three divisions: positive, negative and neutral (Neppalli et al., 2017). Although valuable, this type of analysis is not sufficient for a complete understanding of the sentiments expressed in posts as a reaction to some complex events such as political elections, catastrophes, or even suicidal thoughts (Birjali et al., 2017). Therefore, some researchers have considered a variety of emotions in order to identify sentiments on Twitter and other platforms (Gaspar et al., 2016). During a crisis situation, citizens usually post on social networks. These posts have different aims: to stand in solidarity, to organize, to request, to complain, or even to protest against the government, organizations, or specific people. In situations of this kind, it is necessary to identify not only the polarity of the publications, but also an analysis of feelings to a greater level of precision.

The aim of this chapter is to contribute to connected government strategies by means of a methodology for sentiment analysis in a crisis. The methodology presented here is an adaptation of the standard approach to sentiment analysis as reported in the literature. However, we expanded the list of sentiments in order to better explain the data. We tested our approach on data regarding an earthquake which occurred in September 2017 in Mexico. The seismic activity was more severe at that time, and there were several strong earthquakes. Two of them were particularly intense, causing damage to buildings and dozens of deaths:

- The first earthquake on September 7 was an oscillatory earthquake and was recorded at 8.2 on the Richter scale. The States of Oaxaca and Chiapas were the worst affected. Over 110,000 properties were damaged, in addition to 96 people who lost their lives (Wade, 2017).
- The second earthquake, on September 19 (19S) was recorded at 7.1 on the Richter scale and caused more damage than the first one, particularly in the States of Oaxaca, Chiapas, Morelos, Guerrero, Puebla, State of Mexico, and Mexico City (Mexico's capital) (Atienza et al., 2017).

For the present study, we monitored trending topics on the earthquake, and analyzed more than 140,000 posts (tweets) related to the topic. After reading and analyzing about 10% of these tweets, we noticed that in general, sentiments in the texts could not be analyzed properly by classifying them into the three categories commonly used in the literature: positive, negative, and neutral. This classification is used in Ekman (1993) and Nakamura (2004). Furthermore, we identified eleven terms or topics that denoted the publications more appropriately. We automatized the identification of these eleven hidden sentiments in the rest of the tweets by applying machine-learning methods. With this approach, we provided more elements for the explanation of the different government, NGOs and civil society reactions during the crisis.

The organization of this chapter is as follows: We divided the remainder of it into six sections. The following section focuses on a literature review; the next section describes the research design and the proposed classification. The following two sections describe the results of our investigation, and present the discussion and findings. The final section presents conclusions and recommendations for improving connected government in Mexico.

LITERATURE REVIEW

The purpose of this section is to provide a theoretical background to our research in terms of emotions and sentiment analysis in situations of crisis.

Emotions

There are multiple approaches to defining emotions: physiological, evolutionary, social, expressive behavioral, among others. Many authors have proposed various definition of emotion; however, most of the definitions are oriented towards emphasizing certain aspects of it (Kleinginna and Kleinginna, 1981). Instead of providing a general definition of emotions, some authors only identified the relevant emotions e.g.:

- Ekman (1993) suggested six basic emotions: surprise, happiness, anger, fear, disgust, and sadness.
- Nakamura (2004) proposed ten types of emotion: excitement, shame, joy, fondness, dislike, sorrow, anger, surprise, fear, and relief.
- Tokuhisa and colleagues (2008) proposed ten emotion classes: happiness, pleasantness, disappointment, unpleasantness, loneliness, sadness, anger, anxiety, fear, and relief.
- Some researchers have used categorization of emotions to classify facial and bodily expressions, or documents. Refer to Calvo and Mac Kim (2013); Strapparava and Mihalcea (2008); and Alm et al. (2005).

Many different kinds of emotions arise in humans. Plutchik and Kellerman suggested the "Wheel of Emotions" in 1980. Using this concept, complex emotions can be represented by combining pairs of emotions from eight primary bipolar emotions (Plutchik and Kellerman, 2013). The latter, which can vary in terms of intensity, are the following: joy versus sadness; anger versus fear; trust versus disgust; and surprise versus anticipation. The number of emotions human beings are able to feel is high. Parrott (2001) organized emotions using a tree structure with three levels: primary, secondary, and tertiary emotions.

More than 100 emotions can be identified in the tree (Parrott, 2001). The use of specific emotions is a requirement for sentiment analysis. For example, the Positive and Negative Affect Schedule (PANAS) was applied in order to determine the urgency of urban issues (Masdeval and Veloso, 2015). PANAS is a 10-item scale used to measure both positive and negative affect (Crawford and Henry, 2004).

Despite the exhaustive categorization of emotions and sentiments, it is insufficient for the accurate explanation of sentiments and expressions in posts on social networks. Therefore, some researchers have proposed new categories of emotions. Jin and colleagues (2014) proposed a scale (anxiety, fear, apprehension, sympathy, guilt, embarrassment, shame, disgust, contempt, anger and sadness) in order to measure emotions in crises; specifically, in organizational crises. Bani-Hani and colleagues (2017) developed an algorithm that translates emotions found in English into different Arabic dialects to understand the sentiment of users toward a particular event.

In sum, the literature shows that a simple classification of emotions such as positive, negative, or neutral is an oversimplification and is therefore unhelpful when trying to understand what human beings feel in complex situations. On the other hand, although there are investigations on sentiment analysis in crisis situations, as far as we know, there is no previous study specifically focused on this type of analysis for Latin American countries. This chapter constitutes an expansion of sentiment analysis methodology.

Sentiment Analysis in Crisis Situations

Sentiment analysis is the field of study that analyzes people's opinions towards entities such as products, services, organizations, individuals, issues, events, topics, and their attributes (Liu, 2012). This type of analysis has been used to study the repercussions of events on social networks (Gonçalves et al., 2013). Although some researchers have defined three categories for sentiments (positive, negative, and neutral), there are different emotional models that could be applied for the classification of social network posts and, this way, improve the results of sentiment analysis in order to identify several expressions according to the event.

Yu and colleagues (2019) proposed a system that extracts and classifies emoticons posted on social networks in China. Machine-learning techniques were used to categorize seven types of emotions: happiness, sadness, fear, anger, disgust, surprise, and fondness. They added a perspective on human emotion to the current sentiment analysis literature. (Zhang et al., 2012) integrated marketing theories with text-mining techniques (sentiment and affect analysis) to propose a set of measures that focuses on sentiment divergence in consumer product reviews, finding that firms should pay special attention to text-content information and measure it when managing social networks.

There are different studies related to sentiment analysis in crisis situations. Vo and Collier (2013) studied earthquake situations in Japan for the purposes of emotion analysis using Nakamura (2004) Japanese emotion dictionary (Vo and Collier, 2013). So as to determine the emotions caused specifically by earthquakes from tweets, Vo and Collier (2013) selected a subset of Tokuhisa's list of emotions.

Earle et al. (2010) found how people feel and respond to earthquakes, finding feelings in their research such as confusion (between exact location, intensity, and magnitude) as well as feelings of humor (Earle et al., 2010). Nair studied how people of Chennai used social networks in response to the country's worst flood, and found that random forest is the best technique to analyze social network data (Nair et al., 2017).

Kim and Hastak (2018) studied the created patterns by aggregating interactions of online social networks used for the propagation of emergency information. They identified three entities: individuals, emergency agencies, and organizations. They found that the core of the social networks consists of numerous individuals who are connected by emergency agencies and organizations. Furthermore, they argued that social capital and leadership in the community are the basic attributes for a rapid recovery from a disaster. In Öztürk and Ayvaz (2018), the authors grouped sentiment scores of tweets into five categories: very negative, negative, neutral, positive, and very positive. The objective was to analyze public opinions and sentiments toward the Syrian refugee crisis. They applied sentiment analysis to 2,381,297 relevant tweets (in Turkish and English) in order to investigate public opinions and sentiments regarding the Syrian refugee crisis. They clustered the tweets into three different categories: politics, war, and humanitarian.

Ma et al. (2014) conducted a study of large fire disasters in three dimensions: acquisition of information regarding public opinion, public opinion dissemination, and coping strategies. They classified emergencies into four categories: natural disasters, accident disasters, social security events, and public health events, as well as 53 sub-types.

Previous research shows this gap clearly that classic sentiment analysis in crisis situations is not enough to explain the multi-faceted nature of human emotions and expressions, nor is it enough to determine behavioral patterns.

PRELIMINARY ANALYSIS OF POSTS IN CRISIS SITUATION IN MEXICO

One of the most recent crisis situations in Mexico was the earthquake on September 19th, 2017. We decided to analyze posts on Twitter, observing how the government responded. The first approach was to apply sentiment analysis to discover the polarity of citizens' opinions. Table 1 shows some of the downloaded tweets.

Table 1. Examples of analyzed tweets

Tweets (Translated into English)
#Now - New death toll is confirmed. At present: 119 in Mexico City, Puebla, Morelos, and EdoMex.
It is not the money of the politicians; it is money of the people ... they must return it in order to help and, if they do, they will obtain my vote.
I really do not know whether to dress casually or wear a suit for #TheEndOfTheWorld
San Antonio Alpanocan, Puebla needs help. They have received little help from nearby communities. #brigades
The Centro Expositor Puebla, located in the area of Los Fuertes, is working as a shelter and collection center #SomosMexico #HelpMexico #Verified19s. #WeAreLookingForYou
Brigadier JESUS MEDINA AGUILAR, 36 years old ... https://t.co/Le6F33G6JM
#TurnOffTelevisa, the old reliable, turn off the TV please https://t.co/ri3aj7mAsO
I'm tired of recycled soap operas #TurnOffTelevisa
Young people born between 1985 and 2000. Those people are of weak character and lack leadership #millenials are the first volunteers
Friends, it looks like hands are no longer needed. If you can, donate to the Red Cross or Amazon. Better not to be in the way #HelpCDMX
If you need a structural engineer to take a look at your house, I will leave this link here: https://t.co/ozkiiKBdzy#PrayForMexico

We began our analysis by classifying tweets into three categories: positive, negative, and neutral. We also classified tweets in accordance with the suggestion by Ekman (1993) and Nakamura (2004). Many tweets were requests for help. Many other posts had a predominant expression of demands. Others were intended to help in the search for lost people. There were also some tweets that were not relevant to the earthquake. After more than ten attempts to assign an emotion to each tweet, we realized that none of the emotions of Ekman (1993) and Nakamura (2004) represented the sentiment of users adequately. From this finding, we observed that in a crisis, people used that platform for much more than merely expressing agreement or disagreement. Therefore, we realized that it was necessary to expand the terms or list of sentiments to apply sentiment analysis techniques adequately.

Rather than forcing each and every tweet into a category in which it did not necessarily belong, we decided to discover the main topics in the data. We read a small portion of tweets carefully to identify the predominant emotion. This approach was first presented by Earle and colleagues (2010). The goal was to identify a sentiment or term that described each tweet more accurately, using, but not limited to, Ekman's (1993) six basic emotions and Nakamura's (2004) emotions. We issued an appropriate list of terms which identified the most frequent terms. We applied the usual steps of sentiment analysis found in the literature and observed the data could be explained in a better way.

As a result of this experience, we propose a different methodology. Although it is a procedure that requires some human intervention along with machine-learning techniques, it provides a better understanding of posts concerning crisis situations.

METHODOLOGY

We summarize the proposed methodology in Figure 1. The explanation of the relevant steps is presented below.

- **Step 1:** Data collection. Posts on Twitter regarding a crisis situation are monitored. For this purpose, tweets related to trending topics have to be downloaded. Tweets are grouped and saved into different files; one for each trending topic.
- **Step 2:** About 1% of tweets are selected randomly and used as data, avoiding re-tweets. For manual analysis, a sample of manageable size is required. It is called SS-1 (Subset 1).
- **Step 3:** This is one of the most laborious steps. Each tweet is read carefully by at least two readers to identify the main topics. The result of this analysis eventually becomes the list of terms that describes the tweets. Afterwards, this list needs to be reduced by mixing terms that are synonyms. The terms that represent a small number of tweets are eliminated.
- **Step 4:** A second subset (SS-2) is obtained from the collected data. SS-2 does not contain re-tweets, nor any element of SS-1. SS-2 is analyzed manually by at least two people (these tweets are different from the ones that formed the basis of the list of terms). The purpose is to tag each tweet with a term from the list obtained in step 3.
- **Step 5:** Cohen kappa coefficient is used to measure the agreement between taggers of SS-1 and SS-2. If the strength of agreement between taggers is either moderate or high, we argue that the list of terms is an adequate representation of the sentiments in the data; otherwise, go to step 2.
- Steps 6 to 9 are the ones normally used for sentiment analysis. First, data is cleaned and then it is transformed into a useful representation for training one or several machine-learning models. The

best model is used to predict the terms that are associated with each one of the missing tweets to be tagged automatically.

- **Step 10:** Examine the actions of the government regarding this situation and compare them against sentiments. It is expected that a connected government has to respond promptly.

Figure 1. Research methodology in brief

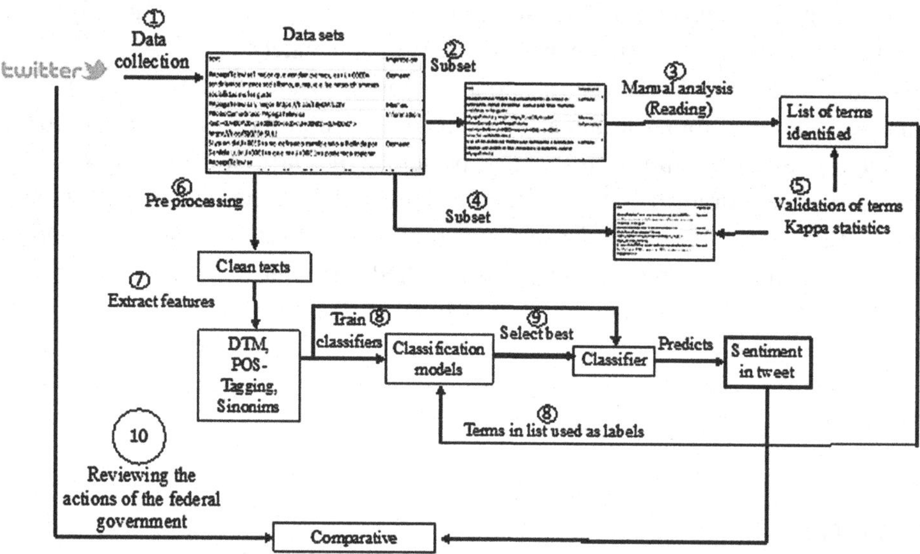

ANALYZING POSTS ON MEXICO'S EARTHQUAKE IN 2017

This section describes the application of the methodology and our findings from Twitter posts.

Data Collection

Our unit of analysis is the earthquake that occurred on September 19, 2017, in Mexico. From that date onward, we monitored related trending topics on Twitter until it was no longer commented. The trending topics are shown in Table 2.

We downloaded 140,988 tweets during the period 09/20/2017 to 09/25/2017. The number of tweets and the trending topics are listed in Table 3.

Identification and Validation of List of Terms

Following the manual analysis of tweets, 137 terms were identified by the taggers. We proceeded to select the most frequent terms and to identify terms that were synonyms. Finally, we chose eleven concepts (or terms), as summarized in Table 4:

Table 2. Trending topics regarding Mexico's earthquake in 2017

Trending Topic	Translation or Brief Explanation
#jojutla	Jojutla is a small town in the State of Morelos, Mexico, which suffered a lot of damage from the earthquake.
#mexicoestadepie	Mexico is standing. Citizens showing support or solidarity.
#partidosdensudinero	Political parties, give your money away. Citizens began demanding that political parties donated a part of their budget for the repair of the damage caused by the earthquake.
#prayformexico	Citizens showing support or solidarity.
#sismo	Earthquake.
#skyalertmx	Sky alert is a seismic alert system in Mexico.
#terremoto	Earthquake.
#millennials	Millennials.
#partidosdennuestrodinero	Political parties, give our money back. Citizens began to claim that the budget of the political parties truly belongs to the people, and should be used to repair the damage caused by the earthquake.
#apagatelevisa	Turn off Televisa. A fake news article broadcast on the "Televisa" television network unleashed the fury of Mexican citizens.
#alertasismica	Seismic alert.
#findelmundo	The end of the world.
#tvaztecamiente	TV Azteca lies. Another fake news article made citizens demonstrate their repudiation towards yet another television network.
#verificado19s	Verified September 19th. This was a digital platform that verified information and managed data to make citizens' responses more efficient after the earthquake.

Table 3. Number of collected tweets for each trending topic

Created	Trending Topic	Tweets Collected
09/20/2017	jojutla	10,000
09/20/2017	mexicoestadepie	20,000
09/20/2017	partidosdensudinero	10,000
09/20/2017	prayformexico	10,000
09/20/2017	sismo	10,000
09/20/2017	skyalertmx	352
09/20/2017	terremoto	10,000
09/21/2017	millennials	4,180
09/21/2017	partidosdennuestrodinero	10,000
09/22/2017	apagatelevisa	10,000
09/23/2017	alertasismica	10,000
09/23/2017	findelmundo	10,000
09/24/2017	tvaztecamiente	6,456
09/24/2017	verificado19s	20,000
	Total	140,988

Table 4. Summary of the identified terms (categories)

Term	Appropriate for Describing This Type of Tweet
Help	Someone is requesting help.
Searching	Searching for someone or something.
Irrelevant	The post is not related to the event.
Support	Support is offered.
Positive	Positive, gratitude, recognition of someone, or something.
Negative	Contempt, jokes in poor taste, denouncing unacceptable behavior.
Information	Information about something.
Demand	Social demand directed at an institution.
Suggestions	Advice or recommendations.
Memes	Positive jokes, reflections, relief memes, sarcasm.
BadNews	Bad news about the situation.

1. **Help is Needed:** When someone asked for help for the rescue of people and/or animals. For instance, when someone requested food, medicine or shovels. We also included requests to remove debris or requests for financial help.
2. **Searching for Someone:** People asked about a lost person or pet.
3. **Irrelevant:** Some tweets were related to another event, or information which was not relevant.
4. **Support is Offered:** Some people, organizations, and institutions offered help or support; for example, food, medicine, water, machinery and tools, cars, Uber, money, among others.
5. **Positive:** This is a typical classification in sentiment analysis; it means gratitude, recognition to someone, or something. What is more, it represents hope and/or unity.
6. **Negative:** Another typical category in sentiment analysis, meaning contempt, jokes in poor taste, denouncing something that someone does, bad behavior, or negative expressions directed at someone.
7. **Information about Something Specific:** Some situation or significant event is reported. Important information for people to take heed of, meet someone or learn about something.
8. **Demand:** A petition or demand made by civil society and directed at the government, politicians, organizations, institutions, or TV stations.
9. **Suggestions:** Some useful tips are given to coordinate volunteer-based support in the best way. Also, suggestions are made in terms of changing rescue strategies and help.
10. **Positive Jokes, Memes, and Reflections:** all information related to memes or jokes that were funny, despite the problems that were caused by the earthquake.
11. **Bad News:** News where dead people or pets were reported. Houses, buildings, or towns collapsed. Poor management of resources and support for victims. More damage caused by earthquakes.

We show a comparison between the identified terms from Ekman's (1993) six basic emotions, and Nakamura's (2004) emotions in Tables 5 and 6. The abbreviation NA (not applicable) means that there is no equivalence between the emotions and the corresponding term in the list. It can also be observed that the term Help is not assigned to any particular emotion or sentiment. Other terms, such as Positive or Negative, are associated with more than one term used by other authors.

Table 5. Identified terms on data sets compared against Ekman's (1993) basic emotions

Terms	Surprise	Happiness	Anger	Fear	Disgust	Sadness
Help	No	No	No	No	No	No
Searching	No	No	No	Maybe	No	Maybe
Support	No	No	No	No	No	No
Positive	Yes	Yes	No	No	No	No
Negative	No	No	Yes	No	Yes	No
Irrelevant	NA	NA	NA	NA	NA	NA
Information	Maybe	Maybe	Maybe	Maybe	Maybe	Maybe
Demand	No	No	Maybe	No	Maybe	No
Suggestions	No	No	No	No	No	No
Memes	Maybe	Maybe	No	No	No	No
Bad News	No	No	Maybe	Maybe	Maybe	Maybe

To test the hypothesis that the eleven identified terms represented the content of tweets properly, 300 tweets were chosen randomly from each data set. These were tagged using the list of identified terms (see Table 6). The frequency of each term is shown in Table 7.

We asked two taggers if the content was correctly represented by any of the terms found for each of the 300 tweets. Table 8 shows a summary of the responses we obtained. Tagger A assured us that in 190 of the 300 tweets, there were terms that correctly described each tweet. In case of tagger B, we were assured of the accuracy of the terms used in describe each tweet in 204 of the 300 cases. We got to the following results by applying the kappa coefficient of kappa = 0.587, SE of kappa = 0.049, and 95% confidence interval from 0.491 to 0.683. The strength of the agreement between taggers was considered to be moderate. Based on these results, we concluded that the list of terms was an appropriate tool for the representation of the collected tweets.

Table 6. Identified terms on data sets compared against Nakamura's (2004) emotions

Terms	Excitement	Shame	Joy	Fondness	Dislike	Sorrow	Anger	Surprise	Fear	Relief
Help	No	No	No	No	No	No	No	No	No	No
Searching	No	No	No	Maybe	No	Maybe	No	No	Maybe	No
Support	No	No	No	Maybe	No	No	No	No	No	No
Positive	Yes	No		Yes	No	No	No	Maybe	No	Yes
Negative	No	Yes	No	No	Yes	No	Yes	No	No	No
Irrelevant	NA	NA	NA	NA	NA	NA	NA	NA	NA	NA
Information	Maybe	Maybe	Maybe	Maybe	Maybe	Maybe	Maybe	Maybe	Maybe	Maybe
Demand	No	No	No	No	Maybe	No	Maybe	No	No	No
Suggestions	No	No	No	Maybe	No	No	No	No	No	Maybe
Memes	No	No	Maybe	Maybe	No	No	No	No	No	Maybe
Bad News	No	No	No	No	Maybe	Maybe	Maybe	Maybe	Maybe	No

Table 7. Frequency of tags set manually on each data set

Dataset	Help	Searching	Irrelevant	Support	Positive	Negative	Information	Demand	Suggestions	Memes	Bad News
jojutla	129	0	12	33	24	0	75	3	18	0	6
mexicoestadepie	51	0	0	18	177	12	33	0	6	3	0
partidosdensudinero	12	0	3	0	6	75	6	183	9	6	0
prayformexico	36	0	24	96	33	12	36	3	18	39	3
sismo	30	3	152	51	120	3	15	3	3	12	3
skyalert	3	0	3	6	9	24	207	0	6	3	39
terremoto	33	3	24	96	30	12	36	3	18	42	3
millennials	0	0	177	0	27	6	66	15	3	6	0
partidosdennuestrodinero	9	3	12	3	15	111	3	135	9	0	0
apagatelevisa	1	0	15	3	6	102	30	99	9	18	0
alertasismica	6	3	15	0	21	27	36	15	30	117	30
findelmundo	6	0	36	3	6	3	27	9	15	195	0
tvaztecamiente	9	0	24	3	6	33	45	141	9	30	0
verificado19s	174	12	9	9	33	36	15	0	12	0	0

Table 8. Tagger responses

		Tagger A		Total
		Yes	No	
Tagger B	Yes	169	35	204
	No	21	75	96
Total		190	110	300

Sentiment Analysis

To manually label all the tweets posted in a crisis is an almost impossible task. Therefore, we first prepared the data for the construction of four classifiers using the labeled data. Classifiers being: Logistic Regression, C4.5, Naive Bayes, and Random Forest.

Preparing Data for Machine Learning

We cleansed data sets in order to remove unusable words and noisy text. This step is in accordance with suggestion by Pak and Paroubek (2010). Then, we made a corpus for each data set. We applied the standard steps for pre-processing of the information, as follows:

- **Accented Vowels:** Accented vowels were replaced by unaccented vowels. All the strings with the pattern < U+???? > and < ed >, URL, and emoticons were removed.
- **Hashtags:** The symbol # was removed, and the words that compose the topic were separated, when necessary.
- **Mentions**: In Twitter, when mentioning someone, he/she is identified by way of the @ symbol followed by a username. We removed all mentions.
- **Stop-words**, punctuation symbols, numbers, and whitespaces were removed.

Once we cleaned the data, we extracted features from the text messages. A document-term matrix (DTM) was computed, and the sparse terms were removed, which lead to the elimination of low-frequency terms. As a second set of features, POS-tagging was applied to the cleaned texts.

We realized that some data sets were unbalanced, i.e., the number of tweets in one category (term) was much larger than the other ones. To avoid the classifier making poor predictions, we applied SMOT (Synthetic Minority Over-sampling Technique) (Chawla et al., 2002). This is a method to generate synthetic instances aimed at balancing the classes in a data set.

We used features and labels to train four classifiers, as mentioned before: Logistic Regression, C4.5, Naive Bayes, and Random Forest. The classification accuracy of each built model is shown in Table 9. We used the classifier with the best performance in order to obtain an automatic classification of all the tweets in each data set.

Table 9. Performance achieved by classification methods on datasets labeled manually

Dataset	Classification Accuracy (%)			
	Logistic Regression	C4.5	Naive Bayes	Random Forest
jojutla	90.37	82.39	84.39	88.70
mexicoestadepie	87.61	87.89	86.20	93.24
partidosdensudinero	94.13	90.61	87.32	95.77
prayformexico	83.93	69.41	81.96	8078
sismo	80.91	70.87	79.88	79.13
skyalertmx	88.22	92.31	84.13	91.35
terremoto	78.99	68.87	77.82	81.32
millennials	89.71	82.55	74.55	86.55
partidosdennuestrodinero	86.91	82.55	74.55	86.55
apagatelevisa	80.74	68.15	70.00	76.30
alertasismica	89.60	78.70	87.01	87.27
findelmundo	87.25	85.49	83.96	89.01
tvaztecamiente	82.25	83.25	86.50	88.25
verificado19s	97.14	92.36	93.79	94.51
19-s	94.92	93.22	85.23	94.67

Automatic Tagging of Tweets

We performed the automatic labeling of the opinions of citizens regarding the earthquake by using the best model generated by way of data training. We also carried out a descriptive analysis based on this labeling. We calculated the number of terms and identified the predominant term of each data set. Table 10 shows this information. The numbers in bold represent the most frequent term.

Table 10. Expressions identified automatically in each dataset

Dataset	Help	Searching	Irrelevant	Support	Positive	Negative	Information	Demand	Suggestions	Memes	Bad News
Jojutla	**7,158**	0	350	448	590	0	691	0	632	0	22
mexicoestadepie	137	0	0	22	**9,209**	51	477	0	4	0	0
partidosdensudinero	16	0	2	0	1	638	1	**8,238**	1	4	0
prayformexico	1,637	0	1,562	**1,827**	1,084	286	1,436	202	607	1,079	181
sismo	1,113	58	**3,130**	1,262	1,593	739	549	57	222	861	224
skyalert	0	0	0	8	8	**9,741**	116	1	1	0	24
terremoto	960	0	1,394	**4,292**	837	957	222	0	263	952	24
millennials	0	0	2,019	0	162	615	129	50	9	**6,917**	0
partidosdennuestrodinero	47	210	184	114	1,344	2,555	4	**5,240**	200	0	0
apagatelevisa	591	0	1,338	53	59	**3,117**	2,006	1,700	648	389	0
alertasismica	216	4	751	0	924	358	828	499	1,471	**2,758**	2,056
findelmundo	38	0	3,882	0	61	1	400	25	26	**5,468**	0
tvaztecamiente	32	0	188	1	3	264	933	**8,029**	13	426	0
verificado19s	**5,527**	110	274	2,484	234	1,109	0	0	161	0	0

Table 10 also serves as a summary of the content of the tweets concerning the situation, and, simultaneously, connecting the government with those citizens who required something specific.

Reviewing the Actions Taken by Federal Government

Finally, we carried out a verification of the federal government's posts in order to ascertain which actions were accomplished, based on each analyzed trending topic. To achieve this, we searched Twitter by using each of the hashtags and the federal government account (@gobmx). The only answers were found in the hashtags: #Jojutla, #sismo, and #alertasismica.

Concerning the hashtag #Jojutla, the president of the republic visited the site the day after the earthquake in order to coordinate rescue and recovery efforts as it was one of the most affected areas in Mexico. Related to the hashtag #sismo, we found recommendations for how to react in case of an earthquake as well as clarification of the fact that earthquakes cannot be predicted and, additionally, information on federal government aid for the entities of Chiapas and Joquicingo. Finally, regarding the hashtag #alertasismica, some recommendations for simulated earthquakes were found.

Discussion and Findings

Sentiment analysis has been used to determine the polarity of sentiments on Twitter. Additionally, emotional models are useful for improving the determination of feelings in texts. However, given the complexity and type of event, there are certain texts that cannot be satisfactorily evaluated by using such models. For this reason, it was necessary to discover the correct categories to classify the type of event and the type of tweets that emerged.

We found, as shown in Table 10. that there is a term that describes most of the tweets in each data set. For example, the #Terremoto (#Earthquake) trending topic had many tweets related to support. On the other hand, the #TemblorMx (#EarthquakeMx) trending topic was used only for memes about the earthquake. The #MexicoEstaDePie (#MexicoIsStanding) trending topic was related to positive posts, like gratitude or recognition to someone or something. These posts usually used positive emotion words such as hope, unity, and good news. Accordingly, the #PartidosDenSuDinero (#Parties,GiveYourMoneyAway) trending topic was related to demanding or requesting that politicians and institutions use their budgets to help victims. The #Jojutla trending topic focused on the help required for this county. Since the diffusion of information and support focused on Mexico City, Jojutla was ignored. This trending topic promoted help for this location based on the awareness created by the platform.

In spite of the situation, many people made jokes. Nonetheless, another portion of Twitter's users made comments aimed at lifting the spirits of the people, as well as to offer and ask for help. A relatively small proportion of the content of these hashtags was related to negative comments, bad news, and suggestions for support. Some other tweets were related to the dissemination of information concerning what to do in an earthquake. Many other tweets were to request help.

Our findings analyzed the evolution of posts on Twitter during a catastrophic event, starting with the dissemination of information regarding the phenomenon and mainly asking for help. Some information was related to support, suggestions, and jokes. Afterwards, some messages were related to demands of and petitions aimed at politicians in addition to information related to news disseminated by TV stations. Some tweets were jokes about the end of the world, reflections, recommendations for future earthquakes, and different ways to help victims until the information about the catastrophe dissipated, and hashtags related to the earthquake disappeared from Twitter.

Our methodological proposal to analyze expressions from tweets posted in emergencies delivers at least six main outcomes. Our data confirms the existence of the patterns proposed by Kim and Hastak (2018) as individuals, emergency agencies, and organizations, as outlined below.

Firstly, we found that reactions to disaster events are at the heart of those posts classified in the "help" category. This may seem obvious for the type of the event. However, social networks, such as Twitter, provided evidence of sending information requesting help and using this tool as the main communication channel. Unfortunately, the current disconnection between government and society came to the fore in this particular case.

Second, we found other contextual terms which better indicated different types of emotions, such as discontent with government, media, and politicians. The number of expressions that are part of this discontent is large and appear in different forms in the sample data sets (e.g., #partidosdensudinero).

Third, the use of hashtags to classify and organize tweets becomes a key element for boosting morale, avoiding despair and focusing on the positive things that society needs in emergency situations. Several hashtags such as #fuerzamexico are part of this trend. This finding supports research by Ma and colleagues (2014), who divided the information on acquisition of public opinion and opinion dissemination.

Fourth, our data revealed that classification is useful for our understanding of the general mood of social networks during crises. Most of the collected expressions provided more support and suggestions rather than criticizing or giving bad news. This analysis can only be carried out by using a different approach; organizing and classifying tweets during crises.

Fifth, the data collection from tweets showed an interesting flow of information. As we can see, the information which was shared offered support in terms of location, casualties, coordination of support, and others. The extraction of terms revealed the sense of urgency and different claims that were part of this research.

Sixth, and finally, the federal government of Mexico carried out some actions to help the areas most affected by the earthquake, but it was surpassed in the petitions and dynamics carried out by the citizens.

CONCLUSION

Our research provides two main contributions to the existing literature. The first contribution is our analysis of data, which clearly shows a disconnection between the government and the civil society in relation to the Mexican earthquake of 2017. In general terms, there is evidence of government disconnection on Twitter, noting that most tweets are complaints, although some tweets are related to seeking help. Our second contribution is our chosen research method. We analyzed tweets using sentiment analysis and machine-learning techniques for the Spanish language.

Our methodological proposal to analyze public sentiments, delivers five main outcomes, as summarized below:

- First, the main difference between our proposal and the standard approach for sentiment analysis is that we created a customized list of eleven key terms that manifested the content of the texts more properly, compared to other sentiment lists. We extracted our list through manual analysis. The terms we discovered provided a more detailed understanding of the discussions and mood of the users. Analyzing Twitter data through sentiment analysis techniques will be useful for the decision-making process in catastrophe events. It will provide key information on topics such as support, supplies, food, tools, and the machinery to remove debris, and concrete walls from the fallen buildings. We expect that this kind of analysis will be useful for our understanding of Twitter messages during different events, because the list of terms is adapted to each situation and context, and based on emotional frameworks.
- Second, we found the evidence that messages sent by Twitter in emergency situations are mostly requests for help. This might seem obvious, however, in previous investigations by other researchers, this could not be detected since the positive, negative and neutral categories did not allow for it.
- Third, we identified a list of terms that form part of an emergency situation context but can be categorized as discontent with the government, mass media, and politicians. The number of expressions related to discontent is diverse in the data sets.

- Fourth, another contribution is that our findings show an evolution of posts on Twitter during the catastrophe, starting with the dissemination of information regarding the phenomenon, mainly requesting support. Some information was related to support, suggestions, and making jokes. Afterward, some messages were related to demands of and petitions aimed at politicians and information related to news disseminated by TV stations. Some tweets were jokes about the end of the world, reflections, recommendations for future earthquakes, and different ways to help victims until the information about the catastrophe dissipated, and hashtags related to the earthquake disappeared from Twitter. These types of different sentiments cannot be identified by means of the positive, neutral, and negative analysis.
- Fifth, the federal government of Mexico needs to issue appropriate actions to improve interaction with citizens and thus provide more efficient solutions in catastrophic situations, such as the September 19 earthquake. Since collaboration with civil society is fundamental for a better-connected government, an important recommendation is to implement big-data and machine-learning technologies to analyze social media for better decision making in crisis situations.

One of the limitations of our work is that the analysis was not carried out in real time. Carrying out this kind of analysis at the time of the events would have been of great help for the decision making. For example, we would have been aware of the places where help was required, as well as having been able to assist the government in making agile, strategic and timely decisions. Because of this, civil society's actions were sometimes faster than government actions. For this reason, in future studies, we will research how to extract the list of relevant terms automatically, using ontologies or the use of deep-learning techniques and unsupervised learning.

We hope our contribution will improve government connection with citizens, allowing a more complete understanding of emotions during crises, and providing a better connected and open government.

ACKNOWLEDGMENT

The authors would like to thank the UAEM for all the support, they kindly provided.

REFERENCES

Alm, C. O., Roth, D., & Sproat, R. (2005, October). Emotions from text: machine learning for text-based emotion prediction. In *Proceedings of the conference on human language technology and empirical methods in natural language processing* (pp. 579-586). Association for Computational Linguistics. 10.3115/1220575.1220648

Atienza, V. M. C., Singh, S. K., & Schroeder, M. O. (2017). ¿Qué ocurrió el 19 de septiembre de 2017 en México? *Revista Digital Universitaria, 18*(7).

Bani-Hani, A., Majdalawieh, M., & Obeidat, F. (2017). The creation of an Arabic emotion ontology based on E-Motive. *Procedia Computer Science*, *109*, 1053–1059. doi:10.1016/j.procs.2017.05.383

Birjali, M., Beni-Hssane, A., & Erritali, M. (2017). Machine learning and semantic sentiment analysis-based algorithms for suicide sentiment prediction in social networks. *Procedia Computer Science*, *113*, 65–72. doi:10.1016/j.procs.2017.08.290

Calvo, R. A., & Mac Kim, S. (2013). Emotions in text: Dimensional and categorical models. *Computational Intelligence*, *29*(3), 527–543. doi:10.1111/j.1467-8640.2012.00456.x

Chawla, N. V., Bowyer, K. W., Hall, L. O., & Kegelmeyer, W. P. (2002). SMOTE: Synthetic minority over-sampling technique. *Journal of Artificial Intelligence Research*, *16*, 321–357. doi:10.1613/jair.953

Crawford, J. R., & Henry, J. D. (2004). The Positive and Negative Affect Schedule (PANAS): Construct validity, measurement properties and normative data in a large non-clinical sample. *British Journal of Clinical Psychology*, *43*(3), 245–265. doi:10.1348/0144665031752934 PMID:15333231

Earle, P., Guy, M., Buckmaster, R., Ostrum, C., Horvath, S., & Vaughan, A. (2010). OMG earthquake! Can Twitter improve earthquake response? *Seismological Research Letters*, *81*(2), 246–251. doi:10.1785/gssrl.81.2.246

Ekman, P. (1993). Facial expression and emotion. *The American Psychologist*, *48*(4), 384–392. doi:10.1037/0003-066X.48.4.384 PMID:8512154

Gaspar, R., Pedro, C., Panagiotopoulos, P., & Seibt, B. (2016). Beyond positive or negative: Qualitative sentiment analysis of social media reactions to unexpected stressful events. *Computers in Human Behavior*, *56*, 179–191. doi:10.1016/j.chb.2015.11.040

Gonçalves, P., Araújo, M., Benevenuto, F., & Cha, M. (2013, October). Comparing and combining sentiment analysis methods. In *Proceedings of the first ACM conference on Online social networks* (pp. 27-38). ACM. 10.1145/2512938.2512951

Jin, Y., Liu, B. F., Anagondahalli, D., & Austin, L. (2014). Scale development for measuring publics' emotions in organizational crises. *Public Relations Review*, *40*(3), 509–518. doi:10.1016/j.pubrev.2014.04.007

Kaczorowski, W. (Ed.). (2004). *Connected Government: Thought Leaders; Essays from Innovators*. Premium Publ.

Kim, J., & Hastak, M. (2018). Social network analysis: Characteristics of online social networks after a disaster. *International Journal of Information Management*, *38*(1), 86–96. doi:10.1016/j.ijinfomgt.2017.08.003

Kleinginna, P. R. Jr, & Kleinginna, A. M. (1981). A categorized list of emotion definitions, with suggestions for a consensual definition. *Motivation and Emotion*, *5*(4), 345–379. doi:10.1007/BF00992553

Liu, B. (2012). Sentiment analysis and opinion mining. *Synthesis Lectures on Human Language Technologies*, *5*(1), 1-167.

Ma, Y. P., Shu, X. M., Shen, S. F., Song, J., Li, G., & Liu, Q. Y. (2014). Study on network public opinion dissemination and coping strategies in large fire disasters. *Procedia Engineering*, *71*, 616–621. doi:10.1016/j.proeng.2014.04.088

Mahmood, Z. (2014). *Emerging Mobile and Web 2.0 Technologies for Connected E-Government*. IGI Global. doi:10.4018/978-1-4666-6082-3

Masdeval, C., & Veloso, A. (2015). Mining citizen emotions to estimate the urgency of urban issues. *Information Systems*, *54*, 147–155. doi:10.1016/j.is.2015.06.008

Nair, M. R., Ramya, G. R., & Sivakumar, P. B. (2017). Usage and analysis of Twitter during 2015 Chennai flood towards disaster management. *Procedia Computer Science*, *115*, 350–358. doi:10.1016/j.procs.2017.09.089

Nakamura, A. (2004). *Kanjō hyōgen jiten* [Dictionary of Emotive Expressions]. Academic Press.

Neppalli, V. K., Caragea, C., Squicciarini, A., Tapia, A., & Stehle, S. (2017). Sentiment analysis during Hurricane Sandy in emergency response. *International Journal of Disaster Risk Reduction*, *21*, 213–222. doi:10.1016/j.ijdrr.2016.12.011

Öztürk, N., & Ayvaz, S. (2018). Sentiment analysis on Twitter: A text mining approach to the Syrian refugee crisis. *Telematics and Informatics*, *35*(1), 136–147. doi:10.1016/j.tele.2017.10.006

Parrott, W. G. (Ed.). (2001). *Emotions in social psychology: Essential readings*. Psychology Press.

Plutchik, R., & Kellerman, H. (Eds.). (2013). *Theories of emotion* (Vol. 1). Academic Press.

Strapparava, C., & Mihalcea, R. (2008, March). Learning to identify emotions in text. In *Proceedings of the 2008 ACM symposium on Applied computing* (pp. 1556-1560). ACM. 10.1145/1363686.1364052

Tokuhisa, R., Inui, K., & Matsumoto, Y. (2008, August). Emotion classification using massive examples extracted from the web. In *Proceedings of the 22nd International Conference on Computational Linguistics-Volume 1* (pp. 881-888). Association for Computational Linguistics. 10.3115/1599081.1599192

Vo, B. K. H., & Collier, N. I. G. E. L. (2013). Twitter emotion analysis in earthquake situations. *International Journal of Computational Linguistics and Applications*, *4*(1), 159–173.

Wade, L. (2017). *Unusual quake rattles Mexico*. Academic Press.

Yu, S., Zhu, H., Jiang, S., Zhang, Y., Xing, C., & Chen, H. (2019). Emoticon Analysis for Chinese Social Media and E-commerce: The AZEmo System. *ACM Transactions on Management Information Systems*, *9*(4), 16. doi:10.1145/3309707

Zhang, Z., Li, X., & Chen, Y. (2012). Deciphering word-of-mouth in social media: Text-based metrics of consumer reviews. *ACM Transactions on Management Information Systems*, *3*(1), 5. doi:10.1145/2151163.2151168

ADDITIONAL READING

López-Chau, A., Valle-Cruz, D., & Sandoval-Almazán, R. (2020). Sentiment Analysis of Twitter Data Through Machine Learning Techniques. In *Software Engineering in the Era of Cloud Computing* (pp. 185–209). Springer. doi:10.1007/978-3-030-33624-0_8

Mckinsey Global Insititute. (2019) Digital India. Technology to transform a connected nation. Online: http://tinyurl.com/yhjwmkq5

Rodríguez-Domínguez, L., Sánchez, I. M. G., & Álvarez, I. G. (2011). From Emerging to Connected E-Government: The Effects of Socioeconomics and Internal Administration Characteristics. *International Journal of Digital Accounting Research, 11.*

Saha, P. (2009). Architecting the connected government: practices and innovations in Singapore. In *ACM International Conference Proceeding Series* (pp. 11-18). 10.1145/1693042.1693046

Saha, P. (Ed.). (2012). *Enterprise Architecture for Connected E-Government: Practices and Innovations: Practices and Innovations*. IGI Global. doi:10.4018/978-1-4666-1824-4

Sandoval-Almazán, R., Valle-Cruz, D., & Kavanaugh, A. L. (2018). The diffusion of social media among state governments in Mexico. *International Journal of Public Administration in the Digital Age*, *5*(1), 63–81. doi:10.4018/IJPADA.2018010104

Valle-Cruz, D. (2019). Public value of e-government services through emerging technologies. *International Journal of Public Sector Management*, *32*(5), 530–545. doi:10.1108/IJPSM-03-2018-0072

Valle-Cruz, D., Alejandro Ruvalcaba-Goméz, E., Sandoval-Almazán, R., & Ignacio Criado, J. (2019, June). A Review of Artificial Intelligence in Government and its Potential from a Public Policy Perspective. In *20th Annual International Conference on Digital Government Research* (pp. 91-99). ACM. 10.1145/3325112.3325242

Valle-Cruz, D., & Sandoval-Almazán, R. (2018). Boosting E-Participation: The Use of Social Media in Municipalities in the State of Mexico. In Optimizing E-Participation Initiatives Through Social Media (pp. 103-125). IGI Global.

Valle-Cruz, D., Sandoval-Almazán, R., & Gil-García, J. R. (2016). Citizens' perceptions of the impact of information technology use on transparency, efficiency and corruption in local governments. *Information Polity*, *21*(3), 321–334. doi:10.3233/IP-160393

KEY TERMS AND DEFINITIONS

Citizen Centricity: Citizen centricity is an approach in which citizen participation, through the explicit or implicit expression of their needs by different means, plays an essential role in the design of strategies.

Document-Term Matrix (DTM): A DTM is a table that describes the frequency of terms that occur in a collection of documents. Typically, DTMs are sparse matrices.

Hashtag: This is a term associated with issues or discussions that are indexed in social networks. The hsh sign (#) is used as a prefix to identify trending topics in posts.

Kappa: Cohen's kappa coefficient is used to determine the degree of agreement or concordance between the categories assigned to each document by two taggers. A kappa coefficient value of 1.0 means complete agreement, lower values indicate more disagreement between taggers.

Micro-Blogging: Technology that allows its registered users to send and publish short messages. Twitter is an example of this platform. On Twitter the number of characters allowed is limited to 280 characters per post or tweet.

NGO: It refers to non-governmental or nongovernment organization that is non-profit making which is independent of any government. Typically, NGOs are mainly created in the name of or for the reasons of fhumanitarian or social support.

PANAS: Positive and Negative Affect Schedule is a self-report questionnaire which is useful for measuring positive and negative affect. The questionnaire used in this study was developed by researchers at the University of Minnesota and Southern Methodist University.

PoS-Tagging (Part-of-Speech Tagging): PoS-tagging is a procedure to assign a grammatical category to each word in a document. The words and categories can be used as input to machine-learning methods.

Sentiment Analysis: Sentiment Analysis is a subfield of artificial intelligence aimed at determining the polarity of opinions expressed by people. This type of analysis allows us to assign a positive, negative or neutral categorization to each document automatically.

Tagger: A tagger is an expert (human being) who reads and analyzes a document in order to identify its polarity and to assign it to a category from a list. The list of categories usually contains the following elements: positive, negative, neutral, or others.

Trending Topic: A trending topic is a word or sentence that becomes popular on a social network or micro-blogging platform. A word or sentence is considered a trending topic if it is frequent and it is novel.

Web 2.0: Web 2.0refers to the second generation of the World Wide Web that focuses on the ability of people to collaborate and share information online. It refers to the transition from static web pages to a more dynamic web.

This research was previously published in Web 2.0 and Cloud Technologies for Implementing Connected Government; pages 162-181, copyright year 2021 by Information Science Reference (an imprint of IGI Global).

Section 2
Development and Design Methodologies

Chapter 7
Integrating Semantic Acquaintance for Sentiment Analysis

Neha Gupta
https://orcid.org/0000-0003-0905-5457
Manav Rachna International Institute of Research and Studies, Faridabad, India

Rashmi Agrawal
https://orcid.org/0000-0003-2095-5069
Manav Rachna International Institute of Research and Studies, Faridabad, India

ABSTRACT

The use of emerging digital information has become significant and exponential, as well as the boom of social media (forms, blogs, and social networks). Sentiment analysis concerns the statistical analysis of the views expressed in written texts. In appropriate evaluations of the emotional context, semantics plays an important role. The analysis is generally done from two viewpoints: how semantics are coded in sentimental instruments, such as lexicon, corporate, and ontological, and how automated systems determine feelings on social data. Two approaches to evaluate sentiments are commonly adopted (i.e., approaches focused on machine learning algorithms and semantic approaches). The precise testing in this area was increased by the already advanced semantic technology. This chapter focuses on semantic guidance-based sentiment analysis approaches. The Twitter/Facebook data will provide a semantically enhanced technique for annotation of sentiment polarity.

INTRODUCTION

Opinions or ideals have become an essential component in making judgment or alternatives for people or businesses. The rapid boom of Web 2.0 over the last decade has improved online organizations and enabled humans to put up their reviews or evaluation on a variety of topics in public domains. This user-generated content (UGC) is an essential statistics supply to help clients make shopping decision,

DOI: 10.4018/978-1-6684-6303-1.ch007

however also provided treasured insights for shops or manufacturers to enhance their marketing strategies and products (Pang & Lee, 2008). Sentiment evaluation deals with the computational treatment of critiques expressed in written texts (Kalra & Agrawal, 2017). In the era of Information explosion, there may be a huge quantity of opinionated statistics generated each day. These generated statistics leads to unstructured records and the analysis of these records to extract useful information is a hard to achieve task. The need to address these unstructured opinionated statistics naturally cause the upward push of sentiment analysis. The addition of already mature semantic technologies to this subject has increased the consequences accuracy. Evaluation of semantic of sentiments is precisely essential method in the internet now a days. Discovering the exact sense and understanding in which a specific sentence was written on the net is very important as there might not be any physical interaction to discover the significance of the sentence. There are a number of techniques to classify the specified sentiment as bad or horrible. This categorization helps us honestly discover the context of a sentence remotely (Gupta & Verma, 2019). The crucial troubles in sentiment evaluation is to express the sentiments in texts and to check whether or not the expressions indicate superb (favorable) or negative (unfavorable) opinions toward the challenge and to evaluate the correctness of the sentences that are classified. The motivation of writing this chapter is to understand the concepts related to sentiment analysis and the importance of semantic in sentiment analysis. The present chapter starts with basic of ontologies and their relation to sentiment analysis. The chapter further discusses semantic ontologies with concept forms and their relationships along with steps to develop a baseline model for simple analysis of sentiment using NLP. At the end of the chapter case study related to the sentiment analysis using R programming on the protests for CAA and NRC in India during December 2019 has been presented. The corpus of the case study has been built by collecting related articles from the Times of India and other leading newspapers of the India. Real time data has been extracted from twitter by applying the most frequent words as hash tags. Finally sentiment analysis techniques have been applied on twitter data to know the opinions of the people of country on the issue of NRC and CAA protest.

ONTOLOGY AND THE SEMANTIC WEB

Today the Internet has become a critical human need. People depend heavily on the Internet for their day-to-day tasks. World Wide Web (WWW) has rapidly become a massive database with some information on all of the interesting things. Most of the web content is primarily designed for human read, computers can only decode layout web pages (Kaur & Agrawal, 2017). Machines generally lack the automated processing of data collected from any website without any knowledge of their semantics.

This has become a concern because users spend a great deal of time comparing multiple websites. Semantic Web provides a solution to this problem. Semantic web is defined as a collection of technologies that enable computers to understand the meaning of metadata based information, i.e., information about the information content. Web Semantic can be applied to integrate information from heterogeneous sources and improve the search process for improved and consistent information (Jalota & Agrawal, 2019). The Semantic technologies allow the ontology to refer to a metadata.

Ontology is a description of a domain knowledge that includes various terminologies of a given domain along with the relationship between existing terms.

Ontology is designed to act as metadata. Ontologies can help to create conceptual search and navigation of semantics for integration of semantically in-order feature. The language structures used to constructs ontologies include: XML, XML Schema, RDF, OWL, and RDF Scheme.

OWL has benefits over other structure languages in that OWL has more facilities to express meaning and semantic than XML and RDF / s. Ontologies built using RDF, OWL etc. are linked in a structured way to express semantic content explicitly and organize semantic boundaries for extracting concrete information (Kalra & Agrawal, 2019).

A semantic ontology can exists as an informal conceptual framework with concept forms and their relationships named and described, if at all, in natural language, Or it may be constructed as a formal semantic domain account, with concept types and systematically defined relationships in a logical language.

However, within the Web environment ontology is not merely a conceptual construct but a concrete, syntactic structure that models a domain's semantics – the conceptual framework – in a machine-understandable language (Gupta & Verma, 2019).

For the purpose of comprehensive and transportable machine understanding, the semantic web relies heavily on the structured ontologies that structure underlying data. Consequently, the performance of the semantic Web is highly dependent on the proliferation of ontology that requires quick and easy ontology engineering and the avoidance of a bottleneck of information gain (Pang & Lee, 2008). Conceptual structures which define the underlying ontology are German to the concept of machine processable data on the semantic Web. By identifying mutual and specific theories of the domain, ontology lets both people and machines interact precisely in order to facilitate semantic exchange. Ontology language editors aid in the development of semantic Web. Thus, the cheap and rapid creation of a domain-specific ontology is crucial to the semantic Web's success.

Limitations of Semantic Ontologies

Ontology helps in delivering solutions for database identification, end-to-end application authentication, authorization, data integrity, confidentiality, coordination and exchange of isolated pieces of information issues (Agrawal & Gupta, 2019). Some of the drawbacks of semantic ontologies are

1. Natural language parsers can function on only single statement at a particular time.
2. It is quite impossible to define the ontology limits of the abstract model of a given domain.
3. Automatic ontology creations, automatic ontology emergence to create new ontologies, and the identification of possible existing relationships between classes to automatically draw the taxonomy hierarchy are needed.
4. Ontology validators are limited and unable to verify all kinds of ontologies, e.g. validation of ontologies on the basis of complex inheritance relations.
5. Domain-specific ontologies are highly dependent on the application domain, and it is not possible to determine the general purpose ontologies from them because of this dependency.
6. The reengineering of semantic enrichment processes for web development consists of relational metadata, which must be built at high speed and low cost based on the abundance of ontologies, which is not currently possible (Agrawal & Gupta, 2019).

Because of these limitations in ontology, it is not currently possible for Semantic Web to achieve the actual objectives of completely structured information over the web in a computer process-able format and making advanced knowledge modeling framework.

NLP AND SENTIMENT ANALYSIS

Sentiment analysis (Pang and Lillian 2008) is a kind of text classiðcation that is used to handle subjective statements. Natural language processing (NLP) is used to gather and study opinion or sentiment words. Determining subjective attitudes in big social data maybe a hotspot in the ðeld of data mining and NLP (Hai et al. 2014). Makers are additionally intrigued to realize which highlights of their items are increasingly well known out in the open, so as to settle on proðtable business choices. There is an immense archive of conclusion content accessible at different online sources as sites, gatherings, internet based life, audit sites and so forth. They are developing, with increasingly obstinate content poured in constantly. In the past, manual strategies are used to investigate millions of sentiments & reviews and aggregated them toward a quick and efficient decision making (Liu, 2006). Sentiment analysis strategies carry out the project via automated procedures with minimum or no consumer support. The datasets that are available online may also comprise of objective statements, which no longer make effective contributions in sentiment analysis. These Type of statements are usually segregated at pre-processing stage. Binary Classification can be used to recommend the outcome of sentiment analysis. It may be considered as a multi-class classiðcation problem on a given scale of likeness. Because text is considered as a complex community of words which might be uniquely related to every sentiment therefore graph based definitely evaluation techniques are used for NLP tasks. Opinion mining involves NLP, to retrieve semantics from phrases and words of opinion. NLP will, however, have open problems that may be too challenging to be handled quickly and correctly up to date. Because sentiment analysis frequently uses NLP really well in large scale, it reflects this complicated behavior (Agrawal & Gupta, 2019). NLP's definitions for categorizing textual source material now don't fit with opinion mining, because they are different in nature. Documents with vastly disproportionate identical frequency of words do not always have the same polarity of sentiment. This is because, a fact can be either morally right or wrong in categorizing textual content, and is commonly accepted by all. Because of its subjective existence, a number of opinions may be incorrect about the same thing. Another distinction is that opinion mining is responsive to individual words, in which an unmarried word like NOT can change the meaning of the entire sentence. The transparent challenging conditions are prepositional phrases without the use of NOT words, derogatory and hypothetical sentences, etc. The latter section includes an in-depth overview of NLP problems surrounding the assessment of sentiments. The online resources consists of subjective content material having basic, composite, or complex sentences. Plain sentences have approximately one product's unmarried view, whereas complex sentences have multiple opinions on it (Agrawal & Gupta, 2019). Long sentences have an implied mean and are difficult to test. Standard assessments pertain only to an unmarried person, even though comparative articles have an object or a variety of its aspects examined as opposed to some other object. Comparative viewpoints may be either empirical or contextual. An example of a subjective comparison sentence is "Game X's visual effects are much better than game Y's," while an example of objective comparison expression is

"Game X has twice as many control options as that of Game Y". Opinion mining anticipates an assortment of sentence types, since individuals follow different composing styles so as to communicate in a superior manner.

Normally, conclusion examination for content information can be figured on a few levels, remembering for an individual sentence level, section level, or the whole archive in general. Frequently, notion is registered on the archive overall or a few collections are done subsequent to processing the supposition for singular sentences. There are two major approaches to sentiment analysis (Gupta & Verma, 2019).

- Supervised machine learning or deep learning approaches
- Unsupervised lexicon-based approaches

Usually we need pre-labeled facts for the first strategy, although we do not also have the luxury of a well-labeled training dataset in the second technique. We would therefore want to use unsupervised approaches to predict sentiment through the use of knowledge bases, ontologies, databases, and lexicons with distinctive details, primarily curated and prepared for analysis of sentiment. A lexicon is an encyclopedia, a wordbook or an e-book. Lexicons, in our case, are special dictionaries or vocabularies created to interpret sentiments (Gupta & Agrawal, 2020). Some of these lexicons provide a list of wonderful and terrible polar terms with a few grades aligned with them along with the use of different techniques such as the position of terms, phrases, meaning, sections of expression, phrases, and so on, . Rankings are given to the text documents from which we need to determine the sentiments. After these scores have been aggregated we get the very last sentiment.

TextBlob, along with sentiment analysis, is an excellent open-supply repository for efficient working of NLP tasks. It is additionally a sentiment lexicon (in the form of an XML file) that enables to offer rankings of polarity as well as subjectivity. The polarity rating is a float inside the [-1.0, 1.0] range. The subjectivity is a float in the range [0.0, 1.0] where zero.0 could be very objective and 1.0 may be very subjective.

Following the trends of artificial intelligence, the number of programs built for the processing of natural languages is growing every day with aid of the day. NLP-developed applications would allow for a faster and more effective implementation of infrastructures to remove human strength in many jobs (Niazi & Hussain, 2009). The following are common examples of NLP applications

- Text Classification (Spam Detector etc)
- Sentiment Analysis & Predictions
- Author Recognition systems
- Machine Translation
- Chatbots

Steps to Develop a Baseline Model for Simple Analysis of Sentiment Using NLP

Following steps needs to be followed to develop a baseline model for analysis of sentiment using NLP. The implementation is in python with standard libraries and tools:

1. Identifcation of Dataset
2. Name of the data set: Sentiment Labelled Sentences Data Set

3. Source of data set: UCI Machine Learning Library
4. Basic Information about the data set: 4.This information kit was generated through a user analysis of 3 websites (Amazon, Yelp, Imdb). Such remarks include impressions of restaurants, movies and goods. Two separate emoticons appear in each record in the data set (PORIA & GELBUKH 2013). These are 1: good, 0: bad.
5. Creation of a model of sentiment analysis with the above-mentioned data.
6. Create a Python based Machine Learning model with the sklearn and nltk library.
7. Code writing by library imports. For instance:
   import pandas as pnd
   import numpy as nmp
   import pickle
   import sys
   import os
   import io
8. Now upload and view the data set. For Example:
   input_file = "../data/amazon_cells_labelled.txt"
   amazon = pnd.read_csv(input_file,delimiter='\t',header=None)
   amazon.columns = ['Sentence','Class']
9. Statistical analysis of the data on the basis of following parameters.
   A) Total Count of Each Category
   B) Distribution of All Categories
10. For a very balanced dataset that is having almost equal number of positive and negative classes then pre processing the text by removing special characters, lower string, punctuations, email address, IP address, stop words etc
11. Data pre-cleaning makes the data inside the model ready for use..
12. Build the model by splitting the dataset to test (10%) and training(90%).
13. Test the model with test data and examine the accuracy, precision, recall and f1 results.
14. To test the accuracy of the calculations, create the confusion matrix. Link to plot a confusion matrix can be seen at

#source: https://www.kaggle.com/grfiv4/plot-a-confusion-matrix

SEMANTIC SEARCH ENGINE

Current keyword-based search engines such as Google can identify internet pages by matching correct tokens or words with tokens or words in internet content inside the consumer's query (Ye & Zang, 2009). There are many disadvantages to this method.

A. Tokens or tokens-like words inside the User Search shall not be taken into account when looking for net sites.
B. The key-word based search engine gives equal importance to all key phrases whereas consumers challenge them as they think of one category of keywords as important.

C. To get the correct applicable end result, customers might also also want to enter numerous synonyms on his very own to get the desired records which would possibly result into the omission of many treasured net pages.
D. Another trouble is of information overloading. The traditional keyword based absolute search engines like google make it very tedious for user to locate the useful facts from a massive list of search results.

To remedy the above mentioned problems that the customers face, Ontology based semantic steps were developed.

Ontology is primarily based on Semantic Search Engine that which recognizes the meaning of the consumer query and gives the results in a comparative sense.

It is not principally easy to return built-in keyword pages but also the pages which can be used to provide the means available by using the Ontological synonym dataset, created using WordNet, to enter keywords from the user. First the Ontology Synonym Collection uses WordNet and then invokes the provider. In addition, if the similarity is 100%, extra keywords are taken into account to provide the user with the appropriate and accurate results. Approximately the meta facts like URL is provided by the meta-processor.

Following are the Components of a Basic Semantic Search Engine

1. **Development of Ontology:** Ontology with. OWL or. DAML extensions are developed in plain text format.
2. **Crawler for Ontology:** Ontology crawler discovers new ontological content on the web and add it to the library of ontology.
3. Ontology notepad: It is used for the purpose of annotating and publishing web pages to ontologies.
4. Web Crawler: Crawls across the web to find Web pages annotated with ontologies and create knowledge base on Ontology instances.
5. Semantic Searching: understands the context and logical reasoning of the content on the website and offers objective results.
6. **Query Builder:** Query builder is used to construct the user search queries.
7. **Query Pre-processor:** It pre-process the queries and send the queries to the inference engine.
8. **Inference Engine:** Reasoning of the search queries using ontology database and the knowledge base is done by the inference Engine.

SEMANTIC RESOURCES FOR SENTIMENT ANALYSIS

Sentiment and Semantic analysis is an important resource in our network today. It is necessary to find a suitable context and meaning for a selected sentence on the internet because the real meaning of the sentence can not be discovered by physical contact (Tsai & Hsu, 2013). There are large variety of methods and techniques used to identify and classify the argument as good or bad in quality. Such classification virtually helps in defining the context of the sentence (Liu, 2006). The essential questions of sentimental analysis is to identify the expressions of feelings in texts and to check whether the expressions indicate wonderful (favorable) or negative (unfavorable) opinions closer to the subject and how successfully and efficaciously sentences are classified. In the detailed interpretation of the meaning of the expression, Semantics plays a critical role. The role of semantics is studied from two perspectives:

1. The manner in which semantics is represented in sentimental tools like lexica, corpora and ontology.
2. The manner in which automatic systems conduct sentiment evaluations of social media data.

For example, context-dependence and a finer detection of feelings that lead to the assignment of feeling values to elements or to the layout and use of an extensive range of effective labels or to the use of current techniques for finer-grained semantical processing. In the case of semantics, lexical elements should be paired with logical and cognitive problems and other aspects that are concerned about emotions.

Many works in sentiment evaluation try to utilize shallow processing techniques. The not unusual element in a lot of these works is that they merely attempt to pick out sentiment-bearing expressions. No effort has been made to discover which expression simply contributes to the overall sentiment of the text.

Semantic evaluation is critical to recognize the exact meaning conveyed inside the textual content. Some words generally tend to mislead the which means of a given piece of text. For Example:

I like awful boys.

Here the phrase 'like' expresses fine sentiments while the word awful represent negative sentiments.

WSD (Word Sense Disambiguation) is a technique that could been used to get the right sense of the word. Syntactic or structural homes of textual content are used in many NLP applications like gadget translation, speech recognition, named entity recognition, etc.

In general, techniques that are using semantic analysis are high-priced than syntax-based techniques because of the shallow processing involved within the latter. Therefore it is incredibly essential for us to ascertain the precise significance of the expression or else it may result in unfortunate knowledge (in many cases altogether different) on the matter. The key issues in the sentiment assessment are the manner in which sentiments are interpreted in texts and how words indicate a positive or negative (unfavorable) view of the subject. In the present situation, feelings of good or bad polarities for particular topics are extracted from a report instead of the whole document being marked as good or bad in order to include a massive quantity of statistics from one individual paper.Most of their applications aim to classify an entire report into a file subject, which is either specifically or implied. For example, the film form evaluates into wonderful or terrible, implies that all the expressions of sentiment in the evaluation directly represent sentiments towards that film and expressions that contradict it. On the contrary, by studying the relationships between expressions of sentiment and subjects, we can investigate in detail what is and is not required (Niazi & Hussain, 2009). These approaches, therefore, provide a wide variety of incentives for different applications to reach beneficial and unfavorable views on particular topics. It provides strong functions for aggressive research, reputation assessment and the identification of undesirable rumours. For example, huge sums are spent on the evaluation and examination of customer satisfaction. However, the efficacy of such surveys is usually greatly limited (Pang and Lee 2008), considering the amount of money and attempts spent on them, both due to sample length limitations and due to the problems associated with making successful questionnaires. There is thus natural preference for detecting and evaluating inclination, instead of making specific surveys, inside online archives, including blogs, chat rooms and news articles. Human views of these electronic files are easy to understand. Therefore there may have been also significant issues for some organisations, as these documents may have an impact on the general public and terrible rumors in online documents. Let us take an example to interpret the realistic application of sentiment investigation: "Product A is good however expensive." This declaration incorporates a aggregation of statements: "Product A is good" "Product A is expensive" We suppose it's smooth to agree that there is one assertion, Product A is good, it gives a good strong impression, and another statement, product A, is expensive and it has a negative thought. Therefore, we seek to extract any assertion of support additionally to research the benefit of the full context and present it to abandon users who use the findings in line with their program requirements. Sentiment Analysis research therefore involves:

- Sentiment expressions recognition.
- Polarity and expressive power.
- Their relation to the subject.

They are interrelated elements. For example, "XXX beats YY" refers to a positive meaning for XXX and a negative sense for YYY. The word "beats" refers to XXX.

SEMANTIC ORIENTATION AND AGGREGATION

Semantic Orientation

The semantic response to a function f shows whether the view is positive, negative or neutral. Here the figure 1 represents the opinion of the user. Wide variety of literature has been studied for semantic approach to sentiment analysis that classifies the semantic orientation into two kinds of approaches, i.e.

1. corpus based
2. Dictionary or lexicon or knowledge based.

Figure 1. Sentiment Classification Techniques

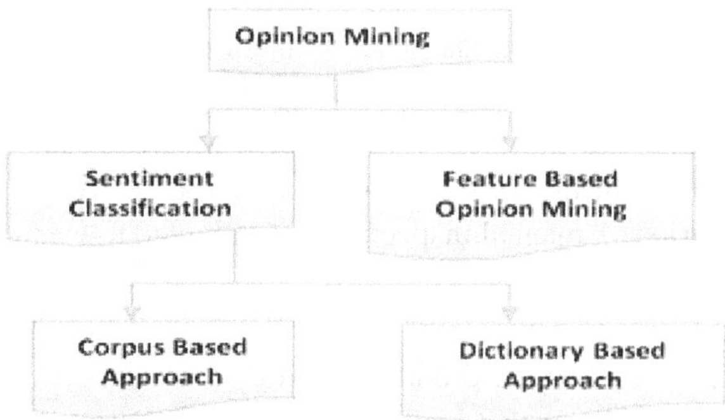

Corpus-based approach suggests data-driven approaches that not only have access to the sentiment labels, but can also be used for the advantage in an ML algorithm. This may simply be a rule-based technique or even a combination of NLP parsing. Corpus also has some specific domain, which will tell the Machine learning algorithm about the variety of the sentiment label for a word depending on its context / domain. Full semantic orientation requires large data sets to satisfy the polarity of the phrases and hence the feeling of the text.

The key drawback with the method is that it is based on the polarity of words contained within the training corpus, and the polarity of word is determined according to the terms in the corpus. Because of the simplification of this approach, this method was well studied in the literature. This method first eliminates sentiment expressions from the unstructured text and then measures the polarity of the words. Most of the sentiment-bearing terms are multi-phrase features in contrast to bag-of-words, e.g., "good movie," "satisfactory cinematography," "satisfactory actors," etc. In literature, the efficiency of a semantic orientation based technology was restricted because of by an insufficient availability of multi-word features.

Dictionary based approach suggests the judging of sentiment based on presence of signaling sentiment words (and perhaps some shorter context, like negations in the front of them) + some kind of counting mechanism to reach at sentiment prediction. In literature, dictionary based method is usually called the most effective (and subsequently of much less accuracy) one. Word based sentiment analysis is a statistical method for evaluating the feeling of a document. In the most successful case, feelings are binary: high or low, but they can be extended to more than one dimension, like anxiety, depression, rage, happiness, etc. This approach is largely based on the predefined list of sentences (or dictionary).

Dictionary-based approach works by identifying the words (for which an opinion has been given), from reviewed textual content then reveals their synonyms and antonyms from dictionary. WordNet or SentiWordNet or any another word network can be used as a dictionary. Corpus based approach helps locate the words of opinion in a particular context orientation, begin with the list of the words of opinion and then locate another word of opinion in a broad corpus. The most useful dictionary to use is SentiWordNet 3.0. It is publicly accessible lexical tools consisting of "synsets," each with a positive and a negative numerical score of 0 to 1. This score is allocated from the WordNet automatically. This uses a semi-supervised learning process and an iterative algorithm for random walks. The above mentioned method works as follows:

First of all, the system needs to collect the simple and easy to understand sentiment words that have well defined positive or negative orientations. This collection is further extended by the algorithm by searching for its synonyms and antonyms in the WordNet or another online dictionary. The words searched by the algorithm are further added into the seed list to enlarge the collection. Included in the seed list are the following terms. The algorithm continues with the iterations. The cycle stops when new words can no longer be identified. A manual inspection is conducted to clean the list after the cycle had been completed.

Semantic Aggregation: Every review related to a product (shall we take an example of a camera) is mapped with its precise polarities in the product ontology. Product attributes that are at the higher level of the tree overpower the attributes that are at the lower level. When a reviewer talks about certain features of the product that are more advantageous or terrible within the ontology, he is weighting that feature more in comparison to other statistics of all child nodes (ex- light, resolution, coloration and compression). This is because the function of the parent class abstracts data and the characteristics of its child class. The value of the function is captured in the ontological tree by increasing the height of the characteristic node. In case of neutral polarity of the parent function, the polarity of the characteristic node is attributed to the polarities of its younger nodes. Thus data in a particular node is generated by his own data and by the weighted information of all its younger nodes.

In order to assess the record content of the base ode and the polarity of the analysis, the accurate propagation is carried out from the bottom to the top.

Let us create an ontology tree TR(V1,E1) where $V1_i \in V1$ which is used for setting up a product attribute.

The attribute set of a product V1i consists of the V1i tuple

$$V1_i = \{f1_i, p1_i, h1_i\}$$

Where $f1_i$ is represented as the feature of the product

$P1_i$ represents the polarity score of the product recieved after the review in relation to $f1_i$ and $h1_i$
$H1_i$ represents the height attribute of the product
$E1_{ij} \in E1$ is s a relationship attribute
$F1_i \in V1_i$,
$F1_i \in V1_j$
$V1_i, V1_j \in V1$.

Let $V1_{ij}$ be the jth child of $V1_i$

The positive sentiment weight (PSW) and negative sentiment weight (NSW) of a vertex $V1_i$ can be calculated using the formula:

$$PSW(V1_i)=h1_i * p1_i$$
$$NSW(V1_i)=h1_i * p1_i$$

The product review polarity is estimated using expected sentiment-weight (ESW) of the ontology tree defined as,

$$ESW (root) = PSW (root) + NSW (root)$$

SEMANTIC APPROACH TO LEXICON ADAPTATION

The sentiment of a term isn't always static, as located in general-cause sentiment lexicons, however rather relies upon at the context wherein the term is used, i.e., it relies upon on its contextual semantics (Liu, 2006). Therefore, the lexicon adaptation technique functions in two predominant step

1. First, given a corpus and a sentiment lexicon, the approach builds a contextual semantic representation for each particular term in the corpus and ultimately uses it to derive the time period's contextual sentiment orientation and strength. The SentiCircle representation version is used to this end. Following the distributional inference, the words co-occurring in specific ways appear to have a common meaning, with certain words within the same corpus, SentiCircle derives the

word's contextual semantics from its co-occurrence-styles. Such patterns are then interpreted as a Geometric Circle & are used to measure the word's conceptual meaning, using simple trigonometric identities. For each single duration m within the corpus in particular, we are constructing a two Dimensional geometric circle, in which the center of the circle is the time span m and each factor is described as a background ci (i.e., a time period that happens with m inside the identical context).

2. Secondly, rules are applied, mostly in line with the correspondent contextual sentiments, in order to change the previous feelings of the words within the lexicon.

The adaptation process uses a series of antecedent-consistent regulations which determine how their previous feelings in Thelwall-Lexicon are to be up to date in accordance with their SentiMedians' positions (i.e. their contextual feelings). For a term m, it checks, particularly,

1. The prior SOS value of the SentiCircle quadrant in Thelwall-Sexicon and
2. The SentiMedian of m.

The method then chooses the most suitable rule to update the previous feeling and/or opinion of the word.

CASE STUDY: SENTIMENT ANALYSIS ON CAA AND NRC PROTESTS IN INDIA - 2019

To perform the sentiment analysis on the protests held for CAA and NRC in India during December 2019, we created one corpus by collecting related articles from the Times of India and other leading newspapers of the India. The corpus was created for the articles of December 2019 and January 2020 during the peak of the protest.

The aim of this case study is to show the technique of sentiment analysis using R programming. The first objective of this study is to plot a word cloud and identify the most frequent words from the corpus along with the sentiments of these words. These words are used as hash tags to extract the data from the twitter. We extracted real time data from twitter by applying the most frequent words as hash tags. Then we applied sentiment analysis on twitter data to know the opinions of the people of country on the issue of NRC and CAA protest.

Installing Packages and Library

First step for implementing sentiment analysis on R is to install the relevant packages and their corresponding libraries. Some of the important packages which are used in sentiment analysis are-tm, SnowballC, SentimentAnalysis and wordcloud. We read the corpus as text file and loaded the data as corpus.

```
docs <- Corpus(VectorSource(text))
```

First few lines of corpus is shown below-

```
<<SimpleCorpus>>
Metadata:  corpus specific: 1, document level (indexed): 0
Content:  documents: 192
  [1] 20-12-2019 25,000 Citizens Protest CAA At August Kranti


  .

  [2] Call for "azaadi" or freedom dominated the student-driven pro-
test of over 25,000 Mumbaikars, including 7,000 women, against the Citi-
zenship Amendment Act (CAA) and the proposed National Register of Cit-
izens (NRC) at the historic August Kranti Maidan at Grant Road on
Thursday. The protest was supported by political parties and activists.


  [3] While organisers said more than one lakh protest-
ers had turned up, police pegged the number at over 25,000.



  [4] Students from Tata Institute of Social Sciences (TISS), IIT-Bombay and
Mumbai University mobilised their peers and other citizens from across the
city. "The first call was given on my Twitter handle on December 11 and though
I have only a few thousand followers, the tweet was seen by over one lakh in-
dividuals," said Fahad Ahmad, PhD student of TISS who was one of the main or-
ganisers. "I am on 24 WhatsApp groups coordinating with students from across
the city."
```

The sample text is an evidence for the extracted article from Times of India dated 20-12-2019. Before applying the text analysis, the text needs to be transformed. Hence text transformation is an important step while analyzing the text. Here we applied the tm_map() function for text transformation to replace the special characters like- "/", "@" and "|" with space in the text. Subsequent to changeover of special characters with space, text cleaning is done with the same tm_map() function where the content_transformer(tolower) is used to convert all capital letters into lowercase letters and removeNumbers is used to remove the digits from the text.

To remove the common stop words, an inbuilt English stopwords dictionary is used by R which can be accessed as –

```
stopwords("english")
```

The common stopwords are-

```
'but' 'if' 'or' 'because' 'as''we\'re' 'they\'re'  'until' 'while' 'of' 'at'
'by' 'for' 'with' 'about' 'against' 'between' 'into' 'i' 'me' 'my' 'myself'
'we' 'our' 'ours' 'ourselves' 'you' 'your' 'yours' 'yourself' 'yourselves' 'he'
```

```
'him' 'his' 'through' 'during' 'before' 'after' 'above' 'below' 'to' 'from'
'up' 'down' 'in' 'out' 'on' 'off' 'over' 'more' 'most' 'other' 'some' 'such'
'no' 'nor' 'not' 'only' 'own' 'same' 'so' 'than' 'too' 'very' 'under' 'him-
self' 'she''her' 'hers' 'herself' 'it' 'its' 'itself' 'they' 'them' 'their'
'theirs' 'themselves' 'what' 'which' 'who' 'whom' 'this''that' 'these' 'those'
'am''is' 'are''was' 'were' 'be' 'been' 'being' 'have' 'has' 'you\'ll' 'he\'ll'
'she\'ll' 'we\'ll' 'they\'ll' 'isn\'t' 'aren\'t''wasn\'t' 'weren\'t' 'hasn\'t'
'haven\'t' 'hadn\'t' 'had' 'having' 'do''does' 'did' 'doing' 'would' 'should'
'could' 'ought' 'i\'m' 'you\'re' 'he\'s''she\'s' 'it\'s' 'i\'ve' 'you\'ve'
'we\'ve' 'they\'ve' 'i\'d' 'you\'d' 'he\'d' 'she\'d' 'we\'d' 'they\'d' 'i\'ll'
'again' 'further' 'then' 'once' 'here' 'there' 'when' 'where' 'why' 'how'
'all' 'any' 'both' 'each' 'few'
'doesn\'t' 'don\'t' 'didn\'t' 'won\'t' 'wouldn\'t' 'shan\'t' 'shouldn\'t'
'can\'t' 'cannot' 'couldn\'t' 'mustn\'t'
'let\'s' 'that\'s' 'who\'s' 'what\'s' 'here\'s' 'there\'s' 'when\'s' 'where\'s'
'why\'s' 'how\'s' 'a' 'an' 'the' 'and'
```

To add more stopwords we need to specify our stopwords as a character vector. In this case we find "said" and "also" as the stopwords and we removed them by applying the following function-

```
docs <- tm_map(docs, removeWords, c("said", "also"))
```

Subsequently punctuation and white spaces are also eliminated. First few lines of the transformed corpus are shown below-

```
<<SimpleCorpus>>
Metadata:  corpus specific: 1, document level (indexed): 0
Content:  documents: 192
  [1]  citizens protest caa august kranti


  [2] call "azaadi" freedom dominated studentdriv-
en protest mumbaikars including women citizenship amendment act
caa proposed national register citizens nrc historic august kranti
maidan grant road thursday protest supported political parties activists

  [3]  organisers one lakh protesters turned police pegged number


  [4] students tata institute social sciences tiss iitbombay mum-
bai university mobilised peers citizens across city " first call giv-
en twitter handle december though thousand followers tweet seen
one lakh individuals" fahad ahmad phd student tiss one main or-
ganisers " whatsapp groups coordinating students across city"
```

```
  [5] apart three institutions organis-
ers got support students st xavier's college internation-
al institute population sciences iips wilson college among others
```

```
  [6] appeals attend rally made protests places " can see people mumbra mira
road govandi bhendi bazaar outraged know allow inequality constitution stop "
activist teesta setalvad
```

To build a term document matrix we applied the following function-

```
D_t_m <- TermDocumentMatrix(docs)
mat <- as.matrix(d_t_m)
var<- sort(rowSums(mat),decreasing=TRUE)
doc <- data.frame(word = names(var),freq=var)
head(doc, 10)
```

This has resulted the output as frequency of each word in descending order. We have shown only first 10 lines of the output by via head().

Table 1. Word frequency table

word	freq	
caa	caa	32
citizenship	citizenship	29
nrc	nrc	28
police	police	27
india	india	26
modi	modi	24
people	people	23
delhi	delhi	23
law	law	20
minister	minister	19

Using this word frequency table we plotted the frequency table of words as shown in figure 2 and generated the word cloud as shown in figure 3 below-

To carry out sentiment analysis of these frequent words we used the SentimentAnalysis package and its library where we used the above generated document term matrix. First few lines of sentiments generated are-

Figure 2. Word Frequency Plot

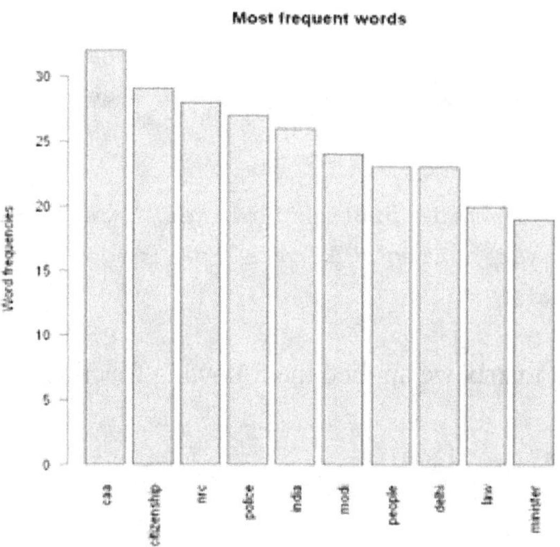

Figure 3. Word cloud

Table 2. Sentiment Analysis of Frequent Words

WordCount	SentimentGI	NegativityGI	PositivityGI
5	-0.20000000	0.20000000	0.00000000
30	0.00000000	0.06666667	0.06666667
8	0.00000000	0.00000000	0.00000000
42	0.04761905	0.00000000	0.04761905
18	0.05555556	0.00000000	0.05555556
24	0.12500000	0.00000000	0.12500000

Every document has a word count, a negativity score, a positivity score, and the overall sentiment score. The distribution of overall sentiment can be seen as-

```
summary(sent$SentimentGI)
```

```
Min.    1st Qu.   Median     Mean    3rd Qu.     Max.      NA's
-0.33333  0.00000  0.00000  0.01538  0.05518  0.33333        34
```

After adding the column of words with the sentiment score-

Table 3. Sentiment score of the words

d[1:6, 1]	WordCount	SentimentGI	NegativityGI	PositivityGI
protest	5	-0.20000000	0.20000000	0.00000000
caa	30	0.06666667	0.10000000	0.16666667
citizenship	8	-0.25000000	0.25000000	0.00000000
india	44	0.06818182	0.00000000	0.06818182
nrc	18	0.11111111	0.00000000	0.11111111
police	26	0.07692308	0.11538462	0.19230769

Performing Sentiment Analysis on Twitter Data based on Hashtags

In 21st century, there has been an exponential rush forward in the online commotion of people across the world. One of the online social platforms is Twitter when people freely express their sentiments. There are several challenges in performing sentiment analysis on the data extracted from the twitter as inhabitants have a dissimilar way of writing and while posting on Twitter, people are least bothered about the correct spelling of words or they may use a lot of slangs which are not proper English words but are used in casual conversations. Hence it has been an interesting research area among researchers from one decade.

By motivating from the above, we have generated the most frequent words from the corpus collected in the above section from various articles in news papers during December 2019 and January 2020 on NRC and CAA and these words have been used as hashtags to extract the relevant data from twitter. Using the twitter API in R we performed data extraction by passing most frequent word as hashtag and extracted top 250 tweets. These tweets were stored as a data frame. First few lines of text of this dataframe can be seen as-

head(tweets.df$text)

1. 'RT @ShayarImran: Participated in KSU protest march and public meeting against #CAA #NRC at Calicutt, Kerala \n@RamyaHaridasMP \n@srinivasiyc…'
2. '@hfao5 @AnjanPatel7 @SyedAhmedAliER @KTRTRS @trspartyonline @TelanganaCMO @asadowaisi Hyderabadi\'s must protest KCR… https://t.co/T53DB7do14'

3. 'RT @GradjanskiO: Novi protest ce obelezititi puteve Vesicevih rusevina.\n\nUrbicid! Mrznja prema gradjanima!\n\n15.02.2020\n\u23f0 18h\nPlato\n\nDo pobede…'
4. 'RT @SwamiGeetika: #DelhiAssemblyElections2020 \n\nYouth gathered in large numbers to protest after TMC barred distributing Hanuman Chalisa an…'
5. 'RT @anyaparampil: Workers w Venezuelan airline Conviasa tell @ErikaOSanoja their protest of Guaidó\'s arrival in Venezuela is part of "defen…'
6. 'RT @JamesRu55311: We've known for a long time that BBC is already lost, and that they were complicit in their own downfall. Watching them s…'

This data frame is first converted into a vector and then preprocessing is applied before sentiment analysis. The function get_nrc_sentiment() is used to identify the positive and negative words. We then computed the total positive and negative words in the twitter text and the a plot is drawn as shown in figure 4 below. This plot shows the sentiments attached with the corresponding text.

Figure 4. Total Positive And Negative Words In The Twitter Text

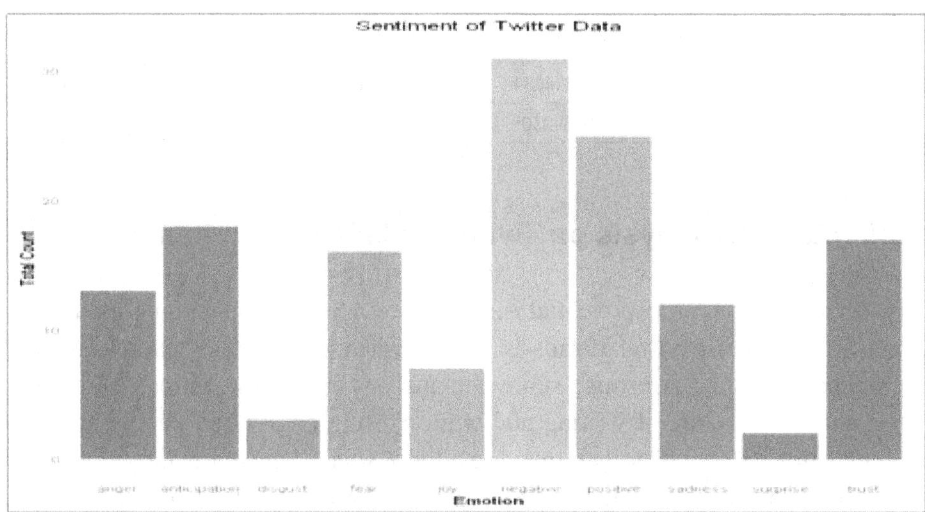

As we can discover here, in the given case more number of negative words are found hence it represents the negative sentiments of the people. Thus we can easily identify and analyse the sentiments of the people based on the key words.

CONCLUSION

The chapter discusses the concepts related to sentiment analysis and the importance of semantic in sentiment analysis. The present chapter has illustrated the basic of ontologies and their relation to sentiment analysis. The chapter has further discussed semantic ontologies with concept forms and their relationships along with steps to develop a baseline model for simple analysis of sentiment using NLP. At the end of the chapter case study related to the sentiment analysis using R programming on the protests for CAA and NRC in India during December 2019 has been presented. The corpus of the case study has been built by collecting related articles from the Times of India and other leading newspapers of the India. Real time data has been extracted from twitter by applying the most frequent words as hash tags. Finally sentiment analysis techniques have been applied on twitter data to know the opinions of the people of country on the issue of NRC and CAA protest. This work can be extended further by applying various sentiment analysis techniques to improve the accuracy of the predicted words. More work is also required to preprocess the data in order to improve the accuracy.

REFERENCES

Agrawal, R., & Gupta, N. (Eds.). (2018). *Extracting Knowledge from Opinion Mining*. IGI Global.

Gupta, N., & Agrawal, R. (2017). Challenges and Security Issues of Distributed Databases. In *NoSQL* (pp. 265–284). Chapman and Hall/CRC.

Gupta, N., & Agrawal, R. (2020). Application and Techniques of Opinion Mining. In *Hybrid Computational Intelligence*. Elsevier.

Gupta, N., & Verma, S. (2019). Tools of Opinion Mining. In *Extracting Knowledge From Opinion Mining* (pp. 179–203). IGI Global.

Hai, Z., Chang, K., Kim, J. J., & Yang, C. C. (2013). Identifying features in opinion mining via intrinsic and extrinsic domain relevance. *IEEE Transactions on Knowledge and Data Engineering*, *26*(3), 623–634. doi:10.1109/TKDE.2013.26

Jalota, C., & Agrawal, R. (2019). Ontology-Based Opinion Mining. In *Extracting Knowledge From Opinion Mining* (pp. 84–103). IGI Global.

Kalra, V., & Aggarwal, R. (2017). Importance of Text Data Preprocessing & Implementation in RapidMiner. In *Proceedings of the First International Conference on Information Technology and Knowledge Management–New Dehli, India* (Vol. 14, pp. 71-75). 10.15439/2017KM46

Kalra, V., & Agrawal, R. (2019). Challenges of Text Analytics in Opinion Mining. In *Extracting Knowledge From Opinion Mining* (pp. 268–282). IGI Global.

Kaur, S., & Agrawal, R. (2018). A Detailed Analysis of Core NLP for Information Extraction. *International Journal of Machine Learning and Networked Collaborative Engineering*, *1*(01), 33–47. doi:10.30991/IJMLNCE.2017v01i01.005

Liu, B. (2006). Mining comparative sentences and relations. In AAAI (Vol. 22). Academic Press.

Medhat, W., Hassan, A., & Korashy, H. (2014). Sentiment analysis algorithms and applications: A survey. *Ain Shams Engineering Journal*, *5*(4), 1093–1113.

Niazi, M., & Hussain, A. (2009). Agent-based tools for modeling and simulation of self-organization in peer-to-peer, ad hoc, and other complex networks. *IEEE Communications Magazine*, *47*(3), 166–173.

Pang, B., & Lee, L. (2008). Opinion mining and sentiment analysis. *Foundations and Trends in Information Retrieval*, *2*(1–2), 1–135. doi:10.1561/1500000011

Poria, S., Gelbukh, A., Hussain, A., Howard, N., Das, D., & Bandyopadhyay, S. (2013). Enhanced SenticNet with affective labels for concept-based opinion mining. *IEEE Intelligent Systems*, *28*(2), 31–38.

Tsai, A. C. R., Wu, C. E., Tsai, R. T. H., & Hsu, J. Y. J. (2013). Building a concept-level sentiment dictionary based on commonsense knowledge. *IEEE Intelligent Systems*, *28*(2), 22–30.

Ye, Q., Zhang, Z., & Law, R. (2009). Sentiment classification of online reviews to travel destinations by supervised machine learning approaches. *Expert Systems with Applications*, *36*(3), 6527–6535.

This research was previously published in Advanced Concepts, Methods, and Applications in Semantic Computing; pages 93-112, copyright year 2021 by Engineering Science Reference (an imprint of IGI Global).

Chapter 8
A Deep Neural Network Model for Cross-Domain Sentiment Analysis

Suman Kumari
Swami Keshvanand Institute of Technology, Management, and Gramothan, Jaipur, India

Basant Agarwal
Indian Institute of Information Technology, Kota, India

Mamta Mittal
https://orcid.org/0000-0003-0490-4413
G.B. Pant Government Engineering College, New Delhi, India

ABSTRACT

Sentiment analysis is used to detect the opinion/sentiment expressed from the unstructured text. Most of the existing state-of-the-art methods are based on supervised learning, and therefore, a labelled dataset is required to build the model, and it is very difficult task to obtain a labelled dataset for every domain. Cross-domain sentiment analysis is to develop a model which is trained on labelled dataset of one domain, and the performance is evaluated on another domain. The performance of such cross-domain sentiment analysis is still very limited due to presence of many domain-related terms, and the sentiment analysis is a domain-dependent problem in which words changes their polarity depending upon the domain. In addition, cross-domain sentiment analysis model suffers with the problem of large number of out-of-the-vocabulary (unseen words) words. In this paper, the authors propose a deep learning-based approach for cross-domain sentiment analysis. Experimental results show that the proposed approach improves the performance on the benchmark dataset.

DOI: 10.4018/978-1-6684-6303-1.ch008

1. INTRODUCTION

Nowadays, online stores are in trend such as such as Amazon (amazon.com), Snapdeal (snapdeal.com). Nowadays numbers of people like to share their views about the product they buy. Whenever any user wants to buy something form online stores the only way to evaluate the product is another user's review about those products. But reading all the review one-by-one and understanding it overall is time consuming. It is attractive if we could have some type of analyser that can analyse reviews automatically. To make this process easy an automatic analyser came into existence which analyse all reviews or opinions and make it easy for the user to make view about the product. This process takes place under the field named as sentiment analysis. Reviewing product is useful for both customer as well as seller; customer can make decision about the product through review whereas seller can understand peoples thinking about the product. If seller sees the negative sentiments it can modify the product and if reviews are positive it can increase the sell accordingly (Jain et al. 2018b).

Sentiment analysis is the field of natural language processing in which computation about opinions, sentiments and emotions expressed in text is analysed (Tai et al. 2015). Sentiment analysis is the way of classification of text where various types of reviews are pre-classified into set of sentiment classes. The document with text can be classified with discrete sentiments value such as rating it on the basis of one to five stars or if the classification is binary, then there are mainly two classes a positive or a negative sentiment. In sentiment analysis, the classifier is trained by using manually labelled user review. For binary classification, the reviews are either divided in positive or negative class or are provided with score of 0 or 1. The whole classification is evaluated on another dataset which is the test dataset. If the classifier is trained using review of one domain and is tested on review of other domain, this is cross-domain sentiment analysis. During the process of training and testing, there are some words which appear in training dataset but do not appear in test dataset. These words which are not in training vocabulary but occur in test dataset are known as unseen words. Cross-Domain sentiment analysis become challenging, because training and testing dataset belongs from different domain, due to which number of unseen words increases and results in decrease of performance of the system. Such as the word '*sharp*', '*durable*' are only related to kitchen domain but will not occur for books in book domain. Dealing with this kind of problem make cross domain sentiment analysis challenging.

For sentiment classification, first, we need to represent words of vocabulary formed during training data in some lower-dimension embedding form. The most popular approach for generation of lower dimension word vector representation is through word embedding. Word embedding is a successful feature representation method in natural language processing (Bengio et al. 2003). The traditional method used for representing word in vector form is one-hot encoding method. Vectors for words were formed in binary format either 1 (if word were found) else 0 (if words were not found). The main limitation of this model is that it does not show the similarity between words. To overcome this limitation word embedding came into popularity. Word embedding forms word representations by considering semantic and syntactic relation between words. Vector representation was formed for only those words which were in vocabulary not for unseen words which are found when evaluation on target dataset is done (Agarwal et al. 2018; Sansanwal et al. 2019).

We proposed a cross-domain sentiment analysis method which has capability of building representation for those unseen words whose synonyms are present in the vocabulary. The proposed method calculates the synonyms of each unseen words and match the calculated synonyms from the words in vocabulary. If a word matches with synonyms the representation of word is provided to unseen word. This method works well as words, its context and its similar words, all lies in same vector space. The whole embedding is processed with deep learning system as it provides dense low dimension embedding. The main contributions of this paper are as follows.

1. We present extensive experimental results for cross-domain sentiment analysis.
2. We propose a deep learning based approach for cross-domain sentiment analysis.

The rest paper is structured as follow: In Section 2, we describe the related work for sentiment analysis, cross domain approaches and word related to embedding of unseen words. In Section 3, we introduce our new improved approach for cross domain sentiment analysis for enhancing vector representation embedding. In Section 4, we evaluated our approach using various parameter of convolutional neural network used for deep learning, and compared it with other basic embedding methods to show effectiveness of proposed model. Finally, in Section 5, we present the conclusion and set directions for future work.

2. RELATED WORK

2.1 Sentiment Analysis

There are various approaches have been proposed in the literature for sentiment analysis with neural network architecture. Socher et al. (2011) proposed an approach based on auto encoder for predicting sentiment distribution. Yoon Kim (2014) performed task wth convolution neural network for sentence level classification which shows improvement in sentiment analysis tasks. Chenet al. (2018) worked on sentiment analysis with dual-channel convolutional neural network to analyse the sentiment related to Chinese short comment. Wu et al. (2018), proposed a novel sentiment analysis model that is based on fusing sentiment knowledge from multiple sources for the domain-specific sentiment analysis.

2.2 Cross Domain Dataset

Blitzer et al. (2007) proposed a domain adaption algorithm named as structural correspondence learning (SCL). Pan et al. (2010) proposed spectral feature alignment (SFA) algorithm that align words from different domain into some cluster by taking help of domain independent word which helps to reduce difference between words in cross domain. Bollegala et al. (2013) worked with cross domain dataset to show how it decreases the performance of the system by applying it for classification. Bollegala et al. (2015) proposed an unsupervised technique for domain specific word representation that precisely catches the domain specific part of word semantics. Besides, they proposed a technique to perform domain adaption utilizing the learned word representation. Bollegala et al. (2016) used cross domain dataset for sentiment classification for learning embedding by forming objective function by capturing properties of pivots from both target and source domain. Heredia et al. (2016) performed sentiment classification with cross domain dataset for reviews and tweets with multinomial naive Bayes and shows that training data with tweets and testing over review shows effectiveness over training data with review and testing with tweets. Bhatt et al. (2016) proposed method for transfer learning for cross domain classification by identifying knowledge from multiple domains which is useful for learning target domain task. Grunigen et al. (2017) worked with cross domain dataset to analyse the performance of system trained with convolutional neural network. Barnes et al. (2018) proposed a method for domain adaption for sentiment analysis by using embedding projection task. Cummins et al. (2018) proposed a method for cross domain sentiment analysis using bag-of–word paradigm which shows gain in performance of the system. Wang et al. (2018) proposed a method for sentiment analysis for short texts by creating sentiment related index so that it can measure association between different elements in specific domain and build some connection between different domains. Khan et al. (2018) proposed an enhanced method for cross domain sentiment classification for find sentiments label by computing weight by cosine similarity measure to SentiWordNet and shows improvement over other contemporary approaches.

2.3 Unseen Words

Kirchhoff et al. (2006) presented a modified neural probabilistic model for prediction of word by learning the mapping into continuous space. Sogaard et al. (2012) proposed method for unseen words, the words which are not found during training and said that they are provided with random embedding and applied the concept of robust optimization to it for perceptron learning. Luong et al. (2013) used morpheme and word level model for unseen words. Soricut et al. (2015) used skip gram model with simple vector arithmetic to calculate vector for unseen words and represented as word pair in same embedding space. Sennrich et al. (2015) proposed an approach that converts unseen words into its character or bytes form and then form its embedding. Madhyastha et al. (2016) worked for a system that uses multi loss objective function to map initial embedding to task specific embedding. Wieting et al. (2016) used n-gram model and represented it as char n gram embedding representation. Cotterell et al.(2016) used morphological resources to generate vectors forwards that are not in training data. A latent variable Gaussian graphical model is presented that infer representation of words not observed in the training corpus and smooth the representation provided for observed words. Zhang et al. (2016) proposed a method for the unseen class data by formulating Zero-Sort recognition with binary prediction problem. Pilehvar and Collier (2017) proposed method for finding embedding for rare words by analysing lexical resources and then providing the embedding with semantic space. Pinter et al. (2017) proposed an approach in which word embedding for words which are not in vocabulary is extracted by learning a function from spellings to distributional embedding named as MIMICK. Bahdanau et al. (2017) worked for embedding of unseen words by considering definition from dictionary. Authors proposed an approach for spam detection using recurrent neural network, and convolutional neural network, further, authors show the improvement in the performance of spam detection using WordNet, and ConceptNet by expanding the initial representation (Jain et al. 2018a).

3. PROPOSED APPROACH

We propose a deep learning based approach for detecting embedding for unseen words. We first preprocess the dataset. Then, the word vector representation of each word from vocabulary is formed. However, there are many words during evaluations which are not in vocabulary or whose embedding is not formed. For these kinds of words, we find their synonyms from WordNet. If synonyms exist in the vocabulary the unseen word is provided with the vector of the word whose synonyms it is. The process is processed on cross domain dataset due to which number of unseen word is more. The updated embedding (embedding of words from vocabulary + embedding of unseen words) are processed with one dimension convolutional layer to get low dimension embedding and efficient classification accuracy. The proposed method mainly includes three steps: pre-processing, embedding, and the network formation that is by convolutional neural network. The embedding is an updated embedding which includes embedding of unseen words which is found by considering synonyms of the words in trained dataset. The flow diagram of the proposed approach is shown in Figure 1.

Figure 1. Flow diagram of the proposed approach

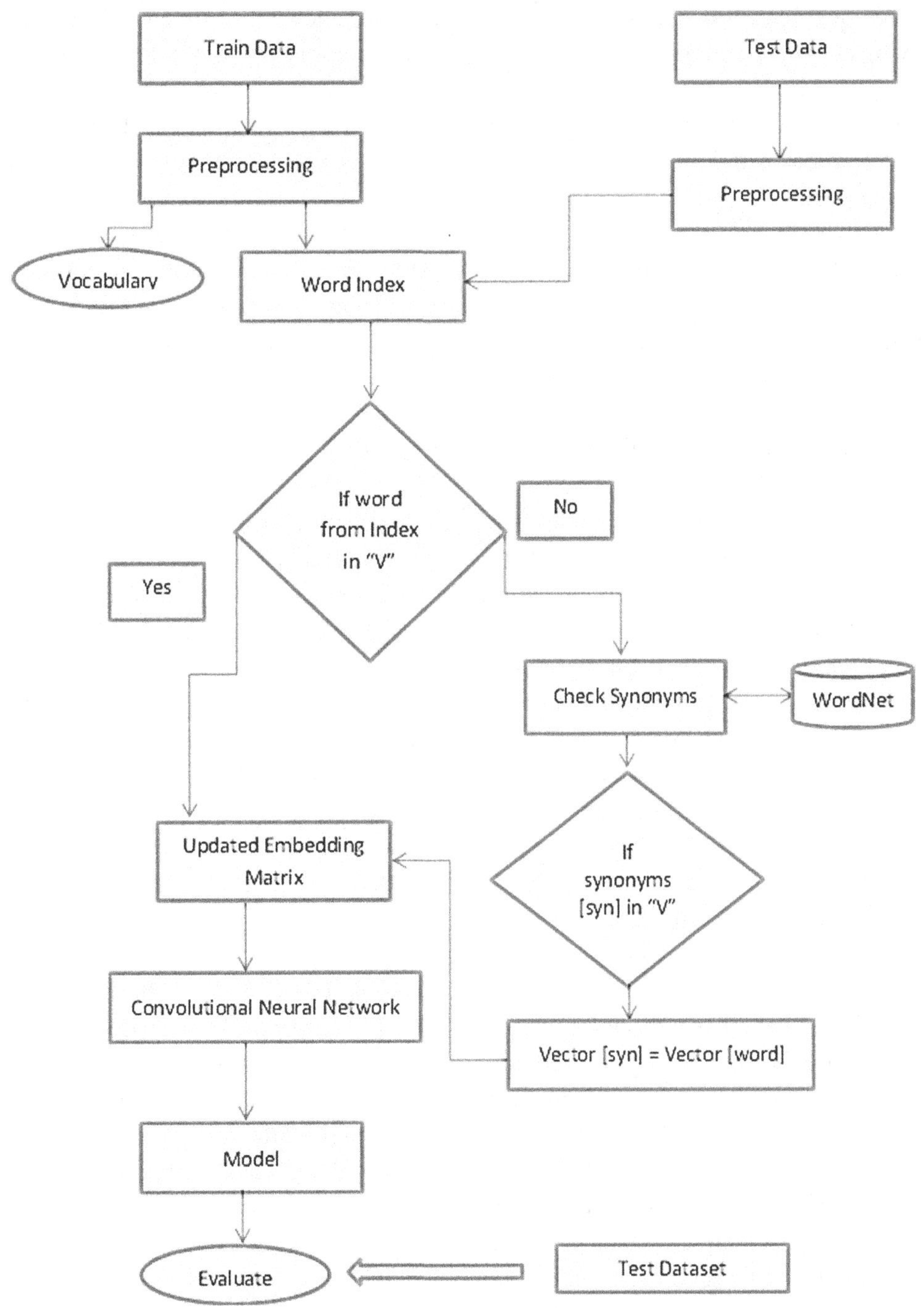

The process starts with pre-processing.

3.1 Pre-Processing

The cross domain dataset is first processed with pre-processing which process is to clean unwanted data and make it prepare for further analysis. The pre-processing step involves, changing content into something that can be processed effectively. Proposed method is processed as:

- **Sentence Segmentation** The step process with splitting the text document into its sentences by following boundary conditions such as full stop (.) and question mark (?). Paragraphs of the data-set are splited into sentences.
- **Tokenization** The segmented texts are further processed for formation of tokens. In this step tokens are formed by dividing the sentences with the help of special symbols such comma (,), space and many others.
- **Stop Word Removal:** There are some words in the sentences which do not contain relevant information. These words can be articles (A, An, The), some functional words, conjunctions, etc. These words are eliminated from document to get efficient word embedding formation.
- **Stemming:** The process of identifying root words by removing suffix and generate its common base. Such as go, goes, gone, going all are formed of same base word go.

3.2 Word Vector Representation

The NLP system treats word as its basic unit. Sentiment analysis is one of the applications of NLP system. The system is trained with source dataset and a word vocabulary is formed.Wordsare stored in that vocabulary without any similarity between them. To provide some similarity we need their vector space representation. Word representation can be done by using one-hot encoding but it provide binary encoding and form high dimensional vector representation. To overcome these problems, word embedding is used for representation. It provide low dimensional vector and provide degree of similarity between words. Word embedding is a way through which we can get associations between words in light of their co-occurrence property in any language. The words that occur in equivalent context end to have similar properties so should be provided with same vector space. Word representation can be done using various words embedding algorithm such as word2vec, GloVe, or FastText.

3.2.1 Word2vec Representation

The first used method for word embedding is word2vec (Mikolov et al. 2013; Bahdanau et al. 2017). Word2vec model shows high quality semantic relation for words and words which are similar are located in same vector space. It inspects the corpus reliably, consistently keeping the window around each word it looks. Each time two words are found having relative context, their affiliation or spatial separations are considered to be together. The more confirmation is found while going through the corpus that two words are essentially indistinguishable, the closer they will be. It uses vector arithmetic for vector calculations. These vector representations can be used in various applications such as document classification, question answering and many more. In order to learn word embedding there are two variants of word2vec model: CBOW (continuous bag of word) and SG (skip gram) model. Both work just inverse of each other CBOW predict word by the use of context while skip gram predict the context for each word. Word2vec with Skip gram model is used for our system. In this the target word is provided to it as input layer generating the output as context word.

3.2.2 Glove

Pennington et al. (2014) suggested a new word representation model that is based on global log bilinear regression model combining the properties of two major models: global matrix factorization and local context window method. Both models have some significant drawbacks. The model that uses global matrix factorization is good with statistical information but is poor for analogy task. Models utilizing context window method are good at analogy task but poorly use the statistics of the dataset. Combining the advantages of both methods, a new method came into existence named as GloVe (global vector for word representation). In this paper, we compared existing glove method with proposed model to see effectiveness of the proposed model.

3.2.3 FastText

FastText is one of latest word embedding method. It is an approach based on skip-gram model. In this approach words are represented in form of bag of character n-grams. It uses the concept of modular embedding i.e. instead of computing vector of each word, a vector of sub words are computed, which is later combined to compute final embedding. The process of embedding retrieval is slower for this algorithm but vocabulary size is smaller for large datasets. The main advantage is that sub word information is captured correctly.

Algorithm 1: Updated embedding

```
Input: A set of pre-processed dataset W (contain the word of both train and
test set), Vocabulary 'v' (from pre-processed training set)
Output: Updated Embedding Matrix E' [i]
E[t] ← Embedding matrix for t.
Syn[t] ←Synonyms for t found from WordNet
Step 1: for each t ∈ W
                If t in v:
                        E [t] ← t
                End if
        End for
Step 2: for each a ∉ W
                If Syn[a] in v:
                        E [a] ← E [Syn[a]]
                End if
        End for
Step 3: E' [i] ← E[t] + E[a]
```

The proposed algorithm is as following: the pre-processed dataset is considered as W and contains words of both training and testing dataset and the formed vocabulary is considered as "v". The vocabulary is formed by training dataset. The algorithm shows output as updated embedding matrix E'[i]. E[t] is embedding for word t and Syn[t] is Synonyms of word t. Now for all words from W if word t is in vocabulary v its E[t] is formed. For the words which are not in vocabulary its synonyms is searched. For word 'a' synonyms is Syn[a]. If Syn[a] is in vocabulary 'v' the embedding of syn[a] which is E[Syn[a]] is provided as embedding of unseen word 'a'. The whole embedding is combined to form updated embedding matrix E'[i].

3.3. Enhancing Embedding

The main motivation behind the proposed approach is find embedding of those words which are unseen. There are unseen words whose synonyms are present in vocabulary, as synonyms are the similar words so will occupy same vector space. The definition of synonyms states that, on substituting on value over other if meaning of the sentence is not changed then words are synonyms. Synonyms for any word can be taken out from WordNet. WorldNet (Miller 1995) is a broad database that gathers English words into the course of action of comparable words called as synsets. In this noun, verb, adjective, and adverbs are gathered together into a set. It can be called as the collection of word reference and thesaurus. For our structure, we use WordNet to find equivalent words for those words which while testing don't occur in the vocabulary. If the synonyms of these unseen words are found in the vocabulary then embedding of these synonyms words are provided to respective unseen word. In our work, we haven't searched synonyms word for the whole corpus but for only those data which are not found in training set. The overview of the proposed model is shown in figure 2.

Figure 2. Flow diagram of the proposed model

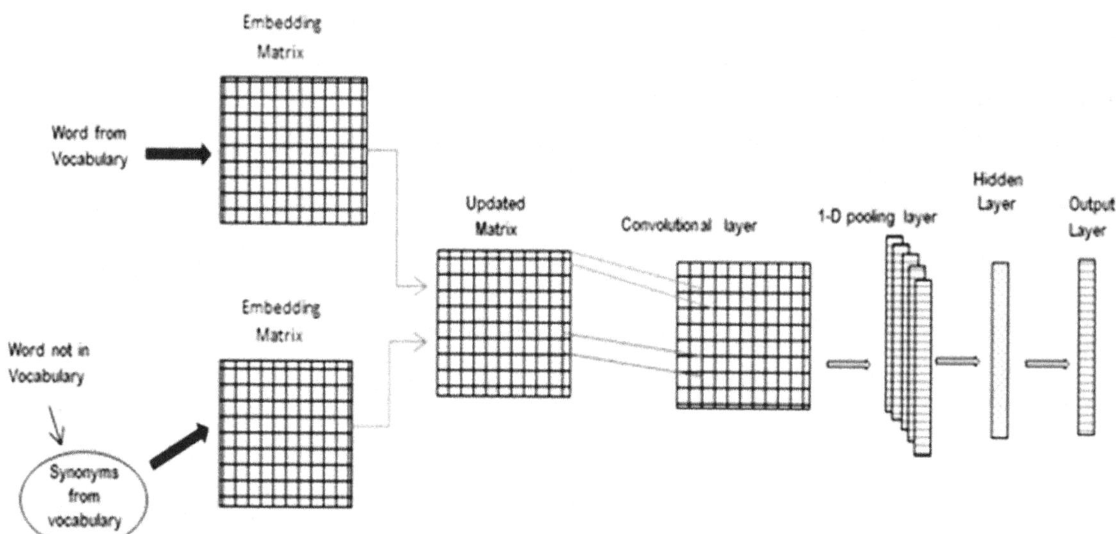

As it is not possible for the word embedding matrix to manage such word which are not in the vocabulary formed during training the dataset. When the model is assessed, the test dataset contains the quantity of words which isn't in vocabulary especially in the case when the training set and the testing dataset isn't from the same domain. For our model, we have considered the dataset which are from cross domain due to which number of unseen words are more. To manage these unseen words we proposed a model which can discover embedding for those words whose similar words are available in vocabulary. Each unseen words look for its synonyms through WordNet database and then search that synonyms value in vocabulary. If the discovered synonyms words are in vocabulary then the vector representation of those synonyms words is provided to the respective unseen word.

3.3 Convolutional Neural Network

The convolutional neural network (CNN) is a neural network made up of neurons. Each neuron receives input value and forwards it to the next layer. It takes input as embedding matrix and uses it for classification. Convolutional neural network consist of input layer, output layer and hidden layer. Input layer receives the data and send it to hidden layer. The hidden layer processes this output and send it to next layer and the output layer give the final classification result. Hidden layer is formed of different types of layers such as: Convolutional layer, pooling, and fully connected layer. The convolution layer contains neuron in the form of the rectangular lattice. The output of the previous layer is the same kind of rectangular matrix containing information. Every neuron is associated just too rectangular segments of the past layer and the weights for this rectangular segment are the same for every neuron. In this way, a convolutional layer is going to complete a convolutional activity of its past layer, where the weights determine the convolution channel. Each convolutional layer has a few networks; every lattice takes contributions from every one of the frameworks of the past layer using some channels. Another essential term of CNN's is pooling. There may be a pooling layer after each convolutional layer. The pooling layer segments the convolutional layer into an arrangement of little non-covering rectangles, for each sub-area, it delivers a single output. The last layer is fully connected layer which is state semantic layers. A completely associated layer interfaces each and every neuron to all neurons in the past layer. It is the last completely associated layer of CNNs, where a softmax loss function is connected to create an appropriation over K fundamentally unrelated classes. There are types of loss function that can be used, such as: a sigmoid cross-entropy loss [0, 1] or a Euclidean loss [-inf, inf].

For our system we have used simplest neuron convolution neural network that work for binary classification by using various parameters of CNN such as: Activation function. The binary activation function can output only 0 or 1. Activation function is centre of neuron that process input to give output. It helps hidden layer to make powerful net. For proposed system we have used ReLU (rectified linear unit) and sigmoid activation function. ReLU range from 0 to maximum positive number and sigmoid range from 0 to 1. We have used various optimizers such as RMSProp, AdaDelta, Adam, AdaGrad. Neural network optimization is the process for minimizing or maximizing the objective function that are dependent on trainable parameter. We have used binary-cross-entropy loss function which is a logarithmic loss function which is used because we are dealing with datasets having binary labels. The fully connected layer sometimes results in over fitting which occur during training. To remove this problem dropout is used. We have experimented with changing dropout to get the best result. While processing data for the training we have to decide number of samples that will be propagating on the network which is defined by batch size. When batch size is provided with some number n, calculations takes initially that n number of data from dataset and trains them. Next, it takes next *n* number from data and prepares processing once more. This mythology continues till all data from dataset is processed as it requires less amount of memory.

4. EXPERIMENT AND RESULT

4.1 Dataset

The dataset for experiment is taken as product review dataset which contain reviews for different products such as electronics, DVD, kitchen, and book (Blitzer et al. 2007). The link to download the dataset is https://www.cs.jhu.edu/~mdredze/datasets/sentiment/index2.html. Total numbers of records are 2,000 out of which each domain has 1,000 positive values based on positive reviews and 1,000 negative values based on negative labelled reviews. Counting these four areas, we get twelve cross domain set but for evaluation we have used only eight pairs. Taking electronics as E, DVD as D, kitchen as K and book as B, the formed pair is as (D_E), (K_E), (E_D), (D_K), (B_D), (E_B), (E_K), (K_B), wherein each set first word relate to the dataset which is utilized for training and the next one is used for testing the model. As in (D_E), D is DVD dataset used as source dataset for training and E is for electronics used as target dataset for testing. Similarly in (K_E), K is for kitchen and is used for training and E is for electronics and is used for testing. As the source dataset and the target dataset is from different domain so there is increase in number of unknown words.

4.2 Result Analysis

The proposed work is analysed with various parameter of deep learning neural network system to check which parameter give the best performance for the chosen dataset. Cross domain dataset sets were taken into consideration to see the effect of the parameters applied to it.

4.2.1. Selection of the Best Optimizer

The convolutional neural network system uses different optimizers for its network. Each optimizer behaves differently when applied to dataset. There is not any fix value of accuracy for the particular optimizer due to its deterministic nature. In first experiment the effect of changing optimizer for a particular set of data set is analysed and a table is provided for it shown in Table 1. There are number of optimizers available but the experiment is done with Adam (i.e. adaptive moment), RMSProp (i.e. root mean square propagation), AdaGrad (i.e. adaptive gradient), and AdaDelta (more robust extension of AdaGrad). Adam requires little memory and is computationally powerful. RMSProp provide way for adaption of learning rate occurs for each parameter. AdaGrad has pre-parameter for learning increments in rate and reducing learning rate of the inadequate parameter. AdaDelta is a novel learning rate strategy that adjusts just first order information and manages minimal computational overhead. The optimizer is used to minimize and maximize the objective functions that depend on trainable parameter. Each combination of dataset shows its highest accuracy for different optimizers. Such as D-E set where D is DVD dataset that is used as training dataset and E is electronics dataset used as testing dataset, they show its highest accuracy for AdaGrad optimizers. Similarly next dataset K-E shows its highest value for AdaDelta. Each set perform differently for optimizers and shows different value.

Table 1. Datasets for finding accuracy with various optimizers

Datasets	Optimizer			
	AdaDelta	RMSProp	AdaGrad	Adam
D-E	60.10	67.80	**70.05**	65.35
K-E	**71.45**	65.35	68.75	72.60
E-D	59.60	59.10	**67.10**	65.65
D-K	67.00	50.60	**69.25**	69.05
B-D	**74.55**	69.35	68.34	60.89
E-B	64.60	58.60	63.35	**65.70**
E-K	76.85	**77.85**	75.85	76.75
K-B	59.90	**66.60**	64.25	65.85

4.2.2. Determination of the Best Dropout Value

In Hidden layer, we can likewise apply dropout as a mean of regularization. Dropout is a strategy used to reduce over fitting. It is somewhat regularization method which lessens the over fitting and gives a capable technique to perform with the neural network. The effect of this dropout change is shown in Table 2. Dropout is one of the main factors which are said as effective method for controlling over fitting which is the issue while training is performed. So we experimented with various dropout measures evaluate the accuracy.

Table 2. Analysis of accuracy by changing dropout parameter

Datasets	Dropout					
	0.2	0.4	0.5	0.6	0.8	0.9
D-E	68.80	**70.05**	68.15	68.05	50.00	63.50
K-E	74.15	**75.65**	73.25	50.00	54.08	56.85
E-D	66.00	**67.25**	63.20	65.60	64.70	67.00
D-K	**69.05**	58.05	61.00	50.00	61.60	50.00
B-D	**68.80**	64.90	58.70	58.10	63.60	50.00
E-B	66.10	**66.35**	61.30	55.85	50.00	50.00
E-K	77.90	**78.30**	74.15	78.15	68.00	71.75
K-B	62.80	**66.85**	54.75	57.00	55.20	50.00

4.2.3. Determine the Number of Hidden Layer

The convolution network has hidden layer as its layer and varying layers in number affect the accuracy for system. We have experimented with 2, 3, 4, and 5 layers and recorded the result for various dataset shown in Table 3.

Table 3. Analysing accuracy when changing the hidden layer

Datasets	2 layers	3 layers	4 layers	5 layers
D-E	**70.05**	65.15	64.35	67.15
K-E	72.60	**75.65**	71.70	68.15
E-D	**67.25**	67.10	64.25	63.85
D-K	67.10	**69.05**	68.25	50.00
B-D	63.30	**69.15**	64.90	68.35
E-B	65.70	63.00	63.70	**66.10**
E-K	**77.90**	77.40	74.00	72.20
K-B	57.55	**66.85**	55.40	56.80

4.2.4. Analysis of Training Data Used to Develop the Model

The all above experiment is with the variation of parameter of the network used for training. The next experiment we performed is with the number of datasets. We divided the dataset which were taken as training into 20%, 40%, 60%, 80%, and finally tested with 100% of data. The experiment shows that as we increase the number of dataset the accuracy percentage increases automatically. So if we perform our model for large set of data it will give more number of accuracy. The graph shown in Table 4 shows the experiment result.

Table 4. Analysing accuracy by % of training data

Datasets	% Data				
	20%	**40%**	**60%**	**80%**	**100%**
D-E	61.30	64.85	67.25	68.60	70.05
K-E	56.30	60.60	72.60	75.30	75.65
E-D	54.05	55.00	64.45	65.00	67.25
D-K	53.10	64.95	66.25	66.75	69.05
B-D	51.25	63.20	65.55	68.05	68.80
E-B	53.05	58.20	59.60	64.45	66.35
E-K	60.15	66.20	74.75	75.15	78.30
K-B	60.00	60.65	61.05	64.55	66.80

4.3. Comparative Analysis

To show the effectiveness of proposed algorithm its comparison is done with some pre-defined algorithms such as FastText, Word2Vec, and Glove. The algorithm defined in this paper provides extension in embedding formed by these previously defined algorithms and on comparison shows its effectiveness by increase in accuracy.

Figure 3. Results for comparison of accuracy variation with FastText

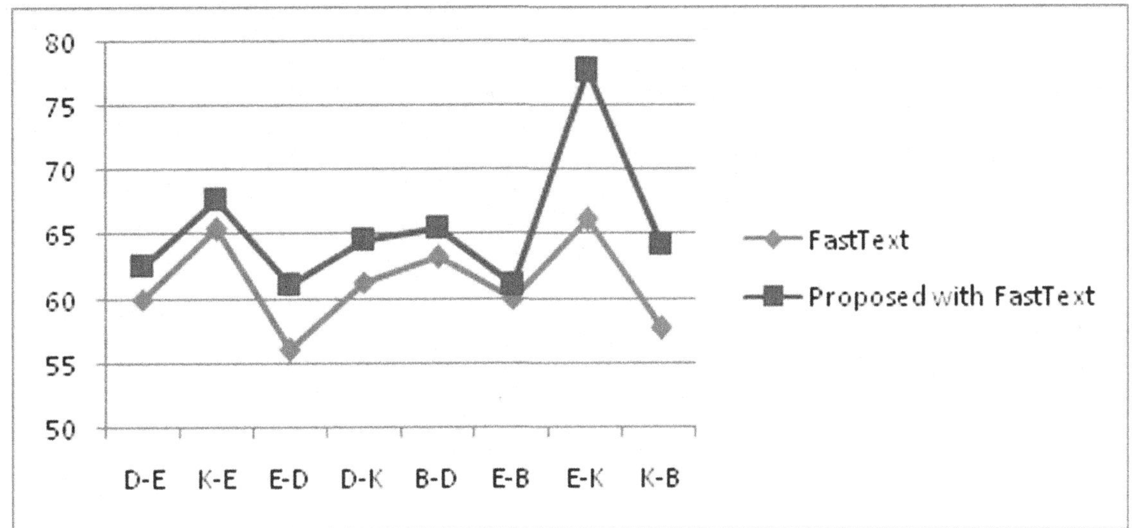

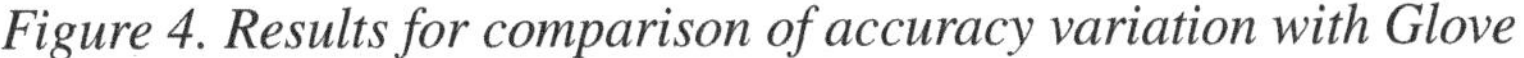

Figure 4. Results for comparison of accuracy variation with Glove

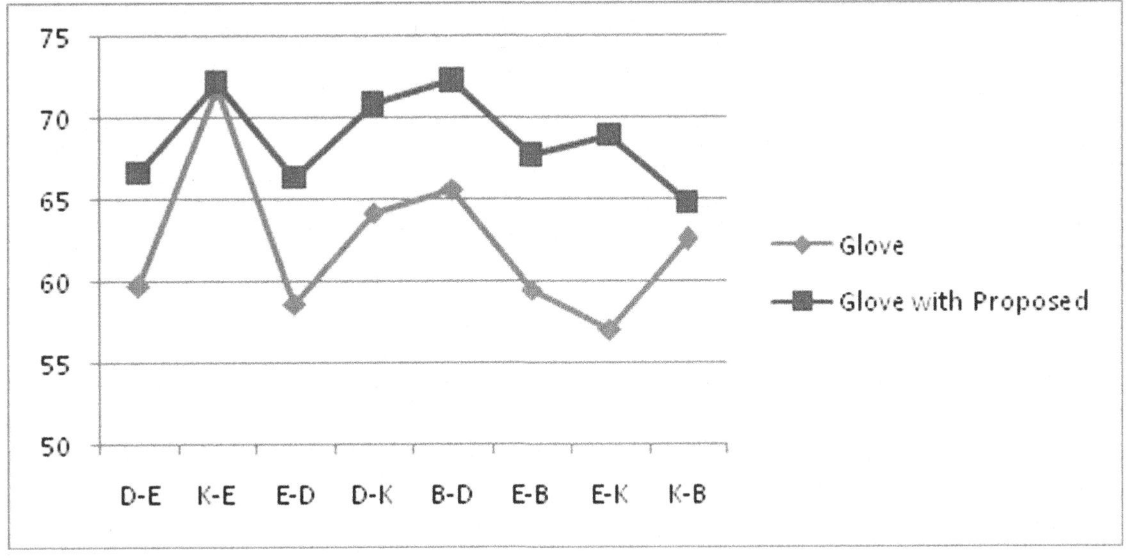

The graphs in Figure 3, Figure 4, and Figure 5 show the effectiveness of the proposed model as it always or every case shows accuracy higher than the model used before. X-axis represents the datasets which are denoted in letters such as B for books dataset, E for electronics dataset, K for kitchen dataset, and D for DVD dataset. So, the graphs show the effectiveness of proposed approach. Sometimes the accuracy variation is not so high that is because the sets considered are of different domain so sometimes it has to deal with some words whose synonyms are not found.

Figure 5. Results for comparison of accuracy variation with word2vec

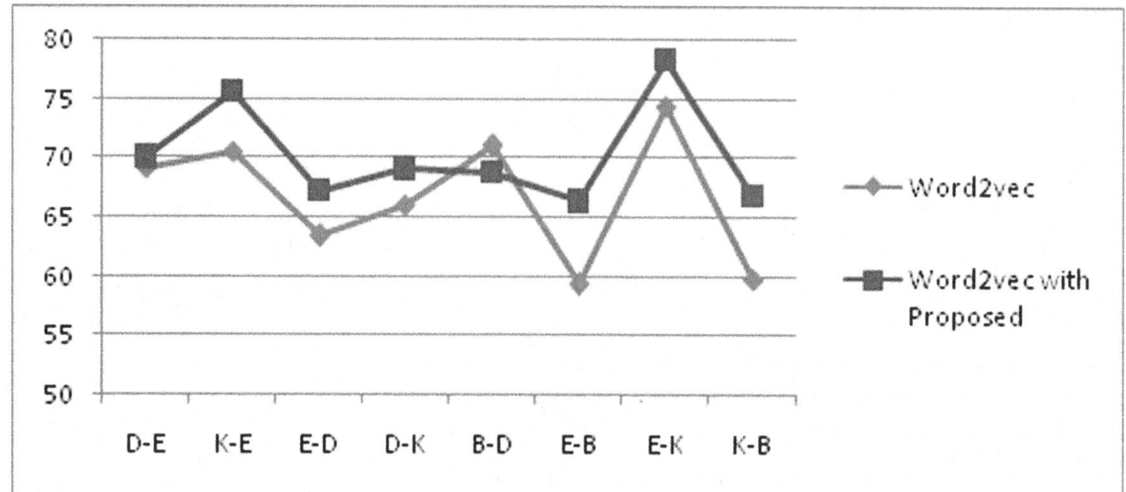

Table 5. Result comparison for proposed approach and existing techniques

	Dataset							
	D-E	K-E	E-D	D-K	B-D	E-B	E-K	K-B
Word2vec	69.20	70.60	63.40	66.10	71.00	59.35	74.40	59.85
Glove	59.70	71.85	58.65	64.25	65.65	59.50	57.05	62.55
FastText	60.00	65.45	56.05	61.30	63.25	60.05	66.20	57.70
Word2vec with proposed method	**70.05**	**75.65**	**67.25**	69.05	68.80	66.35	**78.30**	**66.80**
Glove with proposed method	66.65	72.20	66.35	**70.85**	**72.30**	**67.70**	68.95	64.80
FastText with proposed method	62.65	67.80	61.10	64.60	65.50	61.15	77.80	64.20

Table 5 shows comparisons between the word embedding algorithms when processed with proposed model. On comparison between three most common algorithms FastText, Glove, word2vec it is clear that word2vec perform well in most of the cases for the proposed model. It shows that word2vec is efficient over FastText and Glove. The set of dataset Electronics and Kitchen show the highest accuracy over all of the other dataset while Kitchen and book cross domain combination shows less accuracy as they have less word in common.

5. CONCLUSION AND FUTURE WORK

A new method is proposed so that embedding for unseen words can be calculated, as these unseen words are the main reason for decrease in performance of classification model. When a cross-domain dataset is used for classification model, it shows less effectiveness, which is due to the increase in number of unseen words. So, a model is developed, which finds embedding of unseen words by finding its synonyms in vocabulary. The embedding of those synonyms is provided to the unseen word whose synonyms it was. The matrix formed is an updated matrix which contains embedding of vocabulary words as well as unseen word. The formed matrix is provided as input to deep learning model to form effective classification model. The proposed work presents one of the effective ways to deal with the unseen words by taking the use of synonyms and find word representation effectively. To show the effectiveness of the proposed work, it is compared with previously defined algorithms and increase in the rate of accuracy is observed. The limitation to the proposed work is that the dataset is limited in size; thus, it would be interesting to see the results of the proposed approach on the bigger dataset. In future, an extension to the proposed work can be applied on a large amount of data and research can be directed and carried out in such a way that it can deal with all unseen words.

REFERENCES

Agarwal, B., Ramampiaro, H., Langseth, H., & Ruocco, M. (2018). A Deep Network Model for Paraphrase Detection in Short Text Messages. *Information Processing and Management, 54*(6), 922-937.

Alexandrescu & Kirchhoff. (2006). Factored neural language models. NAACL.

Bahdanau, Bosc, Jastrze, Grefenstette, Mila, & Bengio. (2017). *Learning to Compute Word Embeddings On the Fly.* arXiv:1706.00286v2.

Barnes, Klinger, & Walde. (2018). *Projecting Embeddings for Domain Adaptation: Joint Modeling of Sentiment Analysis in Diverse Domains.* arXiv: 1806.04381v2 [cs.CL].

Bengio, Y., Ducharme, R., & Vincent, P. (2003). Neural Probabilitistic Language Model. *Journal of Machine Learning Research*, 1137–1155.

Bhatt, H. S., Sinha, M., & Roy, S. (2016). Cross-domain Text Classification with Multiple Domains and Disparate Label Sets. *Proceedings of the 54th Annual Meeting of the Association for Computational Linguistics*, 1641–1650. 10.18653/v1/P16-1155

Blitzer, J., Dredze, M., & Pereira, F. (2007). Biographies, bollywood, boom-boxes and blenders: Domain adaptation for sentiment classification. Proceedings of Association for Computational Linguistics, 440–447.

Bollegala, D. (2015). Unsupervised Cross-Domain Word Representation Learning. Academic Press.

Bollegala, D., Weir, D., & Carroll, J. (2013). Cross-domain sentiment classification using a sentiment sensitive thesaurus. *IEEE Transactions on Knowledge and Data Engineering*, *25*(8), 1719–1731. doi:10.1109/TKDE.2012.103

Bollegala & Goulermas. (2016). Cross-Domain Sentiment Classification Using Sentiment Sensitive Embeddings. *IEEE Transactions on Knowledge and Data Engineering*, *28*(2).

Chen, S., Ding, Y., Xie, Z., Liu, S., & Ding, H. (2018). Chinese Weibo sentiment analysis based on character embedding with dual-channel convolutional neural network. *IEEE 3rd International Conference on Cloud Computing and Big Data Analysis (ICCCBDA),* 107-111. 10.1109/ICCCBDA.2018.8386495

Cotterell, Schutze, & Eisner. (2016). Morphological smoothing and extrapolation of word embeddings. In *Proceedings of the 54th Annual Meeting of the Association for Computational Linguistics*, (pp.1651–1660). Berlin, Germany: Academic Press.

Cummins, Amiriparian, Ottl, Gerczuk, Schmitt, & Schuller. (2018). Multimodal bag-of-words for cross domains sentiment analysis. *IEEE ICASSP*.

Heredia, Prusa, & Crawford. (2016). Cross-Domain Sentiment Analysis: An Empirical Investigation. *IEEE 17th International Conference on Information Reuse and Integration*.

Jain, G., Sharma, M., & Agarwal, B. (2018a). Optimizing Semantic LSTM for Spam Detection. In *International Journal of Information Technology*. Springer. doi:10.100741870-018-0157-5

Jain, G., Sharma, M., & Agarwal, B. (2018b). Spam Detection on Social Media using Semantic Convolutional Neural Network. *International Journal of Knowledge Discovery in Bioinformatics, 8*(1), 12-26.

Khan, F. H., Qamar, U., & Bashir, S. (2018). Enhanced cross-domain sentiment classification utilizing a multi-source transfer learning approach. *Soft Computing*.

Kim. (2014). *Convolutional Neural Networks for Sentence Classification*. arXiv:1408.5882v2 [cs.CL].

Luong. (2013). Better Word Representations with Recursive Neural Networks for Morphology. Academic Press.

Madhyastha. (2016). Mapping Unseen Words to Task-Trained Embedding Spaces. Academic Press.

Mikolov, T., Chen, K., Corrado, G., & Dean, J. (2013). Efficient estimation of word representations in vector space. *ICLR Workshop*.

Miller, G. A. (1995). WordNet: A Lexical Database for English. *Communications of the ACM*.

Pan, Ni, Sun, Yang, & Chen. (2010). Cross-domain sentiment classification via spectral feature alignment. *Proceedings of the 19th international conference on World Wide Web, WWW '10*, 751–760.

Pennington, J., Socher, R., & Manning, C. (2014). Glove: Global vectors for word representation. *Proceedings of the 2014 conference on empirical methods in natural language processing (EMNLP)*, 1532–1543.

Pilehvar & Collier. (2017). *Inducing Embeddings for Rare and Unseen Words by Leveraging Lexical Resources*. Academic Press.

Pinter, Guthrie, & Eisenstein. (2017). *Mimicking Word Embeddings using Subword RNNs*. Academic Press.

Sansanwal, K., Mittal, M., & Goyal, L. M. (2020). Prediction of Rise in Violence Inclined Opinions: Utility of Sentiment Analysis in the Modern World. In J. Bansal, M. Gupta, H. Sharma, & B. Agarwal (Eds.), *Communication and Intelligent Systems. ICCIS 2019. Lecture Notes in Networks and Systems* (Vol. 120). Springer.

Sennrich, R., Haddow, B., & Birch, A. (2015). *Neural machine translation of rare words with sub word units*. arXiv preprint arXiv: 1508.07909.

Socher, R., Pennington, J., Huang, E. H., Ng, A. Y., & Manning, C. D. (2011). Semi supervised recursive autoencoders for predicting sentiment distributions. *Proceedings of the Conference on Empirical Methods in Natural Language Processing*, 151–161.

Søgaard & Johannsen. (2012). Robust learning in random subspaces: Equipping NLP for OOV effects. *Proceedings of COLING 2012: Posters*.

Soricut, R., & Och, F. (2015). Unsupervised Morphology Induction using Word Embeddings. *Proceedings of NAACL*.

Tai, K. S., Socher, R., & Manning, C. D. (2015). Improved semantic representations from tree-structured long short-term memory networks. *Proceedings of the 53rd Annual Meeting of the Association for Computational Linguistics and the 7th International Joint Conference on Natural Language Processing*. 10.3115/v1/P15-1150

Wang, L., Niu, J., Song, H., & Atiquzzaman, M. (2018). SentiRelated: A cross-domain sentiment classification algorithm for short texts through sentiment related index. *Journal of Network and Computer Applications*, *101*, 111–119. doi:10.1016/j.jnca.2017.11.001

Weilenmann, M., Deriu, J., Cieliebak, M., & von Grünigen, D. (2017). *Potential and Limitations of Cross-Domain Sentiment Classification*. doi:10.18653/v1/W17-1103

Wieting, J., Bansal, M., Gimpel, K., & Livescu, K. (2016). *Charagram: Embedding words and sentences via character n-grams*. arXiv preprint arXiv: 1607.02789.

Wu, F., Huang, Y., & Yuan, Z. (2017). Domain-Specific Sentiment Classification via Fusing Sentiment Knowledge from Multiple Sources. *Information Fusion*, *35*, 26–37.

Zhang & Saligrama. (2016). *Zero-Shot Learning via Joint Latent Similarity Embedding*. arXiv:1511.04512v3.

This research was previously published in the International Journal of Information System Modeling and Design (IJISMD), 12(2); pages 1-16, copyright year 2021 by IGI Publishing (an imprint of IGI Global).

Chapter 9
A Comparative Study of Different Classification Techniques for Sentiment Analysis

Soumadip Ghosh
https://orcid.org/0000-0003-4817-5363
Academy of Technology, Kolkata, India

Arnab Hazra
Academy of Technology, Kolkata, India

Abhishek Raj
https://orcid.org/0000-0002-8121-3440
Academy of Technology, Kolkata, India

ABSTRACT

Sentiment analysis denotes the analysis of emotions and opinions from text. The authors also refer to sentiment analysis as opinion mining. It finds and justifies the sentiment of the person with respect to a given source of content. Social media contain vast amounts of the sentiment data in the form of product reviews, tweets, blogs, and updates on the statuses, posts, etc. Sentiment analysis of this largely generated data is very useful to express the opinion of the mass in terms of product reviews. This work is proposing a highly accurate model of sentiment analysis for reviews of products, movies, and restaurants from Amazon, IMDB, and Yelp, respectively. With the help of classifiers such as logistic regression, support vector machine, and decision tree, the authors can classify these reviews as positive or negative with higher accuracy values.

DOI: 10.4018/978-1-6684-6303-1.ch009

1. INTRODUCTION

Sentiment analysis or opinion mining (Neethu M. et al., 2013) refers to emotions and opinions by analysis of texts, processing of natural languages to methodically identify, extract, count, and study some interesting information. Sentiment analysis has gained popularity in the recent past. The idea of performing analysis on texts is important for marketing research, where analysts wish to find out some useful information from customer feedback. It is vastly applied to various forms of customer feedback such as reviews and survey responses found on the web and social media. Commercial websites such as Amazon, eBay, Yelp and IMDb provide users the platform required to express their opinions towards any specific product or subject. Individuals post reviews of movies they have watched on websites like IMDb.

Performing analysis of sentiments from various data sources found on the web is valuable for any organization to maintain quality control of their products. For instance, getting user feedback means requesting people with surveys on every aspect the organization is interested in. One of the sources of doing this is web blogs and another one is electronic discussion boards, where individuals can talk about different types of topics or can request other people's views. This approach is beneficial for numerous reasons. Primarily, the people who share their views usually have more noticeable opinions than the average, which are furthermore convincing others to read them. Secondarily, product and service reviews obtained from commercial web sites also help us to choose which products to buy and which services to use. Furthermore, the individual reviews obtained from personal blogging sites are mostly unbiased and have individual experience towards a specific product or service. Mining these opinions is thus carrying valuable information for the improvement of the business.

Opinion mining is a technique of categorizing opinions articulated in the text sentences (Manning et al., 2008) obtained from several data sources. Basically, text sentences carry personal review or attitude concerning any specific product or subject. Opinion mining of small texts is thought-provoking because they are contextually limited. Decisions are to be made based on the inadequate texts provided by the user. We refer to this method as a supervised learning technique as it can categorize each user review correctly (Pang, Lee, & Vaithyanathan, 2002).

Machine learning (ML) (Witten I. H. et al., 2011) based classification models are trained with data sets containing text sentences and their performances are evaluated as well. Classification techniques such as Logistic Regression (LR) (Cramer J. S., 2002), Support Vector Machine (SVM) (Cortes C., & Vapnik V., 1995) and Decision Tree (DT) (Quinlan J. R.,1987) from ML domain can be applied to text data for performing sentiment analysis. These research studies (Kamal S. et al, 2016, 2017, 2018) contributed some methods which we have applied in our work.

The different sections of the research paper are as follows. In the first section, we have introduced about sentiment analysis and described its importance in business. Section 2 provides literature reviews that worth mentioning in this domain. Section 3 presents the data set description which is followed by the proposed methodology in section 4. Section 5 describes and analyzes results with explanations. Finally, section 6 is attributed to the conclusion and future works.

2. LITERATURE REVIEW

There are several ML-based types of research available to classify sentiments from the text. Some of them are listed below.

ML consists of several classification models such as Artificial Neural Network (ANN), SVM, decision tree, Logistic Regression, etc. These techniques are employed to categorize reviews of products. The research study (Mejova Y. et al., 2009) showed that using the presence of every character, frequency of occurrences of every character, text sentence containing negation, etc. as the features to build feature vector. He also showed that using unigram and bigram approaches one could create feature vectors efficiently in Sentiment analysis.

The research work (Domingos P., 1997) proposed that the Naive Bayes classifier could do well using dependent features for a certain problem. This work (Niu Z. et al., 2012) developed a new classifier based on the Bayesian algorithm. The model employed some effective approaches for the selection of a feature, computation of weight and classification. The research study (Barbosa L., & Feng J., 2010) designed a two-step analysis method which was an automatic sentiment analysis for classifying tweets. In the first step, tweets were classified into subjective and objective tweets. Then, in the second step, subjective tweets were classified as positive and negative tweets.

The research work (Celikyilmaz A. et al., 2010) developed a word clustering method based on the pronunciation of words. This method is applicable for normalizing noisy tweets. There are some words with the similar pronunciation but dissimilar meanings. So, to eliminate this kind of conflict, methods were developed. In the stated method, words having the same pronunciation were clustered and assigned with common tokens. This study (Wu Y., & Ren F., 2011) recommended a model to analyze the sentiments in tweets. In this study, if a user idea is found in the tweet, it took prompt action to help towards influence probability.

The research work (Pak A., & Paroubek P., 2010) established a method for sentiment analysis using some automatic twitter texts. This work designed a Naïve Bayes classifier for sentiment analysis which used emotions in the texts as a feature. Some researchers developed methods to recognize public opinion about movies, news, etc. from tweets. The research study (Peddinti V. et al., 2011) had taken the information from other publicly available databases such as IMDB and Blippr for review analysis.

3. ABOUT THE DATA SET

The data set is taken from the UCI (Kotzias D., 2015). It contains three data sets namely *yelp_labelled*, *imdb_labelled* and *amazon_cells_labelled* data set. In this data set, Score for review is measured either by value 1 (for positive review) or 0 (for negative review). The texts are originated from three different websites namely yelp.com, imdb.com, and amazon.com. For each of these websites, there are 500 positive and 500 negative texts. These are selected randomly from larger review data sets. We have selected sentences that have a positive or negative review. No neutral reviews are considered here. These attributes are essentially texts, extracted from reviews of products, movies, and restaurants from Amazon, IMDB and Yelp respectively.

4. METHODOLOGY

Sentiment analysis is all about analyzing texts. These texts can be of books, reviews and all sorts of texts of some HTML webpages that we extract from web scrapping. By using Natural Language Processing

(NLP) (Khurana D. et al., 2017) with regular expressions based operations we can perform predictive analysis on text. The workflow of our methodology is shown in Figure 1.

Figure 1. Workflow of the proposed methodology

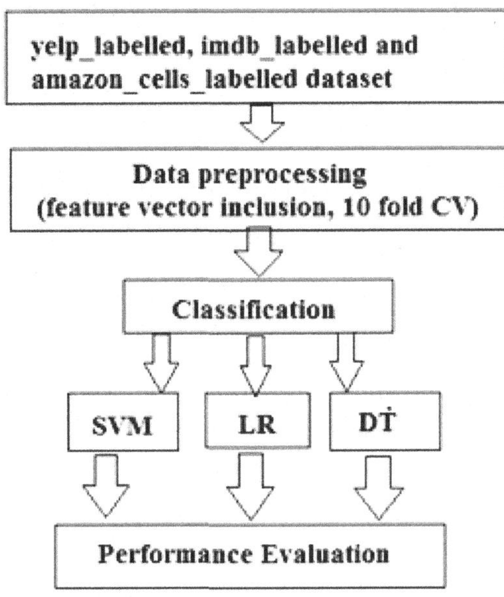

4.1. Step 1: Data Pre-Processing

Data pre-processing is a significant phase in this process. Data are stored in a plain text format along with positive and negative reviews. The data set contains lots of informal words or noises which should be taken care of before being suitable for a model. Therefore, data pre-processing is essential to extract all important or meaningful text that will be relevant for training the model. It also contains different forms of verbs of a particular word which has to be converted into one specific form. To deal with this problem, the concept of feature vector has been brought in. But, before using it, pre-processing is done on each review. Then, features are extracted in two phases: the first phase deals with the extraction of the review specific word. Then, they are removed from the given text. The extracted feature vector is then converted to normal text.

After that, features are extracted from the review which is the normal text without any informal words. These extracted features are then added to develop the feature vector.

4.2. Step 2: Separating Training and Testing Data Set

In ML, we generally split our original data set into two sub-sets namely training set and testing set, and then fit our model on the train data, to make predictions on the test data. For these data sets, we have used *k-fold cross-validation (CV)* (here k=10) for splitting the original data sets into training and testing sets.

The training set contains a known output and the model is trained on this data in order to be generalized to other data later on. Then, we have the testing data set to test the prediction capabilities of these models.

4.3. Step 3: Training the Model

Classification is a method to categorize our data into a desired and separate number of classes where we can assign a label to each class. We have used three different classification models namely Support Vector Machine (SVM), Decision Tree and Logistic Regression for our study.

The present work uses an *SVM classifier* using a *Gaussian RBF kernel* with kernel function *K* as:

$$K\left(x_i, x_j\right) = \phi\left(x_i\right) \cdot \phi\left(x_j\right) \tag{1}$$

Here $\varphi(x)$ is a mapping function applied on the training instances. The SVM classifier can be defined as:

$$K\left(x_i \cdot x_j\right) = e^{\frac{-\left\|x_i - x_j\right\|^2}{2\sigma^2}} \tag{2}$$

Here, we employ the *Classification and Regression Trees (CART)* algorithm which uses the *Gini index* for selection of attribute. This can be represented as:

$$Gini(D) = 1 - \sum_{i=1}^{m} p_i^2 \tag{3}$$

Logistic regression forecasts the probability of an outcome that is having two values. This technique is used when the dependent variable (i.e. target variable) is categorical. It can be seen as:

Output = 1 or 0

Hypothesis such that: $Z = WX + B$ (4)

h*Θ(x) = sigmoid (Z)

We have compared the performance of these algorithms considering the reviews of products, movies, and restaurants from Amazon, IMDB and Yelp respectively.

4.4. Step 4: Testing the Model

Finally, the model is applied to the testing phase. The results of this phase are evaluated against well-known metrics such as RMSE (Armstrong JS., & Collopy F., 1992), Kappa statistic (Carletta J., 1996), and Confusion matrix (Stehman S. V., 1997) based metrics namely Accuracy, Precision, Recall and F1-Measures for performance analysis.

5. RESULT AND DISCUSSION

We have applied three classifiers namely Support Vector Machine, Logistic Regression, and Decision tree to the given UCI data sets for reviews of products, movies, and restaurants from Amazon, IMDB and Yelp respectively. We have divided each of the data sets into two sub-sets namely training set and testing set. The results described here are based on the simulation experiment developed in Python. Several comparisons of these classifiers are done based on some performance measures like classification accuracy, root-mean-square error (RMSE), and kappa statistic values. We have also performed detailed accuracy checking for these classifiers using Precision, Recall and F1-Measure values derived from the confusion matrix of each classifier. Classifiers (SVM, LR, and DT) are applied to a test set for classification after completion of the training phase on each of these data sets.

5.1. YELP Labelled Data Set

Performance comparisons of the three classifiers are presented in Table 1.

Table 1. Performance evaluation based on predicted class level

Classifier	Classification Accuracy (%)	RMSE	Kappa Statistic
SVM	76.5	0.4847	0.5318
Logistic Regression	83.5	0.4062	0.6699
Decision Tree	77.0	0.4795	0.54

We have used classification accuracy, RMSE and kappa statistic values for each of the classifiers in Table 1 for the YELP Labelled Data set. By analyzing Table 1, we see that the Logistic Regression has the highest accuracy and Kappa statistic values and lowest RMSE value among these three classifiers.

Next, we have computed Precision, Recall and F1-measure from the confusion matrix. The result of each of the parameters for each classifier for the Yelp Labelled data set is shown in Table 2.

Table 2. Performance evaluation based on confusion matrix

Classifier	Precision	Recall	F1-Measure
SVM	77%	77%	76%
Logistic Regression	84%	83%	83%
Decision Tree	77%	77%	77%

By analyzing Table 2, we can see that the Precision, Recall and F1-measure values of Logistictic Regression are highest. Values of Logistictic Regression are 84%, 83%, and 83% respectively.

5.2. IMDB Labelled Data Set

Performance comparisons of the three classifiers are described in Table 3.

Table 3. Performance evaluation based on predicted class level

Classifier	Classification Accuracy (%)	RMSE	Kappa Statistic
SVM	77.0	0.4795	0.5403
Logistic Regression	79.5	0.4527	0.59
Decision Tree	74.0	0.5099	0.48

We have calculated classification accuracy, RMSE and kappa statistic values for each of the classifiers in Table 3 for the IMDB Labelled Data set. By analyzing Table 3, we see that the Logistic Regression is having the highest accuracy and Kappa statistic values and lowest RMSE value among these three classifiers used.

Next, we have computed Precision, Recall and F1-measure values from the confusion matrix. The result of each of the parameters for each classifier for IMDB Labelled Data set is shown in Table 4.

Table 4. Performance evaluation based on confusion matrix

Classifier	Precision	Recall	F1-Measure
SVM	77%	77%	77%
Logistic Regression	80%	80%	79%
Decision Tree	76%	74%	73%

By analyzing Table 4, we can see that the Precision, Recall and F1-measure values of Logistictic Regression are highest. These values for Logistictic Regression are 80%, 80%, and 79% respectively.

5.3. AMAZON CELLS Labelled Data Set

Performance comparisons of the three classifiers are given in Table 5.

Table 5. Performance evaluation based on predicted class level

Classifier	Classification Accuracy (%)	RMSE	Kappa Statistic
SVM	83.0	0.4123	0.6599
Logistic Regression	82.5	0.4183	0.6492
Decision Tree	78.0	0.469	0.5578

We have presented classification accuracy, RMSE and kappa statistic values for each of the classifiers in Table 5 for the AMAZON CELLS Labelled Data set. By analysing the Table 5, we can see that SVM has the highest accuracy and Kappa statistic values and lowest RMSE value among these three classifiers.

Next, we have computed Precision, Recall and F1-measure from the confusion matrix. The result of each of the parameters for each classifier for AMAZON CELLS Labelled Data set is shown in Table 6.

Table 6. Performance evaluation based on confusion matrix

Classifier	Precision	Recall	F1-Measure
SVM	83%	83%	83%
Logistic Regression	82%	82%	82%
Decision Tree	78%	78%	78%

By analyzing Table 6, we can see that the Precision, Recall and F1-measure values of SVM are highest. SVM is having the same value i.e. 83% for each of these evaluation metrics.

6. CONCLUSION AND FUTURE WORKS

We can conclude that machine learning-based techniques can be applied to analyze reviews of products, movies, and restaurants from Amazon, IMDB and Yelp data sets. Sentiment analysis is thought-provoking as it is difficult to detect the words that reveal emotion form reviews and also due to the presence of informal words, hast tags, etc. To deal with this problem, the concept of feature vector has been brought in. Before introducing feature vector pre-processing is done on each review. Then features are extracted in two phases: First phase deals with the extraction of the review specific word. Then, they are removed from the given text. The extracted feature vector is then converted to normal text.

After that, features are extracted from the review which is the normal text without any informal words. These extracted features are then added to develop the feature vector. Finally, different ML-based classifiers are applied to the pre-processed data set for classifying the reviews. From our results, we have shown that LR, SVM, and DT based classifiers perform well and also provide higher accuracy. The result shows that the Logistic Regression classifier performs better than the other classifiers considering all scenarios. In the future, the Logistic Regression based classifier can be used for other kinds of sentiment analysis such as to stop spreading rumors against some sensitive issues or to prevent terrorism.

REFERENCES

Armstrong, J.S., & Collopy, F. (1992). Error measures for generalizing about forecasting methods: Empirical comparisons. *International Journal of Forecasting, 8*(6980).

Barbosa, L., & Feng, J. (2010). Robust Sentiment Detection on Twitter from Biased and Noisy data. *23rd International Conference on Computational Linguistics: Posters*, 3644.

Carletta, J. (1996). Assessing agreement on classification tasks: The kappa statistic Computational Linguistics. *MIT Press.*

Celikyilmaz, A., Hakkani-Tur, D., & Feng, J. (2010). Probabilistic Model-Based Sentiment Analysis of Twitter Messages. *Spoken Language Technology Workshop (SLT)*, 7984. 10.1109/SLT.2010.5700826

Cortes, C., & Vapnik, V. (1995, September). Support-vector networks. *Machine Learning*, *20*(3), 273–297. doi:10.1007/BF00994018

Cramer, J. S. (2002). The origins of logistic regression (Technical report). *Tinbergen Institute.*, *119*, 167–178.

Domingos, P., & Pazzani, M. (1997). On the optimality of the Simple Bayesian classifier under zero-one loss. *Machine Learning, 29*, 2–3.

Kamal, M.S., Chowdhury, L., Khan, M.I., Ashour, A.S., Tavares, J.M.R.S., & Dey, N. (2017). Hidden Markov Model and Chapman Kolmogrov for Protein Structures Prediction from Images. Computational Biology and Chemistry, 68, 231–244. doi:10.1016/j.compbiolchem.2017.04.003

Kamal, S., Dey, N., Nimmy, S. F., Ripon, S. H., Ali, N. Y., Ashour, A. S., & Shi, F. (2018). Evolutionary framework for coding area selection from cancer data. *Neural Computing & Applications*, *29*(4), 1015–1037. doi:10.100700521-016-2513-3

Kamal, S., Ripon, S. H., Dey, N., Ashour, A. S., & Santhi, V. (2016). A MapReduce approach to diminish imbalance parameters for big deoxyribonucleic acid data set. *Computer Methods and Programs in Biomedicine*, *131*, 191–206. doi:10.1016/j.cmpb.2016.04.005 PMID:27265059

Khurana D., Koli A., Khatter K., & Singh S. (2017, Mar. 25). *Natural Language Processing*. Natural Language Processing RSS.

KotziasD. (2015). *UCI*. https://archive.ics.uci.edu/ml/data sets/Sentiment+Labelled+Sentences

Mejova, Y. (2009). Sentiment analysis: An overview. Academic Press.

Neethu, M. S., & Rajasree, R. (2013). Sentiment analysis in Twitter using Machine Learning Techniques. *4th ICCCNT.*

Niu, Z., Yin, Z., & Kong, X. (2012). Sentiment classification for microblog by machine learning. *Computational and Information Sciences (ICCIS), 2012 Fourth International Conference on*, 286–289. 10.1109/ICCIS.2012.276

Pak, A., & Paroubek, P. (2010). Twitter as a Corpus for Sentiment Analysis and Opinion mining. *Proceedings of LREC.*

Pang, B., Lee, L., & Vaithyanathan, S. (2002). Thumbs up! Sentiment classification using machine learning techniques. *Proceedings of the 2002 Conference on Empirical Methods in Natural Language Processing*, 79-86.

Peddinti, V., Chintalapoodi, P., & Kiran, V. M. (2011). Domain adaptation in sentiment analysis of twitter. In *Analyzing Microtext Workshop*. AAAI.

Quinlan, J. R. (1987). Simplifying decision trees. *International Journal of Man-Machine Studies*, *27*(3), 221234. doi:10.1016/S0020-7373(87)80053-6

Schütze, H., Manning, C. D., & Raghavan, P. (2008). *Introduction to information retrieval*. Cambridge University Press.

Stehman, S. V. (1997). Selecting and interpreting measures of thematic classification accuracy. *Remote Sensing of Environment*, *62*(1), 7789. doi:10.1016/S0034-4257(97)00083-7

Witten, I. H., Eibe, F., & Hall, M. A. (2011). Data Mining: Practical Machine Learning Tools and Techniques (3rd ed.). Morgan Kaufmann.

Wu, Y., & Ren, F. (2011). Learning sentimental influence in twitter. *Future Computer Sciences and Application (ICFCSA), 2011 International Conference, 119-122.*

This research was previously published in the International Journal of Synthetic Emotions (IJSE), 11(1); pages 49-57, copyright year 2020 by IGI Publishing (an imprint of IGI Global).

Chapter 10
Use of Novel Ensemble Machine Learning Approach for Social Media Sentiment Analysis

Ishrat Nazeer
School of Computer Science and Engineering, Lovely Professional University, Jalandhar, India

Mamoon Rashid
https://orcid.org/0000-0002-8302-4571
School of Computer Science and Engineering, Lovely Professional University, Jalandhar, India

Sachin Kumar Gupta
School of Electronics and Communication Engineering, Shri Mata Vaishno Devi University, Jammu, India

Abhishek Kumar
School of Computer Science and IT, Jain University, Bangalore, India

ABSTRACT

Twitter is a platform where people express their opinions and come with regular updates. At present, it has become a source for many organizations where data will be extracted and then later analyzed for sentiments. Many machine learning algorithms are available for twitter sentiment analysis which are used for automatically predicting the sentiment of tweets. However, there are challenges that hinder machine learning classifiers to achieve better results in terms of classification. In this chapter, the authors are proposing a novel feature generation technique to provide desired features for training model. Next, the novel ensemble classification system is proposed for identifying sentiment in tweets through weighted majority rule ensemble classifier, which utilizes several commonly used statistical models like naive Bayes, random forest, logistic regression, which are weighted according to their performance on historical data, where weights are chosen separately for each model.

DOI: 10.4018/978-1-6684-6303-1.ch010

INTRODUCTION TO SENTIMENT ANALYSIS

In the current world of technology everyone is expressive in one or other way. People want to express their opinions about various issues be it social, political, economic or business. In this process social media is helping people in a great way. Social networking sites like Facebook, twitter, WhatsApp and many others thus become a common tool for people to express themselves. Analyzing the opinions expressed by the people on different social networking sites to get useful insights from them is called social media analytics. The insights gained can then be used to make important decisions. Among all the networking sites twitter is becoming most powerful wherein people express their opinions in short textual messages called tweets. Analyzing the tweets to retrieve insight information is called twitter sentiment analysis (SA) or opinion mining. Sentiment analysis classifies the sentiment of a tweet into three classes of positive negative and neutral (Ahuja, Ret al. 2019). Twitter sentiment analysis is helping the modern world in a great way as an example SA can help a company in knowing the customer reviews about a particular product and will help customers to select the best product based on opinion of people.

Figure 1 shows five main steps required in Sentiment Analysis.

Figure 1. General steps in Twitter sentiment analysis process

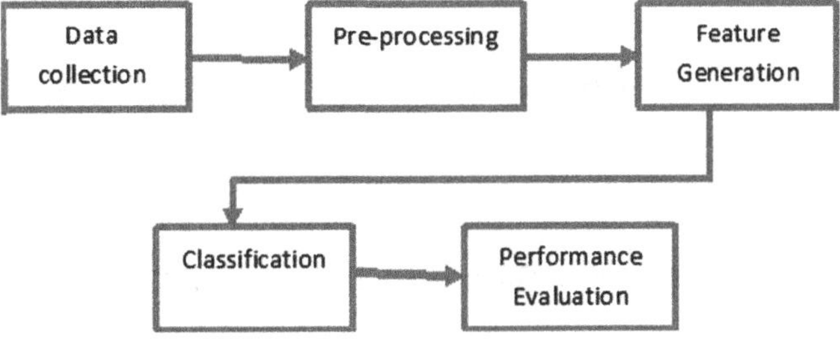

1. **Data Collection**: Process of SA begins by collecting the tweets from twitter using Application Programming Interface (API). API will allow us to interact with the twitter and extract the tweets in a programmatic way. The extracted tweets are then used for further processing,
2. **Pre-Processing**: Data preprocessing is done to remove extra features from the tweets. It decreases the size of tweets and makes them suitable for classification (Rane, A et al. 2018). The feature that are removed include following:
    a. The user name which is preceded by @ symbol.
    b. The retweets which are preceded by RT.
    c. Hashtags denoted by #.
    d. Slang words are replaced with words of equivalent meanings.
3. **Feature Extraction**: Feature extraction steps are responsible for extracting the features from the tweets. Different types of features are there like twitter specific features (includes features like hashtags, retweets, user names, URL), textual features (includes feature like length of tweet and length of words, emoticons, number of question marks), Parts Of Speech (features like nouns, verbs, adverbs, adjectives etc.), Lexicon Based features (comparison of positive and negative word percentages)(Permatasari, R. Iet al. 2018).

4. **Classification**: This step is responsible for determining whether the tweet expresses a positive, negative or neutral sentiment. There are three main approaches to classify the sentiment of a tweet they are, machine learning approach, lexicon based approach and deep learning approach. All these methods classify the polarity of the tweet with varying accuracy levels.
5. **Performance Evaluation**: This step is useful in determining the accuracy of the particular classifier used in the classification stage of the process. Performance is usually determined in terms of accuracy, precision, recall, and f-measure (Gamal, D et al. 2019).

Classification of Sentiment Analysis

Sentiment analysis is done at three different levels they are as follows:

1. **Document Level:** In document level sentiment analysis a document is analysed and the review got from it is classified as being positive negative or neutral. In document level sentiment analysis each document expresses opinion on a single entity (1 from proposal page).
2. **Sentence Level:** In sentence level sentiment analysis a sentence rather than a document is analyzed and classified as being positive negative or neutral. Sentences can be of two types subjective (sentence with opinion) or objective (sentence with factual knowledge). In sentence level classification the type of sentence is first identified and then if it contains an opinion it is classified (Behdenna, Set al. 2018).
3. **Aspect Level:** In aspect level sentiment analysis each aspect of a tweet or sentence is classified individually. The process first identifies the entity and its aspects then classifies the identified aspects.

Use of Twitter Micro-blogging for Sentiment Analysis

Twitter has become an important source of knowledge for people. It acts as a platform where people express themselves using short text messages called tweets. Sentiment analysis is mostly performed on twitter data because of the following reasons:

- It is the most popular micro-blogging site.
- It has 240+ million active users.
- About 500 million tweets are generated each day.
- Tweets are small in length and thus easy to analyze.
- It has variety of users.

Challenges in Twitter Sentiment Analysis

The task of sentiment analysis on twitter data is most challenging. The most common challenges associated with twitter sentiment analysis are as follows:

1. Use of highly unstructured and non-grammatical language in tweets.
2. Use of slang words.
3. Use of sarcasm in tweets.

4. Use of words which have subjective context in one sentence and objective in another.
5. Use of negative words to oppose the sentiment of tweet.
6. Use of acronyms and abbreviations.
7. Use of out of vocabulary words.

INTRODUCTION TO MACHINE LEARNING

Machine learning is a branch of artificial intelligence that gives machines the ability to learn from their own experience without being programmed. Machine learning is trying to impart human learning in computers. Humans learn by reasoning while computers learn by using algorithms. Based on the approach of learning used algorithms are classified into following general categories.

- **Supervised Learning**: Supervised learning algorithms are fed with a labelled dataset. Labelled dataset contains both input and output. The algorithm uses this dataset to train itself. After the training is over the algorithm is tested on a testing dataset, which is similar in dimensions to the training dataset, for predication or classification.
- **Unsupervised Learning**: Unsupervised learning algorithms are fed with an unlabeled dataset. Unlabeled dataset contains only input data and no information about the outputs. The algorithm has to learn by itself as no training is involved (Portugal, I et al. 2018). The algorithm classifies the data based on similarities or differences or patterns present in it.
- **Semi Supervised Learning**: Semi supervised learning algorithms are fed with a labelled dataset which is not complete and has missing information. The algorithm although goes through training but has to learn by itself as well because of the missing information (Portugal, I et al. 2018).
- **Reinforcement Learning**: Reinforcement learning is based on rewards. In this type of learning if algorithm makes a correct decision it is rewarded else it is punished. This type of learning is mostly used in game playing. In game playing if the algorithm makes a correct move the step will be repeated and learned however if an incorrect move is made then the step won't be repeated.

Overview of Machine Learning Classifiers

The different types of machine learning algorithms are given below:

- **Naive Bayes**: Naive Bayes algorithm is a statistical model of classification based on conditional probability. Conditional probability defines the probability of an event given that some other event has already occurred. The formula of Naive Bayes is given by:

$$P(H / X) = \frac{P(X / H)P(H)}{P(X)}$$

- **Support Vector Machine (SVM):** SVM classifier is mostly used for binary classification as shown in Figure 2. SVM is based on the construction of a hyperplane which acts as decision boundary between the two classes to be classified. The hyperplane is defined by w*x+b=0. Where w is the weight vector and b is the bias. Data point with w*x+b>=0 will be classified into a positive category and if w*x+b<0 then it is classified into a negative category (B, V et al. 2016).

Figure 2. Binary classification using SVM
(Mubaris NK, 2017)

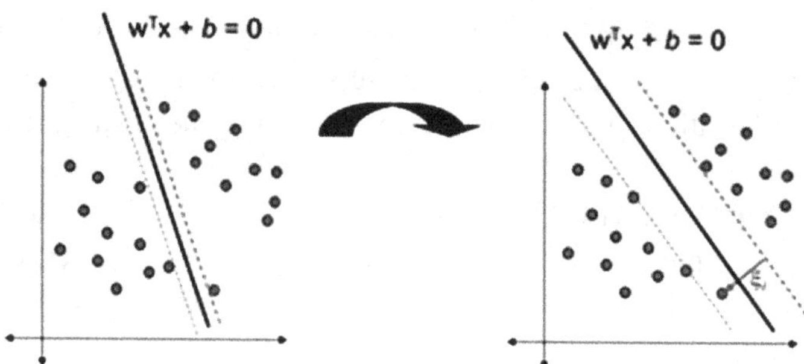

- **Random Forest**: Random forest algorithm builds a multitude of decision trees from the given dataset as shown in Figure 3. It then uses the result of each tree to find the class of data point using majority voting method (Rane, Aet al. 2018).

Figure 3. Illustration of Random forest
(Brendan Tierney, 2018)

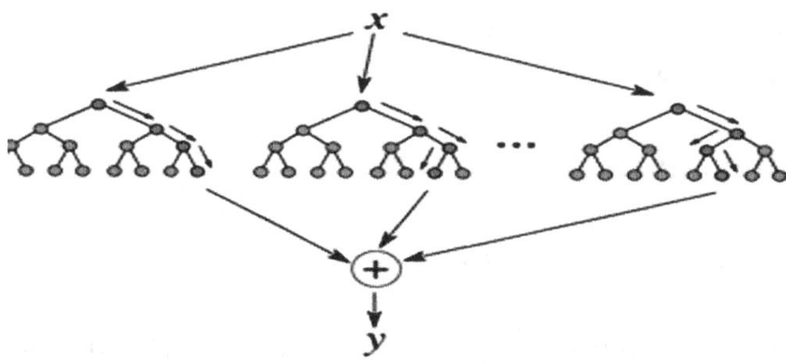

- **Decision Tree**: Decision tree algorithm works by constructing a decision tree from the given data. Each node of the tree represents the attribute of data and branch represents the test on attributes. Leaf nodes of the tree represent the final classes. Decision tree is constructed using the information gain of each node. Figure 4 shows the decision tree constructed for the shown dataset.

Figure 4. Classification of data set using Decision tree classifier
(Upasana Priyadarshiny, 2019)

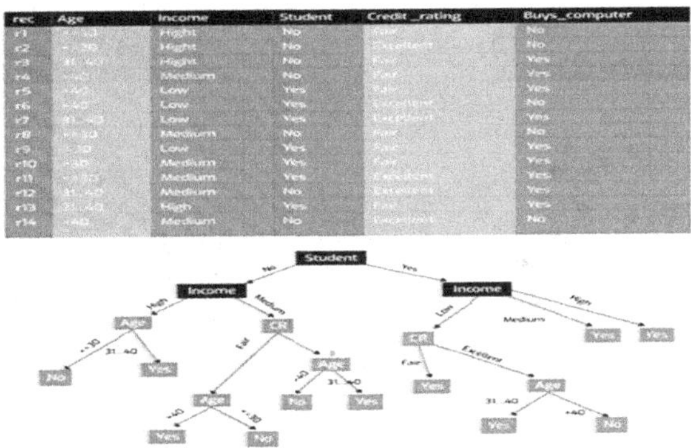

- **K Nearest Neighbour (KNN)**: KNN classifier can be used for classification and regression and its illustration is shown in Figure 5. It is based on similarity index. The algorithm first identifies the K nearest neighbors of a data point using a distance measure like Euclidian distance. The data point is then assigned to the class that is most common among its K neighbours.

Figure 5. Classification of a data point using KNN classifier
(Avinash Navlani, 2018)

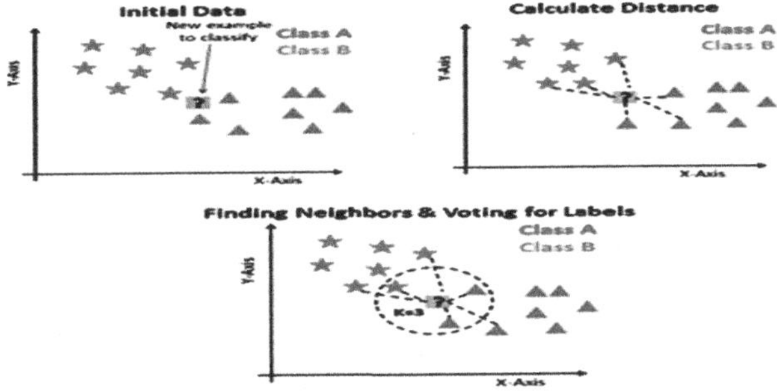

- **K Means Clustering**: K means clustering is an unsupervised learning technique. In this algorithm each data point is assigned to a cluster to which it resembles the most. The grouping of data points in clusters is shown in Figure 6. K represents the number of distinct clusters formed (Dey, A. 2016)

Applying Machine Learning Classifiers for Twitter Analysis

Machine learning involves a set of methods used to identify the features of text. Machine learning enables a computer to learn from the patterns of data and experiences. Thus the computer needs not be programmed explicitly. Machine learning has been successfully used in twitter sentiment classification. Machine learning classifiers have shown a good rate of accuracy in sentiment classification. Some of the recent works done on twitter sentiment analysis are mentioned below.

Figure 6. Grouping of data points into three different clusters
(Arun Manglic, 2017).

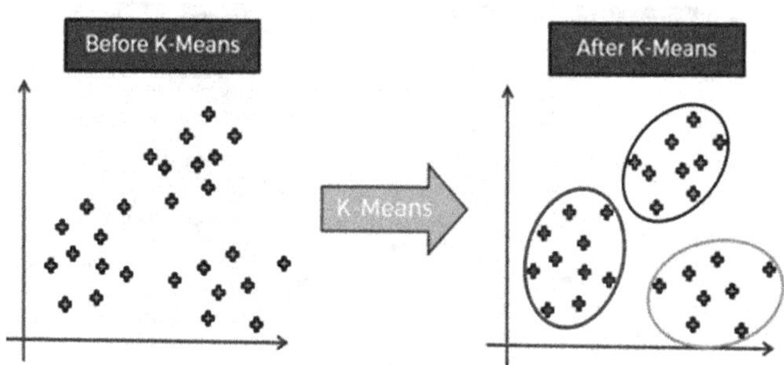

(Nanda, Cet al. 2018) used machine learning algorithms on movie review tweets to classify the tweets into positive and negative. The algorithms used were Support Vector Machine (SVM) and Random Forest (RF). An accuracy of 91.07 and 89.73 was achieved by RF and SVM respectively. (Rathi, M et al. 2018) used an ensemble machine learning algorithm. Ensemble was created by using merging SVM and Decision Tree (DT) algorithms. The algorithm achieved an accuracy of 84% which was greater than the accuracy provided by the individual SVM and DT. (El-Jawad, M. H. A et al. 2018) compared different machine learning and deep learning algorithms. They developed a hybrid model using Naive Bayes, Decision Tree, Convolution Neural Network (CNN) and Recurrent Neural Network (RNN). The model gives an accuracy of 83.6%. (Arti et al. 2019) used Random Forest algorithm on tweets related to Indian Premier League 2016. The classifier achieved an accuracy of 81.69%. (Alrehili, A et al. 2019) combined Naive Bayes, SVM, Random Forest, Bagging and Boosting to create ensemble algorithm for the customer reviews about a product. (Naz, S et al. 2018) used sentiment analysis on SemEval twitter dataset. The machine learning algorithm was SVM which uses multiple features of data to perform better accuracy. (Goel, A et al. 2016) used Naive Bayes algorithm to classify a movie review twitter dataset. (Jose, R et al. 2016) combined machine learning classification approach with lexicon based sentiment classification. The authors combined SentiWordNet classifier, Naive bayes classifier and hidden Markov model classifier to achieve better accuracy.An attempt to fetch twitter data has been done by (Rashid, M et al. 2019). This research used Hadoop distributed file system for storage of data which were fetched with the help of flume. Decision Tree and Naïve Bayes classifiers were used for sentiment analysis. The clustering approach has been used for managing web news data in (Kaur, S et al. 2016). This research has used Back Propagation Neural Network and K-Means Clustering for classifying the news data.

DATA EXTRACTION AND FEATURE SELECTION

When twitter sentiment analysis is done using machine learning approach, feature extraction plays an important role. Features represent the information that can be extracted from the data. Features define the unique property of a data sample. In Machine Learning the feature of data are projected on a higher dimensional feature space. To achieve better accuracy in classification higher dimensional data needs to be mapped onto low dimensional feature space. Feature extraction acts as a dimensional reduction technique. Each machine learning classifier uses most appropriate feature set to classify the sentiment of tweet as positive, negative or neutral (Avinash, M et al. 2018).

El-Jawad, M. H. A *et al.*, (2018) in their study divides features into following categories.

1. **Bag of Words (BOW):** BOW is basically a feature representation technique wherein tweets are commonly converted into an array of numbers. It first learns all the words present in a tweet and then describes the presence of words in a tweet. BOW uses ngram_range as a parameter. ngram range represents number of words taken together. Range can be 1 (unigram), 2 (bigram) or multiple.
2. **Lexicon Based Feature:** In this feature representation technique a comparison is made between percentage of positive and negative words present in a tweet. Positive words include words like good, great, excellent etc. Negative words include words like bad, poor, dangerous etc.
3. **Parts of Speech Feature Representation:** In this feature representation technique the count of nouns, verbs, adverbs, adjectives present in the tweet is determined. By identifying each word of tweet as a different POS it becomes easy to get the context in which each word is used thus helping in analyzing the sentiment of tweet.
4. **Emoticon Based Feature Representation:** Emoticons are used in tweets to represent the feeling an individual has related to a particular event. The number of emoticons present in each tweet represents its feature set. Emoticon based features have been used by many researchers to effectively classify the tweets.

Feature Selection

Feature selection technique is used to select the relevant features and eliminate the irrelevant ones from a tweet. It thus helps in reducing the feature dimensionality of a data set. Lower dimensional feature space provides better accuracy in classification. There are different feature selection methods some of them are discussed below.

1. **Information Gain (IG):** Information gain is used to measure dependencies between the class and the feature. If dependencies are present we select the feature else not. If x is a feature and c1 and c2 are the two classes then the information gain is given by:

$$IG(x) = -\sum_{j=1}^{2} P(C_j)\log(P(C_j)) + P(x)\sum_{j=1}^{2} P(C_j \mid x)\log(P(C_j \mid x))$$
$$+P(\overline{x})\sum_{j=1}^{2} P(C_j \mid \overline{x})\log(P(C_j \mid \overline{x}))$$

2. **Chi- Square:** Chi square is used when tweets contain categorical features. Chi square is used calculated between feature and the class. The features with best chi-square scores are selected. Chi–square is calculated as follows

$$c^2 = \sum_{i=1}^{k}\left[\frac{(O_i - E_i)^2}{E_i}\right]$$

Here O denotes the observed frequency, E denotes expected frequency and “i” denotes “ith” position in the contingency table. Expected frequency is the number of expected observations of class when there is no relationship between the feature and the target class and observed frequency is the number of observations of class.

3. **Minimum Redundancy method:** in this method of feature selection the features which are highly dependent on class and minimally dependent on other features are selected. It is also called as Minimum Redundancy Maximum Relevance feature selection. If two features possess redundant information then if only one is selected it does not affect the classification accuracy much.

Training and Testing Machine Learning Classifier for Twitter Sentiment Analysis

Once the data is pre-processed and ready, the next step is train this data to classifier for model preparation. However to evaluate the performance of model, it is very important to split the given data into training and test parts where the performance will be evaluated later by comparing the predictions from machine learning model with that of the target values in outcome variable of testing data. In some cases, separate datasets are to be used for training and tests purposes which is critical in correctly assessing the performance of classifier. The training and testing datasets. Keeping this challenge under consideration, we can use same dataset for training and testing iterations. The concept of k-fold cross validation is to be used where the data is divided into k units or blocks and then classifier is trained for all units except one unit which is to be used for testing purposes and later this process is repeated for all other units. If the value of K is equal to the number of observations, then this process is called as leave one out cross validation. Leave out one validation is turning biased for large value of K. However 10 fold cross validation is always a good choice (Hastie, T et al. 2009).

PROPOSAL OF NOVEL ENSEMBLE MACHINE LEARNING FOR TWITTER SENTIMENT ANALYSIS

In classical machine learning approach a single classifier is applied on the training data at once for classification. This produces different results of accuracy for different classifiers on same training dataset. Moreover if we have a set of classifiers all of which are providing a good accuracy result on same training dataset. Choosing a single classifier will not give us best and generalized results on unseen data. Thus using a single classifier will not help in selecting a best classifier among the competing ones. Also it is difficult to say which realization of a particular classifier will be best set to training data. All of these problems were solved by ensemble learning. Ensemble learning is a Machine Learning methodology in which different base models are combined to produce an optimal classification model. The optimal classification model formed is known as Ensemble classifier. Ensemble classifier combines output of different models to give best and generalized results in classification. The general ensemble classification approach is shown in Figure 7.

Figure 7. General ensemble classification approach

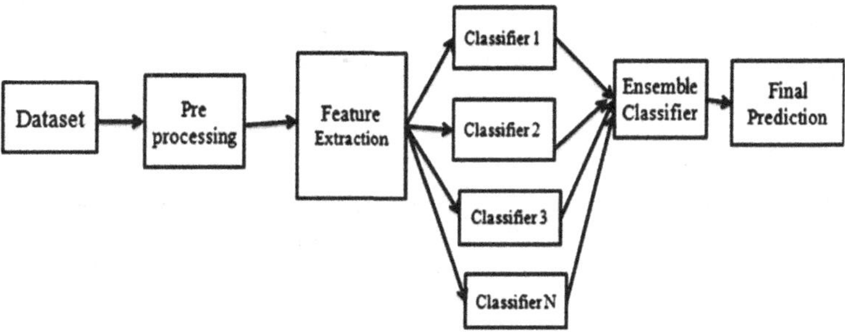

The outputs of different base classifiers are combined in multiple ways to get the final prediction. The different approaches by which the outputs of base classifiers can be combined are;

1. **Majority Voting:** In majority voting method the prediction is made by each base classifier. These predictions are deemed as votes. The final output of the ensemble classifier will be the prediction that is most common among the individual classifier predictions. For example if we are using three classifiers in the ensemble if two classifiers are predicting the tweet as positive and one as negative the final output of ensemble will be positive. Majority voting method is shown in Figure 8.

Figure 8. Majority voting method to classification using Ensemble classifier

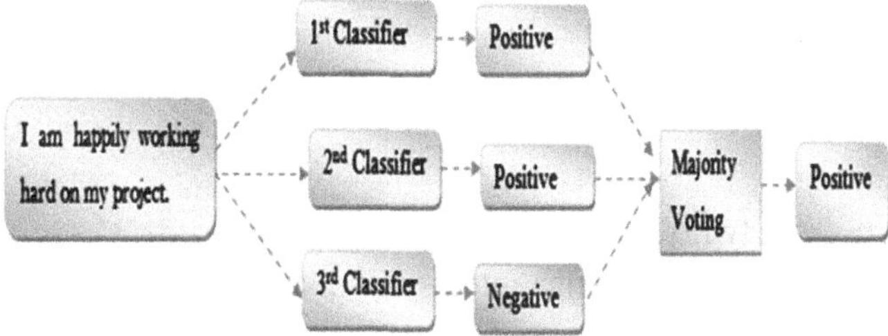

2. **Maximum Probability:** In maximum probability rule the individual predictions of base classifiers are averaged. The final output of the ensemble classifier is the class with maximum average value. In case of Twitter Sentiment Analysis for each tweet probability of positive as well negative class is calculated. The ensemble classifier then finds the average of probabilities of all classes of each classifier and the class with maximum probability is assigned to the tweet. Maximum probability rule of ensemble classification is shown in Figure 9.

Figure 9. Maximum Probability method to classification using Ensemble classifier

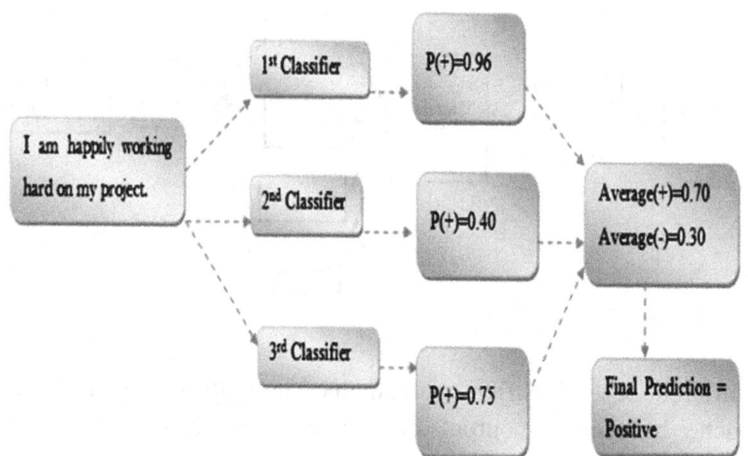

3. **Weighted Average:** Weighted average method is similar to the maximum probability rule however in weighted average rule the base models are assigned with some weights. The weights are given according to the importance of each predictive model. The models which are more effective for a particular dataset will be assigned with larger weights and the models which are less effective are assigned comparatively smaller weights.

The algorithm for ensemble classification is as follows.

ALGORITHM

Step 1: Extraction of data from twitter using twitters API.
Step 2: Pre-processing the data to remove unwanted symbols and words which are of no use in predicting the sentiment of the tweet.
Step 3: Extracting the features from preprocessed tweets using Bag of Words technique.
Step 4: Applying each individual classifier on the extracted features to get individual predictions.
Step 5: Using majority voting technique on the individual predictions to get the final prediction by ensemble classifier.
Step 6: Output the sentiment of the tweet.

CONCLUSION AND FUTURE DIRECTIONS

In this chapter, the authors proposed novel machine learning approach for the sentiment analysis classification. This proposed algorithm is based on ensemble approach which will identify sentiment in tweets through - Weighted Majority Rule Ensemble Classifier where several commonly used statistical models like Naive Bayes, Random forest, Logistic regression will be utilized and weighted according to their performance on historical data and weights will be chosen separately for each model. In future, this proposed ensemble model will be used for training datasets for the classification of sentiments. This model will also be extended by the application of optimization algorithms for further refining the feature set for better results of classification in sentiment analysis.

REFERENCES

Ahuja, R., Chug, A., Kohli, S., Gupta, S., & Ahuja, P. (2019). The Impact of Features Extraction on the Sentiment Analysis. *Procedia Computer Science*, *152*, 341–348. doi:10.1016/j.procs.2019.05.008

Alrehili, A., & Albalawi, K. (2019). Sentiment Analysis of Customer Reviews Using Ensemble Method. *2019 International Conference on Computer and Information Sciences (ICCIS)*. 10.1109/ICCISci.2019.8716454

Arti, D. K. P., & Agrawal, S. (2019). An Opinion Mining for Indian Premier League Using Machine Learning Techniques. *2019 4th International Conference on Internet of Things: Smart Innovation and Usages (IoT-SIU)*. doi: 10.1109/iot-siu.2019.8777472

Avinash, M., & Sivasankar, E. (2018). A Study of Feature Extraction Techniques for Sentiment Analysis. *Advances in Intelligent Systems and Computing Emerging Technologies in Data Mining and Information Security*, 475–486. doi:10.1007/978-981-13-1501-5_41

B., V., & M., B. (2016). Analysis of Various Sentiment Classification Techniques. *International Journal of Computer Applications, 140*(3), 22–27. doi:10.5120/ijca2016909259

Behdenna, S., Barigou, F., & Belalem, G. (2018). Document Level Sentiment Analysis: A survey. *EAI Endorsed Transactions on Context-Aware Systems and Applications*, *4*(13), 154339. doi:10.4108/eai.14-3-2018.154339

Dey, A. (2016). Machine learning algorithms: A review. *International Journal of Computer Science and Information Technologies*, *7*(3), 1174–1179.

El-Jawad, M. H. A., Hodhod, R., & Omar, Y. M. K. (2018). Sentiment Analysis of Social Media Networks Using Machine Learning. *2018 14th International Computer Engineering Conference (ICENCO)*. doi: 10.1109/icenco.2018.8636124

Gamal, D., Alfonse, M., El-Horbaty, E.-S. M., & Salem, A.-B. M. (2019). Implementation of Machine Learning Algorithms in Arabic Sentiment Analysis Using N-Gram Features. *Procedia Computer Science*, *154*, 332–340. doi:10.1016/j.procs.2019.06.048

Goel, A., Gautam, J., & Kumar, S. (2016). Real time sentiment analysis of tweets using Naive Bayes. *2016 2nd International Conference on Next Generation Computing Technologies (NGCT)*. doi: 10.1109/ngct.2016.7877424

Hastie, T., Tibshirani, R., Friedman, J., & Franklin, J. (2005). The elements of statistical learning: Data mining, inference and prediction. *The Mathematical Intelligencer*, *27*(2), 83–85. doi:10.1007/BF02985802

Jose, R., & Chooralil, V. S. (2016). Prediction of election result by enhanced sentiment analysis on twitter data using classifier ensemble Approach. *2016 International Conference on Data Mining and Advanced Computing (SAPIENCE)*. 10.1109/SAPIENCE.2016.7684133

Kaur, S., & Rashid, E. M. (2016). Web news mining using Back Propagation Neural Network and clustering using K-Means algorithm in big data. *Indian Journal of Science and Technology*, *9*(41). Advance online publication. doi:10.17485/ijst/2016/v9i41/95598

Manglic, A. (2017). *Artificial Intelligence and Machine/ Deep Learning*. Retrieved from http://arun-aiml.blogspot.com/2017/07/k-means-clustering.html

Mubaris, N. K. (2017). *Support Vector Machines for Classification*. Retrieved from https://mubaris.com/posts/svm

Nanda, C., Dua, M., & Nanda, G. (2018). Sentiment Analysis of Movie Reviews in Hindi Language Using Machine Learning. *2018 International Conference on Communication and Signal Processing (ICCSP)*. 10.1109/ICCSP.2018.8524223

Navlani, A. (2018). *KNN Classification using Scikit-learn*. Retrieved from https://www.datacamp.com/community/tutorials/k-nearest-neighbor-classification-scikit-learn

Naz, S., Sharan, A., & Malik, N. (2018). Sentiment Classification on Twitter Data Using Support Vector Machine. *2018 IEEE/WIC/ACM International Conference on Web Intelligence (WI)*. 10.1109/WI.2018.00-13

Permatasari, R. I., Fauzi, M. A., Adikara, P. P., & Sari, E. D. L. (2018). Twitter Sentiment Analysis of Movie Reviews using Ensemble Features Based Naïve Bayes. *2018 International Conference on Sustainable Information Engineering and Technology (SIET)*. 10.1109/SIET.2018.8693195

Portugal, I., Alencar, P., & Cowan, D. (2018). The use of machine learning algorithms in recommender systems: A systematic review. *Expert Systems with Applications*, *97*, 205–227. doi:10.1016/j.eswa.2017.12.020

Priyadarshiny, U. (2019). *How to create a Perfect Decision Tree*. Retrieved from https://dzone.com/articles/how-to-create-a-perfect-decision-tree

Rane, A., & Kumar, A. (2018). Sentiment Classification System of Twitter Data for US Airline Service Analysis. *2018 IEEE 42nd Annual Computer Software and Applications Conference (COMPSAC)*. doi:10.1109/compsac.2018.00114

Rashid, M., Hamid, A., & Parah, S. A. (2019). Analysis of Streaming Data Using Big Data and Hybrid Machine Learning Approach. In *Handbook of Multimedia Information Security: Techniques and Applications* (pp. 629–643). Springer. doi:10.1007/978-3-030-15887-3_30

Rathi, M., Malik, A., Varshney, D., Sharma, R., & Mendiratta, S. (2018). Sentiment Analysis of Tweets Using Machine Learning Approach. *2018 Eleventh International Conference on Contemporary Computing (IC3)*. 10.1109/IC3.2018.8530517

Silva, N. F. D., Hruschka, E. R., & Hruschka, E. R. (2014). Tweet sentiment analysis with classifier ensembles. *Decision Support Systems*, *66*, 170–179. doi:10.1016/j.dss.2014.07.003

Tierney, B. (2018). *Random Forest Machine Learning in R, Python and SQL - Part 1*. Retrieved fromhttps://blog.toadworld.com/2018/08/31/random-forest-machine-learning-in-r-python-and-sql-part-1

This research was previously published in Analyzing Global Social Media Consumption; pages 16-28, copyright year 2021 by Information Science Reference (an imprint of IGI Global).

Chapter 11
Approaches to Sentiment Analysis on Product Reviews

Vishal Vyas
Pondicherry University, India

V. Uma
https://orcid.org/0000-0002-7257-7920
Pondicherry University, India

ABSTRACT

Purchase decisions are better when opinions/reviews about products are considered. Similarly, reviewing customer feedback help in improving the sale and ultimately benefit the business. Web 2.0 provides various platforms such as Twitter, Facebook, etc. where one can comment, review, or post to express his/her happiness, anger, disbelief, sadness toward products, people, etc. To computationally analyze the sentiments in text requires a better understanding of the technologies used in sentiment analysis. This chapter gives a comprehensive understanding about the techniques used in sentiment analysis. Machine learning approaches are mostly used for sentiment analysis. Whereas, as per the text and required results, lexicon-based approaches are also used for the same purpose. This chapter includes the discussion on the evaluation parameters for the sentiment analysis. This chapter would also highlight ontology approach for sentiment analysis and outstanding contributions made in this field.

Keywords: Sentiment Analysis, Product reviews, Supervised learning, Unsupervised learning, Social networking websites, Ontology

INTRODUCTION

Expression of thought is not only significant for an individual, but there is a necessity for an automated system to get an opinion from it. For a human being mostly it is straightforward to sense the sentiment in the text using the trained mind. Human beings have trained their mind by learning through experiences. An intelligent system should have an automated method that can identify the sentiment in opinions.

DOI: 10.4018/978-1-6684-6303-1.ch011

Although there is a massive advancement in natural language processing (NLP) and machine learning (ML), automated systems still have not achieved 100% accuracy in dealing with sarcasm or finding the polarity of the text. With the advancements in the field of NLP and ML in the last decade, there is a growing need for sentiment analysing systems to help humans in getting an accurate opinion which could subsequently assist them in decision-making. Rosenthal (2017) explains how sentiment analysis involves detecting the positive, negative and neutral expressions in the text.

Deep understanding of the speaker is possible through sentiment analysis (SA). Sentiment analysis is a task that is becoming increasingly important for many companies because of the emergence of social media viz. Facebook, Twitter, e-commerce websites and the other trillions of them. Nearly, 500 million tweets/day is a massive data to analyse.

Big data related to customer posts/ reviews in social networking, e-commerce websites, etc. is quite unmanageable. An automated system that gives the aggregate inclination of belief and intensity towards entities such as organizations, manufactured items, occasion and their elements is Sentiment analysis / Opinion mining. For the better understanding of the topic/product, Sentiment Analysis is the need of the hour. Opinions are valuable both at personal and professional level. Either we ask for advice, or we get influenced by the advertisement that business organizations put on the Internet after colossal research.

Summarizing product reviews using Sentiment Analysis helps in determining the product features that need improvement. Extracting sentiment from product reviews makes it easy for the brand marketing team to reach its customers who need extra care and hence, benefits the business.

Sentiment analysis is performed at various levels, and these levels are defined in definition section of sentiment analysis. Product review contains unwanted words which have no participation in the sentiment orientation. Such words are removed in preprocessing. The clean data is created after preprocessing. The chapter contains brief explanation of various techniques involved in preprocessing of online product reviews

Feature selection is essential while performing Sentiment Analysis. Feature selection methods will be explained in this chapter. In the supervised learning approach for the Sentiment analysis, text features act as labels and help in classifying the text into different polarities. Ultimately, the sentiment in the text is measured considering different polarities such as positive, negative and neutral. Product reviews are present in text form. SA is a classification task by which text is categorized based on the sentiment orientation. Frequently used approaches in supervised learning for text categorization viz. Naive Bayes, Maximum Entropy and Support vector machine are explained in the discussion section of the chapter. Mostly, sentiment analysis is performed using supervised learning techniques. But, there are few instances where unsupervised learning is preferred. A brief explanation of unsupervised learning approaches is presented in same section. Lexicon based approach is classified as the Dictionary and Corpus-based approaches. Corpus-based method is further divided into semantic and statistical approaches. Lexicon-based procedures are used for lexicon acquisition and developing a corpus which helps in achieving high accuracy in Sentiment analysis. The chapter will explain all the performance measures that are used to evaluate the capability of learning classifiers. While performing sentiment analysis on twitter posts is done using Machine learning approaches, it comes with a drawback that it considers the whole post has a uniform statement and assigns a sentiment score for the entire post. To overcome this issue, Ontology-based technique is applied. It divides twitter post into a set of aspects and assigns sentiment score to each distinct aspect (Kontopoulos et al., 2013). There is a detailed explanation on ontology-based approach in this chapter. This chapter will comprehensively present the approaches to Sentiment Analysis and will contribute towards better understanding of the procedures.

DEFINITION OF SENTIMENT ANALYSIS

Sentiment analysis starts with identifying whether the sentence is subjective or objective. Subjective sentences are those which have feeling/emotion towards an entity. For example, the sentences "New phone in the market has excellent specifications, I will probably buy it" (Positive feeling) and "I wonder why the company has made this mobile with such a bad battery life" (Negative feeling) are subjective sentences. An objective sentence contains facts and figures.

Sentiments are derived from subjective sentences. In subjective sentences, we come across one more kind of opinion viz. neutral sentiment. This chapter will elaborate classification of positive and negative phrases by using several techniques. Till 2002, many research works were based on topic categorization, which categorises the article based on topics such as sports, politics, movies, etc. Topic categorization is considered to be an easy task as compared to sentiment analysis because classification of an article based on a topic is done by calculating the majority of keywords to a definite problem.

There are specific approaches to Sentiment Analysis that are important to understand in designing a system that gives accurate result while performing Sentiment Analysis. These approaches are Document-level sentiment analysis, Sentence level sentiment analysis, Aspect-based sentiment analysis and Comparative-based sentiment analysis.

The vital component in the sentiment analysis architecture is Document analysis. In this module, the processed document is annotated with sentiment polarities. Notations are coupled to the data as per the level of sentiment analysis. Sentiment analysis is classified into following four levels.

1. In Document level Sentiment Analysis, entire document is considered as single information unit. Document is then categorized as positive, negative or neutral which indicates the sentiment polarity. Supervised learning and unsupervised learning are the main approaches in performing document level Sentiment Analysis.
2. Sentence level Sentiment Analysis considers each sentence as one information unit. Before the real analysis of polarity, each sentence is determined to be Subjective or Objective. Only subjective sentences are further analysed. The sentiment polarity of the whole document is known after examining each sentence.
3. In Aspect-based Sentiment Analysis, classification of sentiment concerns particular Aspect/Entity. Firstly, aspects and their entities are identified. For instance, in the opinion about a car "Mileage of the car is very low but it is equipped with high-end safety features", "Mileage" and "Safety features" are two aspects of the entity "Car."
4. In comparative-based Sentiment Analysis, rather than having a direct opinion about a product, text has comparative opinions such as "Most of the features in Audi car are better than BMW." Firstly, comparative sentences are identified in the text and then preferred entities are extracted. Focus on words like "more", "less", "most", "better", "superior" etc. help in identifying comparative sentences.

DISCUSSION: TECHNIQUES INVOLVED IN SENTIMENT ANALYSIS

The process of sentiment analysis on product reviews starts with extracting reviews from E-commerce websites, online review corpus etc. Figure 1 exhibits the process flow of SA.

Figure 1. Process flow of Sentiment Analysis

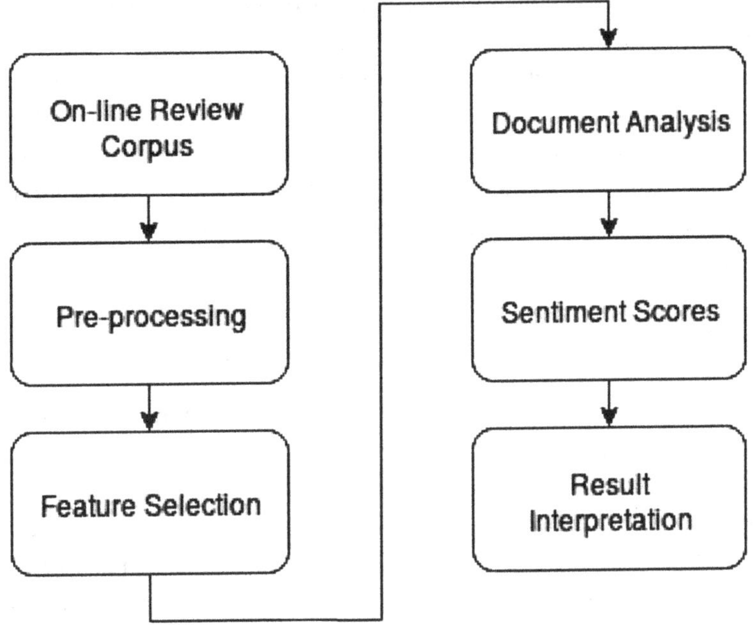

Preprocessing

Preparation of non-redundant text for the process of sentiment analysis is preprocessing. Online reviews which are used for sentiment analysis consist of noise and abundant data which does not have any impact on sentiment analysis. Preprocessing reduces the data dimensionality which leaves only essential data for the study. Noiseless data improves the performance of classifier and makes the sentiment analysis more accurate.

Preprocessing involves several steps namely Tokenization, Stop word removal, Stemming, POS- tagging and Feature Extraction.

Tokenization is a task of cleaving a character order into bits (tokens). The review "Samsung is giving good competition to Apple in mobile market" after tokenization each word becomes a token.

In stop word removal, words "is", "am", "are", etc. in retrieved data which does not have any impact on the orientation of the text are removed. It helps in the reduction of a large data set. These variables if considered increases the complexity of the model. This component of preprocessing removes some of the tokens and hence the review becomes "Samsung giving good competition Apple mobile market". Sometimes a catalogue of stop words unused in one document may have some importance in the other. IDF (Inverse Document Frequency) is another approach that deals with stop words. It assigns a weighted score to the word as per its occurrence in the document. Weight score is increased for less used words and decreased for the words that are frequently used. Tf (term frequency – how often a word occurs) is combined with IDF to calculate Tf-ID, which tells the importance of the word. Tf-IDF approach is a useful approach in text mining.

In online reviews, a word is used in various forms. For, e.g., categorization, categorize, categorizing and categories, etc. Stemming transforms the words into its base form. Porter's algorithm (Porter,

1980) is found to be very useful for stemming characters. POS tagging is assigning words in the text to a particular part of speech. With the tag, a word is identified as a noun, adjective, verb, etc. Brill (1992) introduced a part of speech tagger which is mostly used for POS tagging till date.

Feature extraction is the dimensionality reduction technique which transforms the significant data into the set of features which is expected to have high impact on sentiment orientation. These features are used by the classifier to distinguish sentiment orientations. Better human interpretations are derived through a proper feature extraction technique. Feature extraction helps in saving memory space by reducing the dataset and hence the complexity gets decreased. It is difficult and the most important phase in the process of sentiment analysis.

Feature Selection

The objective to create a predictive model for sentiment analysis can be fulfilled by machine learning algorithms. Feature selection plays a significant role in these algorithms. Better feature selection not only produces accurate results but it also reduces the time complexity. In-depth knowledge of the problem domain is a prerequisite in feature selection. It is advisable not to confuse feature selection with dimensionality reduction as both are entirely different terms. Modification of words is done in both the above said methods, but in feature selection, addition and reduction of attributes/features/variables on the dataset are done by preserving the characteristics of data. Dimensionality reduction is done by the creation of new combinations of variables/attributes.

Online product reviews are mostly in the form of text. Sentiment analysis is the sub class of Sentiment classification (Medhat et al., 2014). To classify the text into different sentiment orientations, text features such as term presence and frequency, part of speech, negation and opinion phrases are used. The contribution of redundant and irrelevant attributes in a predictive model is null and in fact, it degrades the accuracy of the model. Feature selection helps in selecting only those characteristics which contribute to the accuracy of the predictive model. Quality attributes not just makes the model easy to understand, but it reduces the complexity to a significant level. Feature selection plays a vital role in achieving an accurate predictive model. There exist few methods which are very important in understanding the concept of feature selection. In this chapter, filter, wrapper and embedded feature selection methods are discussed, and various techniques which fall under these categories are presented in a table form.

Filter Method

Filter methods benefit by utilizing statistical measures. Through these actions, scores are assigned to each feature. This method remains independent from machine learning classifier in deciding features for the predictive model. Accepted features with high scores are considered for the generation of the predictive model for sentiment analysis.

Wrapper Method

These methods are dependent on the classifiers. Various set of features are used to check the accuracy of a classifier and the combinations which give the best accuracy are selected for the predictive model. In wrapper method, the different combinations of features are prepared, as per the evaluated accuracy and scores are assigned to each combination. These methods give better predictive models but require computational resources in high number. The complex model created through wrapper method becomes difficult to understand. To get rid of the complexity a new approach is evolved which is known as Embedded/Hybrid method.

Embedded Method

In Embedded methods feature selection and classification is done simultaneously.

Table 1. Frequently used feature selection methods in sentiment analysis

Feature Selection		
Filter Method	**Wrapper Method**	**Embedded Method**
Chi-Square test	Forward selection	LASSO
Information Gain	Backward Selection	Elastic net
Correlation coefficient score	Recursive feature elimination algorithm	Ridge Regression
LDA (Linear coefficient analysis)		
ANOVA		

MACHINE LEARNING APPROACH

Machine learning approach for sentiment analysis was firstly utilized by Pang et al. (2002) in classifying movie reviews into positive and negative orientation. In performing sentiment analysis, supervised and unsupervised machine learning techniques are used. Supervised learning employs a large number of human-labelled reviews. When it is hard to identify labels, then unsupervised learning approach is utilized. Further subsections will explain ML techniques in detail.

Supervised learning algorithms which are found to be the best for text categorization are Support vector machine, Naive Bayes, and Maximum Entropy. These three frequently used classifiers are explained in the next section.

Figure 2. Machine learning approach for Sentiment Analysis

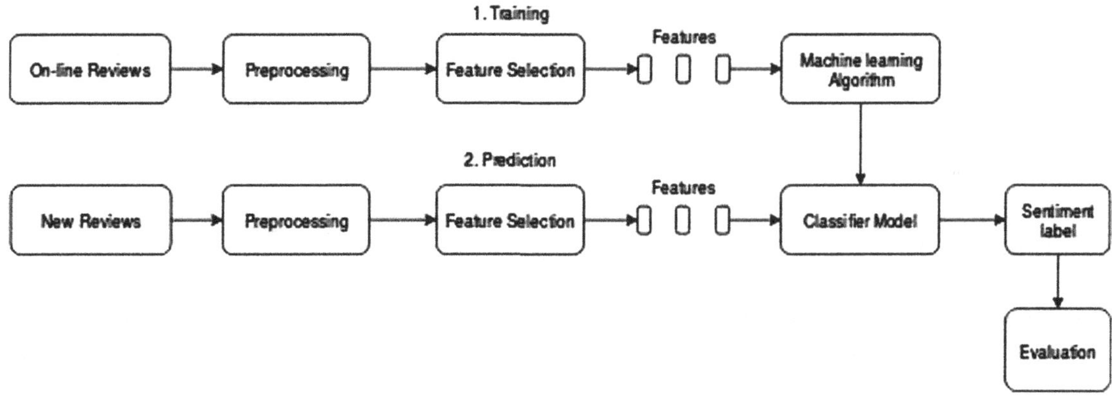

Supervised Learning

Supervised learning approach depends on the pre-defined labelled training documents. Star rating (1-5) of product reviews is used as the training data. Reviews with a score less than three are considered as negative and more than three are labelled as positive. Product reviews with neutral sentiment are identified by examining all reviews with a rating equal to 3.

Naive Bayes

This approach is simple and is frequently used in the area of text categorization. Naive Bayes classifier outperforms a number of machine learning models. The model allocates document "d" to the class:

$$c^* = \arg\max_c P(\frac{c}{d}) \tag{1}$$

Naive Bayes ignores the context of the text, whereas, whole document is considered as bag of words (BOWs).

Bayes theorem is utilized to estimate the probability that given feature set in the document belongs to a particular label defined in the class.

$$P_{NB}\left(\frac{label}{feature}\right) = \frac{P\left(label\right)P\left(\frac{label}{feature}\right)}{P\left(feature\right)} \tag{2}$$

Naive Bayes assumes the document as BOWs. Hence appending equation (2) by considering all independent features 1 to m we get,

$$P_{NB}\left(\frac{label}{featue}\right) = \frac{P\left(label\right)\left(\prod_{i=1}^{m} P\left(\frac{f_i}{label}\right)^{\left(n_i\left(feature\right)\right)}\right)}{P\left(feature\right)} \tag{3}$$

Regardless of the simplicity, independence assumption is not applicable in real world situation. Domingos and Pazzani (1997) showed the optimality of naive bayes on problems with highly dependent features. Kang, Yoo, and Han (2012) proposed an improved naive bayes classifier. They applied this algorithm on restaurant reviews and showed improved precision and recall.

Maximum Entropy (ME)

This approach is also known as a conditional exponential classifier or Maxent classifier. By entropy maximization, it ensures that no bias is introduced into the model. Unlike Naive Bayes this classifier does not assume feature independence. Pang, Lee, and Vaithyanathan (2002, July) utilized ME for sentiment analysis. The accuracy of ME is evaluated over several features such as part of speech (POS), unigram and bigram. Berger et al. (1996) proved the effectiveness of ME in NLP problems. Being a supervised learning technique, labelled feature sets are available. The encoded feature set is converted into vectors. Each feature weight is calculated using encoded feature vector. In prediction phase, the class for feature set is determined by using weight of each feature vector. ME can deal with incomplete information (less training data) and is efficient in acquiring information from natural language text.

Probability "P(c|d)" that the document belongs to particular class is given by following the exponential form:

$$P_{ME}\left(c_j \mid d\right) = \frac{1}{Z\left(d\right)} exp\left(\sum_i \lambda_i f_i\left(d, c_j\right)\right) \tag{4}$$

$P(c_j|d)$ shows class occurrence for the given document.
Z(d) is the normalization function.

λ_i makes sure that observed features matches the expected features in the given set. It is a feature weight parameter. f_i is the function of feature (Kaufmann, 2012) utilized in this approach with a small number of training sample for the detection of parallel sentences in any language pair. This utilization paved a road towards the creation of parallel corpora for new languages.

Support Vector Machine (SVM)

The principle behind SVM is that it linearly classifies the document in the search space using a hyperplane $\vec{w}$. The hyper plane identified during training procedure, not only separates document "d" into different classes but also considers a large margin. It outperforms naive Bayes in the classification of traditional text. The sparse nature of text makes it best suitable for SVM. Chen and Tseng (2011) used SVM for classifying product reviews in term of quality. In this work, information quality framework is utilized to classify digital camera and MP3 reviews in term of quality.

The equation of hyper plane is written as follows:

$$\vec{w} := \sum_i \alpha_i c_i \vec{d_i}, \alpha_i \geqslant 0 \tag{5}$$

Where, $\alpha_i's$ are acquired by solving a dual optimization problem. C_i is the class to which the document belongs. $\vec{d}'s$ which contribute to $\vec{w}$ are called support vectors and for those vectors α_i is greater than zero.

Classification of product reviews on the basis of sentiment orientation is achieved by determining which side of $\vec{w}$ (hyper plane) they are present.

Li and Li (2013) utilized SVM to classify opinion in micro blogs. They proposed a mechanism of numeric summarization of opinions. They found that opinion subjectivity and user integrity is vital for averaging micro blog opinion.

Unsupervised Learning

Unsupervised learning is a domain-independent approach where learning occurs through the grouping of documents/sentences/aspects with similar sentiment orientation. Manual annotation (label) of large domain-independent data is a time consuming task. Unsupervised learning is considered to be cost effective as compared to supervised learning because it is easy to get unlabelled training data. Turney (2002) introduced an unsupervised learning approach to determine sentiment orientation (SO) using point wise mutual information (PMI). This approach consists of three steps:

Step 1: Pattern of POS tags is used to extract a set of two consecutive words (Brill, 1992). POS-tags such as JJ - adjective, NN – nouns, RB - adverbs, VB – verbs, NNP - singular nouns, NNPS - plural proper nouns are utilized to extract two consecutive words which conforms the patterns described by Turney, (2002). Noun (NNP or NNPS) as a third word is not extracted because it does not have any impact on the classification.

Step 2: (Turney, 2002) this step utilizes PMI to estimate SO of extracted phrases:

$$PMI\left(Ext.term_1, Ext.term_2\right) = log_2\left(\frac{P\left(Ext.term_1 \wedge Ext.term_2\right)}{P\left(Ext.term_1\right)P\left(Ext.term2\right)}\right) \tag{6}$$

Here,

$P(Ext.term_1 \wedge Ext.term_2)$ is the probability that Ext.term$_1$ and Ext.term$_2$ co-occur.

$P(Ext.term_1)\,P(Ext.term_2)$ represents that phrases Ext.term$_1$ and Ext.term$_2$ co-occur if they are statistically independent.

In equation 7, sentiment orientation (SO) of the extracted terms is computed by considering their association with positive (Excellent) and negative (Poor) reference words. Reference words "Excellent" and "Poor" resembles the very high and very low star rating respectively.

SO(phrase)=PMI(phrase,"excellent") - PMI(phrase, "poor") (7)

PMI is estimated by querying Alta Vista search engine. Number of "hits" is monitored as each query returned the number of relevant documents. Turney (2002) used Alta Vista search engine because of NEAR operator that constraint the search to document that contain word within ten words of one another in either order.

Let hits (query) are the number of hits returned. Equation 6 and 7 are used to derive the estimation of SO:

$$SO(phrase) = \log_2\left(\frac{hits\left(phrase\ NEAR\,"excellent"\right)\left(hits\left("poor"\right)\right)}{hits\left(phrase\ NEAR\,"poor"\right)\left(hits\left("excellent"\right)\right)}\right) \tag{8}$$

Step 3: Average SO of all extracted phrases is calculated and with the corresponding binary values, text is categorized as positive or negative.

Using the above unsupervised learning approach (Turney, 2002, July) achieved 84% and 66% accuracy in classifying automobile and movie reviews respectively.

LEXICON BASED APPROACH

Another approach to extract sentiment from the text is a lexicon-based approach. Lexicon is a dictionary of sentiment words which also contains sentiment polarity and strength value for each word. Dictionary can be created manually or automatically. In manual lexicon creation, each word with respective items is stored physically in the dictionary. Automatic lexicon creation is done with "seed words" (words with strong sentiment polarity like "excellent", "bad" etc.) and extended list is made using synonym and antonyms of seed words. (Miller, 1995) introduced WordNet to get synonyms and antonyms as it a lexicon database for the English language.

Figure 3. Lexicon-based Approach for Sentiment Analysis

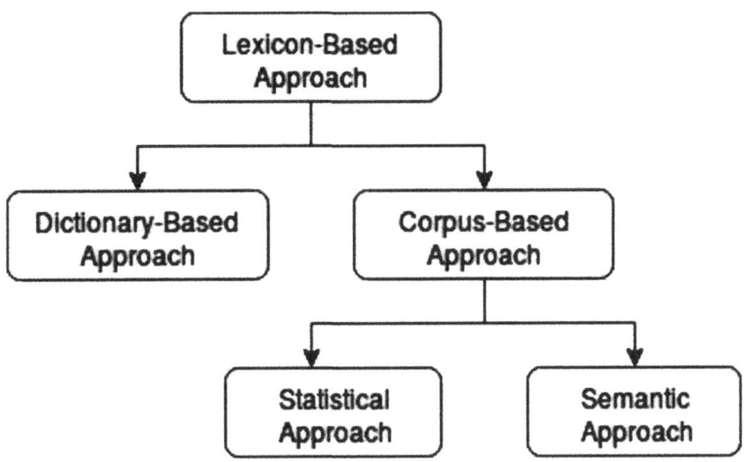

Words with sentiment orientation (positive or negative) are significant for sentiment analysis. Words viz. joy, good and beautiful are positive words; these words assure some quality. Negative words such as loss, weak, terrible and ill convey some undesired nature. In addition to sentiment words, phrases and idioms also have sentiment orientation. For e.g., *"you're genius, you've solved a difficult problem"* is a positive phrase.

Lexicon is a glossary of such words, phrases, etc. with different sentiment orientations. Figure 3 represents the various approaches to create a lexicon for sentiment analysis.

Dictionary-Based Approach

This approach uses synonym and antonym which are present in the dictionary along with the meaning of the word. Necessary words with known sentiment orientation are collected manually from product reviews. In this approach, these words are known as "seed words". List of seed words is expanded by incorporating the glossary viz. WordNet, Thesaurus etc. The process runs iteratively and stops when no further word is found for list extension. Kamps et al. (2004) introduced a more advanced approach to determine the sentiment polarity using WordNet. They evaluated the sentiment polarity of an objective through distanced based approach. The relative distance of seed term (good and bad) is used to assess the SO of term "t".

$$SO\left(t\right) = \frac{\left(d\left(t, bad\right) - d\left(t, good\right)\right)}{d\left(good, bad\right)} \tag{9}$$

term "t" is positive if SO(t)>0 else negative.

Dictionary-based approach does not consider the context and domain to find sentiment. Qui Gang et al. (2010) used this method to find sentiment sentences in a contextual advertisement. They utilized web forum and demonstrated the productivity of proposed approach to ad selection.

The approach is quick, but manual cleanup in-case of errors is an extra effort required. The issue of not considering the context and domain of data is solved in corpus-based approach.

Corpus-Based Approach

This approach uses the method of determining sentiment polarity of new words by utilizing co-occurrence of pattern together with the seed list of sentiment words. This approach uses convention on connectives to recognize more adjective words with sentiment orientation from the vast and diverse corpus. This approach was proposed by Hatzivassiloglou and McKeown (1997). Their idea exploited the set of linguistic rules such as conjunction AND, which means if two sentences are joined using "and" then both have the same polarity. "The new apple phone is robust and its features are incomparable". If "Robust" is known to be positive in the lexicon, "features" is referenced as positive. Similarly, other linguistic constraints such as EITHER-OR, OR, BUT and NEITHER-NOR are utilized. Applying this knowledge to a broad corpus, it is determined whether two conjoined adjectives are of the same polarity or not. Adjective as nodes and interlinks form a graph. Clustering on the graph gives set of words with polarities: Positive and Negative.

Kanayama and Nasukawa (2006) extended corpus approach to Japanese text by utilizing concepts of intra-sentential and inter-sentential. Statistical and Semantic approaches are subcategories of corpus-based approach. Statistical approach namely "latent semantic analysis" is used to produce meaningful patterns in the document.

Pointwise mutual indexing is also utilized in statistical approach for determining the polarity of the new word which co-occurs frequently with the known word.

The other application of statistical approach in sentiment analysis is the identification of manipulated reviews. Hu Nan et al. (2012) worked on Amazon.com reviews and found that 10.3% of product reviews are manipulated. In semantic approach, semantic relationship plays an important role in deriving the sentiment from the review. In this approach, the similarity between words is computed using WordNet. Maks and Vossen (2012) described the application of semantic approach in building lexicon and utilized Dutch WordNet to identify the attitude of the speaker. Zhang et al. (2012) mixed both statistical and semantic approaches to identify the product weakness from online review. They identified the aspect polarity at the sentence level of sentiment analysis and the aspect with high negative scores is marked as unsatisfied. They collaborated statistical approach with PMI to find the weakness of the product and achieved high accuracy.

PERFORMANCE MEASURES

Confusion matrix is used to evaluate the parameters that signifies the performance of the model used for sentiment analysis (Giachanou & Crestani, 2016). It is called so because it is easy to tell whether the classifier is confusing the sentiment orientation (positive and negative) or not. The actual sentiments and predicted sentiment cases are on the X and Y axis respectively.

- **True Positive:** TP is actual positive that has been predicted to be positive.
- **True Negative:** TN is actual negative that has been predicted to be negative.
- **False Positive (Type I Error):** FP is actual negative that has been classified or predicted as positive.
- **False Negative (Type II Error):** FN is actual positive that has been classified or predicted as negative.

Terms in confusion matrix are used for calculating Accuracy, Recall, Precision and Specificity, which ultimately are used for measuring the performance of any algorithm used for sentiment analysis.

Accuracy: It is the proximity between Predicted and actual values.

$$\text{Accuracy} = (TP+TN)/\ (TP+TN+FP+FN) \tag{10}$$

Precision / Positive predictive value (PPV):

$$\text{Precision} = TP/\ (TP+FP) \tag{11}$$

Specificity / False positive rate (FPR):

$$\text{Specificity} = TN/N = TN/\ (TN+FP) \tag{12}$$

Recall / Sensitivity / True positive rate (TPR):

$$\text{Recall} = TP/P = TP/\ (TP+FN) \tag{13}$$

Equation 10 measures the degree of closeness of computationally measured sentiment to the actual sentiment. Equation 11 shows the closeness of sentiment among the predicted sentiments. Equation 12 represents Specificity/FPR which measures the ability to correctly detect the sentiment. Equation 13 measures Recall/sensitivity which is the fraction of relevant sentiments that are successfully predicted.

ONTOLOGY-BASED APPROACH

Ontology is the formal representation of domain knowledge and interrelation of concepts. Ontology organizes information and limits the complexity. OWL or RDF formats are used to store ontology models. Simple queries are used to retrieve information from ontology model. In this section, different ontology creation approaches will be explained. (Kontopoulos et al., 2013) The two approaches that are used to create a domain ontology are Formal concept analysis (FCA) (Wille, 2005) in which a new ontology is generated from scratch and Ontology learning.

1. **Formal Concept Analysis (FCA):** It is a mathematical data analysis theory mainly used in knowledge representation and information management. Obitko et al. (2004) applied FCA to derive ontology. To utilize FCA for the creation of ontology excellent mathematical skills are required. Ontology created using this approach is of appropriate size, design and is domain specific.
2. **Ontology Learning:** This is an automatic ontology creation technique. Ontology is created by extracting concepts and relations from a data set using ontology editors such as Protege, OntoGen, Vitro, Knoodl etc. Kontopoulos et al. (2013) used OntoGen to create ontology from tweets.

After the creation of ontology model following three actions are performed for sentiment analysis from tweets regarding product and aspects:

Ontology utilization: Object-attribute pair is extracted from the tweets. Retrieval is done through JENA which is JAVA API for ontology management (Rajagopal, 2005).

Relevant tweet retrieval: Relevant tweets are extracted by submitting a query in the form of "#object,#attribute". The query is submitted to Twitter4J (Twitter API) which returns the tweets with relevant keywords. Another phase in this step is preprocessing of retrieved tweets that is well explained in the earlier section.

Sentiment Analysis: A web service to tag each retrieved tweet with opinion and sentiment is utilized in this step. Kontopoulos et al. (2013) used OpenDover and obtained excellent results. This step classifies tweets with different sentiment orientations.

Noy and McGuinness (2001) has given a brief insight to build ontology model which has been used by various researchers in several applications. Chatwin (2013) proposed an ontology-based model for sentiment analysis of reviews on the electronic product. In similar manner, Freitas and Vieira (2013) utilized ontology-based approach to analyse viewers inputs on a Portuguese movie.

FUTURE RESEARCH DIRECTIONS

In online product reviews it is hard to identify whether the review is authentic or fake. For better sentiment analysis, the elimination of spam content is necessary. Sentiment detection of the writer is important to get the accurate opinion from the online review. It ultimately tells the reputation of the writer. Identification of duplicates, sentiment detection of writer/reviewer from outliners by knowing the reputation of the content generator is still a challenging task in sentiment analysis.

CONCLUSION

Sentiment analysis is an approach to get the deep understanding of the text. Web 2.0 has provided various platforms where people eagerly express themselves by posting comments, reviews, posts, etc. toward a product, people, organization and other entities. Extracting sentiment from product reviews makes it easy for the brand marketing team to reach its customers who need extra care and hence, benefits the business.

The chapter discussed the approaches to sentiment analysis on product reviews and highlighted the processes involved in Sentiment analysis. The processes such as preprocessing, feature extraction and feature selection were explained. The chapter also provided details regarding Tokenization, stop word removal, stemming and feature selection which are the sub-processes in preprocessing. The chapter also provides details about the analysis of non-redundant data using several approaches such as Machine learning based approach and Ontology-based approach. The Machine learning based approaches namely supervised, unsupervised learning and lexicon based approaches were elaborated. The application of ontology-based approach in sentiment analysis was discussed. The chapter concludes by highlighting the challenges involved in Sentiment Analysis.

REFERENCES

Berger, A. L., Pietra, V. J. D., & Pietra, S. A. D. (1996). A maximum entropy approach to natural language processing. *Computational Linguistics*, *22*(1), 39–71.

Brill, E. (1992, February). A simple rule-based part of speech tagger. In *Proceedings of the workshop on Speech and Natural Language* (pp. 112-116). Association for Computational Linguistics. 10.3115/1075527.1075553

Chen, C. C., & Tseng, Y. D. (2011). Quality evaluation of product reviews using an information quality framework. *Decision Support Systems*, *50*(4), 755–768. doi:10.1016/j.dss.2010.08.023

Domingos, P., & Pazzani, M. (1997). On the optimality of the simple Bayesian classifier under zero-one loss. *Machine Learning*, *29*(2), 103–130. doi:10.1023/A:1007413511361

Freitas, L. A., & Vieira, R. (2013, May). Ontology based feature level opinion mining for portuguese reviews. In *Proceedings of the 22nd International Conference on World Wide Web* (pp. 367-370). ACM. 10.1145/2487788.2487944

Giachanou, A., & Crestani, F. (2016). Like it or not: A survey of twitter sentiment analysis methods. *ACM Computing Surveys*, *49*(2), 28. doi:10.1145/2938640

Hatzivassiloglou, V., & McKeown, K. R. (1997, July). Predicting the semantic orientation of adjectives. In *Proceedings of the eighth conference on European chapter of the Association for Computational Linguistics* (pp. 174-181). Association for Computational Linguistics. 10.3115/979617.979640

Hu, N., Bose, I., Koh, N. S., & Liu, L. (2012). Manipulation of online reviews: An analysis of ratings, readability, and sentiments. *Decision Support Systems*, *52*(3), 674–684. doi:10.1016/j.dss.2011.11.002

Kamps, J., Marx, M., Mokken, R. J., & De Rijke, M. (2004, May). *Using WordNet to Measure Semantic Orientations of Adjectives* (Vol. 4). LREC.

Kanayama, H., & Nasukawa, T. (2006, July). Fully automatic lexicon expansion for domain-oriented sentiment analysis. In *Proceedings of the 2006 conference on empirical methods in natural language processing* (pp. 355-363). Association for Computational Linguistics. 10.3115/1610075.1610125

Kang, H., Yoo, S. J., & Han, D. (2012). Senti-lexicon and improved Naïve Bayes algorithms for sentiment analysis of restaurant reviews. *Expert Systems with Applications*, *39*(5), 6000–6010. doi:10.1016/j.eswa.2011.11.107

Kaufmann, M. (2012, December). JMaxAlign: A Maximum Entropy Parallel Sentence Alignment Tool. In *COLING* (pp. 277–288). Demos.

Kontopoulos, E., Berberidis, C., Dergiades, T., & Bassiliades, N. (2013). Ontology-based sentiment analysis of twitter posts. *Expert Systems with Applications*, *40*(10), 4065–4074. doi:10.1016/j.eswa.2013.01.001

Li, Y. M., & Li, T. Y. (2013). Deriving market intelligence from microblogs. *Decision Support Systems*, *55*(1), 206–217. doi:10.1016/j.dss.2013.01.023

Maks, I., & Vossen, P. (2012). A lexicon model for deep sentiment analysis and opinion mining applications. *Decision Support Systems*, *53*(4), 680–688. doi:10.1016/j.dss.2012.05.025

Medhat, W., Hassan, A., & Korashy, H. (2014). Sentiment analysis algorithms and applications: A survey. *Ain Shams Engineering Journal*, *5*(4), 1093–1113. doi:10.1016/j.asej.2014.04.011

Miller, G. A. (1995). WordNet: A lexical database for English. *Communications of the ACM*, *38*(11), 39–41. doi:10.1145/219717.219748

Noy, N. F., & McGuinness, D. L. (2001). *Ontology development 101: A guide to creating your first ontology*. Academic Press.

Obitko, M., Snasel, V., Smid, J., & Snasel, V. (2004, September). Ontology Design with Formal Concept Analysis. CLA, 128(3), 1377-1390.

Pang, B., Lee, L., & Vaithyanathan, S. (2002, July). Thumbs up?: sentiment classification using machine learning techniques. In *Proceedings of the ACL-02 conference on Empirical methods in natural language processing-Volume 10* (pp. 79-86). Association for Computational Linguistics. 10.3115/1118693.1118704

Porter, M. F. (1980). An algorithm for suffix stripping. *Program*, *14*(3), 130–137. doi:10.1108/eb046814

Qiu, G., He, X., Zhang, F., Shi, Y., Bu, J., & Chen, C. (2010). DASA: Dissatisfaction-oriented advertising based on sentiment analysis. *Expert Systems with Applications*, *37*(9), 6182–6191. doi:10.1016/j.eswa.2010.02.109

Rajagopal, H. (2005). JENA: A Java API for ontology management. *IBM Corporation, Colorado Software Summit*, 23-28.

Rosenthal, S., Farra, N., & Nakov, P. (2017). SemEval-2017 task 4: Sentiment analysis in Twitter. *Proceedings of the 11th International Workshop on Semantic Evaluation (SemEval-2017)*, 502-518. 10.18653/v1/S17-2088

Sam, K. M., & Chatwin, C. R. (2013). Ontology-based sentiment analysis model of customer reviews for electronic products. *International Journal of e-Education, e-Business, e-Management Learning*, *3*(6), 477.

Turney, P. D. (2002, July). Thumbs up or thumbs down?: semantic orientation applied to unsupervised classification of reviews. In *Proceedings of the 40th annual meeting on association for computational linguistics* (pp. 417-424). Association for Computational Linguistics.

Wille, R. (2005). Formal concept analysis as mathematical theory of concepts and concept hierarchies. *Formal Concept Analysis, 3626*, 1-33.

Zhang, W., Xu, H., & Wan, W. (2012). Weakness Finder: Find product weakness from Chinese reviews by using aspects based sentiment analysis. *Expert Systems with Applications*, *39*(11), 10283–10291. doi:10.1016/j.eswa.2012.02.166

This research was previously published in Sentiment Analysis and Knowledge Discovery in Contemporary Business; pages 15-30, copyright year 2019 by Business Science Reference (an imprint of IGI Global).

Chapter 12
Classification Approach for Sentiment Analysis Using Machine Learning

Satyen M. Parikh
Ganpat University, India

Mitali K. Shah
Ganpat University, India

ABSTRACT

A utilization of the computational semantics is known as natural language processing or NLP. Any opinion through attitude, feelings, and thoughts can be identified as sentiment. The overview of people against specific events, brand, things, or association can be recognized through sentiment analysis. Positive, negative, and neutral are each of the premises that can be grouped into three separate categories. Twitter, the most commonly used microblogging tool, is used to gather information for research. Tweepy is used to access Twitter's source of information. Python language is used to execute the classification algorithm on the information collected. Two measures are applied in sentiment analysis, namely feature extraction and classification. Using n-gram modeling methodology, the feature is extracted. Through a supervised machine learning algorithm, the sentiment is graded as positive, negative, and neutral. Support vector machine (SVM) and k-nearest neighbor (KNN) classification models are used and demonstrated both comparisons.

INTRODUCTION

Sentiment Analysis

The word opinion mining is utilized in many different applications for sentiment analysis. Its purpose is to check the opinion of the people on the product's benefits and product's characteristics (features). Essentially, an evaluation of opinion is a kind of common approach used to determine whether or not

DOI: 10.4018/978-1-6684-6303-1.ch012

people are interested in the product. The emotions or feelings of people are expressed textually. These aspects are obtained from different sites or mobile applications. (Duygulu et al., 2002)

Analysis of sentiment is used to keep in touch or show the feelings of people. People give product's positive and negative opinion for the services of item. When making any choice for purchase the product, these opinions are very valuable for the customer (Zhang et al., 2013). It is very difficult to correctly interpret the right view in the sense of large textual data set and unstructured data sets. To identify the characteristics of an unstructured dataset, it is essential to structure a productive technique (Yu et al., 2010).

Preprocessing, feature extraction and classification are three main parts and analysis methods for sentiment analysis (Xu et al., 2013). Some association only works with positive and negative text. They skip the neutral text recognition. Such texts use the binary classification limits. Several researchers introduce polarity problems for perform three classes (Ren & Wu, 2013). For entropy and SVM classifiers, the neutral classes, presentation etc. are very essential. This improves the accuracy of overall classification. These principles ought to be considered by the neutral classes for the execution. The first algorithm understands the concept of neutral language and extracts people's remaining opinions. In simply single phase, this algorithm completes the three-level classification (Poria et al., 2013).

In every class, in the next methodology, the probability and distribution are calculated (Garcia-Moya et al., 2013). When the data is the most neutral with the variance between positive and negative outcomes, it becomes more difficult to implement this methodology (Cheng et al., 2013). Sentiment analysis is used in some various ways. It is useful for marketers to measure the credibility and accomplishment of some new product dispatch and to see what edition of the product is in demand and show the new product's famous highlights (Hai et al., 2013)

The below are some of the key features of tweets:

- Message Length
- Writing technique
- Availability
- Topics
- Real time

Benefits of Using Sentimental Analysis

Sentiment analysis has many benefits given to different business and organization. It helps and gives their business valuable insights that how people feel about their service and brand. It will allow user to identify potential of their products to create more influence on social media. Hence, it will be used to identify negative threads that are emerging online regarding your business, thereby allowing you to be practical in dealing with it more quickly. Some of the benefits are as follow:

- Marketing strategy
- Enlarge product quality
- Improve customer service
- Crisis management

Challenges of Sentimental Analysis

In case of sentiments analysis there are several challenges faced by user in order to tackle their issues, related to their daily life. Natural language processing and text analysis techniques are used to identify and extract the subjective information available in the applied in the practice of sentiment analysis. These challenges become obstacles in analyzing the accurate meaning of sentiments and detecting the suitable sentiment polarity.

Some challenges are as follow:

- Speaker's emotional state
- Multiple thoughts
- Fake Opinion
- Challenge in applying
- Language problem

SENTIMENT ANALYSIS TECHNIQUES

There are two main techniques for sentiment analysis: machine learning based, and lexicon based. Few research studies have also combined these two methods and gain relatively better performance.

1. **Lexicon Based Approach:** opinion lexicon for sentiment classification is based on the insight that the polarity of a piece of text can be obtained on the grounds of the words which compose it. This approach is of two types: positive or negative opinions. Positive opinion is used to show the desired stage and negative stage is used to show undesired stage. Opinion lexicon is also known as opinion phrases or idioms.(Hussein, 2018)
   a. **Dictionary Based Approach:** The resources used are lexicographical, initial method is to collect the seeds of the sentiment words and their orientation to find their antonyms and synonyms to expand their set. When no more words left this iteration stops. This approach is unable to extract opinions with domain specific orientations which are counted as its disadvantage.
   b. **Corpus-Based Approach:** It can help to find domain specific opinion words and their orientation if a corpus from only the specific domain is used in the discovery process. It resolves the problem of dictionary-based approach and also explores the idea of intra-sentential and inter-sentential sentiment. Despite showing domain dependent words it showed the same word having different contexts even in the same domain.
2. **Machine Learning Approach**: Machine learning approach has been used to solve the sentence classifications problems that totally based on the algorithms. It trains a text classifier on a human labeled training dataset. Two approaches were used that is supervised leaning approach and unsupervised learning approach. Bulk of labeled training document is known as supervised learning and further it is of two types: Naïve Baye's algorithm and Maximum Entropy Classifier. (Astya, 2017)
   a. **Naïve Baye's Algorithm:** Naive Baye's provides good result in spite of having low Naïve Baye's Classification probability. It is a supervised machine learning approach. It is totally based on Baye's Theorem.

b. **Maximum Entropy Algorithm:** It is widely used in the field of computer vision for the prediction, using machine learning technique which is known as multinomial logic model. The advantage of using this algorithm is that, it will provide us with extra semantic, syntactic feature and very much flexible in use.

c. **SVM Classifier:** This classifier has enormous edge for classification. Hyper plane technique is used to separates the tweets using comparison difference between the tweet and hyper plane. The discriminative function used by SVM classifier is defined as:

$$g(X) = wT\varphi(X) + b \quad (1)$$

In the above given equation (1), feature vector is denoted by "X", weight vector denoted by "w" and bias vector is "b". Linear kernel is used for classification as it maintains the gap between two classes.

TYPES

Sentiment analysis is a new field of research born in Natural Language Processing (NLP), aiming at detecting subjectivity in text and/or extracting and classifying opinions and sentiments. Sentiment analysis studies people's sentiments, opinions, attitudes, evaluations, appraisals and emotions towards services, products, individuals, organizations, issues, topics events and their attributes. In sentiment analysis text is classified according to the following different criteria:

- the polarity of the sentiment expressed (into positive, negative, and neutral);
- the polarity of the outcome (e.g. improvement versus death in medical texts)
- agree or disagree with a topic (e.g. political debates)
- good or bad news;
- support or opposition;
- pros and cons

APPLICATION

When consumers have to make a decision or a choice regarding a product, important information is the reputation of that product, which is derived from the opinion of others. Sentiment analysis can reveal what other people think about a product. The first application of sentiment analysis is thus giving indication and recommendation in the choice of products according to the wisdom of the crowd. When you choose a product, you are generally attracted to certain specific aspects of the product. A single global rating could be deceiving. Sentiment analysis can regroup the opinions of the reviewers and estimate ratings on certain aspects of the product.

Another utility of sentiment analysis is for companies that want to know the opinion of customers on their products. They can then improve the aspects that the customers found unsatisfying. Sentiment analysis can also determine which aspects are more important for the customers.

Finally, sentiment analysis has been proposed as a component of other technologies. One idea is to improve information mining in text analysis by excluding the most subjective section of a document or to automatically propose internet ads for products that fit the viewer's opinion (and removing the others). Knowing what people think gives numerous possibilities in the Human/Machine interface domain. Sentiment analysis for determining the opinion of a customer on a product (and consequently the reputation of the product) is the main focus of this paper. In the following section, we will discuss solutions that allow determining the expressed opinion on products.

STEPS FOR THE SENTIMENT ANALYSIS

- Data Collection
- Data Preparation
- Develop Model
- Train and Update

VARIOUS FACES OF SENTIMENT ANALYSIS

- Data Extraction
- Data Pre-processing
- Feature Extraction
- Sentiment Classification

WHY MACHING LEARNING NEEDS?

- Nearly 80% of the world's digital data is unstructured, and data obtained from social media sources is no exception to that. Since the information is not organized in any predefined way, it's difficult to sort and analyze. Fortunately, thanks to the developments in Machine Learning and NLP, it is now possible to create models that learn from examples and can be used to process and organize text data.
- Twitter sentiment analysis systems allow you to sort large sets of tweets and detect the polarity of each statement automatically. And the best part, it's fast and simple, saving times valuable hours and allowing them to focus on tasks where they can make a bigger impact. By training a machine learning model to perform sentiment analysis on Twitter, you can set the parameters to analyze all your data and obtain more consistent and accurate results.

RESEARCH GAP

Following are the various research gap of this study:-

Figure 1. Data Extraction
(Source: ICACSE-2019, p. 92)

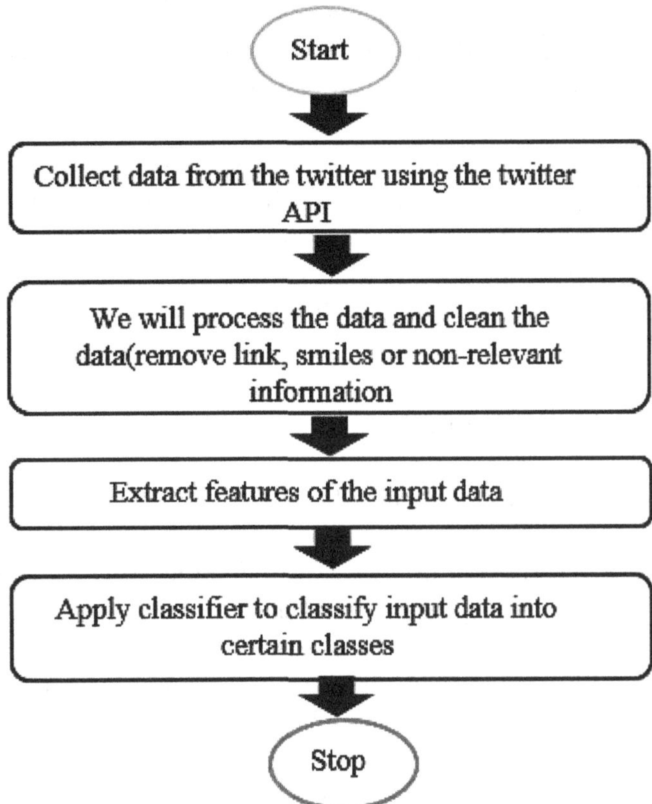

- The sentiment analysis is the type of approach which is applied to analysis the sentiments. In the previous research, the technique of lexical analysis is applied for the sentiment analysis. The techniques which are designed previously are proposed on the small size data, when the size of the data gets increase parametric value gets reduced at steady rate. The accuracy parametric value also describes other values like precision, recall and f-measure which also get affected.
- The techniques of classification are applied for the sentiment analysis. The techniques of classification can be applied without the feature extraction due to which it gives less accuracy. The sentiment analysis approaches need to handle large quantity of historical information to train the model. While handling such large amount of data, the execution time is increased which affects performance
- In the previous years, much work is done on the various types of techniques for the feature extraction and classification which are too complex, it directly increase the execution of the model. The sentiment analysis can be done using the lexical analysis phase; the technique of lexical analysis can be done using the priority phases. The threshold value can assign by taking average of the priority values which affect efficiency of the proposed model. The approach is required which have the both techniques of feature extraction and the classification when combined it improve accuracy of classification

PROBLEM STATEMENT

Sentiment analysis is a way to study the opinion of the users towards an entity, like products, services, brands, movies, events, and so on. Sentiment analysis is applied on the comments posted by users on micro blogging sites, social networking websites, online user review portals etc. In this method, the features of the input data are extracted using pattern matching algorithm and the extracted features are classified using classification techniques. In the existing method, N-gram technique is used for feature extraction and SVM classifier is used for feature classification. In this work two issues may arise. N-gram algorithm extracts the color features from the posts and to improve its efficiency textual features also need to be analyzed. The second issue is when classification is done using SVM classifier, the complexity increases which increase the execution time.

SIGNIFICANCE OF PURPOSE WORK

'Sentiment' literally means 'Emotions' of an individual. Sentiment analysis, also known as opinion mining, is a type of data mining that refers to the analysis of data obtained from micro blogging sites, social media updates, online news reports, user reviews etc., in order to study the sentiments of the people towards an event, organization, product, brand, person etc.

With the expansion of users posting their viewpoints in micro blogging sites, sentiment analysis of the posted texts has turned into a happening field of research, as it serves as a potential source for studying the opinions held by the users towards an entity.

In this work, sentiment classification is done into three categories, namely positive, negative and neutral. The data used for analysis has been taken from twitter, it being the most popular micro blogging site. The source data has been extracted from twitter using python's Tweepy. N-gram modeling technique is used for feature extraction and the supervised machine learning algorithm k-nearest neighbor is used for sentiment classification into positive, negative and neutral classes. The implementation of the proposed approach has been done in python language.

LITERATURE REVIEW

Endang wahyu pamungkas, et.Al (2016) performed lexicon-based sentiment analysis of Indonesian language (Pamungkas et al., 2016). The classification of sentiment data was carried out in three sentiments such as positive, negative, and neutral. The tested outcomes demonstrated that the recommended approach achieved classification accuracy of 0.68. In general, the recommended approach achieved good results in sentiment classification. This work detected some problems as well. It was possible to use these issues as a base to carry out more research work. Initially, a non-standard language was detected in the dataset. The next issue was related to the dissatisfaction of expectation event. The very last issue was related to vagueness.

Shahnawaz, et.Al, (2017) presented that sentiment analysis is the process to identify the opinion or feelings expressed in the opinioned data, in order to find the attitude of writer towards the particular topic whether it is positive, negative or neutral. It provides idea to the customer to identify the product or service is satisfactory or not before the customer buys it. Public opinions on different types of social media are the major concern of the scientific communities and business world to gather and extract public views. Inadequacy accuracy, inability to perform well in different domain and performance are the main issues in the current techniques. Author concluded, by using semi-supervised and unsupervised learning based models, it will be easy minimize lack of labeled data if sufficient amount of unlabeled data is available. (Astya, 2017)

Pulkit garg, et.Al, (2017) as surveyed that social media has becoming a medium for online sharing by the increase of more number of people coming online. In this paper, we study post- terror attack tweets by extracting it from twitter. The flow data posted on twitter is used to study factors like last retweet, number of retweets and number of favorites. Maximum number of retweets indicates maximum reach. It creates widespread reaction on the social media. Governments are concentrating on digitalizing the whole nation. Due to increase in number of people, huge data is generated. Author discussed the Uri terror attacks that show more negative tweets tend to survive as compare to positive tweets, although their amount is low. It will lead to public unrest if people start targeting a community and provide negative information. Misleading information, the trends of retweets and number of favorites are the future scope to study its flow and survival (Garg et al., 2017).

Ana valdivia et.Al, (2017) researchers working in the field of natural language processing and text mining received a lot of attention on sentiment analysis. To operate all domains there was lack of annotated data being used that hampered the accuracy of sentiment analysis. The issue is geared up after attempting many attempts. In this paper, authors' provided techniques and systematic literature review on cross-domain sentiment analysis. According to author there was no perfect solution hence to solve the problems of cross domain sentiment analysis different techniques, methods and approaches had been used in order to develop more accurate data in near future. The fuzzy majority based on aggregating polarity for several sentiment analyses the use of induced ordered weighted is proposed. Author's main focused on removing those neutral reviews labeled by accord of collections (Valdivia et al., 2017).

Wei zhao, ziyu guan et.Al, (2017) to ease new buyers in making good decisions products review are necessary. A new technique has been introduced for opinion mining which help us to determine the positive and negative of a post or review. For solving sentiment classification problems deep learning has effective means and without using human efforts a neutral network represents. Success of deep learning solely depends on the large-scale training data. In this paper, they had given a review on different sentiment classification using purposed deep learning framework that employs commonly existing rating. Adding a classification layer and learning a high level representation are the two steps consists in purposed framework. In order to achieve supervised fine tunings a level sentences are used and on the top of embedding layer a classification layer is added on the other hand in the first step rating information is used to capture the general sentiment distribution. The long short memory and conventional feature extractors are used for low level network structure that helps in modeling review sentences. The Amazon data sets have been used that contained 1.1 weakly review sentences and 11,754 labeled review sentences. To check the proposed framework different experiments have been performed that show its superiority over baselines (Zhao, 2017)

Kulkarni, D. S., Et.Al, (2018) presented sentiment analysis is broadly utilized in a large portion of real time applications. The exact recognizable proof of content features collected from the unstructured textual information is significant research challenge. A few strategies which present the extraction of sentiment-based component in dataset mining patterns are utilized by single survey corpus and avoid by the non-trivial uniqueness in the word of distributional attributes of sentiment feature. Such techniques are not comfortable to predict the people feedback effectively. Sentiment analysis is an alternate strategy directly from mining classification to advance sentiment analysis. To start with, traditional procedures were examined for taking care of the issue of sentiment analysis. At that point they examined the ongoing technique for sentiment features, classification and information recovery. They likewise examined the near investigation among every one of these methods. At last, they watched and saw the present research issues of interest based on expanded study of ongoing techniques. From their investigation, they can reason that sentiment analysis is an attraction in numerous researchers. (Kulkarni & Rodd, 2018).

Soonh Taj, et.al (2019) proposed a lexicon-based approach for sentiment analysis of news articles. It was observed that categories of business and sports had more positive articles, whereas entertainment and tech had a majority of negative articles. The experiments have been performed on BBC news dataset, which expresses the applicability and validation of the adopted approach. Future work in this regard will be based on sentiment analysis of news using various machine learning approaches with the development of an online application from where users can read news of their interests. Also, based on sentiment analysis methods, readers can customize their news feed. (Taj et al., 2019)

Annet John, et.al (2019) studied that the lexicon based approaches plays an active role regarding the aforementioned aspects. Here handling of contextual polarity of text was the major focus wherein which the prior polarity of the term expressed in the lexicon may be different from the polarity expressed in the text. The hybrid lexicon eliminates such hurdles. Not all problems are handled by the usage of hybrid lexicon; certain other problems such as negation, emoticons and modifiers adversely affect the sentiment score of textual data. Experimental results give evidence in the performance improvement of the proposed system in terms of accuracy, recall and precision when compared with the existing systems. (John et al., 2019)

Farkhund Iqbal, et.al (2019) proposed a novel Genetic Algorithm (GA) based feature reduction technique. By using this hybrid approach, it was possible to reduce the feature-set size by up to 42% without compromising the accuracy. Furthermore, our sentiment analysis framework was evaluated on other metrics including precision, recall, F-measure, and feature size. In order to demonstrate the efficacy of GA based designs, a novel cross-disciplinary area of geopolitics was also proposed as a case study application for our sentiment analysis framework. The experiment results have shown to accurately measure public sentiments and views regarding various topics such as terrorism, global conflicts, social issues etc. The applicability of proposed work was evaluated in various areas including security and surveillance, law-and-order, and public administration.(Iqbal et al., 2019)

Korovkinas, et.al, (2019) submitted that ascent of social networks and spread of Internet-related smart gadgets contraptions was trailed by explosion in data available for assortment and making, offering certified mechanical and computational troubles together with new alluring results in research, appointment and utilization of new and existing data science and machine learning procedures. Author closed; by propose a hybrid procedure to enhance SVM characterization accuracy utilizing training data set and hyper parameter tuning. The proposed system uses clustering to select training data and tuning parameters to enhance the viability of the classifier. The paper reports that advance results have been achieved using this proposed method in all analysis compared to previous results showing the work of the technique (Korovkinas et al., 2019).

Priyanka tyagi, et.Al, (2019) presented that any sentiment of a people through which the emotions, attitude and thoughts can be communicated is known as opinion. The sorts of information examination which is accomplished from the news reports, client surveys, social media updates or micro blogging sites are called sentiment analysis which is otherwise called opinion mining. The surveys of people towards specific occasions, brands, item or organization can be known through sentiment analysis. The reactions of overall population are gathered and improvised by specialists to perform evaluation. The fame of sentiment analysis is developing today since the quantities of perspectives being shared by public on the micro blogging sites are additionally expanding. Every one of the opinions can be ordered into three distinct classifications called positive, negative and neutral. Twitter, being the most well-known micro blogging web page, is utilized to gather the information to perform examination. Tweepy is utilized to extract the source information from twitter. Python language is utilized in this exploration to execute the algorithm on the gathered information. Author concluded using n-gram modeling method the features are to be extracted. The opinion is ordered among positive, negative and neutral utilizing a supervised learning algorithm known as k-nearest neighbor. (Tyagi et al., 2019)

Mondher bouazizi et.Al,(2019) presented that most of the work related to sentiment analysis of texts focuses on the binary and ternary classification of these data, the task of multi-class classification has received less attention. Multi-class classification has always been a challenging task given the complexity of natural languages and the difficulty of understanding and mathematically "quantifying" how humans express their feelings. In that work, they study the task of multi-class classification of online posts of twitter users, and show how far it is possible to go with the classification, and the limitations and difficulties of that task. Nonetheless, they propose a novel model to represent the different sentiments and show how this model helps to understand how sentiments are related. The model is then used to analyze the challenges that multi-class classification presents and to highlight possible future enhancements to multi-class classification accuracy. (Bouazizi et al., 2019)

MeghaRathi, et.al (2018) studied that previously, researchers were using existing machine learning techniques for sentiment analysis but the results showed that existing machine learning techniques were not providing better results of sentiment classification. In order to improve classification results in the domain of sentiment analysis, this research used ensemble machine learning techniques for increasing the efficiency and reliability of proposed approach. For the same, Support Vector Machine was merged with Decision Tree and experimental results prove that our proposed approach is providing better classification results in terms of f-measure and accuracy in contrast to individual classifiers. (Rathi et al., 2018)

Mohammed H. Abd El-Jawad, et.al (2018) compared the performance of different machine learning and deep learning algorithms, in addition to introducing a new hybrid system that uses text mining and neural networks for sentiment classification. The dataset used in this work contains more than 1 million tweets collected in five domains. The system was trained using 75% of the dataset and was tested using the remaining 25%. The results show a maximum accuracy rate of 83.7%, which shows the efficiency of the hybrid learning approach used by the system over the standard supervised approaches. (El-Jawad et al., 2018)

PROPOSED METHODOLOGY

Twitter data sentiment analysis is the main purpose of this research work. In the existing framework, a classification model called SVM is used to classify input data into seven classes using the SANTA Tool. The research suggested substitutes the system of classification SVM with the model of classification KNN. This model of classification classifies seven classes of input data. On the basis of accuracy, the performance analysis of both approaches is carried out.

SVM Classifier for Sentiment Analysis

To achieve the prime objective of the classification, SVMs was introduced and it was utilized in that direction, down time use case of SVMs was extended for reference learning and regression. Mainly SVMs algorithm is working on the binary classifier style same as how computer interpret the data. SVMs classifier achieves learned function in terms of positive or negative output (Juneja & Ojha, 2017). Same way by making use of multiple binary classifiers and as core pair-wise coupling, multiclass classification can be implemented. The mapping is made from input space to feature space by SVM to support the constraints related to non-linear classification.

The kernel trick of the mapping function is utilized by preventing accurate formulation. This generates the curse of dimensionality. Such approach makes the linear classification in new space equal to the non-linear classification in original space. With Input vector of SVMs classifier mapping is done.

For instance, there are N training data points $\{(x_1,y_1), (x_2,y_2) \ldots (x_N,y_N)\}$. Here, $x_i \in R^d$ and $y_i \in \{+1, -1\}$. Equation (1) shows the issue of identifying a maximum margin that separates the hyperplane as:

$$\min_{w,b} \frac{1}{2} w^T w \; subject\; to\; y_i \left(w^T x_i - b\right) \geq i = 1, \ldots N$$

In general, this is a convex quadratic programming problem. Lagrange multipliers α is introduced to achieve Wolfe dual in the given equation:

$$maximize_{\alpha} \mathcal{L}_D \equiv \sum_{i=1}^{N} \alpha_i - \frac{1}{2} \sum_{i,j} \alpha_i \alpha_j y_i y_j x_i . x_j \tag{1}$$

Subject to

$$\alpha \geq 0, \sum_i \alpha_i y_i = 0 \,.$$

Following is the equation (2) of providing primary solution:

$$w = \sum_{i=1}^{N} \alpha_i y_i x_i \tag{2}$$

KNN Classifier for Sentiment Analysis

K Nearest Neighbor (KNN) comes under a non-parametric classifier. In many aspects this algorithm seems quite simple and effectual. Because of its effectiveness and competent outcomes, KNN is one of most common neighborhood classifiers in pattern recognition. The feature of this classifier can be used easily. There are number of application where such algorithm is used. As example consider pattern recognition, machine learning, text categorization, data mining, object recognition etc. (Hassan et al.,

2017). as each algorithm has its own advantages and limitation, KNN also has limitation when It comes to memory requirement and time complexity due to dependency on each instance in training set. One advance feature of using this algorithm is that it resolves the issue if clustering. With compare to another complex algorithm, KNN is bit easy to understand and simple to implement. It's kind of unsupervised learning algorithm. Fixed number of simple clusters is used and also same can be efficiently classified by given data earlier.

This technique can be considered as on the distance function as these algorithms can be implemented During the non-existence labeled data. In the same range this technique normalized the overall features. As this is the This is a conventional non-parametric classification model, K-nearest neighbor classification model computes the optimum performance of the best values of k. This technique assigns this pattern within the k nearest patterns (Astya, 2017). based on individual attribute by combining local distance functions, A global distance function can be computed. The easiest method is to add the values as described by the given equation:

$$dist\left(x,q\right)=\sum_{i=1}^{N} dist_{A_i}\left(x.A_i,q.A_i\right). \tag{3}$$

The global distance is identified as the weighted sum of local distances. For calculating the overall distance, there are different levels of importance provided by weight w_i. The values amongst zero and one are sometimes the weight of values. A completely irrelevant attribute might be generated by the weight of zero. Therefore, the modified form of equation (3) can be inscribed as:

$$dist\left(x,q\right)=\sum_{i=1}^{N} w_i \times dist_{A_i}\left(x.A_i,q.A_i\right). \tag{4}$$

There is a common weighted average which is given as in equation (5):

$$dist\left(x,q\right)=\frac{\sum_{i=1}^{N} w_i \times dist_{A_i}\left(x.A_i,q.A_i\right)}{\sum_{i=1}^{n} w_i}. \tag{5}$$

FACILITIES REQUIRED FOR PURPOSE WORK

Following are the various software and hardware requirements:-

1. Hardware Requirements
    a. Dual core Processor
    b. 2 GB RAM
2. Software Requirements
    a. Anaconda
    b. Microsoft Word

Figure 2. Proposed research plan

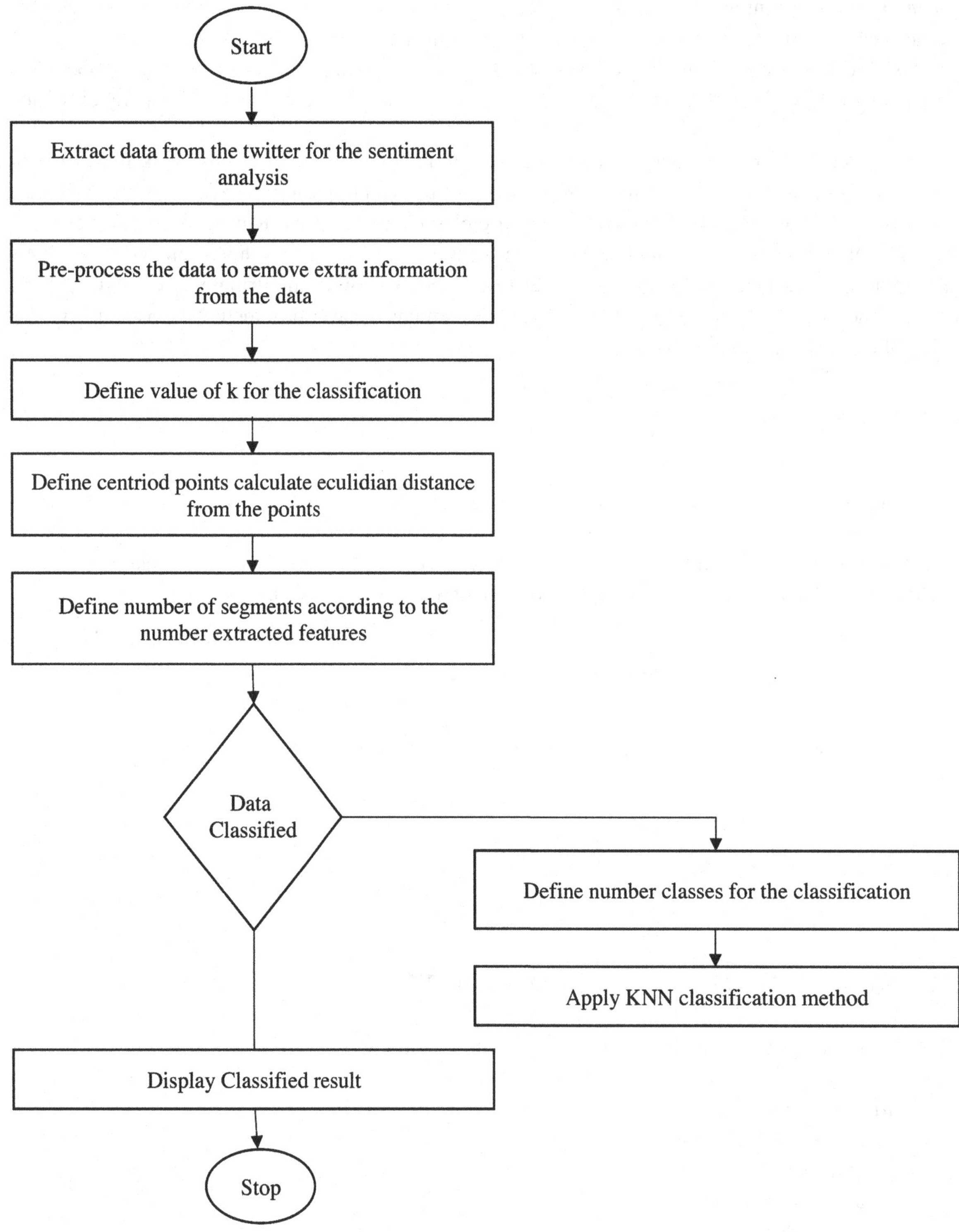

PROPOSED RESEARCH PLAN

This research aims at sentiment analysis of text, namely tweets, taken from Twitter. The complete approach for sentiment analysis consists of the following steps:

Step 1: Data Extraction: The input data set consists of real time tweets that have been extracted from Twitter using Tweepy.
Step 2: Data Pre-processing: In the pre-processing phase, the input data set is cleaned and transformed into a form suitable for feature extraction.
Step 3: Feature Extraction: The pre-processed data is fed as input to the feature extraction algorithm. In this step weights are assigned to the keywords thus preparing them for classification. In this paper N-Gram modeling technique has been used for designing the feature extraction algorithm.
Step 4: Sentiment Classification: In based on their polarity. In this work, machine learning technique k-nearest neighbor classifier has been used for classification into positive, negative and neutral classes.

RESULT AND DISCUSSION

Python is a language of programming at the highest level. This tool includes semantics that are dynamic. Within the data structures, this language is created. Thanks to the incorporation of data structures and adaptive typing and linking, the Rapid Application Development can effectively use this tool. In this method, scripting interrelates the previously available components. Therefore, since this language is incredibly simple and easy to understand, it can easily be read. This also minimizes the program's maintenance cost.

The classification parameters, such as precision, recall and f-measure, are calculated as shown in figure 3. The precision recall and f-measure is calculated as positive, negative for each class. That parameter's values are plotted as a figure.

The figure4 shows the examination of WDE-LSTM and KNN as far as accuracy. KNN classification model shows preferred accuracy over WDE-LSTM for sentiment examination.

The figure 5 shows the examination of WDE-LSTM and KNN regarding precision, recall. The estimations of the precision and recall are appeared in the above figure.

Figure 6 demonstrates the f-measure relation between WDE-LSTM and KNN. KNN classification system has a higher f scale of sentiment analysis than WDE-LSTM

Figure 3. Classification report plotting

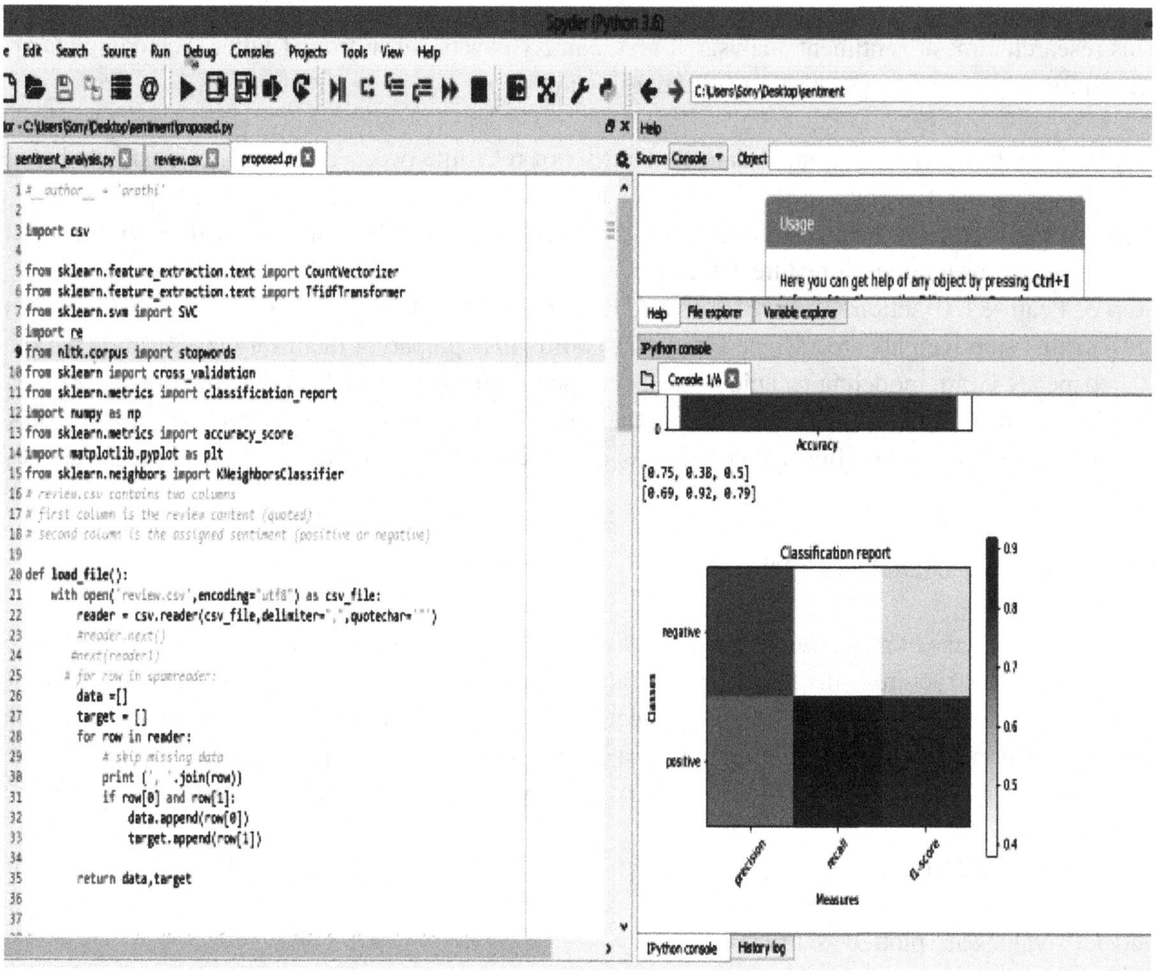

```
# __author__ = 'prothi'

import csv

from sklearn.feature_extraction.text import CountVectorizer
from sklearn.feature_extraction.text import TfidfTransformer
from sklearn.svm import SVC
import re
from nltk.corpus import stopwords
from sklearn import cross_validation
from sklearn.metrics import classification_report
import numpy as np
from sklearn.metrics import accuracy_score
import matplotlib.pyplot as plt
from sklearn.neighbors import KNeighborsClassifier
# review.csv contains two columns
# first column is the review content (quoted)
# second column is the assigned sentiment (positive or negative)

def load_file():
    with open('review.csv',encoding='utf8') as csv_file:
        reader = csv.reader(csv_file,delimiter=',',quotechar='"')
        #reader.next()
        #next(reader1)
        # for row in spamreader:
        data =[]
        target = []
        for row in reader:
            # skip missing data
            print (', '.join(row))
            if row[0] and row[1]:
                data.append(row[0])
                target.append(row[1])

        return data,target
```

```
[0.75, 0.38, 0.5]
[0.69, 0.92, 0.79]
```

Figure 4. Accuracy analysis

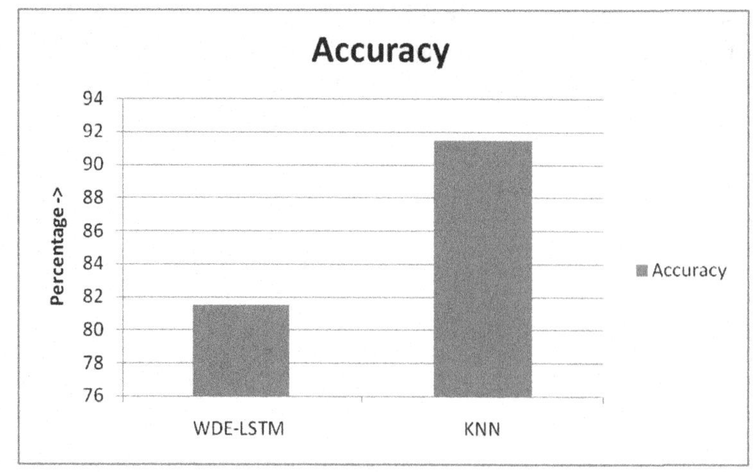

Figure 5. Precision-recall analysis

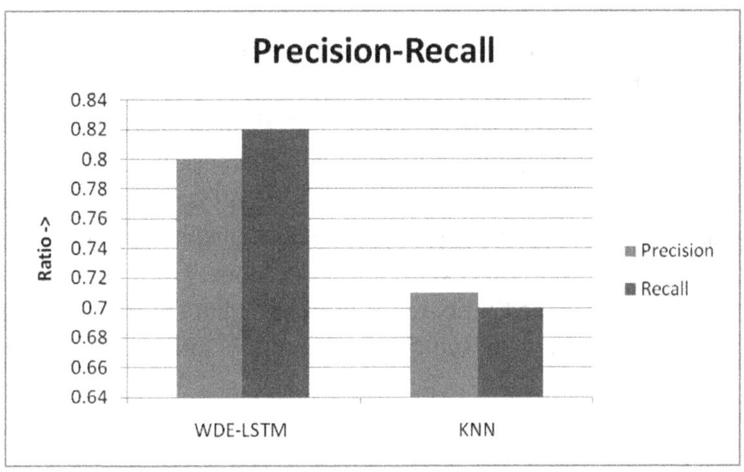

Figure 6. F-measure analysis

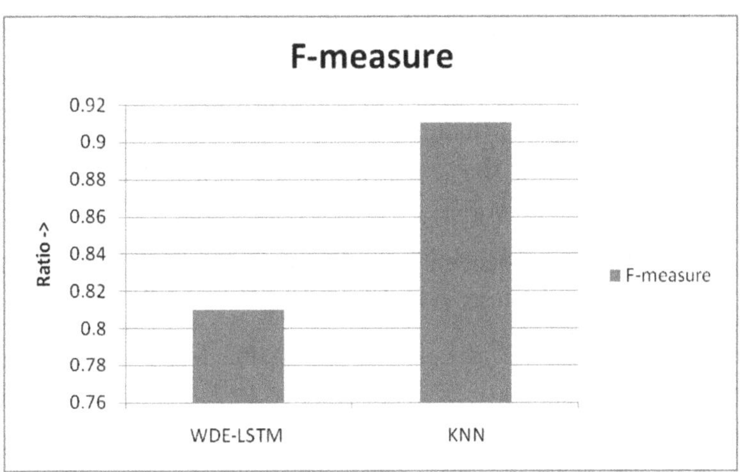

Table 1. Performance analysis

Parameter	WDE-LSTM	KNN
Accuracy	81.51	91.45
Precision	0.80	0.71
Recall	0.82	0.70
F-measure	0.81	0.91

CONCLUSION

Prior of this work was done for twitter data to study the sentiments of users by considering mainly two algorithms named as one is N-Gram technique used for feature extraction and one another is K-Nearest Neighbor classifier used for classification of the tweets into positive, negative and neutral classes. The performance scores of the proposed approach in terms of accuracy, precision, recall and F1 score are respectively. Numerous approaches have been designed in the recent years for sentiment analysis. However complete efficiency has not been achieved so far. The main challenges that come up are named entity recognition, anaphora resolutions, negation expressions, sarcasms, abbreviations, misspellings, etc. The main challenges that come up are named entity recognition, anaphora resolutions, negation expressions, sarcasms, abbreviations, misspellings, etc. Using huge amount of labeled data for improving results.

REFERENCES

Astya, P. (2017, May). Sentiment analysis: approaches and open issues. In *2017 International Conference on Computing, Communication and Automation (ICCCA)* (pp. 154-158). IEEE.

Bouazizi, Mondher, & Ohtsuki. (2019). Multi-class sentiment analysis on twitter: classification performance and challenges. *Big Data Mining and Analytics, 2*(3), 181-194.

Cheng, V. C., Leung, C. H., Liu, J., & Milani, A. (2013). Probabilistic aspect mining model for drug reviews. *IEEE Transactions on Knowledge and Data Engineering, 26*(8), 2002–2013. doi:10.1109/TKDE.2013.175

Clavel, C., & Callejas, Z. (2015). Sentiment analysis: From opinion mining to human-agent interaction. *IEEE Transactions on Affective Computing, 7*(1), 74–93. doi:10.1109/TAFFC.2015.2444846

Duygulu, P., Barnard, K., de Freitas, J. F., & Forsyth, D. A. (2002, May). Object recognition as machine translation: Learning a lexicon for a fixed image vocabulary. In *European conference on computer vision* (pp. 97-112). Springer.

El-Jawad, M. H. A., Hodhod, R., & Omar, Y. M. (2018, December). Sentiment Analysis of Social Media Networks Using Machine Learning. In *2018 14th International Computer Engineering Conference (ICENCO)* (pp. 174-176). IEEE. 10.1109/ICENCO.2018.8636124

Garcia-Moya, L., Anaya-Sánchez, H., & Berlanga-Llavori, R. (2013). Retrieving product features and opinions from customer reviews. *IEEE Intelligent Systems, 28*(3), 19–27. doi:10.1109/MIS.2013.37

Garg, Pulkit, Garg, & Ranga. (2017). Sentiment analysis of the uri terror attack using twitter. In *2017 international conference on computing, communication and automation (ICCCA)*. IEEE.

Go, A., Bhayani, R., & Huang, L. (2009). Twitter sentiment classification using distant supervision. CS224N Project Report, Stanford, 1(12), 2009.

Hai, Z., Chang, K., Kim, J. J., & Yang, C. C. (2013). Identifying features in opinion mining via intrinsic and extrinsic domain relevance. *IEEE Transactions on Knowledge and Data Engineering, 26*(3), 623–634. doi:10.1109/TKDE.2013.26

Hassan, A. U., Hussain, J., Hussain, M., Sadiq, M., & Lee, S. (2017, October). Sentiment analysis of social networking sites (SNS) data using machine learning approach for the measurement of depression. In *2017 International Conference on Information and Communication Technology Convergence (ICTC)* (pp. 138-140). IEEE. 10.1109/ICTC.2017.8190959

Hussein, D. M. E. D. M. (2018). A survey on sentiment analysis challenges. *Journal of King Saud University-Engineering Sciences*, *30*(4), 330–338. doi:10.1016/j.jksues.2016.04.002

Iqbal, F., Hashmi, J. M., Fung, B. C., Batool, R., Khattak, A. M., Aleem, S., & Hung, P. C. (2019). A Hybrid Framework for Sentiment Analysis Using Genetic Algorithm Based Feature Reduction. *IEEE Access: Practical Innovations, Open Solutions*, *7*, 14637–14652. doi:10.1109/ACCESS.2019.2892852

John, A., John, A., & Sheik, R. (2019, April). Context Deployed Sentiment Analysis Using Hybrid Lexicon. In *2019 1st International Conference on Innovations in Information and Communication Technology (ICIICT)* (pp. 1-5). IEEE. 10.1109/ICIICT1.2019.8741413

Juneja, P., & Ojha, U. (2017, July). Casting online votes: to predict offline results using sentiment analysis by machine learning classifiers. In *2017 8th International Conference on Computing, Communication and Networking Technologies (ICCCNT)* (pp. 1-6). IEEE. 10.1109/ICCCNT.2017.8203996

Kennedy, A., & Inkpen, D. (2006). Sentiment classification of movie reviews using contextual valence shifters. *Computational Intelligence*, *22*(2), 110–125. doi:10.1111/j.1467-8640.2006.00277.x

Korovkinas, K., Danėnas, P., & Garšva, G. (2019). SVM and k-Means Hybrid Method for Textual Data Sentiment Analysis. *Baltic Journal of Modern Computing*, *7*(1), 47–60. doi:10.22364/bjmc.2019.7.1.04

Kulķarni & Rodd. (2018). Extensive study of text based methods for opinion mining. In *2018 2nd international conference on inventive systems and control (ICISC)*. IEEE.

Pamungkas, Wahyu, & Putri. (2016). An experimental study of lexicon-based sentiment analysis on Bahasa Indonesia. In *2016 6th international annual engineering seminar (INAES)*. IEEE.

Poria, S., Gelbukh, A., Hussain, A., Howard, N., Das, D., & Bandyopadhyay, S. (2013). Enhanced SenticNet with affective labels for concept-based opinion mining. *IEEE Intelligent Systems*, *28*(2), 31–38. doi:10.1109/MIS.2013.4

Rathi, M., Malik, A., Varshney, D., Sharma, R., & Mendiratta, S. (2018, August). Sentiment Analysis of Tweets Using Machine Learning Approach. In *2018 Eleventh International Conference on Contemporary Computing (IC3)* (pp. 1-3). IEEE. 10.1109/IC3.2018.8530517

Ren, F., & Wu, Y. (2013). Predicting user-topic opinions in twitter with social and topical context. *IEEE Transactions on Affective Computing*, *4*(4), 412–424. doi:10.1109/T-AFFC.2013.22

Spencer, J., & Uchyigit, G. (2012, September). Sentimentor: Sentiment analysis of twitter data. In SDAD@ ECML/PKDD (pp. 56-66). Academic Press.

Taj, S., Shaikh, B. B., & Meghji, A. F. (2019, January). Sentiment Analysis of News Articles: A Lexicon based Approach. In *2019 2nd International Conference on Computing, Mathematics and Engineering Technologies (iCoMET)* (pp. 1-5). IEEE. 10.1109/ICOMET.2019.8673428

Tyagi, Priyanka, & Tripathi. (2019). A review towards the sentiment analysis techniques for the analysis of twitter data. Academic Press.

Valdivia, Luzíón, & Herrera. (2017). Neutrality in the sentiment analysis problem based on fuzzy majority. In *2017 IEEE international conference on fuzzy systems (FUZZ-IEEE)*. IEEE.

Xu, X., Cheng, X., Tan, S., Liu, Y., & Shen, H. (2013). Aspect-level opinion mining of online customer reviews. *China Communications*, *10*(3), 25–41. doi:10.1109/CC.2013.6488828

Yu, X., Liu, Y., Huang, X., & An, A. (2010). Mining online reviews for predicting sales performance: A case study in the movie domain. *IEEE Transactions on Knowledge and Data Engineering*, *24*(4), 720–734. doi:10.1109/TKDE.2010.269

Zhang, X., Cui, L., & Wang, Y. (2013). Commtrust: Computing multi-dimensional trust by mining e-commerce feedback comments. *IEEE Transactions on Knowledge and Data Engineering*, *26*(7), 1631–1643. doi:10.1109/TKDE.2013.177

Zhao. (2017). Weakly-supervised deep embedding for product review sentiment analysis. *IEEE Transactions on Knowledge and Data Engineering, 30*(1), 185-197.

This research was previously published in Applications of Artificial Neural Networks for Nonlinear Data; pages 94-115, copyright year 2021 by Engineering Science Reference (an imprint of IGI Global).

Chapter 13
Applications of Ontology-Based Opinion Mining

Razia Sulthana
SRM Institute of Science and Technology, India

Subburaj Ramasamy
SRM Institute of Science and Technology, India

ABSTRACT

Ontology provides a technique to formulate and present queries to databases either stand-alone or web-based. Ontology has been conceived to produce reusable queries to extract rules matching them, and hence, it saves time and effort in creating new ontology-based queries. Ontology can be incorporated in the machine learning process, which hierarchically defines the relationship between concepts, axioms, and terms in the domain. Ontology rule mining has been found to be efficient as compared to other well-known rule mining methods like taxonomy and decision trees. In this chapter, the authors carry out a detailed survey about ontology-related information comprising classification, creation, learning, reuse, and application. The authors also discuss the reusability and the tools used for reusing ontology. Ontology has a life cycle of its own similar to the software development life cycle. The classification-supervised machine learning technique and clustering and the unsupervised machine learning are supported by the ontology. The authors also discuss some of the open issues in creation and application of ontology.

8.0 INTRODUCTION

Ontology is widely used in machine learning. It is used for instance, in the following applications:

- Classification of customers' reviews of items such as books, movies or any product or service.
- Sentiment analysis using text retrieved from social media.
- Rule mining in semantic web.

DOI: 10.4018/978-1-6684-6303-1.ch013

With the advent of Web 2.0, the number of Internet users is growing and thereby contribute data to the common pool of global resources. Social networks are important sources of data which can be gainfully used with the help of machine learning techniques for sentiment analysis, product market analysis, changing opinion of the consumers for products etc. The increasing velocity, variety and volume of the data which is popularly known as big data (Xia, Wang, Berkele & Liu, 2017; Padhy, Mishra & Panigrahi, 2012) has resulted in advanced research in machine learning techniques. Usage of Ontology with big data provides significant savings in efforts, cost and efficiency.

8.1 ONTOLOGY

Ontology is a hierarchical representation system. Ontology finds wide use in genetic algorithms, medical databases and machine learning. Since the early 2000s, ontology is applied in semantic web. In the early 1990s ontology was defined by Gruber as "a formal, explicit specification of a shared conceptualization" (Gruber, 1993). It provides a formal and shared conceptualization of a domain that helps in ensuring communication amongst people and supports interactions among application systems.

Creating ontology for an application enables the following:

- A formal documented vocabulary.
- A formal representation understandable by machine.
- Understanding concepts of application domain such as supermarket application.
- Reusing of concepts.
- Sharing of concepts.

8.1.1 Ontology Classification

Ontology can be classified based on the following:

- Creation methodology adopted
- Application

8.1.1.1 Ontology Classification Based on Creation Methodology

The ontologies can be classified into the following based on the methodology adopted for their creation.

- Supervised
- Unsupervised
- Upper / top ontology
- Domain ontology
- Metadata ontology
- User-defined ontology

The creation of ontology can be manual, semi-automatic or automatic. The reference to the research articles discussing the three types are given in Table 1.

Table 1. Articles classified based on Ontology Creation types.

	Ontology Types	Reference to Articles
1	Automated Ontology	(Park & Kang, 2012; Park & Lee, 2007; Pearl, 1984; Park, Kang, & Kim, 2007; Golbreich, 2004; Lin & Pantel, 2001; Szpektor, Tanev, Dagan, & Coppola, 2004; Velardi, Navigli, Cuchiarelli, & Neri, 2005; Navigli & Velardi, 2004; Weng, Tsai, Liu, & Hsu, 2006; Köhler, Philippi, Specht, & Rüegg, 2006; Ma et al., 2012; Faure & Nédellec, 1998; Stumme & Maedche, 2001; Jiang & Tan, 2005; Du, Li, & King, 2009; Yue, Zuo, Peng, Wang, & Han, 2015; Shi & Setchi, 2012)
2	Semi - Automated Ontology	(Li, Du, & Wang, 2005; Cimiano & Völker, 2005; Maedche, & Staab, 2000; Gacitua, Sawyer, & Rayson, 2008; Bisson, Nédellec, & Canamero, 2000; Gal, Modica, & Jamil, 2004; Fan, Luo, Gao, & Jain, 2007; Chi, Lin, & Hsieh, 2014, Sanchez-Pi, Martí, & Garcia, 2016)
3	Manual Ontology	(Maedche & Staab, 2000)

8.1.1.2 Ontology Classification Based on Application

The ontology is classified into various types based on the application in which it is used (Navigli & Velardi, 2004). The reference to the research articles of the various types of ontology based on its application is given in Table 2.

Table 2 Articles classified based on Ontology application

	Ontology types based on application	Reference to Articles
1	Domain Ontology	(Park & Kang, 2012; Park & Lee, 2007; Park, Kang, & Kim, 2007; Velardi, Navigli, Cuchiarelli, & Neri, 2005; Navigli & Velardi, 2004; Weng, Tsai, Liu, & Hsu, 2006; Köhler, Philippi, Specht, & Rüegg, 2006; Ma et al., 2012; Faure & Nédellec, 1998; Stumme & Maedche, 2001; Jiang & Tan, 2005; Du, Li, & King, 2009; Yue, Zuo, Peng, Wang, & Han, 2015; Li, Du, & Wang, 2005; Cimiano & Völker, 2005; Maedche, & Staab, 2000; Gacitua, Sawyer, & Rayson, 2008; Gal, Modica, & Jamil, 2004; Chi, Lin, & Hsieh, 2014; Sanchez-Pi, Martí, & Garcia, 2016; Maedche & Staab, 2000)
2	Corpus Based Ontology	(Bisson, Nédellec, & Canamero, 2000)
3	User Ontology	(Shi & Setchi, 2012; Fan, Luo, Gao, & Jain, 2007)

8.1.2 Ontology in Semantic Web

Semantic web can be visualized as three layer architecture as represented in Figure 1. The top layer is user layer, middle is domain layer and the bottom layer is storage layer. The user layer consists of end users and web service components. The domain layer encompasses a set of tools and languages to support semantic web and ontology uniquely for every service. The storage layer acts as a miniature data warehouse with a collection of structured and unstructured files or documents.

Ontology (Gruber, 1995) plays a major role in knowledge sharing and communications among technologies in the web. Ontologies were also developed based on the domains for which the application is developed, which are listed below.

Figure 1. Ontology in Web

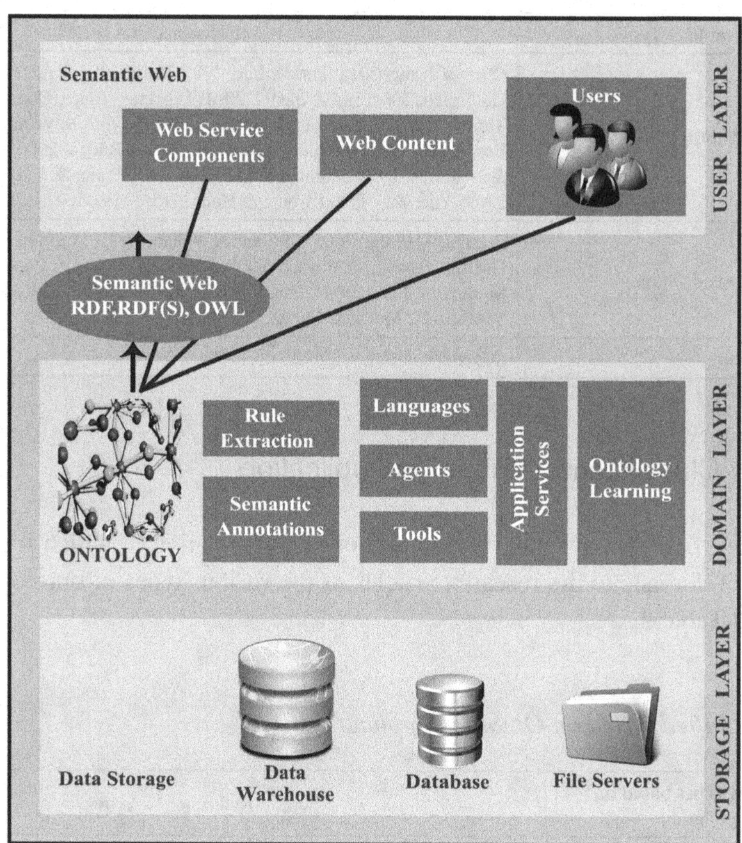

- Cyc (Lenat & Guha, 1989), and MicroCosmos (Mahesh & Nirenburg, 1996), SUMO (http://ontology.teknowledge.com) are generic ontologies.
- WordNet (Fellbaum, 1998) is a lexical ontology.
- Gene Ontology (Gene Ontology Consortium, 2001) and UMLS (Lindberg, 1990) for life sciences.

8.1.3 Ontology Development Process

Ontology has been developed for each domain of the application and Ontology Development (Li, Martínez, & Rubio, 2016) process is an iterative process. Ontology development process is represented in Figure 2.

Ontology development process is a continuous life cycle, and it involves the following steps:

Step 1: Initially, the requirement to design the ontology is gathered. E.g. Domain, Application: Real-time or static.

Step 2: Identify the scope and domain of the application for which ontology is created.

Step 3: Identify the candidate relationship between the entities.

Step 4: To ensure ontology reuse in future, the components are made independent of the underlying software.

Step 5, 6: Identify the terms and the entities. Entities are a composite collection of terms.

Figure 2. Ontology development process

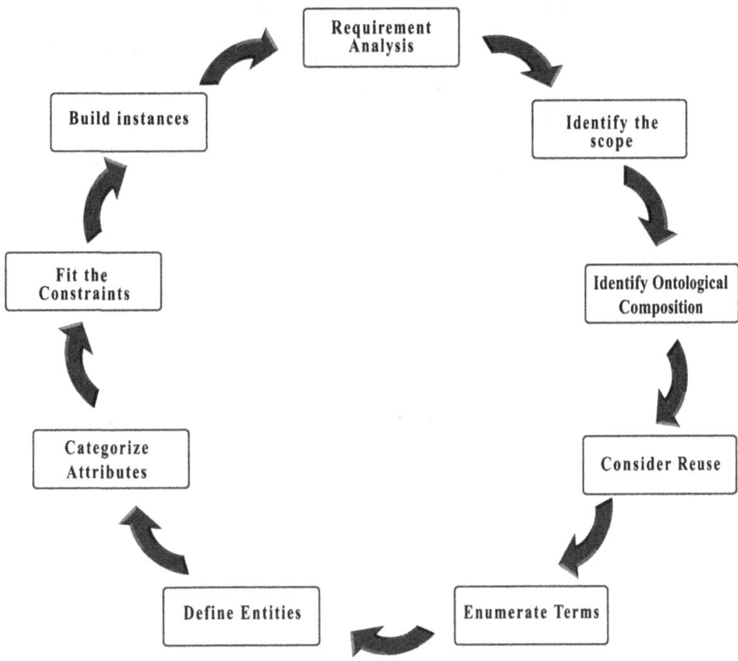

Step 7: The entities are then categorized based on their similarity and grouped under a domain.

Step 8: The entire process starts with a set of rules as a constraint. These constraints restrict the number of terms and entities to pick. It restricts them to be under a common domain.

Step 9: The instances of the ontology are now built, and each hierarchical flow is checked before deployment. This ensures an increase in process accuracy.

This survey has grouped the information under different types of ontology, approaches, applications and the ontology languages supporting them. Section 3 discusses the classical usage of ontology as rules: Rule ontology. Section 4 addresses the state-of-the-art of ontology learning listing the types and algorithms used. Section 5 discusses the role of ontology in the extraction process. Section 6 briefs the usage of ontology in clustering, classification, data analytics. Section 7 lists the performance measures used in validating the ontology system. Section 8 discusses the open issues. Conclusions are in Section 9.

8.2 RULE ONTOLOGY

Rule ontology (Park & Kang, 2012) automatically extracts rules from web sites based on the similar rules extracted from other sites using Breadth First Search (BFS) algorithm. There are different ways of extracting rules from textual information in the semantic web. The rules extracted may be inference rules or entailment rules based on the application. Entailment rules represent the directional information between the components. Inference rules represent the logical relationship between components.

A semi-automatic ontology (SOAM) (Li, Du, & Wang, 2005) extracts rule from a relational database. It extracts the necessary data from the database and then builds an ontology structure. The similar rules are extracted in Park, Kang, and Kim (2007) using ontology based on the semantic similarity measure. An automatic rule acquisition method: OntoRule encapsulates rule components and its structure. It first identifies the rule, and in the second stage, the composition of the rule is determined. A hyponym hierarchy method is used to find the semantic similarity distance. A graph based breadth first search method is used for identifying the relationship in the ontology. A method in Gasse and Haarslev, (2008) uses protégé plugin (Golbreich, 2004) to rewrite the axioms written in Ontology Web Language (OWL) to Description Logics (DL) during rule extraction.

Intelligent search strategies using automated rule extraction and breadth first search method are described in Pearl (1984). Using this method, the nodes in the graph are traversed in layers of depth, and it follows first in first out policy.

Generally, BFS is used for construction of ontology and a set of works are listed below

- Extracts inference rules from similar web sites. Uses OWL to generate RDF graph (Park & Kang, 2012).
- Uses XMRL to identify the rule components (Park & Lee, 2007).
- Enlightens the heuristics method to solve the graph based problems (Pearl, 1984).
- Extracts similar rules from web sites (Park, Kang, & Kim, 2007).
- Extracts rule from the relational database uses OWL (Li, Du, & Wang, 2005).

Extensive research has been carried out in automated ontology development. An automated ontology (Park & Lee, 2007) along with XRML (eXtensible Rule Markup Language) identifies the rule component from texts and tables. It recognizes the variables, classes, and the value of the variable and omitted variables. The similar rules are extracted from the same domain based on simple similarity measure based on synonyms using the bottom-up approach.

8.3 ONTOLOGY LEARNING

Ontology learning (Maedche, 2002) refers to set of data-driven techniques that support ontology engineering. Ontology is widely used in web applications. Ontology learning procedures are classified into four categories (Weng, Tsai, Liu, & Hsu, 2006), they are text clustering, association rules and knowledge based and Formal Conceptual Analysis(FCA).

Ontology can either exist as a separate module or part of web applications. Ontology has evolved from taxonomy (Hakeem & Shah, 2004; Van Rees, 2003; Hoxha, Jiang, & Weng, 2016; Niu & Issa, 2015) providing the advantage of optimally reducing the effort and time taken to carry out an operation in data stores.

Ontology Hierarchy vs. Taxonomical Hierarchy

- Taxonomy is purely hierarchical and is a top-down representation, whereas ontology represents some relationships between the entities. E.g. parent –child relation, sibling relation, child of parent1 can be connected with a grandchild of parent 2.
- Taxonomy contains parent-child relationship, and ontology contains many user-defined varying relationships.

The major advantage of ontology is its reusability. This facilitates creating a repository of ontology which can be dynamically and continuously expanded. Developing ontology can be achieved with the following tools OntoLearn (Navigli & Velardi, 2004), ASIUM system (Faure & Nédellec, 1998), Text-ToOnto (Maedche, & Staab, 2000), the the Mo'k Workbench (Bisson, Nédellec, & Canamero, 2000), OntoLT (Buitelaar, Olejnik, & Sintek, 2004), DODDLE II (Yamaguchi, 2001), WEB->KB (Craven et al., 2000) which reuse the existing ontology that minimizes the time taken for its construction. Integrating these tools with the application has compatibility issues as these are restricted to otology models, and more importantly, the user interaction is minimal. This can be overcome by use of Text2Onto (Cimiano & Völker, 2005). OntoLT, Text2Onto and DODDLE tools automatically extract the ontology from the web. It works seamlessly with ontology tools.

The tool support for ontology can be grouped into the following categories

- Tools for Ontology Learning.
- Tools for Ontology construction.

KAON (KArlsruhe Ontology and Semantic web infrastructure) is a tool that helps in managing the ontology and its application. TextToOnto (Maedche, & Staab, 2000) is an ontology learning system applied in KAON. This methodology builds a modeler for an underlying corpus. Many effective algorithms are inbuilt in this system with its own parameters. Ontobuilder (Gal, Modica, & Jamil, 2004) is a tool which extracts ontology from web sources. It encompasses many matching algorithms to identify the structure similarity. More information on ontology learning can be drawn from the ontology learning workshops (ECAI, 2002; K-CAP, 2003; Staab, Maedche, Nedellec, & Wiemer-Hastings, 2000; Maedche, Staab, Hovy, & Nedellec, 2001; ECAI-02, 2002)

The well-known ontology learning tools, the algorithms and the learning methods used by them are given in Table 3.

Ontology learning is the process of understanding existing ontologies. There are two methods for ontology construction. They are listed below:

1. Modifying an existing ontology.

The existing ontology is learned, the data is extracted and necessary refinement is carried out to suite the new applications. A detailed study about the association among entities has to done to modify an existing ontology. Ontology alignment (Noy & Musen, 1999, 2000) is one of the requirements during the ontology extraction process, and it helps in identifying the association between concepts.

2. Constructing a new ontology

When a new ontology is created, tools such as protégé are used. Constructing ontology requires deep knowledge about the domain, the entities and the relationship between them.

As a first step, before we consider creating a new ontology it is advisable to learn the existing ontologies. When the user's interest or the rule query changes dramatically, it is better to create a new ontology and when the changes are marginal, then existing ontology can be reused and can be extended to suite the new query.

Table 3. Ontology learning tools and its construction methods

Paper	Ontology Learning tool and Nomenclature	Principle of operation	Algorithms	Construction Method (Ontology Learning Methods)
(Navigli & Velardi, 2004)	Ontolearn:	Extracts domain ontology from websites and documents hosted by virtual environments.	Structural semantic interconnection: It performs semantic interpretation based on the domain words extracted from the web documents	Knowledge base
(Weng, Tsai, Liu, & Hsu, 2006)	Ontology learning	Builds a map for related ontological concepts that helps the user to search relevant information. Uses FCA and conceptual relationship between term and document for ontology learning	Formal Conceptual Analysis Performs conceptual analysis among ontological concepts	FCA (Formal Concept Analysis)
(Faure & Nédellec, 1998)	ASIUM Ontology Learning	Parses text in natural language, clusters them conceptually developing into generality graph	ASIUM clustering algorithm for learning ontologies. ASIUM follows Bottom-up and best-first method	Corpus-based
(Cimiano & Völker, 2005)	Text 2Onto	Learning from web pages dynamically	Ontology Learning Algorithms Model implemented in Probabilistic Object (POM) It Supports handling RDFS, OWL, F-logic	knowledge base
(Maedche, & Staab, 2000)	TexttoOnto	Determining conceptual structures and engineering ontologies from text	Generalized association rule algorithm: Identity relationship between concepts and determine the appropriate level of abstraction	Association rules
(Bisson, Nédellec, & Canamero, 2000)	Mo'k Workbench:	Develops a workbench that recognizes the clustering method and builds ontology	Uses NLP methods and calculates the similarity distance	Corpus-based text clustering
Gal, Modica, & Jamil, 2004	Ontobuilder:	Learning from web pages and reservation systems.	Word similarity algorithms, String matching algorithms, Value normalization and Value matching	Knowledge base

3. The developed ontology has to be maintained so as to extract the necessary, timely information from it. An approach to maintaining the developed ontology is noted in Gašević, Zouaq, Torniai, Jovanović, and Hatala (2011) which use collaborative tags for visualization and user interaction. The intuitiveness of the proposed method in relating the folksonomy and taxonomy is measured quantitatively and qualitatively using statistical measures.

8.4 ONTOLOGY CREATION

Ontology has been found to be suitable for rule mining, in both in the web and offline applications. The steps in building ontology are given below

- Determine the scope and domain for which ontology is to be constructed.
- Identify the important terms/concepts from the corpus or relational database.
- Determine the class attributes and frame a class hierarchy. A high-quality dynamic ontology can be built if meaningful, correct and minimally redundant class attributes are extracted.
- Identify the relationship between the class attributes i.e. cardinality, intersection, union, complement, etc. which has to be represented in the ontology.
- Filter out the properties of the classes.
- Finally, identify the individual names

The created ontology is stored in the repository and is modified to suit the needs of the application. The co-occurrence frequency of the word is used to detect the non-taxonomic relationship in Concept Relation Concept Tuple-based Ontology Learning (CRCTOL) (Jiang & Tan, 2005) and texttoonto (Maedche, & Staab, 2000). The precision of CRCTOL is 99.7%, and texttoonto is 99.1%. A difference of 0.6% can be seen between them. CRCTOL performs efficiently than texttoonto in multi-word term extraction.

The automatic extraction of ontology from web ensures the quality or continuity of web pages chosen. Most of the web pages on the web are themselves organized in a taxonomical hierarchy or ontological hierarchy. Ontology extraction from web pages that are aligned in ontological hierarchy eases the extraction process. Ontology can be constructed for web sites that have same URL base. Moreover, this makes the navigation process easier. Thus it becomes ontology directed web pages. The specific content from the web pages can be extracted when a thorough study of the web page structure. The ontology can also be created by comparing multiple existing ontologies. A divide and conquer approach (Hu, Qu, & Cheng, 2008) matches two related ontologies from the web by developing a structure based partitioning algorithm and using clustering. The technology governing ontology follows a systematic path comprising of well-defined processes. We call this as ontology life cycle represented in Figure 3. While there may be many variations of Ontology Life cycle (OLC) we portray a simple OLC consisting of 4 phases as explained below:

1. **Creation of Ontology:** The creation of ontology can be either from scratch or modify the existing ontology from the same domain. The ontology creation involves the following:
    a. Choosing the ontology type.
    b. Choosing the construction type.
    c. Creation of new ontology versus modifying existing ontology.
2. **Using the Ontology:** The ontology can be applied in various applications by programming in any one of the following languages:
    a. OQL (Ontology query language).
    b. RDF (Resource Description Framework).
    c. RDFS (Resource Description Framework Schema).

Figure 3. Ontology Life cycle

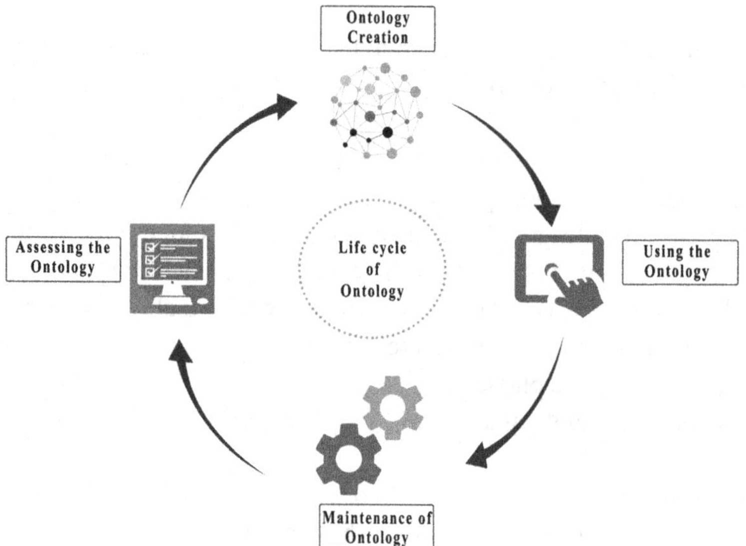

3. **Maintenance of Ontology:** The ontology is reusable. The reusability can be achieved by the following:
   a. Automatic update
   b. Semi-automatic update
   c. Manual update

   The ontology structure is designed for reusability
4. **Assessing the Ontology:** Ontology can be called in an application for rule mining to extract knowledge from the data stores. The ontology creation stage has some components and is shown in Figure 4.

The steps in ontology creation are explained below:

1. **Choosing the Ontology Type:** The foremost step is to choose the type of ontology. The different types of ontology include:
   a. **Domain Ontology:** Developed for a particular application.
   b. **Upper Ontology:** Works in the upper layer and groups all the domain ontologies.
   c. **Metadata Ontology:** Developed with the metadata information of an application. It eases the search process.
   d. **User-Defined:** Developed based on user–defined rules.
2. **Choosing the Construction Type:** Ontology can be constructed in 3 ways:
   a. **Top-Down Ontology:** Built from top to bottom, where the top level entities are identified following which sub-entities are identified.
   b. **Bottom-Up Ontology:** Built from bottom to top, where the low-level entities are identified following which its parents are identified
   c. **Middle-Out Ontology:** Built-in any fashion, where all the entities are identified, and grouped together and linked by finding the relationship between them.

Figure 4. Expanded stages of Ontology creation

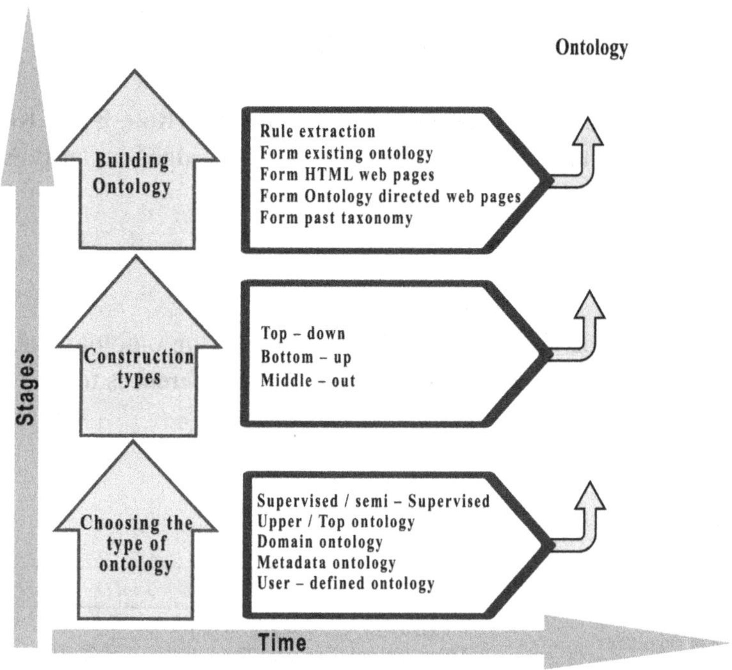

3. Creation of new ontology versus modifying existing ontology.
4. The ontology is created using ontology languages or modified by extracting from other ontologies.

8.4.1 Ontology-Based Information Retrieval From Semantic Web

In the past, information from the web pages was extracted using matching algorithms. An improved way for information retrieval is by using ontologies. Ontology-based information retrieval identifies the relationship between the text documents and the contents of the web page in a better way. A scalable mode of information retrieval is proposed in Fernández et al. (2011) for ontology-based information retrieval of web contents. A list of similarity measures used for information retrieval is given below. Similarity measures were used to find the relationship between the query given by the user and the text in the document in a vector space.

- The geometric average of two attributes (Lin & Pantel, 2001).
- Distributional similarity principle (Szpektor, Tanev, Dagan, & Coppola, 2004).
- Rule-based and algebraic methods (Navigli & Velardi, 2004).
- Latent semantic indexing (Ma et al., 2012; Shi & Setchi, 2012).
- Cosine similarity (Yue, Zuo, Peng, Wang, & Han, 2015; Hu, Qu, & Cheng, 2008).
- Lexical similarities based on edit distance (Li, Du, & Wang, 2005).
- The skewed divergence of two attributes (Cimiano & Völker, 2005).
- Log-likelihood (Gacitua, Sawyer, & Rayson, 2008).
- Similarity computation matrix (Bisson, Nédellec, & Canamero, 2000).

- Levenshtein distance (Fernández et al., 2011).
- Dice's coefficient: Identifies the similarity between two strings (Du, Li, & King, 2009).
- Pearson's similarity Measure (Su, Yeh, Philip, & Tseng, 2010).

A set of algorithms used in similarity measure calculation includes Rule-Based Knowledge Similarity Calculation System (RBKSCS) and Conditional Probability Knowledge Similarity Algorithm (CPKSA) (Huang & Cheng, 2008).

8.4.2 Ontology Tools

During the last few decades tools have been developed for creating ontology and ontology learning. These tools provide ease of creation of ontologies. Table 4 lists references to the articles published on the ontology tools used.

Table 4. List of ontology tools and its purpose

Paper	Purpose	Tool
1	Construction of Ontology	1. CODE (Li, Du, & Wang, 2005) 2. Protege tool (Yue, Zuo, Peng, Wang, & Han, 2015; Cimiano & Völker, 2005)
2	Ontology reasoning tools	1. Jena (Reynolds, 2004) 2. F-OWL (Zou, Finin, & Chen, 2004) 3. KAON (Volz, Oberle, Staab, & Motik, 2003) 4. OntoBroker (Decker, Erdmann, Fensel, & Studer, 1999)
3	Miner tool	1. Rule Miner (Park, Kang, & Kim, 2007)
4	Reasoning tools with OWL	1. RACER, Jess (Golbreich, 2004)
5	Ontology learning tools	1. OntoLearn (Navigli & Velardi, 2004) or OntoLT (Buitelaar, Olejnik, & Sintek, 2004) 2. ASIUM system (Faure & Nédellec, 1998) 3. TextToOnto (Maedche, & Staab, 2000) 4. Ontolancs (Gacitua, Sawyer, & Rayson, 2008) 5. Mo'k Workbench (Bisson, Nédellec, & Canamero, 2000) 6. DODDLE II (Yamaguchi, 2001) 7. WEB->KB (Craven et al., 2000)
6	Manual Ontology Tools	1. FCA-Merge (Stumme & Maedche, 2001) 2. SMART (Noy & Musen, 1999) 3. PROMPT (Noy & Musen, 2000) 4. Chimera (McGuinness, Fikes, Rice, & Wilder, 2000)
7	Web based ontology description tools	1. SOAM (Li, Du, & Wang, 2005) → Uses SHOE, RDF(S), DAMN+OIL, OWL

8.5 ONTOLOGY IN VARIOUS APPLICATIONS

8.5.1 Ontology-Based Clustering

It is an unsupervised methodology of machine learning approach where the groups are not pre-determined. It is used in information retrieval and exploratory data mining. Ontology is used in clustering approaches (Faure & Nédellec, 1998; Bisson, Nédellec, & Canamero, 2000) either to restrict the relevant features or to identify the similarity between the grouping items when they are large in number. Most of the existing clustering algorithms are formulated for handling the English texts where the delimiters can be easily identified. In languages where delimiters or stop words are not cited, clustering methods fail to group them even approximately. Few methods were proposed to cluster documents written in natural language.

An Ontology-based Text Mining (OTMM) approach is used in Ma et al. (2012) for clustering documents written in native Chinese language. The words/concepts and their relationship are stored in ontology repository. It clusters the research proposals together to identify a particular research project. It has also discussed on the challenges faced during clustering, and these are listed below:

- Identifying the features
- Identifying the relationship between the documents
- Minimizing the features selected
- Reducing the dimensionality of data
- Fixing the borderline of the cluster

Few of these challenges in ontology clustering are handled in Yue, Zuo, Peng, Wang, and Han (2015) where a domain specific ontology is constructed for feature selection. The clustering here is done with the help of domain ontology. It has given better clustering results as it reduces the dimensionality of the data by identifying the correlation factor which indicates the dependency between the terms. The domain ontology is then constructed for feature selection. It reduces noise and outliers from the data.

Table 5. Different clustering methods using ontology

	Clustering Method	Clustering Objective	Application
1	Self-Organized Mapping (SOM) (Ma et al., 2012)	Neural network algorithm, clusters data based on similarities	It groups the research proposals based on similarity.
2	ASIUM (Faure & Nédellec, 1998)	Conceptual clustering method. This method has restricted forming a maximal of two clusters	It improves the efficiency of syntactic parser
3	Fuzzy Clustering (Yue, Zuo, Peng, Wang, & Han, 2015)	It reduces the dimensionality of the feat are set and improves the clustering result. It outperforms latent semantic analysis and bisection K-means.	It clusters similar documents in food safety supervision domain of government.
4	K-means clustering (Shi & Setchi, 2012)	A semantic information management system that identifies the semantic relationship among stored memories using K-means clustering and singular value decomposition.	Automatic management of stored memories of royal families.
5	Mo'K workbench (Bisson, Nédellec, & Canamero, 2000)	Conceptual clustering method	It supports ontology building process
6	K-means clustering (Trappey, Wang, Hoang, & Trappey, 2013)	A patent clustering method that takes correlation matrix as input and forms clusters applying the k-means algorithm.	Identifies the life span of dental implant patent technologies.
7.	Bisecting *K*-means algorithm (BISK) (Zanjani, Dastjerdi, Asgarian, Shahriyari, & Kharazian, 2015)	Bisection K-Means algorithm	Clustering Persian text using semantic relationship

Ontology is used in combination with topic identification to identify the semantic relation between the entities (Shi & Setchi, 2012). The topic identification from the documents is done using OntoSVD and K-Means methods. It identifies the semantic relation by combining the terms and named entities. The named entities are semantic indexes. It compares the topic identification performance of SVD approach and OntoSVD approach and has proven that the OntoSVD has given good performance than SVD. The various clustering methods are given in Table 5.

8.5.2 Ontology-Based Classification

It is a supervised machine learning approach where the grouping is done based on class labels. A classifier is built by testing the classification algorithm with multiple training sets. It is uncertain to predict the performance of classification algorithm, as the behavior of classifier depends on the input data and the chosen class label. In cases, where a document falls under multiple categories with equal probability leading to ambiguous classification, ontology based classification helps in classifying the documents in using a hierarchy. The characteristics or attributes are aligned in a hierarchy in the ontology which eases the classification by allocating it to the nearest parent or relevant child attribute. Table 6 lists the classification methods using ontology.

Ontology assists in classifying both text information and video.

Context based ontology (Fan, Luo, Gao, & Jain, 2007) helps in classification of video using hierarchical boosting classification algorithm.

Ontology-based text classification (Chi, Lin, & Hsieh, 2014) is used to enhance the solution space during development of an application-job hazard analysis. The ontology was used in mapping the unsafe scenarios and safe solutions. A domain dependent text classification using ontology (Sanchez-Pi, Martí, & Garcia, 2016) is used for text classification. It compares ontology classifier and term relevance ontology classifier. Support vector machines (SVM) are supervised learning models that perform non-linear classification of data was introduced in 1995 by Vapnik. It is used in many real-time applications to classify data (Ali, Kwak, Kim, 2016 ; Bi, Zhou, Lu, & Wang, 2007; Zhang, Yoshida, & Tang, 2008).

Table 6. Classification methods using ontology

	Classification Methods	Application
1	Hierarchical boosting (Fan, Luo, Gao, & Jain, 2007)	Video classification
2	Principal component analysis and document vectorization (Chi, Lin, & Hsieh, 2014)	Job hazard analysis
3	Term relevance ontology classifier algorithm (Sanchez-Pi, Martí, & Garcia, 2016)	Occupational health and security application
4	Support vector machines (Ali, Kwak, Kim, 2016 ; Bi, Zhou, Lu, & Wang, 2007; Zhang, Yoshida, & Tang, 2008).	Online review classification, Gene ontology, Text classification

8.5.3 Ontology in Machine Learning

Machine learning helps in providing knowledge to the computer to learn and understand things on its own. An increasing emphasis on social media application has overwhelmed the growth of machine learning, neural network, fuzzy logics and artificial intelligence.

1. Ontology using Fuzzy logics

A fuzzy based sentiment analysis (Lau, Li, & Liao, 2014) is implemented on customer reviews for extracting marked intelligence. This system has outperformed the opinion finder (Wilson, 2005) with an overall accuracy of 79.10%. Ontology and Fuzzy sets are used together in knowledge extraction in Huang, Lee, Wang, and Kao (2014); and Liu (2013).

2. Ontology in handling Big data

Ontology web language (OWL) is modified in García, García-Nieto, and Aldana-Montes (2016) for consolidating the tracked data in web source. A series of analysis were made with data from Google Analytics and Piwik digital foot prints. The data were converted into a standard format and stored in the RDF repository. The data from multiple sources were sorted, and ontology helps in fusing the data in RDF (Resource Description Framework).

8.5.4 Ontology-Driven Knowledge Maintenance

Ontology is used in knowledge discovery and data mining (KDD facilitating the task of mining data. The ontology also contributes to the evaluation of a system.

- In the traditional method of data mining, the keywords given by the user were used for KDD, and a revised model is proposed in Hilario, Nguyen, Do, Woznica, and Kalousis, (2011) which rely on both data and algorithm.
- The automated process of data mining and KDD (Bernstein, Hill, & Provost, 2002) uses Intelligent Discovery Assistants (IDA) which works effectively in validating the state change using ontology.
- Ontology validates the knowledge discovery workflow in Záková, Kremen, Zelezny, and Lavrac, (2011). It is done by mapping the input to the expected output using ontology workflow.

Ontology development (López, Gómez-Pérez, Sierra, & Sierra, 1999; Suárez-Figueroa et al., 2008) describes the different methods of constructing the ontology for applications. Table 7 lists a couple of ontology used on other domain.

Table 7. Ontology in other domains

	Methodologies for building ontologies	Scope and Focus	Ontology Representation
1	METHONTOLOGY – (López, Gómez-Pérez, Sierra, & Sierra, 1999)	Chemical Ontology	Uses ODE(ontology design environment) to generate code in into lingua
2	NeON - (Suárez-Figueroa et al, 2008)	Distributed network	OWL-DL

8.6 PERFORMANCE MEASURES FOR RESULT VALUATION

In the field of information retrieval and machine learning, a set of performance measures is used to assess the quality of the system. The articles which use the performance measures are listed in Table 8.

- **Precision:** Or positive predicted value is the fragment of retrieved instances that are relevant. Precision defines "How valuable the results are?" and signifies the quality of the system.
- **Recall:** Or true positive rate is the fragment of relevant instances that are retrieved. Recall defines "How complete the results are?" and quantifies the system.
- **F-Measure:** Is the harmonic mean of precision and recall
- **Accuracy:** Is the measure of precision and recall weighted by bias and prevalence.
- **TF-IDF:** (Term Frequency – Inverse Document Frequency) Defines "How informative is a word in a corpus inclosing many documents?"
- **Entropy** is an attribute selection measure which measures the homogeneity of the sample.

Table 8. Articles and the performance measures

	Performance Measures	Papers
1	Precision	(Lin & Pantel, 2001; Szpektor, Tanev, Dagan, & Coppola, 2004; Velardi, Navigli, Cuchiarelli, & Neri, 2005; Navigli & Velardi, 2004; Weng, Tsai, Liu, & Hsu, 2006; Köhler, Philippi, Specht, & Rüegg, 2006; Ma et al., 2012; Jiang & Tan, 2005; Du, Li, & King, 2009; Yue, Zuo, Peng, Wang, & Han, 2015; Shi & Setchi, 2012; Cimiano & Völker, 2005; Gacitua, Sawyer, & Rayson, 2008; Bisson, Nédellec, & Canamero, 2000; Fan, Luo, Gao, & Jain, 2007; Chi, Lin, & Hsieh, 2014, Sanchez-Pi, Martí, & Garcia, 2016; Maedche & Staab, 2000; Ali, Kwak, Kim, 2016; Lau, Li, & Liao, 2014; Kuptabut & Netisopakul, 2016; Guo, Tang, & Kao, 2014; Sulthana & Subburaj, 2016; Sulthana & Ramasamy, 2017)
2	Recall	(Velardi, Navigli, Cuchiarelli, & Neri, 2005; Navigli & Velardi, 2004; Weng, Tsai, Liu, & Hsu, 2006; Köhler, Philippi, Specht, & Rüegg, 2006; Ma et al., 2012; Jiang & Tan, 2005; Du, Li, & King, 2009; Shi & Setchi, 2012; Cimiano & Völker, 2005; Gacitua, Sawyer, & Rayson, 2008; Fan, Luo, Gao, & Jain, 2007; Chi, Lin, & Hsieh, 2014; Sanchez-Pi, Martí, & Garcia, 2016; Maedche & Staab, 2000; Ali, Kwak, Kim, 2016; Lau, Li, & Liao, 2014; Kuptabut & Netisopakul, 2016; Guo, Tang, & Kao, 2014; Sulthana & Subburaj, 2016; Sulthana & Ramasamy, 2017)
3	F-measure	Ma et al., 2012; Faure & Nédellec, 1998; Jiang & Tan, 2005; Sanchez-Pi, Martí, & Garcia, 2016; Zhang, Yoshida, & Tang, 2008; Zhang, Yoshida, & Tang, 2008; Kuptabut & Netisopakul, 2016; Guo, Tang, & Kao, 2014; Sulthana & Subburaj, 2016; Sulthana & Ramasamy, 2017)
4	TF-IDF	(Weng, Tsai, Liu, & Hsu, 2006; Cimiano & Völker, 2005; Maedche, & Staab, 2000)
5	Entropy	(Yue, Zuo, Peng, Wang, & Han, 2015; Shi & Setchi, 2012; Cimiano & Völker, 2005)

8.7 OPEN ISSUES

Furthermore, after an elaborate study on state of the art of the system, it is observed that certain issues still exist in this domain which is depicted below:

- **Making System Understands:** The information collected from various sources is highly unstructured. The system has to validate the information before processing them. Ontologies are used in knowledge sharing and reuse between human and computer. Ontology plays a major role in assisting the computers in speeding up the access and to reduce the waiting time of the user.
- **Implement Machine Learning:** Design the project/ontology to understand the system by executing the training set multiple times. Making the system understand what the user wants, by mitigating the biases and inconsistencies made by human
- **Ontology Representation:** The representation of ontology is designed so as to include the quantified concepts/ attributes, which minimizes the time to access.
- **Ontology Maintenance:** An incremental update to evolve ontology over time has to be done periodically.
- **Identifying the Relations:** The relationships between the concepts are identified using ontology. The identified concepts are inter-connected through the discovered relations. Candidates that represent the domain are identified and are sorted according to the strength of the relations. Co-occurrence patterns of the concepts are studied to identify the n-ary relations.
- **Big data and Ontology:** The senses of ontology have to be fine-tuned to handle the V's of big data.
- **Valuation Yardstick:** The performance benchmark of ontology has to be identified to know its quality.

8.8 CONCLUSION

Ontology is emerging as a powerful technique and is used in semantic web, knowledge discovery and machine learning. In this chapter, we have given an overview of ontology types, ontology application, and ontology in the web, rule ontology, etc. The interesting feature of ontology is its extensibility and reusability. We discuss the same and also the ontology learning tools and the creation of ontology. Ontology-based classification and clustering are also discussed in this paper. We carry out measures so as to compare its efficiency and accuracy. We have listed the performance measures and their references used in conjunction with ontology. This chapter although not comprehensive but extensive.

REFERENCES

Ali, F., Kwak, K. S., & Kim, Y. G. (2016). Opinion mining based on fuzzy domain ontology and Support Vector Machine: A proposal to automate online review classification. *Applied Soft Computing*, *47*, 235–250. doi:10.1016/j.asoc.2016.06.003

Bernstein, A., Hill, S., & Provost, F. (2002). *Intelligent assistance for the data mining process: An ontology-based approach*. Academic Press.

Bi, R., Zhou, Y., Lu, F., & Wang, W. (2007). Predicting Gene Ontology functions based on support vector machines and statistical significance estimation. *Neurocomputing*, *70*(4-6), 718–725. doi:10.1016/j.neucom.2006.10.006

Bisson, G., Nédellec, C., & Canamero, D. (2000, August). Designing Clustering Methods for Ontology Building-The Mo'K Workbench. In ECAI workshop on ontology learning (Vol. 31). Academic Press.

Buitelaar, P., Olejnik, D., & Sintek, M. (2004, May). A protégé plug-in for ontology extraction from text based on linguistic analysis. In *European Semantic Web Symposium* (pp. 31-44). Springer. 10.1007/978-3-540-25956-5_3

Chi, N. W., Lin, K. Y., & Hsieh, S. H. (2014). Using ontology-based text classification to assist Job Hazard Analysis. *Advanced Engineering Informatics*, *28*(4), 381–394. doi:10.1016/j.aei.2014.05.001

Cimiano, P., & Völker, J. (2005, June). text2onto. In *International conference on application of natural language to information systems* (pp. 227-238). Springer.

Consortium, T. G. O. (2001). Creating the gene ontology resource: Design and implementation. *Genome Research*, *11*(8), 1425–1433. doi:10.1101/gr.180801 PMID:11483584

Craven, M., DiPasquo, D., Freitag, D., McCallum, A., Mitchell, T., Nigam, K., & Slattery, S. (2000). Learning to construct knowledge bases from the World Wide Web. *Artificial Intelligence*, *118*(1-2), 69–113. doi:10.1016/S0004-3702(00)00004-7

Decker, S., Erdmann, M., Fensel, D., & Studer, R. (1999). Ontobroker: Ontology based access to distributed and semi-structured information. In *Database Semantics* (pp. 351–369). Boston, MA: Springer. doi:10.1007/978-0-387-35561-0_20

Du, T. C., Li, F., & King, I. (2009). Managing knowledge on the Web–Extracting ontology from HTML Web. *Decision Support Systems*, *47*(4), 319–331. doi:10.1016/j.dss.2009.02.011

Du, T. C., Li, F., & King, I. (2009). Managing knowledge on the Web–Extracting ontology from HTML Web. *Decision Support Systems*, *47*(4), 319–331. doi:10.1016/j.dss.2009.02.011

ECAI-02. (2002). *Ontology Learning Tools Workshop*. Retrieved from http://www-sop.inria.fr/acacia/WORKSHOPS/ ECAI2002-OLT /accepted-papers.html

ECAI-02. (2002). *Workshop on Machine Learning and Natural Language Processing for Ontology Engineering*. Retrieved from http://www-sop.inria.fr/acacia/WORKSHOPS/ECAI2002-OLT/

Fan, J., Luo, H., Gao, Y., & Jain, R. (2007). Incorporating concept ontology for hierarchical video classification, annotation, and visualization. *IEEE Transactions on Multimedia*, *9*(5), 939–957. doi:10.1109/TMM.2007.900143

Faure, D., & Nédellec, C. (1998, May). A corpus-based conceptual clustering method for verb frames and ontology acquisition. In LREC workshop on adapting lexical and corpus resources to sublanguages and applications (Vol. 707, No. 728, p. 30). Academic Press.

Fellbaum, C. (1998). *WordNet: An Electronic Lexical Database (Language, Speech, and Communication)*. Academic Press.

Fernández, M., Cantador, I., López, V., Vallet, D., Castells, P., & Motta, E. (2011). Semantically enhanced information retrieval: An ontology-based approach. *Journal of Web Semantics*, *9*(4), 434–452. doi:10.1016/j.websem.2010.11.003

Gacitua, R., Sawyer, P., & Rayson, P. (2008). A flexible framework to experiment with ontology learning techniques. *Knowledge-Based Systems*, *21*(3), 192–199. doi:10.1016/j.knosys.2007.11.009

Gal, A., Modica, G., & Jamil, H. (2004, March). Ontobuilder: Fully automatic extraction and consolidation of ontologies from web sources. In *Data Engineering, 2004. Proceedings. 20th International Conference on* (p. 853). IEEE.

García, M. D. M. R., García-Nieto, J., & Aldana-Montes, J. F. (2016). An ontology-based data integration approach for web analytics in e-commerce. *Expert Systems with Applications*, *63*, 20–34. doi:10.1016/j.eswa.2016.06.034

Gašević, D., Zouaq, A., Torniai, C., Jovanović, J., & Hatala, M. (2011). An approach to folksonomy-based ontology maintenance for learning environments. *IEEE Transactions on Learning Technologies*, *4*(4), 301–314. doi:10.1109/TLT.2011.21

Gasse, F., & Haarslev, V. (2008, April). DLRule: A Rule Editor plug-in for Protege. OWLED (Spring).

Golbreich, C. (2004, November). Combining rule and ontology reasoners for the semantic web. In *International Workshop on Rules and Rule Markup Languages for the Semantic Web* (pp. 6-22). Springer. 10.1007/978-3-540-30504-0_2

Gruber, T. R. (1993). A translation approach to portable ontology specifications. *Knowledge Acquisition*, *5*(2), 199–220. doi:10.1006/knac.1993.1008

Gruber, T. R. (1995). Toward principles for the design of ontologies used for knowledge sharing? *International Journal of Human-Computer Studies*, *43*(5-6), 907–928. doi:10.1006/ijhc.1995.1081

Guo, Y. W., Tang, Y. T., & Kao, H. Y. (2014). Genealogical-Based Method for Multiple Ontology Self-Extension in MeSH. *IEEE Transactions on Nanobioscience*, *13*(2), 124–130. doi:10.1109/TNB.2014.2320413 PMID:24893362

Hakeem, A., & Shah, M. (2004, August). Ontology and taxonomy collaborated framework for meeting classification. In *Pattern Recognition, 2004. ICPR 2004. Proceedings of the 17th International Conference on* (*Vol. 4*, pp. 219-222). IEEE. 10.1109/ICPR.2004.1333743

Hilario, M., Nguyen, P., Do, H., Woznica, A., & Kalousis, A. (2011). Ontology-based meta-mining of knowledge discovery workflows. In *Meta-learning in computational intelligence* (pp. 273–315). Berlin: Springer. doi:10.1007/978-3-642-20980-2_9

Hoxha, J., Jiang, G., & Weng, C. (2016). Automated learning of domain taxonomies from text using background knowledge. *Journal of Biomedical Informatics*, *63*, 295–306. doi:10.1016/j.jbi.2016.09.002 PMID:27597572

Hu, W., Qu, Y., & Cheng, G. (2008). Matching large ontologies: A divide-and-conquer approach. *Data & Knowledge Engineering*, *67*(1), 140–160. doi:10.1016/j.datak.2008.06.003

Huang, C. J., & Cheng, M. Y. (2008). Similarity Measurement of Rule-based Knowledge Using Conditional Probability. *Journal of Information Science and Engineering*, *24*(3).

Huang, H. D., Lee, C. S., Wang, M. H., & Kao, H. Y. (2014). IT2FS-based ontology with soft-computing mechanism for malware behavior analysis. *Soft Computing*, *18*(2), 267–284. doi:10.100700500-013-1056-0

Jiang, X., & Tan, A. H. (2005, November). Mining ontological knowledge from domain-specific text documents. In *Data Mining, Fifth IEEE International Conference on* (pp. 4-pp). IEEE. 10.1109/ICDM.2005.97

K-CAP. (2003, October 26). *Knowledge mark-up and Semantic Annotation workshop.* Retrieved from http://km.aifb.kit.edu/ws/semannot2003/

Köhler, J., Philippi, S., Specht, M., & Rüegg, A. (2006). Ontology based text indexing and querying for the semantic web. *Knowledge-Based Systems*, *19*(8), 744–754. doi:10.1016/j.knosys.2006.04.015

Kuptabut, S., & Netisopakul, P. (2016). Event Extraction using Ontology Directed Semantic Grammar. *Journal of Information Science and Engineering*, *32*(1), 79–96.

Lau, R. Y., Li, C., & Liao, S. S. (2014). Social analytics: Learning fuzzy product ontologies for aspect-oriented sentiment analysis. *Decision Support Systems*, *65*, 80–94. doi:10.1016/j.dss.2014.05.005

Lenat, D. B., & Guha, R. V. (1989). *Building large knowledge-based systems; representation and inference in the Cyc project*. Academic Press.

Li, M., Du, X., & Wang, S. (2005, October). A semi-automatic ontology acquisition method for the semantic web. In *International Conference on Web-Age Information Management* (pp. 209-220). Springer. 10.1007/11563952_19

Li, X., Martínez, J. F., & Rubio, G. (2016). A new fuzzy ontology development methodology (FODM) proposal. *IEEE Access: Practical Innovations, Open Solutions*, *4*, 7111–7124. doi:10.1109/ACCESS.2016.2621756

Lin, D., & Pantel, P. (2001, August). DIRT@ SBT@ discovery of inference rules from text. In *Proceedings of the seventh ACM SIGKDD international conference on Knowledge discovery and data mining* (pp. 323-328). ACM. 10.1145/502512.502559

Lindberg, C. (1990). The Unified Medical Language System (UMLS) of the National Library of Medicine. *Journal of the American Medical Record Association*, *61*(5), 40–42. PMID:10104531

Liu, C. H., Lee, C. S., Wang, M. H., Tseng, Y. Y., Kuo, Y. L., & Lin, Y. C. (2013). Apply fuzzy ontology and FML to knowledge extraction for university governance and management. *Journal of Ambient Intelligence and Humanized Computing*, *4*(4), 493–513. doi:10.100712652-012-0139-6

López, M. F., Gómez-Pérez, A., Sierra, J. P., & Sierra, A. P. (1999). Building a chemical ontology using methontology and the ontology design environment. *IEEE Intelligent Systems & their Applications*, *14*(1), 37–46. doi:10.1109/5254.747904

Ma, J., Xu, W., Sun, Y. H., Turban, E., Wang, S., & Liu, O. (2012). An ontology-based text-mining method to cluster proposals for research project selection. *IEEE Transactions on Systems, Man, and Cybernetics. Part A, Systems and Humans, 42*(3), 784–790. doi:10.1109/TSMCA.2011.2172205

Maedche, A., & Staab, S. (2000, August). The text-to-onto ontology learning environment. In *Software Demonstration at ICCS-2000-Eight International Conference on Conceptual Structures* (Vol. 38). Academic Press.

Maedche, A., & Staab, S. (2000). Mining ontologies from text. *Knowledge Engineering and Knowledge Management Methods, Models, and Tools,* 169-189.

Maedche, A., Staab, S., Hovy, E., & Nedellec, C. (2001). The IJCAI-2001 Workshop on Ontology Learning. *Proceedings of the Second Workshop on Ontology Learning-OL'2001.*

Maedche, A. D. (2002). *Ontology learning for the semantic Web.* Kluwer Academic Publishers.

Mahesh, K., & Nirenburg, S. (1996). Meaning representation for knowledge sharing in practical machine translation. *Proceedings of the FLAIRS Track on Information Interchange.*

McGuinness, D. L., Fikes, R., Rice, J., & Wilder, S. (2000, April). *An environment for merging and testing large ontologies.* Academic Press.

Navigli, R., & Velardi, P. (2004). Learning domain ontologies from document warehouses and dedicated web sites. *Computational Linguistics, 30*(2), 151–179. doi:10.1162/089120104323093276

Niu, J., & Issa, R. R. (2015). Developing taxonomy for the domain ontology of construction contractual semantics: A case study on the AIA A201 document. *Advanced Engineering Informatics, 29*(3), 472–482. doi:10.1016/j.aei.2015.03.009

Noy, N. F., & Musen, M. A. (1999, October). SMART: Automated support for ontology merging and alignment. *Proc. of the 12th Workshop on Knowledge Acquisition, Modelling, and Management (KAW'99).*

Noy, N. F., & Musen, M. A. (2000, August). Algorithm and tool for automated ontology merging and alignment. *Proceedings of the 17th National Conference on Artificial Intelligence (AAAI-00). Available as SMI technical report SMI-2000-0831.*

Padhy, N., Mishra, D., & Panigrahi, R. (2012). *The survey of data mining applications and feature scope.* arXiv preprint arXiv:1211.5723

Park, S., & Kang, J. (2012). Using rule ontology in repeated rule acquisition from similar web sites. *IEEE Transactions on Knowledge and Data Engineering, 24*(6), 1106–1119. doi:10.1109/TKDE.2011.72

Park, S., Kang, J., & Kim, W. (2007, June). A framework for ontology based rule acquisition from web documents. In *International Conference on Web Reasoning and Rule Systems* (pp. 229-238). Springer. 10.1007/978-3-540-72982-2_17

Park, S., & Lee, J. K. (2007). Rule identification using ontology while acquiring rules from Web pages. *International Journal of Human-Computer Studies, 65*(7), 659–673. doi:10.1016/j.ijhcs.2007.02.004

Pearl, J. (1984). *Heuristics: intelligent search strategies for computer problem solving.* Academic Press.

Reynolds, D. (2004). *Jena 2 inference support.* Retrieved from http://jena. sourceforge. net/inference/ index. html

Sanchez-Pi, N., Martí, L., & Garcia, A. C. B. (2016). Improving ontology-based text classification: An occupational health and security application. *Journal of Applied Logic*, *17*, 48–58. doi:10.1016/j.jal.2015.09.008

Shi, L., & Setchi, R. (2012). User-oriented ontology-based clustering of stored memories. *Expert Systems with Applications*, *39*(10), 9730–9742. doi:10.1016/j.eswa.2012.02.087

Staab, S., Maedche, A., Nedellec, C., & Wiemer-Hastings, P. (2000). ECAI'2000 Workshop on Ontology Learning. *Proceedings of the First Workshop on Ontology Learning-OL'2000.*

Stumme, G., & Maedche, A. (2001, August). FCA-Merge: Bottom-up merging of ontologies. *IJCAI (United States)*, *1*, 225–230.

Su, J. H., Yeh, H. H., Philip, S. Y., & Tseng, V. S. (2010). Music recommendation using content and context information mining. *IEEE Intelligent Systems*, *25*(1), 16–26. doi:10.1109/MIS.2010.23

Suárez-Figueroa, M. C., de Cea, G. A., Buil, C., Dellschaft, K., Fernández-López, M., Garcia, A., ... Villazon-Terrazas, B. (2008). NeOn methodology for building contextualized ontology networks. *NeOn Deliverable D*, *5*, 4–1.

Sulthana, A. R., & Subburaj, R. (2016). An improvised ontology based K-means clustering approach for classification of customer reviews. *Indian Journal of Science and Technology*, *9*(15).

Sulthana, R., & Ramasamy, S. (2017). Context Based Classification of Reviews Using Association Rule Mining, Fuzzy Logics and Ontology. *Bulletin of Electrical Engineering and Informatics*, *6*(3), 250–255.

Szpektor, I., Tanev, H., Dagan, I., & Coppola, B. (2004). Scaling web-based acquisition of entailment relations. *Proceedings of the 2004 Conference on Empirical Methods in Natural Language Processing.*

Trappey, C. V., Wang, T. M., Hoang, S., & Trappey, A. J. (2013). Constructing a dental implant ontology for domain specific clustering and life span analysis. *Advanced Engineering Informatics*, *27*(3), 346–357. doi:10.1016/j.aei.2013.04.003

Van Rees, R. (2003). Clarity in the usage of the terms ontology, taxonomy and classification. *CIB REPORT*, *284*(432), 1–8.

Velardi, P., Navigli, R., Cuchiarelli, A., & Neri, R. (2005). Evaluation of OntoLearn, a methodology for automatic learning of domain ontologies. *Ontology Learning from Text: Methods, evaluation and applications, 123*(92).

Volz, R., Oberle, D., Staab, S., & Motik, B. (2003, May). KAON SERVER-A Semantic Web Management System. WWW (Alternate Paper Tracks).

Weng, S. S., Tsai, H. J., Liu, S. C., & Hsu, C. H. (2006). Ontology construction for information classification. *Expert Systems with Applications*, *31*(1), 1–12. doi:10.1016/j.eswa.2005.09.007

Wilson, T., Hoffmann, P., Somasundaran, S., Kessler, J., Wiebe, J., Choi, Y., . . . Patwardhan, S. (2005, October). OpinionFinder: A system for subjectivity analysis. In Proceedings of hlt/emnlp on interactive demonstrations (pp. 34-35). Association for Computational Linguistics.

Xia, F., Wang, W., Bekele, T. M., & Liu, H. (2017). Big scholarly data: A survey. *IEEE Transactions on Big Data*, *3*(1), 18–35. doi:10.1109/TBDATA.2016.2641460

Yamaguchi, T. (2001, August). Acquiring Conceptual Relationships from Domain-Specific Texts. In *Workshop on Ontology Learning* (*Vol. 38*, pp. 69-113). Academic Press.

Yue, L., Zuo, W., Peng, T., Wang, Y., & Han, X. (2015). A fuzzy document clustering approach based on domain-specified ontology. *Data & Knowledge Engineering*, *100*, 148–166. doi:10.1016/j.datak.2015.04.008

Záková, M., Kremen, P., Zelezny, F., & Lavrac, N. (2011). Automating knowledge discovery workflow composition through ontology-based planning. *IEEE Transactions on Automation Science and Engineering*, *8*(2), 253–264. doi:10.1109/TASE.2010.2070838

Zanjani, M., Dastjerdi, A. B., Asgarian, E., Shahriyari, A., & Kharazian, A. A. (2015). Short Paper_. *Journal of Information Science and Engineering*, *31*, 315–330.

Zhang, W., Yoshida, T., & Tang, X. (2008). Text classification based on multi-word with support vector machine. *Knowledge-Based Systems*, *21*(8), 879–886. doi:10.1016/j.knosys.2008.03.044

Zou, Y., Finin, T., & Chen, H. (2004, April). F-owl: An inference engine for semantic web. In *International Workshop on Formal Approaches to Agent-Based Systems* (pp. 238-248). Springer. 10.1007/978-3-540-30960-4_16

This research was previously published in Extracting Knowledge From Opinion Mining; pages 149-177, copyright year 2019 by Engineering Science Reference (an imprint of IGI Global).

Chapter 14
Deep Learning Approaches for Textual Sentiment Analysis

Tamanna Sharma
Department of Computer Science and Technology, Guru Jambheshwar University of Science and Technology, Hisar, India

Anu Bajaj
https://orcid.org/0000-0001-8563-6611
Department of Computer Science and Engineering, Guru Jambheshwar University of Science and Technology, Hisar, India

Om Prakash Sangwan
Department of Computer Science and Technology, Guru Jambheshwar University of Science and Technology, Hisar, India

ABSTRACT

Sentiment analysis is computational measurement of attitude, opinions, and emotions (like positive/negative) with the help of text mining and natural language processing of words and phrases. Incorporation of machine learning techniques with natural language processing helps in analysing and predicting the sentiments in more precise manner. But sometimes, machine learning techniques are incapable in predicting sentiments due to unavailability of labelled data. To overcome this problem, an advanced computational technique called deep learning comes into play. This chapter highlights latest studies regarding use of deep learning techniques like convolutional neural network, recurrent neural network, etc. in sentiment analysis.

INTRODUCTION

Sentiment analysis is a subset of natural language processing used in association with text mining techniques for the extraction of subjective information from social media sources. Collection of documents, reviews, blog posts, data from microblogging sites like tweets from twitter, status and news articles. Basically sentiments are analysed for certain product, domain, people and try to quantify the polarity of

DOI: 10.4018/978-1-6684-6303-1.ch014

that particular information. In other words, Sentiment analysis means mining of text for finding out the actual meaning/essence/attitude behind the text. It is also called as opinion mining. It is both science and art because of its complex context. Correct identification of hidden polarity behind the text is the key of success for any sentiment analysis task. Some of the reasons which make sentiment analysis a tough job in text are:

- Understanding the context of language for human is easy but teaching the same thing to machine is a complicated task.
- Vast variety of languages and grammar usage of every language is different.
- Usage of unstructured text like slangs, abbreviated form of text and grammar nuances make it more difficult to analyse.

Figure 1 shows the general framework of sentiment analysis. With the advent of web and social media lots of information is present for opinion mining like blog posts, data from microblogging sites, news posts etc. Most of this data is in textual form and for computation we need to transform it in to vector form. Natural language processing come up with loads of models like bag of words vector, vector space models, word embedding etc. Mining technique is chosen after that according to application for example if we want to analyse movie reviews we have rating and text as our dataset etc. Correct feature extraction is necessary for the training and testing accuracy of any machine learning model.

Now a days, deep learning models do not required hand coded features but they are data hungry techniques and need loads of data for training. Training is accomplished with the help of labelled data. After that trend or pattern is analysed by machine learning technique called knowledge. At last this knowledge with some mathematical function will be used for predictions of unlabelled data.

Sentiment analysis plays a greater role in gaining the overview of wider public opinion and social media interactive dataset is the best source for it. Gaining deeper insights from dataset make it more useful for forecasting applications like stock market in which correct sentiment identification make it more predictable for investors. Market research for maintaining the quality of product can be accomplished with the help of sentiment analysis. Opinion mining of customer review helps in knowing the current status of our product and its competitors.

Natural language processing (NLP) is one of the promising domain which makes our day to day life easier like keyboard auto completion, speech recognition, dictionary prediction etc. Amalgamation of machine learning with NLP brings awesome results in various applications and sentiment analysis is one of them. Sentiment analysis become talk of the town day by day because of its deep business insights which help in taking further decisions. Sentiment information is taken from customer reviews, posts from microblogging sites like twitter, rediff etc. and computational intelligence based techniques are applied for mining, analysing and forecasting of trend information.

Major limitation in sentiment analysis is the strict classification of polarity in to three buckets called positive, negative and neutral. While human emotions are not so quantifiable every time sometime it is ambiguous and chaotic in nature. While in future researchers are trying to move from one dimensional monotonous scaling of positive to negative to multidimensional scaling. Involvement of deep learning techniques opens a new line of research in sentiment analysis which is described in last part of this chapter. In next section we presented a simple case study of sentiment classifier using Naïve Bayes machine learning algorithm for understanding the general flow of model.

Figure 1. General framework of sentiment analysis

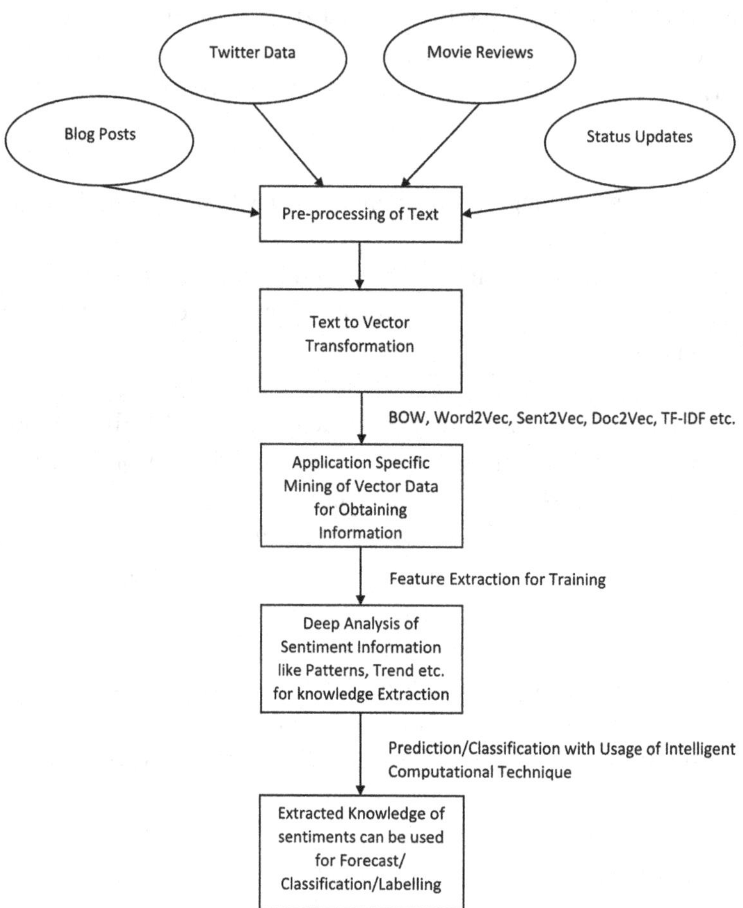

This chapter is arranged as follows. Second section tells about basic machine learning based sentiment analysis with the help of tabular representation. Third section discusses supervised based sentiment classifier. Fourth section is all about revolutionary change bought by next generation of learning (deep) techniques in accuracy of sentiment analysis with the help of existing studies followed by conclusion in the last section.

Case Study Of Naïve Bayes Based Sentiment Classifier

In this small and simple case study our attempt was to make a sentiment classifier based on movie review dataset. In this model firstly we have labelled set of sentiments (positive, negative and neutral) used for training of classifier. After training of classifier unlabelled set of movie reviews are taken for testing. Naïve Baye's model was chosen as classifier for classification task. Let's have some basic idea about Baye's formula first:

$$P[a/b] = [P[b/a]*P[a]]/P[b] \tag{1}$$

Equation 1st is the basic Bayes formula consist of b is the document and a is the class and objective is to find out the probability of class b given by document a. So numerator is composed of likelihood and prior information and denominator consist of normalization constant. Mapping of Bayes algorithm in this problem is followed as: Prior information is original label (L.H.S part) which model come to know at training time and after that testing is done on unlabelled reviews and try to predict the correct labels. Naïve Bayes works on this principle and termed as multinomial Naïve Bayes in text classification problems.

Natural language toolkit was used for importing dataset and further computations. Argmax function was employed which returns probability of polarity with respect to class and help in finding out the class of unlabelled reviews. Trained and fine-tuned model was employed on unlabelled data with best possible parametric setting for this model. Accuracy measure was used for assessment of overall performance. It was observed that seventy to seventy five percent of accuracy was achieved. Top ten words are shown with predicted labels in Table 1.

Accuracy obtained: 82%

Table 1. Most valuable information ten features

Word(unimaginative) = T	n: p =	8.3: 1.0
Word(shoddy) = T	n: p =	6.9: 1.0
Word(schumacher) = T	n: p =	6.9: 1.0
Word(singers) = T	n: p =	6.4: 1.0
Word(turkey) = T	n: p =	6.3: 1.0
Word(suvari) = T	n: p =	6.3: 1.0
Word(mena) = T	n: p =	6.3: 1.0
Word(wasted) = T	n: p =	6.3: 1.0
Word(atrocious) = T	n: p =	5.8: 1.0
Word(justin) = T	n: p =	5.8: 1.0

True = T, Negative = n, Positive = p

It can be concluded that basic machine learning techniques works good but doesn't have brilliant performance. Last three years of research shows a deflection towards NLP with deep learning. It is one of the emerging fields with enormous applications and improving accuracy. In this chapter our aim is to explain the drift of Basic learning based sentiment analysis to advanced learning based sentiment analysis. We tried to explain the power of deep learning based sentiment analysis with the help of detailed review of existing research studies.

MACHINE LEARNING BASED SENTIMENT ANALYSIS

Due to exponential increase in digital world (like social networking sites and online marketing sites) decision making becomes logical. In previous times people use their intution or data was not the biggest power that time. But now prediction becomes easy due to vast availability of data like reviews, blogs etc.

Sentiment analysis is one of the major tool in business analytics because it helps in knowing the doamin, needs and trend of target users. Machine learning based approaches plays a great role in classification and analysis of sentiments for example labelling of unstructured reviews with the help of labelled one. Some of the machine learning based sentiment analysis studies are described and summarised with the help of table 2.

Table 2. Basic learning based sentiment analysis

Reference	Machine Learning Technique Used	Purpose
Neethu & Rajasree, 2013	Naïve Bayes, Support Vector Machine, Maximum Entropy, Ensemble learning	Classification efficiency is improved by using feature extraction technique
Maas et al., 2011	Vector space model, Probabilistic latent topic Model, Linear SVM	Extended unsupervised model with semantic information in association with lexical information
Gautam & Yadav, 2014	Naïve Bayes, Maximum entropy and Support vector machine, Semantic analysis	Naïve Bayes outperform maximum entropy and SVM in classification of reviews with the help of twitter dataset
Mudinas, Zhang, & Levene, 2012	Support Vector Machine, Sentiment strength detection.	Integrates lexicon and learning based approaches and shows better results on CNET and IMDB movie reviews as compared to individual learning or lexicon based models
Tripathy, Agrawal, & Rath, 2016	Stochastic Gradient Descent, Naïve Bayes, Maximum Entropy,	Text conversion in to vector is accomplished with the Combination of count vectorizer and TF-IDF, also compare N-Gram with POS techniques. It was shown that as N increases after two accuracy starts decreasing
Rosenthal, Farra, & Nakov, 2017	Support Vector Machine, word2vec	Cross lingual training was explored with the help of Arabic language and shows improved results in irony and emotion detection
Cambria, 2017	Gated Multimodal Embedding Long short term memory	Use of temporal attention layer proved to be very beneficial in dealing of acoustic and visual noise
Chen, Xu, He, & Wang, 2017	Divide and Conquer, Neural Network	Sentence level sentiment analysis was accomplished with convolutional neural network at sentence level
Appel, Chiclana, Carter, & Fujita, 2016	Naïve Bayes, Maximum Entropy	Semantic orientation of polarity was utilized with the help of NLP based hybrid technique and shows improved results than NB and ME
Kolchyna, Souza, Treleaven, & Aste, 2015	Support Vector machine, Naïve Bayes, Lexicon based ensemble method	Naïve Bayes and SVM outperforms the lexicon based methods
Toh & Su, 2016	Feed forward Neural Network	Two step approach was employed, single layer feed forward network for domain classification, DNN for sequential classification
Kanakaraj & Guddeti, 2015	Decision Tree, Random Forest, Extremely Randomized Trees	Experimented with ensemble based learning which have kind of approaches depend on application and training data provided.
Chalothom & Ellman, 2015	Naïve Bayes, Support Vector Machine, Senti Strength and Stacking	Different flavour of supervised and semi supervised ensemble classifiers was explored in association with lexicons and shows better results than BOW
Dey, Chakraborty, Biswas, Bose, & Tiwari, 2016	Naïve Bayes, K- Nearest Neighbour	Two supervised learning approaches were used by focussing on sentence polarity and subjective style on movie and hotel reviews. Results were application specific.

DEEP LEARNING BASED SENTIMENT ANALYSIS

Sentiment analysis aim is to analyse people's sentiments or opinions according to their area of interest. Sentiment analysis becomes a hot topic among researchers with the rapid growth of online generated data and equally powerful processing techniques like natural language processing, machine learning and deep learning etc. As we already discussed machine learning techniques in previous section in association with supervised learning based case study. Results are still not satisfactory with basic learning techniques. In this section we will study advance learning techniques called deep learning and studies which accomplished these techniques in sentiment analysis and opinion mining.

Word embedding is one of the crucial step in deep learning based sentiment analysis technique. As described in (Tang et al., 2016) "Word embedding is a representation in which each word is represented as a continuous, low-dimensional and real valued vector". Basic concept behind word embedding is the utilization of context information. For example words like good and bad will be mapped in to same space and beneficial in many NLP applications (POS tagging etc.) but proved to be a disaster in case of sentiment analysis because of their opposite polarity. Therefore, extra information called sentiment embedding is needed for increasing the effectiveness of word context. Semantic embedding is composed of labelled information called sentiment polarity and able to differentiate between words which have opposite polarity. The authors (Tang et al., 2016) uses two neural networks one for prediction (predict polarity of words) and another for ranking (provide real valued sentiment score for word sequence with fixed window size). Empirical study was carried out with three models (Dist + Ngrams, SVM+ Ngrams, SVM + Text Features) on twitter dataset. Effectiveness of sentiment embedding was experimented on three levels word, sentence and lexical. End results concluded sentiment embedding and proved to be a milestone on three levels; word level shows sentiment similarity between words, sentence level for discriminative features and lexical level for sentiment lexicon.

Another approach was proposed by (Chen, Sun, Tu, Lin, & Liu, 2016) for same problem: absence of sentiment information. This approach utilizes the document –level sentiment information which deals with complete information about a product instead of just local level text information. This model was built on hierarchical neural network in association with global user and product based information. Hierarchical long short term memory model was employed to generate sentence and document embedding. Sometime due to vague ratings and complex statement of reviews sentiment analysis degrades its accuracy. At that time user and product information played a significant role in improving the accuracy of model.

Customer reviews is one of the major factor for accessing the opinionated quality of any product. Traditionally it was accomplished with manual steps like lexicon construction, feature engineering etc. But revolutionary change in computation come up with deep learning techniques which reduces the human efforts of feature selection and make this work automated with high demand of large data. Deep learning techniques intrinsically learn mappings from large scale training data. The authors (Guan et al., 2016) proposed a new framework in association with deep learning which is composed of two steps. First one is to learn embedding from rating of customer reviews and second one is the addition of classification layer for supervised fine tuning of labelled sentences. Learning of embedding is based on the concept of sentences with same labels are ranked closer while sentences with opposite labels are ranked farther from each other. Weakly supervised deep learning embedding (WDE) was employed with the help of convolutional neural network. Effectiveness of WDE was measured with the help of amazon reviews and it was concluded that framework based on weakly labelled set of sentences outperforms existing baseline models.

Employment of deep learning in sentiment analysis make it easier to extract contextual information from complex short texts like reviews, posts of microblogging sites etc. Joint model was proposed by (Wang, Jiang, & Luo, 2016) was built with convolutional neural network (CNN) and recurrent neural network (RNN). CNN took the advantage of coarse grained local features while RNN learned via long term distance dependencies. Windows of different length and involvement of various weight metrics was employed in CNN and max pooling was used from left to right. Pipeline of framework was composed of word and sentence embedding after that convolutional and pooling layers, RNN layer support with concatenation layer and final output with softmax output. Results was computed on three benchmark datasets 1) Movie Review 2) Stanford sentiment treebank1 (SST1) with all kind of reviews 3) SST2 with binary labels only. This joint model outperforms the CNN and RNN models alone.

One of the best application which exploits deep learning is financial sentiment analysis. Stock price forecasting is of great interest for investors before investing their money. Financial sentiment analysis comes under financial technology also called as Fin Tech (Day & Lee, 2016) is one of the growing research field. Exploration of deep learning for improving accuracy of forecasting make it more interesting for investors. Stock attributes is composed of information like firm specific news articles, public sentiments which affects decision and impact of media information on firms. This means same information may leads to different decisions for different investors. Deep learning model was employed with three non-linear activation functions called Sigmoid, TanH and rectified linear Unit (ReLu). Result shows that inclusion of deep learning techniques proved to be a turning stone in increasing the forecasting accuracy of Fin Tech models.

Deep learning techniques are data hungry and therefore they work best in case of big data analytics. Big investment banks like Goldman Sachs, Lehman Brothers and Salomon brothers uses the financial advice as their backbone. StockTwits and SeekingAlpha is one of the growing social media for investors and stock information. Long short term memory, doc2vec and CNN model was employed by (Sohangir, Wang, Pomeranets, & Khoshgoftaar, 2018) for finding out the hidden knowledgeable patterns from StockTwits network. Performance was evaluated with accuracy, precision, recall, F-measure and AUC. It was concluded from results that CNN outperforms logistic regression, doc2ve and LSTM for StockTwits dataset.

Most of the sentiment analysis models are based on English generated texts, the authors (Vateekul & Koomsubha, 2016) evaluated the deep learning based sentiment analysis on Thai generated twitter data. Two efficient deep learning techniques was employed one is long short term memory (LSTM) and another is dynamic convolutional neural networks (DCNN) except maximum entropy. Effect of word orders was also taken in to consideration of experimental study. LSTM and DCNN outperforms basic machine learning models for Thai based twitter data. Comprehensive experimental study was carried out for parametric adjustments and results as computed on best parametric settings. It was concluded that DCNN followed by LSTM give best results and shuffling of word orders strongly influence sentiment analysis.

In traditional sentiment analysis (around 2005) statistical models used words with their sentiment scores called lexicons, as their features. But now a days due to involvement of word embedding, use of lexicons become invisible and almost obsolete. The authors (Shin, Lee, & Choi, 2016) tried to explore the combination of word embedding with lexicons. Weather it is a useful combination and if it is what is the best path of using both in association. Experimental study was carried out on two datasets SemEval-2016 Task 4 and Stanford sentiment treebank. Word2Vec from google skip-gram model and six types of lexicon embedding was employed. CNN in association with attention vectors (importance of each word and lexicon) was used as deep learning layer. Integration of lexicons with word embedding helps in improving the efficiency of traditional CNN model.

Sarcasm detection is one of the crucial task in sentiment analysis. Sarcasm consist of ambiguous and reversible statements whose polarity can't be classified positive or negative easily. Therefore, powerful NLP techniques are required for analysis of sarcastic statements. CNN based deeper analysis of sarcastic tweets was accomplished by (Poria, Cambria, Hazarika, & Vij, 2016). CNN was used because it doesn't need any hand crafted features and build its global feature set by taking local features which is good for learning context. Macro-F1 was used as efficacy measure and experiments was accomplished on both CNN and CNN-SVM in which extracted features from CNN, fed to SVM for classification.

Similar to sarcasm there is one more information called hate speech detection. It is useful in various business decisions. Hateful tweets are imposed of abusive language and a targeted domain may be product, gender, racism, Gay community etc. Multiple classifiers was employed by (Badjatiya, Gupta, Gupta, & Varma, 2017) in association with three deep learning embedding called Fast Text, CNN and LSTM for detection of hateful sentiments. Comprehensive analysis of numerous embedding was accomplished like TF-IDF values, Bag of words model, GLoVe model and deep learning based embedding. Precision, recall and F1 measure was used as evaluation metrics. It was observed that deep learning based embedding outperform baseline embedding models and gradient boosted decision tree shows best accuracy values.

Composition of sentiment plays an important role in detecting the sentiment polarity. Extended approach of layer-wise relevance propagation was used with recurrent neural network (RNN) (Arras, Montavon, Müller, & Samek, 2017). RNN was employed with one hidden layer of bi-directional long short term memory and five class sentiment prediction. Trained LSTM was compared on two decomposition methods sensitivity analysis and LRP. It was concluded from our experiments, LRP based LSTM supports best classification decision as compared to gradient based decomposition.

Lexical and syntactic features are one of the turning stones in improving the accuracy of sentiments. Unsupervised learning (Jianqiang, Xiaolin, & Xuejun, 2018) was used in association with latent contextual semantic relationship and co-occurrence relationship between tweets. Feature set was obtained through word embedding with n-gram features and polarity score of word sentiments. Feature set was propagated to deep convolution neural network was for training and prediction of sentiment labels. Accuracy and F1 measure on five twitter datasets (STSTd, SE2014, STSGd, SED, SSTd) clearly shows GloVe - DCNN model outperform baseline N-gram model, BoW and SVM classifier.

With the advent of deep learning models traditional approaches become invisible while they also have good computational powers. The authors (Araque, Corcuera-Platas, Sanchez-Rada, & Iglesias, 2018) explores combination of both traditional surface approaches and deep learning. Baseline model was formed with word embedding and linear machine learning approach. Ensemble of (classifiers and features) models was formed from these varied feature set and experimented on six public datasets. Friedman test was used for empirical verification of results and it was observed that ensemble of features and classifiers outperforms basic models.

One of the major issue in sentiment analysis is their language because not all tweets are monolingual, and at that time translation incurs extra cost. Machine learning based approaches needs extra effort of machine translation. Deep learning based models was proposed by (Wehrmann, Becker, Cagnini, & Barros, 2017) which learn latent features from all languages at the time of training. Word level and character level embedding was explored with CNN. Four different language tweets (English, Spanish, Potuguese and German) was analysed. Results was compared with machine translation based techniques with three polarities (Positive, Negative, Neutral) with the help of accuracy and F-Measure. Proposed approach works on character level networks so independent of machine translation technique, word embedding, less pre-processing steps and took only half of memory space. Summary of deep learning techniques used in sentiment analysis is presented Table 3.

Table 3. Deep learning in sentiment analysis

Authors	Algorithm	Dataset	Text 2 vec	Efficacy Measures	Language
Tang et al., 2016	Sentiment Embedding+KNN	Twitter Data (SemEval, RottenTomatoes)	WE, SE, word2veec	Accuracy	English
Guan et al., 2016	SVM, SVM+NB, CNN	Amazon Customer Review	Word2vec	Accuracy, Macro F1	English
Wang et al., 2016	CNN, CNN+RNN	Movie Reviews, Stanford Sentiment Treebank (SST1) and SST2	Word2vec	Accuracy	English
Chen et al., 2016	Hierarchical LSTM	IMDB, Yelp 2013, Yelp 2014	Sentence level embedding	Accuracy, RMSE	English
Day & Lee, 2016	Deep neural network with sigmoid, tanH and ReLu function	News data (Now News, Apple Daily, LTN and Money DJ finance)	Lexicon based embedding	ROI Heatmap	Chinese
Vateekul & Koomsubha, 2016	LSTM and DCNN	Thai tweet corpus	Word2vec	Accuracy	Thai
Shin et al., 2017	CNN	SemEval'16 Task 4 and SST	Word2vec, lexicon embedding	F1 score, Accuracy	English
Poria et al., 2017	CNN, CNN-SVM	Sarcastic tweets	Word2vec	F1 score	English
Badjatiya et al., 2017	CNN, LSTM	Hate related tweets	BOWV, N-gram, GloVe, FastText	Precision, Recall, F1 measure	English
Arras et al., 2017	Bi-directional LSTM	SST, movie reviews	Word2vec	Accuracy	English
Jianqiang et al., 2017	Deep convolution neural network	STSTd, SemEval2014, Stanford twitter sentiment gold, SED, SSTd	GloVe, BOW	Precision, Recall, F1 score	English
Araque et al., 2017	Ensemble of classifiers	Microblogging data and movie reviews	Word2vec, GloVe	F1 score	English
Wehrmann et al., 2017	CNN, LSTM	1.6 million annotated tweets	Word and character level embedding	Accuracy, F-measure	English, German, Portuguese, Spanish
Sohangir et al., 2018	LSTM, CNN	StockTwits posts	Doc2vec	Accuracy, Precision, AUC	English

CONCLUSION

Sentiment analysis is one of the evolving research area with an ample amount of applications and getting matured day by day. It is concluded from above studies that accuracy of sentiment analysis models are not up to the mark till now. One of the main reason behind lacking of accuracy is complex structure of data. While, it is also observed that drift from machine learning to deep learning techniques with natural language processing shows promising results. Unstructured nature of data is very difficult for training and accuracy achieved by basic machine learning algorithms were very low. Correct feature extraction is the heart of machine learning algorithms. But this problem is very much solved by the use of deep learning algorithms due to automatic selection of features with large availability of data. And it is estimated that understanding the contextual behaviour of data (ratings, reviews etc.) with deep learning and other computational techniques make it more likable for more applications in future.

REFERENCES

Appel, O., Chiclana, F., Carter, J., & Fujita, H. (2016). A hybrid approach to the sentiment analysis problem at the sentence level. *Knowledge-Based Systems, 108*, 110–124. doi:10.1016/j.knosys.2016.05.040

Araque, O., Corcuera-Platas, I., Sanchez-Rada, J. F., & Iglesias, C. A. (2017). Enhancing deep learning sentiment analysis with ensemble techniques in social applications. *Expert Systems with Applications, 77*, 236–246. doi:10.1016/j.eswa.2017.02.002

Arras, L., Montavon, G., Müller, K.R., & Samek, W. (2017). *Explaining recurrent neural network predictions in sentiment analysis*. Academic Press.

Badjatiya, P., Gupta, S., Gupta, M., & Varma, V. (2017). Deep learning for hate speech detection in tweets. *Proceedings of the 26th International Conference on World Wide Web Companion*, 759-760. 10.1145/3041021.3054223

Cambria, E. (2016). Affective computing and sentiment analysis. *IEEE Intelligent Systems, 31*(2), 102–107. doi:10.1109/MIS.2016.31

Chalothom, T., & Ellman, J. (2015). Simple approaches of sentiment analysis via ensemble learning. In Information science and applications. Springer. doi:10.1007/978-3-662-46578-3_74

Chen, H., Sun, M., Tu, C., Lin, Y., & Liu, Z. (2016). Neural sentiment classification with user and product attention. *Proceedings of the 2016 conference on empirical methods in natural language processing*, 1650-1659. 10.18653/v1/D16-1171

Chen, T., Xu, R., He, Y., & Wang, X. (2017). Improving sentiment analysis via sentence type classification using BiLSTM-CRF and CNN. *Expert Systems with Applications, 72*, 221–230. doi:10.1016/j.eswa.2016.10.065

Day, M. Y., & Lee, C. C. (2016). Deep learning for financial sentiment analysis on finance news providers. *2016 IEEE/ACM International Conference on Advances in Social Networks Analysis and Mining*, 1127-1134. 10.1109/ASONAM.2016.7752381

Dey, L., Chakraborty, S., Biswas, A., Bose, B., & Tiwari, S. (2016). *Sentiment analysis of review datasets using naive bayes and k-nn classifier.* arXiv preprint arXiv:1610.09982

Gautam, G., & Yadav, D. Sentiment analysis of twitter data using machine learning approaches and semantic analysis. In *2014 Seventh International Conference on Contemporary Computing (IC3)*. IEEE. 10.1109/IC3.2014.6897213

Guan, Z., Chen, L., Zhao, W., Zheng, Y., Tan, S., & Cai, D. (2016). *Weakly-Supervised Deep Learning for Customer Review Sentiment Classification*. IJCAI.

Jianqiang, Z., Xiaolin, G., & Xuejun, Z. (2018). Deep convolution neural networks for Twitter sentiment analysis. *IEEE Access: Practical Innovations, Open Solutions*, *6*, 23253–23260. doi:10.1109/ACCESS.2017.2776930

Kanakaraj, M., & Guddeti, R. M. R. Performance analysis of Ensemble methods on Twitter sentiment analysis using NLP techniques. In *Proceedings of the 2015 IEEE 9th International Conference on Semantic Computing*. IEEE. 10.1109/ICOSC.2015.7050801

Kolchyna, O., Souza, T. T. P., Treleaven, P., & Aste, T. (2015). *Twitter sentiment analysis: Lexicon method, machine learning method and their combination.* arXiv preprint arXiv:1507.00955

Maas, A. L., Daly, R. E., Pham, P. T., Huang, D., Ng, A. Y., & Potts, C. Learning word vectors for sentiment analysis. In *Proceedings of the 49th annual meeting of the association for computational linguistics: Human language technologies*. Association for Computational Linguistics.

Mudinas, A., Zhang, D., & Levene, M. (2012). Combining lexicon and learning based approaches for concept-level sentiment analysis. In *Proceedings of the first international workshop on issues of sentiment discovery and opinion mining*. ACM. 10.1145/2346676.2346681

Neethu, M. S., & Rajasree, R. Sentiment analysis in twitter using machine learning techniques. In *2013 Fourth International Conference on Computing, Communications and Networking Technologies*. IEEE. 10.1109/ICCCNT.2013.6726818

Poria, S., Cambria, E., Hazarika, D., & Vij, P. (2016). *A deeper look into sarcastic tweets using deep convolutional neural networks.,* arXiv preprint arXiv:1610.08815

Rosenthal, S., Farra, N., & Nakov, P. (2017). SemEval-2017 task 4: Sentiment analysis in Twitter. *Proceedings of the 11th international workshop on semantic evaluation (SemEval-2017)*, 502-518. 10.18653/v1/S17-2088

Shin, B., Lee, T., & Choi, J. D. (2016). *Lexicon integrated cnn models with attention for sentiment analysis.* arXiv preprint arXiv:1610.06272

Sohangir, S., Wang, D., Pomeranets, A., & Khoshgoftaar, T. M. (2018). Big Data: Deep Learning for financial sentiment analysis. *Journal of Big Data*, *5*(1), 3. doi:10.118640537-017-0111-6

Tang, D., Wei, F., Qin, B., Yang, N., Liu, T., & Zhou, M. (2016). Sentiment embeddings with applications to sentiment analysis. *IEEE Transactions on Knowledge and Data Engineering*, *28*(2), 496–509. doi:10.1109/TKDE.2015.2489653

Toh, Z., & Su, J. (2016). Nlangp at semeval-2016 task 5: Improving aspect based sentiment analysis using neural network features. *Proceedings of the 10th international workshop on semantic evaluation*, 282-288. 10.18653/v1/S16-1045

Tripathy, A., Agrawal, A., & Rath, S. K. (2016). Classification of sentiment reviews using n-gram machine learning approach. *Expert Systems with Applications*, *57*, 117–126. doi:10.1016/j.eswa.2016.03.028

Vateekul, P., & Koomsubha, T. (2016). A study of sentiment analysis using deep learning techniques on Thai Twitter data. *2016 13th International Joint Conference on Computer Science and Software Engineering*, 1-6. 10.1109/JCSSE.2016.7748849

Wang, X., Jiang, W., & Luo, Z. (2016). Combination of convolutional and recurrent neural network for sentiment analysis of short texts. *Proceedings of COLING 2016, the 26th International Conference on Computational Linguistics: Technical Papers*, 2428-2437.

Wehrmann, J., Becker, W., Cagnini, H. E. L., & Barros, R. C. (2017). A character-based convolutional neural network for language-agnostic Twitter sentiment analysis. *2017 International Joint Conference on Neural Networks (IJCNN)*, 2384-2391. 10.1109/IJCNN.2017.7966145

This research was previously published in the Handbook of Research on Emerging Trends and Applications of Machine Learning; pages 171-182, copyright year 2020 by Engineering Science Reference (an imprint of IGI Global).

Chapter 15
Public Security Sentiment Analysis on Social Web:
A Conceptual Framework for the Analytical Process and a Research Agenda

Victor Diogho Heuer de Carvalho
https://orcid.org/0000-0003-2369-7317
Universidade Federal de Alagoas, Brazil

Ana Paula Cabral Seixas Costa
Universidade Federal de Pernambuco, Brazil

ABSTRACT

This article presents (1) the results of a literature review on social web mining and sentiment analysis on public security; (2) the idea of a framework for the analytical process involved in the literature review themes; and (3) a research agenda with a perspective for future studies, considering some elements of the analytical process. The literature review was based on searches of five databases: Scopus, IEEE Xplore, Web of Science, ScienceDirect, and Springer Link. Search strings were applied to retrieve literature material of four kinds, without defining an initial time milestone, to get the historical register of publications associated with the main thematic. After some filtering, primary and secondary findings were separated, enabling the identification of elements for the framework. Finally, the research agenda is presented, containing a set of three research artifacts related to the proposed framework.

INTRODUCTION

The great amount of information available through the social web signals to organizations an analytical perspective aligned with a social need to view human behavior to understand preferences, opinions, emotions, and feelings (Bjurstrom, 2015). The emergence of the concept of Big Data, related to an enormous amount of data in several formats and retrievable by various sources (Poleto, Carvalho, & Costa, 2017),

DOI: 10.4018/978-1-6684-6303-1.ch015

only tends to reinforce this need. It also makes evident the tendency to combine artificial intelligence with data science (Sapountzi & Psannis, 2018).

While there are enormous amounts and varieties of data possible to retrieve and use—for instance, on decision-making (Tien, 2013)—the mining process is not trivial and requires a suitable technological toolbox for different purposes (Dobre & Xhafa, 2014).

In the organizational context, public services have many advantages to derive from both the massive amount of information and the analytical tools to ensure that stakeholders' expectations can be met within the appropriate time, and generating processes are satisfactorily attended (Charalabidis, Koussouris, & Ramfos, 2011).

The organizational management is the main beneficiary since the related technological resources can make new knowledge discoveries, combine them with those already existing, and disseminating the results to the organization to promote continuous process improvement (Caione, Guido, Martella, Paiano, & Pandurino, 2016; Handzic, 2011). Knowledge discovery may apply in different data-structuring contexts, but it is important to emphasize that unstructured data are common in Big Data, and in this case, specific tools are required for web mining, text mining, and natural language processing (NLP) (Carvalho & Costa, 2019; Usai, Pironti, Mital, & Aouina Mejri, 2018).

Organizational knowledge management, decision support systems, big data, and data science have all become more integrated, and organizations, in turn, make use of this integration to drive strategic change. The main link among these elements is the need for information technology in the organization, promoting suitable means for sharing information and knowledge, even as they enable decision-making aligned with operational needs to ensure efficient troubleshooting (Navarro, Ruiz, & Peña, 2017; Wang & Noe, 2010).

One of the most critical sectors of public services that may benefit from data analysis is public security. The use of data from different sources (including the social web) and the application of analytical tools could lead, for instance, to the concept of the "smart city," defined by Manjunatha & Annappa (2018) as a milestone of urban planning and development that integrates information technology with people's routines, promoting sustainability and quality of life. Public security benefits from this integration insofar as it can make use of data such as past criminal registers, historical registered cases, and real-time information, enabling forecasting of events that threaten the public welfare.

Social web mining and sentiment analysis are areas from text mining dedicated to retrieve users-published records (social web mining) and to analyze these records to classify them according to polarity (sentiment analysis) expressed by the user (Kamel et al., 2010; He et al., 2015). Both have interesting toolkits that grant analytical power to be explored by areas such as public security to assess, for example, the level of satisfaction of people in social networks regarding the actions of policing, investigations, tracking of criminal activity, application, and maintenance of security policies in general (Carvalho & Costa, 2019). In this sense, related tools and their applications in public security deserve to be evidenced through a literature review identifying what is being applied and for what purposes, in other words, demonstrating what types of problems they are solving.

This article aims to: (i) present the results of a literature review about social web mining and sentiment analysis in public security; (ii) present the concept of a framework for the analytical process involved in the literature thematic; and (iii) define an agenda to support future research based on the analytical process. The emphasis is on the public-security area as a critical sector with absolute social repercussions, since it directly deals with the protection of people acting as social agents themselves, the main information providers, using several kinds of platforms (notably the social web).

The rest of this article is organized as follows: Section 2 presents the research procedure. Section 3 contains a summary of the literature findings. Section 4 contains the literature review. Section 5 proposes the framework. Section 6 establishes the research agenda. Finally, Section 7 contains the conclusions.

RESEARCH PROCEDURE

The reported research has a descriptive character, involving social web mining and sentiment analysis related to social impressions of public security. Its first part was a literature search to clarify which elements are necessary to formulate a framework for the analytical process involved.

Social web mining exists to extract people's registers on several social web sources as weblogs, forums, personal websites, news sites, and social networks, revealing a field of computational applications with abundant techniques (Ravi & Ravi, 2015; Stieglitz, Mirbabaie, Ross, & Neuberger, 2018). This makes the understanding of social web mining principles and purposes fundamental for using them adequately in the social field of interest (for instance, public security).

Figure 1 presents the flow of the research procedure, in three phases: first, literature research on the themes of interest, identifying available analytical techniques/tools and data sources; second, the proposal of the framework, based on the literature findings; and third, the definition of an agenda to support future research.

Figure 1. Research flow in three phases

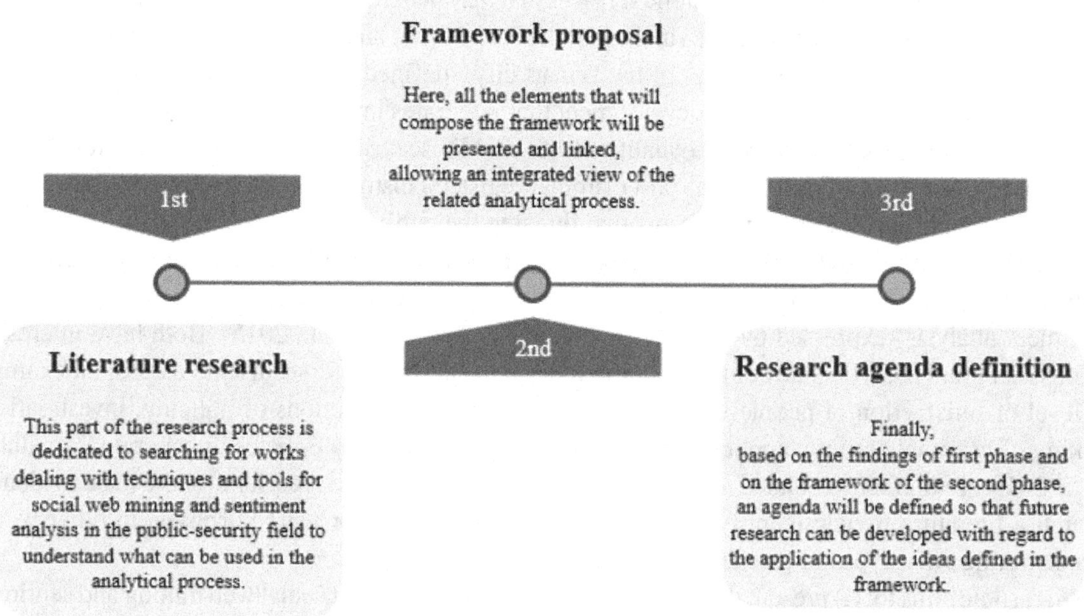

The first phase detail follows, still within this methodological section, and its results will be presented subsequently. The literature directly influenced the second and third phases, so the framework proposal and the research agenda will be presented after the literature review section.

Literature Research Procedure

The literature review was developed based on the procedures described by Kitchenham and Charters (2007), Akter et al. (2019), and Sundermann, Domingues, Sinoara, Marcacini, and Rezende (2019). Definitions there should include (i) objectives, (ii) research questions, (iii) inclusion and exclusion criteria, (iv) search and selection strategies, and (v) filtering and evaluation of the findings. Figure 2 presents the related workflow.

Figure 2. Workflow for literature research and review

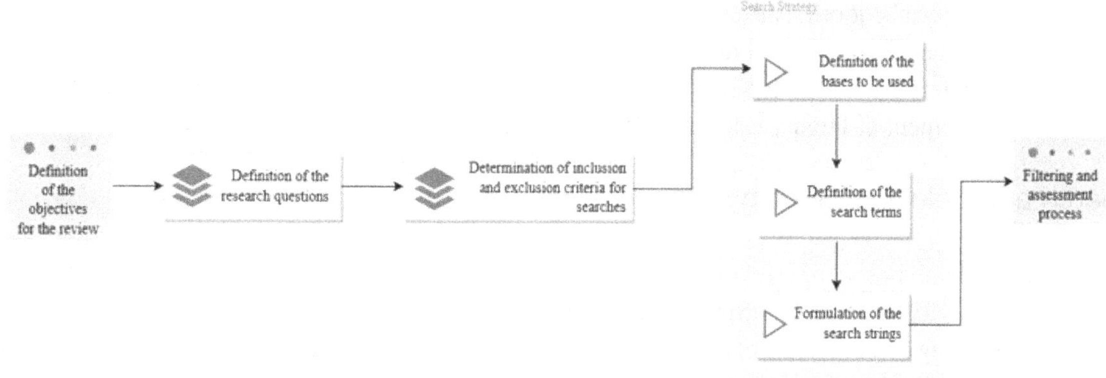

Objectives

To identify and select studies about techniques and tools for social web mining and sentiment analysis in the public-security field is the main objective of the literature review.

Research Questions

Q1: Which tools can be applied to retrieve data from the social web and to analyze the feelings related to public security?

Regarding "tools", the idea here is to identify methods, techniques, software, or any other type of technology that can be applied throughout the analytical process represented in the framework proposal. There are different tools for extracting textual records, preprocessing, identifying topics, and classifying sentiments, for example, so it is important to have a sense of what literature findings are applying for specific purposes.

Q2: Which data sources and informational elements should be considered for collection and analysis in the process?

In this case, the idea is to identify the data sources used by the literature findings and which informational elements were considered for application in the analysis. These elements, for example, can be user data (gender, age), date of publication of texts, and location.

Inclusion/Exclusion Criteria

These criteria were defined to limit the results, filtering them based on the language, kinds of materials, and publication period:

- Studies about web mining and sentiment analysis;
- Studies about public sentiment on security;
- Only studies in English;
- Kind of materials: journal articles, conference articles, books and book chapters;
- Period: all material published until April 2019;
- Access: material available to search through the Research Portal of the Brazilian Coordination for the Improvement of Higher Education Personnel and open-access materials.

Search and Selection Strategy

The following databases were used to ensure the quality of the search results: Scopus, Web of Science, Science Direct, IEEE Xplore, and Springer Link. For each database, using its specific notation, search strings with varying combinations of the terms were applied: "public security," "social networks," "social web," "sentiment analysis," and "opinion mining." All the searches were done by "titles, abstracts, and keywords" (or the equivalent composition, depending on the database).

Findings Filtering

The findings filtering was done in a first moment using the initial search results to identify duplicated material, and since the number of findings was small, this was an easy task. Then, the literature findings were evaluated to identify which materials made a relevant contribution to knowledge about the research themes (i.e., web mining and sentiment analysis).

FINDINGS

Before the presentation of the literature review itself, it is interesting to present an overview of the results obtained by using the procedure previously described. Table 1 contains the strings applied with their respective results (i.e., the number of materials per database).

Regarding the kind of material, defined by the inclusion/exclusion criteria, four kinds of publications were searched. Noteworthy is that Springer Link categorizes book conference articles as well as book chapters. Figure 3 contains the percentage found for each kind.

Table 1. Strings and number of findings per database

Strings	Bases				
	Scopus	**IEEE Xplore**	**Web of Science**	**Science Direct**	**Springer Link**
String 1: "public security" AND "web mining" AND ("sentiment analysis" OR "opinion mining")	0	4	0	0	2
String 2: "public security" AND ("social networks" OR "social web") AND ("sentiment analysis" OR "opinion mining")	1	12	0	1	20
String 3: "public security" AND ("social networks" OR "social web") AND "web mining" AND ("sentiment analysis" OR "opinion mining")	0	3	0	0	0

Journal articles predominate, followed by conference papers and book chapters. On the latter two kinds, the graph shows that the hybrid kind "chapter and conference article" is an intermediate element that, added to either "chapter" or "conference paper," does not change the order of predominance.

The largest number of findings occurred from the Springer Link database, and it was easy to verify that there were no duplicates between the two strings that presented results. The total amount of findings from Springer Link was 22.

IEEE Xplore was the second-ranked database on the number of findings, with a total of 19. For this database, the strategy to eliminate the duplicates was based on a little Python script, using Pandas to handle data frames and Glob libraries to read multiple data files in comma-separated values (csv) format for the case reported here. The filtering resulted in 14 unique findings at the intersection of each string for this database. However, the search on IEEE Xplore returned two lists of content in conference proceedings that were eliminated, resulting in 14 unique findings.

Scopus and ScienceDirect each returned just one result and only for the second string, and it was also easy to detect that both results referred to the same finding. Web of Science did not return any findings for the three strings.

With thirty-five findings (twenty-two from Springer Link, twelve from IEEE Xplore and one from Scopus/ScienceDirect), new analyses were performed. Figure 4 presents the count of findings per year.

Figure 3. Percentages per kind of findings

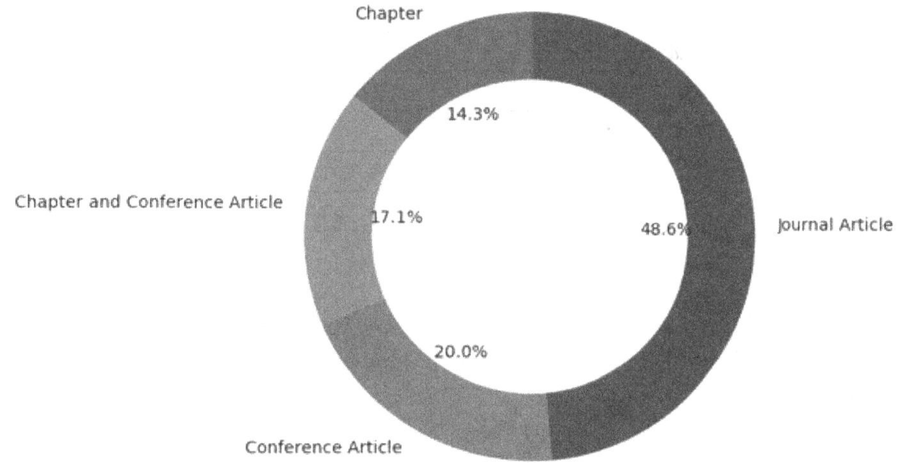

Figure 4. The number of findings per year

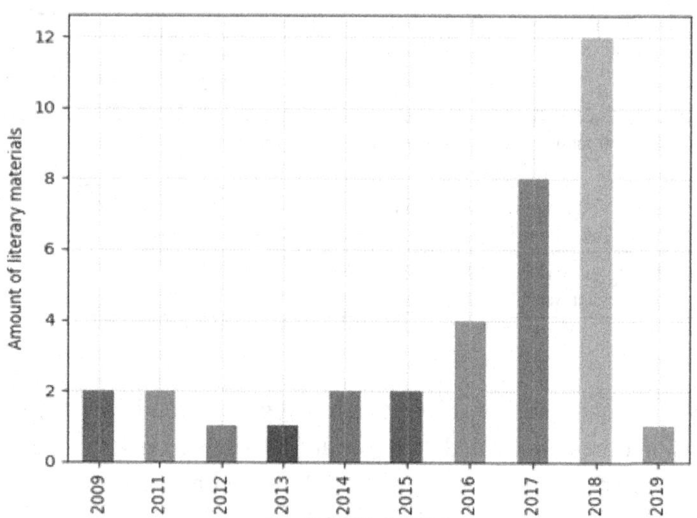

The year 2018 presented the largest number of literature items (twelve findings) about the researched themes, followed by 2017, with eight findings. The third was for 2016 (four findings), followed by 2009, 2011, 2014, and 2015 (each with two findings). Finally, the smaller amounts were for 2012, 2013, and 2019, each with only one finding. Since no initial time/period restrictions were applied, 2009 can be taken as the starting point for the publications on the thematic of the present article.

The last analysis filtered the materials for their accessibility. Although the searches had presented a last filtered amount of 35 findings, not all materials were accessible by the means defined in the inclusion/exclusion criteria. So, even though their abstracts could partially contain some findings, it was judged that using only the information contained in these abstracts did not guarantee an analysis that would be sufficiently good to define the alignment of the works with the research. Based on this, the literature review was done using a final count of twenty-four texts. Table 2 presents the classification of these findings, according to their kind.

Table 2. The number of accessible findings per kind

Kind	Amount
Journal article	16
Book chapter	1
Conference article	7
Total	**24**

Table 3 presents the count related to the databases where the materials were found.

Figure 5 presents the count of the ten most frequent keywords related to these 24 final findings.

Table 3. The number of accessible materials per database

Base	Amount
Springer Link	11
IEEE Xplore	12
Scopus/ScienceDirect	1
Total	**24**

Figure 5. The ten most frequent keywords related to the final twenty-four findings

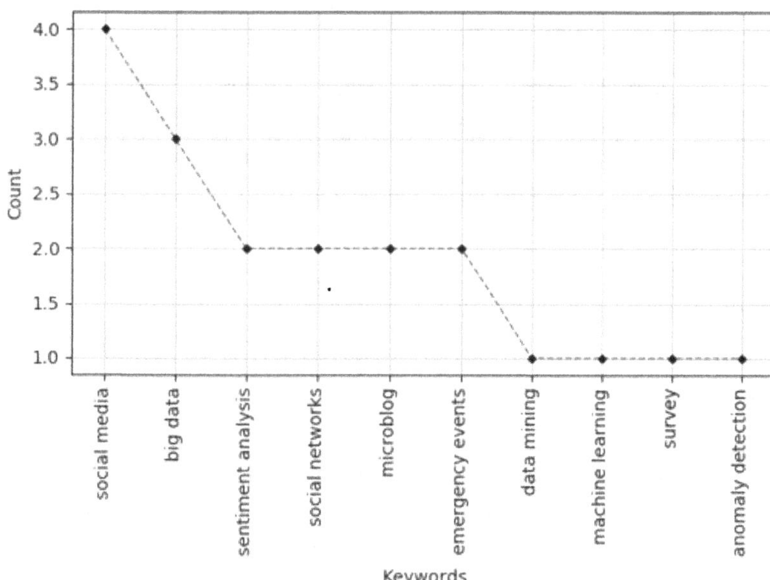

The final count revealed a total of 111 keywords, and the first six were the most frequent terms since from the seventh until the last one, the frequency is unitary. A word cloud also could be elaborated based on the keywords, as Figure 6 shows.

This last graph allows an understanding of the recurrence of words based on their size, adjusted according to the number of occurrences. All the keywords were broken into their atomic terms to construct this cloud, so the counting is quite different from that presented in Figure 5.

The final analysis of these twenty-four findings intended to determine which of them had direct alignment with the research objectives. Nine articles were considered primary because they deal directly with public security, using the researched tools/techniques; fifteen articles were considered secondary because they were not dedicated exclusively to the theme, although they made some mention of public security.

Figure 6. Word cloud extracted from the keywords of the 24 final findings

LITERATURE REVIEW

The secondary findings point out several developments on social web mining and sentiment analysis used to study behavior patterns or to describe people's impressions of events that reverberate on the social web. Sentiment analysis that has demonstrated its value to public security is supported by machine learning, data mining, NLP, and computational linguistics tools (Yue, Chen, Li, Zuo, & Yin, 2018).

Different topics within the field of public security have been dealt with from data mining and analysis point-of-view, helping the authorities to monitor situations that can threaten people's security. The study by Bisio et al. (2015) on social networks sought to identify unscheduled events on Twitter, based on the service traffic analysis, by fielding an experiment with three different scenarios, two of which were unexpected and involved the security of the participants. They tested techniques based on semantic clustering or text mining and demonstrated the performance metrics for each scenario.

In general, not only the public-security area but all public administration is a fertile field for applications related to data mining, social network analysis, sentiment analysis, and related tools. Charalabidis et al. (2011) proposed an online platform to boost open-innovation initiatives in public services, considering elements of the creative process within web 2.0, such as wikis, blogs, social networks, and web 3.0, responsive to users' actions and able to perform forecasting and make suggestions. These authors suggest the presence of open and connected repositories to be used in the creative process.

Predicting the social-web user's behavior has received attention from public-security authorities aware that digital communication platforms are a means of data extraction, to indicate behavior trends that aid in anticipating actions and avoiding risk situations (Cui et al., 2016).

In this field of behavior prediction, the bibliographic research found interesting studies:

- Lin, Mao, and Zeng (2017) worked on refining the classification of feelings based on personality trends, using data extracted from a Chinese microblog service;
- Bao et al. (2009) proposed a model based on the association of emotion and terms or topics of users to perform socio-affective text mining;
- Jin, Zhang, and Zhang (2018) formulated an index to assess the negativity of users' moods related to events receiving comment on social networks;
- Chen, Cai, Huang, and Jiao (2016) worked with the identification of users hired to make floods of posts on social networks, based on their behavior patterns.

In parallel to public security, the literature aided to detect the transportation area as deserving of the attention of researchers on sentiment analysis. For instance, Cao, Wang, and Lin (2018) developed a study using semantic information extracted from Chinese social networks to support the analysis of vehicle traffic conditions based on users' registers. The authors highlight that threatening situations may be detected according to the conditions and kinds of traffic occurrences reported by users. Lv, Chen, Zhang, Duan, and Li (2017) carried out a bibliographical survey of the transportation area and detected that social web/social networks, web mining, text mining, and sentiment analysis are recurrent topics.

Big Data and Internet of Things are themes of great interest in urban planning and development, mainly related to the idea of "smart cities." According to Manjunatha and Annappa (2018), public security, transportation/traffic control, and monitoring, health, agricultural production, and public governance are where potential users of analytical tools typically associated with data science and analysis should be sought.

Xu et al. (2017) developed an interesting study that presented a method based on spatial-temporal graphs to describe semantic relations among various concepts. Their study provides an analytical methodology for both punctual analyses as well as analytical software development. The authors sought to validate the method's accuracy through an experiment using a movie database. The application of spatial-temporal graphs in the experiment was based on the semantic relation "person co-acted with person" in movies. An accuracy rate of 96.7% was verified using the extracted data.

Other media than texts for use in the analysis were also detected. For instance, techniques such as cluster analysis may be used to extract characteristics of images available on the social web (Wazarkar & Keshavamurthy, 2019). This kind of technique can help in detecting social events or suspect activities registered on users' images and videos. Peng et al. (2017) surveyed state-of-the-art techniques, based on the joint analysis of several kinds of media describing a kind of application (iMonitor) with which some intelligent systems have been designed and implemented to enable media monitoring: PRISM (United States), Tempora (United Kingdom), and Golden Shield (China).

Zheng et al. (2017) comment that there are still many unsolved problems, highlighting those related to machine understanding of the fuzzy elements on human language, especially to detect and avoid risks, mentioning possible applications in criminal justice.

Primary Literature

Since the secondary findings highlighting the wide range of analytical tools and strategies appeared at the opening of the literature review, now the focus shifts to the primary findings and applications directly associated with public security. Table 4 presents a synthesis of the identified articles sorted as primary literature about social web mining and sentiment analysis applied to public security.

Table 4. Primary findings, with specific application to public security

Authors	Main Application	Techniques/ Technologies	Research Problem	Data Sources	Elements for Analysis
Sun, Zhang, Ding, & Quan (2018)	Detecting abnormal opinions, sentiments, patterns, or aspects of such patterns	Convolutional Neural Network Long and Short-Term Memory for Sentiment Analysis using the multivariate Gaussian model	The main problem in this work is to assess the method applied, demonstrating how accurate it is and validating its applicability for detecting abnormal behaviors on social networks.	Users of a social network	Messages shared on the social network
Leventakis & Kokkinis (2018)	Community policing	- Geospatial processing and analysis - Semantic information extraction by multimedia analysis - Sentiment analysis - Case-based reasoning - Data warehousing and Decision Support Systems	This work presents a set of modules developed within a project dedicated to community policing. The main problem here is to identify what are the technological elements to support the related policing actions.	- Users of dedicated mobile app and web portal - Community policing communications channels in the social web	Messages shared via mentioned channels
Zhang, Zhu, & Wang (2018)	Public emergency events	- Word2Vec - SO-PMI algorithm - Social web mining - Language Technology Platform (LTP) - Recurrent Neural Network (RNN)	This work is concerned with some issues related to the existing lexicons for sentiment classification. Based on these issues, the article's problematic is to propose an alternative procedure using the mentioned technologies, measuring its accuracy.	- Users of a social network - NLP&CC2013 dataset	Messages shared on the social network
Yang, Liu, Liu, & Cui (2018)	Predictions about the occurrences of collective actions	- Social web mining - Sentiment analysis - Collective Emotional Contagion Model - Deep neural networks (DNN) - TensorFlow (to implement DNN)	Here, the main problem is the prediction of the probability of collective actions every day in a next month, ensuring early decision-making about them.	- Users of social networks - Arab Spring dataset	Messages shared on the social network
Tang (2013)	- Harmonious society measurement - Societal risks identification	The work identifies some forms to measure a harmonious society: - Gini coefficient - Legatum Prosperity Index - Happiness Indices - GDP Quality Index - Harmony Indices - Tightness Score On the other hand, it identifies computational techniques to measure the risk perception: - Computational linguistics/NLP	This work defines the measurement of a harmonious society as its main problem, seeking to identify indices for this to be possible.	Social Web in general	Words extracted from people's messages/texts on the social web
Zuo, Wu, Zhang, Wang, & Xu (2018)	Public opinion analysis, with an application in public security	- CAMEL* that uses maximum entropy and latent Dirichlet allocation - Alternatively, a non-parametric alternative to CAMEL, that uses - coupled Dirichlet Processes *Cross-collection Auto-labeled Max Ent-LDA	This work states cross-media aspect-opinion mining as a challenge to be addressed since there are various types of online media. The main problem here is how to deal with the cross-media aspect-opinion mining.	- Social web - News portals	- Online reviews (for experimental purpose) - News texts - Messages shared on microblogs service
Xu et al. (2016)	Detect and describe urban emergency events	Spatial-temporal mining using heuristics associated with the 5W Model (When, Why, What, Where, Who)	The main problem in this work is to provide a good description of an urban emergency event.	Users of a social network	Messages shared on the social network
Jin, Li, Fu, Zhang, & Ding (2017)	Governmental emergency events management	- Social web mining - Opinion mining	The central problem explored in this article is how the government uses opinions on microblogging services to generate alerts, orientations, and promote control in emergencies.	Users of a social network	Messages shared on the social network during the life cycle of emergency events
Koot et al. (2014)	Support for security officers	Web crawling and data extraction using Python's frameworks and libraries, namely: - Django for web development - OAuth 2.0 for social networks authentication - BeautifulSoup for HTML parsing - urllib for URL handling - AJAX for the front-end	The problem explored in this paper is the use of social network analysis tools to partially automate the activities of security agents in extracting information from user profiles, assisting, for example, criminal investigations.	Users of multiple social networks	Personal data in social networks users' profiles

The table notes that the primary findings have their techniques, methods, or technologies distributed according to the typology commented upon by Yue et al. (2018), and the social web mining is present as a feeder for the set of techniques. The typology is divided into the following sets:

- Natural language processing (NLP) set contains techniques for the extraction of useful information from unstructured texts as data sources, and the sentiment analysis is a typical example of a problem that may be solved using these techniques (Lv et al., 2017; Sun et al., 2018).
- Machine learning set contains techniques that enable computers to learn about a specific subject and make inferences analogously to humans. Support vector machines (SVM), naïve Bayes classifiers, maximum entropy method, neural networks, and deep learning, are machine learning techniques that gained notoriety in the literature about sentiment analysis, as they allow better refinement of the data and the process results (Yang & Chen, 2017; Song, Kim, Lee, Kim, & Youn, 2017).

The next subsections will present a synthesis based on the primary findings in Table 4, using this typology.

Natural Language Processing and Computational Linguistics

The article by Zhang et al. (2018) presents applications of these tools in the context of public security for emergencies, aiming to create a comprehensive lexicon of emotions, with data extracted from a Chinese microblog social network. Initially, the authors relied on an existing ontological dictionary from which they extracted words related to emotional situations used on the network. The Word2Vec tool was used to transform the messages/postings into a vector of words, applying the SO-PMI algorithm to calculate the value of pointwise mutual information in a new word, and another defined for comparison to get the emotional tendency of the new word in the process. This procedure was performed several times, enabling the construction of the lexicon. The final value of the text sentiment was left to the Language Technology Platform, which implements automatic routines for processing and treatment of input texts. While NLP is the basis of the initially described procedure, the authors also applied machine-learning concepts to achieve refinements.

Tang (2013) presents applications relating to the concept of "harmonious society," proposed by Chinese leaders to define a balanced society in terms of the number of people, their quality of life, and the balanced distribution of wealth. Several indexes can be used to measure harmony (authors cite examples such as the Gini coefficient, the index of prosperity related to the Legatum Institute, the happiness index, greed GDP, and green GDP quality index). The final proposition of the authors was measuring the perception of online societal risks as a means of detecting societal hazards, according to a codification done by the Institute of Psychology of the Chinese Academy of Science. The use of computational linguistics and NLP is noteworthy, as is the use of users' registers mined from social-web channels, such as microblogs, to identify and sort potential societal risks through postings on these media.

The study by Jin et al. (2017) was applied to the social networks' users in emergency events. The objective of the work was to provide references so that the emergency services could monitor public opinion to aid the government in dealing with emergencies. Four periods define an emergency event, using an earthquake as the basis for the analysis.: incubation, development, decline, and calm. These periods reflect how public opinion manifests itself in response to warnings about the emergency events disseminated on the social web. Although the article does not mention the techniques applied, only reporting the application of sentiment analysis/opinion mining, in the theoretical development of the material are listed techniques/methods such as signal analysis theory, intuitionistic fuzzy inference, Bayesian networks, and the fuzzy comprehensive method.

Koot et al. (2014) developed a study to support public-security agents with intelligent analysis using the information provided by the Internet, specifically by social networks. The authors proposed an analytical tool architecture for the public profile of social networks' users to perform web mining. They describe all the technological framework for the tool development: Python language and related technologies, such as OAuth, to manage social networks' API authentications, BeautifulSoul for HTML parsing, urllib to handle the URLs, Ajax (another programming language) for the front-end development, and all this combined through the object-oriented framework Django, widely applied in web development. They also point out the interest in engaging NPL tools for analyzing sentiments, modeling topics, analyzing trends, and providing results visualization.

Leventakis and Kokkinis (2018) deal with applications for communitarian policing identifying technological elements able to support policial decisions and actions for public-security maintenance. In their article, they present the INSPC^{2}T project, developed by the European Union, as the main goal for presenting researched contributions to enabling the collaboration of police and society on several levels. The project includes modules related to mobile applications and web portals for citizens' use; events geospatial processing; multimedia analysis; business intelligence (notably with the use of web mining and NLP for sentiment analysis); the application of case-based reasoning to develop expert systems; measuring data aging; application of data warehousing and decision support systems; use of security portals; and simulating trainings for communitarian policing.

Xu et al. (2016) propose in their article a method for urban emergency events, using social networks as the main data sources, specifically collecting users' messages. The method is based on the "five W" questions—who, where, why, when, and what—to look for spatial-temporal information (i.e., spatial-temporal mining) and semantic information provided by the users' crowd in digital social networks. In this work, the authors do not name any NLP technique, but its use is supposed by the semantic nature mentioned in the method's architecture.

Machine Learning

Sun et al. (2018) sought to detect anomalous behavior using social-network users' messages. In order to verify the behavior pattern, the authors applied analysis involving the Gaussian multivariate distribution, using deep learning based on convolutional neural networks to make the detection. Zhang et al. (2018) used recurrent neural networks to refine the treatment that started with NLP. The objective, in this case, was to improve the sentiments classifications over word vectors extracted from users' registers on social networks.

Yang et al. (2018) present in their work a form to make forecasts about collective actions using deep learning and communications on social media. They define certain kinds of collective actions as possible threats to social welfare, containing several risks, especially when they occur during social conflicts, which can affect economic, social, and public-safety levels. Therefore, using deep neural networks, the authors model a forecasting framework for collective actions whose data sources are social media. In this case, deep neural networks were applied to perform binary classification, based on a training set. The work also uses the models as the species competitions and epidemic propagation, to make predictions about the emotional contagion leading to collective events on social media.

The work of Zuo et al. (2018) is the last of the primary findings that describe the application of analytical tools to public security. This material purposed the Cross-collection Auto-labeled MaxEnt-LDA (CAMEL), described as a novel model that makes use of the maximum entropy method and the Dirichlet latent allocation to do complimentary aspects-based opinion mining in asymmetric collections. The work also presents a nonparametric proposal based on Dirichlet processes for estimating a specific number of topics, which would be extremely difficult using only the CAMEL (parametric).

FRAMEWORK FOR THE ANALYTICAL PROCESS

The literature review made it possible to understand the technological trends associated with the researched themes, helping to obtain answers to the two research questions presented in the research-procedure section. The answers are the basis for the framework construction related to the analytical process.

Which Tools Can Be Applied to Retrieve Data From the Social Web and Tt Analyze the Feelings Related to Public Security?

The understanding of which analytical tools should be used for the composition of the framework revolves around what can be defined as analytical moments, following initial indications realized by Stieglitz et al. (2018). The first moment within the framework is the choice of the data sources, i.e., which kinds of social media should be used for mining. This determination aims to establish whether the search will focus on (for example) news sites, e-commerce sites, blogs, search engines, social networks, or combined types. Once the basic typology is defined, the specific platforms can be selected—for example, in the case of social networks, platforms such as Twitter, Facebook, YouTube, or LinkedIn.

The second moment is the search for and constant extraction of raw data. Search and extraction strategies will depend on the previous choice since each platform will have a specific API. Consequently, this strategy will define which technological tools to use. Fundamentally, web crawling and scraping are the starting strategies for the mining and analytical process, dealing here with the web-mining process (Sapountzi & Psannis, 2018). The strategy for storing extracted (unstructured) raw data should be established and big data schemas may be chosen if the amount of data demands it (Manjunatha & Annappa, 2018; Xu et al., 2016).

The extracted and stored data are the starting point for the third moment within the framework, where the raw data will be preprocessed to ensure that they receive a suitable format for subsequent processing. The application of NPL-based preprocessing techniques, such as tokenization, stemming, stop-words removal, extraction, and weighting of characteristics, is emphasized (Ravi & Ravi, 2015; Yang & Chen, 2017). The preprocessed data, already in a format adjusted for analysis, should be stored in adequate databases to enable the sequence.

The fourth moment contains the routines for refining the preprocessed data (Zhang et al., 2018), enabling the sentiment analysis in the fifth moment. In this part of the framework, the machine-learning techniques enter to find hidden patterns in the treated and formatted data (Sun et al., 2018) as well as to perform topics modeling and extract only textual registers related to the desired topics (Bao et al., 2009). The refined data also require proper storage, ensuring their availability for the next moments.

On the fifth moment, the sentiment analysis uses the refined data, the main goal of the framework. As mentioned, this analysis is a typical NLP problem; however, the machine-learning techniques may be used here too. The fundamental result of this moment is to obtain measures of polarity and subjectivity related to sentiment about a theme (Zhang et al., 2018). Indicators can also be obtained on the robustness of the analysis of feelings: accuracy, precision, recall, and the F1 score (Hailong, Wenyan, & Bo, 2014).

The sixth and final moment is dedicated to the results visualization, user-friendly interfaces presenting the classification/pattern of the extracted sentiments (Koot et al., 2014; Leventakis & Kokkinis, 2018).

Which Data Sources and Informational Elements Should Be Considered for Collection and Analysis in the Process?

Virtually all the literature findings easily answer this question. First, data sources are the users themselves who feed the social web with their records in a variety of formats, but mainly through social networks' posts. Second, the informational element for sentiment analysis is the user's textual register—for instance, the shared messages in social networks, expressing in an unstructured way the user's sentiment about some theme or event that creates repercussions on the social web. The whole process, described in answer to the first question, revolves around users' registers, so the entire process is about their extraction, treatment, and refinement, as well as the analysis to measure the expression of the feelings.

Figure 7 presents the schema of the framework, following the moments described in answer to the first question.

Figure 7. Framework for the analytical process

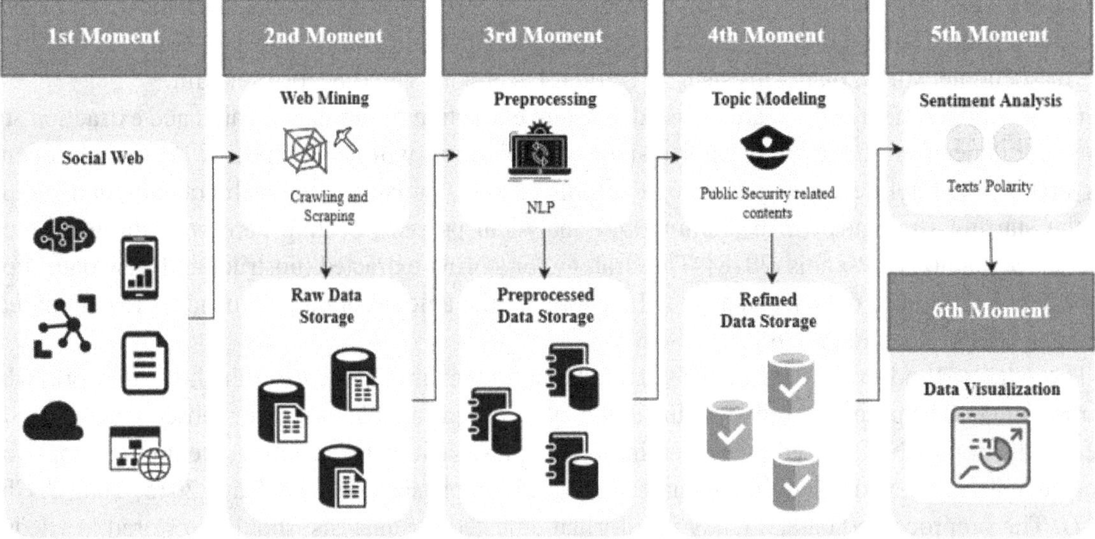

Fairly close approaches also appear in works such as those by Charalabidis et al. (2011), Koot et al. (2014), Lin et al. (2017), Manjunatha and Annappa (2018), and Xu et al. (2016), however, it should be clear that the proposed framework is dedicated to sentiment analysis related to public security issues.

This specification is evident in its fourth moment, where the main refinement of the process is devoted to topic modeling, helping to identify textual records on public security and related topics.

The proposed framework provides methodological guidelines for future applications, enabling (i) the development of sentiment analysis on public security and (ii) the development of a dashboard for use by the agents of public-security management. With that, it only remains to define a research agenda, presenting topics for future research.

RESEARCH AGENDA

From the literature review and the framework, this section presents ideas for applications related to the analysis of feelings dedicated to public security. Among the possible forms of presentation of research agendas, elements related to Design Science in Information Systems research was chosen (Hevner, March, Park, & Ram, 2004), where guidelines are defined for conducting structured and systemic research with well-defined objectives; and a structure for future proposals, based on the article by Loebbecke and Picot (2015).

Artifacts—elements related to the analytical process—could be identified as referrals within the research agenda, indicating possibilities of advances in the applications treated from the theoretical and conceptual point of view. Three possible artifacts for future developments are described below.

Artifact 1: Analytical Process Addressed to Governmental Agencies of Public Security and Safety Management

Notably, the studies of Charalabidis et al. (2011) and Manjunatha and Annappa (2018) point out that certain nations have been developing for some time projects designed to carry out diverse analyses based on the social web. They aim to verify opinions or evaluate popular sentiment about events that may have social repercussions for the actions of public-management agencies, regardless of the orientation of these projects.

The framework defined above shows an analytical process that comprises seeking technical and technological tools for mining the social web, preprocessing raw data collected and necessary refinements leading to sentiment analysis, generating reports for government agencies in public-security management, and allowing the development of systems with interfaces dedicated to the interactive and configurable presentation of the results by decision-makers.

Artifact 2: Decision Dashboard for Configuration of Sentiment Analysis Parameters and Results Visualization

This artifact will specifically require the combination of web mining, artificial-intelligence tools, software engineering, and interface design to construct a sentiment analysis/opinion-mining decision-support dashboard on social-networking platforms. Some of the findings of the bibliographic research also point out developments in this regard, namely, the works of Manjunatha and Annappa (2018) and Peng et al. (2017).

The dashboard aims to reflect and expand the possibilities associated with the previous artifact (analyses for government agencies in public-security management). This artifact is intended for public managers; however, the provision of information open to the general population should also be considered, as it is the main recipient of government actions, as well as the primary provider of information needed for such analyses.

Artifact 3: Spatial and Temporal Analysis of the Sentiment Trends About Public Security

The third and last artifact is the specific development of spatial and temporal analyses of the general feeling related to public security, following the tendencies that Leventakis and Kokkinis (2018) and Xu et al. (2017) point out. This artifact could be linked to the previous two, but its highlight is the incorporation of interfaces with geographic information systems and the use of georeferenced information combined with sentiment analysis (Reinoso, Farooq, & Forum, 2015; Song & Xia, 2016). Various intersections can emerge, for example, the discovery of patterns of crime occurring in certain regions (Nepomuceno & Costa, 2019), with the expression of the population's feelings from georeferenced records in social networks.

CONCLUSION

This paper aimed to achieve three interconnected goals: (i) review of the literature on analytical tools applied to understand people's feelings/sentiments about public security; (ii) design of an analytical framework for analyzing feelings/sentiments about public security, according to perceived trends in the literature findings; and (iii) definition of an agenda for presenting to the community the developments related to the theme, indicating elements (artifacts) for further research, generated from the concepts searched with specific application to public security.

The literature search results may seem rather restrictive when compared to other researches (mainly systematic reviews). However, there are two interpretations of this perception. First, protocol definitions were quite restrictive. Additions to the inclusion and exclusion criteria could have been made, just as more databases could have been used to perform the searches, and other configurations could have been devised within the strings to increase the number of findings. Second, there is a gap in the research to be filled in terms of real-world applications of sentiment-analysis tools concerning public security, which signals the positive path that this research initiated and can take from here.

Regarding the first interpretation, although terms referring directly to analytical tools and data sources have been used, the use of the term "public security" may have been restrictive. Other terms associated with the theme could also result in a greater number of literature findings; a systematic review could also be considered as an extension of the research agenda.

Although it does not add new features to the web mining or sentiment analysis fields, the proposed framework is fundamental for the description and fulfillment of the defined agenda, representing the basic concepts to be used, as well as providing guidelines for the selection of specific tools for upcoming developments, among those that were presented in the literature review. This research tends to consider this framework as a divider of the theoretical-conceptual from the practical moments, the latter of which will be the fruit of its unfolding. The research can also determine that its structure is conceptually satisfactory since it is aligned with the tendencies of the associated areas, as well as other works reported in the literature review, pointing to developments with methods and architectures similar to the one used in the framework proposed here.

The agenda presents three interconnected possibilities for future research, ensuring that researchers have a vision of niches to be worked with government agencies in public-security management and providing decision-support tools for the formulation of strategies aligned with social needs in this area.

The framework proposed in this article should be applied to collect text from social network users in order to extract from these texts those related to public security issues such as policing, violence and crime control, and other actions. This application will be made in the metropolitan region of Recife (Pernambuco, Brazil). With the extracted texts, sentiment analysis will be applied to initially provide local public security management agencies with feedback on how people judge security actions taken. Secondly, a dashboard will be delivered so that both the authorities and the interested citizens can hold consultations. This instrument is expected to serve as a support tool for public security decisions, adding public opinion directly to the associated planning.

FUNDING

This work was financed in part by the Coordination for the Improvement of Higher Education Personnel (Brazil) – Finance Code 001, and by the National Council for Scientific and Technological Development (Brazil).

REFERENCES

Akter, S., Bandara, R., Hani, U., Fosso Wamba, S., Foropon, C., & Papadopoulos, T. (2019). Analytics-based decision-making for service systems: A qualitative study and agenda for future research. *International Journal of Information Management*, *48*(January), 85–95. doi:10.1016/j.ijinfomgt.2019.01.020

Bao, S., Xu, S., Zhang, L., Yan, R., Su, Z., Han, D., & Yu, Y. (2009). Joint Emotion-Topic Modeling for Social Affective Text Mining. In *2009 Ninth IEEE International Conference on Data Mining* (pp. 699–704). IEEE. 10.1109/ICDM.2009.94

Bisio, F., Meda, C., Zunino, R., Surlinelli, R., Scillia, E., & Ottaviano, A. (2015). Real-time monitoring of Twitter traffic by using semantic networks. *2015 IEEE/ACM International Conference on Advances in Social Networks Analysis and Mining (ASONAM)*, 966–969. 10.1145/2808797.2809371

Bjurstrom, S. (2015). Sentiment Analysis Methodology for Social Web Intelligence. In *Proceedings of the Twenty-first Americas Conference on Information Systems* (pp. 1–12). Puerto Rico: Association for Information Systems.

Caione, A., Guido, A. L., Martella, A., Paiano, R., & Pandurino, A. (2016). Knowledge base support for dynamic information system management. *Information Systems and e-Business Management*, *14*(3), 533–576. doi:10.100710257-015-0294-3

Cao, D., Wang, S., & Lin, D. (2018). Chinese microblog users' sentiment-based traffic condition analysis. *Soft Computing*, *22*(21), 7005–7014. doi:10.100700500-018-3293-8 de Carvalho, V. D. H., & Costa, A. P. C. S. (2019). Social Web Mining as a Tool to Support Public Security Sentiment Analysis. In P. S. Freitas, F. Dargam, R. Ribeiro, J. M. Moreno, & J. Papathanasiou (Eds.), *5th International Conference on Decision Support System Technology* (pp. 164–169). Funchal: EURO Working Group on Decision Support Systems. Retrieved from https://icdsst2019.files.wordpress.com/2019/06/icdsst2019_proceedings_final.pdf

Charalabidis, Y., Koussouris, S., & Ramfos, A. (2011). A cloud infrastructure for collaborative digital public services. *Proceedings - 2011 3rd IEEE International Conference on Cloud Computing Technology and Science, CloudCom 2011*, 340–347. 10.1109/CloudCom.2011.53

Chen, G., Cai, W., Huang, J., & Jiao, X. (2016). Uncovering and Characterizing Internet Water Army in Online Forums. In *2016 IEEE First International Conference on Data Science in Cyberspace (DSC)* (pp. 169–178). IEEE. 10.1109/DSC.2016.77

Cui, P., Liu, H., Aggarwal, C., Wang, F., Cao, L., Yu, P. S., ... Qiang, Y. (2016). Uncovering and Predicting Human Behaviors. *IEEE Intelligent Systems*, *31*(2), 77–88. doi:10.1109/MIS.2016.37

Dobre, C., & Xhafa, F. (2014). Intelligent services for Big Data science. *Future Generation Computer Systems*, *37*, 267–281. doi:10.1016/j.future.2013.07.014

Hailong, Z., Wenyan, G., & Bo, J. (2014). Machine learning and lexicon based methods for sentiment classification: A survey. *Proceedings - 11th Web Information System and Application Conference, WISA 2014*, 262–265. 10.1109/WISA.2014.55

Handzic, M. (2011). Integrated socio-technical knowledge management model: An empirical evaluation. *Journal of Knowledge Management*, *15*(2), 198–211. doi:10.1108/13673271111119655

He, W., Wu, H., Yan, G., Akula, V., & Shen, J. (2015). A novel social media competitive analytics framework with sentiment benchmarks. *Information & Management*, *52*(7), 801–812. doi:10.1016/j.im.2015.04.006

Hevner, A. R., March, S. T., Park, J., & Ram, S. (2004). Design Science in Information Systems Research. *Management Information Systems Quarterly*, *28*(1), 75. doi:10.2307/25148625

Jin, R., Zhang, H.-L., & Zhang, Y. (2018). The social negative mood index for social networks. In *2018 IEEE Third International Conference on Data Science in Cyberspace (DSC)* (pp. 1–5). IEEE. 10.1109/DSC.2018.8570298

Jin, X., Li, H., Fu, H., Zhang, J., & Ding, B. (2017). A study on early-warning response of emergency events network public opinion based on analysis of Microbloggers' Behaviors. *PIC 2016 - Proceedings of the 2016 IEEE International Conference on Progress in Informatics and Computing*, 753–756. 10.1109/PIC.2016.7949599

Kamel, M. N., Sanfilippo, A. P., Corley, C. D., & Wheeler, S. (2010). Social Web mining and exploitation for serious applications: Technosocial Predictive Analytics and related technologies for public health, environmental and national security surveillance. *Computer Methods and Programs in Biomedicine*, *100*(1), 16–23. doi:10.1016/j.cmpb.2010.02.007 PMID:20236725

Kitchenham, B., & Charters, S. (2007). *Guidelines for performing Systematic Literature Reviews in Software Engineering. EBSE Technical Report EBSE-2007-01.*

Koot, G., Veld, M. A. A. H. I. T., Hendricksen, J., Kaptein, R., De Vries, A., & Van Den Broek, E. L. (2014). Foraging online social networks. *Proceedings - 2014 IEEE Joint Intelligence and Security Informatics Conference, JISIC 2014*, 312–315. 10.1109/JISIC.2014.62

Leventakis, G., & Kokkinis, G. (2018). Developing and Assessing Next Generation Community Policing Social Networks with THOR Methodology. In G. Leventakis & M. R. Haberfeld (Eds.), *Community-Oriented Policing and Technological Innovations* (pp. 47–62). Springer International Publishing. doi:10.1007/978-3-319-89294-8_6

Lin, J., Mao, W., & Zeng, D. D. (2017). Personality-based refinement for sentiment classification in microblog. *Knowledge-Based Systems, 132*, 204–214. doi:10.1016/j.knosys.2017.06.031

Loebbecke, C., & Picot, A. (2015). Reflections on societal and business model transformation arising from digitization and big data analytics: A research agenda. *The Journal of Strategic Information Systems, 24*(3), 149–157. doi:10.1016/j.jsis.2015.08.002

Lv, Y., Chen, Y., Zhang, X., Duan, Y., & Li, N. L. (2017). Social media based transportation research: The state of the work and the networking. *IEEE/CAA Journal of Automatica Sinica, 4*(1), 19–26. doi:10.1109/JAS.2017.7510316

Manjunatha, & Annappa, B. (2018). Real Time Big Data Analytics in Smart City Applications. In *2018 International Conference on Communication, Computing and Internet of Things (IC3IoT)* (pp. 279–284). IEEE. doi:10.1109/IC3IoT.2018.8668106

Navarro, J. L. A., Ruiz, V. R. L., & Peña, D. N. (2017). The effect of ICT use and capability on knowledge-based cities. *Cities (London, England), 60*, 272–280. doi:10.1016/j.cities.2016.09.010

Nepomuceno, T. C. C., & Costa, A. P. C. S. (2019). Spatial visualization on patterns of disaggregate robberies. *Operations Research*, (0123456789). Advance online publication. doi:10.100712351-019-00479-z

Peng, Y., Zhu, W., Zhao, Y., Xu, C., Huang, Q., Lu, H., Zheng, Q., Huang, T., & Gao, W. (2017). Cross-media analysis and reasoning: Advances and directions. *Frontiers of Information Technology & Electronic Engineering, 18*(1), 44–57. doi:10.1631/FITEE.1601787

Poleto, T., de Carvalho, V. D. H., & Costa, A. P. C. S. (2017). The Full Knowledge of Big Data in the Integration of Inter-Organizational Information. *International Journal of Decision Support System Technology, 9*(1), 16–31. doi:10.4018/IJDSST.2017010102

Ravi, K., & Ravi, V. (2015). A survey on opinion mining and sentiment analysis: Tasks, approaches and applications. *Knowledge-Based Systems, 89*, 14–46. doi:10.1016/j.knosys.2015.06.015

Reinoso, G., Farooq, B., & Forum, C. T. R. (2015). Urban Pulse Analysis Using Big Data. In *Canadian Transportation Research Forum 50th Annual Conference* (p. 16). Montreal: Transportation Association of Canada (TAC). Retrieved from https://trid.trb.org/view/1417784

Sapountzi, A., & Psannis, K. E. (2018). Social networking data analysis tools & challenges. *Future Generation Computer Systems, 86*, 893–913. doi:10.1016/j.future.2016.10.019

Song, J., Kim, K. T., Lee, B., Kim, S., & Youn, H. Y. (2017). A novel classification approach based on Naïve Bayes for Twitter sentiment analysis. *Transactions on Internet and Information Systems (Seoul), 11*(6), 2996–3011. doi:10.3837/tiis.2017.06.011

Song, Z., & Xia, J. (2016). Spatial and Temporal Sentiment Analysis of Twitter data. In *European Handbook of Crowdsourced Geographic Information* (Vol. 25, pp. 205–221). Ubiquity Press. doi:10.5334/bax.p

Stieglitz, S., Mirbabaie, M., Ross, B., & Neuberger, C. (2018). Social media analytics – Challenges in topic discovery, data collection, and data preparation. *International Journal of Information Management, 39*(December), 156–168. doi:10.1016/j.ijinfomgt.2017.12.002

Sun, X., Zhang, C., Ding, S., & Quan, C. (2018). Detecting anomalous emotion through big data from social networks based on a deep learning method. *Multimedia Tools and Applications*, (420), 1–22. doi:10.100711042-018-5665-6

Sundermann, C. V., Domingues, M. A., Sinoara, R. A., Marcacini, R. M., & Rezende, S. O. (2019). Using opinion mining in context-aware recommender systems: A systematic review. *Information (Switzerland), 10*(2), 1–45. doi:10.3390/info10020042

Tang, X. (2013). Exploring on-line societal risk perception for harmonious society measurement. *Journal of Systems Science and Systems Engineering, 22*(4), 469–486. doi:10.100711518-013-5238-1

Tien, J. M. (2013). Big Data: Unleashing information. *Journal of Systems Science and Systems Engineering, 22*(2), 127–151. doi:10.100711518-013-5219-4

Usai, A., Pironti, M., Mital, M., & Aouina Mejri, C. (2018). Knowledge discovery out of text data: A systematic review via text mining. *Journal of Knowledge Management, 22*(7), 1471–1488. doi:10.1108/JKM-11-2017-0517

Wang, S., & Noe, R. A. (2010). Knowledge sharing: A review and directions for future research. *Human Resource Management Review, 20*(2), 115–131. doi:10.1016/j.hrmr.2009.10.001

Wazarkar, S., & Keshavamurthy, B. N. (2019). A soft clustering technique with layered feature extraction for social image mining. *Multimedia Tools and Applications, 78*(14), 20333–20360. Advance online publication. doi:10.100711042-018-6881-9

Xu, Z., Liu, Y., Yen, N., Mei, L., Luo, X., Wei, X., & Hu, C. (2016). Crowdsourcing based Description of Urban Emergency Events using Social Media Big Data. *IEEE Transactions on Cloud Computing, 7161*(c), 1–1. doi:10.1109/TCC.2016.2517638

Xu, Z., Xuan, J., Liu, Y., Choo, K. K. R., Mei, L., & Hu, C. (2017). Building spatial temporal relation graph of concepts pair using web repository. *Information Systems Frontiers, 19*(5), 1029–1038. doi:10.100710796-016-9676-4

Yang, P., & Chen, Y. (2017). A survey on sentiment analysis by using machine learning methods. In *2017 IEEE 2nd Information Technology, Networking, Electronic and Automation Control Conference (ITNEC)* (pp. 117–121). IEEE. 10.1109/ITNEC.2017.8284920

Yang, W., Liu, X., Liu, J., & Cui, X. (2018). Prediction of collective actions using deep neural network and species competition model on social media. *World Wide Web (Bussum)*. Advance online publication. doi:10.100711280-018-0655-1

Yue, L., Chen, W., Li, X., Zuo, W., & Yin, M. (2018). A survey of sentiment analysis in social media. *Knowledge and Information Systems*, 1–47. doi:10.100710115-018-1236-4

Zhang, W., & Zhu, Y. Chun, & Wang, J. Peng. (2018). An intelligent textual corpus big data computing approach for lexicons construction and sentiment classification of public emergency events. *Multimedia Tools and Applications*. Advance online publication. doi:10.100711042-018-7018-x

Zheng, N., Liu, Z., Ren, P., Ma, Y., Chen, S., Yu, S., Xue, J., Chen, B., & Wang, F. (2017). Hybrid-augmented intelligence: Collaboration and cognition. *Frontiers of Information Technology & Electronic Engineering*, *18*(2), 153–179. doi:10.1631/FITEE.1700053

Zuo, Y., Wu, J., Zhang, H., Wang, D., & Xu, K. (2018). Complementary Aspect-Based Opinion Mining. *IEEE Transactions on Knowledge and Data Engineering*, *30*(2), 249–262. doi:10.1109/TKDE.2017.2764084

This research was previously published in the International Journal of Decision Support System Technology (IJDSST), 13(1); pages 1-20, copyright year 2021 by IGI Publishing (an imprint of IGI Global).

Chapter 16
Towards a Sentiment Analysis Model Based on Semantic Relation Analysis

Thien Khai Tran
Faculty of Computer Science and Engineering, Ho Chi Minh City University of Technology - VNU-HCM, Hồ Chí Minh, Vietnam & Faculty of Information Technology, Ho Chi Minh City University of Foreign Languages and Information Technology, Hồ Chí Minh, Vietnam

Tuoi Thi Phan
Faculty of Computer Science and Engineering, Ho Chi Minh City University of Technology - VNU-HCM, Hồ Chí Minh, Vietnam

ABSTRACT

Sentiment analysis is an important new field of research that has attracted the attention not only of researchers, but also businesses and organizations. In this article, the authors propose an effective model for aspect-based sentiment analysis for Vietnamese. First, sentiment dictionaries and syntactic dependency rules were combined to extract reliable word pairs (sentiment - aspect). They then relied on ontology to group these aspects and determine the sentiment polarity of each. They introduce two novel approaches in this work: 1) in order to "smooth" the sentiment scaling (rather than using discrete categories of 1, 0, and -1) for fined-grained classification, then extract multi-word sentiment phrases instead of sentiment words, and 2) the focus is not only on adjectives but also nouns and verbs. Initial evaluations of the system using real reviews show promising results.

1. INTRODUCTION

The task of sentiment analysis was first formulated in the early 2000s, particularly in the work of Dave, Lawrence, and Pennock (2003) as well as that of Nasukawa and Yi (2003). In the past fifteen years, a great deal of research has sought to analyse and evaluate opinions on products and services in media sources (Singh, Sharma, Dey, 2015). As elaborated in Sentiment Analysis and Subjectivity. Handbook of Natural Language Processing, Second Edition (2010), there are three levels of analysis worth considering:

DOI: 10.4018/978-1-6684-6303-1.ch016

(i) document-level, (ii) sentence-level, and (iii) aspect-level. In reference to document level analysis, the research of Sharma, Nigam, and Jain (2014), Sharma, Hoque, and Chandra (2016), Tang, Qin, Liu, and Yang (2015), and Xia, Xu, Yu, and Qi, (2016) need to be taken into consideration. Significant works which discuss sentence-based sentiment analysis include Marcheggiani, Tackstrom, Esuli, and Sebastiani (2014) and Yang and Cardie, (2014). Our core research interest is in aspect-based sentiment analysis, the focus of several important studies, including those of Chinsha and Joseph (2015) and Wang, Jiang, Lan, and Wu, (2017). The challenge of sentiment analysis is that the opinions which users provide on various topics are often complex and multifaceted. The sentiment valence of a word can change depending on its specific context, a phenomenon which is referred to as contextual valence shifting (Polanyi and Zaenen, 2006). Contextual valence shifting has made traditional methods, such as machine learning with bag of words or n-gram models, ineffective, as the latter tend to tackle single words, assigning them a positive or negative polarity based on pre-defined sentiment lexicons. In contrast, the most widely used techniques in sentiment analysis tend to account for contextual valence shifting by paying considerable attention to semantic elements, namely words or phrases which are factors giving rise to polarity shifting (Carrillo de Albornoz, Plaza, & Gervas, 2010; Jia, Yu, & Meng, 2009; Tran & Phan, 2018).

In the present paper we propose an aspect-based sentiment analysis model for Vietnamese reviews, which combines an opinion dictionary and syntactic dependency rules to extract reliable word pairs (sentiment - aspect). Using domain-specific ontologies we grouped these aspects and determined the sentiment polarity of each.

The key innovations presented here are as follows:

- We have provided an effective model for solving the sentiment analysis problem by combining an opinion dictionary, domain-specific ontologies, and syntactic dependency rules.
- We have extracted multi-word sentiment phrases (instead of individual words) for fine-grained (multi-class) classification, including extracting nouns and verbs which bear emotional factors, rather than adjectives alone.

The remainder of this paper is organized as follows: In Section 2 related work is summarised. In Section 3 the proposed sentiment analysis model is outlined. In Section 4 the experiments used to evaluate the model are described. Finally, the results of the paper are summarized and avenues for future work are discussed.

2. RELATED WORK

In this section, we will present the various types of sentiment analysis problem: i) document-level sentiment analysis; ii) sentence-level sentiment analysis; iii) aspect-based sentiment analysis. Document- level sentiment analysis is the simplest form of opinion mining. This technique identifies users' reviews as positive, negative or neutral using the assumption that each review is written regarding one object by only one holder. Opinion classification uses each opinion as a document, reducing the opinion classification process to document classification. Opinions are divided into three categories: positive, negative or neutral. Using this model allows a wide variety of document classification algorithms to be effectively applied to opinion classification problems. Machine learning represents one class of widely used document classification algorithms. Pang et al., (2002) applied naïve Bayes, maximum entropy and support vector machines to classify film reviews as either positive or negative. Their results showed that a SVM using unigram gave the highest accuracy (82.9%). In the case of Vietnamese text, Tran et al., (2016) have made use of a similar method accompanied by a multilabel classification approach.

The more fine-grained sentiment-level analysis is based on the understanding that a document can contain many different opinions, even regarding the same object/entity. To fully analyse the opinions in a review document, researchers need to perform sentiment analysis at the sentence level. This involves two main tasks: 1) classification of the sentence as a subjective sentence or an objective sentence, and 2) identification of the sentiment polarity of the subjective sentence. Yu and Hatzivassiloglou, (2003) adopted the naïve Bayes and multiple naïve Bayesian methods to tackle the first task. For the second task, Matsumoto et al., (2005) extracted subtrees from the dependency parsing trees for classification of the features. The authors showed that subtrees yielded richer semantic information than n-grams and word sequences.

Aspect-based sentiment analysis involves two core tasks: extracting sentiment aspects and identifying their sentiments. In Liu, Hu, and Cheng, (2005) the authors proposed a method of extracting infrequent aspects based on the observation that "sentiments tend to appear together with aspects." They identified infrequent aspects using the following procedure: if a sentence contains no frequent aspects but features sentiment words, then the nearest noun or noun phrase to the sentiment word is treated as an infrequent aspect. This method is useful for extracting important aspects and features not captured by sentiment words. In Hu and Liu (2004), an association rule method with the Apriori algorithm is adopted to identify the aspects. In Li, Huang, and Zhu, (2010) combined two models, sentiment LDAs and dependency sentiment LDAs, to identify opinion targets; their polarities were positive and negative, respectively. Zhao et al., (2010) proposed a hybrid model that combined maximum entropy and LDA to take advantage of syntactic characteristics and identify the aspects and their associated opinion words. Recently, deep learning has emerged as an outstanding model as a result of its ability to produce data representation at a variety of hierarchy levels, as demonstrated in Wu, Gu, Sun, and Gu (2016).

3. SENTIMENT ANALYSIS MODEL

We proposed a model for extracting targets and opinion words for aspect-based sentiment analysis. The distinctive innovation of this model is that we combine ontologies, sentiment dictionaries, and extraction rules based on mining the semantic relations between the words in sentences.

3.1. Proposed Model

The combination of sentiment dictionary and syntactic dependency rules allows us to extract reliable pairs (sentiment - aspect). Using ontologies, we grouped these aspects and determined the sentiment polarity of each. The model involves these components:

- Vietnamese Sentiment Dictionary (VNSD) – for looking up sentiments of individual words.
- Domain ontology – for managing semantic relationships between entities and entity attributes.
- Extraction Rules – for extracting reliable word pairs (sentiment - aspect).

The model is presented in Figure 1. When applying this model, online reviews were first preprocessed. Next, the data were passed into a dependency parser, generating a dependency tree with semantic relations and part-of-speech tagging of the words in the texts. The extraction rules were subsequently applied and combined with the sentiment dictionary to extract the pairs (sentiment - aspect). Finally, the aspect grouping task was conducted based on the ontologies and their sentiment was identified by the SO-CAL method (Taboada, Brooke, Tofiloski, Voll & Stede, 2011). The output of the whole process consists of a sentiment summary of each aspect.

Figure 1. Aspect-based sentiment analysis model

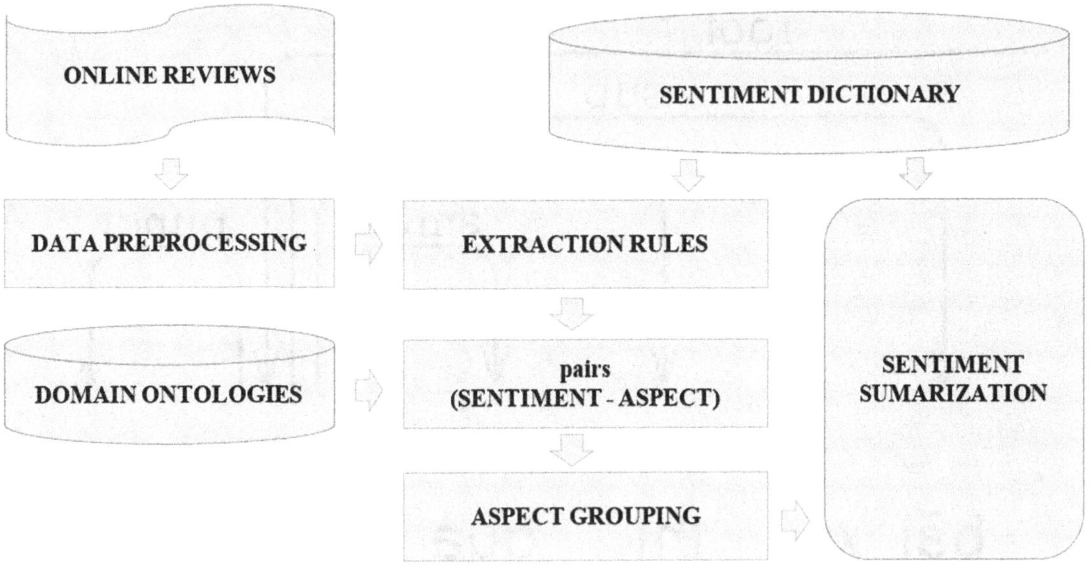

ONLINE REVIEWS
SENTIMENT DICTIONARY
DATA PREPROCESSING
EXTRACTION RULES
DOMAIN ONTOLOGIES
pairs (SENTIMENT - ASPECT)
SENTIMENT SUMARIZATION
ASPECT GROUPING

3.2. Extraction Rules

We exploited the semantic relationships between words in natural language texts to extract pairs (sentiment - aspect) from opinion reviews similar to (Tran and Phan, 2017). All possible combinations of pairs of part-of-speech taggings in Vietnamese were examined to create complete extraction rules: noun-noun, noun-verb, noun-adjective, noun-adverb, verb-verb, verb-adjective, and verb-adverb, etc. We used the following tools in the preprocessing stage: 1) VnTokenizer (Hong, Nguyen, & Roussanaly, 2012) for word segmentation tasks 2) RDRPOST (Nguyen, Nguyen, Roussanaly, 2012) for POS tagging tasks, and 3) VNDP (Nguyen & Pham, 2014) for analysing syntactic dependency. The most common VNDP dependency labels are *sub* (a noun phrase that is the syntactic subject of a clause), *vmod* (verb modifier), *dobj* (direct object of a verbal phrase), *pobj* (direct object of a prepositional phrase), and *conj* (conjunction).

The 12 rules were proposed and installed are as follows:

Rule 1: If a noun phrase is the subject that directly affects an adjective then we extract this word pair.

T → T-Dep → S

S ∈ SentiDict, T-Dep ∈ {*sub*},

POS(T) ∈ {N}, POS(S) ∈ {A}

For example: Bãi_xe thì quá nhỏ. *(The parking is too small.)*

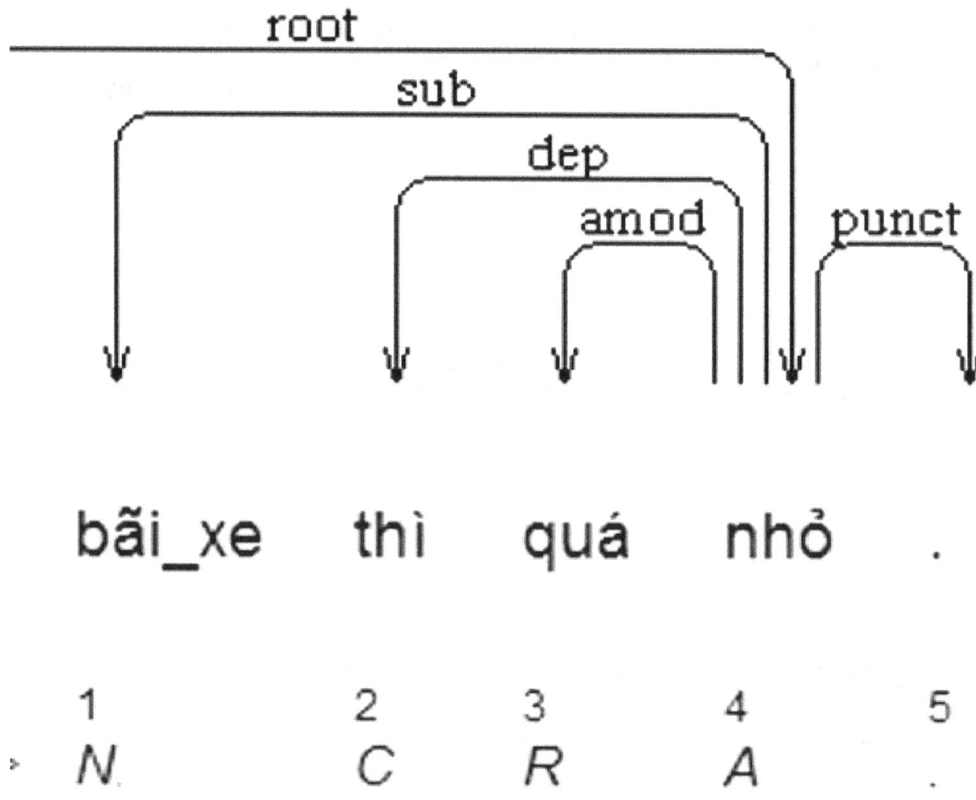

Output: pair(nhỏ $_{small}$ – bãi_xe $_{parking}$).

Rule 2: If a noun phrase is the subject that directly affects a sentiment verb then we extract this word pair.

T → T-Dep → S

S ∈ SentiDict, T-Dep ∈ {*sub*},

POS(T) ∈ {N}, POS(S) ∈ {V}

For example: Học_phí tăng hoài. *(The tuition fee is always rising.)*

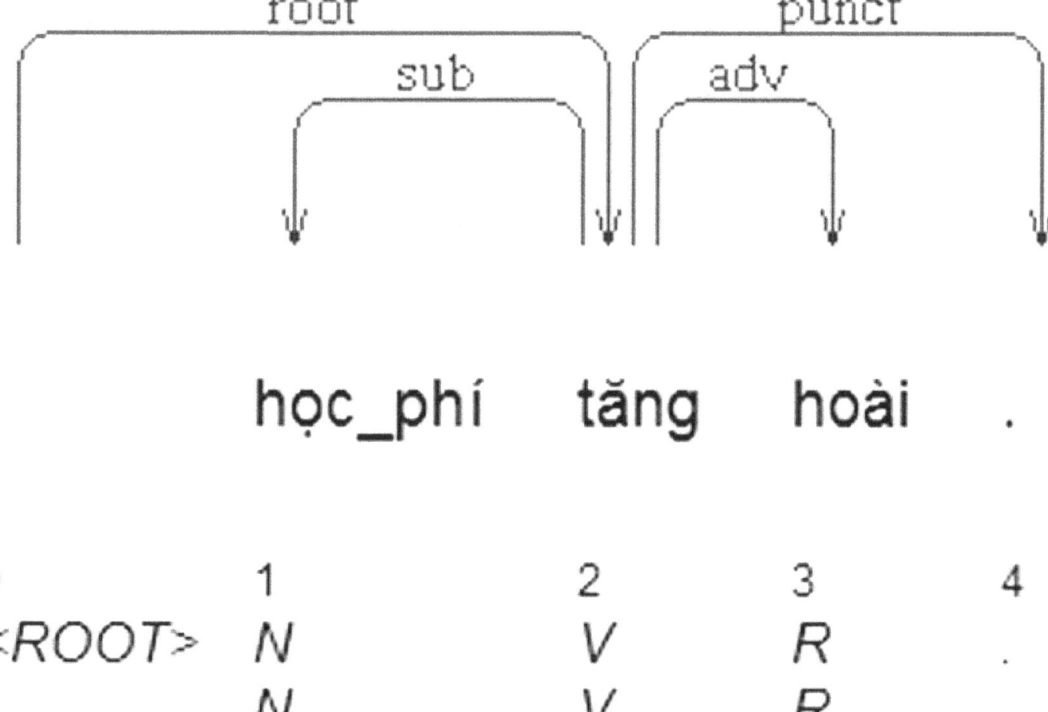

Output: pair(tăng $_{rising}$ – học_phí $_{tuition\ fee}$).

Rule 3: If a noun phrase T is the subject of word H and word H has a verb modifier relation (vmod) with a sentiment word S then we extract the pair(S-T).

T → T-Dep → H ← S-Dep ← S

S ∈ SentiDict, T-Dep ∈ {*sub*}, S-Dep ∈ {*vmod*},

POS(T) ∈ {N}, POS(S) ∈ {A}

For example: Lớp học nhìn sạch. *(The classroom looks clean.)*

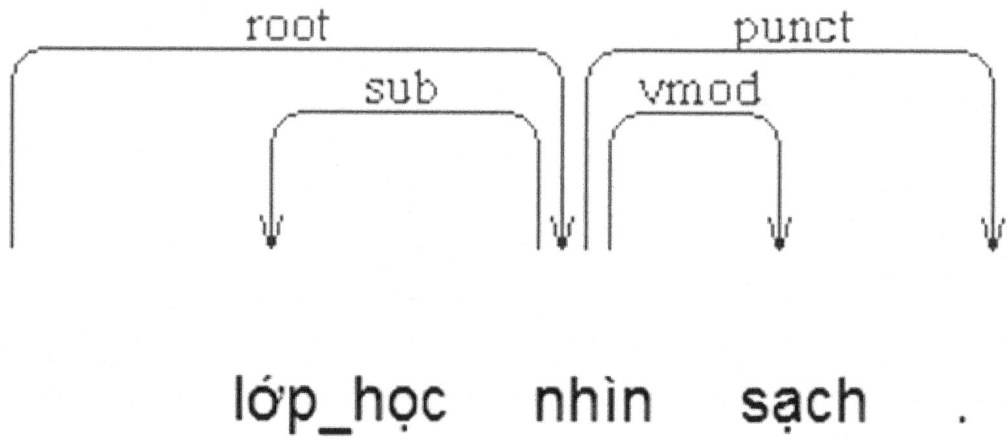

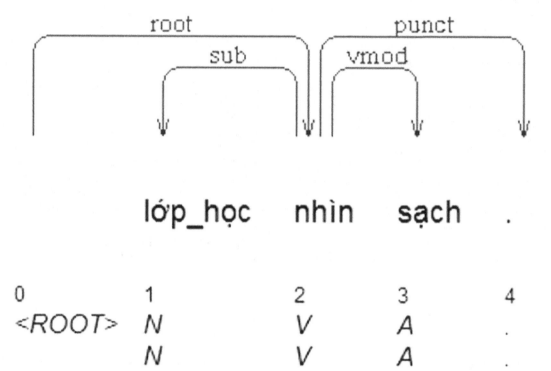

Output: pair(sạch $_{clean}$ – lớp_học $_{classroom}$).

Rule 4: If a noun phrase T is the subject of word H and word H has a direct object relation (dob) with a sentiment word S then we extract the pair(S-T).

$T \rightarrow$ T-Dep $\rightarrow H \leftarrow$ S-Dep $\leftarrow S$

$S \in$ SentiDict, T-Dep $\in \{sub\}$, S-Dep $\in \{dob\}$,

POS(T) $\in \{N\}$, POS(S) $\in \{N\}$

For example: Máy_chiếu hay gặp sự_cố. *(The projector often has problem.)*

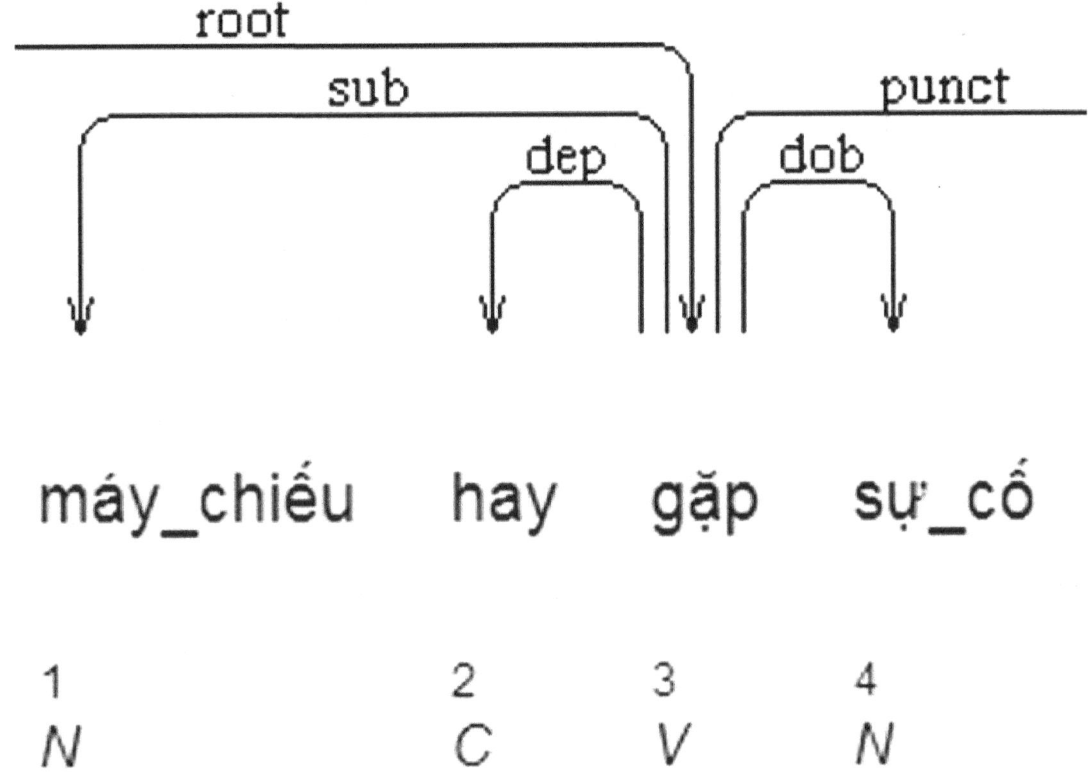

Output: pair(sự_cố $_{\text{problem}}$ – máy_chiếu $_{\text{projector}}$).

Rule 5: If a sentiment adjective has a noun modifier relation (nmod) with a noun phrase then we extract this word pair.

S → S-Dep → T

S ∈ SentiDict, S-Dep ∈ {*nmod*},

POS(T) ∈ {N}, POS(S) ∈ {A}

For example: Trường có cơ_sở_vật_chất tốt. *(School has good facilities.)*

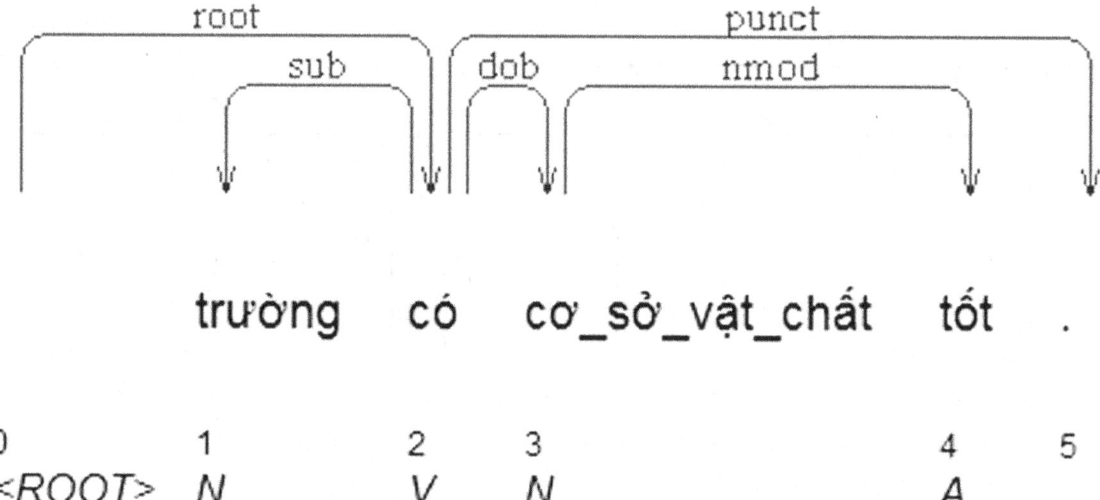

Output: pair(tốt $_{good}$ – cơ_sở_vật_chất $_{facilities}$).

Rule 6: If a noun phrase has a direct object relation (dob) with a sentiment verb then we extract this word pair.

T → T-Dep → S

S ∈ SentiDict, T-Dep ∈ {*dob*},

POS(T) ∈ {N}, POS(S) ∈ {V}

For example: Chúng_em không cần thành_tích. *(We do not need achievement.)*

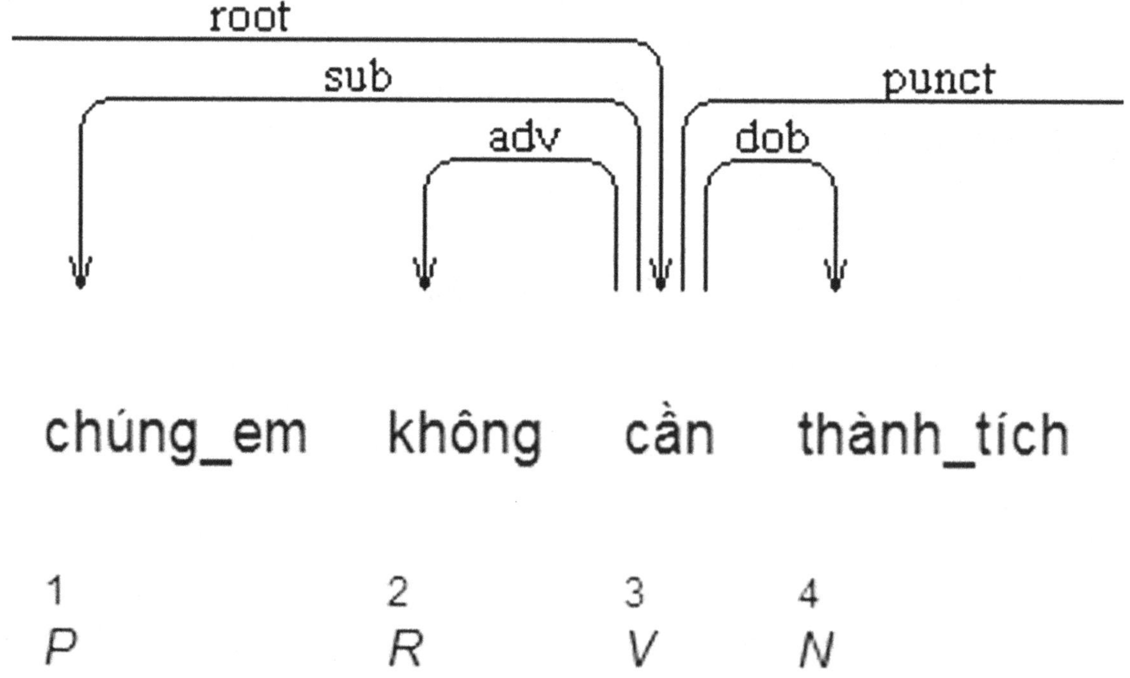

Output: pair(không cần $_{\text{do not need}}$ – thành_tích $_{\text{achievement}}$).

Rule 7: If a noun phrase has a direct object relation (dob) with a sentiment adjective then we extract this word pair.

T → T-Dep → S

S ∈ SentiDict, T-Dep ∈ {*dob*},

POS(T) ∈ {N}, POS(S) ∈ {A}

For example: Tôi thích khách_sạn này. *(I like this hotel.)*

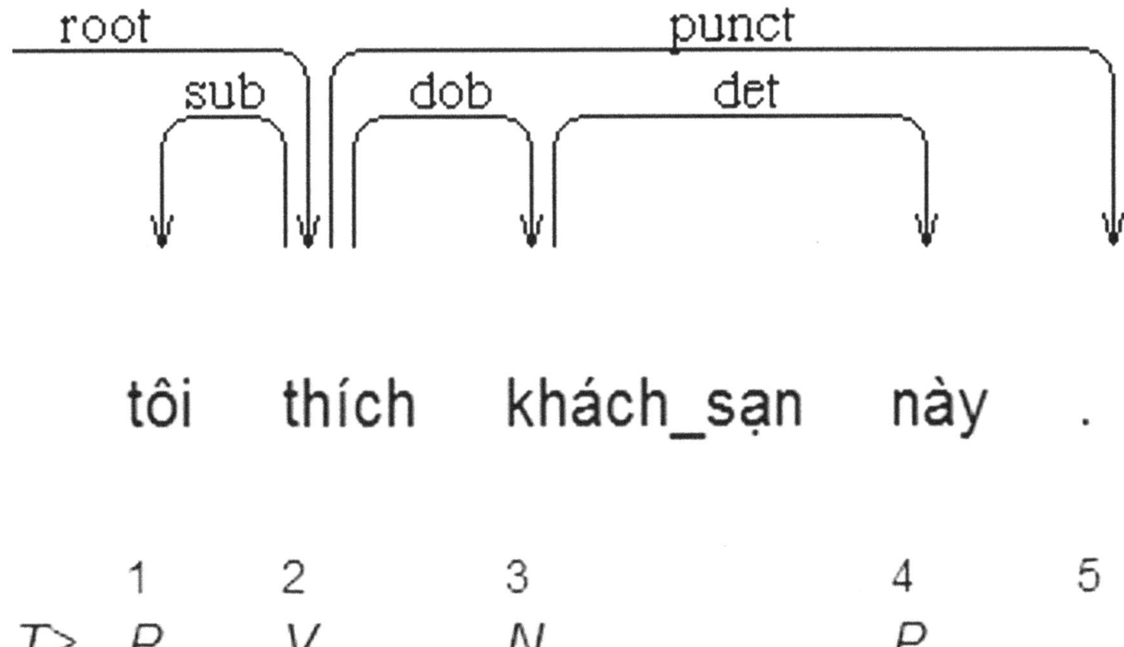

Output: pair(thích $_{\text{like}}$ – khách_sạn $_{\text{hotel}}$).

Rule 8: If many noun phrases are linked to each other by conjunctions, such as "and", "or", etc., then we extract these noun phrases and sentiment words linked to them.

T_i → T_i-Dep → H → T_j-Dep → T_j

T_i-Dep ∈ {*coord*},

T_j-Dep ∈ {*conj*}, POS($T_{i(j)}$) ∈{N}

For example: Tôi thích cảnh_vật và con_người nơi_đây. *(I like the landscape and people here.)*

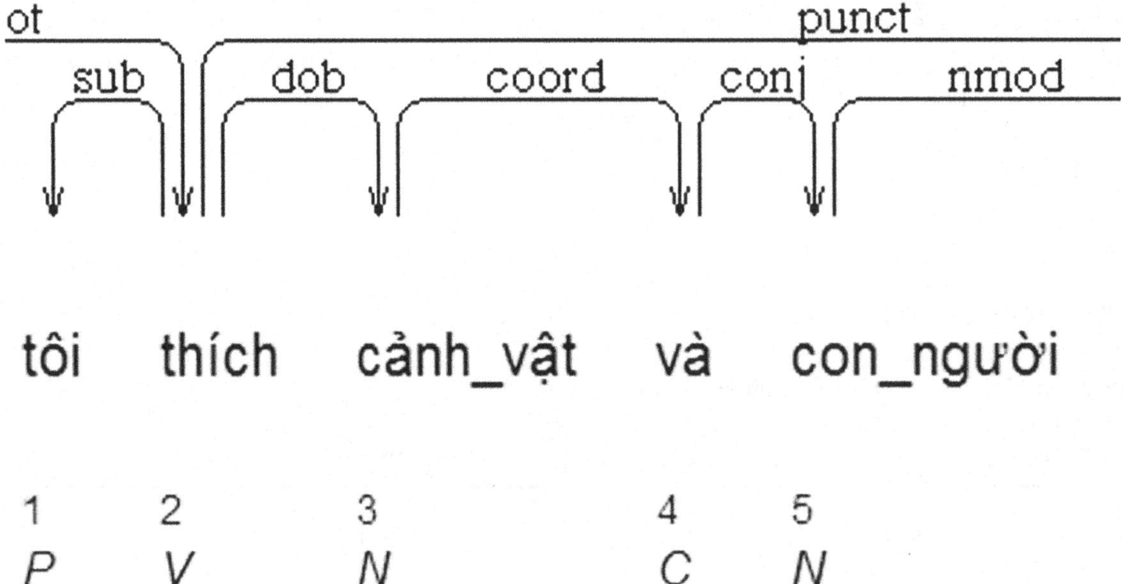

Output: pair(thích $_{\text{like}}$ – cảnh_vật $_{\text{landscape}}$), pair(thích $_{\text{like}}$ – con_người $_{\text{people}}$).

Rule 9: If many sentiment words are linked to each other by "nhưng", "tuy", etc., then we extract these words and targets linked to them.

$S_i \rightarrow S_i\text{-Dep} \rightarrow H \rightarrow S_j\text{-Dep} \rightarrow S_j$

$S_{i(j)} \in \text{SentiDict}$, $S_i\text{-Dep} \in \{conj\}$,

$S_j\text{-Dep} \in \{coord\}$, $\text{POS}(S_{i(j)}) \in \{A\}$

For example: Trường nhỏ nhưng đẹp. *(School is small but nice.)*

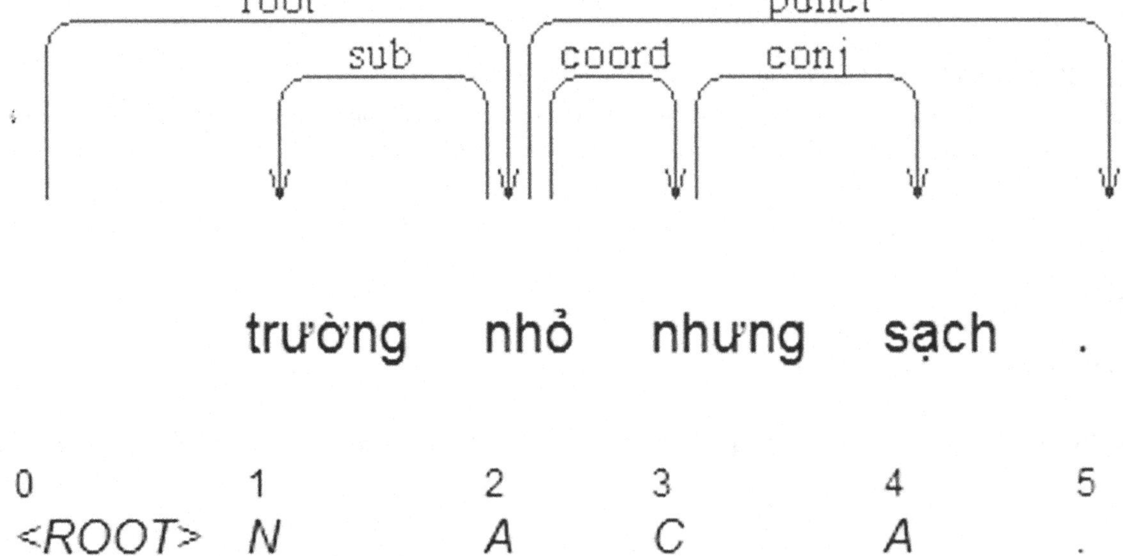

Output: pair(nhỏ $_{\text{small}}$ - trường $_{\text{schoole}}$), pair(đẹp $_{\text{nice}}$ – trường $_{\text{school}}$)

Rule 10: If a sentiment verb has a verb modifier relation (vmod) with a other verb then we extract this word phrase and targets linked to them.

$S_i \rightarrow$ S-Dep $\rightarrow S_j \leftarrow$ T-Dep $\leftarrow$ T

$S_{i(j)} \in$ SentiDict, POS($S_{i(j)}$) $\in \{V\}$

S-Dep $\in \{vmod\}$, T-Dep $\in \{dob\}$

For example: Trường cần giảm học_phí. *(School need to reduce fee.)*

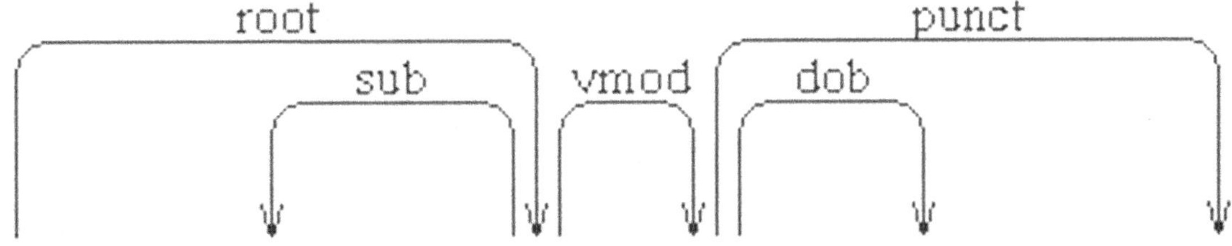

Output: pair(cần giảm $_{\text{need to reduce}}$ – học_phí $_{\text{fee}}$).

Rule 11: If there is an adverb in the sentence then we extract it and the sentiment word that it modifies.

RC $\rightarrow$ RC-Dep $\rightarrow$ S

POS(RC) $\in \{R\}$,

POS(S) $\in \{A\}$, RC-Dep $\in \{amod\}$

For example: Trường khá ổn. *(School is rather good.)*

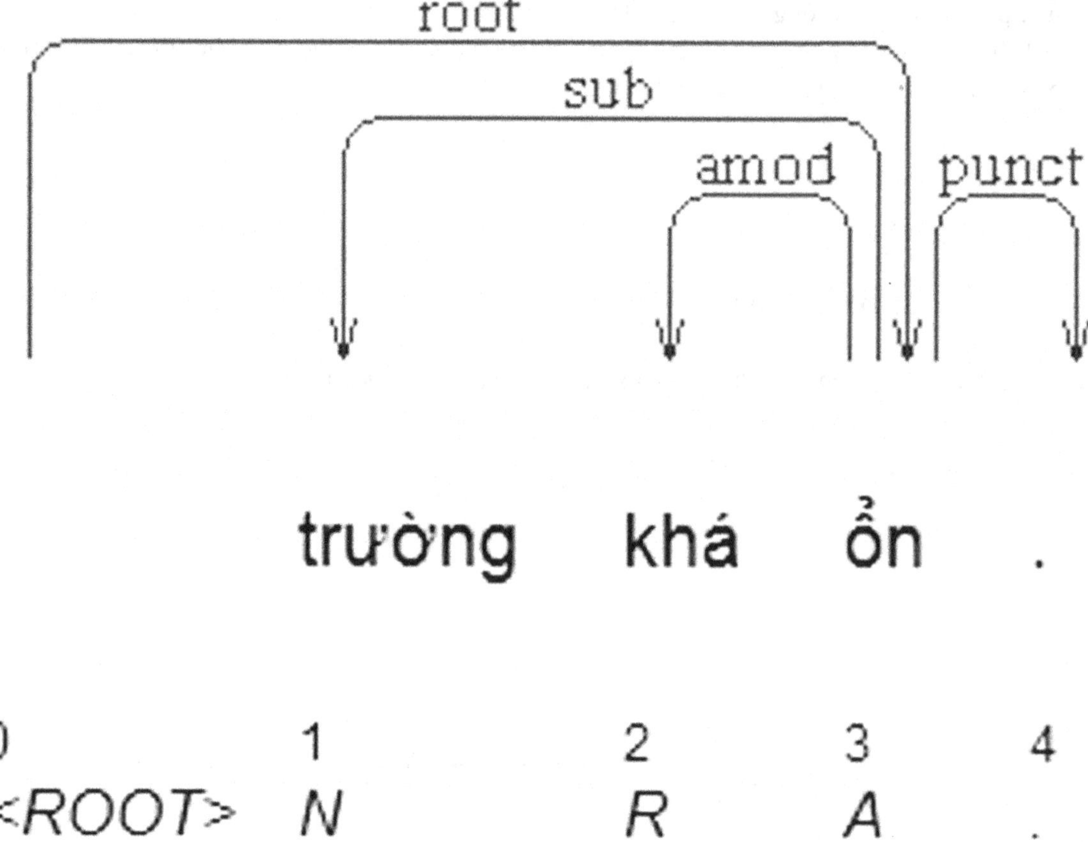

Output: pair(khá ổn $_{\text{rather}}$ – trường $_{\text{school}}$).
Rule 12: If the sentence has "no" pattern than we extract "no" and the noun phrase.
For example: Không máy_lạnh! *(No air conditioner!)*
Output: pair(không $_{\text{no}}$ – máy_lạnh $_{\text{air conditioner}}$).

Meaning of symbols:

- {S} (or T) and S-Dep (or T-Dep): the sentiment word (or aspect) and dependencies of S (or T).
- H: any words.
- POS(S) or POS(F): S or F POS tags.
- {N}, {A}, {R} etc.: the set of POS tags of a candidate word.
- *sub, amod, dob, nmod, sub, conj, coord*, etc.: the dependency relationship under the VNDT.

3.3. Computing Sentiment Scores Of The Aspects

We used an algorithm similar to the SO-CAL method described in (Taboada et al., 2011) which computes the individual scores of all sentiment words or phrases of each aspect. For each review, we sum all the sentiment scores of each aspect to give its polarity. If the total score is zero, then the aspect is classified as neutral. If it is greater than zero, then the aspect is classified as positive; otherwise, negative.

4. EXPERIMENTS

4.1. Review Database

To verify the efficiency of the approach, we conducted experiments on real data. In this research, we considered a review database of the university. 320 Vietnamese reviews of the Huflit university were studied. This review database was executed during the time from October the first 2015 to January 10 2016. It was preprocessed to get rid of wrong spellings, correct words in shorthand, teen slang, signs, logos. We finished putting positive/negative labels on this review database. The Table 1 will depict its information.

Table 1. Labelled information from hotel review database

Number of reviewers	320
Number of favorable reviews	160
Number of depreciative reviews	160
Number of words	8,042
Uploading review time	from October the first 2015 to January 10 2016

4.2. Sentiment Dictionary

We use the VNSD sentiment dictionary developed by Tran et al. (2018) that contains approximately 5,000 sentiment adjectives, 2,000 sentiment verbs, and 300 sentiment nouns. VNSD provides the fuzzy rules which can compute the score of a whole phrase of text. In Table 2, some of the opinion words that appear in this dictionary are described.

Table 2. Fragment of VNSD sentiment dictionary

ID	Term	Score
1	không đẹp $_{\text{no beautiful}}$	0
2	tin phải $_{\text{trust (a bad guy)}}$	- 0.60
3	không tốt $_{\text{no fine}}$	- 0.37
4	hơi đẹp rồi $_{\text{pretty well already}}$	0.06
5	đẹp cực_kỳ $_{\text{beautiful extremely}}$	0.93

4.3. Specific-Domain Ontology

For the experiment tasks, we built an ontology to provide formal representations of knowledge about the university in order to manage semantic relationships between entities and entity attributes. By identifying these semantic relations, we can easily group the aspects which were collected in Section 3. We show a fragment of the university ontology in Figure 2. Most university domain information was described in terms of the entities concerned, their attributes, and their relationships. We organized these pairs into a hierarchical tree structure. Each node represents a concept and each concept is a specialisation of its parent.

In this system, we defined the pairs based on the Quality Assessment at the University of Vietnam Ministry of Education & Training. There were eight main pairs: Chương trình đào tạo (Curricula); Con người (People); Cơ sở vật chất (Facilities and Infrastructure); Hoạt động đào tạo (Teaching and Learning Processes); Hỗ trợ tư vấn (Student Advice and Support); Tài chính (Finance); Tổ chức (Organization) và Vui chơi giải trí (Union Association and Entertainment). The current version contains 85 pairs.

Figure 2. A fragment of the university ontology

4.4. Evaluation

We built a core standard for all (sentiment - aspect) labels that appeared in the corpus. Then, we computed Term Precision (P), Term Recall (R) and F-measure (F_1) scores. CT is the core standard term set of the label, and T is the term set discovered by the dependency rules.

The experiments results were presented in Table 3.

Table 3. Experiments results

CT	T	CT ∩ T	P	R	F_1
453	395	320	81,01%	70,06%	75,14%

Comparison with the regular expression method: We also made a comparison to the regular expression method suggested by Tran and Phan, (2015). Some regular expression rules implemented in GATE/JAPE:

<adv> + <word in dictionary> → <sentiment word> (1)

<sentiment word> (<conj.><sentiment word>)* → <sentiment words> (2)

<reverse word> <positive word (negative word)> → <negative word (positive word)> (3)

with:

- <adv> can be "rất $_{very}$", "khá $_{rather}$", "siêu $_{super}$", etc. (positive) or "bị $_{undergo}$", "hơi $_{rather}$", "gây $_{casuse}$", etc. (negative);
- <reverse word> can be "không $_{no}$", "chả $_{not}$", "chẳng $_{don't}$", etc.

We evaluated how well two systems could identify opinion words and their associated aspects. 437 hotel reviews in Tran and Phan, (2015) were used as testing data.

The results of two extraction systems were reported in Table 4 and Figure 3.

Table 4. Test result of opinion word recognition and aspects evaluation

Methods	P	R	F_1
Regular expression method proposed with 437 hotel reviews in Tran and Phan (2015) were used as testing data.	73%	71%	72%
This system (syntactic dependency method) with 437 hotel reviews in Tran and Phan (2015) were used as testing data.	72%	76%	74%

Figure 3. Comparison of the syntactic dependency method and the regular expression method

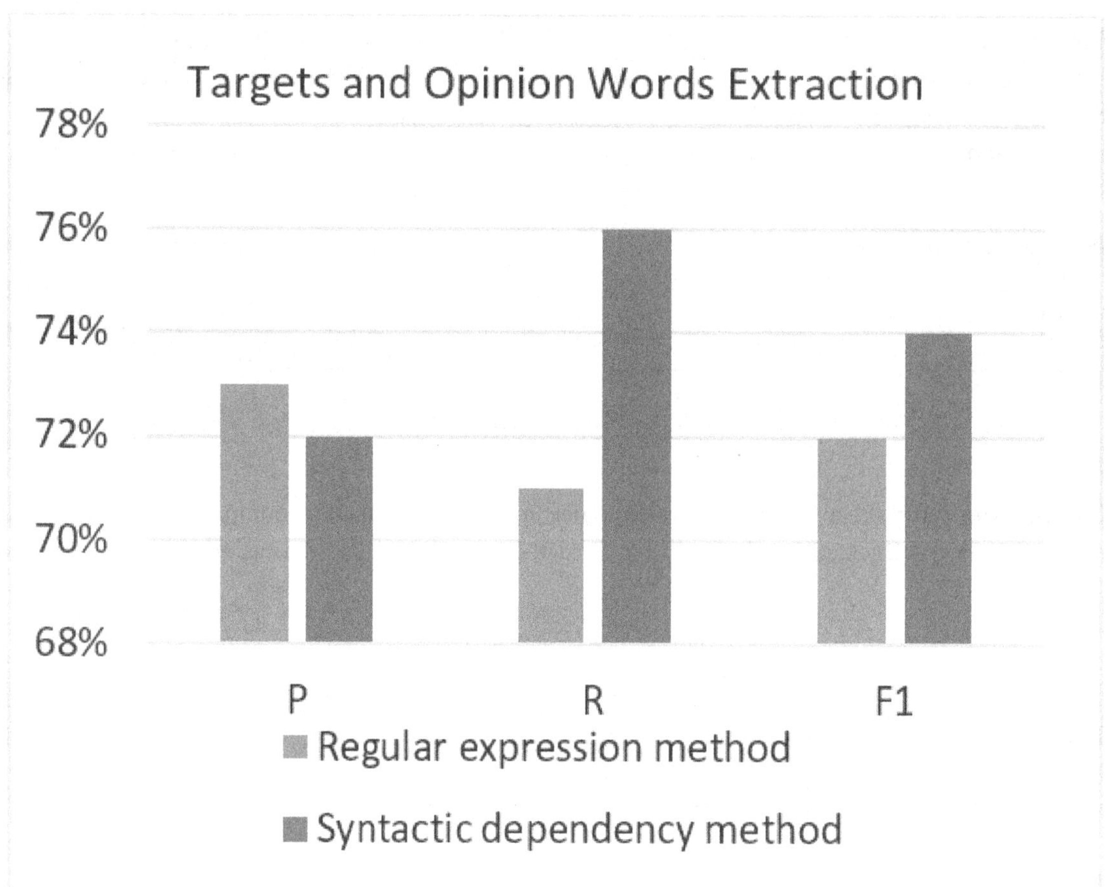

The results in Figure 3 show that the regular expression method seems to achieve better accuracy but a worse recall and F-measure. This is unsurprising, since the regular expression method depends far more on lexicons and sequences. A slight irregularity in the input can easily lead to incorrect results, whereas the syntactic dependency method can handle these irregularities much better, owing to its identification of semantic relations. Additionally, the syntactic dependency method outperforms the regular expression method in its ability to automatically recognise aspects by extracting rules. Following analysis of the error system, we discovered a large number of incorrect results could be accounted for by the inefficiency of the dependency parser. Once the preprocessing components are developed and upgraded, we expect that the system's efficiency will be noticeably improved. In other respects, sentiments of sentences and texts are defined by the syntactic dependency method in agreement with the fine-grained method. This will be discussed in detail as part of the case-study in section 4.5.

Finally, to understand the scientific value of the study, we compare this model with other contemporary research. Tables 5 and 6 present the model's results in comparison with those of the studies in Tran and Phan, (2015); Qiu, Liu, Bu, and Chen, (2009) (2001); Le, Le, and Pham, (2015); Van and Dau, (2014); Ha, and Vu, Pham, and Luu, (2011).

Table 5. Comparisons of our model with state-of-the-art sentiment analysis models

Study	Model/Method	Extracted words	Language	Number of Rules
Qui, G. et al., (2009 and 2011)	Exploring of the dependency relations between sentiment words and targets to extract one when knowing the other.	Adjective	English	8 double propagation rules
This model	Exploring of the dependency relations between sentiment words and targets and combining with sentiment dictionary to extract sentiment pairs. Using specific-domain ontologies for grouping the targets/ features	Adjective, verb, and noun	Vietnamese	12 extracting rules

Table 6. Comparisons of our model with latest Vietnamese sentiment analysis models

Study	Model/Method	Weaknesses	Strengths
Le et al., (2015)	Semi-supervised learning GK-LDA to extract and classify aspect-terms in the Vietnamese language	A long time for the execution when using machine learning.	The semi-supervised learning GK-LDA proves to have better performance than the traditional topic modeling LDA.
Van et al., (2014)	A crossed-domain sentiment analysis system that can capture the sentiment of career-related messages from Twitter and Facebook.	Dependent on the special domain	The experiment could identify the favorite careers which enjoy the highest positive/negative sentiment. The precision of the proposed system was over 85%.
Ha et al., (2011)	Feature words and opinion words were extracted based on some Vietnamese syntactic rules. Extracted feature words were grouped using semi-supervised classification.	A long time for the execution when using machine learning. Depending on the special domain.	Implicit product features and co-reference were resolved using some Vietnamese rules.
Tran et al. (2015)	Regular expression method implemented in GATE/JAPE framework.	Worse Recall and F-measure ratio. The model can only capture adjective.	Better Precision ratio.
This model	Hybrid approach: using dependency rules, sentiment dictionary and domain ontology for extracting opinion word and target pairs. Extracted feature words (targets) were grouped by using specific-domain ontology.	The objective error of the dependency parser VnDP did significantly reduce the accuracy of the system.	The extracting rules are not dependent on the special domain or language. The model can capture all types of sentiment words (adjective, verb, noun)

4.5. Case Study: Vietnam Hotel Information Inquiry

Problem: Building a system searching for users' reviews on domestic hotels.
Script: A possible scenario of the system can take place as follows:

User: Could you please give me information about the hotel ABC in Nha Trang?

System: The hotel ABC in Nha Trang has received 234 reviews, out of which:

- *Price: 100 positive reviews and 65 negative reviews;*
- *Room: 155 positive reviews and 40 negative reviews;*
- *View: 56 positive reviews and 36 negative reviews.*

To realize the functions in observing the above scenario, the system must be composed of following components:

- UI: The user interface.
- Vietnamese Language Processor: resolve the syntax and semantic representations of all the command sentences or query sentences of user.
- Central Processor: Transform the semantic representations of the queries into the SQL commands and execute it, and then, filter, organize, and return the results to user.
- Hotel Knowledge Base: Contain the hotel reviews that were analyzed based on our proposed model in Section 3.1.

Our system architect is presented in Figure 4.

Figure 4. The system architect

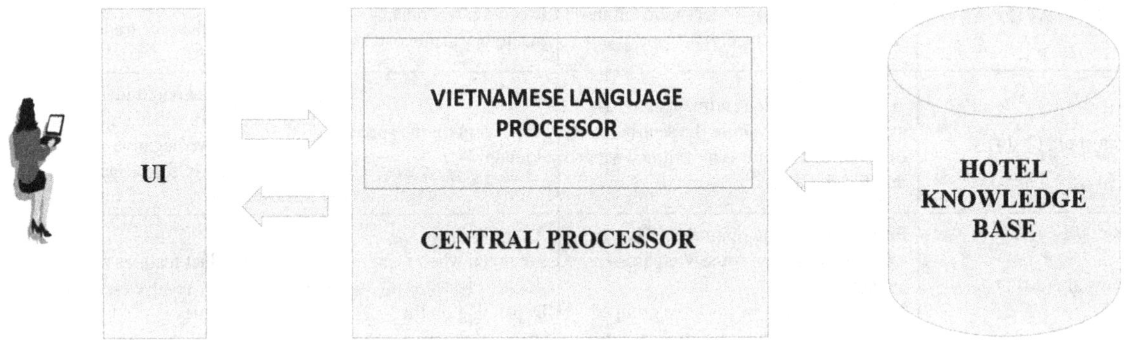

The application is founded on the web base using PHP language and database system MySQL containing review information about 120 hotels.

4.5.1. *Building the Hotel Knowledge Base*

- **Hotel corpus**: - Hotel corpus: A crawler is built in JavaScript to automatically collect 14,460 reviews about 120 hotels. This review information has been posted on agoda.vn and mytour.vn from August 2nd, 2010 to June 29th, 2017.
- **Extracting rules**: we use the method which proposed in Section 3.2.
- **Sentiment dictionary**: we adopt the VNSD proposed in Tran et al. (2018).
- **Hotel ontology**: Hotel-domain ontology is built as a support for the application. To evaluate a hotel, six aspects are taken into account:
  - Room associated with entities, such as surface, conditioners, beds, blankets, bed sheets, pillows, TV, internet, toilet, water heaters, washbasins, bath tubs, hair dryers, telephones, towels, soap, shampoo.
  - Location associated with entities such as neighbourhood, surroundings, areas.

- Prices associated with entities such as room price, rate, service fee, expenses, and some key words like expensive, cheap.
- Services associated with entities such as mini-bar, staff, reception, room service, beauty salon, casino, swimming pool, restaurant.
- Overview associated with entities such as hotel, this place, as well as some key words: beautiful, noisy.
- View associated with scenery, balcony.

4.5.2. *Contructing the Vietnamese Language Processor*

Swi-Prolog is utilised to execute commands created out of Definite Clause Grammar (DCG) and create the semantic representations of the queries like those in the work of Tran et al., (2015). In obedience to this application, 5 semantic structures are shown in the Table 7.

Table 7. Comparisons of our model with latest Vietnamese sentiment analysis models

ID	Semantic presentation
1	query(hotel, place, aspect)
2	query(hotel, place)
3	query(hotel,)
4	query(hotel, place, attribute)
5	query(hotel, attribute)

Example: With the query "Khách sạn Y ở Hà Nội như thế nào?" (How about the hotel Y in Ha Noi?). The syntactic and semantic rules in DCG are defined as below:

```
query(query(Hotel, Place)) --> n_hotel, n_hotel(Hotel), v_at, n_place(Place),
w_how.
n_hotel --> [khách, sạn].
n_hotel(hotel(KS)) --> n_hotels(KS).
n_hotels(y) --> [y].
v_at --> [ở].
n_place(place(Place)) --> n_places(Place).
n_places(hanoi) --> [hà, nội].
w_how --> [như, thế, nào].
```

These syntactic and semantic rules determine the semantic structure of this command as: ***query(hotel(y), place(hanoi))***. This semantic structure is the structure 2 in Table 6.

These semantic structures will be converted to SQL commands for querying the database. A screenshot of the application is presented by Figure 5.

Figure 5. A screenshot of the application

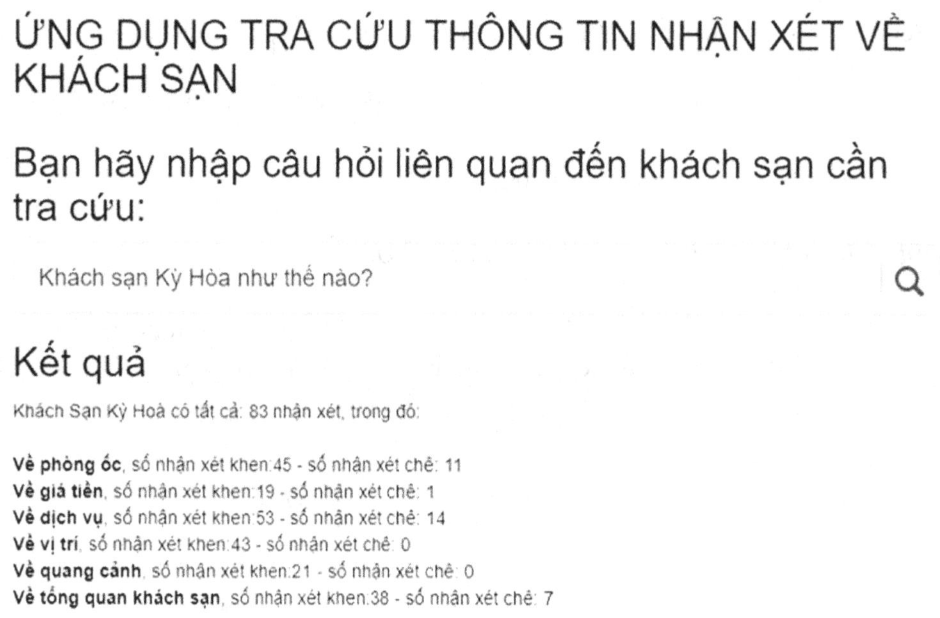

ỨNG DỤNG TRA CỨU THÔNG TIN NHẬN XÉT VỀ KHÁCH SẠN

Bạn hãy nhập câu hỏi liên quan đến khách sạn cần tra cứu:

Khách sạn Kỳ Hòa như thế nào?

Kết quả

Khách Sạn Kỳ Hoà có tất cả: 83 nhận xét, trong đó:

Về phòng ốc, số nhận xét khen:45 - số nhận xét chê: 11
Về giá tiền, số nhận xét khen:19 - số nhận xét chê: 1
Về dịch vụ, số nhận xét khen:53 - số nhận xét chê: 14
Về vị trí, số nhận xét khen:43 - số nhận xét chê: 0
Về quang cảnh, số nhận xét khen:21 - số nhận xét chê: 0
Về tổng quan khách sạn, số nhận xét khen:38 - số nhận xét chê: 7

4.6. Discussion

Nowadays, most websites publishing reviews, such as agoda.com, are equipped with a scoring function together with free-text reviews, though these two are not always in complete agreement. Figure 6 shows an example of a negative review for which the user offered a positive score (6/10). Using our proposed system, inconsistencies such as this would be corrected, as the system takes scrupulous care of semantic structures which create valence shifting, such as negation structures, euphemisms or dysphemisms. The evaluation of fine-grained sentiments of these phrases is carried out with the help of the VNSD dictionary.

A key innovation of this work is our ability to extract aspects based on the analysis of semantic relations in Vietnamese, which are very complicated. Owing to the extraction rules, these aspects can be automatically discovered and grouped by domain-specific ontologies. These aspects, and sentiment phrases relating to them, are calculated and synthesized by the SO-CAL method and VNSD dictionary.

Figure 6. A screenshot of a hotel review "The room is rather small, cramped." with positive score

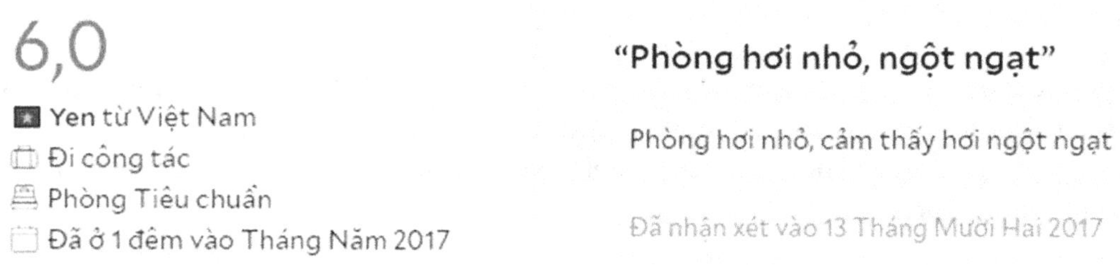

6,0

Yen từ Việt Nam
Đi công tác
Phòng Tiêu chuẩn
Đã ở 1 đêm vào Tháng Năm 2017

"Phòng hơi nhỏ, ngột ngạt"

Phòng hơi nhỏ, cảm thấy hơi ngột ngạt

Đã nhận xét vào 13 Tháng Mười Hai 2017

5. CONCLUSION AND FUTURE WORK

In this paper, we presented and explained a model for extracting and grouping pairs of aspects and sentiment words in a Vietnamese aspect-based sentiment analysis. The evaluation phase of our study demonstrates the effectiveness of our approach which combines ontologies, a sentiment dictionary, and syntactic dependency rules. To the best of our knowledge this is the first work to adopt dependency grammar for Vietnamese sentiment analysis. This technique could also be adapted to other languages.

In future work we plan to develop more syntactic dependency rules and build further specific-domain ontologies, as well as considering, selecting, and upgrading the preprocessing tools.

REFERENCES

Carrillo de Albornoz, J., Plaza, L., & Gervas, P. (2010). A hybrid approach to emotional sentence polarity and intensity classification. *CoNLL*, *10*, 153–161.

Chinsha, T. C., & Joseph, S. (2015). A syntactic approach for aspect based opinion mining. In *IEEE international conference on semantic computing* (pp. 24–31). ICSC.

Dave, K., Lawrence, S., & Pennock, D. M. (2003). Mining the peanut gallery: opinion extraction and semantic classification of product reviews. In *Proceedings of the 12th international ACM conference on World Wide Web* (pp. 519–528).

Ha, Q. T., Vu, T. T., Pham, H. T., & Luu, C. T. (2011). An Upgrading Feature-Based Opinion Mining Model on Vietnamese Product Reviews. In N. Zhong, V. Callaghan, A. A. Ghorbani, & B. Hu (Eds.), *Active Media Technology. AMT 2011, LNCS* (Vol. 6890). Springer; . doi:10.1007/978-3-642-23620-4_21

Hong, P. L., Nguyen, T. M. H., & Roussanaly, A. Vietnamese Parsing with an Automatically Extracted Tree-Adjoining Grammar. In *Proceedings of the 9th IEEE RIVF International Conference on Computing & Communication Technologies, Research, Innovation, and Vision for the Future*. IEEE; . doi:10.1109/rivf.2012.6169832

Hu, M., & Liu, B. (2004). *Mining opinion features in customer reviews* (pp. 755–760). AAAI.

Jia, L., Yu, C., & Meng, W. (2009). The effect of negation on sentiment analysis and retrieval effectiveness. *CIKM*, *09*, 1827–1830.

Jiang, M., Wang, J., Lan, M., & Wu, Y. (2017). An effective gated and attention-based neural network model for fine grained financial target-dependent sentiment analysis. In *International Conference on Knowledge Science, Engineering and Management* (pp. 42–54). Springer. doi:10.1007/978-3-319-63558-3_4

Le, H.S., Le, T.V., Pham, T.V. (2015). Aspect analysis for opinion mining of Vietnamese text. In 2015 international conference on advanced computing and applications *ACOMP*.

Li, F., Huang, M., & Zhu, X. (2010). Sentiment Analysis with Global Topics and Local Dependency. In M. Fox, & D. Poole (Ed.), *Proceedings of the 24th AAAI Conference on Artificial Intelligence, AAAI 2010*, Atlanta, GA, July 11-15. AAAI Press.

Liu, B. (2010). *Sentiment Analysis and Subjectivity. Handbook of Natural Language Processing* (N. Indurkhya & F. J. Damerau, Eds.). 2nd ed.). Chapman & Hall.

Liu, B., Hu, M., & Cheng, J. (2005). Opinion observer: analyzing and comparing opinions on the Web. In *WWW '05: Proceedings of the 14th international conference on World Wide Web* (pp. 342-351). doi:10.1145/1060745.1060797

Marcheggiani, D., Täckström, O., Esuli, A., & Sebastiani, F. (2014). Hierarchical multi-label conditional random fields for aspect-oriented opinion mining. In M. de Rijke & ... (Eds.), *Advances in information retrieval. ECIR 2014, LNCS* (Vol. 8416, pp. 273–285). Cham: Springer; . doi:10.1007/978-3-319-06028-6_23

Matsumoto, S., Takamura, H., & Okumura, M. (2005). Sentiment classification using word sub-sequences and dependency sub-trees. In *Proceedings of PAKDD* (pp 301–311). doi:10.1007/11430919_37

Nasukawa, T., & Yi, J. (2003). Sentiment analysis: Capturing favorability using natural language processing. In *Proceedings of the 2nd International Conference on Knowledge Capture* (pp. 70–77). ACM; . doi:10.1145/945645.945658

Nguyen, Q. D., Nguyen, Q. D., Pham, D. D., & Pham, B. S. (2014). RDRPOSTagger: A Ripple Down Rules-based Part-Of-Speech Tagger. In *Proceedings of the Demonstrations at the 14th Conference of the European Chapter of the Association for Computational Linguistics* (pp 17-20). doi:10.3115/v1/E14-2005

Nguyen, Q. D., Nguyen, Q. D., Pham, D. D., Pham, B. S., Nguyen, P. T., & Nguyen, L. M. (2014). From Treebank Conversion to Automatic Dependency Parsing for Vietnamese. In *Proceedings of 19th International Conference on Application of Natural Language to Information Systems, NLDB'14* (pp 196-207). Springer. doi:10.1007/978-3-319-07983-7_26

Pang, B., Lee, L., & Vaithyanathan, S. (2002). Thumbs up?: sentiment classification using machine learning techniques. In *Proceedings of the ACL-02 conference on Empirical methods in natural language processing* (Vol. 10, pp. 79-86). doi:10.3115/1118693.1118704

Polanyi, L., & Zaenen, A. (2006). *Contextual valence shifters.* In *Computing attitude and affect in text: Theory and applications* (pp. 1–10). doi:10.1007/1-4020-4102-0_1

Qiu, G., Liu, B., Bu, J., & Chen, C. (2009). Expanding Domain Sentiment Lexicon through Double Propagation. In C. Boutilier (Ed.), *IJCAI* (pp. 1199–1204).

Qiu, G., Liu, B., Bu, J., & Chen, C. (2011). Opinion Word Expansion and Target Extraction through Double Propagation. *Computational Linguistics*.

Sharma, R., Nigam, S., & Jain, R. (2014). Opinion mining of movie reviews at document level. *International Journal on Information Theory*, *3*(3).

Sharma, S. K., Hoque, X., & Chandra, P. (2016). Sentiment Predictions Using Deep Belief Networks Model for Odd-Even Policy in Delhi. *International Journal of Synthetic Emotions*, *7*(2), 1–22. doi:10.4018/IJSE.2016070101

Singh, A., Sharma, A., & Dey, N. (2015). Semantics and agents oriented web personalization: State of the art. *International Journal of Service Science, Management, Engineering, and Technology*, *6*(2), 35–49.

Taboada, M., Brooke, J., Tofiloski, M., Voll, K., & Stede, M. (2011). Lexicon-Based Methods for Sentiment Analysis. *Computational Linguistics*, *37*(2), 267–307. doi:10.1162/COLI_a_00049

Tang, D., Qin, B., Liu, T., & Yang, Y. (2015) User modeling with neural network for review rating prediction. In *Proceedings of IJCAI* (pp 1340–1346).

Tran, T. K., & Phan, T. T. (2015). An upgrading SentiVoice-a system for querying hotel service reviews via phone. In *International Conference on Asian Language Processing* (pp. 115–118). IALP; . doi:10.1109/IALP.2015.7451545

Tran, T. K., & Phan, T. T. (2016). Multi-class Opinion Classification for Vietnamese Hotel Reviews. *International Journal of Intelligent Technologies and Applied Statistics*, *9*(1), 7–18.

Tran, T. K., & Phan, T. T. (2017). Mining opinion targets and opinion words from online reviews. *Int. J. Inf. Technol.*, *9*(3), 239–249.

Tran, T. K., & Phan, T. T. (2018). A hybrid approach for building a Vietnamese sentiment dictionary. *Journal of Intelligent & Fuzzy Systems*, *35*(1), 967–978.

Van, A. T. T., & Dau, H. X. (2014) A crossed-domain sentiment analysis system for the discovery of current careers from social networks. In *Proceedings of the fifth symposium on information and communication technology (SoICT 14)*, New York (pp. 226–231). doi:10.1145/2676585.2676614

Wu, H., Gu, Y., Sun, S., & Gu, X. (2016). Aspect-based opinion summarization with convolutional neural networks. In *2016 International Joint Conference on Neural Networks (IJCNN)* (pp. 3157-3163). IEEE. doi:10.1109/IJCNN.2016.7727602

Xia, R., Xu, F., Yu, J., Qi, Y., & Cambria, E. (2016). Polarity shift detection, elimination and ensemble: A three-stage model for document-level sentiment analysis. *Information Processing & Management*, *52*(1), 36–45. doi:10.1016/j.ipm.2015.04.003

Yang, B., & Cardie, C. (2014) Context-aware learning for sentence-level sentiment analysis with posterior regularization. In *ACL* (no 1, pp. 325-335). doi:10.3115/v1/P14-1031

Yu, H., & Hatzivassiloglou, V. (2003). Towards Answering Opinion Questions: Separating Facts from Opinions and Identifying the Polarity of Opinion Sentences. In Proceedings of the 2003 Conference on Empirical Methods in Natural Language Processing (pp. 129-136). The Association for Computer Linguistics. doi:10.3115/1119355.1119372

Zhao, W. X., Jiang, J., Yan, H., & Li, X. (2010). Jointly modeling aspects and opinions with a MaxEnt-LDA Hybrid. In *Proceedings of the 2010 Conference on Empirical Methods in Natural Language Processing, EMNLP 2010*, MIT Stata Center, MA, October 9-11 (pp. 56-65). The Association for Computer Linguistics.

This research was previously published in the International Journal of Synthetic Emotions (IJSE), 9(2); pages 54-75, copyright year 2018 by IGI Publishing (an imprint of IGI Global).

Chapter 17
A Novel Aspect Based Framework for Tourism Sector with Improvised Aspect and Opinion Mining Algorithm

Vishal Bhatnagar
Department of Computer Science and Engineering, Ambedkar Institute of Advanced Communication Technologies and Research, New Delhi, India

Mahima Goyal
Ambedkar Institute of Advanced Communication Technologies and Research, New Delhi, India

Mohammad Anayat Hussain
Ambedkar Institute of Advanced Communication Technologies and Research, New Delhi, India

ABSTRACT

With the growth of e-commerce web sites, the demand of writing reviews on these portals have gained huge popularity. This huge data must be mined to analyze the opinion and for making better decisions in different domains. In this paper, we have proposed an aspect based opinion mining algorithm for the tourism domain. It first determines the aspects, and then extracts the opinion words related to the aspects. The opinion words are provided a score based on the Senti-Wordnet and the final score of each aspect is calculated by the summation of the scores of the opinions. The final score is visualized depicting ranking of scores of different aspects for different hotels.

INTRODUCTION

With the growth of the world wide web in the recent years, the demand of expressing different opinions and experiences on different media has grown exponentially. The different media include reviews, blogs, forum and twitter. This opinionated data, in large volumes, has to be analyzed to make better decisions about different products and services. For instance, customer check reviews of restaurants on web plat-

DOI: 10.4018/978-1-6684-6303-1.ch017

forms before checking to a restaurant. Users also check the review of a product before buying a product and manufacturers need to understand a review to know about the sales performance of a product. The huge information from twitter can also be used to analyze political trends and popularity of a brand. Although, it appears interesting to analyze the available opinionated texts, it is quite challenging to estimate such kind of problems. People write a lot of objective sentences in their review which don't directly affect the opinion of the product. Thus, these sentences must be eliminated while analyzing the reviews.

Most of the authors have focused on classifying the reviews as positive or negative classes (Turney, 2002). For instance, a restaurant review can be classified into positive or negative based on the different data mining techniques. The different machine learning algorithms employed by the authors are Naive Bayes and SVM (Support Vector Machine) (Zhang et al., 2011). However, the aspect or feature based opinion mining (M. Hu and B. Liu, 2004) gives a broader and clearer picture of what the user wants. In this type, different features of the product and services are mined. The opinion is identified for the mined features and results are visualized according to the different features. This type of visualization allows potential customers to look for the features in which they are interested. For example, consider a hotel review in which customers usually comment about the features like food, staff, ambience and the other facilities of the hotel. In this, customer would like to know about the particular features in which one is interested. Thus, the aspect based opinion evaluation gives an insight, depth of these aspects. Moreover, this type of opinion mining has fascinated a lot of authors in the recent times because of its customization according to the aspects.

In this paper, we put forward a novel aspect based opinion mining approach using SentiWordNet by arranging the aspects of different reviews in the tourism domain. A lot of authors have applied opinion mining in product reviews, movie domain and political tweets, but very few have focused on the tourism domain. This domain is not a physical product review, but an intangible service as pointed by Taylor et al. (2014). An algorithm is proposed to extract the explicit aspects of the hotel reviews downloaded from the TripAdvisor site. The opinion is searched for each explicit aspect and those aspects which have an opinion are provided a score based on the Sentiwordnet. The cumulative score for each aspect is calculated and the results are visualized in the form of a graph. For example, consider the sentences- (1) The staff is helpful and friendly. (2) The staff enables you to find your bearings by providing a trishaw facility. In the first sentence, opinion 'helpful' and 'friendly' is extracted for the aspect 'staff'. In the second sentence, no opinion is extracted for the word 'staff'. The different techniques used in opinion mining are sentiment classification, subjectivity analysis, lexicon based, statistical based, dictionary based and semantic based. In this paper, we have used unsupervised dictionary based approach where the dictionary is SentiWordNet to extract explicit

This paper has been classified into different sections. Section 2 elucidates the description of related work. Section 3 describes the proposed framework and its architectural details. Section 4 describes an experimental view in tourism domain. Section 5 illustrates its evaluation and section 6 provides the conclusion with the future scope of the proposed system.

RELATED WORK

Bhatnagar (2010, 2013), Acharjee (2013), and Radhwan (2015) reviewed the different data mining techniques for data analysis. The method of capturing market intelligence has been shown by Li (2013). Ripon et al. (2016) found different automated machine learning techniques and compared them. Opinion mining refers to analyzing of different sentiments, opinions from different product reviews and services. Pang and Lee (2008) discussed different techniques of opinion mining in their book. The term 'opinion mining' and 'sentiment analysis' can be used interchangeably as they both have the same meanings. It can be categorized into three levels- Document Level, Sentence Level and Aspect Level.

The Document level (Pang et al., 2002) states that every document can be classified into two classes –positive or negative. It uses different data mining techniques to classify the document into two levels. Naïve Bayes and SVM machine learning techniques were used by Zhang et al. (2013) to classify restaurant reviews. Moraes (2013) also implemented the data mining algorithm by comparing SVM and ANN (Artificial Neural Network). A supervised machine learning algorithm using SVM was implemented by Ghiassi (2014). In this, the twitter was used as a platform for performing the analysis. Van de camp (2014) showed the application of biography by implementing SVM. Word selection method was used by Carroll (2008) to implement sentiment classification of product reviews. Kang et al. (2011) classified the reviews based on traditional machine learning techniques. Goyal and Bhatnagar (2016) used an unsupervised approach to classify the opinions in tourism domain.

In sentence level Kim and Hovy (2004) has proposed a bootstrapping method which applies a seed opinion to find synonyms and antonyms from wordnet. In the 'Sentence level', each sentence will be classified as objective or subjective (Weibe et al., 2003). Esuli and Sebastiani (2006) coined the importance of subjectivity and orientation in their paper. They used semi supervised machine techniques to show the subjectivity in their paper. The review will then be classified according to the subjective sentences. Some of the authors have used statistical based approach as stated by Coling (2010) while some have applied semantic based approach discussed by Ding et al (2008). Rui (2013) discussed various data mining algorithms to find how movie sales are affected by the various tweets in the twitter.

Aspect or feature level was first coined by Hu and Liu (2004). It showed that reviews can be mined according to the different features of a product. It lets the customer know about what he likes or dislikes about a product. This information is very useful as users are not always interested in knowing whether the product is positive or negative. They want to know about the different features of the product such as size, battery, price of a camera. Thus, this level has been attracted by a lot of researchers in the recent times. This level follows four types of approaches-lexicon, statistical, semantic and dictionary based. A lexicon based approach Pang et al. (2002) identifies the opinion words to find the orientation of the sentence on a feature. A statistical approach has been elucidated in Coling (2010). Dictionary based approach is quite popular according to Miller (1995) and semantic based approach has been shown in Ding et al. (2008).

Several other authors (Liu 2007; Decker & Trusov, 2010) have also focused on aspect based opinion mining in different fields. Moghaddam and Ester (2012) also implemented aspect based opinion mining in product reviews. Parkhe and Biswas (2014) showed aspect based opinion mining in movie reviews. Manek et al. (2016) implemented aspect based opinion mining in movie domain using SVM. Thet et al. (2010) showed aspect based opinion mining in movie domain using grammatical dependency structure. Taylor et al. (2014) has worked on this in tourism domain, but, their work is different. They have used lexicon based approach to calculate the orientation of the opinion words while we are using a dictionary based approach (Sentiwordnet) to find the score of the opinions. Baccianella et al. (2010) discussed the basics of Sentiwordnet. The explicit features are found using the algorithm described in Hu and Liu (2004). Ahmad and Doja (2012) worked on the aspect based opinion mining in product domain. A dictionary based approach was used by them but the negation words were not taken into account. In this paper, we have tried to incorporate the negation words which reverses the polarity of the word.

The extensive review of different papers show that aspect based opinion mining has fascinated a lot of potential researchers in the recent years. We have followed the same footsteps and proposed an aspect based opinion mining algorithm for the tourism domain to rank the features according to their scores. It is somehow different to deal with the tourism domain, since different users respond differently to different type of products.

The sentiment scores of each aspect are found using SentiWordNet in which a dictionary based approach is followed rather than a lexicon based approach as in Taylor et al. (2014). Bhatnagar et al. (2016) have taken into account implicit as well as explicit aspects while we have only considered explicit aspects in this paper as it was not possible to take implicit aspects as well into the account.

PROPOSED FRAMEWORK AT ASPECT BASED LEVEL

Opinion mining is an important concept which has become immensely popular in the recent years. Moreover, the aspect based opinion mining has gained more popularity as it caters to the needs of users and help them to take important decisions in the correct manner. This drives us to propose a framework which not only automates this cumbersome process of manually reading the reviews but provide the results which are improved on its own. The proposed framework is able to perform the different tasks and provide the ranking of scores for different aspects. We are performing the ranking of aspects since it is an interesting way to know which aspects customer are really interested in. We have tried, not only to extract the different aspects, but the different opinions corresponding to an aspect. The proposed framework has been described in Figure 1. The proposed framework describes about the overall methodology of the working of our model. It consists of three modules. Data Extraction, Opinion Mining and Data Visualization module. Each of these modules contains sub components as described in the further section.

Data Extraction Module

This module contains two sub-components. 'Review Extraction' and' word Tagger'. The main functionality of this module is to download the data set in the form of reviews from the website 'www.Tripadvisor.in' and perform searching of nouns and adjectives from the retrieved files.

Review Extraction

This component performs the function of downloading different hotel reviews from the TripAdvisor site and storing the reviews in .txt files.

Word Tagger

This component searches for nouns and adjectives from the SentiWordNet and collects them in two files called NounCollection.txt and AdjectiveCollection.txt respectively. A Java Program is written to search the nouns and adjectives from the SentiWordNet file. We have chosen nouns and adjectives as it is observed that most of the times nouns in the reviews correspond to the aspects and adjectives are represented by opinions.

Figure 1. Proposed Framework for Aspect Based Opinion Mining

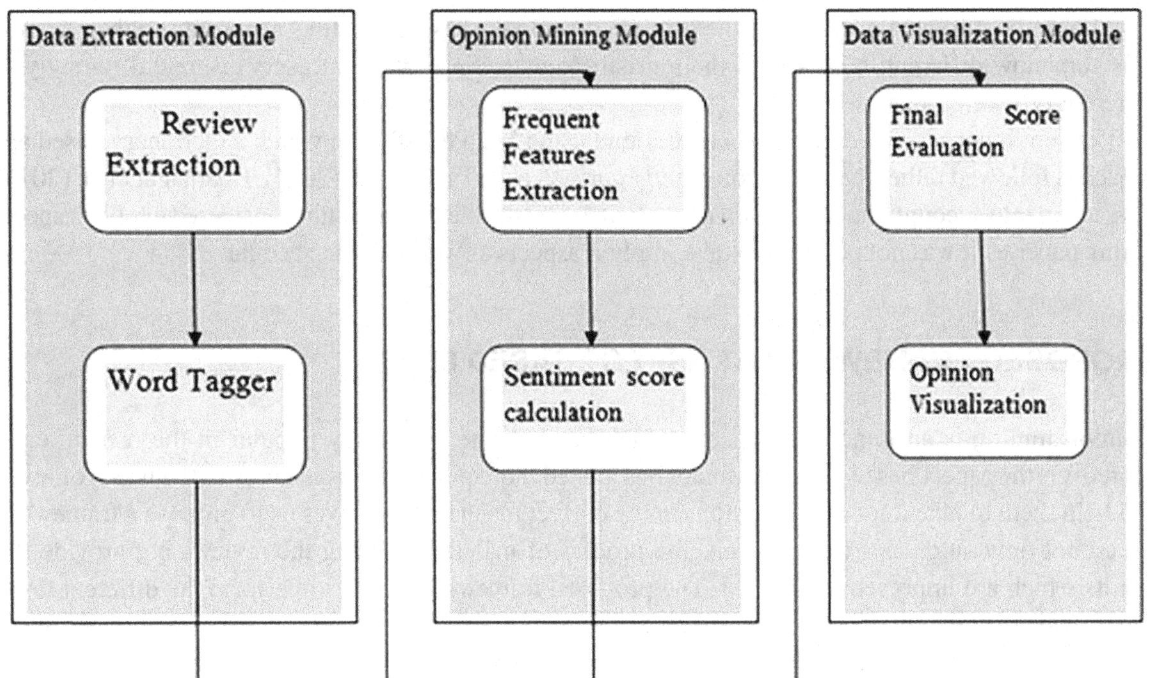

Opinion Mining Module

This module is responsible for implementing the extraction of aspects and sentiment score calculation. The output of this module would be the score of different features which are extracted by frequent feature extraction phase. This module is bifurcated into two phases- Frequent Feature phase and Sentiment Score calculation phase which is explained below: -

Frequent Features or Aspect Extraction

It is very important to extract features of a product or service since we need to know which features are being liked and disliked by the customers. Moreover, as it is aspect based opinion mining so extraction of features become an important task. While deciding for the features to be extracted, frequent nouns are made the features of the scenario as it tells that people are talking about those features very frequently. Such features are called explicit aspects (Hu & Liu, 2004). Explicit features or aspects are chosen because these can be clearly identified by a human, some features are such that they are embedded in the meaning of the sentences for example, "*The staff worked very swiftly*" here in this example "*staff*" is of course explicit feature as they are being addressed but "*swiftly*" is containing an implicit aspect also, which is "*performance of staff*". In this paper, feature and aspect will, by default refer to explicit features or aspects only. The nouns that appear frequently in the review will be marked as features. The frequent features which come in the review are the most talked about things which must be mapped to know the interest of the user. The frequent nouns will be found out by comparing the frequency of the noun with a threshold. The threshold taken here is 1% of noun phrases as considered in Hu and Liu (2004). The nouns that are above the threshold will be extracted in the feature list. The algorithm described below gives the explanation of extracting the frequent nouns which will be mapped to explicit aspects.

Algorithm 1. Aspects Extraction

Input: review file, NounCollection.txt
Output: Extracted features in the list
1. for each line in review file
2. Compare([NounCollection.txt], [review file])
3. If (noun found) then
4. collect[list]<-noun
5. End if
6. End for
7. If (frequency of each noun in collect[list]>threshold) then
8. Feature[list]<-noun
9. Else
10. Discard noun
11. End if

Sentiment Score Calculation

The sentiment or opinion of each feature can be calculated by considering the adjectives in the sentences. It is because adjectives describe the best meaning of what people like or not. For example-nice, good, friendly, etc. This component searches for the collected features in the file and find the adjective sentence by sentence for that particular feature. The adjectives may be found in near proximity of the feature only. Proximity here is a human decided value because a sentence as a whole can be very large and it may contain adjectives about the feature in immediate proximity or very far away from feature or may not contain any adjective about feature at all. This proximity is decided by the average value of the length of sentence and the number of files tested on a system. The scores of the adjectives are extracted from the SentiWordNet and the final score is calculated by summation of score for each extracted feature. If any negation word is found for the adjective as in "not good" or "don't like it" or "not bad" then the polarity of the adjective is reversed with its opposite score in the SentiWordNet. This is done because a negation word reverses the opinion eg- consider the sentence 'The staff is not good'. This sentence consider opinion 'good' which is positive but adding 'not' before it changes its orientation. Thus, we have introduced negation rules in our algorithm to improve the accuracy. The below algorithm describes the opinion score calculation for each aspect. Line 5 and 6 takes into account the negation words by swapping the adjective score.

Algorithm 2. Opinion Calculation

Input: Feature[list], review.txt, Sentiwordnet
Output: final score for each feature
1. for each Feature j=1 to N

2. for each sentence in review.txt
3. find nearest adjective
4. for each found adjective i= 1 to n
5. if (found negation word) then
6. Si=swap (adjective score (positive,negative)
7. else
8. Si=adjective score(positive)
9. end if
10. end for
11. end for
12. fscore $_j$+=score
13. end for

A partial list of extracted aspects for the hotel China Haidain is given in Table 1. It depicts the different extracted aspects along with the sentiment or opinion of that aspect. The opinion is calculated by finding the adjectives in the vicinity of the extracted aspects.

Table 1. Partial List of Aspects Extracted with Their Opinion

Hotel	Feature	Opinion
China Haidian	Gym	Small
	Buffet	Okay, good
	Internet	Wireless, reliable, free, comfortable
	Staff	helpful, friendly, incompetent
	Room	Nice, spotless, better

Data Visualization Module

This module performs the final score evaluation of the sentiment and visualization of opinion in the form of the graph. This module is classified into two phases-Final Score Evaluation and Opinion Visualization phase. The two phases are described as below: -

Final Score Evaluation

The final score is calculated by summation of the individual sentiment scores of each aspect or feature. The formula is given as follows:

$$fscore_j = \sum_{i=1}^{n} (Si)$$

where $fscore_j$ represents the final score for the aspect where j = 1, 2, 3… N and N = total no. of features or aspects in the list.

Here Si represent the score of the opinions calculated where i = 1, 2, 3… n and n = total no. of adjectives for each aspect.

$fscore_{staff} = S_{helpful} + S_{friendly} + S_{incompetent}$
$= (0.687 + 0.25 + 0.18)$
$= 1.117$

Opinion Visualization

Figure 2 has been formed by plotting the aspects with their sentiment scores. The aspects with their scores are stored in a .csv file as shown in Figure 3. Graphical representation makes the concept more clear to the viewer and one can easily see what things about what are good, moderate, and bad. Thus, final aspects are displayed along with their scores in the form of the graph visualizing the different levels of aspects. Users can themselves decide which aspect is important for them and accordingly choose the aspect based on the score of the opinions. A graph is shown where all the features are plotted on the X-axis and the fscore of the opinion of each feature is plotted on y-axis

Figure 2 shows that hotel, room, staff, buffet are the features that are mostly liked by the users, whereas gym, breakfast and bed are not that popular among customers. This figure visualizes different extracted aspects with their final score. This graph describes that hotel aspect is the most liked by the

Figure 2. Graph of Features vs Opinion Score of the Feature

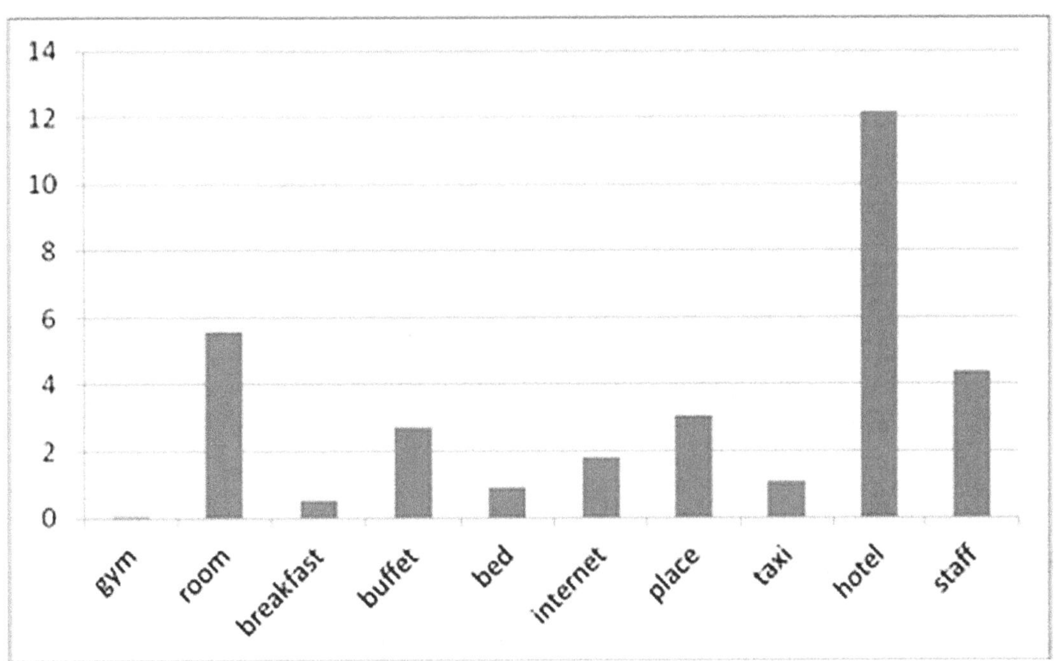

consumers as its score is highest among the other aspects whereas the aspect gym is least liked since it has a minimum score.

VALIDATION

In this section, we present an application where the proposed algorithm was implemented using Java. The dataset was downloaded from TripAdvisor site where reviews of 5 hotels of China were collected in .txt file. Each of the hotel contains some 30 reviews so a total of almost 100 reviews was tested on the applied algorithm. While extracting the aspects, we have only considered explicit aspects debarring implicit aspects. The sentiment score was taken from SentiWordNet 3.0 which is open-source and can be downloaded freely. Table 2 shows the partial results of opinion score with their extracted opinion words for some aspects

In Figure 3 the output of the features with their final score is shown in .csv file. A graph is visualized for clear understanding of the scores using these values as described in Figure 2. The implemented algorithm when run gives the output in .csv file as shown in Figure3.It contains two columns- feature

Table 2. Sentiment Value of Opinion Word Corresponding to Each Feature

Features	Opinion word	Score
Gym	Small	0.0125
Buffet	Okay	0.375
Buffet	Good	2.317
Internet	Reliable	0.833
Internet	Free	0.441
Internet	Comfortable	0.545
Staff	Friendly	0.687
Staff	Helpful	0.25
Staff	Incompetent	0.218
Room	Spotless	0.5
Room	Nice	1.712
Room	Better	1.562

and opinion value which describes the opinion or final score (fscore) for each extracted feature of the input file.

PERFORMANCE EVALUATION

The performance of the whole system is evaluated by considering the performance of extraction of features and opinion through the entire process. The downloaded reviews were stored in .txt files. Each

Figure 3. Opinion Score of Extracted Features in .csv File

	A	B
1		
2	Features	opinion value
3	gym	0.0125
4	room	5.58125
5	breakfast	0.5
6	buffet	2.69154427
7	bed	0.925
8	internet	1.821130952
9	place	3.043154762
10	taxi	1.0625
11	hotel	12.17892187
12	staff	4.36875

file was manually reviewed by an expert in linguistics. Sentences which appeared really difficult were asked from second human experts. Thus, for measuring the evaluation of the system the accuracy of the system can be checked by calculating the precision and recall of the system. Here TP (True positive) is the number of features that are correctly identified by the system FP (False positive represents the number of incorrect features that are correctly identified by the system. TN (true negative represents the incorrect features that the system has identified as incorrect. FN (False negative represents number of correct features that the system has failed to identify as correct. The formula for precision, recall and F1-measure is given below as stated by Kang and Han (2009).

$$Precision\ P = \frac{TP}{\left(TP + TN\right)}$$

$$Recall\ R = \frac{TP}{\left(TP + FN\right)}$$

$$F1 - measure = \frac{\left(2 * P * R\right)}{\left(P + R\right)}$$

Table 3 summarizes the precision, recall and F1-measure of 5 hotels of China on which algorithm was implemented.

It is quite evident from the table that a very high value of recall has been evaluated. It states that the system was able to extract the correct aspects. This is because the number of occurrences of FN becomes low as there are very few correct features which the system fails to identify as correct. This makes the recall value, high as shown in the table. Moreover, it points out that our system is able to determine most of the correct features which is the major and the first requirement in any aspect mining algorithm. However, the precision value is lower than recall. It is due to the fact that a lot of features which are redundant must be filtered out by the system. It is due to the fact that every domain requires its corresponding corpus to evaluate the results such as the product domain will have its own dictionary of words. The corpus of product domain will be different from the movie or the tourism domain as the words used to elucidate the opinion will vary according to the domain. The threshold taken is more than 1% of the total noun phrases. We have chosen this threshold because when we were taking the threshold less than 1% the number of aspects extracted were redundant and inconsistent. However, when we take the threshold more than 1%, then, various important aspects were missed. Hence, we found that we got the best aspects at threshold 1%.

Table 3. Performance Evaluation of Extraction of Feature Opinion

Hotel Name		Precision	Recall	F1-Measure
Hotels	Century towers	0.625	0.55	0.585
	Bamboo garden	0.15	0.96	0.25
	Garden Courtyard	0.26	0.80	0.39
	Ascott	0.224	0.92	0.36
	Haidain	0.28	0.69	0.39
Average		0.30	0.784	0.395

IMPLICATION OF RESEARCH

The aspect based opinion mining gives the insight about the features that are mostly liked by the users. It is also the systematic way of understanding the needs of the customers by plotting the graph of the features with their sentiment scores. This graph gives us the ranking of the features according to the parameter of their scores. The sentiment scores of each aspect are calculated using Sentiwordnet3.0, a popular dictionary which is open source available. The negation words like 'not', couldn't' etc. are also taken into account as these words changes the polarity of the word.

LIMITATIONS

As it is evident from the precision and recall, that the system is able to find a large number of relevant features. However, it also discovers other features which are less relevant to the given context and domain. The proposed algorithm doesn't take under consideration the diversity of various domains. For example, here the tourism domain has been taken and its collection of features are different from that of product domain or vehicle domain or movie domain reviews. There are implicit aspects which are again not in the scope of this algorithm and thus are not considered in this paper. The same word can sometimes be a noun as well as verb or adjective e.g. "*can*". Here the word "*can*" can be a "helping verb" or it can also be a noun if it is used in context of a "metal container". So, the context of the sentences has not been evaluated for this paper. The contextual polarity of the words is not taken into account as it was beyond the scope of the paper.

CONCLUSION

In this paper, we have proposed a framework and algorithm for aspect based opinion mining system in tourism domain. The proposed algorithm extracts features and opinions from the different reviews in the tourism sector. The opinion score for different aspects gives the idea what features are mostly liked or disliked by the users. It is observed that the resale value of the system is high, but the precision value is quite low. This is due to the fact that every domain requires its corresponding corpus to evaluate the results such as the product domain will have its own dictionary of words. The corpus of product domain will be different from the movie or the tourism domain as the words used to describe the opinion will vary according to the domain.

It is required to filter the dictionary according to the tourism domain to increase the precision of the system. In the future, we would try to create a new corpus of the opinion mining framework in tourism domain. We would also like to remove the different ambiguities present while calculating the opinion score by considering the different senses in the Sentiwordnet.

REFERENCES

Acharjee, S., Dey, N., Biswas, D., Das, P., & Chaudhuri, S. S. (2012, November). A novel Block Matching Algorithmic Approach with smaller block size for motion vector estimation in video compression. In *Proceedings of the 12th IEEE International Conference on Intelligent Systems Design and Applications (ISDA)* (pp. 668-672). 10.1109/ISDA.2012.6416617

Ahmad, T., & Doja, M. N. (2012). Ranking system for opinion mining of features from review documents. *IJCSI International Journal of Computer Science Issues*, *9*(4), 1694–0814.

Baccianella, S., Esuli, A., & Sebastiani, F. (2010, May). *SentiWordNet 3.0: An Enhanced Lexical Resource for Sentiment Analysis and Opinion Mining* (Vol. 10, pp. 2200–2204). LREC.

Bai, X. (2012). Predicting consumer sentiments from online text. *Decision Support Systems*, *50*(4), 732–742. doi:10.1016/j.dss.2010.08.024

Bhatnagar, V. (2013). Data mining-based big data analytics: Parameters and layered framework. *International Journal of Computational Systems Engineering*, *1*(4), 265–276. doi:10.1504/IJCSYSE.2013.057224

Bhatnagar, V., Goyal, M., & Hussain, M. A. (2016). A Proposed framework for improved identification of implicit aspects in tourism domain using supervised learning technique. In *Proceedings of the ACM International Conference on Advances in Information Communication Technology & Computing*, Bikaner. 10.1145/2979779.2979835

Bhatnagar, V., & Ranjan, J. (2010). Principles for successful mobile CRM in organisations from data mining perspective. *International Journal of Electronic Customer Relationship Management*, *4*(3), 280–301. doi:10.1504/IJECRM.2010.035967

Carroll, T. Z. J. (2008, January). Unsupervised Classification of Sentiment and Objectivity in Chinese Text. In *Proceedings of the Third International Joint Conference on Natural Language Processing*.

Cruz, F. L., Troyano, J. A., Enríquez, F., Ortega, F. J., & Vallejo, C. J. (2013). Long autonomy or long delay? The importance of domain in opinion mining. *Expert Systems with Applications*, *40*(8), 3174–3184. doi:10.1016/j.eswa.2012.12.031

Ding, X., Liu, B., & Philip, S. Y. (2008). A Holistic Lexicon-Based Approach to Opinion Mining. In *Proceedings of the first ACM International Conference on Web search and Data Mining (WSDM'08)*, California, USA (pp. 231-240). 10.1145/1341531.1341561

Esuli, A., & Sebastiani, F. (2006, April). *Determining Term Subjectivity and Term Orientation for Opinion Mining* (Vol. 6, p. 2006). EACL.

Esuli, A., & Sebastiani, F. (2006). SentiWordNet: A publicly available lexical resource for opinion mining. In *Proceedings of LREC-06, the 5th Conference on Language Resources and Evaluation*, Genova (pp. 417-422).

Ghiassi, M., Skinner, J., & Zimbra, D. (2013). Twitter brand sentiment analysis: A hybrid system using n-gram analysis and dynamic artificial neural network. *Expert Systems with Applications*, *40*(16), 6266–6282. doi:10.1016/j.eswa.2013.05.057

Goyal, M., and Bhatnagar, V. (2016). Classification of Polarity of Opinions using Unsupervised Approach in Tourism Domain. *International Journal of Rough Sets and Data Analysis, 3*(4).

Hu, M., & Liu, B. (2004). Mining and Summarizing Customer Reviews. In *Proceedings of ACM SIG-KDD International Conference on Knowledge Discovery and Data Mining (KDD'04)* (pp. 168-177).

Kang, H., Yoo, S. J., & Han, D. (2009). Accessing positive and negative online opinions. In *Universal Access in Human-Computer Interaction* (pp. 359–368). Applications and Services.

Liu, B. (2012). Sentiment analysis and opinion mining. *Synthesis Lectures on Human Language Technologies*, *5*(1), 1–167. doi:10.2200/S00416ED1V01Y201204HLT016

Manek, A. S., Shenoy, P. D., Mohan, M. C., & Venugopal, K. R. (2016). Aspect term extraction for sentiment analysis in large movie reviews using Gini Index feature selection method and SVM classifier. *World Wide Web (Bussum)*.

Marrese-Taylor, E., Velásquez, J. D., & Bravo-Marquez, F. (2014). A novel deterministic approach for aspect-based opinion mining in tourism products reviews. *Expert Systems with Applications*, *41*(17), 7764–7775. doi:10.1016/j.eswa.2014.05.045

Miller, G. A., & Fellbaum, C. (1991). Semantic networks of English. *Cognition*, *41*(1), 197–229. doi:10.1016/0010-0277(91)90036-4 PMID:1790654

Moghaddam, S., & Ester, M. (2012). Aspect-based opinion mining from product reviews. In *Proceedings of the 35th international ACM SIGIR conference on Research and development in information retrieval* (pp. 1184-1184).

Moraes, R., Valiati, J. F., & Neto, W. P. G. (2013). Document-level sentiment classification: An empirical comparison between SVM and ANN. *Expert Systems with Applications*, *40*(2), 621–633. doi:10.1016/j.eswa.2012.07.059

Panda, M., Hassanien, A. E., & Abraham, A. (2016). Hybrid Data Mining Approach for Image Segmentation Based Classification. *International Journal of Rough Sets and Data Analysis*, *3*(2), 65–81. doi:10.4018/IJRSDA.2016040105

Pang, B., & Lee, L. (2008). Opinion mining and sentiment analysis. *Foundations and trends in information retrieval, 2*(1-2).

Pang, B., Lee, L., & Vaithyanathan, S. (2002). Thumbs up? Sentiment Classification Using Machine Learning Techniques. In *Proceedings of the 2002 Conference on Empirical Methods in Natural Language Processing (EMNLP'02)* (pp. 79 – 86).

Parkhe, V., & Biswas, B. (2014, September). Aspect based sentiment analysis of movie reviews: finding the polarity directing aspects. In *Proceedings of the 2014 International Conference on Soft Computing and Machine Intelligence (ISCMI)* (pp. 28-32). 10.1109/ISCMI.2014.16

Radhwan, A., Kamel, M., Dahab, M. Y., & Hassanien, A. E. (2015). Forecasting Exchange Rates: A Chaos-Based Regression Approach. *International Journal of Rough Sets and Data Analysis*, *2*(1), 38–57. doi:10.4018/ijrsda.2015010103

Riloff, E., & Wiebe, J. (2003). Learning extraction patterns for subjective expressions. In *Proceedings of the conference on Empirical methods in natural language processing* (pp. 105-112).

Ripon, S. H., Kamal, S., Hossain, S., & Dey, N. (2016). Theoretical Analysis of Different Classifiers under Reduction Rough Data Set: A Brief Proposal. *International Journal of Rough Sets and Data Analysis, 3*(3), 1–20. doi:10.4018/IJRSDA.2016070101

Rui, H., Liu, Y., & Whinston, A. (2013). Whose and what chatter matters? The effect of tweets on movie sales. *Decision Support Systems, 55*(4), 863–870. doi:10.1016/j.dss.2012.12.022

Thet, T. T., Na, J. C., & Khoo, C. S. (2010). Aspect-based sentiment analysis of movie reviews on discussion boards. *Journal of Information Science*.

Tsytsarau, M., & Palpanas, T. (2013). Survey on mining subjective data on the web. *Data Mining and Knowledge Discovery, 24*(3), 478–514. doi:10.100710618-011-0238-6

Turney, P. (2002). Thumbs Up or Thumbs Down? Semantic Orientation Applied to Unsupervised Classification of Reviews. In *Proceedings of the 40th Annual Meeting on Association for Computational Linguistics (ACL'02)* (pp. 417 – 424).

This research was previously published in the International Journal of Rough Sets and Data Analysis (IJRSDA), 5(2); pages 119-130, copyright year 2018 by IGI Publishing (an imprint of IGI Global).

Chapter 18
Analyzing Social Emotions in Social Network Using Graph Based Co-Ranking Algorithm

Kani Priya
Hindustan University, Chennai, India

Krishnaveni R.
Hindustan University, Chennai, India

Krishnamurthy M.
KCG College of Technology, Chennai, India

Bairavel S.
KCG College of Technology, Chennai, India

ABSTRACT

Twitter has become exceedingly popular, with hundreds of millions of tweets being posted every day on a wide variety of topics. This has helped make real-time search applications possible with leading search engines routinely displaying relevant tweets in response to user queries. Recent research has shown that a considerable fraction of these tweets are about "events," and the detection of novel events in the tweet-stream has attracted a lot of research interest. However, very little research has focused on properly displaying this real-time information about events. For instance, the leading search engines simply display all tweets matching the queries in reverse chronological order. Online content exhibits rich temporal dynamics, and diverse real-time user generated content further intensifies this process. However, temporal patterns by which online content grows and fades over time, and by which different pieces of content compete for attention remain largely unexplored. This article describes tracking and analyzing public sentiment on social networks and finding the possible reasons causing these variations. It is important to find the decision from public views and opinion in different domain. They can be used to discover special topics or aspects in one text collection in comparison with another background text collection. The implemented method attains the 95% accuracy while predict the sentiments from the social websites and the 96.3% of the opinion rate with minimum time.

DOI: 10.4018/978-1-6684-6303-1.ch018

1. INTRODUCTION

Micro blogging is an increasingly popular form of communication on the web. It allows users to broadcast brief text updates to the public or to a selected group of contacts. Micro blog posts, commonly known as tweets, are extremely short in comparison to regular blog posts, being at most 140 characters in length. The micro blog works by using the actual and aggregated data files which is differ from the traditional blogs. In addition to this, the micro blog helps to transmit the information's in terms of short sentences, videos, images, links and so on which are called as the micro posts. Along with the information transmission, the micro blog provides the information security mechanisms for user details and other web-based interfaces such as instant messaging, text messaging, e-mail, digital video and audio. Recently Twitter launches the popularized communication web in October 2006 for making the effective communication or interaction systems. Users of these online communities use micro blogging to broadcast different types of information. During the communication process, social emotions are placed in a vital role because its depends on the individual feelings, actions, thoughts of the particular situation or activities. The sample social emotions are happiness, sadness, envy, pride, shame, embarrassment, jealousy and so on. These described emotions are combined with the social cognition which helps to detect the people mental situations. Along with the social emotions which help to create the morality that used to take the moral decision of the particular problem.

So, the sentiment analysis plays a vital role in citation context extraction using supervised learning Precision. Citation classification is the important part for identifying the quality reference article. A recent analysis of the Twitter network revealed a variegated mosaic of uses including a) daily chatter, e.g., posting what one is currently doing, b) conversations, i.e., directing tweets to specific users in their community of followers, c) information sharing, e.g., posting links to web pages, and d) news reporting, e.g., commentary on news and current affairs Sentiment analysis (also known as opinion mining) refers to the use of natural language processing, text analysis, and computational linguistics to identify and extract subjective information in source materials. During the analyze process different techniques such as support vector machine, artificial neural networks, linear discriminate analysis, decision tree, etc., are used to derive the decision about the moralities in the Twitter based social sites. Along with the supervised techniques, several optimized method, such as genetic algorithms, particle swarm optimization methods, ant bee colony, and fireflies algorithm, are used to improve the efficiency while detecting the social emotions from the social sites. Based on these algorithms, several research use the different machine learning algorithm for detecting the social emotions which are explained as follows. Then the rest of the section is organized as follows, section 2 analyze the various surveys about the sentiment analysis, section 3 describes the relevant materials and methods about the Latent Dirichlet Allocation (LDA) based sentiment emotion detection process, section 4 analyze the excellence of the Latent Dirichlet Allocation (LDA) method and concludes in section 5.

2. RELATED WORKS

In this section analyze the various authors opinion involved in the sentiment examination process in social sites. Shulong Tan et al. (2014) proposes a Latent Dirichlet Allocation (LDA) based model. To distill foreground topics and filter out longstanding background topics, Foreground and Background LDA (FB-LDA) was used. To rank them with respect to their "popularity" within the variation period,

Reason Candidate and Background LDA (RCB-LDA) was used. Alexandre Trilla et al. (2013) proposes the work focuses on categorization of a plain input text to inform a TTS system about the most appropriate sentiment (+ve, -ve, neutral) to automatically synthesize expressive speech at the sentence level. Alena Neviarouskaya et al. (2011) proposes the Latent Semantic Analysis (LSA) which assumes that words that are close in meaning will occur in similar pieces of text. Analyzing relationships between a set of documents and the terms contain in it. Parisa Lak et al. (2014) proposes the online product/service reviews serve as sources of product/service-related information star ratings provide a quick indication of tone of a review. In some cases, it is not available or detailed enough. Sentiment analysis automatically detect the polarity of text, i.e. more refined analysis.

Neethu et al. (2013) recognizing the various opinions and sentiments from social Medias which is done with the help of the machine learning method. The social media consists of several updates, posts, blog which is continuously monitored by the millions of users. The author examines the Twitter for analyze the opinion of the user depending on the posts for detecting their morality related emotions. So, the author retrieve their emotions from mobile, laptop based electronic gadgets texts which is processed by the machine learning techniques. The technique examines the positive negative tweets while analyzing the sentiments. Then the excellence of the system is analyzed using the experimental results. (Geetika Gautam et al., 2014) analyze the sentiments from the number of tweets which are collected in Twitter. The collected tweets are examined in both structured and unstructured manner for retrieving the positive and negative tweets. The retrieved tweets related feature vector is extracted which is fed into the different machine learning techniques such as maximum entropy, Naïve Bayes method, support vector machine. These classifiers analyze the semantic orientation-based features according to the similarity manner which successfully retrieve the features. Then the excellence of the system is evaluated with the help of the experimental results. According to the analysis, different machine learning techniques are used to detect the sentiments from the collection of emotions which are discussed as follows.

3. METERIALS AND METHODS

3.1. Interpreting the Public Sentiment Variations on Twitter

This paper proposed two Latent Dirichlet Allocation (LDA)-based models: (1) Foreground and Background LDA (FB-LDA); and (2) Reason Candidate and Background LDA (RCB-LDA), to analyze public sentiment variations and mine possible reasons behind these variations.

3.2. Sentence-Based Sentiment Analysis for Expressive Text-to-Speech

This section explains about the porter stemming algorithm which removes the inflection of words for indexing purposes semantically related words should map to the same stem, base or root form. This paper also proposes multinomial Naïve Bayes (MNB), a base line method used in sentiment analysis which assigns class label to problem instance, represented as vectors of features values, where class labels are drawn from finite set.

3.3. Sentiful: A Lexicon for Sentiment Analysis

This section discuses about the Latent Semantic Analysis (LSA/LSI) which assumes that the words that are close in meaning will occur in similar pieces of text. Analyzing relationship between a set of documents and the term contains in it. The techniques used for finding new sentiment conveying words includes, the synonymy: different words have different meaning, e.g. doctor and physician; polysemy: same word has different meaning, e.g. book refers text book and booking a room; antonyms: related words which have opposite meanings, e.g. long and short; and hyponymys: a relationship between general terms and a more specific term, e.g. color to blue, red, pink, etc.

3.4. Star Ratings Versus Sentiment Analysis – A Comparison of Explicit and Implicit Measures of Opinions

This section deals that the comparison of online product/service reviews and star ratings. Online product/service reviews serve as sources of product/service-related information. Star ratings provide a quick indication of tone of a review.

In some cases, it is not available or detailed enough. Sentiment analysis automatically detect the polarity of text[24] (i.e.) more refined analysis. Extreme ratings (5 star/ 1 star) are more useful than moderate ratings (3 star). This paper uses the several tools such as Lexalytics web demo: tool used to analyze tweets (not exceed 20,000 words), Sentistrength: estimates the strength of +ve and –ve sentiment in short text, Sentiment 140: used to analyze document whose size is less than 140 words and Lymbix: works similar to lexalytics, and for the document larger than tweets.

3.5. Proposed Latent Dirichlet Allocation (LDA) With Graph Based Co-Ranking System

It is observed that the emerging topics (named foreground topics) within the sentiment variation periods are highly related to the genuine reasons behind the variations. A novel approach based on the partially supervised alignment model, which regards identifying opinion relations as an alignment process. Then a graph-based co-ranking algorithm is exploited to estimate the confidence of each candidate. Finally, candidates with higher confidence are extracted as opinion targets or opinion words.

Figure 1 describes that the general architecture of the Latent Dirichlet Allocation (LDA) based sentiment examination process in Twitter. The Twitter consists of collection of information's such as politics, sports, news, films, media and etc. People may Tweet their opinion mostly in the above described areas such as, sports, news and politics. So, their social emotions are easily retrieved from these areas successfully. From the areas, different sentiment related queries are raised and their sentiment has been derived with the help of Latent Dirichlet Allocation (LDA) method and the detail explanation of the working process is explained as follows. The method works by constructing the graph by using the user opinion which are done with the help of the Graph based Co-ranking Algorithm.

Figure 1. System architecture diagram

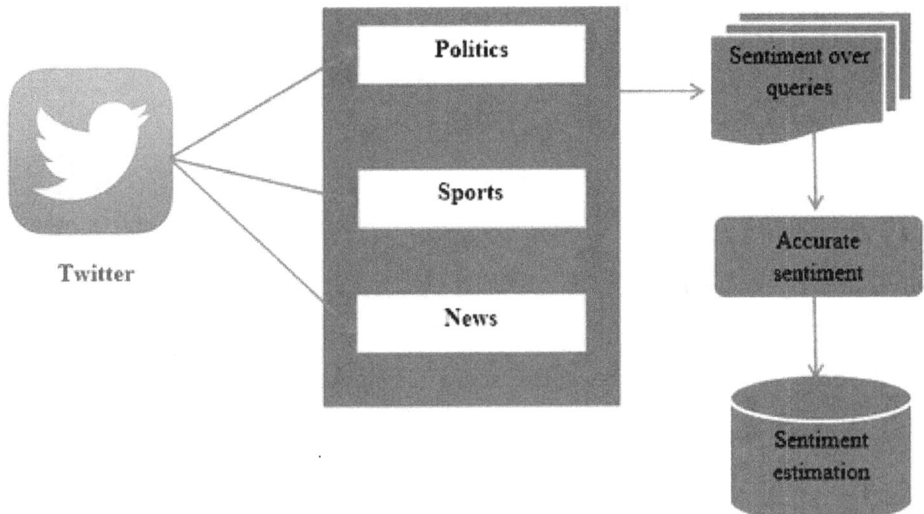

3.5.1. Graph Based Co-Ranking Algorithm

In order to apply the graph based co-ranking algorithms, we convert the text document into a graph. We extract words (except stop-words) from each sentence and represent them as nodes of our graph. Each pair of related words (lexically or semantically) forms the edges. We use SentiWordNet (a publicly available lexically or semantically) to determine the sentiment polarity of each node (signature word). SentiWordNet assigns to each synset of WordNets, three sentiment scores: positivity, negativity, and objectivity. We choose the highest (most common) sentiment polarity of a word as the bias. Edge weights are determined by the total outgoing edges from the node. If there is a {not, no, though, but, etc.} present between word (A) and word (B), the edge weight receives the opposite sign of bias (a). Our algorithm performs the following:

1. **Build the text graph:** The first step is text graph construction process. During this process, the signature words are collected from the tweets. Then the link between words are examined and form the edges between the words. After that the related weight value is assign for each edge which is updated continuously while new edges are add to the graph. At last assign a random value as rank to all the nodes of the graph (initially all nodes are on the same level). After that he ranking model is applied to constructed graph;
2. **Apply ranking model:** Apply formula over the graph until the rank value converges;
3. **Find ranked word vectors, and extract sentences:** Then the rank has been computed depending on the positive and negative words such as Create a positive word vector, W(pos) of keywords by selecting all positively ranked words, create a negative word vector, W(neg) of keywords by selecting all negatively ranked words. Then use W(pos) and W(neg) to determine the weight and orientation of the sentences. Group top k (can be determined by the user) negatively (positively) oriented sentences as anti-summary(summary);

4. **Estimate the confidence of candidate:** After constructing the graph with relevant ranks, the confidence value of each candidate has been computed as follows:
   a. Find the opinion target candidate:

$$C_t^{k+1} = (1-\mu)\times M_{to}\times C_o^k + \mu\times I_{t,} \tag{1}$$

   b. Find the opinion word candidate:

$$C_t^{k+1} = (1-\mu)\times M_{to}^K\times C_t^k + \mu\times I_{o,} \tag{2}$$

   c. Make the positive score and negative score of opinion words:

$$s_i^{(0)} = \begin{cases} s_i^{(0)} \Big/ \sum_{j\in D_{mrg}^U}\left(-s_j^{(0)}\right), & if\, s_i^{(0)} < 0 \\ s_i^{(0)} \Big/ \sum_{j\in D_{poi}^U} s_j^{(0)}, & if\, s_i^{(0)} > 0 \end{cases} \tag{3}$$

   d. We give "-1" to *si*(0) if *di*'s label is "negative", and "1" if "positive". So we obtain the initial sentiment score vector *S*(0) for both domain data.

Based on the above process, the successful graph has been created depending on the sentiment values and related weighted values. According to the graph the opinion of the particular situation is examined with successful manner. Then the excellence of the system is evaluated with the help of the experimental results which is explained as follows.

4. RESULTS AND DISCUSSION

In this section discusses about the experimental analysis of the Latent Dirichlet Allocation (LDA) for examining the sentiments in the social web site commonly referred as Twitter. The efficiency is evaluated using by asking different type of queries which is discussed as follows.

4.1. Tweets Extraction Related to Query Issue

To extract tweets related to the target, we go through the whole dataset and extract all the tweets which contain the keywords of the target. Compared with regular text documents, tweets are generally less formal and often written in an ad hoc manner. Sentiment analysis tools applied on raw tweets often achieve very poor performance in most cases. Therefore, preprocessing techniques on tweets are necessary for obtaining satisfactory results on sentiment analysis: (1) Slang words translation; (2) Non-English tweets filtering; (3) URL removal.

4.1.1. Modeling Sentiment Over Queries

This solution is not optimal since the optimization goal of the topic modeling step does not take into account the tweet-candidate association at all. We propose to measure the quality of a topic using word entropy: the conditional entropy of the word distribution given a topic, which is similar to the topic entropy. Entropy measures the average amount of information expressed by each assignment to a random variable. If the topic's word distribution has low word entropy, it means that topic has a narrow focus on a set of words. Therefore, a topic modeling method with a low average word entropy generates topics with high clarity and interpretability.

4.1.2. Selection of Accurate Sentiment

Twitter Sentiment is based on a Maximum Entropy classifier. It uses automatically collected 160,000 tweets with emoticons as noisy labels to train the classifier. Then based on the classifier's outputs, it will assign the sentiment label (positive, neutral or negative) with the maximum probability as the sentiment label of a tweet. Though these two tools are very popular, their performance on real datasets are not satisfactory because a large proportion of tweets still contain noises after preprocessing. We randomly picked 1,000 tweets and manually labeled them to test the overall accuracy of these two tools. It turns out that Senti Strength and Twitter Sentiment achieve 62.3% and 57.2% accuracy on this testing dataset, respectively. By analyzing more cases outside the testing set, we found that Twitter Sentiment is very inclined to mis-judge a non-neutral tweet as neutral, while SentiStrength is highly likely to make a wrong judgment when Final Score is close to 0.

4.1.3. Extract Sentiment Variation Point

After obtaining the sentiment labels of all extracted tweets about a target, we can track the sentiment variation using some descriptive statistics. In this work, we are interested in analyzing the time period during which the overall positive (negative) sentiment climbs upward while the overall negative (positive) sentiment slides downward. In this case, the total number of tweets is not informative any more since the number of positive tweets and negative tweets may change consistently. The system adopts the percentage of positive or negative tweets among all the extracted tweets as an indicator for tracking sentiment variation over time. Based on these descriptive statistics, sentiment variations can be found using various heuristics.

4.1.4. Extract Foreground Topics

It can filter out background topics and extract foreground topics from tweets in the variation period, with the help of an auxiliary set of background tweets generated just before the variation. Then it will associate each remaining tweet in the variation period with one reason candidate and rank the reason candidates by the number of tweets associated with them. To mine foreground topics, we need to filter out all topics existing in the background tweets set, known as background topics, from the foreground tweets set.

4.2. Performance Metrics and Result Analysis

In this section discusses about the various performance metrics such as time, accuracy, opinion mining rate that helps to discusses the excellence of proposed Latent Dirichlet Allocation (LDA) and Graph based Co-ranking approach while extracting the sentiment related emotions from the social sites. Each and every performance metric is discussed as follows.

4.2.1. Time

Time is the important metric because the emotion or sentiment should examined with minimum time. That is user emotions are recognized immediately when the user suggesting their reviews or opinions in the social sites.

4.2.2. Accuracy

Accuracy is other metric which helps to determine, how exactly the system recognize the user correct emotion on particular situation in social sites.

4.2.3. Opinion Mining

The next metric is opinion mining which is used to measure right opinion used by the user while sharing their emotions in social sites.

Depending on the above performance metric, the obtained result has been shown in the Table 1.

Table 1. Performance analysis of time

S. No.	Algorithms	Time Efficiency (ms)
1	Apriori	45
2	Fp-Growth	36
3	Graph Based Co-ranking	12

Table 1 clearly shows that the Graph Based Co-ranking algorithm attains minimum time while estimating the sentiment from the social web sites which is very low when compared to the other two algorithms such as Apriori and Fp-Growth. Then the obtained value graph representation is shown in Figure 2.

Figure 2 depicted that the time value of the graph based co-ranking algorithm which predicts the user sentiments with minimum time (12 ms) compared to other two algorithms such as Apriori (45ms) and Fp-Growth (36ms). Even though the algorithm predicts the sentiments with minimum time it has higher accuracy and the obtained value is shown in Table 2.

Table 2 clearly shows that the Graph Based Co-ranking algorithm attains higher accuracy while estimating the sentiment from the social web sites which is higher when compared to the other two algorithms such as Apriori and Fp-Growth. Then the obtained value graph representation is shown in Figure 3.

Figure 2. Time

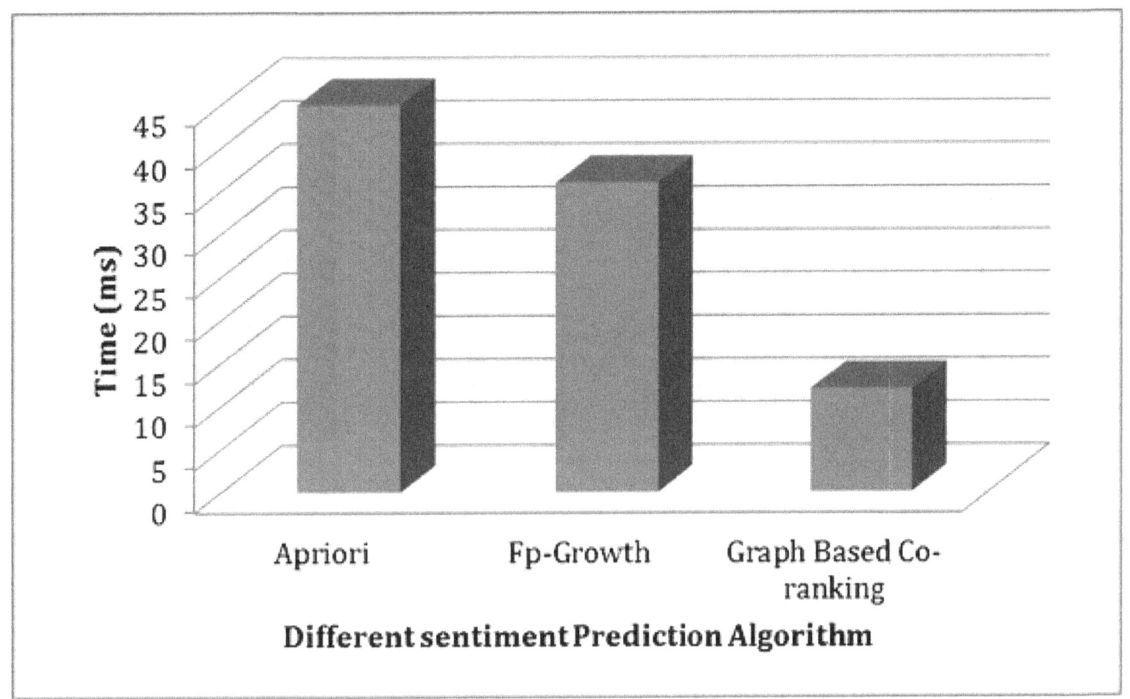

Table 2. Performance analysis of accuracy

S. No.	Algorithms	Accuracy (%)
1	Apriori	75
2	Fp-Growth	82
3	Graph Based Co-ranking	93

Figure 3 depicted that the accuracy value of the graph based co-ranking algorithm which predicts the user sentiments with higher accuracy (95%) compared to other two algorithms such as Apriori (75%) and Fp-Growth (82%). Even though the algorithm predicts the sentiments with minimum time and higher accuracy, it effectively predicts the user opinion with effective manner and the obtained value is shown in Table 3.

Table 3 clearly shows that the Graph Based Co-ranking algorithm attains higher accuracy which helps to improve overall opinion recognition rate while estimating the sentiment from the social web sites which is very high when compared to the other two algorithms such as Apriori and Fp-Growth. Then the obtained value graph representation is shown in Figure 4.

Figure 4 depicted that the opinion rate of the graph based co-ranking algorithm which predicts the user sentiments with higher accuracy (96.3%) compared to other two algorithms such as Apriori (80%) and Fp-Growth (86%). Thus, the proposed Graph Based Co-ranking algorithm effectively predicts the sentiments with high accuracy when compared to the other methods.

Figure 3. Accuracy

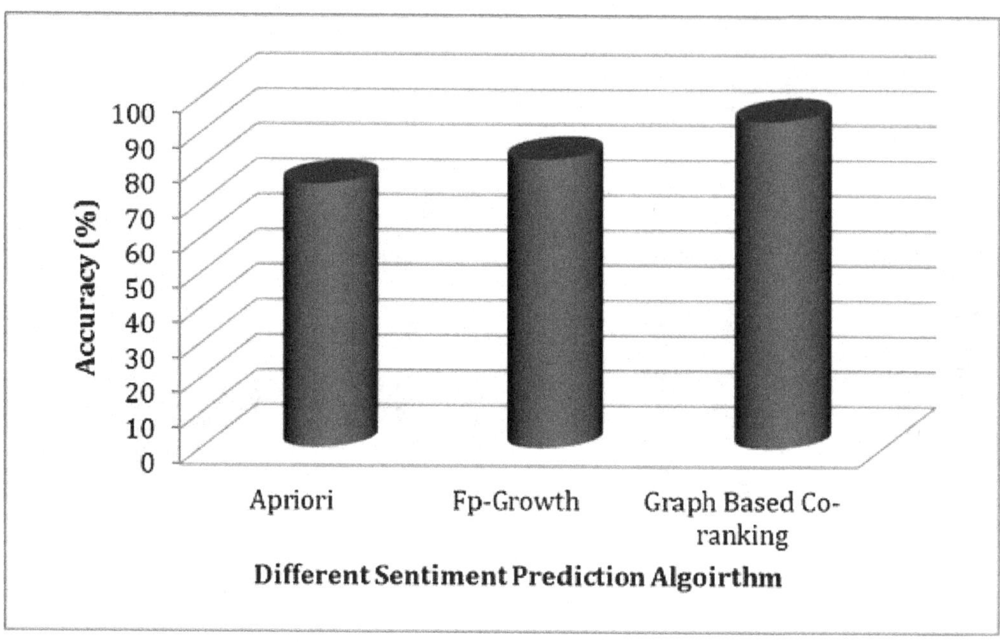

Table 3. Performance analysis of opinion rate

S. No.	Algorithms	Opinion Rate (%)
1	Apriori	80
2	Fp-Growth	86
3	Graph Based Co-ranking	96.3

Figure 4. Opinion rate

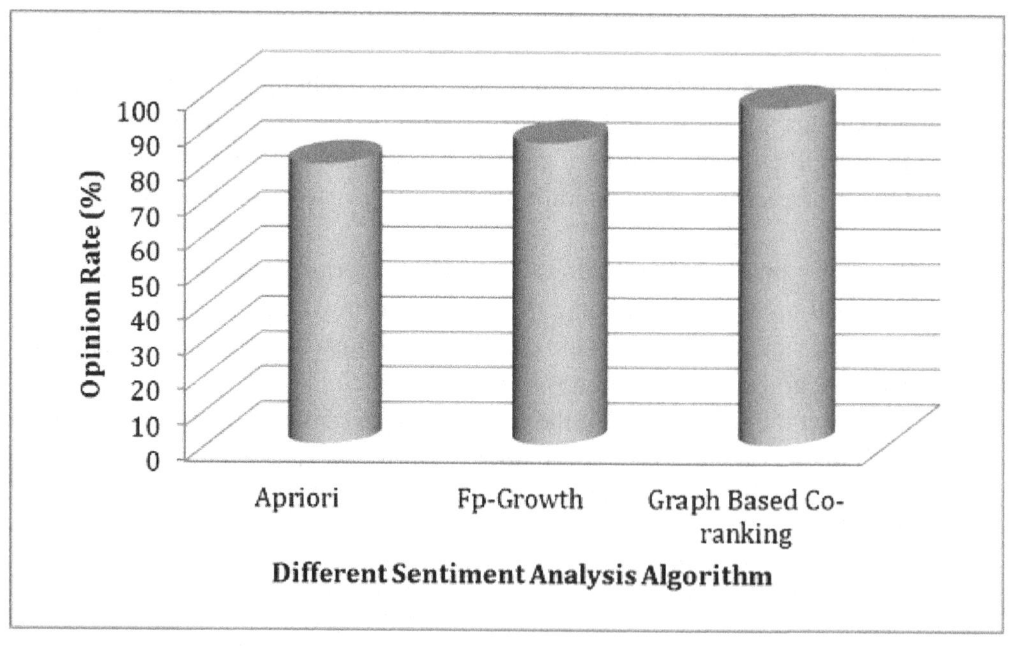

5. CONCLUSION

The problem of analyzing public sentiment variations and finding the possible reasons causing the variations are find out. To solve this problem two Latent Dirichlet Allocation (LDA) based model that namely Foreground and Background LDA(FB-LDA) and Reason Candidate and Background LDA(RCB-LDA) are developed. The FB-LDA model can filter out background topics and then extract foreground topics to reveal possible reasons. The RCB-LDA model can rank on candidates expressed in natural language to provide sentence-level reasons.

Table 4. Basic statistics for the 50 sentiment variations

Sentiment Variations	"Obama"	"Apple"
#Negative cases	14	11
#Positive cases	12	13

This system can mine possible reasons behind sentiment variations. These models are general and can be used to discover special topics or aspects in one text collection in comparison with another background text collection. It is important to find the decision from public views and opinion in different domain.

REFERENCES

Alías, F., Sevillano, X., Socoró, J. C., & Gonzalvo, X. (2008, September). Towards high-quality next-generation text-to-speech synthesis: A multidomain approach by automatic domain classification. *IEEE Transactions on Audio, Speech, and Language Processing*, *16*(7), 1340–1354. doi:10.1109/TASL.2008.925145

Argamon, S., Bloom, K., Esuli, A., & Sebastiani, F. (2007). Automatically Determining Attitude Type and Force for Sentiment Analysis. *Proc. Third Language and Technology Conf.* Academic Press.

Blei, D. M., Ng, A. Y., & Jordan, M. I. (2003). Latent dirichlet allocation. *Journal of Machine Learning Research*, *3*(Jan), 993–1022.

Bollen, J., Mao, H., & Pepe, A. (2011). Modeling public mood and emotion: Twitter sentiment and socio-economic phenomena. *Proc.5th Int. AAAI Conf. Weblogs Social Media*, Barcelona, Spain. AAAI Press.

Bollen, J., Mao, H., & Zeng, X. (2011, March). Twitter mood predicts the stock market. *Journal of Computational Science*, *2*(1), 1–8. doi:10.1016/j.jocs.2010.12.007

Calix, R., Mallepudi, S., Chen, B., & Knapp, G. (2010, October). Emotion recognition in text for 3-D facial expression rendering. *IEEE Transactions on Multimedia*, *12*(6), 544–551. doi:10.1109/TMM.2010.2052026

Campbell, N. (2006, July). Conversational speech synthesis and the need for some laughter. *IEEE Transactions on Audio, Speech, and Language Processing*, *14*(4), 1171–1178. doi:10.1109/TASL.2006.876131

Chakrabarti, D., & Punera, K. (2011). Event summarization using tweets. *Proc. 5th Int. AAAI Conf. Weblogs Social Media*, Barcelona, Spain. AAAI Press.

Gautam, G., & Yadav, D. (2014, August). Sentiment analysis of twitter data using machine learning approaches and semantic analysis. *Proceedings of the 2014 Seventh International Conference on Contemporary Computing (IC3)* (pp. 437-442). IEEE.

Hatzivassiloglou, V., & McKeown, K. R. (1997). Predicting the Semantic Orientation of Adjectives. *Proc. 35th Ann. Meeting of the Assoc. for Computational Linguistics and the Eighth Conf. European Chapter of the Assoc. for Computational Linguistics* (pp. 174-181). Academic Press.

Lak, P., & Turetken, O. (2014, January). Star ratings versus sentiment analysis--a comparison of explicit and implicit measures of opinions. *Proceedings of the 2014 47th Hawaii International Conference on System Sciences* (pp. 796-805). IEEE.

Liu, B. (2012). Sentiment analysis and opinion mining. *Synthesis Lectures on Human Language Technologies*, *5*(1), 1–167.

Mahalakshmi, G. S., Siva, R., & Sendhilkumar, S. (2015). *Context Based Retrieval of Scientific Publications via Reader Lens. In Computational Intelligence in Data Mining* (Vol. 3, pp. 583–596). Springer India.

Mudambi, S.M. & Schuff, D. (2010). What makes a helpful online review? A study of customer reviews on Amazon.com. *MIS Quarterly*, *34*(1), 185-200.

Neethu, M. S., & Rajasree, R. (2013, July). Sentiment analysis in twitter using machine learning techniques. Proceedings of the 2013 Fourth International Conference on Computing, Communications and Networking Technologies (ICCCNT) (pp. 1-5). IEEE. doi:10.1109/ICCCNT.2013.6726818

Neviarouskaya, A., Prendinger, H., & Ishizuka, M. (2011). SentiFul: A lexicon for sentiment analysis. *IEEE Transactions on Affective Computing*, *2*(1), 22–36.

Pavlou, P. & Dimoka, A. (2006). The Nature and Role of Feedback Text Comments in Online Marketplaces: Implications for Trust Building, Price Premiums, and Seller Differentiation. *Information Systems Research*, *17*(4), 392-414.

Poston, R., & Speier, C. (2005). Effective Use of Knowledge Management Systems: A Process Model of Content Ratings and Credibility Indicators. *Management Information Systems Quarterly*, *29*(2), 221–244.

Reilly, J., & Seibert, L. (2003). Language and Emotion. In R. J. Davidson, K. R. Scherer, & H. H. Goldsmith (Eds.), *Handbook of Affective Science* (pp. 535–559). Oxford Univ. Press.

Skowron, M., Pirker, H., Rank, S., Paltoglou, G., Ahn, J., & Gobron, S. (2011). No peanuts! Affective cues for the virtual bartender. *Proc. FLAIRS'11*. Academic Press.

Strapparava, C., & Valitutti, A. (2004). WordNet-Affect: An Affective Extension of WordNet. *Proc. Int'l Conf. Language Resources and Evaluation* (pp. 1083-1086). Academic Press.

Tan, S., Li, Y., Sun, H., Guan, Z., Yan, X., Bu, J., ... He, X. (2014, May). Interpreting the Public Sentiment Variations on Twitter. *IEEE Transactions on Knowledge and Data Engineering*, *26*(5), 1158-1170.

Trilla, A., & Alias, F. (2012). Sentence-based sentiment analysis for expressive text-to-speech. *IEEE Transactions on Audio, Speech, and Language Processing*, *21*(2), 223–233.

Turetken, O., & Olfman, L. (2013). Introduction to the Special Issue on Human-Computer Interaction in the Web2.0 Era. *AIS Transactions on Human-Computer Interaction*, *5*(1), 1–5.

Wilson, T., Wiebe, J., & Hoffmann, P. (2005). Recognizing Contextual Polarity in Phrase-Level Sentiment Analysis. *Proc. Human Language Technology Conf. and Conf. Empirical Methods in Natural Language Processing* (pp. 347-354). 10.3115/1220575.1220619

Wilson, T., & Hofer, G. (2011, February). Using linguistic and vocal expressiveness in social role recognition. In IUI (pp. 419-422). doi:10.1145/1943403.1943480

This research was previously published in the International Journal of Technology and Human Interaction (IJTHI), 16(2); pages 23-33, copyright year 2020 by IGI Publishing (an imprint of IGI Global).

Chapter 19
Using Computational Text Analysis to Explore Open-Ended Survey Question Responses

Shalin Hai-Jew
Kansas State University, USA

ABSTRACT

To capture a broader range of data than close-ended questions (often defined and delimited by the survey instrument designer), open-ended questions, such as text-based elicitations (and file-upload options for still imagery, audio, video, and other contents) are becoming more common because of the wide availability of computational text analysis, both within online survey tools and in external software applications. These computational text analysis tools—some online, some offline—make it easier to capture reproducible insights with qualitative data. This chapter explores some analytical capabilities, in matrix queries, theme extraction (topic modeling), sentiment analysis, cluster analysis (concept mapping), network text structures, qualitative cross-tabulation analysis, manual coding to automated coding, linguistic analysis, psychometrics, stylometry, network analysis, and others, as applied to open-ended questions from online surveys (and combined with human close reading).

INTRODUCTION

The popularization of online surveys has meant that a wide range of different questions are ask-able, with the integration of still visuals, audio, video, web links, and other elements. Invisible or hidden questions enable the collection of additional information, such as time spent per question, devices used to access the survey, geographical information, and other data. File upload question types enable respondents to share imagery, audio, video, and other digital file types as a response. Integrations with online tools enable outreaches through social media for broader audiences through crowd-sourcing and commercial survey panels. Automation enables customizing survey experiences with uses of names, question an-

DOI: 10.4018/978-1-6684-6303-1.ch019

swers, piped text from a number of sources, expanded question elicitations (like through loop & merge techniques, and others), branching logic, and randomizers, among others. And many online research suites, designed as all-in-one shops, enable the automated analyses of text, quantitative data in cross-tabulation analyses, and other approaches.

Yet, in the midst of all these changes, a simple confluence of technological capabilities has suggested an even more fundamental change: the sophistication of computational text analysis (computer-aided text analysis) means that open-ended text-based survey question responses may be better harnessed and exploited for information than in the recent past. Computational text analysis enables the identification of a range of data patterns: matrix queries, theme extraction (topic modeling), sentiment analysis, cluster analysis (concept mapping), network text structures, qualitative cross-tabulation analysis, manual coding to automated coding, linguistic analysis, psychometrics, stylometry, network analysis, and others. These computational text analysis approaches harness quantitative, qualitative and mixed methods approaches, and all include "humans in the loop" for the analyses.

While some all-in-one online survey systems are expanding to built-in text analyses, the available tools look to be simplistic presently, with commercial software tools enabling more sophisticated text analysis. Those with the technology skills and statistical know-how stand to exploit the capabilities of open-ended survey questions and freeform respondent comments and insights. Going to "machine reading" (or "distant reading" through various forms of computational text analysis) does not remove the human from the loop. There is still the need for human "close reading" of the findings and of some of the original raw data. (In some cases, all of the original text may be read depending on the size of the text corpus.)

Technology Tools Used

The software tools highlighted in this work include Qualtrics®, NVivo 12 Plus, Linguistic Inquiry and Word Count (LIWC2015), and Network Overview, Discovery and Exploration for Excel (NodeXL).

REVIEW OF THE LITERATURE

The main strength of surveys is that they capture elicited information from human respondents, but that fact is also its main weakness. There is a wide body of literature that shows that people's responses to surveys may depend on social relationships, design features of how questions are presented and asked, the types of technologies used, and other factors, which "intervene" and "interfere" with respondents' offering their truest thinking. Besides these factors, the respondent himself/herself has limitations, in terms of built-in cognitive biases (confirmative bias, anchoring biases, priming effects, and others) and limited working memory. And yet, surveys are sometimes the only way to capture respondent experiences, preferences, imaginations, and opinions, even with the limitations of self-reportage.

Surveys are delivered in various ways. Surveys may be delivered in person or remotely, to respondents who are alone or in the company of others. They may be other-administered or self-administered. They may be delivered through various modalities: via telephone (Arnon & Reichel, Apr. 2009) or paper (postal or face-to-face) or computer, offline or online, and so on. There are some survey sequences that involve various mixes of the prior variables. Some classic Delphi survey methods began with face-to-face (F2F) meetings followed by distance-based interactions, for example.

Modalities and Respondent Responsiveness

Researchers have studied to understand differences between various modalities of surveys, such as between mail (postal) and web ones (Kwak & Radler, 2002). Various studies have found some differences in response rates to surveys based on their modality, but others have found "no significant differences"—but these vary depending on the specific research contexts and respondents. The differences in survey modes are generally thought to be a source of instability in terms of responses, with potential effects on both respondents and on responses. The ideal is to achieve "measurement equivalence" (Andrews, Nonnecke, & Preece, 2003, p. 190), so modality does not affect outcomes.

In early years, researchers found wide discrepancies between open-ended vs. closed questions in a postal survey (Falthzik & Carroll, 1971), with only 27% responding to open-ended questions and 78% for closed question. Each approach has its strengths and weaknesses. One study suggests that the "mode effect" between paper and electronic surveys did not result in any statistically significant difference in the length of answers to open-ended questions (Denscombe, Aug. 2008). One study that found that fifth graders responded more in-depth to open-ended questions on computerized versions than paper ones (Love, Butz, Usher, & Waiters, 2018), which may be a result of generational differences.

In-person open-ended survey responses may be unduly influenced by the interviewer and his / her preferences, resulting in measurement error:

The average survey has a vast number of opportunities for measurement error resulting from the interaction between an interviewer and a respondent. Even in the case of simple forced-choice questions, subtle cues delivered by the interviewer become a part of the stimulus situation and lend credibility to the hypothesis that the responses solicited in the interview are due, in part, to the particular interviewer who collected them. In the case of open-ended survey questions the opportunities for interview bias increase substantially, since such questions give rise to a prolonged social interaction in which cues are actively sought and parsimoniously delivered. (Shapiro, Autumn 1970, p. 412)

Those who would build survey instruments will not be interacting with the survey respondents directly, but the constructed survey instrument may have unplanned effects on respondent feedback. To mitigate for this, research on survey designs has focused on such influences, such as the order of response options (ascending or descending), user interface effects, question layout (horizontal and vertical), and sizes of answer boxes for open-ended questions (Maloshonok & Terentev, 2016, pp. 506 - 507). One research team studied the prior elements to see if these aspects of survey questions affect "data quality" (based on whether responses are "substantive" or informational, and the amounts of feedback in open-ended questions) (p. 507). Radio buttons in the survey design work better to lower the selection of non-substantive answers like "Don't know" than slider response and text-box interfaces (p. 506). While some researchers suggest that the "primacy effect" influences the ratings that people apply to scalar questions, such as that going from negative ratings to positive ones (ascending order) "significantly reduces the share of positive answers," this effect was not found in another study (p. 507). There is also the idea that descending (from positive to negative scale measures) order format "increases the number of respondents who choose neutral response categories" p. 507). Larger text boxes do seem to encourage more commentary for native speakers of the survey language for "narrative questions" (Maloshonok & Terentev, 2016, pp. 514 - 515).

In an earlier study, just the availability of "more space for responses to an open-ended question produced marginally more words and ideas per response, but did not generate a greater total number of ideas" (Gendall, Menelaou, & Brennan, 1996, p. 1). So more contents do not mean more quality responses per se. The uses of encouragement to respondents "to write positive or negative comments to an open-ended question did not produce either more words or more ideas" (Gendall, Menelaou, & Brennan, 1996, p. 1). The question cue does influence "the number and content of the responses received" (Gendall, Menelaou, & Brennan, 1996, p. 1), which suggests the importance of thoughtful question design and testing of those designs for responsiveness and data quality. A later study found that the sizes of answer boxes with "extra verbal instructions" had an effect on response quality, with quality defined as including "response length, number of themes reported, elaboration on themes, response time, and item nonresponse" (Smyth, Dillman, Christian, & McBride, May 2009, p. 5).

To avoid low response rates, survey designers need to avoid creating "high-burden Web interactions" that may lower response rates to online surveys (Crawford, Coupler, & Lamias, Summer 2001, p. 146). Some interventions to encourage response include the following: "a progress indicator, automating password entry, varying the timing of reminder notices to nonrespondents, and using a prenotification report on the anticipated survey length" to "vary the burden (perceived or real) of the survey request" (Crawford, Coupler, & Lamias, Summer 2001, p. 146).

Another test of modality potentially affecting responses focused on sequences—such as beginning from the quantitative methods to the qualitative and then vice versa, to see if the respective survey respondent groups responded differently. They found: "The sequence of data collection did not greatly affect the participants' responses to the close-ended questions (survey items) or the open-ended questions (interview questions)" (Covell, Sidani, & Ritchie, 2012, p. 664). That is not to say that the researchers did not find some risks of unduly influencing some open-ended question results:

That is, participants' descriptions of the phenomenon of interest will be affected by the domains, dimensions, and / or aspects captured and / or covered by those assessed with the quantitative measure; therefore, the qualitative responses may not accurately or solely reflect their perspective. These recommendations are logical; however, they are not empirically based. No empirical evidence could be found from investigations that supports or refutes the influence of the sequence of data collection in concurrent mixed methods designs on the participants' responses to close-ended questions (e.g., items on surveys) or open-ended questions (e.g. interview questions) when data are collected at the same phase of a study. (Covell, Sidani, & Ritchie, 2012, p. 665)

How questions are set up can also frame respondent understandings of the purposes of the questions and the scope. "Response alternatives" frame understandings for respondents and affect their provided answers (Schwarz, Feb. 1999, p. 95) and help respondents contextualize their own behavior (Schwarz, Hippler, Deutsch, & Strack, Autumn 1985, p. 389). Response scales to close-ended questions are informational to survey respondents Schwarz, Hippler, Deutsch, & Strack, Autumn 1985, p. 394), and they systematically affect respondent choices: "An examination of respondents' behavioral reports indicates that those who were presented the low range scale tended to choose categories in the middle of the list, whereas respondents who were presented the high range scale tended to endorse the first category provided" Schwarz, Hippler, Deutsch, & Strack, Autumn 1985, p. 390). When offered a list of numbers, most survey respondents tend to choose those "near the middle of the list" (Payne, 1951, p. 80, as cited in Schwarz, Hippler, Deutsch, & Strack, Autumn 1985, p. 389), with respondents preferring "usual" behavior (and not the polar extremes). Researchers note that question design requires some directiveness, so respondents understand what researchers are interested in, but the options should be inclusive of the range of alternatives without unduly leading respondents to certain responses.

Survey question design involves defining objectives for the question and creating question cues that achieve those objectives without bias.

Uses of Open-Ended Questions in Online Surveys

Historically, the most common open-ended question in surveys were as a catch-all question. However, while this information was captured, researchers apparently did not always analyze these.

The habitual 'any other comments' general open question at the end of structured questionnaires has the potential to increase response rates, elaborate responses to closed questions, and allow respondents to identify new issues not captured in the closed questions. However, we believe that many researchers have collected such data and failed to analyze or present it. (O'Cathain & Thomas, 2004, p. 1)

Researchers suggest that if survey designers are more strategic in building "general open questions at the end of structure questionnaires," they may more effectively elicit useful insights (O'Cathain & Thomas, 2004, p. 1). They identify four basic types of open-ended questions—to extend existing close-ended questions (such as with "Other, please specify"), to substitute for a closed question, to expand on an answer given to a prior close-ended question, and to "elaborate on their general experience in relation to the overall topic of the survey" (O'Cathain & Thomas, 2004, p. 3). These refer to open-ended questions in relationship to close-ended ones. In more recent work, open-ended survey questions are strategically designed to capture original insights not available otherwise, without any necessary direct tie to close-ended questions.

Open-ended questions may serve various question roles. In one study, they were used to assess respondent senses of the questionnaire, and one involved eliciting information conceived as private in many cultures (Leidich, Jayaweera, Arcara, Clawson, Chalker, & Rochat, 2018). Open-ended questions may be used to measure non-expert respondent competence (Brugidou, 2003; Reynolds, Bostrom, Read, & Morgan, 2010). Another study used open-ended questions to identify "sub-corpora by group" which may inform on segments of the respondents (Deneulin, Le Fur, & Bavaud, 2016, p. 289), or audience / consumer category / population segmentation.

A core feature is that open-ended questions enable a wide range of responses for questions about which the survey designer may not directly anticipate the full range of possible responses.

In one study, researchers identified a negativity bias in open-ended responses (in terms of employee surveys) (Poncheri, Lindberg, Thompson, & Surface, July 2008). To balance against "strategic misrepresentations of values in open-ended stated preference surveys," researchers have explored positive and negative reinforcement to mitigate these tendencies (Dit Sourd, Zawojska, Mahieu, & Louviere, 2018, p. 153). Interventions have included sharing of information, recoding values, structuring incentives (for "consequential" surveys with opportunities for gain or loss), and other efforts.

Manifest or Latent Information

An important differentiation is to understand whether the online survey research is in pursuit of manifest or latent information, which some have referred to as "breadth" vs. "depth." The research team explains:

Another methodological question at the outset is whether a study will examine the **manifest** *(visible at the surface level or literally present in the text) or* **latent** *(having a deeper meaning implied in the text) content of the text or a combination. Manifest content is identified using coding and key word searches and can be recorded in frequencies such as word counts. Latent content, although amenable to objective coding processes, is more complex and requires developing constructs and drawing conclusions to add broader meaning to the text. It is generally easier to conduct a CA (content analysis) of the manifest content of a message, but latent content is often the more interesting and debatable aspect of communication. (Kondracki, Wellman, & Amundson, 2002, p. 225)*

In some ways, making a case for what is manifest may be somewhat easier than what is latent, but there are data analytics methods and software tools that make the latter easier and more arguable.

Who Responds to Online Surveys?

A range of methodological studies suggest varying reasons why people do or do not respond to surveys in general and to open-ended questions in particular. In terms of who will respond to online surveys, this depends on various factors, such as the types of research, the incentives designed into the survey, the access to information, and other factors. In some cases, targeted surveys may go out to an organization's membership, and there may be higher response rates to these than to others. Non-response error affects how representative the captured data sample is.

In theory, the Internet enables access to all those who are engaged online, but Internet research surveys have strengths and weaknesses. While online surveys may seem more efficient in "cost and speed," that may not be so accurate in terms of a "significantly shorter survey fielding period" (Fricker & Schonlau, 2012, p. 356). A common challenge may be a "coverage error" for representative population (Fricker & Schonlau, 2012, p. 357), and because there are some "hard-to-involve Internet users" who are "non-public participants of online communities (also known as 'lurkers')" (Andrews, Nonnecke, & Preece, 2003, p. 185). Online it is difficult to distinguish one's survey from others (Fricker & Schonlau, 2012, p. 365). People who are highly motivated to engage in a particular topic are found to respond to web surveys (Holland & Christian, May 2009, p. 196), but that characteristic already suggests some bias in the data collected. Internet penetration does not reach all possible respondents who may have insights on a topic because of the simple reality that "not all persons in the United States can be reached using the Internet" (Crawford, Coupler, & Lamias, Summer 2001, p. 146). There is also the reality that many surveys online are incentivized by micropayments, which may attract people who are willing to share their thoughts for very small amounts of money. Sampling options for electronic surveys include the following: "non-probabilistic methods: self-selection; volunteer panels of Internet users; probability-based methods: intercept; list-based, high coverage; mixed-mode design with choice of completion method; prerecruited panels of Internet users; (and) probability samples of full populations" (Couper, 2000, as cited Andrews, Nonnecke, & Preece, 2003, p. 185). [Non-probabilistic approaches deal with samples that are not necessarily "representative," and many of these are convenience samples. Self-selection methods include opt-in to participate in advertised surveys. Volunteer panels are those who opt-in based on expertise or micropayments, or other incentives. The probabilistic methods include the following: "Intercept surveys target visitors at a particular Web site, asking every nth visitor to participate, similar to an election exit poll. Invitation presentation timing problems may increase nonresponse. With the sampling option, list-based sampling, everyone on a list is sent an invitation to increase coverage. However, this approach does not address nonresponses. With prerecruited Internet user panels, panel members are recruited using probability sampling methods such as random digital dialing. Here, nonresponse can occur at any stage of the recruitment and survey process. The last sampling method, probability samples of full populations, requires that participants can be provided with the PCs and Internet access necessary to participate (Andrews, Nonnecke, & Preece, 2003, p. 190).]

More Responsive "Types" to Open-Ended Questions

Multiple studies suggest that particular demographic features may predispose some to be more sensitive to some survey design features than others. Open-ended questions allow respondents to reply "in their own words" (Glasow, April, 2005, p. 2-7), which requires some contemplation and effort. The cognitive load required is higher than for making selections from pre-defined options.

A different research team suggests that "large answer boxes earn higher item nonresponse than small answer boxes regardless of the usage of a motivation text" (Zuell, Menold, & Körber, 2015, p. 115). One explanation for this is that open-ended questions incur a "higher cognitive burden" for respondents even as these help "gain additional, more sophisticated information from respondents" (Zuell, Menold, & Körber, 2015, p. 115). In this study, those from the "social sciences" as a field of study and females… were more responsive to the open-ended questions (Zuell, Menold, & Körber, 2015, p. 115).

For example, "interactive probing" (elicitations for further elaboration) with web surveys seems to work well in particular contexts only and particular respondents:

We find that respondents' interest in the question topic significantly affects the responses to open-ended questions, and interactively probing responses to open-ended questions in web surveys can improve the quality of responses for some respondents, particularly for those very interested in the question topic. Nonresponse remains a significant problem for open-ended questions; we found high item nonresponse rates for the initial question and even higher nonresponse to the probe, especially for those less interested in the topic of the question. (Holland & Christian, May 2009, p. 196)

Text and Textual Analysis

Once open-ended questions have been designed and presented in as non-biased ways as possible, and sufficient responses captured, it is important to analyze the responses based on research design, particularly the intent and objectives of the open-ended questions. Textual data is fairly high dimensional in terms of semantic or meaning-bearing terms. It carries information through orthography, the conventions for writing a language (including spelling, punctuation, capitalization, and others). It carries information by author hands (signatures of authors). Researchers suggest that text analysis is not directly linked to a particular theoretical framework but cuts across multiple types. They write:

The assumption about the nature of text refers to the relationship between text data and reality. Positivist approaches assume language corresponds to an objective reality; that is, meaning is assumed to be objective—researchers merely need to find it. Linguistic approaches assume that language is not a neutral description of reality but rather an act that shapes reality. Linguistic approaches assume that reality emerges through language because reality does not exist independent of language. Interpretivist approaches assume that the meaning of language is subjective—the speaker, listener, and observer may all ascribe different meanings to language. (Lacity & Janson, Fall 1994, p. 139) (Note: The numerical citations have been removed from the prior paragraph.)

A text analysis approach encapsulates these different types of approaches depending on the researcher, the theoretical frameworks, the research context, and other factors. Regardless of the initial text analysis findings, validity checks are assumed to follow (Lacity & Janson, Fall 1994, p. 141). More modern approaches assume some level of validation checking as well.

Concurrent Mixed Methods Research

Classic survey data was generally quantitative and amenable to a variety of statistical analysis methods. With the inclusion of open-ended questions, capturing "interview" data, the data also became qualitative, amenable to qualitative analytics methods through interpretive lenses and without claims of objectivity.

Sufficient Data

A quality response, generically, is seen as achieving "data saturation" [described as the point at which few other changes are made to the codebook (Trans, Porcher, Falissard, & Ravaud, 2016, p. 88) or the point that no new information is available]. In one meta-analytic study, data saturation was achieved with greater than 150 participants for the full range of identifiable themes (Tran, Porcher, Falissard, & Ravaud, 2016). This study was based on Monte Carlo simulations on data:

In the literature, 85% of researchers used a convenience sample, with a median size of 167 participants (interquartile range [IQR] = 69 – 406). In our simulation study, the probability of identifying at least one new theme for the next included subject was 32%, 24%, and 12% after the inclusion of 30, 50, and 100 subjects, respectively. The inclusion of 150 participants at random resulted in the identification of 92% themes (IQR = 91 – 93%) identified in the original study. (Trans, Porcher, Falissard, & Ravaud, 2016, p. 88)

Having sufficient respondents enables quality because these may help mitigate over-estimations and under-estimations, to get closer to accurate data.

Depth of Responses

Another data quality approach involves the depth or complexity of the textual responses, with research indicating that it is better in some cases and worse in others, in case-based studies. In self-administered questionnaires, open-ended questions involved reduced responses as compared to the same questions in face-to-face interviews (Sudman & Bradburn, 1974, pp. 35 – 36). Open-ended questions elicited more of a response when the subject matter was "threatening" (Sudman & Bradburn, 1974, p. 47). And open-ended questions seemed to be more protected against social desirability effects (Sudman & Bradburn, 1974, p. 47).

One study focused on recognizing respondent motivations (not as "mono" or single-channel but multi-channel) (Espina & Figueroa, 2017). To achieve these, the question cues need to enable respondents to process information at the semantic or meaning-based levels (not the orthographic or the phonological ones, or the ones based on language rules or sounds) (Burgess & Weaver, 2003, as cited in Gardner, 2018, p. 7).

In online survey systems, there is coding of text data done in system for close-ended questions but not open-ended ones (Van Selm & Jankowski, 2006), but this may be changing with later-generation systems. A common approach to summative content analysis involves "counting and comparisons, usually of key-words or content" (Hsieh & Shannon, Nov. 2005, p. 1277). Frequency counts may seem simplistic on the surface, but such an approach enables some pithy research insights. The data from open-ended surveys are also analyzed using concept mapping to summarize the text responses in the aggregate (Jackson & Trochim, Oct. 2002). In offline qualitative analytics software, the enablements may include the following: "*text impor*t and management; *exploration*; *dictionaries, categorization schemes, and coding*; and *export operations"* (Kondracki, Wellman, & Amundson, 2002, p. 227), and more.

COMPUTATIONAL TEXT ANALYSIS TO EXPLORE OPEN-ENDED SURVEY QUESTION RESPONSES

Before focusing on the various available types of computational text analyses for open-ended survey question responses, it helps to explore the steps to setting up an online survey with open-ended questions. This segment integrates some of the research findings addressed in the prior section and information related to some of the functionalities in Qualtrics®. Setting up a research survey generally involves the following eight somewhat-recursive semi-sequential steps:

1. Research Design
2. Survey Design
3. Deployment
4. Data Capture
5. Data Cleaning
6. Data Analysis
7. Write-up
8. Presentation

These related steps are depicted in Figure 1, with the nominal steps highlighted. The respective steps will require different amounts of effort and time depending on the research context and focus. A brief summary of each step follows. (This summary is not to replace more thorough works describing various aspects of the work but is intended merely to set a context for the discussion of computational text analysis of open-ended questions from online surveys.)

A brief summary of the eight steps follow.

Figure 1. General online survey design, development, and deployment sequence

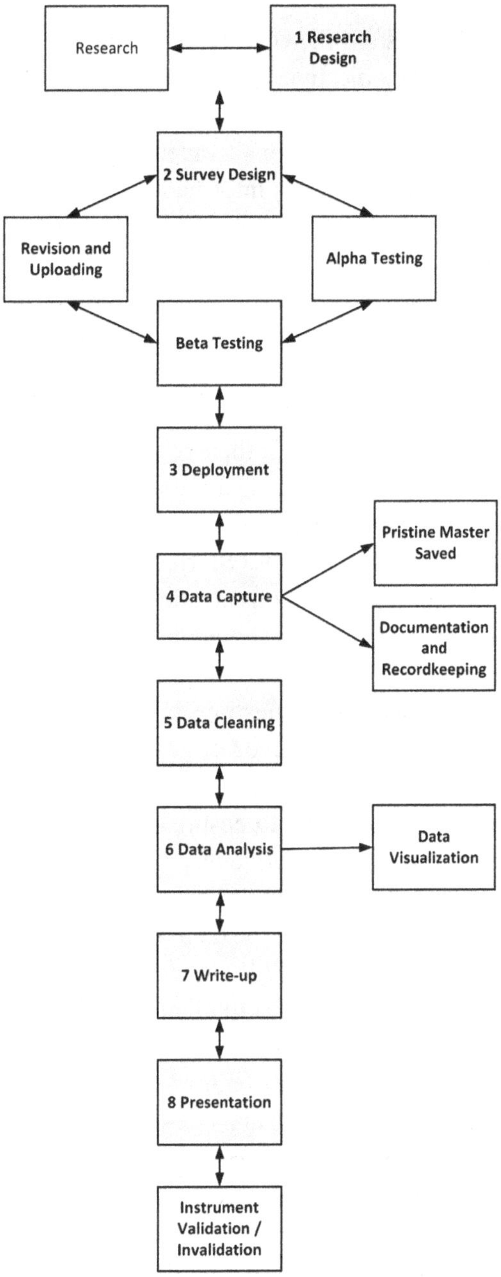

Research

1 Research Design

2 Survey Design

Revision and Uploading

Alpha Testing

Beta Testing

3 Deployment

Pristine Master Saved

4 Data Capture

Documentation and Recordkeeping

5 Data Cleaning

6 Data Analysis

Data Visualization

7 Write-up

8 Presentation

Instrument Validation / Invalidation

General Online Survey Design, Development, and Deployment Sequence

1. Research Design

The design of an online survey requires the definition of some basic elements, which may be addressed in part by the following questions:

- **Published Research:** What sorts of prior published research inform the research design, and why?
- **Research Objectives:** What is/are the objective/s of the survey? (If the survey is part of more complex research, what are the objectives of that research, and how does the survey part fit within that larger context?)
- **Data and Information:** What informational content is needed?
    - What are optimal ways to attain this information?
    - Are there extant survey instruments that are available for use to elicit this information? If not, what are the unique needs for this particular research?
- **Target Respondents:** Who are the target respondents for the survey research?
    - Do the respondents have access the requisite information?
    - How will these respondents be reached? How will they be sufficiently sampled for statistical power in the research? For sufficient data saturation?
    - What incentives will be used to elicit their responses?
    - Are there vulnerable populations being accessed? How can their interests be protected?
- **Designed Elicitations:** What sorts of questions, prompts, and elicitations will be most effective in this context? Will there by hypotheticals? Stories? Vignettes? Images? Video? Simulations?
    - What are ways to ensure that questions are single-barreled for easier analytics?
    - If in-depth prompts are needed, how should these be designed? What stimuli should be used? What (non-leading) memory aids?
    - When will different modalities of questions be deployed, and why?
    - What sequences will be most effective?
    - If there are branching logic sequences, what are the rationales for these, and how should these be designed? What are ways to ensure that the branches are fitting and do not fail to capture information from the respective respondents?
    - If latent or hidden understandings and patterns are a focus, how will these be elicited? How will the data be captured? How will the data be analyzed?
    - Will demographic data be captured? If so, which ones? Why, or why not? How will demographic data be used? What are ways to elicit such data without turning off survey respondents (or creating a sense of invasion of privacy)?
- **Accessibility:** How can the online survey be made fully accessible for all potential respondents (and in alignment with federal laws requiring accessibility)?
- **Ethical, Legal, and Professional Considerations:** What are ethical considerations for this survey? Legal ones? Professional requirements considerations?
- **Data Handling:** How will the data be managed? Why?
- **Data Analytics:** How will the data be analyzed? Why?
    - What sorts of quantitative, qualitative, and mixed methods analytics methods will be applied, and why?
    - What statistical techniques will be applied, and why?
    - How will the data be value-coded? Why?
    - What data visualization techniques will be applied, and why?
- **Pilot Testing:** How will the survey instrument be pilot tested? Which subject matter experts may be brought in for the testing? Which target respondents?
    - How will the instrument be validated/invalidated?

- How will its reliability be tested?
- How will potential response biasing be identified and mitigated for?
- How will the neutrality of the survey instrument be ensured?

- **Technology Identification:** How well will this survey be deployed on the particular online research platform, and why? What functionalities will be required for the particular platform?
  - What about the technologies needed for the computational text analyses?

Depending on the ambitions of the research, other questions may also need to be included.

2. Survey Design

Based on the prior research design, the survey is set up with the elicitations. The open-ended questions may be included in any part of the designed sequences (Figure 2). The sequences matter because the prior contents of the survey may set up respondents to address particular issues or to have particular thoughts top-of-mind. A survey, in all its parts—from the name, the informed consent, the textual and other descriptors, the questions, the prompts, the sequences—inform respondents about what is relevant and what the researcher(s) wants to know. If poorly designed, the information will be leading and affect the acquired feedback.

Figure 2. Some variations on placements of open-ended questions in online surveys

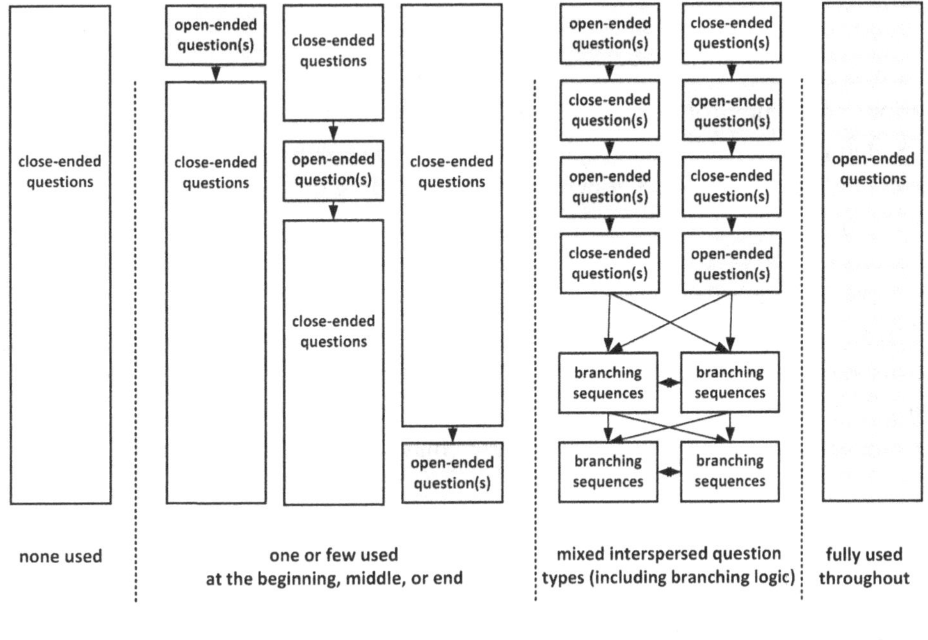

In general, conceptually, open-ended questions may appear in various ways in survey sequences. There may be none used; one or few used, such as at the end, beginning, or middle of a survey; interspersed open-ended and close-ended questions in surveys, or surveys with open-ended questions used throughout. If there were a typical use case, it might be those in the two middle categories of Figure 2, where a few are placed at the beginning, middle, or end, or a few are interspersed with close-ended questions.

When the draft instrument is completed and polished, it is uploaded to the survey platform and tested for all functionalities (including with faux auto-created data…to ensure that the information will be captured in a usable format). Then, a live link is sent to pilot testers. Content experts evaluate the instrument to ensure that it is sufficiently comprehensive and representational of the constructs under study. Target respondents experience the survey to ensure that it is understandable and adaptable to their respective experiences. To test for undue design influences, variants of the survey may be tested to assess for systematic biases based on question types, question sequences, answer designs for close-ended questions, and other details. How to test open-ended questions requires a little more work than for close-ended ones because of the polysemous nature of language and the openness of a text box-based response. Auto-generated data only creates garble text on online research systems, so both experts and target respondents engaged in the pilot test would do well to fully flesh out their responses in open-ended questions, and avoid placeholder text.

Once the researcher or research team has acquired the Institutional Review Board (IRB) approval for the work (or exemption from oversight), and gone through other approvals based on the local authorizing environment, then the actual research can proceed.

3. Deployment

The deployment phase involves launching the online survey—via a closed list or an open-access link (with invites to various populations of possible respondents). The respondents should come from the defined populations suitable for the survey. This phase also involves inviting participation. In some cases, this may include conducting randomized drawings for the awarding of prizes to participants.

Some monitoring is required during the deployment given the changeability of cloud-based survey platforms. Changes made by the company hosting the survey may affect the survey's availability and performance. (Author note: For example, when Qualtrics retracted its "conjoint analysis" feature in September 2018, a number of surveys using this feature were rendered inoperable. The company had not given its users any warning that they had decided to retract this feature and move it to a different conjoint analysis suite.)

In some multi-phased research, the deployment may involve multiple iterations of survey phase deployments.

4. Data Capture

The captured data from online surveys consist of both structured and semi-structured and unstructured data. Structured data refers to labeled data, such as those in a classic data table (Table 01). The column data are demographic data and question data. The row data represent each of the respondents. Structured data can be downloaded as comma separated values (.csv), tab-separated values (.tsv), extensible markup language (.xml), and data formats for common statistical analysis tools like SPSS (.sav), and others. More complex questions like ranking questions, matrix table questions, slider questions, may have their data downloaded separately for more in-depth analysis. Visual questions like hotspot questions and heat map questions, which enable selection of particular regions on a 2D image or map or figure also do well with unique per question data downloads for enriched data analytics and visual representations of the summary data.

Semi-structured and unstructured data refers to imagery, text, audio, video, and multimodal data formats. The capturing of this data requires their artful downloading to maintain their formatting and ride-along metadata.

The data capture phase should include archival of the pristine master sets of data with proper labeling, so that if lossy methods of data cleaning and manipulation occur, there is always a pristine unedited master set to draw from.

Table 1. Typical data structure of online survey responses

	Demographic Data	Question 1	Question 2	Question 3	Question 4...
Respondent 1					
Respondent 2					
Respondent 3					
Respondent 4					
Respondent 5					
Respondent 6					

5. Data Cleaning

Data cleaning for quantitative data generally involves removing multiple responses if one individual responded multiple times. It involves managing incomplete responses (because some statistical analysis techniques and machine learning techniques cannot run with blanks in data fields). For textual data, data cleaning may involve correction of misspellings, interpretation of confusing text, and other factors. If some text files are uploaded portable document format (.pdf) files, these have to be machine readable, so some of these will have to be run through optical character recognition (OCR) scans if these were captured as image files.

In addition to the data cleaning, how the various text sets are thin-sliced will affect the types of askable questions about the textual data (with some of the software tools). For example, some of the lighter-weight software tools require the manual separation of the content in respective text sets to enable comparisons and contrasts. To ask other questions of the text, the various granular text corpora may have to be recombined with others. For example, if a researcher wanted to compare how female and male respondents engaged a particular question, using a lighter weight text analysis software tool, then there has to be a text set representing each group (female and male respondents) for the particular question. With the respective sets, various analyses may be run. (More on this will follow.)

More sophisticated qualitative analytics tools enable the coding of contents into separate nodes, which can then be compared and contrasted (such as through matrix table queries, sentiment analysis, qualitative cross-tabulation analysis, and other tools).

For audio and video, these have to be transcribed for the text analysis to be applied. Likewise, imagery has to be turned into an informational textual format to be queried, coded, and included in qualitative computational text analysis.

Some tools treat text analyses somewhat naively. N-grams (contiguous sequences of words) may not be accurately recognized and coded. For example, some do not see words as more than unigrams or one-grams; they do not consider bi-grams or digrams (two words in contiguous order like "computational linguistics"), tri-grams (three words in contiguous order like "Latin numerical prefixes"), four-grams (four words in contiguous order like "longest common substring problem"), and others. If words are treated in a non-sticky way, names and phrases cannot be coded in a way that more accurately reflects the natural language usage in the world. Another naïve point is how sentiment is analyzed. More sophisticated algorithms will recognize negatives, and they will recognize irony and sarcasm. Many of the off-the-shelf qualitative analytics software tools lack such sophistication at present.

6. Data Analysis

In terms of open-ended text-based-response questions, computational text analysis enables multiple ways to approach the data: (1) exploratory queries, (2) manual coding, (3) auto-coding, and (4) mixed sequence analysis.

(1) "Exploratory" queries enable running of various text analytics methods against the text to provide overall summative data and descriptions of the data. Researchers can also zoom-in to particular terms, symbols, phrases, or other elements in the text and explore the contextual usage of every instance of the particular term (such as in an interactive word tree). Simple explorations may include word frequency counts (which may be depicted as word clouds, treemap diagrams, sunburst diagrams, Pareto charts, bar charts, and others). Word frequency counts may be explored not only for the most popular semantic terms used but also for the "long tail" or outlier topics with single or few mentions. Such outliers may shed light on unique topics of interest.

(2) "Manual" coding involves a researcher-created codebook or "codeframe" by which raw data may be coded for insights. A codebook may be created in a top-down way, based on theories, models, or frameworks. Or they may be created from the available data in a bottom-up way, based on "grounded theory" approaches. Or they may be created in a mixed top-down and bottom-up way, informed by concepts and by the available data. A manual codebook may be automated if there are sufficient examples of coded text to each codebook category and subcategories (nodes and subnodes). A researcher can code, say, 10% of the raw textual data and then have the computer code the rest of the data (with a Cohen's Kappa of 1, with very high interrater reliability). Manually created codebooks may be exported and used in other similar research contexts. These codebooks should contain the following, at minimum: the comprehensive list of codes, and the definitions for what belongs within each code category. It also helps to have a few paragraphs describing the origins of the manual codebook. All who contributed to the codebook should be listed based on their respective roles. The codebook should have a disambiguated and unique name for easy reference.

(3) "Autocoding" (in various forms of machine learning) may be applied to understand topic modeling, sentiment, psychometrics, stylometry, and other aspects of text. Topic modeling or theme extraction identifies the main topics and subtopics in a text set, and this method also captures a sense of the topic prevalence (based on counted mentions). Sentiment analysis involves the identification of how positive or negative non-neutral expressions are in the text set (and around particular topics). Psychometrics are

measures of the amount of psychology related insights. Stylometry involves counts of various points of grammar and syntax that may be indicative of an author hand (as a "tell"). More on these will follow. The basic power of such auto coding is that such results are reproducible and repeatable (important values in quantitative data analysis).

(4) "Mixed sequence" analysis involves combining any of the prior in a mix of different queries. For example, computational sentiment analysis may be run on individual responses to a particularly controversial issue, and then those autocoded text sets (for very negative, moderately negative, moderately positive, and very positive) may be analyzed to explore different topics emplaced in the respective sentiment categories. Frequency counts may be run against the sets to understand the frequency of mentions in the respective sentiment sets. Or a cluster diagram (concept map) may be created from a word-frequency-based dendrogram to understand how related topics are interconnected, and the main categories may be analyzed to understand what is being discussed in relation to particular popular topics (and fat nodes). Or demographic data may be used to separate people by gender, class, geography, professions, age, and / or other features, to see how these might affect their perceptions of particular issues raised in the survey. (This may be done with qualitative cross-tabulation analyses, matrix queries, and others.)

Computational text analysis methods transform unstructured and semi-structured data into quantitative structured data. The questions asked in such computational methods are rich, and they shed light on issues that may not be capturable in other ways. The output data are representable in human-interpretable data visualizations. Further, these approaches enable the handling of vast amounts of data well beyond the capabilities of human close reading and human manual coding, so the scale factor is an important one.

Some Computational Text Analysis Approaches (by Function)

While it is beyond the purview of this work to describe the nuances of the various computational text analysis techniques, some of the more common methods are described here.

Matrix Queries

Matrices are rectangular arrays of quantities and / or expressions. A matrix query involves the definition of contents for any of the variables in columns or rows and the viewing of the resulting overlapping data cells to understand frequencies. For example, the cell which is the overlap between Column Header A and Row Header A will be populated with frequency data, and matrices will represent as color intensity-highlighted cells to show the interrelationships. To create such matrices, the data have to be properly set up and coded. (Table 2)

Theme Extraction (Topic Modeling)

Theme extraction or topic modeling is an automated process by which the software program extracts the main focuses (topics and related subtopics) of particular text sets (whether documents, articles, text corpora, or other).

Table 2. An empty generic data matrix

	Column Header A	Column Header B	Column Header C	Column Header D
Row Header A				
Row Header B				
Row Header C				
Row Header D				

Sentiment Analysis

Sentiment is conceptualized as a polar dimension, either positive or negative. While a majority of natural language is not sentiment-laden but "neutral," the text in a text set that is seen to carry a sentiment value is coded in a pre-existing dictionary with a certain direction (positive or negative) and intensity, and the comparison of words in a text set against this dictionary enables coding to sentiment (either as a binary positive or negative category, or as a continuum, such as the "very negative, moderately negative, moderately positive, and very positive" categories mentioned earlier).

Cluster Analysis (Concept Mapping)

Concept mapping by showing interrelationships between main semantic terms in a text set provides an aggregate summary sense of the text. Clustering can be used in other ways, too, with individuals sharing messaging on a social media platform clustered based on "shared messaging" and shared interests (or at least shared engagement around particular topics). Clustering is based on a number of different algorithms, some identifying likeness, others identifying word proximities, and so on.

Network Text Structures

Network text structures capture structured relationships of various types. Social relationships may be those between individuals intercommunicating across a social media platform or a learning management system or an online survey research platform (with collaborative surveying). Or it may indicate relationships between co-occurring folk tags on an image sharing platform. Or it may show relationships between co-occurring terms within a certain size proximity. Essentially, network text structures are comprised of terms and their interrelationships.

Qualitative Cross-Tabulation Analysis

A qualitative cross-tabulation analysis enables the identification of large-scale patterns in survey data including open-ended text-response questions. One form of this analysis is to use the captured demographic features of the respondents in the row headers to find what relationships there may be among those dimensions and particular commenting on certain topics, certain sentiments, and other variables in the research. (Table 3)

Table 3. One setup of a qualitative cross-tabulation analysis

Demographic Features of Respondents	Topic	Topic	Topic	Sentiment	Other Variables

Another common setup of a qualitative cross-tabulation analysis has the respective individual cases in the row headers column. The qualitative cross-tabulation analysis does not use the calculations of chi-squared calculations and degrees of freedom and critical values found in the quantitative version, but the cells are mostly filled with straight counts.

Manual Coding to Automated Coding

Manual codebooks and codeframes may highlight particular aspects of the raw data as a form of systematic content analysis, "coding raw messages (ie, textual material, visual images, illustrations) according to a classification scheme" (Kondracki, Wellman, & Amundson, 2002, p. 224).

Linguistic Analysis

Computational text analysis tools enable the capturing of various dimensions of textual contents. For example, normed scores for text features may be captured to understand how analytic, clout or authoritative-based, authentic (emotionally warm), and positive (tone) a particular text or text set may be normed against known corpora. There are various types of linguistic analyses for particular general and customized purposes.

Psychometrics

Some tools have built-in psychometric assessments (backed up by validity and reliability scores), for positive and negative emotions, social focuses, cognitive processes, perceptual features, bodily references, human drives, time references, physics relativity references, lifestyle references, informalisms, and netspeak, among others.

Stylometry

Basic linguistic analyses may be run for basic counts of various word types and punctuation types, to enable stylometry (the metrics of style), to understand authorship. Each human writer's authorship is composed of a particular mix of word combinations, in a way that is often hidden to the unique author (and so is less directly manipulate-able).

Network Analysis

Multiple tools enable the capturing of interrelationships between words, people inter-communicating, folk tags, and other relational angles.

Query Sequences

Each of the above computational text analyses techniques may be applied in different sequential orders to ask particular questions and acquire particular informational data.

In each of the sequences above, there are various options for data cleaning, parameter setting, data visualizations, and other ways to customize the approaches.

7. Write-Up

In terms of the write-up of the text analyses, the methods should be described in depth, along with the parameter settings and the technologies used (and the versions of the technologies. Certainly, the findings need to be human-analyzed and the findings and implications of those findings described in depth.

8. Presentation

The prior section gives a sense of some of the capabilities of commercial and freeware tools for text analysis. These are not from a comprehensive list of software, and there are many others out in the public space. Still, this gives a sense of some of the approaches to the analysis of text responses from online surveys. Many of the findings are reproducible (and repeatable) in terms of outcomes, which is an important part of quantitative data analytics.

DISCUSSION

Many who design surveys usually use close-ended questions (T/F, multiple-choice, ranking, and other structured alternative options) to elicit responses from respondents because the responses are easy to represent and the summary data are readily available on most online survey platforms. On occasion, one of the multiple-choice selections may include "Other" and text fill-in options. Using close-ended questions can be limiting, however, based on the initial conceptualizations by the survey instrument creator. The potential of open-ended questions enriches what may be learned from survey respondents beyond the initial expectations of survey instrument creators. There is some early work on how to create elicitations that encourage more in-depth engagement by respondents. Some of these come from the learning space, with open-ended questions designed to develop cognitive skills and express their rationales for particular concepts (Lee, Kinzie, & Whittaker, 2012).

Applying computational text analytics to responses by the respective respondents not only informs on the target topic, but it may suggest ways to improve the survey instrument for later deployments. The answers may help survey designers elicit valuable data, ask difficult questions, iterate to acquire more in-depth data, encourage effusiveness (and data leakage) in respondents, trigger the subconscious and unconscious, and ultimately attain a wider range of textual responses.

Certainly, survey designs are not only evaluated for potential biasing from its structure, but there are implications external to the instrument. Researchers have to consider how to handle "sensitive" responses ethically from responses to open-ended questions (Lloyd & Devine, 2015). And political surveys have been found to have effects on the political opinions and actions of voters (Biondo, Pluchino, & Rapisarda, 2018), which have external implications on the research work.

If textual data is multi-faceted and informationally rich, "images are much higher dimensional, and typically more noisy than pure text" (Wu, Teney, Wang, Shen, Dick, & van den Hengel, 2017, p. 22). Further, "...images capture more of the richness of the real world, whereas natural language already represents a higher level of abstraction" (Wu, Teney, Wang, Shen, Dick, & van den Hengel, 2017, p. 22). Automated analyses of image sets, such as "visual question answering," which enables structured annotations of an image show a sense of promise for the future. The prompts to computers involve "an image and a question in natural language" (Wu, Teney, Wang, Shen, Dick, & van den Hengel, 2017, p. 21), and the computer programs combine machine vision and natural language processing to provide annotation of the images, with impressive accuracy. (In this context, the question to be answered was not created until runtime.)

The literature review, the description of the eight steps to building a survey with open-ended questions, and the cursory summary of some of the software tool functionalities for text analysis suggest that designing a survey purposefully with an understanding of how the data may be analyzed once captured is critical. At each of the eight steps, important knowledge and skills are required, to ensure that an online survey is comprehensive, ethical, professional, and effective.

FUTURE RESEARCH DIRECTIONS

This work makes a simple assertion that online surveys may be designed with more usable open-ended questions because of the computational text analyses that are possible. Eight steps have been suggested for the building of surveys based on quantitative, qualitative, and mixed methods approaches, specifically including open-ended questions.

1. Research Design
2. Survey Design
3. Deployment
4. Data Capture
5. Data Cleaning
6. Data Analysis
7. Write-up
8. Presentation

This work has addressed some common approaches, but there is a number of other tools in the commercial and open-source space that offer other ways to extract insights. Sequential ways of processing texts and conducting queries, and creating data visualizations may enable richer insights.

As various computational text analysis methods are harnessed for end-to-end online survey systems, their capabilities may also be studied for knowability.

With the prevalence of custom text analysis dictionaries and other light programs, the capabilities of these tools may also contribute to the field.

Another worthwhile angle may be to study the design of fully open-ended question surveys.

Visual question answering and other more sophisticated computational analysis techniques may enable the computational assessment of "file upload" questions, with the analysis of imagery and text with machine vision. These computational text and image analytics capabilities do not restrict human close reading, and the computational findings are still analyzed by the researcher. There is still the "human in the loop".

CONCLUSION

This chapter suggests that a broader strategic usage of open-ended questions in online surveys is warranted given the ability to manage and analyze such texts using computational text analyses.

REFERENCES

Andrews, D., Nonnecke, B., & Preece, J. (2003). Electronic survey methodology: A case study in reaching hard-to-involve Internet users. *International Journal of Human-Computer Interaction*, *16*(2), 185–210. doi:10.1207/S15327590IJHC1602_04

Arnon, S., & Reichel, N. (2009, April). Closed and open-ended question tools in a telephone survey about 'The Good Teacher.'. *Journal of Mixed Methods Research*, *3*(2), 172–196. doi:10.1177/1558689808331036

Biondo, A. E., Pluchino, A., & Rapisarda, A. (2018). Modeling surveys effects in political competitions. *Physica A*, *503*, 714–726. doi:10.1016/j.physa.2018.02.211

Brugidou, M. (2003). Argumentation and values: An analysis of ordinary political competence via an open-ended question. *International Journal of Public Opinion Research*, *15*(4), 413–430. doi:10.1093/ijpor/15.4.413

Covell, C. L., Sidani, S., & Ritchie, J. A. (2012). Does the sequence of data collection influence participants' responses to closed and open-ended questions? A methodological study. *International Journal of Nursing Studies*, *49*(6), 664–671. doi:10.1016/j.ijnurstu.2011.12.002 PMID:22204811

Crawford, S. D., Coupler, M. P., & Lamias, M. J. (2001, Summer). Web surveys: Perceptions of burden. *Social Science Computer Review*, *19*(2), 146–162. doi:10.1177/089443930101900202

Deneulin, P., Le Fur, Y., & Bavaud, F. (2016). Study of the polysemic term of minerality in wine: Segmentation of consumers based on their textual responses to an open-ended survey. *Food Research International*, *90*, 288–297. doi:10.1016/j.foodres.2016.11.004 PMID:29195884

Denscombe, M. (2008, August). The length of responses to open-ended questions: A comparison of online and paper questionnaires in terms of a mode effect. *Social Science Computer Review*, *26*(3), 359–368. doi:10.1177/0894439307309671

Dit Sourd, R. C., Zawojska, E., Mahieu, P.-A., & Louviere, J. (2018). Mitigating strategic misrepresentation of values in open-ended stated preference surveys by using negative reinforcement. *Journal of Choice Modelling*, *28*, 153–166. doi:10.1016/j.jocm.2018.06.001

Espina, A., & Figueroa, A. (2017). Why was this asked? Automatically recognizing multiple motivations behind community question-answering questions. *Expert Systems with Applications*, *80*, 126–135. doi:10.1016/j.eswa.2017.03.014

Falthzik, A. M., & Carroll, S. J. Jr. (1971). Rate of return for closed versus open-ended questions in a mail questionnaire survey of industrial organizations. *Psychological Reports*, *29*(3_suppl), 1121–1122. doi:10.2466/pr0.1971.29.3f.1121

Fricker, R. D., & Schonlau, M. (2012). Advantages and disadvantages of Internet research surveys: Evidence from the literature. In J. Hughes (Ed.), SAGE Internet Research Methods. London: SAGE Publications.

Gardner, M. K. (2018). The psychology of deep learning. In Z. Robert (Ed.), *Zheng's Strategies for Deep Learning with Digital Technology* (pp. 3–36). Hauppauge, NY: Nova Science Publishers, Inc.

Gendall, P., Menelaou, H., & Brennan, M. (1996). Open-ended questions: Some implications for mail survey research. *Marketing Bulletin*, *7*, 1–8.

Glasow, P.A. (2005, Apr.). Fundamentals of survey research methodology. *MITRE*, 1-1 to DI-1.

Holland, J. L., & Christian, L. M. (2009, May). The influence of topic interest and interactive probing on responses to open-ended questions in web surveys. *Social Science Computer Review*, *27*(2), 196–212. doi:10.1177/0894439308327481

Hsieh, H.-F., & Shannon, S. E. (2005, November). Three approaches to qualitative content analysis. *Qualitative Health Research*, *15*(9), 1277–1288. doi:10.1177/1049732305276687 PMID:16204405

Jackson, K. M., & Trochim, W. M. K. (2002, October). Concept mapping as an alternative approach for the analysis of open-ended survey responses. *Organizational Research Methods*, *5*(4), 307–336. doi:10.1177/109442802237114

Kondracki, N.L., Wellman, N.S., & Amundson, D.R. (2002). *Content analysis: Review of methods and their applications in nutrition education*. Report.

Kwak, N., & Radler, B. (2002). A comparison between mail and web surveys: Response pattern, respondent profile, and data quality. *Journal of Official Statistics*, *18*(2), 257–273.

Lacity, M. C., & Janson, M. A. (1994, Fall). Understanding qualitative data: A framework of text analysis methods. *Journal of Management Information Systems*, *11*(2), 137–155. doi:10.1080/07421222.1994.11518043

Lee, Y., Kinzie, M. B., & Whittaker, J. V. (2012). Impact of online support for teachers' open-ended questioning in pre-k science activities. *Teaching and Teacher Education*, *28*(4), 568–577. doi:10.1016/j.tate.2012.01.002

Leidich, A., Jayaweera, R., Arcara, J., Clawson, S., Chalker, C., & Rochat, R. (2018). Evaluating the feasibility and acceptability of sending pregnancy and abortion history surveys through SMS text messaging to help reach sustainable development goal 3. *International Journal of Medical Informatics*, *114*, 108–113. doi:10.1016/j.ijmedinf.2017.10.017 PMID:29100753

Lloyd, K., & Devine, P. (2015). The inclusion of open-ended questions on quantitative surveys of children: Dealing with unanticipated responses relating to child abuse and neglect. *Child Abuse & Neglect*, *48*, 200–207. doi:10.1016/j.chiabu.2015.03.021 PMID:25952476

Love, A. M. A., Butz, A. R., Usher, E. L., & Waiters, B. L. (2018). Open-ended response from early adolescents: Method matters. *Journal of Adolescence*, *67*, 31–34. doi:10.1016/j.adolescence.2018.05.007 PMID:29890346

Maloshonok, N., & Terentev, E. (2016). The impact of visual design and response formats on data quality in a web survey of MOOC students. *Computers in Human Behavior*, *62*, 506–515. doi:10.1016/j.chb.2016.04.025

O'Cathain, A., & Thomas, K. J. (2004). 'Any other comments?' Open questions on questionnaires—a bane or a bonus to research? *BMC Medical Research Methodology*, *4*(25), 1–7. PMID:15533249

Poncheri, R. M., Lindberg, J. T., Thompson, L. F., & Surface, E. A. (2008, July). A comment on employee surveys: Negativity bias in open-ended responses. *Organizational Research Methods*, *11*(3), 614–630. doi:10.1177/1094428106295504

Reynolds, T. W., Bostrom, A., Read, D., & Morgan, M. G. (2010). Now what do people know about global climate change? Survey studies of educated laypeople. *Risk Analysis*, *30*(10), 1520–1538. doi:10.1111/j.1539-6924.2010.01448.x PMID:20649942

Schwarz, N. (1999). Self-reports: How the questions shape the answers. *The American Psychologist*, *54*(2), 93–105. doi:10.1037/0003-066X.54.2.93

Schwarz, N., Hippler, H.-J., Deutsch, B., & Strack, F. (1985, Autumn). Response scales: Effects of category range on reported behavior and comparative judgments. *Public Opinion Quarterly*, *49*(3), 388–395. doi:10.1086/268936

Shapiro, M. J. (1970, Autumn). Discovering interviewer bias in open-ended survey responses. *Public Opinion Quarterly*, *34*(3), 412–415. doi:10.1086/267819

Smyth, J. D., Dillman, D. A., Christian, L. M., & McBride, M. (2009, May). Open-ended questions in web surveys: Can increasing the size of answer boxes and providing extra verbal instructions improve response quality? *Public Opinion Quarterly*, *73*(2), 325–337. doi:10.1093/poq/nfp029

Sudman, S., & Bradburn, N. M. (1974). *Response effects in surveys: A review and synthesis.* Chicago: Aldine Publishing Company.

Tran, V.-T., Porcher, R., Falissard, B., & Ravaud, P. (2016). Point of data saturation was assessed using resampling methods in a survey with open-ended questions. *Journal of Clinical Epidemiology*, *80*, 88–96. doi:10.1016/j.jclinepi.2016.07.014 PMID:27492788

Van Selm, M., & Jankowski, N. W. (2006). Conducting online surveys. *Quality & Quantity*, *40*(3), 435–456. doi:10.100711135-005-8081-8

Wu, Q., Teney, D., Wang, P., Shen, C., Dick, A., & van den Hengel, A. (2017). Visual question answering: A survey of methods and datasets. *Computer Vision and Image Understanding*, *163*, 21–40. doi:10.1016/j.cviu.2017.05.001

Zuell, C., Menold, N., & Körber, S. (2015). The influence of the answer box size on item nonresponse to open-ended questions in a web survey. *Social Science Computer Review*, *33*(1), 115–122. doi:10.1177/0894439314528091

KEY TERMS AND DEFINITIONS

Close-Ended Questions: Questions that may be responded to with true/false, yes/no, or other multiple-choice options.

Cluster Analysis: Any of a class of statistical analysis techniques that group various contents (like words or data points) based on similarity or other forms of connectedness (often depicted in node-link graphs).

Codebook (Codeframe): The thematic categories that may be coded to that are relevant to a particular phenomenon or research target of interest (and these may be created from top-down coding as well as bottom-up coding).

Computational Text Analysis: The application of various counting, statistical analysis, dictionary comparison, and other techniques to capture information from natural language texts (and transcribed speeches).

Concept Map: A 2D diagram that shows interrelationships between words and concepts.

Coverage Error: A sampling error in survey deployment that does not involve sufficient random representation of the complete population's members.

Dendrogram: A data visualization that shows clustered words in structured interrelationships as branches on a tree (may be horizontal or vertical).

Dimensionality: The state of having multiple characteristics or attributes (with high dimensionality indicating many dimensions and low dimensionality indicating few dimensions).

Elicitation: The drawing out of information.

File-Upload Questions: Questions that may be responded to with the upload of any number of digital file types.

High-Burden: A descriptive term suggesting the level of investment needed for a survey respondent to engage with a survey instrument.

Linguistic Analysis: The scientific study of language.

Modality: A form or type (of survey, such as face-to-face, in-person; by telephone; by postal mail; by computer face-to-face; by paper face-to-face; online; mixed modal, and others).

N-Gram: A contiguous sequence of "n" items (words), from unigram (one-gram) to bigram, three-gram, four-gram, and so on.

Network Analysis: The depiction of objects and relationships.

Non-Substantive Option: A response of "don't know" on a survey that does not offer much in the way of informational value; the equivalent of avoiding an opportunity to answer or skipping an elicitation.

Open-Ended Questions: Questions that may be responded to with a variety of text responses (only limited by the length of the text).

Polysemous: Many-meaninged.

Population Segmentation: The partitioning of a human population to particular sub-groups with specified characteristics and preferences.

Psychometric: The objective measurement of various aspects of human personality.

Qualitative Cross-Tabulation Analysis: The integration of a cross-tabulation table with interview subjects/focus group speakers/survey respondents in the row data, and variables and themes in the column data to enable the identification of data patterns through computational means.

Semantic: Meaning-bearing (as in words in a language).

Sentiment Analysis: The labeling of words and phrases as positive or negative (in a binary way) or in various categories of positive to negative (on a continuum).

Stylometry: The statistical analysis (metrics) of style.

Text Corpus: A collection of written texts selected around particular topics and standards.

Theme Extraction: The identification of main ideas and/or topics from a text or collection of texts.

Topic Modeling: The extraction of topics within a piece of writing or set of written texts.

Treemap Diagram: A data visualization indicating the frequency of occurrence of particular words and/or n-grams.

Visual Question Answering: A new computational data analytics technique that enables computers to analyze an image or image sequence or set using computer vision and making observations of the target images.

Word Frequency Count: A computational technique that enables computers to count how many words of each time occur in a piece of writing or collection or text set.

Word Tree: A data visualization that depicts a target word or ngram/phrase and a number of lead-up and lead-away words to the target term to provide human users with a sense of the target word/phrase use contexts (for semantic meaning).

This research was previously published in Online Survey Design and Data Analytics; pages 148-180, copyright year 2019 by Engineering Science Reference (an imprint of IGI Global).

Chapter 20
A Probabilistic Deep Learning Approach for Twitter Sentiment Analysis

Mostefai Abdelkader
Dr. Tahar Moulay University of Saida, Algeria

ABSTRACT

In recent years, increasing attention is being paid to sentiment analysis on microblogging platforms such as Twitter. Sentiment analysis refers to the task of detecting whether a textual item (e.g., a tweet) contains an opinion about a topic. This paper proposes a probabilistic deep learning approach for sentiments analysis. The deep learning model used is a convolutional neural network (CNN). The main contribution of this approach is a new probabilistic representation of the text to be fed as input to the CNN. This representation is a matrix that stores for each word composing the message the probability that it belongs to a positive class and the probability that it belongs to a negative class. The proposed approach is evaluated on four well-known datasets HCR, OMD, STS-gold, and a dataset provided by the SemEval-2017 Workshop. The results of the experiments show that the proposed approach competes with the state-of-the-art sentiment analyzers and has the potential to detect sentiments from textual data in an effective manner.

1. INTRODUCTION

It is very important to business industries and organizations to know opinions, thoughts, emotions, or sentiments expressed in texts by peoples using microblogging platforms such as twitter since it allows better decision making (Giachanou et al. 2016). This activity is commonly referenced as sentiment analysis (i.e., opinion mining) and it is an active area of research in recent years.

Sentiment analysis is a research field in the area of text mining and natural language processing that aims at analyzing texts that express opinions, sentiments and emotions of people's about a topic (e.g., services, individuals, products, issues) (Giachanou et al. 2016; Abbasi et al. 2008; Nasukawa & Yi, 2003).

DOI: 10.4018/978-1-6684-6303-1.ch020

If the analyzed text holds a sentiment, then it is viewed as polar (positive or negative), otherwise, it is viewed neutral (Zimbra, 2018). The analysis process consists of automatically predicting such polarity.

Nowadays, large textual data expressing people 's opinions and thoughts on products, services, or any topic can be found on social media platforms such as twitter which is a widely known microblogging platform. Thus it is not necessary to get them using traditional approaches such as surveys that are costly processes.

This situation constitutes a valuable opportunity for organizations to know about the quality of their services and products by analyzing user's texts to infer their opinions (Zimbra et al. 2015, Forman et al. 2008).

To organizations and business industries, tweets are viewed as the medium that contains evaluations of business and society works (Jansen et al. 2009; Gleason, 2013). For example, Organizations conduct sentiment analysis processes to study product sales (Rui et al. 2013), stock market movements (Bollen et al. 2011), and so on.

Unfortunately, While it is very easy to collect textual data that express user's opinions on a topic on twitter, It still is very difficult to analyze them to get information about people's sentiments. The achieved accuracies by the proposed techniques were found under 70%, which limits their applicability in real situations (Zimbra, 2018; Minghui et al. 2020; Kiritchenko et al. 2014; Santos et al.2014; Hassan et al. 2017). The difficulty Sources are tweet length, the used abbreviations, the problem of spelling errors, and the existence of special characters(Hassan et al. 2017; Kiritchenko et al. 2014).

So far, many approaches have been proposed to infer sentiments from textual data. These approaches are classified into three classes machine-learning approaches that include deep learning one, Lexicon-based and hybrid (Gupta & Joshi, 2019; Musto et al. 2014; Zimbra, 2018; Giachanou et al. 2016; Turney, 2002; Kim & Hovy, 2004; Tang et al. 2015).

Deep learning approaches which are class of neural networks with multi-hidden layers such as a convolutional neural network (CNN) have been found effective in many areas such as computer vision, natural language processing(Graves et al. 2013; Kalchbrenner et al. 2014). Due to this success, many deep learning approaches have been proposed to replicate this success in the sentiment analysis domain (Zhang et al. 2018). The performance of these deep learning models is dependent on many hyperparameters and an important one of them is the choice of the word embeddings model which is a vector representation of data (Bengio et al. 2003; Zhang et al. 2018; Kim, 2014).

This paper proposes a probabilistic deep learning approach for sentiments analysis. The deep learning model used is a Convolutional Neural Network (CNN). The main contribution of this work is a new probabilistic representation of the textual data (tweet) to be fed to the CNN. This representation is a matrix composed of two vectors. The first vector stores for each word composing the message the probability that it belongs to a positive class. The second one stores for each word composing the message, the probability that it belongs to a negative class. The system is evaluated on four well-known datasets: HCR OMD and STS-gold, and a dataset provided by the SemEval-2017 Workshop(subtask B). The results of the experiments show that the proposed approach can compete with the state of the art tools for sentiment analysis.

The rest of the paper is organized as follow: section2 introduces the deep learning and convolutional neural networks, section 3 presents Related Works, section 4 presents the approach proposed for SA, section 5 presents the empirical study, presents and analyzes the obtained results and section 6 concludes and presents future works.

2. DEEP LEARNING

Deep learning is an active area of research in the machine learning domain. Deep learning or Deep Neural networks are a class of neural networks with multiple hidden layers of nonlinear processing units able to extract representations or features at different layers directly from data. In general, building a data-mining solution using classical approaches, such as support vector machines, logistic regression, artificial neural networks(ANNs) and decision rules requires a high-quality feature engineering process. This process is expert dependent, costly, and must be done carefully to get the best features to represent the problem. It is also seen as the weakest point of classical machine-learning algorithms(Kantardzic, 2019). Deep learning approaches are a promising solution to this problem. They can automatically learn good multilayers representations or best features directly from data which makes the learning algorithms less dependent on a feature engineering process. The learned representations are hierarchical and at many levels(Kantardzic, 2019; Zhang et al. 2018). Examples of deep learning models are Convolutional Neural Network (CNN), Recurrent Neural Network (RNN), Long Short Term Memory network (LSTM), Recursive Neural Network (RecNN), Attention Mechanism and so on.

2.1. CNN

The Convolutional Neural Network (CNN) is well known deep neural networks. CNNs are a type of feedforward neural networks. The CNN was proposed in 1989 by LeCun (1989) and was found effective in machine vision and speech recognition (Krizhevsky et al. 2012; Graves et al. 2013; Kalchbrenner et al. 2014).

CNN architecture is composed of an input layer, one or more hidden layers, a fully connected output layer. The hidden layers include convolutional, non-linearity layer, and pooling layers for data reduction. These layers aim at detecting features or representations of data. The convolutional filters are learned during backpropagation.

The convolutional layer aims at detecting features and representations. In the sentiments detection problem, convolutional filters can get semantic and syntactic features of sentiments(Kim. 2014; Collobert et al. 2011)

The Pooling layer takes outputs of the convolutional layer after they are passed by the activation function and it aims at reducing data.

An example of a CNN is presented in Figure 1.

3. RELATED WORKS

Deep learning approaches have been found effective in many areas such as image recognition and natural language processing, speech recognition, computer vision, and information retrieval(Krizhevsky et al. 2012; Graves et al. 2013; Kalchbrenner et al. 2014). Due to this success, many deep learning approaches have been proposed to repeat this success in the sentiment analysis domain (Zhang et al. 2018).

In the field of sentiment analysis, many solutions based on deep learning have been investigated (Tang et al. 2015; Severyn & Moschitti, 2015). Convolution neural networks (CNN) with word embeddings have been implemented for text classification (Kim 2014) and have achieved state-of-the-art results in SemEval 2015 (Severyn & Moschitti, 2015).

Figure 1. An example of a CNN (Collobert et al. 2011)

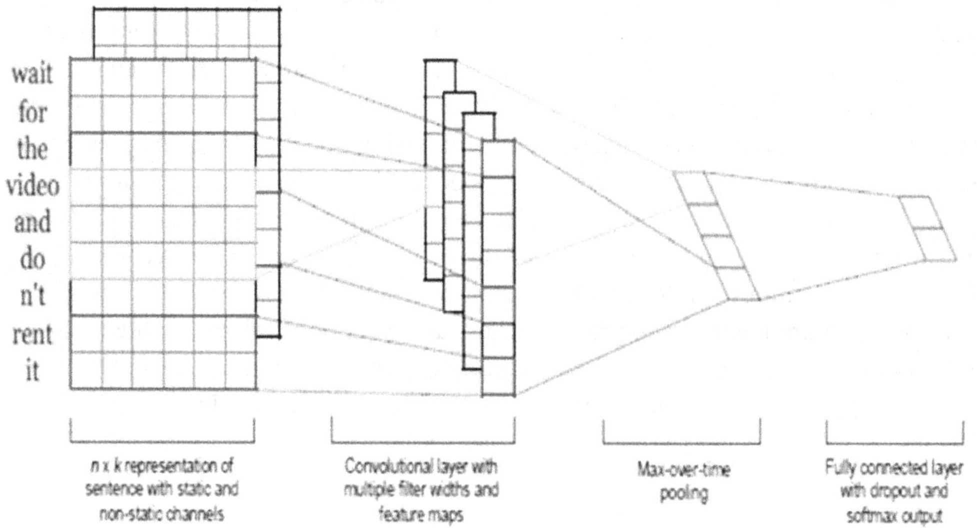

Alharbi & Doncker (2019) used a CNN with user behavioural information existing in tweets to ameliorate the results of the sentiment analysis process based on a CNN. The approach was evaluated on two datasets provided by the SemEval-2016 Workshop. The results showed that the approach outperforms tools based on Naive Bayes and Support Vector Machines.

Severyn & Moschitti (2015) presented a model for initializing the parameter weights of the CNN. In this model, initial word embeddings are trained based on an unsupervised neural language model. Then, a fine refinement of these embeddings is done using the deep learning model based on a distant supervised corpus.

In (dos Santos & Gatti, 214) the authors presented the Character to Sentence Convolutional Neural Network (CharSCNN) to analyze sentiments. The proposed approach exploits information existing in character- to sentence level. its main components are two convolutional layers to extract good features.

In (Minghui et al. 2020) The authors proposed the Sentiment Convolutional Neural Network (SentiCNN) model to extract opinions from sentences. The analysis process is based on the contextual information and sentiment information of sentiment words. The contextual one is derived from word embeddings and the sentiment information is derived from lexicons. The empirical study conducted on two well-known datasets showed that sentiment words, the Highway Network, and LBAMs affect the result of the process of sentiment analysis.

Akhtar et al. (2016) proposed a hybrid deep learning method for sentiment analysis. In this method, first, sentiment embedded vectors are learned using a Convolutional Neural Network (CNN) and augmented by a set of optimized features calculated using a multi-objective optimization (MOO) approach. Then, an SVM approach based on these representations is conducted to extract sentiment.

In (Hassan & Mahmood, 2017) the ConvLstm neural network architecture is presented. This model is a combination of a hybrid deep learning model. The model is CNN that uses a Long Short-Term Memory (LSTM) in place of a pooling layer. The model is used with a top of pre-trained word vectors. The achieved results were comparable to the state of the art tools for sentiment analysis.

Salinca (2017) used a CNN based word embeddings to classify business reviews. The author compared the results of CNN when with pre-trained word embeddings and end-to-end vector representations. the experiments showed that the approach is promising.

In (Zhou et al. 2016) the authors presented an attention-based bilingual representation learning model able to get the distributed documents semantics in the source and the target languages. they used a Long Short Term Memory (LSTM) network to represents the documents.

In (Santos & Gatti, 214) the authors presented the Character to Sentence Convolutional Neural Network (CharSCNN) to analyze sentiments. The proposed approach takes advantage of information from character- to sentence level and its architecture is composed of two convolutional layers to extract good features.

Yu & Liu (2018) Presented the sliced recurrent neural networks (SRNNs), a faster deep neural network than RNN, as a solution to the difficulty of parallelization of RNN. The experiments conducted on sentiment analysis datasets proved that SRNNs are accurate than RNNs.

4. THE PROPOSED APPROACH

4.1. The Architecture of The Deep Learning Model

The proposed deep learning model for analyzing and extracting sentiments from textual data is a CNN (convolutional neural network). This model is presented in Figure 2. It is composed of two convolutional layers followed by a non-linearity, average pooling, and another convolutional layer followed by a non-linearity, average pooling, and a sigmoid classification layer.

The input to fed to the CNN is a message (tweet) matrix. This matrix is composed of message word representations and is computed from the training corpus. This representation is explained in the following section.

4.2. Convolutional Layer

This layer is a fundamental component of CNNs. It is a mathematical operation (i.e., convolution) that multiplies(i.e., dot product) an input with a filter (i.e., kernel) which is a set of weights. The filter is of smaller size than the input data and is passed across it to produce a feature map .

While it is possible to design such filters by an expert to detect features, the power of CNN is in its ability to automatically learn such filters.

4.3. Pooling Layer

A pooling layer come after a convolutional layer. This layer works on the feature map by reducing its size using a pooling operation. Generally, the feature map is divided into regions and the pooling operation is applied to each region. The most used pooling functions by designer are:

Average Pooling: Compute the average value of the values existing in a region .

Maximum Pooling (or Max Pooling): Compute the maximum value between all values found in a region.

Figure 2. The architecture of the proposed CNN

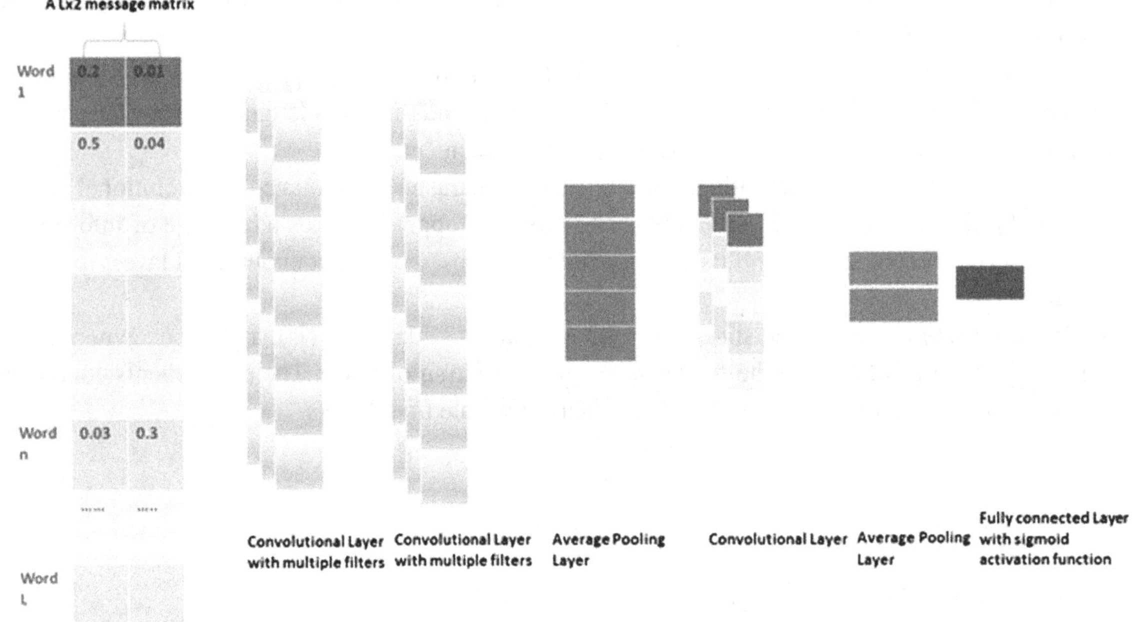

4.4. Message Matrix

A message or a tweet is a textual data composed of a sequence of words $w_1 \ldots w_N$ of length N. Each message is represented by an Lx2 matrix M where L is the largest length found between all messages composing the training corpus or it can be fixed to largest possible message. This representation is a concatenation of two vectors of dimension Lx1, V_1 and V_2. Formally, $M = V_1 \oplus V_2$ where $\oplus$ is the concatenation operator. The first vector V_1 stores for each word W_i composing the message the probability that it belongs to a positive class. The second vector V_2 stores, for each word W_i composing the message, the probability that it belongs to a negative class. Formally, let T denote a message composed of a sequence N-words $W_1 \ldots . W_N$.

Let C denote the class of the message which is positive or negative. The vector $V_1 = (P_{11}, \ldots, P_{1L})$ where $P_{1i} = P(W_i|C=\text{positive})$ is the probability that W_i belongs to a positive class. The vector $V_2 = V_1 = (P_{21}, \ldots, P_{2L})$ where $P_{2i} = P(W_i|C=\text{negative})$ is the probability that Wi belongs to a negative class. L is the largest length found between all messages composing the training corpus or the largest possible message.

If N <L the remaining last L-N elements are padded(filled) with 0. Padding is a common approach used to handle missing elements (Dumoulin & Visin, 2016). Probabilities are calculated using frequencies in the training corpus.

To calculate the probability P(W|C) that a word W belongs to a class C (positive or negative), First the training corpus is split into two sets SP, SN. The set SP contains only positive polar messages. The second set SN contains only negative polar messages. Next messages of the two sets are pre-processed. The pre-processing activity consists of the following steps. First a tokenization step divides the activity label into words. Next a noise removal step removes numbers, special characters, and meaningless words. A word is meaningless if it does not influence the analysis process. Examples of such words are prepositions (e.g., are, in, and, or, there). Meaningless words are removed based on a stop word list. Then, a normalization step transforms each word in a lowercase form. Finally tokens are stemmed and lemmatized. After this process, the probabilities are calculated using the following formulas:

$$P(W_i|C=positive)= \frac{count(w_i,SP)}{\sum_{w\in V} count(W,SP)}.$$

V is the set of the vocabulary V composed of all distinct words found in messages of the two classes.

$$P(W_i|C=negative)= \frac{count(w_i,SN)}{\sum_{w\in V} count(W,SN)}.$$

It is important to note that a word WM that does not appear in one or in the two classes, its probability is calculated using the following formulas:

$$P(WM_i|C=positive)= \frac{1}{\sum_{w\in V} count(W,SP)+|V|}$$

$$P(WM_i|C=negative)= \frac{1}{\sum_{w\in V} count(W,SN)+|V|}.$$

5. EMPIRICAL STUDY

5.1. Design

To conduct the empirical study, a tool named PCNNSA (Probabilistic CNN sentiment analyzer) is developed using Python language and with the help of a set of packages that implement machine learning algorithms such as sklearn, Keras and nltk.

The main logic and the components of the tool are presented in Figure 3.

The tool takes a training corpus as input and pre-process it. Next the pre-processed corpus is split into positive and negative sets. Next, a representation of each word composing the corpus is created following the proposed method in section 4.2. Then the CNN is trained to classify sentiments into positive or negative. Finally, the obtained model is evaluated on test datasets.

The aim of this study is the evaluation of the performance of the proposed approach. The main hypothesis is that a CNN with a probabilistic representation of short textual data is suitable for analyzing and extracting sentiments from them. More specifically, the study aims at answering the following research question.

Figure 3. The architecture of the proposed tool PCNNSENT

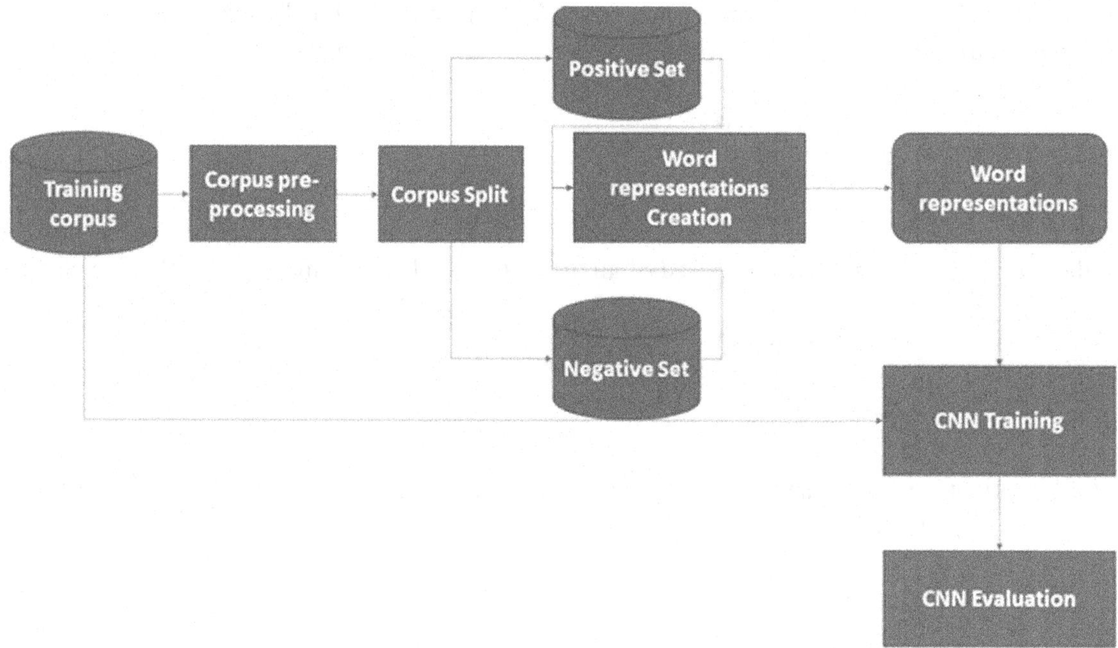

RQ1: Can the proposed approach be effective in analyzing and extracting sentiments from short textual data.

To answer RQ1, CNN is trained on a training corpus, then it is evaluated on a test dataset. This process is conducted on four well-known datasets. The used datasets are described in the following section. The obtained results on the test datasets are analyzed using four metrics. Precision, Recall, F-measure, and Accuracy. These metrics are widely used to evaluate sentiment analysis tools(Rosenthal et al. 2017).

The tool results are classified as either true-positive (TP) which is a number of positive messages that were correctly predicted as positive, False-positive (FP) is the number of negative messages that were incorrectly predicted as positive. True-negative (TN) and False-negative (FN) have the same meaning but for the negative class.

Based on this classification, Precision, Recall, F-measure, and Accuracy are calculated using the following formulas:

$$\text{Precision}=\frac{TP}{TP+FP}.$$

$$\text{Recall}=\frac{TP}{TP+FN}.$$

$$\text{F-measure}=\frac{2*precision*recall}{precision+recall}$$

$$\text{Accuracy}=\frac{TP+TN}{TP+FP+TN+FN}$$

5.2. The Datasets

The proposed deep learning model is trained on four well-known datasets. These datasets are the Obama-McCain Debate (OMD), Health Care Reform(HCR), the Stanford Twitter Sentiment Gold Standard (STS-Gold) dataset (saif et al. 2013; Da Silva, 2014; Krouska et al. 2017) and a twitter dataset provided by SemEval-2017(Rosenthal et al. 2017). Table 1. presents statistics about these datasets in terms of the total number of tweets, number of positive and negative tweets.

Table 1. Statistics about the used Datasets

Dataset	#tweets	#positive tweets	#number of negative tweets
OMD	1904	709	1195
HCR	1922	541	1381
STS-Gold	2034	632	1402
SemEval-2017	16225	12789	3436

5.3. Results

5.3.1. Parameters Setting

The results were obtained, in all cases, using the following parameters: A rectified linear units(ReLu) as an activation function in hidden layers, filter size = 5 for the two first convolutional layers, and 1 for the last one. A sigmoid activation function in the output layer. The number of filters was set to 100. A dropout approach was used to avoid the overfitting of the model with a rate of 0.4 and applied only to the second convolutional layer. The batch size was 70. Early stopping on the validation dataset was used to halt the training process.

5.3.2. Results Analysis

To study the quality of the obtained results by the proposed approach. These results need to be compared with sentiment analyzers proposed in the literature. Thus, the results obtained by the proposed approach were compared with approaches based on classical machine learning tools used for sentiments analysis (Saif et al. 2013; Krouska et al. 2017), a well-known lexicon approach and with the state of the art tool (Rosenthal et al. 2017).

The classical tools are Support Vector Machine (SVM), Naïve Bayes (NB), Logistic Regression (LR), C4.5, and k- Nearest Neighbor (KNN) and Maximum Entropy classifier (MaxEnt).

The lexicon approach is SentiStrengh (Thelwall, 2010) and the state of the art tools are the tools that participated in SemEval-2017 contest (Rosenthal et al. 2017).

Table 2 presents the obtained results on the four used datasets. The table shows the achieved Precision, Recall, F-measure on each dataset. The table presents also that the achieved accuracy in each case.

This table shows that the averagePrecision, averageRecall, averageF-measure, and the Accuracy achieved was 0.66, 0.57, 0.55 and 0.66 in the case of the OMD dataset.

In the case of the HCR dataset these values were 0.73,0.64, 0.67 and 0.80.

In the case of the STS-Gold dataset, these values were respectively 0.73, 0.69, 0.70 and 0.89.

In the case of the SemEval2017 dataset, these values were respectively 0.66, 0.58, 0.59 and 0.78.

Table 3 compares the accuracy of all classical methods and the lexicon one (SentStrenght) on the first three datasets.

This table shows that the proposed approach is effective than all the others on two cases of three (HCR and STS-Gold). The achieved accuracy was 0.803 and 0.886 in the case of the HCR and STS-Gold datasets respectively. These values are very high in comparing to the values of other approaches. In the case of OMD, the achieved accuracy was 0.66 and this value is better than values obtained by SS and KNN.

Table 2. Results of the proposed method on the four used datasets

	Positive			Negative			ALL (macro average)			
Dataset	**Precision**	**Recall**	**F-measure**	**Precision**	**Recall**	**F-measure**	**Precision**	**Recall**	**F-measure**	**Accuracy**
OMD	0.65	0.22	0.33	0.66	0.93	0.77	0.66	0.57	0.55	0.66
HCR	0.64	0.35	0.45	0.83	0.94	0.88	0.73	0.64	0.67	0.80
STS-Gold	0.92	0.95	0.94	0.53	0.42	0.47	0.73	0.69	0.70	0.89
SemEval 2017	0.81	0.94	0.87	0.51	0.22	0.31	0.66	0.58	0.59	0.78

Table 4 compares the accuracy of the proposed approach with state of the art tools that participated in SemEval2017 subtask B (Rosenthal et al. 2017). This table shows that our approach (PCNNSA) achieved an accuracy of 0.78. This value ranks our approach in the place 16 of 24.

In general, These results show that the proposed approach outperformed many classical machine learning approaches and it competes with the recent state of the art tools for sentiment analysis.

Consequently, RQ 1 is answered as follows: The proposed approach has the potential to detect sentiments from textual data in an effective manner.

6. CONCLUSION

This paper presented an approach for analyzing and extracting sentiments from textual data.

The proposed approach is a probabilistic deep learning approach. This approach uses a Convolutional neural network as a deep learning model with probabilistic word representations. The input of the CNN is a matrix composed of two vectors. The first vector stores for each word composing the message the probability that it belongs to a positive class. The second one stores for each word composing the message, the probability that it belongs to a negative class. The CNN architecture was composed of two convolutional layers followed by a non-linearity, average pooling, and another convolutional layer followed by a non-linearity, average pooling, and a sigmoid classification layer.

Table 3. Comparison of the accuracy of the proposed method to accuracies classical sentiment analyzers

Method	datasets		
	OMD	**HCR**	**STS-Gold**
NB	0.811	0.767	0.820
SVM	0.812	0.77	0.786
KNN	0.640	0.73	0.708
C4.5	0.753	0.742	0.743
LR	0.743	0.726	0.767
SS(SentiStrength)	0.656	0.703	0.821
MaxENT	0.823	0.787	0. 857
PCNNSENT	0.66	0.801	0.880

Table 4. Comparison of the accuracy of the proposed method to accuracies of the state of the art sentiment analyzers (subtask B)

#	System	Accuracy
1	BB_twtr	0.897
2	DataStories	0.869
3	Tweester	0.863
4	TopicThunder	0.854
5	WarwickDCS	0.843
6	TakeLab	0.840
7	Ti-Senti	0.838
8	funSentiment	0.827
8	CrystalNest	0.827
10	YNU-HPCC	*0.818*
11	SINAI	0.809
12	Amobee-C-137	0.802
13	NRU-HSE	0.790
13	ELiRF-UPV	0.790
15	NileTMRG	0.789
16	*PCNNSA*	*0.780*
17	EICA	0.777
18	OMAM	0.764
19	DUTH	0.607
20	ej-za-2017	0.518
20	SSN MLRG1	0.518
22	YNUDLG	0.499
23	TM-Gist	0.444
24	SSK JNTUH	0.412

An empirical study is conducted on four well-known datasets HCR, OMD, STS-gold, and a dataset provided by the SemEval-2017 Workshop. The results of the experiments show that the proposed approach can achieve competitive results with the state of the art tools for sentiment analysis and has the potential to detect sentiments from textual data in an effective manner.

In the future, advanced deep learning models and advanced probabilistic representations will be evaluated in the context of sentiment analysis.

REFERENCES

Agarwal, B. (2020). *Deep Learning-Based Approaches for Sentiment Analysis.* Springer Nature.

Akhtar, S., Kumar, A., Ekbal, A., & Bhattacharyya, P. (2016). A hybrid deep learning architecture for sentiment analysis. *Proceedings of COLING 2016, the 26th International Conference on Computational Linguistics: Technical Papers*, 482–493.

Alharbi, A. S. M., & De Doncker, E. (2019). Twitter sentiment analysis with a deep neural network: An enhanced approach using user behavioral information. *Cognitive Systems Research*, *54*, 50–61. doi:10.1016/j.cogsys.2018.10.001

Alsaeedi, A., & Khan, M. Z. (2019). A Study on Sentiment Analysis Techniques of Twitter Data. *Int. J. Adv. Comput. Sci. Appl.*, *10*(2), 361–374. doi:10.14569/IJACSA.2019.0100248

Baccianella & Sebastiani. (2010). SentiWordNet 3.0: An enhanced lexical resource for sentiment analysis and opinion mining. *Proceedings of LREC*, 10, 2200–2204.

Bengio, Y., Ducharme, R., & Vincent, P. (2003). Neural Probabilistic Language Model. *Journal of Machine Learning Research*, *3*, 1137–1155.

Cambria, E. (2014). *Senticnet 3: A common and common-sense knowledge base for cognition-driven sentiment analysis*. AAAI.

Cambria, E. (2016). Affecting computing and sentiment analysis. *IEEE Intelligent Systems*, *31*(2), 102–107. doi:10.1109/MIS.2016.31

Cliche, M. (2017): BB twtr at SemEval-2017 Task 4: Twitter Sentiment Analysis with CNNs and LSTMs. *Proceedings of the 11th International Workshop on Semantic Evaluation. Vancouver, Canada, SemEval '17*, 572–579.

Collobert, R., Weston, J., Bottou, L., Karlen, M., Kavukcuglu, K., & Kuksa, P. (2011). Natural Language Processing (Almost) from Scratch. *Journal of Machine Learning Research*, *12*, 2493–2537.

Da Silva, N. F. F., Hruschka, E. R., & Hruschka, E. R. Jr. (2014). Tweet sentiment analysis with classifier ensembles. *Decision Support Systems*, *66*, 170–179. doi:10.1016/j.dss.2014.07.003

da Silva, N. F. F., Hruschka, E. R., & Hruschka, E. R. Jr. (2014, October 1). Tweet sentiment analysis with classifier ensembles. *Decision Support Systems*, *66*, 170–179. doi:10.1016/j.dss.2014.07.003

Dos Santos, C. N., & Gatti, M. (2014): Deep Convolutional Neural Networks for Sentiment Analysis of Short Texts. *Proceedings of the 25th International Conference on Computational Linguistics (COLING)*.

dos Santos, C. N., & Gatti, M. (2014). Deep convolutional neural networks for sentiment analysis for short texts. *Proceedings of the International Conference on Computational Linguistics (COLING)*.

Dumoulin, V., & Visin, F. (2016). *A guide to convolution arithmetic for deep learning*. arXiv 1603.07285

Forman, C., Ghose, A., & Wiesenfeld, B. (2008). Examining the Relationships Between Reviews and Sales: The Role of Reviewer Identity Disclosure in Electronic Markets. Info. Systems Research, 19(3).

Ghosh, S., Hazra, A., & Raj, A. (2020). A Comparative Study of Different Classification Techniques for Sentiment AnalysisIn *International Journal of Synthetic Emotions, 11(1)*. doi:10.4018/IJSE.20200101.oa

Giachanou, A., & Crestani, F. (2016). Like it or not: A survey of twitter sentiment analysis methods. *ACM Computing Surveys*, *49*(2), 1–41. doi:10.1145/2938640

Graves, A., Mohamed, A., & Hinton, G. (2013). Speech recognition with deep recurrent neural networks. *Proceedings of ICASSP 2013*. 10.1109/ICASSP.2013.6638947

Gupta & Joshi. (2019). Enhanced Twitter Sentiment Analysis Using Hybrid Approach and by Accounting Local Contextual Semantic. Journal of Intelligent Systems, 29(1).

Hassan, A., Abbasi, A., & Zeng, D. (2013). Twitter sentiment analysis: A bootstrap ensemble framework. In *SocialCom* (pp. 357–364). IEEE. doi:10.1109/SocialCom.2013.56

Hassan, A., & Mahmood, A. (2017). Deep learning approach for sentiment analysis of short texts. *Proceedings of the Third International Conference on Control, Automation and Robotics (ICCAR)*, 705–710. 10.1109/ICCAR.2017.7942788

Huang, M., Xie, H., Rao, Y., Liu, Y., Poon, L. K. M., & Fu, L. W. (2020). Lexicon-Based Sentiment Convolutional Neural Networks for Online Review Analysis. *IEEE Transactions on Affective Computing*, 1. doi:10.1109/TAFFC.2020.2997769

Kalchbrenner, Grefenstette, & Blunsom. (2014). *A convolutional neural network for modelling sentences*. CoRR abs/1404.2188.

Kantardzic, M. (2019). *Data Mining Concepts, Models, Methods, and Algorithms* (3rd ed.). Wiley-IEEE Press. doi:10.1002/9781119516057

Kim, S., & Hovy, E. (2004). Determining the Sentiment of Opinions. *Proc. of Intl. Conf. on Computational Linguistics*, 1-8.

Kiritchenko, S., Zhu, X., & Mohammad, S. M. (2014). Sentiment analysis of short informal texts. *Journal of Artificial Intelligence Research*, *50*, 723–762. doi:10.1613/jair.4272

Kolchyna, O., Souza, T. T. P., Treleaven, P., & Aste, T. (2016). Twitter sentiment analysis: lexicon method, machine learning method and their combination. Handbook of Sentiment analysis in Finance.

Krizhevsky, I. S., & Hinton, G. (2012). ImageNet Classification with Deep Convolutional Neural Networks. *Proceedings of NIPS 2012*.

Krouska, A., Troussas, C., & Virvou, M. (2017). Comparative evaluation of algorithms for sentiment analysis over social networking services. *Journal of Universal Computer Science*, *23*(8), 755–768.

LeCun, Y., Boser, B., Denker, J. S., Henderson, D., Howard, R. E., Hubbard, W., & Jackel, L. D. (1989). Backpropagation applied to handwritten zip code recognition. *Neural Computation*, *1*(4), 541–551. doi:10.1162/neco.1989.1.4.541

Lin, J., & Kolcz, A. (2012). Large-scale machine learning at twitter. In *Proceedings of the 2012 ACM SIGMOD International Conference on Management of Data*. ACM. 10.1145/2213836.2213958

Mohammad, S. M., & Turney, P. D. (2010). Emotions evoked by common words and phrases: Using Mechanical Turk to create an emotion lexicon. In *Proceedings of the NAACL HLT 2010 workshop on computational approaches to analysis and generation of emotion in text* (pp. 26-34). Association for Computational Linguistics.

Musto, C., Semeraro, G., & Polignano, M. (2014). *A comparison of lexicon based approaches for sentiment analysis of microblo posts* (Vol. 59). Information Filtering and Retrieval.

Rosenthal, S., Farra, N., & Nakov, P. (2017). SemEval-2017 Task 4: Sentiment Analysis on Twitter. *Proceedings of the 11th International Workshop on Semantic Evaluation (SemEval-2017),* 502–518. 10.18653/v1/S17-2088

Saif, H., Fernandez, M., He, Y., & Alani, H. (2013). Evaluation datasets for twitter sentiment analysis. *Proc. 1st Workshop on Emotion and Sentiment in Social and Expressive Media.*

Saleh, M. R., Martín-Valdivia, M. T., & Montejo-Ráez, A. (2011). Experiments with SVM to classify opinions in different domains. *Expert Systems with Applications*, *38*(12), 14799–14804. doi:10.1016/j.eswa.2011.05.070

Salinca, A. (2017). *Convolutional neural networks for sentiment classification on business reviews.* arXiv preprint arXiv:1710.05978

Severyn, A., & Moschitti, A. (2015). Twitter sentiment analysis with deep convolutional neural networks. In *Proceedings of the 38th International ACM SIGIR Conference on Research and Development in Information Retrieval*. ACM. 10.1145/2766462.2767830

Strapparava & Valitutti. (2004). Wordnet affect: An affective extension of wordnet. LREC, 4, 1083–1086.

Sumanth, C., & Inkpen, D. (2015): How much does word sense disambiguation help in sentiment analysis of micropost data? *Proceedings of the 6th Workshop on Computational Approaches to Subjectivity, Sentiment and Social Media analysis*, 115–121. 10.18653/v1/W15-2916

Taboada, M., Brooke, J., Tofiloski, M., Voll, K., & Stede, M. (2011). Lexiconbased methods for sentiment analysis. *Computational Linguistics*, *37*(2), 267–307. doi:10.1162/COLI_a_00049

Tang, D., Qin, B., & Liu, T. (2015). Document Modeling with Gated Recurrent Neural Network for Sentiment Classification. *Proc. 2015 Conf. Empir. Methods Nat. Lang. Process.*, 1422–1432. 10.18653/v1/D15-1167

Tang, D., Qin, B., & Liu, T. (2015). Deep learning for sentiment analysis: Successful approaches and future challenges. *Wiley Interdisciplinary Reviews. Data Mining and Knowledge Discovery*, *5*(6), 292–303. doi:10.1002/widm.1171

Turney, P. (2002). Thumbs Up or Thumbs Down? Semantic Orientation Applied to Unsupervised Classification of Reviews. *Proc. of Annual Meeting of ACL*, 417–424.

Wang, Yu, Lai, & Zhang. (2016). *Dimensional Sentiment Analysis Using a Regional CNN-LSTM Model*. Academic Press.

Wang, J., Yu, L.-C., Lai, R. K., & Zhang, X. (2016). Dimensional sentiment analysis using a regional CNN-LSTM model. *Proceedings of the Annual Meeting of the Association for Computational Linguistics (ACL 2016)*. 10.18653/v1/P16-2037

Wiebe, J., Wilson, T., & Cardie, C. (2005). Annotating expressions of opinions and emotions in language. *Language Resources and Evaluation*, *39*(2-3), 165–210. doi:10.100710579-005-7880-9

Yu, Z., & Liu, G. (2018). Sliced recurrent neural networks. *27th International Conference on Computational Linguistics*.

Zhang, L., Wang, S., & Liu, B. (2018). Deep learning for sentiment analysis: A survey. *Wiley Interdisciplinary Reviews. Data Mining and Knowledge Discovery*, *8*(4), 1253. doi:10.1002/widm.1253

Zhou, X., Wan, X., & Xiao, J. (2016). Attention-based LSTM network for cross-lingual sentiment classification. *Proceedings of the Conference on Empirical Methods in Natural Language Processing (EMNLP)*. 10.18653/v1/D16-1024

Zimbra, D., Abbasi, A., Zeng, D., & Chen, H. (2018). The state-of-the-art in twitter sentiment analysis: A review and benchmark evaluation. *ACM Trans. Manage. Inf. Syst., 5*.

Zimbra, D., Chen, H., & Lusch, R. F. (2015). Stakeholder Analyses of Firm-Related Web Forums: Applications in Stock Return Prediction. ACM Trans. on Management Information Systems, 6(1).

This research was previously published in the International Journal of Distributed Artificial Intelligence (IJDAI), 12(2); pages 21-34, copyright year 2020 by IGI Publishing (an imprint of IGI Global).

Chapter 21
Opinion Mining of Twitter Events using Supervised Learning

Nida Hakak
Maharshi Dayanand University, Haryana, India

Mahira Kirmani
Maharshi Dayanand University, Haryana, India

ABSTRACT

Micro-blogs are a powerful tool to express an opinion. Twitter is one of the fastest growing micro-blogs and has more than 900 million users. Twitter is a rich source of opinion as users share their daily experience of life and respond to specific events using tweets on twitter. In this article, an automatic opinion classifier capable of automatically classifying tweets into different opinions expressed by them is developed. Also, a manually annotated corpus for opinion mining to be used by supervised learning algorithms is designed. An opinion classifier uses semantic, lexical, domain dependent, and context features for classification. Results obtained confirm competitive performance and the robustness of the system. Classifier accuracy is more than 75.05%, which is higher than the baseline accuracy.

1. INTRODUCTION

Opinion mining is used to refer to the task of automatically determining the opinion expressed in text, phrases, sentences or any piece of writing. However, more generally it is used to determine one's attitude towards a particular event or reaction to an event. Here, attitude means qualitative opinion, feeling or reaction to some situation that triggered the event. Opinion measurement and sentiment analysis for Twitter data are attracting much research both in academia and industry. Millions of users of Twitter are posting tweets about their daily life, write opinions on a variety of issues. Twitter is easily accessible through smartphones and other web services and thus is a preferred media for communication. Hence internet users are shifting from traditional communication tools like blogs and mailing lists to twitter.

DOI: 10.4018/978-1-6684-6303-1.ch021

More specifically, as Twitter users are expressing their opinions about several issues including religious matters, political views, and reviews of e-services, products or even movie reviews twitter has become a viable source for opinion measurement and detection. Such data is extremely potent for the industry for feedback and political parties to frame their policies and strategies.

Dey, Babo, Ashour, Bhatnagar & Bouhlel (2018) presented a detailed implementation of strategies and challenges to social network intelligence in their study. Twitter posts are 240 characters long messages called tweets. Java, Song, Finin & Tseng (2007) in their study suggest that users use Twitter for following reasons (1) for information source (2) to be in touch with family and friends and (3) seeking information about trends happing worldwide. Opinion mining involves data mining and Natural Language Processing (NLP) techniques to uncover hidden information and opinions from social web's substantial textual sources. Opinion mining from the text written in natural languages is challenging as it requires a deep understanding of explicit and implicit, regular and irregular, syntactic and semantic rules of language. Therefore, opinion mining is a challenge for NLP researchers for taking utilizing tools of NLP for efficient and effective opinion mining systems and thus leading to substantial practical impact.

Most of the companies are using opinion mining systems to create and automatically maintain reviews written by their customers for their popular products. Opinion mining can also be used by companies to improve customer relationship. Opinion mining also finds its applications in the recommender systems used by e-commerce sites. Moreover, opinion mining can play an essential part in the anti-spam policy drafting. Political parties also use opinion mining to know if the people support their decisions and programs or not and use feedback to frame their policies and strategies for future.

Opinion mining involves tracking users perception towards the brand or an event so as to capture mood of the public towards the brand or some political movement. Automatic opinion mining uses the NLP tools and machine learning techniques to effectively extract sentiments in text. Several studies exist in literature which have used machine learning to automatically detect the opinion like (Mohammad, Zhu, Kiritchenko & Martin, 2015; Yan, Turtle & Liddy, 2016; Gore, Diallo & Padilla, 2015). Pak & Paroubek (2010) used multinomial Naıve Bayes classifier with linguistic features to perform opinion analysis of collected twitter corpus. Grigori Sidorov (Sidorov, Miranda-Jiménez, Viveros-Jiménez, Gelbukh, Castro-Sánchez, Velásquez, & Gordon, 2012) used several machine learning algorithms for automatic detection of opinions in a Spanish language Tweet corpus.

In this paper, we discuss opinion mining of Twitter event done used state-of-art NLP techniques and machine learning tools. We show how to use Twitter for the corpus of opinion detection system. We have collected a corpus of 4,928,436 tweets about event namely Kashmir Unrest 2016 downloaded from the twitter from 10, July 2016 to 31, December 2016. We then preprocess tweets cleaning noise and performing other text transformations. Then the state-of-art linguistic analysis is performed using NLP techniques and then built an opinion classifier using supervised learning algorithms. We have also developed a rich opinion corpus using crowd-sourcing.

1.1. Contribution

The contributions of our research are:

1. We present a method for efficient preprocessing of text for removing and replacing slangs and to correct misspelled words.
2. We have built a vibrant opinion mining corpus for supervised learning algorithms.

3. We have used state-of-art NLP techniques for linguistic analysis of text to uncover explicit and implicit, regular and irregular, and syntactical and semantic language rules.
4. Built a supervised opinion classifier capable of mining opinions in Twitter.
5. Performed evaluation experiments that confirm competitive performance and robustness of our system.
6. Crowd-sourcing is used to create the opinion corpus where each tweet was labeled with five judgments and then majority voting was chosen and label agreed by at least three judges is given to the tweet.

2. RELATED WORK

Since the growth of social media, research in the field of opinion mining and sentiment analysis has grown many folds. Opinion mining is done at two levels: document level opinion mining and sentence level opinion mining. Pang and Lee (2008) presented a survey of existing approaches an techniques for opinion mining in textual systems. In their survey the authors present the detailed survey of the existing techniques and approaches of information retrieval using opinion analysis.

Another approach employed by Go, Bhayani and Huang (2009) uses machine learning algorithms to opinion detection in textual data streams. Their approach uses Twitter as a platform to collect the data for training. Training set is created using distant supervision. They used positive and negative emoticons for automatically creating dataset. Das, Borra, Dey and Borah (2018) presented movie recommendation system with good results. Turney (2002) used the average semantic orientation of phrases to calculate documents polarity. He used point wise mutual similarity to compute semantic orientation between documents and extracted phrases. Turney and Littman (2003) used cosine similarity and Latent semantic analysis at document level for opinion analysis. Dave, Lawrence and Pennock (2003) used term frequencies on uni-gram, bi-gram, and tri-gram to classify reviews on Amazon. Das and Chen (2001) used financial documents to classify sentiment polarity. Pang, Lee and Vaithyanathan (2002) used state-of-art machine learning algorithms to classify movie reviews for their sentiment polarity. They also used subjectivity with minimum graph cuts along with machine learning to detect sentiment in movie reviews as document-based opinion classification. Pang and Lee (2004) work is entirely different from these approaches as they have used sentence level opinion classification with state-of-art machine learning algorithms using feature classifiers. Kamal, Dey, Ashour, Ripon, Balas and Kaysar (2017) designed an automated system for monitoring Facebook data. Lan, Wang, Fong, Liu, Wong and Dey (2018) presented a survey of data mining and deep learning in bioinformatics. Zhuang, Jing and Zhu (2006) used sentence level classification using high-frequency keywords and high-frequency opinion keywords for classification of movie reviews. They used dependency graphs to identify feature-opinion pairs, along with a fixed set of keywords and thus their system was limited. Kouloumpis, Wilson and Moore (2011), Saif, He and Alani (2012), Sarlan, Nadam and Basri (2014), Balabantaray, Mohammad and Sharma (2012) based strategies, however, do not produce satisfactory results when used for opinion mining at the sentence level. Several works have suggested extending emotion lexicons with distribution semantic algorithms like Word2Vec (Mikolov, Chen, Corrado, & Dean, 2013) for classification (Canales, Strapparava, Boldrini & Martnez-Barco, 2016).

All these works focus on sentiment analysis, opinion mining or emotion detection at the fine-grained or coarse-grained level, however, and they lack subjectivity and domain dependent features. Domain dependent features describe the opinion that is currently being mined. All the work in the literature are general in nature and miss the crucial aspect of the current opinion being mined. The novelty of this work is that the domain dependent features are being introduced for the task of emotion mining. We capture the domain dependent features by creating an initial seed set by the domain experts. The opinions that are to mined require subject experts for identification of opinion terms; that act as the initial seed set for lexicon creation. The lexicon is then used by the automatic classifier for the opinion classification.

In this work, we will be using domain dependent features and show how they help in improving the efficiency of the classifier. Also, we have built an opinion corpus that can be used by other classifiers.

3. METHODOLOGY

In this section, a novel opinion classifier is proposed built using supervised classifier. The supervised classifier is built using lexical, contextual, semantic, domain dependent and morphological features. We have used pre-processing to normalize the dataset by reducing noise and correct misspelled words. Our classifier clarifies tweeter feed into six opinion classes viz; anti-India, pro-India, anti-Kashmir, pro-Kashmir, anti-Pakistan, pro-Pakistan and neutral depending on the opinion described in the tweet. We have built an opinion corpus of 9818 tweets that is useful for several opinion related tasks.

4. DATASET

We used twitter streaming API[1] and twitter4j[2] to download our dataset for opinion mining task. Dataset was downloaded to automatically for mining opinion during Kashmir unrest 2016[3]. Violent protests erupted in the Kashmir valley (J&K India) during summer of 2016 due to the killing of Hizbul Mujahidin commander, Burhan Wani. Burhan got killed on 8th July 2016. On 12th July 2016, we started downloading the tweets about the event until 31st December 2016. The dataset had 4,928,436 tweets. The downloaded dataset has non-English tweets as well we removed them and kept English only tweets, re-tweets were also discarded. Figure 1 show timeline of event where the frequency is plotted against date. Table 1 shows a sample of tweets downloaded.

5. AUTOMATIC OPINION CLASSIFICATION

Our automatic opinion classifier is developed using supervised classifier. We have used multiclass Support Vector Machine ($SVM_{multiclass}$) (Joachims, Finley & Yu, 2009). Our automatic classification algorithm consists of following parts:

1. Twitter scrapping module
2. Pre-processing
3. Lexicon generation
4. Feature selection

5. Generation of opinion corpus
6. Automatic classifier
7. Proposed Algorithm.

We discuss each of the sub-processes in following subsections. Figure 2 shows overall functioning of our system.

Figure 1. Time series of the event

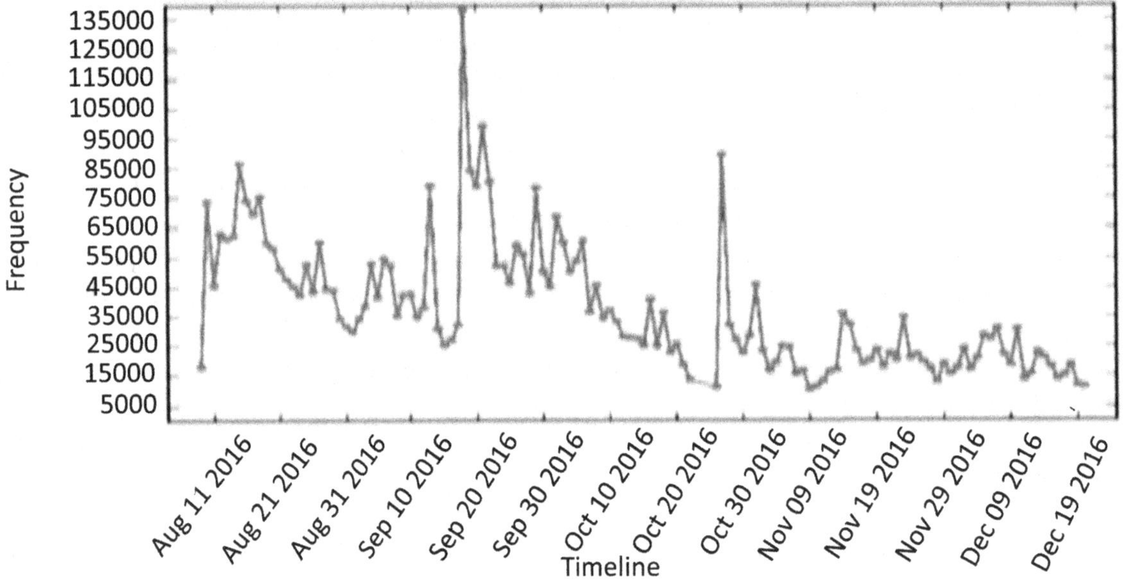

Table 1. Sample Tweets

Serial number	Tweet
1	createdAt:Wed Oct 26 14:28:10 CEST 2016, location: Bangalore, tweet: RT @Username: 19 schools burnt down in Kashmir in 3 months. Dear @username, pls confirm if schools were useless because they didn't have a\u2026", lang: en, rtweet: true, tid:791255097766350849, username: username
2	createdAt:Wed Oct 26 14:28:11 CEST 2016, location: India, tweet: Burning schools is new way of celebrating \#Diwali \#kashmir, lang: en, rtweet:false, tid:791255101570555905, username: username
3	createdAt: Wed Oct 26 14:28:12 CEST 2016, tweet: RT @maulinshah9: @username During the unnatural alliance of \#PDP_BJP in the state and NDA in the Center, \#Kashmir has faced maximum days of \u2026, lang: en,rtweet: true, tid:791255105563570176, username: username
4	{"tweet":"@saysdiyanag @CatchNews This one statement made me worry more about his wife than the jawans in Kashmir. So much power", "tid":791255101570556914}
5	{"tweet":"@TimesNow i get stunned when u still trying to get consensus over Kashmir..it is never going to take place..the Q is why gov. (1)", "tid":763044533558874113}
6	{"tweet":"Anyone watching Times Now?Better not. Hell break loose over Kashmir & la ilaaha illalla.Where are these debates taking us2. Shameful indeed.","tid", 763046521180790784}

Figure 2. Overall working of the System

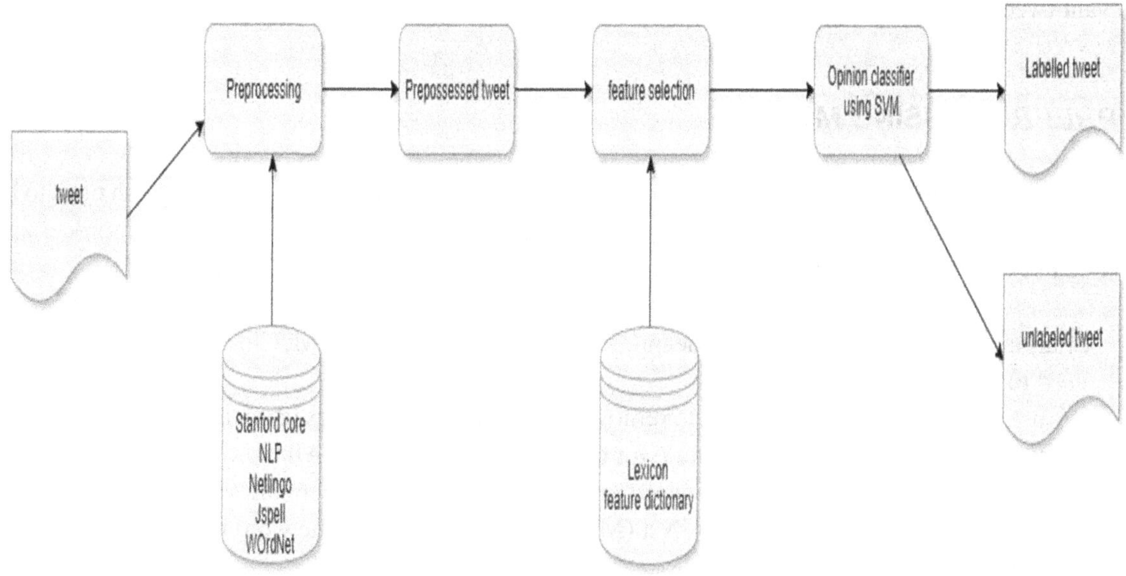

5.1. Twitter Scrapping Module

We made a scraper for collecting tweets related to the unrest. Scrapper was developed using twitter4j and twitter streaming API. Figure 3 shows the architecture of our scrapping module.

Figure 3. Scrapping module architecture

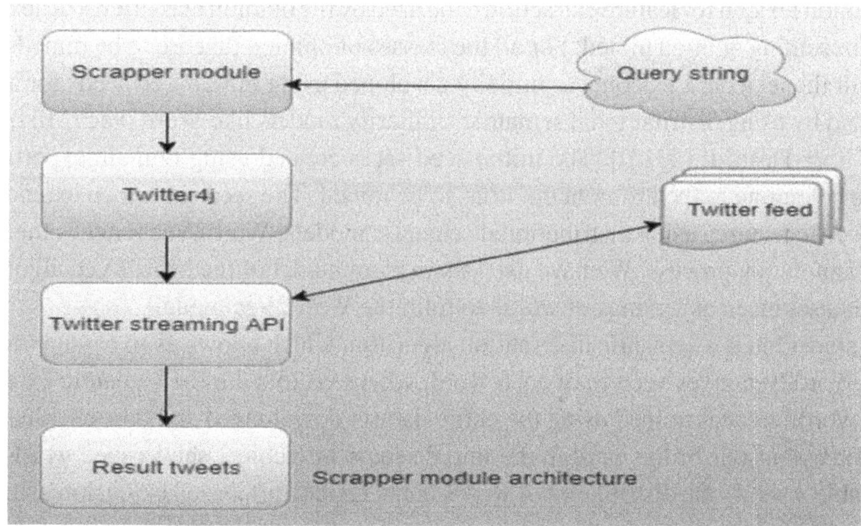

Our scrapping module receives a set of query string words which are probed to twitter for retrieving relevant tweets.

6. PREPROCESSING MODULE

Our preprocessing module removes noise from tweets. Tweets are unstructured a noisy which need to be cleaned for processing before passing to the supervised classifier for classification. Our preprocessing module use following steps to clean the tweet.

1. Stanford core NLP (Manning, Surdeanu, Bauer, Finkel, Bethard & McClosky, 2014) package is used to tokenize tweets into words.
2. We use English dictionary modules to remove slangs and abbreviations from the tweet. All words of the tweet are feed to dictionary module for retrieving their meaning. All words that have no proper meaning returned are passed to the word replacer module for replacement with proper meanings. The dictionary module is used WordNet (Miller, 1995) and Jspell. The word replacer module uses Netlingo and urban dictionary.
3. Stemming from each word in the tweet is done using potter stemmer (Van Rijsbergen, Robertson & Porter, 1980).
4. Stop words removed.
5. Usernames and URL's removed.
6. The case of tweet changed to lowercase.

7. LEXICON GENERATION

We built an opinion lexicon for feature extraction to be used by the opinion classifier. The lexicon contains seed words representing opinion mined. For all the classes of opinion that are to be mined in the Twitter dataset, we built the lexicon. Lexicon was initially developed using initial seed seeds for all classes and later on extended by using distributional semantic similarity models like Word2vec [Mikolov, T., Chen, K., Corrado, G., & Dean, J. (2013)]. The initial seed set is created using domain experts who choose the seed words belonging to the different opinions to be mined. The seed set is then extended to capture the domain specific features using distributional semantic models. Word2Vec reduces the bias that may creep into the annotation process. We have used Skip-gram model of the Word2Vec algorithm. To this model entire dataset given as lemmas of words to train the Word2Vec model.

Word2vec algorithm is a semantic distribution algorithm which allows us to capture domain dependent features. Word2vec gives vectors of each word, where vectors are the semantic extensions of the word probed. Word2vec was trained using the entire dataset downloaded and thus enabled us to capture domain-specific extensions of the word in the initial seed sets. Table 2 shows seed words in the initial seed set and Table 3 shows the distribution of words in the lexicon after seed extension using Word2Vec.

Table 2. Seed words in lexicon

Class	Seed words	# seed words
O1	Kashmir, prison, war, school, burn, pellet, blind, kill, child, grave, crpf, beat, force, human, right, violate, blood, fire, gun, curfew, Muslim, injury, force, occupy, shell, child, police, India	29
O2	education, effect, mask, youth, damage, problem, young, terrorist, religion, separatist, stone, pellet, throw, Geelani, unrest, want, state, Kashmir, militant, evacuate, dirty, illiterate, direction, dismiss, local	26
O3	Pakistan, ceasefire, violate, Nawaz, Taliban, isis, terrorist, Balochistan, illegal, fuel, unrest, terror, state, train, camp., pok, blackday, destabilize, claim, Kashmir, bomb, unrest, Nawaz, trouble	25
O4	Kashmir, referendum, dispute, territory, uno, resolve, issue, protest, separatist, love, silent, Burhan, hero, martyr, demand, freedom, Kashmir, develop, Congress, Abdullah, Azadi, Nehru, support, Burhan, Geelani	28
O5	Pakistan, valley, beauty, flag, banayaga, love, zindabad, support, Pakistani, fake, strike, China, support, Kashmiri, Jinnah, Jeeva, zindabad, Muslim, raise, issue, peace, peaceful, Islamic, poster	26
O6	part, India, Kashmir, with, celebrate, Diwali, legal, accession, army, job, accede, home, protect, love, Modi, PDP, Indian, Hindustani, discipline, win, bjp, Modi, game	26

Table 3. Distribution after extension

Class	# seed words after extension
O1	231
O2	137
O3	97
O4	225
O5	40
O6	98

8. FEATURE SELECTION

Features were extracted using java. We used following features for our classification:

1. **Unigrams**: Unigrams are nouns, adjectives, noun verbs from the corpus.
2. **Bigrams**: bigrams are the randomly selected two unigrams.
3. **Trigrams**: Trigrams are the three words. The word after and before the middle word depends on the middle word. The middle word is chosen from the seed set, after reading the tweet if the seed word exists there we choose words before and after the seed word in the tweet to form the trigram.
4. **Adjective**: Adjectives are extracted from the corpus using the Stanford NLP toolkit
5. **POS-Bigrams**: using the same NLP toolkit we extracted adjectives and proper nouns from the corpus to generate the POS-bigrams.
6. **Opinion lexicon**. We use opinion lexicon as a domain dependent features. The opinion lexicon serves as a domain dependent features as they are related to the mining of opinion directly and are more correlated with the opinion to be mined.

9. OPINION CORPUS

Any corpora annotations are reliable only when we have multiple annotations for the same tweet by multiple judges. We used five annotators to annotate our corpus. A total of 12,000 tweets randomly selected from the dataset were chosen for annotation. Annotators did not receive any training but were shown samples to make them understand what kinds of annotation were required. Each annotator has to label a tweet with a category among the six opinion classes namely: O1, O2, O3, O4, O5, O6 or Neutral if no opinion is found. Thus, an opinion corpus has seven labels, six opinion classes plus neutral. From the 12,000 tweets, we choose only those tweets where at least three annotators have agreed, and thus our opinion corpus has 9,818 tweets. Table 4 shows the distribution of opinion classes in the opinion corpus. Figure 4 shows the percentages of opinion classes in manually annotated opinion corpus.

Table 4. Distribution of opinion classes in the manually annotated corpus

Class	# of instances in manually annotated opinion corpus
O1	2544
O2	1638
O3	1562
O4	2534
O5	171
O6	837
neutral	532
Total	9818

Figure 4. Percentages of opinion classes in manually annotated opinion corpus

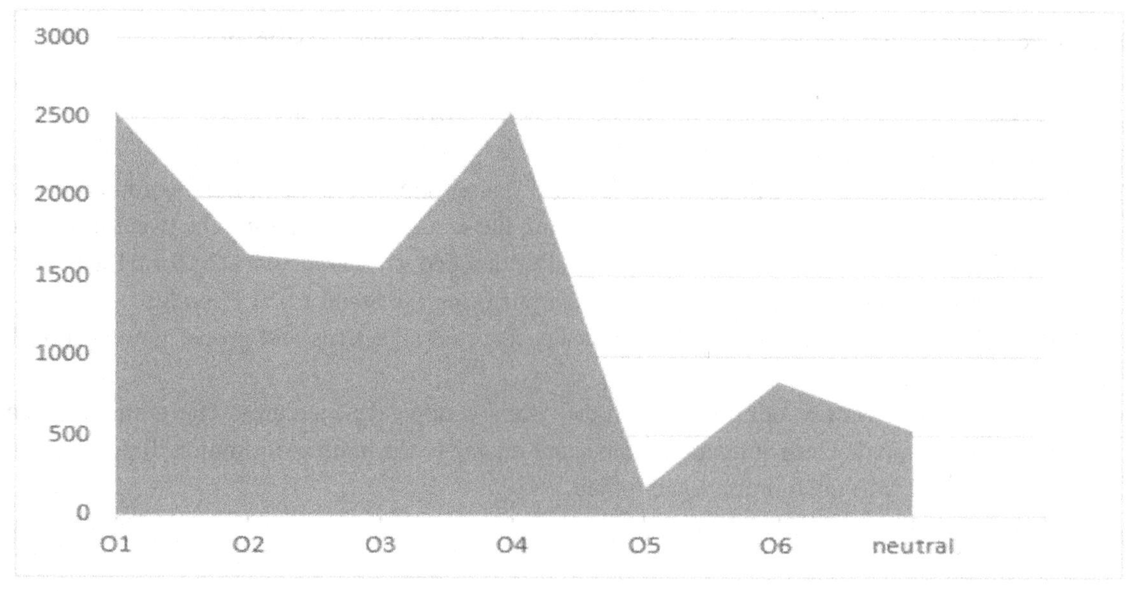

10. AUTOMATIC CLASSIFIER

Our automatic opinion classifier uses Support vector machine ($SVM^{multiclass}$) for classification. It processes input as vectors in a feature weight combination. We transform features generated in the preceding phase into vectors for classification. We have used different combinations of features to test our classification.

$SVM^{multiclass}$ uses multiclass formulization described in [22], but it optimizes it with an algorithm that is fast in linear case For a training set (x1, y1) ... (xn,yn) with labels yi in [1..k], it finds the solution of the following optimization problem during training.

$$\min 1/2\Sigma i=1..k\ wi*wi + C/n\ \Sigma i=1..n\ \xi i$$

$$\text{for all } y \text{ in } [1..k]: [\ x1 \bullet wyi\ ] >= [\ x1 \bullet wy\ ] + 100*\Delta(y1,y) - \xi 1$$

$$\text{for all } y \text{ in } [1..k]: [\ xn \bullet wyn\ ] >= [\ xn \bullet wy\ ] + 100*\Delta(yn,y) - \xi n$$

C is the usual regularization parameter that trades off margin size and training error. Δ(yn,y) is the loss function that returns 0 if yn equals y, and 1 otherwise.

The opinion classifier takes as input the set of tweets and the set of labels which are opinions that are to be mined and returns the set of tweets labelled with the opinion classes. The pinion classifier uses the features for opinion extraction and creates a model using $SVM^{muticlass}$ based on the features and then the model is used for inference of opinion for the unknown test examples.

10.1. Proposed Algorithm

The algorithm of the opinion classifier is as follows:

1. Use domain experts to generate seed words for the opinion classes.
2. Train Word2Vec model using the corpus for which mining is to be done.
3. Extend the seed set generated in step (a) with the trained Word2Vec model to obtain the extended seed set to obtain the opinion lexicon
4. Preprocess the training corpus generated using crowd-sourcing to obtain the preprocessed training corpus.
5. Generate the features for opinion mining.
6. Convert features into numbers for the $SVM_{muticlass}$ training.
7. Preprocess, generate features and convert them into numbers of the test set for classification.

11. EVALUATION AND RESULTS

Our opinion classifier takes as input the set of tweets and six opinion classes named 01,02, ...O6 and the output of the classifier is the tweet along with the opinion label for the tweet or Neutral otherwise. We tested our classifier on the opinion corpus and got the accuracy of **75**.05% with macro-average of 72.32%, 67.72% and 68.71% for precision, recall and f1-score respectively.

Confusion matrices, accuracy, F_1- score, precision, and recall were used to evaluate the proposed opinion classifier. Confusion matrices are a good indicator of measuring the efficiency of the multi-class classifier. The general structure of a confusion matrix is shown in Table 5. The diagonal elements represent the true positives (correctly classified) of the classification process, represented by tp in the table and other elements in the corresponding row represent the false positives. Elements of the corresponding column represent the false negatives. Misclassifications are both false positives and false negatives.

Table 5. General structure of confusion matrix

		Predicted class			
		A	B	C	D
Known class	A	tp_A	eAB	eAC	eAD
	B	eBA	tp_B	eBC	eBD
	C	eCA	eCB	tp_C	eCD
	D	eDA	eDB	eDC	tp_D

Precision is the ratio of true-positives to the sum of false negatives and true positives. Mathematically, the precision of class A is defined as:

$$Precison\ A = \frac{tpA}{tpA + fpA}$$

Where tp_A is the true positives of class A and fp_A is the false positives of all classes corresponding to class A. The recall is the ratio of true positives to the sum of true positives and false negatives. Mathematically, recall of class A is defined as

Where tp_A is the true positives of class A and fn_A is the false negatives of all classes corresponding to class A.The harmonic mean of both precision and recall gives F-score of the classifier. Mathematically F_1-score of classifier is

$$\text{Fl} - \text{score} = 2 * \frac{\text{precision} * \text{recall}}{\text{precision+recall}}$$

Accuracy is the ratio of correct classifications to the total classifications. Mathematically,

$$\text{Accuracy} = \frac{tpc}{total}$$

There tpc is the sum of all true positives and total is the total no of classifications. We used leave one out validation for the evaluation purpose.

Table 6 shows the confusion matrix and results of our classifier. Figure 5 shows the graph of our precision, recall and f-score for different opinion classes classified by our classifier.

Table 6. Confusion matrix and evaluation

	Confusion matrix							Results		
	O1	**O2**	**O3**	**O4**	**O5**	**O6**	**Neutral**	**Precision**	**Recall**	**F1-score**
O1	1658	56	220	119	10	26	19	66.23	75.52	70.57
O2	49	1008	65	108	0	102	12	64.53	75.56	69.41
O3	139	0	1102	0	0	180	17	67.27	76.63	71.64
O4	63	192	74	810	0	220	19	96.77	58.70	73.13
O5	21	14	0	5	110	9	0	64.32	67.90	66.06
O6	493	209	73	15	13	1623	23	64.04	66.27	65.13
Neutral	80	97	84	15	12	185	442	83.08	53..21	65.09
Macro-average								72.32	67.72	68.71
Accuracy								75.05%		

Figure 5. Precision, recall and F1-score of different opinion classes

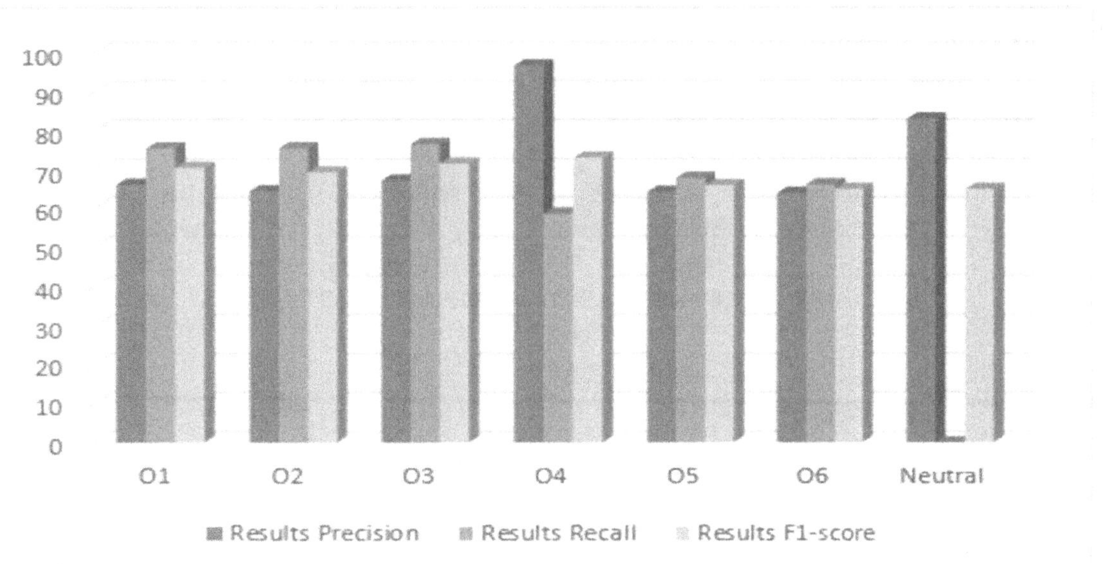

12. DISCUSS AND COMPARATIVE ANALYSIS

In this section, we will discuss results of our algorithm and compare our proposed approach with other similar techniques. We have achieved accuracy of 75.05% with macro-average of 72.32%, 67.72% and 68.71% for precision, recall and f1-score respectively. While the agreement between results of our proposed algorithm and manual annotation was found to be having accuracy of 75.05%. Using initial seed set as starting point, which was created by domain experts, the domain specific word extension was done using word2vec algorithm. Table 7 and Figure 6 compares the results of our opinion classifier with the similar studies results.

Table 7. Comparative analysis

Technique	Accuracy
Proposed algorithm	75.05%
Canales, Strapparava, Boldrini & Martnez-Barco, 2016	59.5%
Mikolov, Chen, Corrado & Dean, 2013	65.2%
Balabantaray, Mohammad, & Sharma, 2012	73.05%

Figure 6. Comparative analysis of different techniques

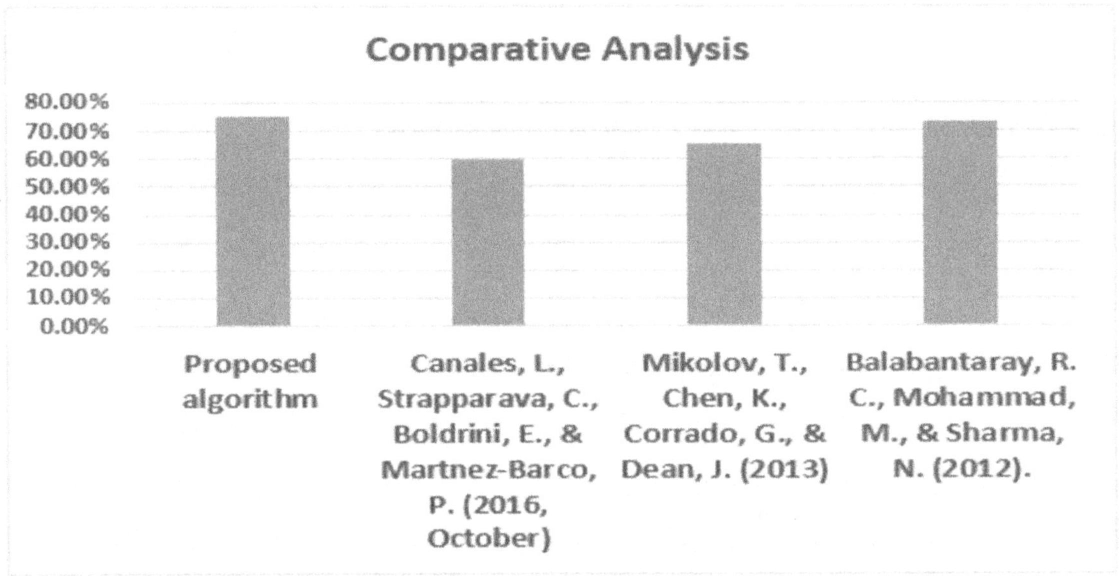

13. CONCLUSION

This research is about the opinion mining using supervised classifiers, use of extensive features to improve the classifier accuracy. This research aims to build an efficient opinion corpus that is usable for opinion mining purpose. The supervised classifier is trained on well-crafted opinion corpus, and results confirm the competitive performance and robustness of the system. Our proposed algorithm achieved an overall accuracy of 75.05%. With the micro-average precision of 72.32%, recall of 67.72% and f1-score of 68.71% which is higher than the baseline accuracy.

In our future work, we will use more lexicographical, and topic modulation features to improve the performance of our supervised classifier. Usage of Glove for lexicon building will also be explored.

REFERENCES

Agarwal, A., Xie, B., Vovsha, I., Rambow, O., & Passonneau, R. (2011, June). Sentiment analysis of twitter data. In *Proceedings of the workshop on languages in social media*(pp. 30-38). Association for Computational Linguistics.

Balabantaray, R. C., Mohammad, M., & Sharma, N. (2012). Multi-class twitter emotion classification: A new approach. *International Journal of Applied Information Systems*, *4*(1), 48–53. doi:10.5120/ijais12-450651

Canales, L., Strapparava, C., Boldrini, E., & Martnez-Barco, P. (2016, October). Exploiting a bootstrapping approach for automatic annotation of emotions in texts. In *2016 IEEE International Conference on Data Science and Advanced Analytics (DSAA)* (pp. 726-734). IEEE. 10.1109/DSAA.2016.78

Das, N., Borra, S., Dey, N., & Borah, S. (2018). Social Networking in Web Based Movie Recommendation System. In *Social Networks Science: Design, Implementation, Security, and Challenges* (pp. 25–45). Cham: Springer. doi:10.1007/978-3-319-90059-9_2

Das, S., & Chen, M. (2001, July). Yahoo! for Amazon: Extracting market sentiment from stock message boards. In *Proceedings of the Asia Pacific finance association annual conference (APFA)* (Vol. 35, p. 43).

Dave, K., Lawrence, S., & Pennock, D. M. (2003, May). Mining the peanut gallery: Opinion extraction and semantic classification of product reviews. In *Proceedings of the 12th international conference on World Wide Web* (pp. 519-528). ACM. 10.1145/775152.775226

Dey, N., Babo, R., Ashour, A. S., Bhatnagar, V., & Bouhlel, M. S. (2018). Social Networks Science: Design. In Implementation, Security, and Challenges From Social Networks Analysis to Social Networks Intelligence.

Go, A., Bhayani, R., & Huang, L. (2009). Twitter sentiment classification using distant supervision. CS224N Project Report, Stanford, 1(12).

Gore, R. J., Diallo, S., & Padilla, J. (2015). You are what you tweet: Connecting the geographic variation in America's obesity rate to twitter content. *PLoS One*, *10*(9). doi:10.1371/journal.pone.0133505 PMID:26332588

Hall, M., Frank, E., Holmes, G., Pfahringer, B., Reutemann, P., & Witten, I. H. (2009). The WEKA data mining software: an update. *ACM SIGKDD explorations newsletter, 11*(1), 10-18.

Java, A., Song, X., Finin, T., & Tseng, B. (2007, August). Why we twitter: understanding microblogging usage and communities. In *Proceedings of the 9th WebKDD and 1st SNA-KDD 2007 workshop on Web mining and social network analysis* (pp. 56-65). ACM. 10.1145/1348549.1348556

Joachims, T., Finley, T., & Yu, C. N. J. (2009). Cutting-plane training of structural SVMs. *Machine Learning*, *77*(1), 27–59. doi:10.100710994-009-5108-8

Kamal, S., Dey, N., Ashour, A. S., Ripon, S., Balas, V. E., & Kaysar, M. S. (2017). FbMapping: An automated system for monitoring Facebook data. *Neural Network World*, *27*(1), 27–57. doi:10.14311/NNW.2017.27.002

Kouloumpis, E., Wilson, T., & Moore, J. D. (2011). Twitter sentiment analysis: The good the bad and the omg! *Icwsm, 11*(538-541), 164.

Krammer, K., & Singer, Y. (2001). On the algorithmic implementation of multi-class SVMs. In *Proc. of JMLR* (pp. 265-292).

Lan, K., Wang, D. T., Fong, S., Liu, L. S., Wong, K. K., & Dey, N. (2018). A Survey of Data Mining and Deep Learning in Bioinformatics. *Journal of Medical Systems, 42*(8), 139. doi:10.100710916-018-1003-9 PMID:29956014

Manning, C., Surdeanu, M., Bauer, J., Finkel, J., Bethard, S., & McClosky, D. (2014). The Stanford CoreNLP natural language processing toolkit. In *Proceedings of 52nd annual meeting of the association for computational linguistics: system demonstrations* (pp. 55-60). 10.3115/v1/P14-5010

Mikolov, T., Chen, K., Corrado, G., & Dean, J. (2013). Efficient estimation of word representations in vector space. arXiv:1301.3781

Miller, G. A. (1995). WordNet: A lexical database for English. *Communications of the ACM, 38*(11), 39–41. doi:10.1145/219717.219748

Mohammad, S. M., Zhu, X., Kiritchenko, S., & Martin, J. (2015). Sentiment, emotion, purpose, and style in electoral tweets. *Information Processing & Management, 51*(4), 480–499. doi:10.1016/j.ipm.2014.09.003

Nakov, P., Ritter, A., Rosenthal, S., Sebastiani, F., & Stoyanov, V. (2016). SemEval-2016 task 4: Sentiment analysis in Twitter. In *Proceedings of the 10th International Workshop on Semantic Evaluation (SemEval-2016)* (pp. 1-18). 10.18653/v1/S16-1001

Pak, A., & Paroubek, P. (2010, May). Twitter as a corpus for sentiment analysis and opinion mining. In LREc (Vol. 10, pp. 1320-1326).

Pang, B., & Lee, L. (2004, July). A sentimental education: Sentiment analysis using subjectivity summarization based on minimum cuts. In *Proceedings of the 42nd annual meeting on Association for Computational Linguistics* (p. 271). Association for Computational Linguistics. 10.3115/1218955.1218990

Pang, B., & Lee, L. (2008). Opinion mining and sentiment analysis. *Foundations and Trends in Information Retrieval, 2*(1–2), 1-135.

Pang, B., Lee, L., & Vaithyanathan, S. (2002, July). Thumbs up?: sentiment classification using machine learning techniques. In *Proceedings of the ACL-02 conference on Empirical methods in natural language processing* (Vol. 10, pp. 79-86). Association for Computational Linguistics. 10.3115/1118693.1118704

Popescu, A. M., & Etzioni, O. (2007). Extracting product features and opinions from reviews. In *Natural language processing and text mining* (pp. 9–28). London: Springer. doi:10.1007/978-1-84628-754-1_2

Saif, H., He, Y., & Alani, H. (2012, November). Semantic sentiment analysis of twitter. In *International semantic web conference* (pp. 508-524). Springer. 10.1007/978-3-642-35176-1_32

Sarlan, A., Nadam, C., & Basri, S. (2014, November). Twitter sentiment analysis. In *2014 International Conference on Information Technology and Multimedia (ICIMU)* (pp. 212-216). IEEE. 10.1109/ICIMU.2014.7066632

Sidorov, G., Miranda-Jiménez, S., Viveros-Jiménez, F., Gelbukh, A., Castro-Sánchez, N., Velásquez, F., . . . Gordon, J. (2012, October). Empirical study of machine learning based approach for opinion mining in tweets. In *Mexican international conference on Artificial intelligence* (pp. 1-14). Springer.

Turney, P. D. (2002, July). Thumbs up or thumbs down?: semantic orientation applied to unsupervised classification of reviews. In *Proceedings of the 40th annual meeting on association for computational linguistics* (pp. 417-424). Association for Computational Linguistics.

Turney, P. D., & Littman, M. L. (2003). Measuring praise and criticism: Inference of semantic orientation from association. *ACM Transactions on Information Systems*, *21*(4), 315–346. doi:10.1145/944012.944013

Van Rijsbergen, C. J., Robertson, S. E., & Porter, M. F. (1980). *New models in probabilistic information retrieval*. London: British Library Research and Development Department.

Yan, J. L. S., Turtle, H. R., & Liddy, E. D. (2016). EmoTweet-28: a fine-grained emotion corpus for sentiment analysis. In *Proceedings of the 10th International Conference on Language Resources and Evaluation. LREC* (pp. 1149-1156).

Zhuang, L., Jing, F., & Zhu, X. Y. (2006, November). Movie review mining and summarization. In *Proceedings of the 15th ACM international conference on Information and knowledge management* (pp. 43-50). ACM.

ENDNOTES

1 https://dev.twitter.com/streaming/overview
2 http://twitter4j.org/en
3 https://en.wikipedia.org/wiki/2016-17-kashmirunrest

This research was previously published in the International Journal of Synthetic Emotions (IJSE), 9(2); pages 23-36, copyright year 2018 by IGI Publishing (an imprint of IGI Global).

Chapter 22
Implementation of Recurrent Network for Emotion Recognition of Twitter Data

Anu Kiruthika M.
Anna University, Chennai, India

Angelin Gladston
Anna University, Chennai, India

ABSTRACT

A new generation of emoticons, called emojis, is being largely used for both mobile and social media communications. Emojis are considered a graphic expression of emotions, and users have been widely used to express their emotions in social media. Emojis are graphic unicode symbols used to express perceptions, views, and ideas as a shorthand. Unlike the small number of well-known emoticons carrying clear emotional content, hundreds of emojis are being used in different social networks. The task of emoji emotion recognition is to predict the original emoji in a tweet. Recurrent neural network is used for building emoji emotion recognition system. Glove is a word-embedding method used for obtaining vector representation of words and are used for training the recurrent neural network. This is achieved by mapping words into a meaningful space where the distance between words is related to semantic similarity. Based on the word embedding in the Twitter dataset, recurrent neural network builds the model and finally predicts the emoji associated with the tweets with an accuracy of 83%.

1. INTRODUCTION

Developing social network platforms has given people a new way of generating and consuming a lot of web-based information (Dixit et. al., 2017). People used to obtain information from portal websites in the past. A large number of websites today provide information on a long list of subjects that vary from politics to entertainment. These traditional online information sources are always useful, but are less efficient since they often contain redundant information. Due to the arrival of online social network

DOI: 10.4018/978-1-6684-6303-1.ch022

platforms, people tend to get information from them in a faster pace and is more efficient. These platforms are available for users to choose the information source they are interested in. To mention, large number of social network platforms such as, Twitter, Google+, and Facebook provide information to users (Geetha et. al., 2019; Xiong et. al., 2018).

The most popular platform for microblogging is Twitter. It is one of the fastest growing social network platforms and has a dominant microblogging position. Every day, more than 500 million registered users post 340 million twitter messages (Dixit et. al., 2017; Mohammad et. al., 2015), sharing their views and activities every day. Twitter posts are much shorter than those on regular microblogging platforms (Pak et. al., 2010; Pennington et. al., 2014). Only 140 characters or less can be posted in one twitter message (Dixit et. al., 2017). This feature makes twitter easier and keeps it distinct from the massive amount of information available online for people to get the main point. In twitter, communication is made through messages commonly referred as the tweets. In this social website, people are allowed to make posts about different things, thus enabling people to get their required information from the massive amount of information available.

Twitter users can follow whatever people and source of information they prefer, depending on the users' needs. Twitter has therefore become a powerful platform with many kinds of information from worldwide breaking news to buying products at home, with all the benefits mentioned above. The information streams on twitter have experienced an incredible increase in the popularity of social network over the past few years. Users have a huge amount of information on various aspects (Unnisa et. al., 2016). Not all the information is useful to users however, and each user has their own interests and preferences. There is urgency for users to have personalized services. Nowadays, more and more personalized services are provided to benefit the users. People need this personalized service to make their fast-paced lives more efficient.

Every day, users are publishing a large amount of information on the twitter platform. Twitter data is related to the behaviour of the user and therefore many research studies focus on twitter and its collection of data. One of the twitter based research is user modelling. Researchers started to explore rankings and recommendations of twitter-referenced web resources to provide a personalized service. Based on their published tweets, a large amount of research focuses on modelling users and interests. Microblogs such as Twitter and SinaWeibo are a kind of popular social media (Pennington et. al., 2014) in which millions of people express their feelings, emotions, and attitudes. Because a large number of microblog posts are generated on a daily basis, the mining of feelings from this data source helps to perform research on various topics, such as analysing brand reputation, predicting the stock market, and detecting abnormal events.

It is therefore crucial to improve the performance of the tasks of sentiment analysis in microblog environments (Li et. al., 2017). In recent years, microblog sentiment analysis (Al-Halah et. al., 2019) has been a hot research area and several important issues have been studied, such as identifying whether a post is subjective or objective, called subjectivity classification, identifying whether a post is positive or negative, i.e. polarity classification, and recognizing emotion in a particular post. Supervised machine learning techniques have been widely adopted for analysing microblog feelings and have proved effective. Different features, such as sentiment lexicons, part-of-speech tags, and microblogging features, were used to reinforce the classifiers. However, due to the large vocabulary adopted by microblog users, the manual labelling of sufficient training posts is extremely labor intensive. Fortunately, different emoticons are often adopted in microblog environments and are usually posted along with emotional words (Xia et. al., 2017). In addition, in many microblog platforms, graphical emoticons, which are more accurate than those composed of punctuation marks, have been introduced. Emoticons can thus serve as an efficient source of emotional signals, enabling tasks for the classification of feelings to be performed without or with a small number of manually labelled posts (Bulut et. al., 2019).

Recognizing the emotion of the user is a major challenge for people and machines alike. On one hand, at certain times, people may not be able to recognize or state their own emotions. On the other hand, machines need precise ground truth for modelling emotions, as well as advanced algorithms for machine learning to develop emotion models. Sensors provide data sources, such as audio, gestures, eye gazes and brain signals that may be relevant to emotion recognition in hard sensing methods. Additional sensors may be attached to the user to provide personal physiological cues such as heart rate sensors, however these wearable sensors are not applicable in practical and natural settings, since they can be obtrusive to the user. Soft sensing methods, on the other hand, extract information from software that already exists with the user, on their phone. Events of positive and negative feelings and overall impressions have been studied in order to understand the nature and usage of such characters (Liu, 2012). Public opinions about global happenings can be analysed as the main resource to investigate the effects and usage of Emoji characters (Colneriĉ & Demsar, 2018) on social network sentiments.

Deep learning has recently shown a lot of success. Previous works have studied only one emotion classification. Working with multiple classifications simultaneously not only enables performance comparisons between different emotion categorizations on the same type of, but also allows us to develop a single model for predicting multiple classifications at the same time. It is better to train recurrent neural networks on sequences of characters than on sequences of words. Recurrent neural networks are connectionist models of sequential data that are naturally applicable to the analysis of emotion in tweets.

Detecting emotion from text is a relatively new classification task and advances in textual analysis have made emotion detection a recent interest in the natural language processing field. (Dixit et. al., 2017; Irsoy et. al., 2014). Every time the text need not contain any emotion indicating words such as anger, fear, shame, but when they have expressed their feelings indirectly, it can also contribute to the user's emotion. Different techniques (Cappallo et. al., 2019; Mohammad et. al., 2015) are used to identify and analyse emotion in such cases.Hence, the combination of text and emoji can be used for the emotion recognition, more accurately even for an indirectly expressed emotion.

The proposed emotion recognition system utilizes the features of emoji for more accurate results so that the emotion expressed, even in a different ways can be recognized. The contributions in this paper are i) the emoji emotion recognition framework, ii) the combined approach utilizing text and emoji for emotion recognition, iii) utilization of glove word embedding for characterizing the emotion, and iv) application of emoji based features to train the RNN based emotion recognition framework along with the experimentation of more than one such for emotion recognition. The remainder of this paper is organized as follows: Section 2 presents discussion on various related works. Section 3 introduces the proposed emotion recognition system in detail. Section 4 provides the experimental results and the discussion on results. Conclusions drawn from the experiments are presented in Section 5.

2. LITERATURE REVIEW

There has been significant progress in the development of emotion recognition, and numerous approaches have been used so far in the literatures. This section presents discussion on various related works and on the research gaps that are present.

In their work, Colneriĉ, & Demsar (2018) suggested a model to detect the emotions in the tweets by using the deep learning methods. Given some text, emotion recognition algorithms detect which emotions the writer wanted to express when composing it. To treat this problem as a special case of text classification, it is necessary to define a set of basic emotions. Although emotions have long been studied by psychologists, there is no single, standard set of basic emotions. Therefore, they worked with the classifications that are the most popular, and have also been used before by the researchers from computational linguistics and natural language processing (NLP). Paul Ekman defined six basic emotions by studying facial expressions. Robert Plutchik extended Ekman's categorization with two additional emotions and presented his categorization in a wheel of emotions. Finally, Profile of Mood States (POMS) is a psychological instrument that defines a six-dimensional mood state representation. Each dimension is defined by a set of emotional adjectives, like bitter, and the individual's mood is assessed by how strongly the person experienced such a feeling in the last month.

Majority of previous studies predict either Ekman's or Plutchiks's classifications, while POMS's adjectives had only been used in simple keyword spotting algorithms are not aware of any studies that tackle the problem of predicting POMS's categories from the text. Methodologically, they mainly used simple classification algorithms, like logistic regression or support vector machines, on top of word and n-gram counts, and other custom engineered features capturing the use of punctuation, the presence or absence of negation, and counts of words from various emotion lexicons.

Irsoy et. al., (2014) suggested an application of deep recurrent neural networks to the task of sentence-level opinion expression extraction. Recurrent neural networks (RNNs) are connectionist models of sequential data that are naturally applicable to the analysis of natural language. Recently, "depth in space" as an orthogonal notion to "depth in time" in RNNs has been investigated by stacking multiple layers of RNNs and shown empirically to bring a temporal hierarchy to the architecture. These deep RNNs are applied to the task of opinion expression extraction formulated as a token-level sequence-labelling task. Experimental results show that deep, narrow RNNs outperform traditional shallow, wide RNNs with the same number of parameters. Furthermore, this approach outperforms previous CRF-based baselines, including the state-of-the-art semi-Markov CRF model, and does so without access to the powerful opinion lexicons and syntactic features relied upon by the semi-CRF, as well as without the standard layer-by-layer pre-training typically required of RNN architectures.

The sentiment analysis proposed in the work, (Liu, 2012) is a growing area of the task of natural language processing at many granularity levels. Starting from being a document level classification task, it was handled at the sentence level and even at the polarity of words and phrases at the phrase level more recently. The informal and specialized language used in tweets and the nature of the micro-blogging domain, however, make Twitter's sentiment analysis a very different task. With the increasing number of blogs and social networks, the analysis of opinion mining and sentiment has become fields of interest for many researches. Researchers have also started to investigate different ways of collecting data on training automatically. Several researchers used emoticons to define training data and hashtags to create training data, but limited their experiments to the classification of sentiment or non-sentiment rather than the multi-way classification of emotions presented in this article. Extending research to many different types of emotions is a very new concept and has not yet been studied extensively. There are currently few examples where researchers have gone beyond the polarity of analysis of sentiment. Predicted feelings of five different dimensions with Pluck's emotion wheel model and a rule-based approach to detecting emotions in the text.

Na'aman et. al., (2017), suggested that emoji was seen primarily as an indicator of feeling by many of the previous work. This is done either explicitly, by considering sentiment directly, or implicitly by considering only popular emoji. The most popular emoji are disproportionately composed of sentiment-laden emoji. Face emojis, thumbs-up, and hearts have high incidence, while fewer emoji such as symbols, objects, and flags have much lower incidence. As a result, any work that considers only the most popular emoji with heavy feeling may have an inherent bias towards emoji. Several works examine the effect that may have on the perception of accompanying text, including emoji. Some find that emoji inclusion increases the perceived level of feeling attached to a message. These works show that emoji can be a useful additional signal for identifying emotions within text messages, but these works focus primarily on face emoji specifically designed for emotion communication. By the time, the effect of non-face emoji is also investigated. They found that even non-face emoji can increase perceived emotion, as well as enhance the clarity of otherwise ambiguous text. When considered alone, some text phrases are ambiguous, but the inclusion of another modality namely emoji may help readers identify the intended meaning.

Analysis of traditional feelings or emotions is an important research task that has attracted many researchers in the field of processing natural language. Li et. al., (2017) focused on the classification of polarities between positive and negative, or extends to the third polarity of neutral, or sometimes adds fine-grained classes such as a very positive and very negative spectrum. Predefined types of emotion are also involved in some work on sentiment analysis, such as happy, sad, and so on, while the classification of emotions might be multi-label at times. Recent years, research work appears to be continuously using these technologies to improve the performance of sentiment analysis with the development of word embedding and neural networks. Since word embedding might well represent its semantic characteristics and latent information, it is natural to add sentiment-specific information to the word embedding while training through neural networks.

In addition, in certain specific scenarios, particularly on social networks, the context of human interaction is considered to improve the analysis of feelings. In addition to using emoji as a kind of remote supervision, emoji or emoticons are also related to the expression of feelings. In plain-text computer-mediated communication, emoticons could indicate sentiment polarities and a sentiment map is established for several hundred types of the most frequently used emoji, both to improve the performance of sentiment analysis.

Despite research work that suggests a multi-modal approach to generating emoji labels for an image, there is still lack of effort to match emoji with plain text. Thus, we propose an emoji emotion recognition system that adjusts the problem of classifying emoji with word embedding learning, which is more complicated than traditional feeling or emotional analysis. The proposed approach builds an RNN based emoji emotion recognition model thereby achieving better recognition performance. Research has become very popular on Twitter these years, in which users post their thoughts on a variety of topics across the globe, discuss current issues, criticise and share many types of feelings. Even so, most of them have not been implemented based on emoticon work, so we are improving emoji prediction work and future strategies that significantly enhance the recognition of many forms of emotions, so that emoji-based work can be used for opinion mining, sentiment and emotion analysis.

Comparing to the works discussed, in this work, for converting the tweets into vector format, the glove word embedding method has been used. Word representations, Glove becomes a global log-bilinear regression model that outperforms other models on word analogy, word similarity, and named entity recognition tasks. Even with little corpus and small vectors, glove provides reasonable output.

3. EXPERIMENTAL DESIGN

This section presents the detailed design of the proposed emotion recognition approach from emojis present in tweets. Twitter is an ever-growing social-media platform where users post tweets, or small messages, for all of their followers to see and react to. Currently, Twitter handles approximately six thousand new tweets every second, so there is plenty of data to be analysed. With a character limit of 140 per tweet, emojis are commonly used to express feelings in a tweet without using extra characters that may be required for more explanation. This is helpful in identifying the mood or state of mind that a person may have been in, when writing their tweet. From a computing standpoint, this makes mood analysis much easier. Rather than analysing the group of words and predicting moods from keywords, we can analyse single or many emojis, and then match those emojis to commonly expressed emotions and feelings. The objective of this work is to gather large amounts of Twitter data and analyse emojis by using the RNN (Colneriĉ & Demsar, 2018) and thereby recognize the emotions expressed. Dataset used in the emoji recognition approach, named emoji dataset, consists of tweets collected from Twitter.

Figure 1 shows the overall diagram of the proposed emoji emotion recognition system, which takes in the tweets with emojis which are collected from Twitter as input. From the collected tweets with emojis, the emojis are extracted using tweet extraction. Glove word embedding is used for arriving at the vector representation of the word. These vectors are fed into RNN which gets trained and the emoji prediction model is built. The model built is a multiclass classification model and its purpose being classification of emoji in the tweets into five classes.

Figure 1. Emoji Emotion Recognition System

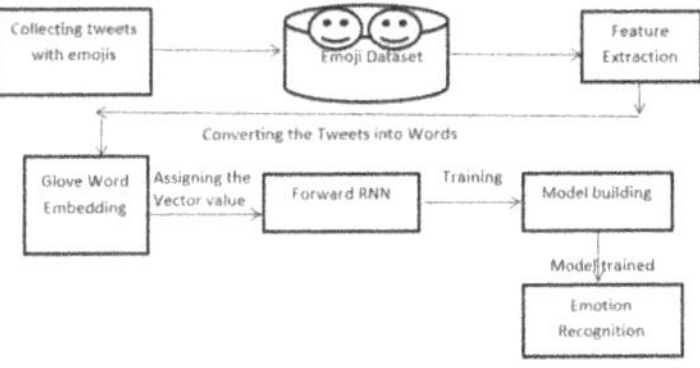

Figure 2 shows the activities involved using an activity diagram of the proposed emoji emotion recognition system. First activity is collection of tweets with emoji from Twitter. Once this collection is completed, extraction activity follows. The tweets are converted into words and the emojis are extracted. Next activity is to use Glove algorithm for assigning into vectors. These vectors are taken as input in the following activity, RNN model generation. Model is built and the model obtained is used to recognize the emojis.

3.1. Glove Word Embedding

Glove word embedding takes the tweets with emojis, converts the tweets into words and assigns each with a vector value thus help arrive the vector form. The Glove algorithm used consists of the following steps: Collect word co-occurrence statistics in the form of a word co-occurrence matrix, X.

Figure 2. Activity Diagram for Emoji Emotion Recognition

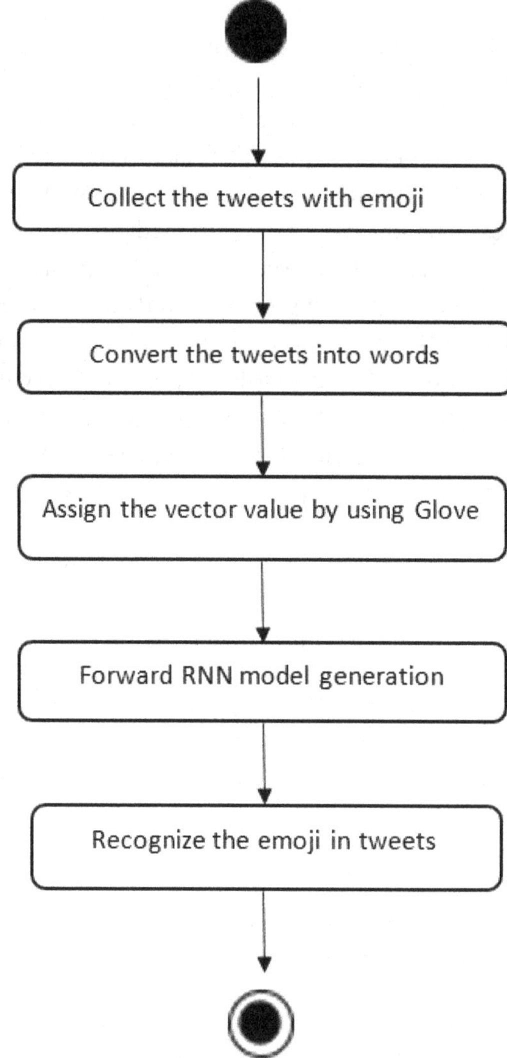

1. Each element X_{ij} of such matrix represents how often word i appears in context of word j.
2. Scanning the corpus in the following manner:
   a. For each term look for context terms within some area, defined by the window size before the, and the window size after the term. Also, less weight are assigned for more distant words as in the Equation (1):

$$decay=1/offset \quad (1)$$

3. Soft constraints for each word pair is defined as in the Equation (2):

$$W_i^T w_j + b_i + b_j = \log(X_{ij}) \quad (2)$$

where:

- w_i - vector for the main word
- w_j - vector for the context word
- b_i, b_j - scalar biases for the main and context words.

Cost function used can be defined as in the Equation (3):

$$J = f(X_{ij})\,(w_i^T w_j + b_i + b_j - \log X_{ij})^2 \tag{3}$$

where f is a weighting function which help us to prevent learning only from extremely common word pairs.

3.2. Emoji Emotion Recognition Model

The vectors obtained are used to train and build the emoji emotion recognition model. Because of its widespread applicability as discussed in the related work section, Recurrent neural networks are used to construct the emoji emotion recognition model. The parameters for RNN are set as follows: the number of classes is initialized as five set of emoji classes, number of training samples is 124 and the dimensions for glove vectors is set as 100. Initializing the network with the right weights is very important for the recurrent neural network to function properly. The weights are ensured whether they fall in a reasonable range before the start of training the network. This is where Xavier initialization comes into picture. Before training, we do not know anything about the data, so it is not sure on how to assign the weights that would work in that particular case. One good way is to assign the weights from a Gaussian distribution. Obviously, this distribution would have zero mean and some finite variance. Let's consider a linear neuron in the equation (4):

$$y = w_1 x_1 + w_2 x_2 + \ldots + w_N x_N + b \tag{4}$$

With each passing layer, the variance need to remain the same. This helps to keep the signal from exploding to a high value or vanishing to zero. In other words, we need to initialize the weights in such a way that the variance remains the same for x and y. This initialization process is known as Xavier initialization. Then the model is developed using forward RNN (Colneriĉ & Demsar, 2018). By using glove word embedding (Pennington et. al., 2014) with dimension 100, all the words are converted into vector form, and are given as the feature set for the RNN. Finally, the emoji in the tweets are recognized using the trained model. This emotion recognition based on emojis help extend the emotion recognition as multimodal, which further can strengthen the emotion recognition. In addition, recognizing emotion from emojis will help rule out confusions in recognizing complex emotions. Emotions expressed in short chats can be well taken for further analysis.

4. RESULTS AND DISCUSSION

This section presents in detail the experiments conducted, dataset used in the experiments, results obtained and the discussion on results. Experiments are conducted to recognize emotion from the emoji using the emoji emotion recognition system built. This is a classification of multiclass text and its aim is to classify the emoji in the tweets into five emoji classes.

4.1. Dataset

In these experiments, we use the emoji dataset consisting of tweets collected from twitter in the form of .csv file and are taken from the Kaggle repository. The dataset is made up of tweets and labels. The datasets are divided into two sub sets, one for training, 90% of dataset is used as training dataset and the other for testing, 10% of dataset is used as testing dataset. The emoji emotion recognition model is built using forward RNN. Each tweet is labelled with the five emoji sets, as given, in Figure 3. Then the dataset is pre-processed for segregating the emojis from the words.

Figure 3. Five emoji set

By using glove word embedding with dimension 100, all words are converted into a vector form which is taken as the RNN feature set. RNN initializes parameters namely, weight, bias, and model construction parameters using Xavier initialization as explained in previous section. Thus the emoji prediction system using RNN is built. The model built is tested with the testing dataset. The emoji associated with the test data are predicted and the results are obtained.

Evaluating the emoji prediction system built is carried out using various evaluation metrics. For evaluating the emoji prediction system, the evaluation metrics, namely, accuracy, precision, recall and f-score are used. Accuracy measures how often the classifier makes the correct prediction. Classification accuracy is the ratio of number of correct predictions to the total number of input samples or the prediction made as given by the Equation (5):

$$\text{Accuracy} = \frac{Number\ of\ correct\ predictions}{Total\ number\ of\ predictions\ made} \tag{5}$$

Table 1. Output for Sample Tweet

Input	Actual Output	Expected Output
I am upset		
Funny lot		
Food is ready		

Table 2. Mis-predicted Output for Sample Tweet

Input	Actual Output	Expected Output
Let us go play baseball	😞	⚾
Why are you feeling bad	😄	😞
I did not have breakfast	⚾	🍴

Table 1 and 2 show the sample output obtained by the emoji emotion recognition system for the cases where the emojis are correctly predicted as well as the emojis are wrongly predicted. As shown in Table 3, for evaluating the emoji emotion recognition system, confusion matrix is arrived at. From this, accuracy, precision, recall, and f-score are computed. True positive (TP) are the correctly predicted positive values which means that the value of actual class is yes and the value of predicted class is also yes. True negative (TN) are the correctly predicted negative values which means that the value of actual class is no and value of predicted class is also no. False positive (FP) are when actual class is no and predicted class is yes but predicted class is yes. False negative (FN) are when actual class is no and predicted class is yes but predicted class is no.

Table 3. Confusion Matrix

PREDICTED	❤	⚾	😄	😞	🍴
ACTUAL					
❤	6	0	0	1	0
⚾	0	8	0	0	0
😄	2	0	16	0	0
😞	1	1	2	12	0
🍴	0	0	1	0	6

In the confusion matrix, correctly predicted emotions are present in the diagonal of the matrix called TP. The sum of all values predicted by the individual class presented in the row of confusion matrix is called FP. A zero in row in confusion matrix shows TN and, in any column, represents the FN:

$$P = TP \div TP + FP \quad (6)$$

$$R = TP \div TP + FN \quad (7)$$

$$2 * P * R \div (P + R) \quad (8)$$

Evaluation metrics, namely precision, recall, and f-score are used to evaluate performance of the emoji emotion recognition system. The emoji prediction system classifies the tweets into the emoji classes and achieved the prediction accuracy of 83%. Figure 3 depicts the recognition of the emoji in the corresponding emoji label. The evaluation metrics used for evaluating the performance of the emoji prediction system are given in the equations (6), (7), and (8). The precision, recall and f-score values obtained for the emoji prediction system are plotted in the Figure 4. The f-score value achieved is 0.68. From these precisions obtained, 0.875, we infer the exactness of the emoji prediction. The achievement of the recall as 0.622, shows the less false negatives. Thus, considering the precision, recall and f-score values obtained for the emoji prediction system, as well the better accuracy achieved as 83% it can be inferred that the proposed emoji prediction system does predict well the emojis from the tweets.

Figure 4. Emoji Recognition across five classes

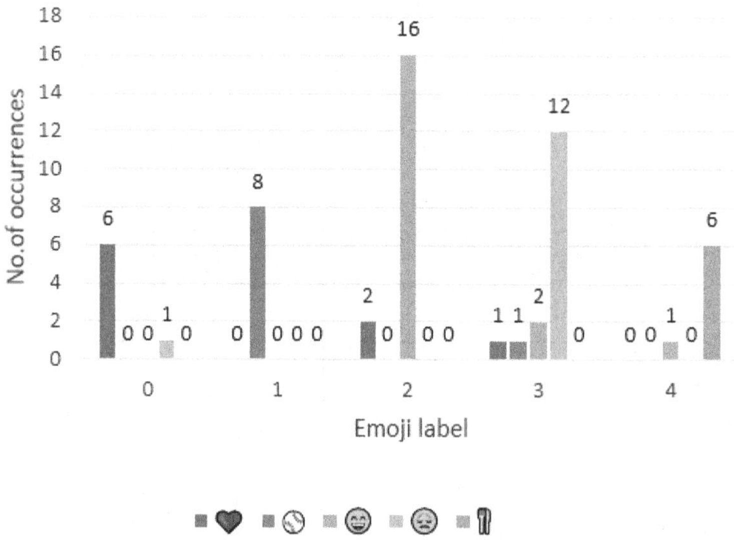

Figure 5. Precision, Recall and F-score

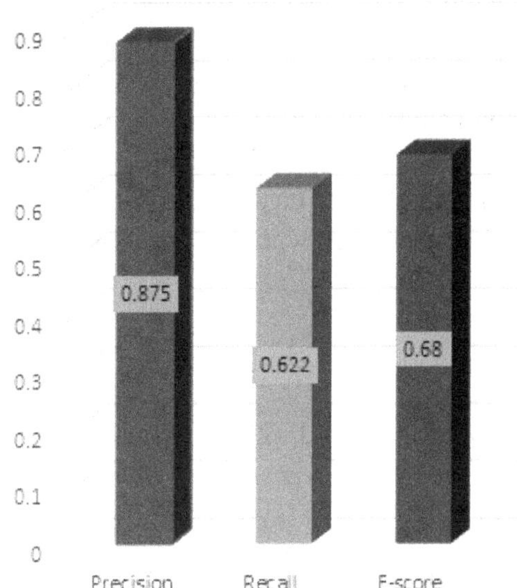

In this work, five emoji labels have been used and the model constructed is used to predict the emoji associated with every message. This work is limited to few emoji labels which could be extended for more emojis in future work. Here, the prediction is focused on the vector value of the embedding word. So, the tweets that belong to five emoji labels are predicted. Our analysis is based on the Twitter dataset, not the tweets that are gathered from Twitter platform and also less tweets are used as a dataset. This work can be extended for real-time tweets. With larger training dataset and also using other word embedding techniques, the model accuracy could increase further.

Working with a noisy dataset was a major part for predicting the emojis. People have different emoji meanings and sometimes mix several emojis with each another. In order to find these interpretations and multimodal emoji, more creativity is required. Future work could also tend to associate emojis and sentiments further. In most cases, emoji are used to extract opinions from user tweets and categorise them into negative, average and positive classes. The study of social media sentiment as an important source of knowledge is currently being used for various purposes, including detecting consumer dissatisfaction or product issues, predicting stock market prices as well as to predict the election outcome ahead.

5. CONCLUSION

Social media provides platforms for the users to share their opinions, feelings, personal contents. However, as it is often difficult to express emotion using text alone, accessibility is available to add non-verbal details such as images to a text. Emojis are one kind of non-verbal data. These emotional transmitters have proliferated over time they are now commonly used on electronic message boards, chat systems, and in e-mails. Microblogging such as on Twitter has today become one of the major types of communication. As a result of its large, diverse, and growing user base, Twitter's containing opinion information has been effectively used for several tasks, such as prediction of stock market trends, political monitoring, and inferring public mood on social events. The large amount of information contained in these websites makes them an attractive source of data for opinion mining and sentiment analysis. Most text-based methods of analysis may not always be useful for sentiment analysis in these domains. Researchers still need novel ideas to make significant progress in this area. Using symbol analysis that makes use of emoticons and emoji characters can significantly increase precision in recognising many kinds of emotions. In this work, presented the neural architecture for predicting the appropriate emoji associated with each post in twitter dataset based on the glove word embedding method with an accuracy of 83%. This work can be further experimented with many emojis as well in multiple categories.

REFERENCES

Al-Halah, Z., Aitken, A., Shi, W., & Caballero, J. (2019). Smile, be happy emoji embedding for visual sentiment analysis. *Proceedings of the IEEE International Conference on Computer Vision Workshops*. 10.1109/ICCVW.2019.00550

Bulut, İ., Erdoğan, M., Gönülal, B., Baş, R., & Kılıç, Ö. (2019, September). Using Short Texts and Emojis to Predict the Gender of a Texter in Turkish. In *2019 4th International Conference on Computer Science and Engineering (UBMK)* (pp. 435-438). IEEE. 10.1109/UBMK.2019.8907198

Cappallo, S., Svetlichnaya, S., Garrigues, P., Mensink, T., & Snoek, C. G. (2019). New Modality: Emoji Challenges in Prediction, Anticipation, and Retrieval. *IEEE Transactions on Multimedia*, *21*(2), 402–415. doi:10.1109/TMM.2018.2862363

Colneriĉ, N., & Demsar, J. (2018). (accepted for publication). Emotion recognition on Twitter: Comparative study and training a unison model. *IEEE Transactions on Affective Computing*.

Dixit, A., Pal, A. K., Temghare, S., & Mapari, V. (2017). Emotion detection using decision tree. *International Journal of Advance Engineering and Research Development*, *4*(2), 145–149.

Geetha, S., & Kumar, K. V. (2019). Tweet Analysis Based on Distinct Opinion of Social Media Users. In *Advances in Big Data and Cloud Computing* (pp. 251–261). Springer. doi:10.1007/978-981-13-1882-5_23

Irsoy, O., & Cardie, C. (2014). Opinion mining with deep recurrent neural networks. In *Proceedings of the 2014 conference on empirical methods in natural language processing (EMNLP)* (pp. 720-728). 10.3115/v1/D14-1080

Li, X., Yan, R., & Zhang, M. (2017, July). Joint emoji classification and embedding learning. In *Asia-Pacific Web (APWeb) and Web-Age Information Management (WAIM) Joint Conference on Web and Big Data* (pp. 48-63). Springer. 10.1007/978-3-319-63564-4_4

Liu, B. (2012). Sentiment analysis and opinion mining. *Synthesis Lectures on Human Language Technologies, 5*(1), 1-167.

Mohammad, S. M., Zhu, X., Kiritchenko, S., & Martin, J. (2015). Sentiment, emotion, purpose, and style in electoral tweets. *Information Processing & Management*, *51*(4), 480–499. doi:10.1016/j.ipm.2014.09.003

Na'aman, N., Provenza, H., & Montoya, O. (2017). Varying linguistic purposes of emoji in (twitter) context. In *Proceedings of ACL 2017, Student Research Workshop* (pp. 136-141). 10.18653/v1/P17-3022

Pak, A., & Paroubek, P. (2010, May). Twitter as a corpus for sentiment analysis and opinion mining. In LREc (Vol. 10, No. 2010, pp. 1320-1326). Academic Press.

Pennington, J., Socher, R., & Manning, C. (2014). Glove: Global vectors for word representation. In *Proceedings of the 2014 conference on empirical methods in natural language processing (EMNLP)* (pp. 1532-1543). 10.3115/v1/D14-1162

Unnisa, M., Ameen, A., & Raziuddin, S. (2016). Opinion mining on Twitter data using unsupervised learning technique. *International Journal of Computers and Applications*, *148*(12), 12–19. doi:10.5120/ijca2016911317

Xia, R., Jiang, J., & He, H. (2017). Distantly supervised lifelong learning for large-scale social media sentiment analysis. *IEEE Transactions on Affective Computing*, *8*(4), 480–491. doi:10.1109/TAFFC.2017.2771234

Xiong, S., Lv, H., Zhao, W., & Ji, D. (2018). Towards Twitter sentiment classification by multi-level sentiment-enriched word embeddings. *Neurocomputing*, *275*, 2459–2466. doi:10.1016/j.neucom.2017.11.023

Yang, G., He, H., & Chen, Q. (2019). Emotion-Semantic-Enhanced Neural Network. *IEEE/ACM Transactions on Audio, Speech, and Language Processing*, *27*(3), 531–543. doi:10.1109/TASLP.2018.2885775

This research was previously published in the International Journal of Social Media and Online Communities (IJSMOC), 12(1); pages 1-13, copyright year 2020 by IGI Publishing (an imprint of IGI Global).

Chapter 23
Impact of Balancing Techniques for Imbalanced Class Distribution on Twitter Data for Emotion Analysis: A Case Study

Shivani Vasantbhai Vora
CGPIT, Uka Tarsadia University, Bardoli, India

Rupa G. Mehta
Sardar Vallabhbhai National Institute of Technology, Surat, India

Shreyas Kishorkumar Patel
Sardar Vallabhbhai National Institute of Technology, Surat, India

ABSTRACT

Continuously growing technology enhances creativity and simplifies humans' lives and offers the possibility to anticipate and satisfy their unmet needs. Understanding emotions is a crucial part of human behavior. Machines must deeply understand emotions to be able to predict human needs. Most tweets have sentiments of the user. It inherits the imbalanced class distribution. Most machine learning (ML) algorithms are likely to get biased towards the majority classes. The imbalanced distribution of classes gained extensive attention as it has produced many research challenges. It demands efficient approaches to handle the imbalanced data set. Strategies used for balancing the distribution of classes in the case study are handling redundant data, resampling training data, and data augmentation. Six methods related to these techniques have been examined in a case study. Upon conducting experiments on the Twitter dataset, it is seen that merging minority classes and shuffle sentence methods outperform other techniques.

DOI: 10.4018/978-1-6684-6303-1.ch023

INTRODUCTION AND MOTIVATION

Information technology is used in every field of human life and make human's life improved and more accessible. This tool became valued elements of life because it opened many doors to individuals. It firmly entrenched in human lives and facilitated their lives. Continuously growing technology strengthens individual creativity, makes our daily life more accessible, and gives us the facility to predict and cater to our needs. A deep understanding of human behavior is needed in machines and computers to understand our needs. The key part of human behavior is about perceiving and communicating emotions. It also motivates to take actions, influence the quality of decision making, and enhance the ability to empathize and communicate. Machines and computers must deeply understand emotions to anticipate human needs (Chatterjee A et al. (2019)). Emotion recognition and detection are closely related to sentiment analysis. Identification of sentiment intends to detect neutral, negative, or positive feelings from the content (Liu, B. (2012)).

In contrast, Emotion Analysis aims to identify and recognize feelings through text phrases, like joy, happiness, anger, disgust, fear, sadness, surprise, and many more (Picard R. W. (2000)). Recently, an identification of emotion has become a popular application of NLP. It has potential applications in Artificial intelligence (Damani S et al. 2018), Psychology (Druckman J. N. et al. 2008), Human-computer interaction (S. Brave et al.2009), Political science (Valentino N. A. et al. 2011) help in preventing suicide, or measuring the communal well-being (Van der Zanden R. et al. 2014), and Marketing (Bagozzi R. P. et al. 1999) etc.

WhatsApp, Facebook, and Twitter are prominent messaging platforms used by many online users to interact with each other. Statics given by (Statista, 2021) – "by the 3rd quarter of 2020, there are around 187 million daily active users of Twitter worldwide." In varied fields like researchers in marketing, analytics for political parties or social scientists look into twitter data in order to study human behavior in physical world. Tweets are rich sources of textual data containing the emotions of users. These data inherit the imbalanced emotion class distribution. In imbalanced dataset, data samples of one class are higher or lower than that of other group of classes. Figure 1 illustrates an imbalanced data. On encountering a imbalance class distribution problem in the training data, the results of classification task is influenced by majority class (Zhao C. et al. 2020).

Most machine learning classification algorithms are unable to manage imbalanced distribution of classes and are likely to get influenced by majority classes (Kothiya, Y. (2020, July 17)).

In the research literature, various approaches are proposed to cater to the imbalance class distribution issues in the data classification. These approaches are broadly categorized as algorithmic centered approaches and pre-processing methods or data level approaches.

Re-sampling techniques (Kotsiantis S. et al. 2006), reducing redundant data (Y.K. (2019, May 15)), and augmentation of text data are data-level approaches that are included as a solution to handle imbalance distribution of classes. The techniques are utilized to obtain an approximately equal count of samples in the classes. Assumptions created to favor the minority class and change the costs to get the balance classes, is the algorithmic-centered approach. (Kotsiantis S. et al. 2006).

In the machine learning (ML) community, the imbalanced class distribution gained extensive attention as it has produced many research challenges. It demands the experimental comparisons of approaches to take care of the imbalanced data set. A case study focuses on various data-level methods to deal with the imbalance distribution of emotion classes in Twitter data.

Figure 1. Imbalance distribution of class (Zhao C. et al. 2020)

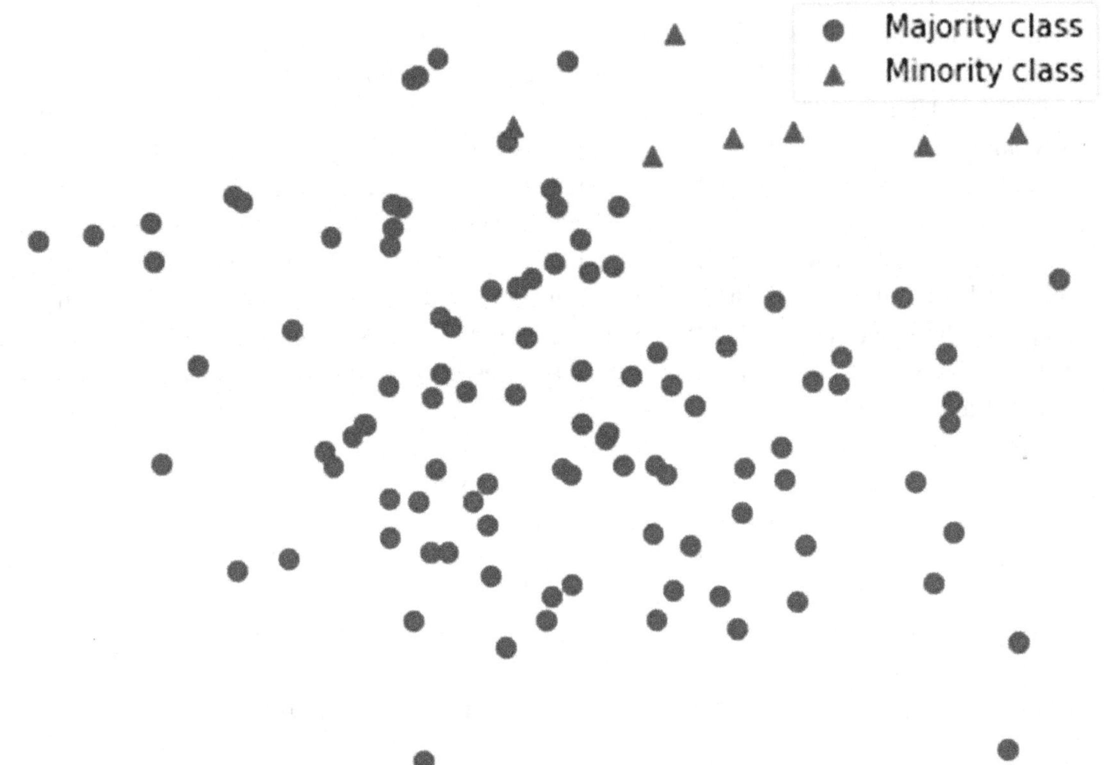

Contribution and Plan of the Report

- A case study focuses on tackling the imbalance multiclass emotion classification of tweets using various techniques such as resampling, reducing redundant data, augmentation of text data. It focuses on effectively processing imbalanced data while including the proposed model that inferred emotions from tweets. The study intends to bridge the gap between imbalanced learning and emotion analysis.
- This study's primary goal is to compare various approaches for balancing classes and enhance the proposed deep learning (DL) based model's efficiency and accuracy.

The rest of this chapter is organized as follows: Section 2 describes a literature review. The Proposed methodology is explained in section 3. Section 4 discusses the experiment setup. The analysis of experimental results is discussed in section5. Section 6 is the conclusion and future work that remarks the findings of this study in the end of the chapter.

LITERATURE REVIEW

In the research literature, Kotsiantis S. et al. 2006 discuss various approaches at the data and the algorithm level for managing class imbalanced data. Many different resampling approaches are proposed at the data level like random over-sampling, Synthetic Minority Over-Sampling (SMOT), and random under-sampling, etc.,. Various classification algorithms and techniques are updated to manage the imbalanced class distribution. Ensemble learning, leveraging the class weights parameter during the training of models, etc., is examples under the latter category.

The study focuses on different data-level methods to deal with imbalanced multiclass emotion analysis for Twitter data. Strategies such as resampling, handling redundant data, data augmentation methods for NLP task are used in the case study for balancing classes and enhance the efficiency and accuracy of the proposed deep learning model.

Twitter Emotion Analysis

Although emotion Recognition based on speech and images has been worked on a lot at this point, text-based emotion detection is in its early stage in natural language processing, including how recently it has drawn ample of attention. The emotion-detection algorithms are at large, put down to two categories, namely, Machine learning (ML) based methods and dictionary based methods.

When the vocabularies such as linguistic rules, ontologies, lexicons, or bags of words are used it is considered as Lexicon based approaches, whereas when the algorithms based on linguistic features, it falls into the category of Machine learning (ML) approaches (Canales L.et al. 2014).

The limitations of lexicon-based methods (Strapparava c. Et al. 2008, ma c. Et al. 2005, Balahur a. Et al. 2011, Sykora m. D. Et al. 2013, Bandhakavi a. Et al. 2017, pp. 102-108, Bandhakavi a. Et al. 2017, pp. 133-142, Chaumartin f. R. 2007, al Masum et al. 2007, Ortony a. Et al. 1988, Neviarouskaya a. Et al. 2010, Deerwester s. Et al. 1990, gill a. J. Et al. 2008, Wang x. Et al. 2013) concerning scalability and domain customization can be overcome by machine learning approaches (Mohri m. Et al. 2012, Hasan m. Et al. 2014, ACM, Sigkdd, Hasan m. Et al. 2014, Wang w. Et al. 2012, Roberts k. Et al. 2012, Suttles j. Et al. 2013, Balabantaray r. C. Et al. 2012, Seol y. S. Et al. 2008, li w. Et al. 2014, lee s. Y. M. Et al. 2010). It can also learn emotional signals that are not explicitly expressed.

The Conventional machine learning techniques required heavy feature engineering as well as a substantial expertise in the domain to create a model to transform raw input into a feature vector which enables a classifier to identify patterns in the input.

Deep learning-based (DL) methods are basically the method of representation learning. It has multiple levels of representation that are obtained by composing non-linear components which transforms a raw input at one level into a abstract higher level (LeCun Y. et al. 2015). The key advantage of deep learning methods is that the layers of features are learned from data using learning procedure. The DL methods perform feature engineering so there is no requirement to design hand-crafted features (LeCun Y. et al. 2015).

Deep learning-based architectures and algorithms have shown considerable success in speech and image domains. They also show favorable results in many NLU tasks such as question answering, topic classification, language translation, and sentiment analysis (LeCun Y. et al. 2015).

Lately, many approaches using deep learning (DL) models for emotion recognition from the text format have been proposed.

In (Zahiri S. M. et al. 2017), the author classifies emotion in a transcript of TV show. Transcripts are well-scripted, but the text data from social media such as tweets and textual dialogue are crowded by internet slang. spell errors etc. Some recent researches are on understanding the various emotions of tweets (Abdul-Mageed M. 2017, Köper M. 2017). In (Felbo B. 2017), authors learn representation based on emojis and uses it for identification of emotions. An author used pretrained LSTM model that is trained with lots of tweets and the emoticons appears in tweets. The work done by Mundra S.2017 is the sole study that addresses the difficulty of emotion identification in textual conversation of English language.

The study says that the deep learning methods give promising results for emotion detection in text. Also, deep learning-based algorithms require very less feature engineering, and so they can conveniently take advantage of available computation and data, as it increases in the amount. It motivated us to move to deep learning approaches for recognized emotion from the text.

Deep Learning Based Emotion Analysis for Imbalanced Class Distribution

Imbalance class distribution is a common problem in classification tasks. Model's performance will degrade due to imbalanced distribution of class. A balanced class distribution is not possible for real-world application domains.

To balance the minority class samples, researchers utilize data over-sampling methods to generate synthetic data from original training data. Method such as synthetic minority oversampling technique (SMOT) performs well for random numerical data (Chawla N. V. et al. 2002) and AdaSyn (He H. et al. 2008). A deep learning model CycleGAN that is the type of generative adversarial networks (GAN) performs well for images (Almahairi, A. et al. 2018). Synthetic text and images generally suffers from semantic or contextual information loss, whereas this is not the case with numeric data. The resulting text frequently turns out to have poor text structure and grammar, thus losing its meaning. Recently, research on tackling imbalanced dataset involves semantic text generation using deep language models. In (Shaikh S. et al. 2021), the authors proposed an LSTM-based model for sentence-level text generation to cater to imbalance distribution of classes in NLP domain applications. Three highly imbalanced datasets from two different domains were used evaluate the performance of LSTM and GPT-2 models for document-level sentence generation. Experimental results show overall improved classification accuracy for the proposed model (Shaikh S. et al. 2021).

In (Cong Q. et al. 2018), authors proposed a model for identification of depression in highly imbalanced social media data. They proposed a deep learning based model (X-A-BiLSTM) that consists of two modules: one is XGBoost module that increases the samples in minority classes and other one is an attention based BiLSTM model that enhances performance of classification task. An author utilizes real-world depression dataset. The dataset used is the Reddit Self-reported Depression Diagnosis (RSDD) dataset. Results illustrate that the approach remarkably performs well with the previous (SOTA) state-of-the-art models on the same dataset.

A research study in (Jamal N. et al. 2019) proposed a hybrid method of a deep learning-based model for emotions recognition on a highly imbalanced tweets data. The proposed model works in four stages:

1. Pre-processing steps are help in getting useful features from raw tweets and filtering out the noisy data.
2. The importance of each feature is computed using entropy weighting method.
3. Further, each class is balanced using a class balancer.

4. Principal Component Analysis (PCA) is applied to get normalized forms from the high correlated features.

At last the TensorFlow with Keras module is recommended to predict good-quality features for identification of emotions. A data set of 1,600,000 tweets that is collected from the 'Kaggle' was analyzed with the suggested methodology. Upon comparing it with the various states of art techniques on various training ratios, it is seen that the recommended methodology outperforms all of them.

Several researchers in different learning settings have studied imbalanced learning for emotion detection. However, we found very few papers that directly address imbalanced emotion classification for Twitter data (Shaikh S. et al. 2021, Jamal N. et al. 2019).

A study focuses on deep learning-based emotion detection for highly imbalanced Twitter data. The next sections describe the methodology used to balance the imbalanced class distribution of text data.

Handle Redundant Data

Twitter dataset comprises of duplicate tweets and a lots of similar tweets. Discarding identical tweets will help to bring down the size of the majority class. Tweet dataset contains multiple tweets with similar semantic meaning. Removing the redundant tweets will help in balancing the classes. One of the beneficial approaches is that the validation set can remove redundant tweets (Kotsiantis S. et al. 2006). There is a range of techniques to represent tweets like word2vec embedding, TF-IDF embedding, BOW representations, etc. The similarity of tweets is measured using different similarity metrics such as Jaccard similarity, cosine similarity, etc. Siamese LSTM models to find out similar tweets have been proposed in the research domain (Cohen E. (2018, September 16)).

Merge minority classes is the approach to merge multiple minority classes that have numerous overlapping features (Multi-Class Emotion Classification for Short Texts, 2018). This trick may help out to enhance the f1-score of the classification task.

Resample Training Dataset

Oversampling the tweets of minority classes or under sampling tweets of majority classes is the straightforward method for balancing the imbalanced tweet data set. Another resampling method is to make new synthetic tweets from minority classes with SMOTE (Synthetic Minority Over-sampling Technique) (Chawla N. V. et al. 2002) algorithm.

Undersampling is an approach to balance the majority classes by eliminating tweets randomly. It may cause information loss from tweets and lead to inadequate model training (Y.K. (2019d, May 15)).

Oversampling is the process to replicate minority class tweets randomly. Random under-sampling suffers with information loss issue and random over-sampling may cause the problem of over fitting. To be precise, if the instances in the dataset are randomly replicated, then the learned model would fit too closely with the training data, resulting into unseen cases to be less generalized (Hoens T. R. et al. 2013).

To conquer this issue, (Chawla N. V. et al. 2002) came up with a SMOTE approach that creates synthetic data instead of taking same samples that already exist in the dataset. In this algorithm, the synthetic instances are introduced to each sample from the minority class, along the line segments connecting any or all of the nearest neighbours of the k minority class (Chawla N. V. et al. 2002). In the feature space, the Euclidean Distance between its data points help evaluates the nearest neighbours, this is essential for the technique. SMOTE works in the feature space such that it selects close examples and draws a line between them, then at a point along this line it draws a new sample.

Data Augmentation

Recently, research on tackling imbalanced dataset involves data augmentation methods of texts. Data augmentation of text can be done by tokenizing documents into a sentence, shuffling and joining them again to generate new sentences. Semantic text generation is also done by replacing adjectives, verbs, etc., with its synonym. A word's synonym is found using any pre-trained word embeddings or lexical dictionaries such as Wordnet, SentiWordNet, etc. ((I. (2019b, March 1)), (T. (2018a, November 16))).

(Zhang X. et al. 2015), Introduced the use of synonyms in their research work. While experimenting, it is found that text augmentation can be done by replacing words or phrases with their synonyms. In a very time effective way a huge amount of data can be generated if there is leverage existing thesaurus. The geometric distribution helps the authors to replace the selected word with its synonym (Zhang X. et al. 2015). Another interesting way was utilization of K-NN algorithm with cosine similarity to find a analogous word for replacement was suggested by (Wang W. Y. et al. 2015).In place of using static word embedding to replace the target word, (Fadaee M. et al. 2017) used the contextualized word embedding. In their work of data augmentation for machine translation with lower resources, they perform text augmentation to validate the model. The experiment proves that by leveraging text augmentation, the machine translation model gets enhanced.

(Kobayashi S. 2018), proposes to employ a bi-directional language model in the research work of data augmentation using contextual word embedding. Upon having selected the target word, the model predicts all probable substitutions by providing the surrounding words. Author applied the language model (LM) approach with sequential model RNN and convolution model CNN on six datasets, and the results turned out to be positive. (Kafle K. et al. 2017) presented an alternate approach for data augmentation. Here, the whole sentence is generated instead of just replacing a single few words.

Machine language translation is another interesting method of data augmentation for text. The technique helps to increase samples of minority classes. The technique used machine translation model to translate English language text to any language text and again converting back to English text. In this way, the essential details of the input texts are preserved, but word order or sometimes new words with similar meanings are introduced as new records, thus increasing the number of insufficient classes ((T. (2020a, September 7)), (Es, S. (2021b, April 9))). It may help out to enhance the f1-score of the classification task.

A case study focuses on tackling the imbalance multiclass emotion classification of tweets using various techniques such as resampling, reduced redundant data, augmentation of text data. It also focuses on effectively processing imbalanced data while including the proposed model that inferred emotions from tweets. The study intends to bridge the gap between imbalanced learning and emotion analysis.

This study's primary goal is to compare different techniques for balancing classes and enhance the proposed deep learning model's efficiency and accuracy.

PROPOSED APPROACH

Emotion recognition from the tweets is an area in Natural Language Processing (NLP), which is the study of interpreting the emotion expressed in text. A study of emotion detection using a deep learning-based approach is shown in Figure 2.

Proposed approach work in two phases. The first phase balances the dataset's class distribution using different data level strategies such as handling redundant data, resampling techniques, and data augmentation approach.

In second phase, pre-processing of a balanced dataset has been done with different methods and tools. Pre-processing techniques replace contraction words with proper words, remove punctuation, numbers, URLs, replace line space and extra white space, replace emoticons with related appropriate words, and demojized the emojis in tweets using emot library available in python.

The proposed model utilized the pre-trained embedding of GloVe (Global Vectors) as weights of the Embedding layer. The Glove Twitter pre-trained model with 200 dimensions is used to embedding the pre-processed Twitter data.

Glove embedding data fed to recurrent neural network (RNN), a deep learning (DL) based model for the text classification task. For twitter classification, the proposed model utilizes the biLSTM model with different layers.

Figure 2. Proposed framework for emotion detection

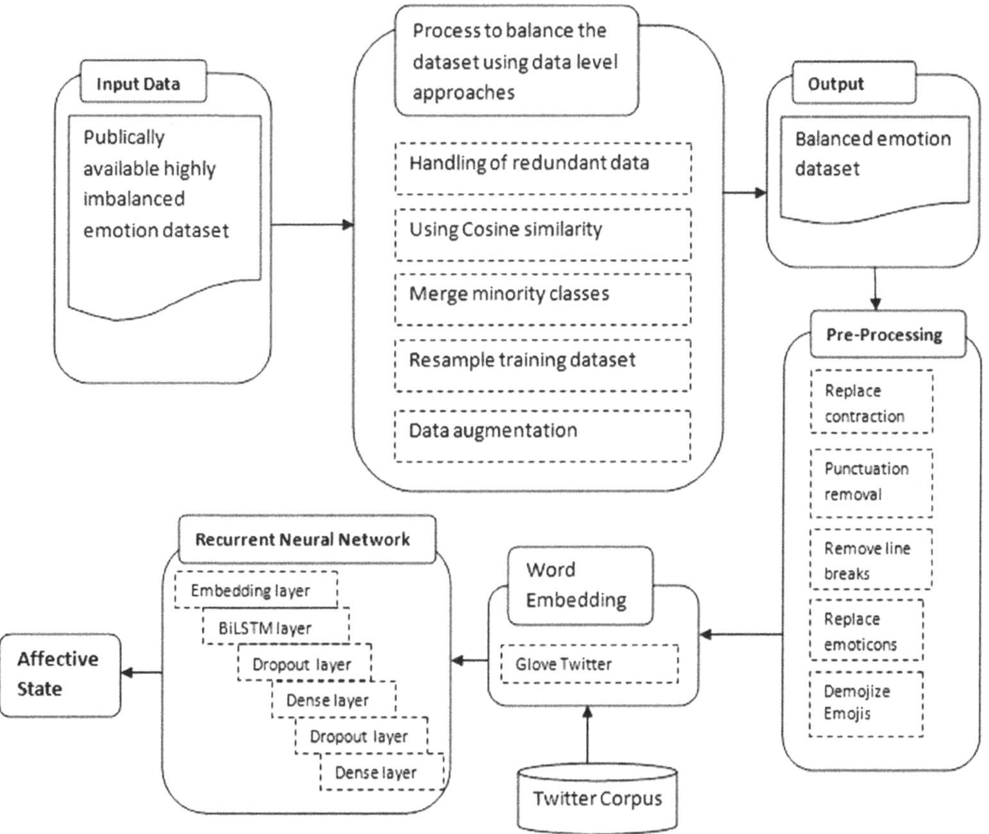

A sequential model RNN is the type of ANN that specialize in the processing the sequential data. RNNs designed to deal with sequential data by sharing their internal weights. The Long Short-Term Memory networks (LSTMs), an extension of the RNN was introduced In 1997. In LSTM, the vanishing and exploding of the gradient issues are avoided by the unique connection of the recurrent cells (Sepp Hochreiter et al. 1997). Generally the LSTMs maintain information from the past because the sequence is processed in only one direction. The bidirectional LSTM (BiLSTM) combine output from two LSTM layers that processed in opposite directions. One processed forward through time, and another processed backwards through time to retrieve information from both states simultaneously (Schuster M. et al. 1997).

EXPERIMENTAL SETUP

Dataset

Experiments performed on a publically available emotion dataset from Kaggle (Emotion, 2020). The emotion dataset has 40,000 tweets with its 13 emotion labels. The dataset is highly imbalanced with a different number of tweets in each emotion category. Detail of imbalanced dataset provided in Table 1.

For the emotion dataset, 80% used for training, 20% for testing and another 20% used for validation. The training dataset has 25,600 tweets, 6400 tweets are in the validation set, and 8000 tweets are in the test set. The cleaning operations are performed on train, validation and test tweets datasets. Details of the dataset are available in Table 2.

Table 1. Class details of emotion dataset

Emotion Classes	# Tweets	Emotion Classes	# Tweets	Emotion Classes	# Tweets
neutral	8504	love	3837	empty	806
worry	8441	surprise	2178	enthusiasm	758
happiness	5206	fun	1774	boredom	178
sadness	5154	relief	1525		
anger	110	hate	1323		

Table 2. Emotion dataset

Dataset	Classes	Train	Validation	Test
Emotion dataset from Kaggle	13 (neutral, worry, happiness, sadness, anger, love, surprise, fun, relief, hate, empty, enthusiasm, and boredom)	25600	6400	8000

Pre-Processing Techniques

Pre-processing techniques replace contraction words with proper words, remove punctuation, numbers, URLs, replace line space and extra white space, replace emoticons with related appropriate words, and demojized the emojis in tweets using emot library available in python. Figure 3 describes the pre-processing techniques.

Removal of Punctuations, Digits, Twitter Handles ('@'), Special Characters

Basically, the twitter users are denoted by their twitter handles that start with a '@' sign. These handles do not give any significant meaning to the text and so they are to be removed. Tweets also contain punctuations, numeric information and special characters. These are also unnecessary as they do not convey many emotions with their meaning. It can quickly be done using Regular Expression available in python libraries. It uses simple methods to find characters and patterns in a string.

Example: "@abc 102 Not out Excellent!!" will become "Not out Excellent

Remove Unicode Strings and Noise

To get a clean dataset is not always possible. The Unicode strings like "\u002c" and "\x06" and some non-English characters were left behind by the crawling method that was used to create the dataset. These strings have to be removed or replaced by some regular expressions.

Replacing Contractions

Yet another approach in pre-processing is to replace the contractions, which is replacing words like "won't" and "don't" by "will not" and "do not", respectively.

Lowercasing

A common pre-processing method is to convert all the words into lowercase. This will merge a lot of words thereby reducing the dimensionality of the problem.

Lemmatization

Lemmatization typically refers to doing things correctly using a vocabulary and morphological examination of words, generally aimed solely at eliminating infection endings and restoring the basic term referenced as a lemma. Lemmatization is done by using different modules and available open-source libraries.

Spell Check

Examining the word's spelling is one of the primary necessities for any form of text processing. There are various paths available in Python to check the spelling of terms and correct their respective words.

Removing Stop Words

The function words that have high frequency that it their presence across all the sentences is high are called stop words. This reduces their importance in getting analyzed because they don't hold much necessary information in regards to the sentiment analysis. This collection of words is never pre-defined; it may change by adding or removing some words, based on the application.

Figure 3. Flow of data pre-processing

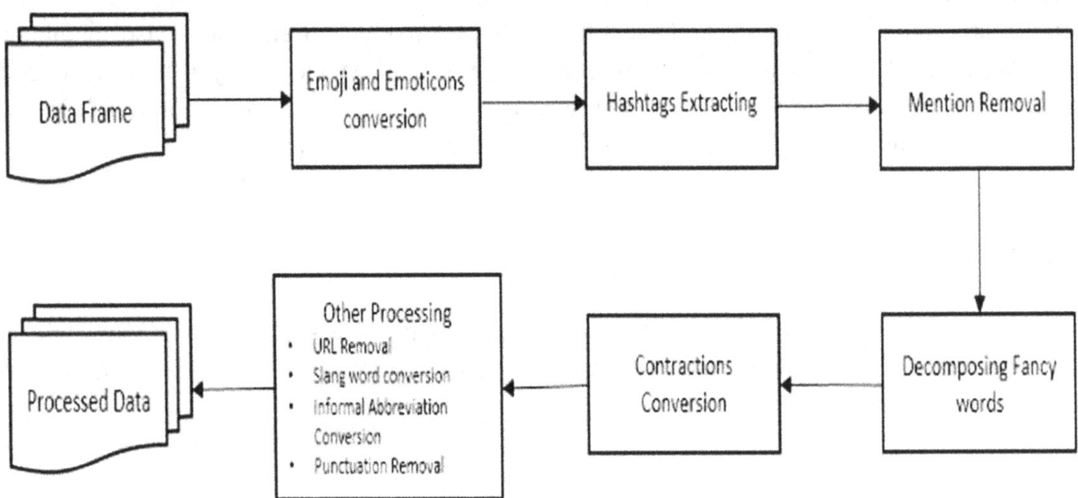

Replacing Elongated Words

Sometimes there are words which have characters that have been wrongly (thought purposely) repeated more than once, e.g. "greeeeat", these are called as elongated words. The need is to replace these words with their source words in order to merge them. If this wasn't done then these different words would never be considered in evaluation due to their low frequency of occurrence.

Replacing Emoticons and Demojized Emojis

An emoji is defined as a unique combination of keyboard characters like letters, numbers and punctuation marks to express a human facial expression. They are like small images that can be fitted into text also express an emotion or idea. The name "emoji" is derived from the Japanese characters 'e' for picture + 'mo' for writing + 'ji' for character, making its literal meaning to be 'picture-character' (Subramanian D. (2020b, January 7)).

Emojis and emoticons play a fundamental role in human computer-mediated communications. They use a proxy of emotional communication to process tweets by considering emoticons information. Emot library available in Python libraries used to replace emoticons with appropriate words. With the help of Demojize function of Python, emojis replaced with suitable words.

Pre-Trained Word Embedding – GloVe

Experiments have been done with Glove that is pre-trained with billions of tweets (Pennington J. et al. 2014) word embedding as an embedding layer of the model.

The proposed model used the pre-trained embeddings of GloVe (Global Vectors) as weights of the Embedding layer. The model used a Glove Twitter pre-trained model with 200 dimensions. The accuracy and complexity of the model increase as the size of training data and vocabulary size increases. The model used GloVe embeddings trained with Twitter data.

Glove Twitter pre-trained model trained with 2B tweets and has 27B tokens and 1.2M vocab. It is available in uncased, 25d, 50d, 100d, & 200d vectors with a size of 1.42 GB. The GloVe Twitter Embedding has a dataset of 27 Billion tokens which contains slangs commonly used while writing a tweet. Hence GloVe Twitter is favorable when dealing with Twitter data.

Classification Model

The experimental study is to create a model whose task is to understand emotions as a multiclass classification problem where for the given input through tweets, the model will provide probabilities of varied emotion classes like – neutral, fear, anger, sadness, and joy and more.

Figure 4 describes the proposed EMOTWEET_TL deep learning model architecture. The neural network's proposed architecture comprising the embedding unit and a (biLSTM) bidirectional LSTM unit (64 dim). The LSTM unit learns semantic and sentiment feature representation. Initially, using the pre-trained word embedding, each tweet is given to the bidirectional LSTM. Text-based transfer learning techniques such as Glove embedding used as embedding layer and leverage them to perform effectively on downstream tasks. To predict the final emotion class label, the features proceed through a dense layer with the Relu non-linear function and then through the output layer with the softmax non-linear function. A dropout layer (Srivastava N. et al. 2014) was added between the bidirectional LSTM layer and to the first dense layer with Relu activation function and another dropout layer was added between the dense layer and the prediction layer (p=0.2) to improve the generalization of the network.

The Adam optimizer is used to train the model. For multiclass classification, the categorical cross-entropy loss function is utilized. F1-score, recall and precision were used as performance measures of the model.

Strategies used for Balancing Imbalanced Data

The experimental study focuses on different data-level methods to deal with imbalance multi-class emotion analysis. The strategies used in experiments are discussed below.

Handling of Redundant Data

For handling redundant tweets, the experiments have performed with two techniques. In the first technique, similar tweets are identified from the majority class. Such tweets are either deleted or added to the validation set to reduce the majority class size. The second technique merges similar minority classes.

Figure 4. EMOTWEET_TL: Proposed model for inferring emotions from tweets

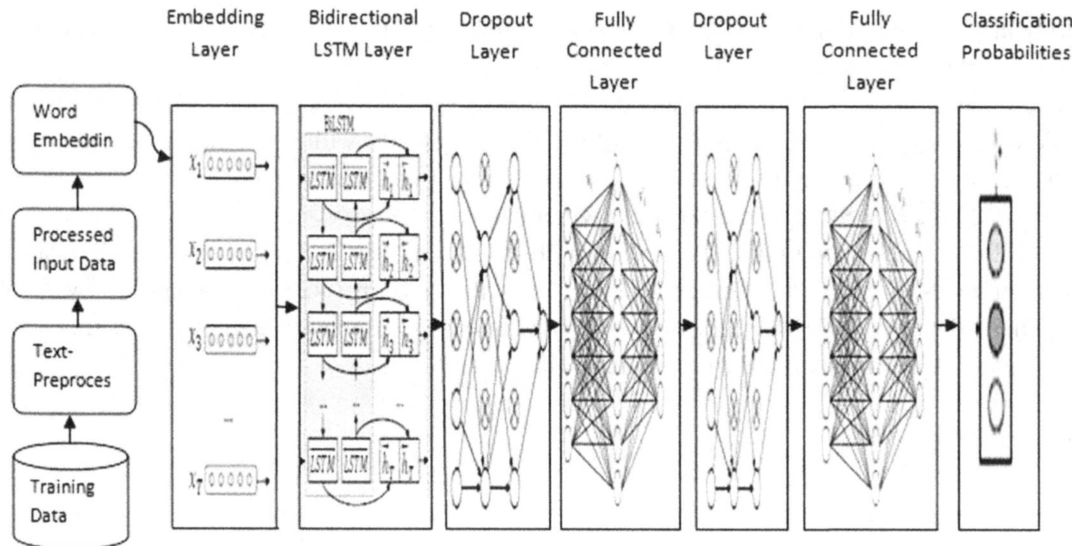

Using Cosine Similarity

tweets with similar semantic meaning or duplicate tweets are finding out using a cosine similarity measure. The tweets are used in validation sets also. Removing such duplicate and similar semantic meaning tweets will aid to reduce the size of the majority classes. In an experimental study, the tweets' similarity is identified using a cosine similarity metric with a threshold of 40% similarity.

Merge Minority Classes

It is the approach to merge multiple minority classes that have numerous overlapping features. The 13 emotions have been converted into 5 emotions such as neutral, happy, sad, hate, and anger. (It will add in handling the redundant data-merge similar classes-The native dataset is consists of 40,000 tweets that are divided into 13 emotion classes. These five classes are also the same as in (Bouazizi M. et al. 2017).

Resample Training Dataset

The experimental study used the SMOTE method to generate synthesized new tweets for minority classes. For creation of a new synthetic minority class instance, begin with randomly selecting a minority class instance namely 'p' and figure out its k-nearest class neighbors. Now randomly choose any one of these k-nearest minority neighbors namely 'q' and connect the two together, making a line segment in the feature space. The convex combination of these instances 'p' and 'q' generate the synthetic instance. Experiments have been performed with k=5. All minority classes have been balanced with the same number of tweets of majority class (here neutral class has maximum tweets - 8504 tweets). SMOTE algorithm is used to generate synthesized new data.

Data Augmentation

Simple data augmentation methods are used to increase similar tweets for minority classes. In the first approach, tokenizing tweets into words, shuffling and joining them again to create new tweets. NLTK library is used to tokenize tweets. The second approach replaces words of tweets with synonyms found using Pydictionary. It is a Dictionary Module for Python to get synonyms, translations, meanings, and Antonyms of words (PyDictionary, 2020). The synonym replacement method is helpful to generate semantic texts.

Performance Metrics

The use of an evaluation metrics is a vital to rate the classification performance of a learning algorithm. The broadly used metrics for evaluating classification algorithm is the accuracy and error. In the imbalances datasets, it seen that there exists a bias towards the majority class while, measuring performance. Therefore, these famous metrics' values do not show the classifier's ability to predict examples from minority classes.

Theoretically, various evaluation metrics like Precision, Recall, and F-measure etc. have been put forward to measure the classifier performance while dealing with imbalanced data problems.

To measure the correctly classified positive class samples, a Precision metric is used and defined as:

$$Precision = \frac{TP}{TP + FP}.$$

where TP and FP stands for the count of true-positive and false-positive respectively.

Now the Recall is used to measure the proportion of correctly identified the real positive samples and is calculated using:

$$Recall = \frac{TP}{TP + FN}.$$

where FN stands for the counts of false-negative.

In general, there is a trade-off between precision and recall. This relationship can give an inherent view of the performance of the classifier using the F-measure metrics. F-measure is basically a harmonic mean of precision and recall (Chicco D. et al. 2020). It is calculated using:

$$F - measure = 2 * \frac{Presicion * Recall}{Precision + Recall}.$$

In the experimental study, a highly imbalanced dataset is used so precision, recall and F-measures are used as evaluation metrics for evaluating model performance.

EXPERIMENT RESULTS AND ANALYSIS

Experiments performed on a highly imbalanced emotion dataset. It is balanced using above mentioned techniques and applied to the proposed model EMOTWEET_TL and infer emotion from it. Results are shown in Table 3.

In the study, an emotion dataset with 13 emotion classes is used. Data distributions of classes are highly imbalanced and described in Table1. To balance data distributions of minority classes, different techniques such as resampling, handling redundant data in majority classes, and data augmentation methods are used. After applying the methods mentioned above, the prepared balanced dataset is fed to the proposed EMOTWEET_TL model that infers tweets' emotion.

The experimental study conducted with the baseline method gives an f1-score 0.17. In the Baseline method, the imbalanced dataset is fed to the proposed model and evaluates its performance. The results of the dataset, balanced with the SMOTE method, give poor performance. F1-score is only 0.028. The performance of the model is decreasing with much difference in F1-score.

One observation of SMOTE algorithm's poor performance is that it does not take neighboring samples from other classes while generating synthetic samples. This can lead to an increase in the overlapping of classes and may introduce additional noise. The literature study indicates that the performance of the SMOTE is degrading with text data because the vectors created from the text data has high dimensions, and SMOTE is not very effective for high dimensional data (Chawla N. V. et al. 2002).

The technique's performance that used cosine similarity to filter out similar tweets from majority classes is almost equal to a baseline method. The F1-score of the method is 0.18. The technique finds similar tweets with a cosine similarity threshold of 40%. Due to the small amount of similar tweets identified with a given threshold, the majority class tweets not reduced much in size. So the impact of the method on this dataset is not much as compared to other techniques. A prior experiment was conducted with 65% threshold but identified a very less number of similar tweets.

Data augmentation methods such as shuffle words, shuffle sentences and replacing synonyms in tweets give better results than the baseline method. Their F1-score are 0.36, 0.48 and 0.38 respectively. Almost it is +0.20 points higher than the baseline method. The new tweets generated using these methods are similar to their class tweets, and it is one of the reasons for better performance. The Shuffle sentence method gives better performance than the shuffle words method. In the shuffle words method, a tweet is tokenized and shuffles these tokens and again joining them may change the context of some tweets and may cause the model's effectiveness. Whereas in the shuffle sentences method, tweets are tokenized by sentences and shuffle sentences to create a new tweet, so the context of sentences did not change, and performance may improve. These prominent methods are performed well as a merging minority classes method. The F1-score of this method is 0.48. Similar minority classes are merged, and as a result, it reduces the number of classes in the dataset. The merging method performs well over other methods of experimental study. Better performance of the methods due to below reasons:

CONCLUSION AND FUTURE WORK

Emotion detection from the Twitter dataset is confronted with the class imbalance problem. Most machine learning and deep learning classification algorithms are not equipped to manage imbalanced distribution of classes and are likely to get influenced by majority classes.

Table 3. Performance of the proposed model for different techniques to balancing class distribution of the dataset

Method		Train			Validation			Test		
		Precision	Recall	F1-score	Precision	Recall	F1-score	Precision	Recall	F1-score
Baseline		0.65	0.2	0.30	0.44	0.10	0.18	0.44	0.10	0.17
Handling Redundant Data	Using cosine similarity	0.71	0.22	0.34	0.39	0.12	0.18	0.39	0.12	0.18
	Merging Minority classes	0.78	0.62	0.69	0.53	0.45	**0.49**	0.53	0.44	**0.48**
Resample Training Dataset	SMOTE	0.69	0.014	0.028	0.67	0.012	0.023	0.70	0.014	0.028
Data Augmentation	Shuffle Words	0.80	0.28	0.42	0.73	0.24	**0.37**	0.72	0.24	**0.36**
	Shuffle sentences	0.84	0.30	0.52	0.78	0.35	**0.48**	0.77	0.35	**0.48**
	Synonym	0.86	0.30	0.44	0.78	0.26	**0.39**	0.77	0.25	**0.38**

- It reduces the number of classes of the dataset.
- It balances the distribution of data in all merged classes.

A way to address this challenge is to use different strategies for balancing imbalance class distribution in a case study are handling redundant dataset, resampling training dataset and data augmentation. Five methods related to the techniques mentioned above examined in a case study. In a case study, experiments are conducted on Twitter dataset collecting from Kaggle to infer emotions from the tweets. A Twitter dataset is in the English language. The obtained results show that merging minority classes with similar classes and shuffle sentence methods for data augmentation give better performance than other techniques.

In future work, we intend to extend our study to incorporate more advanced techniques for data augmentation, such as generating new semantic tweets using biLSTM models and using machine language translation techniques.

Reduce the majority classes' size by filtering out semantically similar tweets using the Siamese LSTM model instead of a cosine similarity measure to get the more accurate and efficient performance of the model. An experimental study will perform with more datasets on the same domain and with different domain datasets.

REFERENCES

Abdul-Mageed, M., & Ungar, L. (2017, July). Emonet: Fine-grained emotion detection with gated recurrent neural networks. In *Proceedings of the 55th annual meeting of the association for computational linguistics* (volume 1*: Long papers)* (pp. 718-728). 10.18653/v1/P17-1067

Al Masum, S. M., Prendinger, H., & Ishizuka, M. (2007, November). Emotion sensitive news agent: An approach towards user centric emotion sensing from the news. In *IEEE/WIC/ACM International Conference on Web Intelligence (WI'07)* (pp. 614-620). IEEE. 10.1109/WI.2007.124

Almahairi, A., Rajeshwar, S., Sordoni, A., Bachman, P., & Courville, A. (2018, July). Augmented cyclegan: Learning many-to-many mappings from unpaired data. In *International Conference on Machine Learning* (pp. 195-204). PMLR.

Bagozzi, R. P., Gopinath, M., & Nyer, P. U. (1999). The role of emotions in marketing. *Journal of the Academy of Marketing Science*, *27*(2), 184–206. doi:10.1177/0092070399272005

Balabantaray, R. C., Mohammad, M., & Sharma, N. (2012). Multi-class twitter emotion classification: A new approach. *International Journal of Applied Information Systems*, *4*(1), 48–53. doi:10.5120/ijais12-450651

Balahur, A., Hermida, J. M., & Montoyo, A. (2011, June). Detecting implicit expressions of sentiment in text based on commonsense knowledge. In *Proceedings of the 2nd Workshop on Computational Approaches to Subjectivity and Sentiment Analysis (WASSA 2011)* (pp. 53-60). Academic Press.

Bandhakavi, A., Wiratunga, N., Massie, S., & Padmanabhan, D. (2017). Lexicon generation for emotion detection from text. *IEEE Intelligent Systems*, *32*(1), 102–108. doi:10.1109/MIS.2017.22

Bandhakavi, A., Wiratunga, N., Padmanabhan, D., & Massie, S. (2017). Lexicon based feature extraction for emotion text classification. *Pattern Recognition Letters*, *93*, 133–142. doi:10.1016/j.patrec.2016.12.009

Bouazizi, M., & Ohtsuki, T. (2017). A pattern-based approach for multi-class sentiment analysis in Twitter. *IEEE Access: Practical Innovations, Open Solutions*, *5*, 20617–20639. doi:10.1109/ACCESS.2017.2740982

Brave, S., & Nass, C. (2009). Emotion in human–computer interaction. In *Human-computer interaction fundamentals* (Vol. 20094635). CRC Press. doi:10.1201/b10368-6

Canales, L., & Martínez-Barco, P. (2014, October). Emotion detection from text: A survey. In *Proceedings of the workshop on natural language processing in the 5th information systems research working days (JISIC)* (pp. 37-43). 10.3115/v1/W14-6905

Chatterjee, A., Gupta, U., Chinnakotla, M. K., Srikanth, R., Galley, M., & Agrawal, P. (2019). Understanding emotions in text using deep learning and big data. *Computers in Human Behavior*, *93*, 309–317. doi:10.1016/j.chb.2018.12.029

Chaumartin, F. R. (2007). UPAR7: A knowledge-based system for headline sentiment tagging. In *SemEval (ACL Workshop)* (pp. pp-422). 10.3115/1621474.1621568

Chawla, N. V., Bowyer, K. W., Hall, L. O., & Kegelmeyer, W. P. (2002). SMOTE: Synthetic minority over-sampling technique. *Journal of Artificial Intelligence Research*, *16*, 321–357. doi:10.1613/jair.953

Chicco, D., & Jurman, G. (2020). The advantages of the Matthews correlation coefficient (MCC) over F1 score and accuracy in binary classification evaluation. *BMC Genomics*, *21*(1), 1–13. doi:10.118612864-019-6413-7 PMID:31898477

Cohen, E. (2018, September 16). *How to predict Quora Question Pairs using Siamese Manhattan LSTM*. Medium. https://blog.mlreview.com/implementing-malstm-on-kaggles-quora-question-pairs-competition-8b31b0b16a07

Cong, Q., Feng, Z., Li, F., Xiang, Y., Rao, G., & Tao, C. (2018, December). XA-BiLSTM: A deep learning approach for depression detection in imbalanced data. In *2018 IEEE International Conference on Bioinformatics and Biomedicine (BIBM)* (pp. 1624-1627). IEEE.

Damani, S., Raviprakash, N., Gupta, U., Chatterjee, A., Joshi, M., Gupta, K., & Mathur, A. (2018). *Ruuh: A deep learning based conversational social agent*. arXiv preprint arXiv:1810.12097.

Deerwester, S., Dumais, S. T., Furnas, G. W., Landauer, T. K., & Harshman, R. (1990). Indexing by latent semantic analysis. *Journal of the American Society for Information Science*, *41*(6), 391–407. doi:10.1002/(SICI)1097-4571(199009)41:6<391::AID-ASI1>3.0.CO;2-9

Druckman, J. N., & McDermott, R. (2008). Emotion and the framing of risky choice. *Political Behavior*, *30*(3), 297–321. doi:10.100711109-008-9056-y

Emotion. (2020, January 7). *Kaggle*. https://www.kaggle.com/icw123/emotion

Es, S. (2021b, April 9). *Data Augmentation in NLP: Best Practices From a Kaggle Master*. Neptune. Ai. https://neptune.ai/blog/data-augmentation-nlp

Fadaee, M., Bisazza, A., & Monz, C. (2017). Data augmentation for low-resource neural machine translation. arXiv preprint arXiv:1705.00440. doi:10.18653/v1/P17-2090

Felbo, B., Mislove, A., Søgaard, A., Rahwan, I., & Lehmann, S. (2017). Using millions of emoji occurrences to learn any-domain representations for detecting sentiment, emotion and sarcasm. arXiv preprint arXiv:1708.00524. doi:10.18653/v1/D17-1169

Gill, A. J., French, R. M., Gergle, D., & Oberlander, J. (2008). Identifying emotional characteristics from short blog texts. In *30th Annual Conference of the Cognitive Science Society* (pp. 2237-2242). Washington, DC: Cognitive Science Society.

Hasan, M., Agu, E., & Rundensteiner, E. (2014). Using hashtags as labels for supervised learning of emotions in twitter messages. ACM SIGKDD workshop on health informatics.

Hasan, M., Rundensteiner, E., & Agu, E. (2014). *Emotex: Detecting emotions in twitter messages*. Academic Press.

He, H., Bai, Y., Garcia, E. A., & Li, S. (2008, June). ADASYN: Adaptive synthetic sampling approach for imbalanced learning. In *2008 IEEE international joint conference on neural networks (IEEE world congress on computational intelligence)* (pp. 1322-1328). IEEE.

Hochreiter, S., & Schmidhuber, J. (1997). Long short-term memory. *Neural Computation*, *9*(8), 1735–1780. doi:10.1162/neco.1997.9.8.1735 PMID:9377276

Hoens, T. R., & Chawla, N. V. (2013). Imbalanced datasets: from sampling to classifiers. *Imbalanced learning: Foundations, algorithms, and applications*, 43-59.

I. (2019b, March 1). *NLP (data augmentation).* Kaggle. https://www.kaggle.com/init927/nlp-data-augmentation#Introduction-to-Data-Augmentation-in-NLP

Jamal, N., Xianqiao, C., & Aldabbas, H. (2019). Deep learning-based sentimental analysis for large-scale imbalanced twitter data. *Future Internet, 11*(9), 190. doi:10.3390/fi11090190

Kafle, K., Yousefhussien, M., & Kanan, C. (2017, September). Data augmentation for visual question answering. In *Proceedings of the 10th International Conference on Natural Language Generation* (pp. 198-202). 10.18653/v1/W17-3529

Kobayashi, S. (2018). Contextual augmentation: Data augmentation by words with paradigmatic relations. arXiv preprint arXiv:1805.06201. doi:10.18653/v1/N18-2072

Köper, M., Kim, E., & Klinger, R. (2017, September). IMS at EmoInt-2017: Emotion intensity prediction with affective norms, automatically extended resources and deep learning. In *Proceedings of the 8th Workshop on Computational Approaches to Subjectivity, Sentiment and Social Media Analysis* (pp. 50-57). 10.18653/v1/W17-5206

Kothiya, Y. (2020, July 17). *How I handled imbalanced text data - Towards Data Science*. Medium. https://towardsdatascience.com/how-i-handled-imbalanced-text-data-ba9b757ab1d8

Kotsiantis, S., Kanellopoulos, D., & Pintelas, P. (2006). Handling imbalanced datasets: A review. *GESTS International Transactions on Computer Science and Engineering, 30*(1), 25–36.

LeCun, Y., Bengio, Y., & Hinton, G. (2015). Deep learning. *Nature, 521*(7553), 436-444.

Lee, S. Y. M., Chen, Y., & Huang, C. R. (2010, June). A text-driven rule-based system for emotion cause detection. In *Proceedings of the NAACL HLT 2010 Workshop on Computational Approaches to Analysis and Generation of Emotion in Text* (pp. 45-53). Academic Press.

Li, W., & Xu, H. (2014). Text-based emotion classification using emotion cause extraction. *Expert Systems with Applications, 41*(4), 1742–1749. doi:10.1016/j.eswa.2013.08.073

Liu, B. (2012). Sentiment analysis and opinion mining. *Synthesis Lectures on Human Language Technologies, 5*(1), 1-167.

Ma, C., Prendinger, H., & Ishizuka, M. (2005, October). Emotion estimation and reasoning based on affective textual interaction. In *International conference on affective computing and intelligent interaction* (pp. 622-628). Springer. 10.1007/11573548_80

Mohri, M., Rostamizadeh, A., & Talwalkar, A. (2012). *Foundations of machine learning*. Academic Press.

Multi-Class Emotion Classification for Short Texts. (2018, March 17). *Github*. https://tlkh.github.io/text-emotion-classification/

Mundra, S., Sen, A., Sinha, M., Mannarswamy, S., Dandapat, S., & Roy, S. (2017, May). Fine-grained emotion detection in contact center chat utterances. In *Pacific-Asia Conference on Knowledge Discovery and Data Mining* (pp. 337-349). Springer. 10.1007/978-3-319-57529-2_27

Neviarouskaya, A., Prendinger, H., & Ishizuka, M. (2010, August). Recognition of affect, judgment, and appreciation in text. In *Proceedings of the 23rd International Conference on Computational Linguistics (Coling 2010)* (pp. 806-814). Academic Press.

Ortony, A., Clore, G. L., & Collins, A. (1988). *The cognitive structure of emotions*. Cambridge University Press.

Pennington, J., Socher, R., & Manning, C. D. (2014, October). Glove: Global vectors for word representation. In *Proceedings of the 2014 conference on empirical methods in natural language processing (EMNLP)* (pp. 1532-1543). 10.3115/v1/D14-1162

Picard, R. W. (2000). *Affective computing*. MIT Press. doi:10.7551/mitpress/1140.001.0001

PyDictionary. (2020, July 9). *PyPI*. https://pypi.org/project/PyDictionary/

Roberts, K., Roach, M. A., Johnson, J., Guthrie, J., & Harabagiu, S. M. (2012, May). EmpaTweet: Annotating and Detecting Emotions on Twitter. In Lrec (Vol. 12, pp. 3806-3813). Academic Press.

Schuster, M., & Paliwal, K. K. (1997). Bidirectional recurrent neural networks. *IEEE Transactions on Signal Processing*, *45*(11), 2673–2681. doi:10.1109/78.650093

Seol, Y. S., Kim, D. J., & Kim, H. W. (2008, July). Emotion recognition from text using knowledge-based ANN. In *ITC-CSCC: International Technical Conference on Circuits Systems, Computers and Communications* (pp. 1569-1572). Academic Press.

Shaikh, S., Daudpota, S. M., Imran, A. S., & Kastrati, Z. (2021). Towards Improved Classification Accuracy on Highly Imbalanced Text Dataset Using Deep Neural Language Models. *Applied Sciences (Basel, Switzerland)*, *11*(2), 869. doi:10.3390/app11020869

Srivastava, N., Hinton, G., Krizhevsky, A., Sutskever, I., & Salakhutdinov, R. (2014). Dropout: A simple way to prevent neural networks from overfitting. *Journal of Machine Learning Research*, *15*(1), 1929–1958.

Strapparava, C., & Mihalcea, R. (2008, March). Learning to identify emotions in text. In *Proceedings of the 2008 ACM symposium on Applied computing* (pp. 1556-1560). 10.1145/1363686.1364052

Subramanian, D. (2020b, January 7). *Emotion analysis in text mining | Towards AI*. Medium. https://pub.towardsai.net/emoticon-and-emoji-in-text-mining-7392c49f596a

Suttles, J., & Ide, N. (2013, March). Distant supervision for emotion classification with discrete binary values. In *International Conference on Intelligent Text Processing and Computational Linguistics* (pp. 121-136). Springer. 10.1007/978-3-642-37256-8_11

Sykora, M. D., Jackson, T., O'Brien, A., & Elayan, S. (2013). Emotive ontology: Extracting fine-grained emotions from terse, informal messages. *IADIS Int. J. Comput. Sci. Inf. Syst*, *2013*, 19–26.

T. (2018a, November 16). *Using Word Embeddings for Data Augmentation*. Kaggle. https://www.kaggle.com/theoviel/using-word-embeddings-for-data-augmentation

T. (2020a, September 7). *Using Google Translate for NLP Augmentation*. Kaggle. https://www.kaggle.com/tuckerarrants/using-google-translate-for-nlp-augmentation

Valentino, N. A., Brader, T., Groenendyk, E. W., Gregorowicz, K., & Hutchings, V. L. (2011). Election night's alright for fighting: The role of emotions in political participation. *The Journal of Politics*, *73*(1), 156–170. doi:10.1017/S0022381610000939

Van der Zanden, R., Curie, K., Van Londen, M., Kramer, J., Steen, G., & Cuijpers, P. (2014). Keshia Curie, Monique Van Londen, Jeannet Kramer, Gerard Steen, and Pim Cuijpers. Web-based depression treatment: Associations of clients' word use with adherence and outcome. *Journal of Affective Disorders*, *160*, 10–13. doi:10.1016/j.jad.2014.01.005 PMID:24709016

Wang, W., Chen, L., Thirunarayan, K., & Sheth, A. P. (2012, September). Harnessing twitter" big data" for automatic emotion identification. In *2012 International Conference on Privacy, Security, Risk and Trust and 2012 International Conference on Social Computing* (pp. 587-592). IEEE.

Wang, W. Y., & Yang, D. (2015, September). That's so annoying!!!: A lexical and frame-semantic embedding based data augmentation approach to automatic categorization of annoying behaviors using# petpeeve tweets. In *Proceedings of the 2015 Conference on Empirical Methods in Natural Language Processing* (pp. 2557-2563). 10.18653/v1/D15-1306

Wang, X., & Zheng, Q. (2013, March). Text emotion classification research based on improved latent semantic analysis algorithm. In *Proceedings of the 2nd International Conference on Computer Science and Electronics Engineering* (pp. 210-213). Atlantis Press. 10.2991/iccsee.2013.55

Zahiri, S. M., & Choi, J. D. (2017). *Emotion detection on tv show transcripts with sequence-based convolutional neural networks*. arXiv preprint arXiv:1708.04299.

Zhang, X., Zhao, J., & LeCun, Y. (2015). *Character-level convolutional networks for text classification*. arXiv preprint arXiv:1509.01626.

Zhao, C., Xin, Y., Li, X., Yang, Y., & Chen, Y. (2020). A heterogeneous ensemble learning framework for spam detection in social networks with imbalanced data. *Applied Sciences (Basel, Switzerland)*, *10*(3), 936. doi:10.3390/app10030936

This research was previously published in Data Preprocessing, Active Learning, and Cost Perceptive Approaches for Resolving Data Imbalance; pages 211-231, copyright year 2021 by Engineering Science Reference (an imprint of IGI Global).

Chapter 24
Unraveling E-WOM Patterns Using Text Mining and Sentiment Analysis

João Guerreiro
Instituto Universitario de Lisboa, Portugal

Sandra Maria Correia Loureiro
https://orcid.org/0000-0001-8362-4430
Instituto Universitário de Lisboa, Portugal

ABSTRACT

Electronic word-of-mouth (e-WOM) is a very important way for firms to measure the pulse of its online reputation. Today, consumers use e-WOM as a way to interact with companies and share not only their satisfaction with the experience, but also their discontent. E-WOM is even a good way for companies to co-create better experiences that meet consumer needs. However, not many companies are using such unstructured information as a valuable resource to help in decision making: first, because e-WOM is mainly textual information that needs special data treatment and second, because it is spread in many different platforms and occurs in near-real-time, which makes it hard to handle. The current chapter revises the main methodologies used successfully to unravel hidden patterns in e-WOM in order to help decision makers to use such information to better align their companies with the consumer's needs.

INTRODUCTION

Today, e-WOM is an extremely important source for Marketing due to its impact on the online reputation of the firms. Consumers are no longer passive bystanders. Following consumer satisfaction expressed through online interactions on Facebook, Twitter, Instagram and other user generated content sites is paramount for effectively implementation of corrective measures that may increase satisfaction and consumer engagement with the brands (Bilro, Loureiro & Guerreiro, 2018).

DOI: 10.4018/978-1-6684-6303-1.ch024

However, although companies have been digitalizing themselves and upgrading their infrastructure to accommodate such Big Data with technology that grabs all the interactions with the consumer in real-time (written or verbal), there is still a long work to do regarding the effective use of such information to unravel hidden patterns of behavior. However, there are some successful examples of using such information to help decision-making. In Tourism, companies such as ReviewPro and Revinate offer complete solutions for firms to grasp the unstructured information written in sites such as TripAdvisor and Booking about their brands and their competitors. Using such information, companies may understand how their online reputation is changing over time and improve guest experience according to their feedback (Nave, Rita & Guerreiro, 2018). However, such information is often offered as a silo of information and not integrated with the company's' remaining key performance indicators (KPIs). To do so, companies must integrate analytical skills and develop internal decision support systems that may able them to integrate both structured (e.g. Financial KPIs, Human Resources KPIs), and unstructured information (e.g. reviews, online posts on the company's Facebook page, verbal complains).

The current chapter analyzes the characteristics of e-WOM and presents a theoretical approach to the most relevant methods used to handle unstructured data. Such information may allow managers to treat e-WOM data in order to uncover hidden patterns of behavior.

BACKGROUND

The emergence of the Web 2.0 has brought a new era of consumer-brand interaction through the spread of electronic word-of-mouth. E-WOM may be defined as "all informal communications directed at consumers through Internet-based technology related to the usage or characteristics of particular goods and services, or their sellers." (Litvin, Goldsmith & Pan, 2008, pp.461).

While in the early days of the Internet, companies had mainly a one way communication with their consumers through institutional web sites, today users interact with companies in a two-way communication. The consumer today is both the listener and the originator of information and such change echoed for the entire decision-making process. Not only in the awareness of need stage, where consumers may interact with viral communication videos and write their opinion or share such communication with their network of friends, but also while searching for alternatives online, where consumers read and form an opinion about the experiences or products in the market, or in the purchase and post-purchase stage, where some consumers are even driven to express their own opinion about the experience. Motivations of such behavior vary from (1) a need to have a platform to spread a message for an assistance, (2) to share negative feelings, (3) by a genuine concern toward other users, (4) for extraversion and self-enhancement, (5) for social and economic benefits, (6) to help the brand or (7) to seek for advices (Hennig-Thurau et al., 2004). Some of them are positive drivers and may help the companies to achieve a better reputation online, but some are negative drivers that may harm the company if not properly addressed.

Companies have been trying to keep up with such progress by (1) setting specialized teams of digital marketers responsible for handling such interaction and (2) investing on Big Data infrastructure that captures all this information in near-real-time for later analysis. E-WOM is usually posted online in the form of textual messages either in social media or in recommendation sites. However, today bloggers also share e-WOM through video, and that information may also have valuable information for brands to understand how are they being viewed and discussed online. Therefore, all public information spread online (text, audio, video) should be captured in Big Data systems (usually also transformed into a single type of media such as text) for helping brands to better align their positioning with the expectations of their consumers.

Despite the recent technological evolution in Big Data infrastructure, allowing information with such volume, variety and velocity to be captured and stored efficiently, there is still a need to analyze information and transform it into useful patterns that may be helpful for decision-making. Text Mining (TM) has been used (along with Natural Language Processing techniques and Sentiment Analysis) to successfully grasp the hidden patterns in data and present the most relevant drivers of behavior stemming from e-WOM data.

TEXT MINING

Sanchez et al. (2008) define text mining as the discovery of non-trivial, previously unknown and potentially useful information from text. TM is a form of semi-structured analysis of unstructured data that dates back to the work of Hearst (1999). Although unstructured data has been around since companies started to keep textual documents in their database systems, only recently, technology allowed the huge amount of information stored in such systems to be thoroughly analyzed. Today, Big Data infrastructures allow companies to gather not only documents but also real-time textual information such as tweets, posts, complains over the call-center or any other type of interaction with the consumer. There are generally two types of textual analysis. The first is a deductive approach which uses a top-down approach following pre-determined associations and relations between words. Such words are included in an ontology or dictionary that determines much of the process of knowledge discovery on data (Hristovski, Peterlin, Mitchel and Humphrey, 2005). The alternative type is a bottom-up approach, were unstructured data is structured into a set of terms that are then used to uncover latent relationships in text or classify specific events (such as for example the event of a fake news or a reputational issue) using machine learning algorithms. Therefore, the second approach combines the use of text mining as a way to structure data and then uses traditional data mining techniques to uncover patterns in the data (Sanchez et al., 2008).

Regarding the use of TM in e-WOM, usually both approaches are combined, particularly because consumers may write anything that comes to their mind and sometimes a formal dictionary may help the analysis on a big collection of data to focus on the most important elements for a specific sector.

In the inductive approach the work starts by extracting the data to a workable set of documents or *corpus*. Usually in e-WOM analysis, each review, tweet or post defines the *corpus* that together sets up the *corpora* (Feinerer, Hornik & Meyer, 2008). After the initial stage of data collection a preparation stage follows. In some cases, e-WOM may be extracted in real-time to feed the next stages.

The preparation stage converts the *corpus* into a set of bag-of-words (a group of relevant terms) for analysis. However, in order to structure the text into relevant terms, its semantic context has to be taken into consideration.

Natural Language Processing

Natural Language Processing (NLP) are a set of techniques that capture the semantic characteristics of text so that later analysis may take such context into consideration. NLP tasks include tokenization, part-of-speech tagging or named entity recognition (Collobert et al., 2011).

Tokenization breaks the text into small tokens that may be single terms or n-terms depending on common relations and context. For example, depending on the semantic context of a review, the expression "alarm clock" may have different meaning if they are assumed to be a single token or two separate tokens "alarm" and "clock". A proper tokenization is then an extremely important part of the deductive analysis of text (Hassler & Fliedl, 2006). Another NLP technique that helps on defining contextual meaning is the part-of-speech (POS) task. POS classifies text tokens according to its syntactic role (noun, verb, adverb). Depending on the context of a review, the same word may have different syntactic roles. For example, the bi-term "fast" expressed in a review may be used as an adjective: "This mobile phone is fast" or as an adverb: "The mobile phone is loosing battery fast". Therefore, a POS transformation technique ensures that when grouping text, only those tokens that are common are grouped to form a relationship between tokens (e.g. words) and documents (e.g. reviews). A final preparation step usually rips text from its *stopwords* (the set of auxiliary terms that are not relevant for analysis after semantic classification is performed). Punctuations and words such as "a", "he", "she", "for" may be removed from text for building the document-term-matrix. In many situations, some techniques to reduce complexity may also be applied such as stemming and lemmatization. Stemming is a heuristic method that reduces each term to its radical term (*stem*) so that words with the same radical term may be analyzed together (Porter, 1980). For example, words such as "run" and "running" may be analyzed together after a stemming procedure. On the other hand, a lemmatization approach takes into consideration vocabulary and morphology and is therefore a more advanced technique.

Document-Term-Matrix and Wordclouds

A first exploratory analysis of text after transformation may be done using the document-term-matrix (DTM) analysis. As the name implies, the DTM is a cross-relation between each document (e.g. a review) and each token. Although a sum approach may be used to fill such matrix (term frequency), the term-frequency-inverse document frequency (TF-IDF) is usually the best approach to reduce the sparsity of the matrix (composed of many zero values on the crossing between reviews and terms) (Grün & Hornik, 2011). The TF-IDF approach weights differently the terms in each document so that the terms that occur more often in a single document but not often in all the documents are more relevant (Delen & Crossland, 2008).

The DTM may be explored using a *wordcloud*, a graphical representation of the weight of each term either by using the absolute frequency or by using the TF-IDF.

Clustering of e-WOM

After an exploratory analysis, the text may be grouped into clusters of words. Although traditional clustering techniques such as k-Means may be used to group text into different groups, a more appropriate approach is the use of mixed-membership clustering techniques such as topic models. Topic models are "probabilistic models for uncovering the underlying semantic structure of a document collection based on a hierarchical Bayesian analysis of the original texts" (Blei & Lafferty, 2007, p. 1). They can be represented as a relationship between an observable N number of words in a D document and a latent set of K variables. A topic (t) is modelled as a multinomial probability distribution over a set of words (w) in a given document, such as $p(w|t)$, for t € $1{:}K$ (Blei, Ng, & Jordan, 2003).

Each latent topic is a distribution over words in the document where each term has a different probability to belong to that underlying topic. Also, they are mixed-membership models, given that each document can belong simultaneous to multiple topics at the same time (Grün & Hornik, 2011). Topics are hidden entities that can be inferred from observable words using posterior inference. By analyzing topics instead of a bag-of-words, text mining can find useful structure in the *corpus* collection of e-WOM information (Blei & Lafferty, 2007). Two of the most commonly used topic model algorithms are Latent Dirichlet Allocation (LDA) (Blei, Ng, & Jordan, 2003) and Correlated Topic Models (CTM) (Blei & Lafferty, 2007).

Latent Dirichlet Allocation

In Latent Dirichlet Allocation, the assumptions relies in a generative process that it is believed to have been used to produce the *corpus* (Blei, Ng, & Jordan, 2003).The algorithm is based on Latent Semantic Indexing and probabilistic Latent Semantic Indexing (Deerwester, Dumais, Landauer, Furnas, & Harshman, 1990; Hofmann, 1999), and assumes that *corpora* are written as follows (see Table 1).

Table 1. Corpora written

a) First, a decision is made about the number of topics the document will have;
b) A second step defines the proportions of each topic in the document, i.e. for example in a review about the service in a restaurant, 80% may be related to staff and 20% may be related to the price;
c) Afterward, words are given proportions according to their importance for each topic;
d) A word is taken according to its importance in the topic, and according to the topic distribution.

Figure 1 shows an example using the abstract of a paper from Strahilevitz & Myers (1998), in which, the histogram to the right represents the topic distribution over the documents that the generative process infers from the text.

Figure 1. Topic models generative process

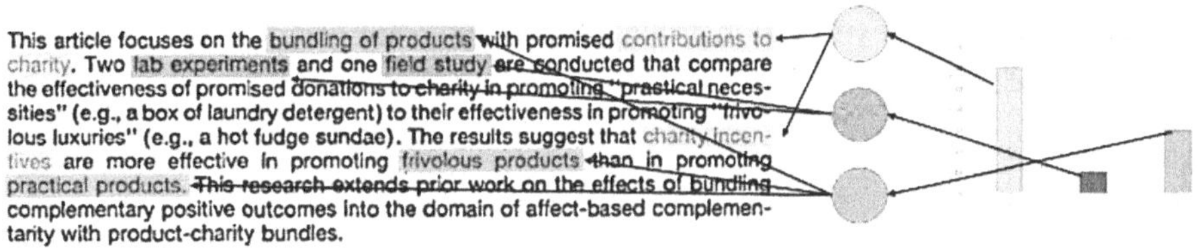

Although this generative process only generates a meaningless bag-of-words, it is useful for the LDA algorithm purposes, which is, to generate a stochastic process that represents the hidden model and then to reverse it using posterior probabilities.

Figure 2 shows the graphical model representation of LDA generation procedure which is described by Blei & Lafferty (2009) as shown in Table 2.

Figure 2. LDA generation procedure (Blei and Lafferty, 2009)

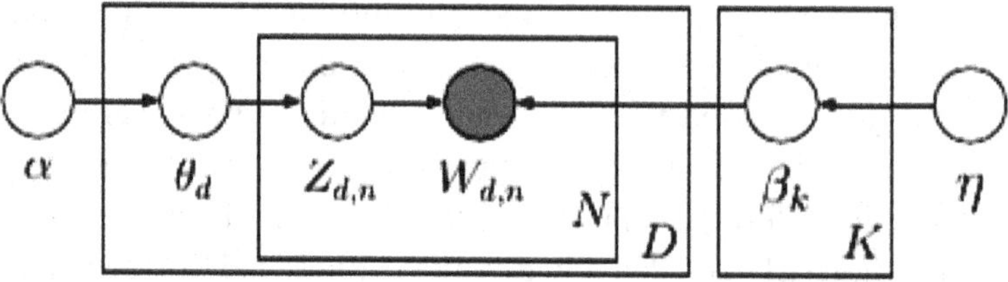

Table 2. Table 2. LDA generation procedure (Blei & Lafferty, 2009)

(1) For each topic K,

a. Draw a distribution over words, $\vec{\beta}_k \; Dir_y\left(\eta\right)$.

(2) For each document D,

a. Draw a vector of topic proportions, $\vec{\theta}_d \sim Dir_y(\vec{\alpha})$.

b. For each word,

i. Draw a topic assignment $Z_{d,n} \sim Mult\left(\vec{\theta}_d\right), Z_{d,n} \in \left\{1 \ldots K\right\}$.

ii. Draw a word $W_{d,n} \sim Mult\left(\vec{\beta} z_{d,n}\right), W_{d,n} \in \left\{1 \ldots V\right\}$.

V is the size of the vocabulary of the corpus document, $\vec{\alpha}$ a positive K-vector and η a scalar.

As the name implies, LDA algorithm uses Dirichlet distribution to design the generative process. While $Dir_y(\vec{\alpha})$ is a V-dimensional Dirichlet, $Dir_y(\eta)$ is the distribution of the distributions using a dimensional symmetric Dirichlet (Blei & Lafferty, 2009). A Dirichlet distribution is used because their properties ensure that the distribution of a Dirichlet distribution is still a Dirichlet distribution with the same characteristics, which is useful for computational purposes. However, the inference over the stochastic process of LDA has some shortcomings. The posterior distribution of the hidden variables is computationally intractable. The effort needed to compute the integral in the normalized distribution used in LDA is NP-hard and must be approximated using an approximate inference technique (Blei & Lafferty, 2009). Multiple techniques have been used to optimize this equation, such as collapsed variational inference (Teh et al., 2006), expectation propagation (Minka & Lafferty, 2002), and Gibbs sampling (Griffiths & Steyvers, 2007).

Correlated Topic Models

Although LDA has been successfully applied to model latent topics in documents, they lack an important characteristic. The Dirichlet distribution assumes that its vector points are nearly independent, which means that when topics are modelled using the Dirichlet distribution, they are assumed to be independent (Blei & Lafferty, 2009). However, in a real-word review, topics are usually correlated. Correlated Topic Models (CTM) builds on LDA but modifies the distribution used to model the topic proportions. Instead of using the Dirichlet distribution, CTM uses a logistic normal distribution (Atchison & Shen, 1980). The logistic normal distribution incorporates the covariance among the topics.

SENTIMENT ANALYSIS

Sentiment analysis goes a step further than identifying the more relevant terms or grouping text into topics. The main purpose of such task is to identify the polarity (or a sentiment scale) of the corpus, the sentences of the corpus or even individual n-grams. Sentiment analysis is a crucial step to extract relevant patterns in eWOM. Other than just knowing what consumers are discussing, managers want to know if they are discussing it in a more positive or negative tone. Such information allows managers to focus on corrective measures to address the problems identified and therefore to increase customer satisfaction.

Sentiment analysis may be developed using a machine learning approach or a lexicon based approach (Medhat, Hassan, & Korashy, 2014). The machine learning approach is usually used to identify polarities (or emotions such as anger, disgust, fear, interest, surprise, etc.) in entire reviews or sentences. Using a training dataset with reviews or sentences already classified with the different emotions, machine learning algorithms such as Artificial Neural Networks (ANN) or Support Vector Machines (SVM) create a model that may be used to predict emotions on a validation dataset. If the model is accurate enough it can be used to predict emotions on a new set of reviews. The second approach (lexicon based) is based on a list of words (a seed list) that contains the word polarity. Such seed lists may be created using a dictionary based approach or a corpus based approach (Feldman, 2013). The dictionary based approach is a top down method that is usually created using a set of starting words and their polarities, which are then expanded through the use of synonyms and antonyms. Wordnet is an example of a lexical database that contains more than 117.000 words and its synonym relations and is often used to expand initial seed of words in sentiment analysis (Fellbaum, Christiane, 2005). Although a bottom-up approach may be used successfully to uncover sentiments in text, it often lacks the specific terms of the different business domains. For example the word "short" may have different sentiment polarities if we are discussing the time spent to serve a customer on a restaurant – positive sentiment, or if it is referring to the size of a shirt – negative sentiment. Therefore, the dictionary based approach is often coupled with the *corpus* based approach that uses the text itself to identify word polarities. The *corpus* based approach also depends on seed lists but then uses them with natural language processing (NLP) techniques to classify the text (Caro & Grella, 2013; Liu & Zhang, 2012). There are several lexicons that are available online to be used for sentiment analysis purposes such as Hamilton, Clark, Leskovec & Jurafsky (2016) domain-specific sentiment lexicon and the AFFIN (Nielsen, 2019), BING (Bing, 2019) and NRC (Mohammad, 2019) lexicons available on the *tidytext* package on R (a statistical tool often used for text mining and sentiment analysis). While BING has a binary classification of positive and negative words, AFFIN has a set of words with sentiments classified between -5 (more negative) to 5 (more positive), and NRC classifies a set of words with ten categories (positive, negative, anger, anticipation, disgust, fear, joy, sadness, surprise and trust).

Issues, Controversies, Problems

Despite the innumerous advantages of using semi-automatic techniques to extract patterns from text, there are still some challenges to overcome in text mining and sentiment analysis. Although there are multiple standard lexicons that may be used in most situations, there are several specific industries were the same word may have a different meaning or a different polarity. As highlighted above, for example, the word "fast" may be a positive thing if the consumer is talking about the waiting time in a restaurant, but a negative thing if the consumer is discussing "fast" food. Also, although NLP has evolved tremendously in the last decade (especially in handling the English language) there are still several issues regarding the understanding of morphologically rich languages (e.g. Arabian, Hebrew) (Kincl, Novák & Přibil, 2019). The identification of irony, sarcasm and humour also still presents a big challenge for scholars in the field (Katyayan & Joshi, 2019; Farias & Rosso, 2017).

SOLUTIONS AND RECOMMENDATIONS

Solutions for the problems presented above include word sense disambiguation, in which machine learning techniques are used to classify terms depending on their context (Vechtomova, 2017). In fact, machine learning techniques have also been used to detect irony and sarcasm. Using pre-classified expressions of irony or sarcasm it is possible to predict new sentences by using algorithms such as support vector machines (SVM), artificial neural networks (ANN) and others. For example, Bharti et al., (2017) used SVM and Naïve Bayes classifiers, while Mukherjee and Bala (2017) used Naïve Bayes and fuzzy clustering to address such issues.

FUTURE RESEARCH DIRECTIONS

The current paper addresses the main methods that have been used to highlight behavior patterns in e-WOM messages. However, there are new approaches that have been recently suggested by scholars and that complement the vision here presented, such as the use of the network relations between the several consumers that share e-WOM messages. The connections between consumers in a network (called a graph) may be important to determine if for example a negative opinion may spread through relations and at what speed. To study such problem, graph mining techniques have been employed recently to detect consumer communities, opinion leaders and to study network dynamic. A good review may be found on the work of Bamakan, Nurgaliev and Qu, 2019, where the authors describe a methodological review of the use of graph mining to handle consumer interactions and how some consumers may lead others in their opinion, making them important actors in the network. A positive opinion leader may become an evangelist of the brand and should therefore be incentivized to share its motivation with its peers, while a negative opinion leader may harm the company's' reputation and firms should be particularly careful when addressing its needs (Bamakan, Nurgaliev & Qu, 2019; Arrami, Oueslati & Akaichi, 2017; Bilici & Saygın, 2017; Chen et al., 2017).

Another new promising direction to handle e-WOM is to use adaptive techniques such as deep learning algorithms to handle unstructured data (Arora & Kansal, 2019). Deep learning algorithms have recently gained traction to support self-driving cars and adapt easily to new variables in the environment (in this case, new words and expressions in e-WOM). Therefore, it is a promising direction to increase e-WOM classification accuracy in the future.

CONCLUSION

e-WOM text starts as a set of unstructured review, comment, post, in the form of free text. However, the value in using such information for understanding consumer behavior lies in trying to make sense on the patterns of data that rely latent in the comments of multiple consumers at the same time. To perform such task, scholars have developed a set of techniques based on natural language processing (NLP) that analyses the semantic relations of the text and structures the most important terms discussed by consumers. A second step aggregates the relevant terms into latent topics using techniques such topic models. Finally, sentiment analysis classifies such information regarding sentiment polarities or emotions that may be used to help managers understand the main drivers of satisfaction or dissatisfaction discussed by consumers.

The current chapter explores the methodologies used to handle the large amounts of unstructured data such as those expressed in e-WOM comments. Although many techniques have been used to treat such data, the current chapter summarizes the techniques that have been used to successfully transform e-WOM into a set of structured patterns. Such patterns may then be used to help decision makers in devising strategies to better meet consumer needs.

REFERENCES

Arora, M., & Kansal, V. (2019). Character level embedding with deep convolutional neural network for text normalization of unstructured data for Twitter sentiment analysis. *Social Network Analysis and Mining*, *9*(18). doi:10.1007/s13278-019-0557-y

Arrami, S., Oueslati, W., & Akaichi, J. (2017). Detection of Opinion Leaders in Social Networks: A Survey. In *International Conference on Intelligent Interactive Multimedia Systems and Services* (pp. 362-370). Berlin: Springer.

Atchison, J., & Shen, S. M. (1980). Logistic-normal distributions: Some properties and uses. *Biometrika*, *67*(2), 261–272. doi:10.1093/biomet/67.2.261

Bamakan, S. M. H., Nurgaliev, I., & Qu, Q. (2019). Opinion leader detection: A methodological review. *Expert Systems with Applications*, *115*, 220–222. doi:10.1016/j.eswa.2018.07.069

Bharti, S. K., Pradhan, R., Babu, K. S., & Jena, S. K. (2017). Sarcasm analysis on twitter data using machine learning approaches. In *Trends in Social Network Analysis* (pp. 51–76). Berlin: Springer. doi:10.1007/978-3-319-53420-6_3

Bilici, E., & Saygın, Y. (2017). Why do people (not) like me?: Mining opinion influencing factors from reviews. *Expert Systems with Applications*, *68*, 185–195. doi:10.1016/j.eswa.2016.10.001

Bilro, R. G., Loureiro, S. M. C., & Guerreiro, J. (2018). Exploring online customer engagement with hospitality products and its relationship with involvement, emotional states, experience and brand advocacy. *Journal of Hospitality Marketing & Management*, *28*(2), 1–25.

Bing, L. (2019). *Opinion Mining, Sentiment Analysis, and Opinion Spam Detection*. Retrieved from https://www.cs.uic.edu/~liub/FBS/sentiment-analysis.html#lexicon

Blei, D. M., & Lafferty, J. D. (2007). A correlated topic model of science. *The Annals of Applied Statistics*, *1*(1), 17–35. doi:10.1214/07-AOAS114

Blei, D. M., & Lafferty, J. D. (2009). Topic models. In Text mining: classification, clustering, and applications (p. 71). Chapman & Hall.

Blei, D. M., Ng, A. Y., & Jordan, M. I. (2003). Latent Dirichlet Allocation. *Journal of Machine Learning Research, 3*, 993–1022.

Chen, Y. C., Hui, L., Wu, C. I., Liu, H. Y., & Chen, S. C. (2017, August). Opinion leaders discovery in dynamic social network. In *Ubi-media Computing and Workshops (Ubi-Media), 2017 10th International Conference on* (pp. 1-6). IEEE. 10.1109/UMEDIA.2017.8074110

Collobert, R., Weston, J., Bottou, L., Karlen, M., Kavukcuoglu, K., & Kuksa, P. (2011). Natural language processing (almost) from scratch. *Journal of Machine Learning Research, 12*(Aug), 2493–2537.

Deerwester, S. C., Dumais, S. T., Landauer, T. K., Furnas, G. W., & Harshman, R. A. (1990). Indexing by latent semantic analysis. *Journal of the American Society for Information Science, 41*(6), 391–407. doi:10.1002/(SICI)1097-4571(199009)41:6<391::AID-ASI1>3.0.CO;2-9

Delen, D., & Crossland, M. D. (2008). Seeding the survey and analysis of research literature with text mining. *Expert Systems with Applications, 34*(3), 1707–1720. doi:10.1016/j.eswa.2007.01.035

Di Caro, L., & Grella, M. (2013). Sentiment analysis via dependency parsing. *Computer Standards & Interfaces, 35*(5), 442–453. doi:10.1016/j.csi.2012.10.005

Farias, D. H., & Rosso, P. (2017). Irony, sarcasm, and sentiment analysis. In B. Liu, E. Messina, E. Fersini, & F. A. Pozzi (Eds.), *Sentiment Analysis in Social Networks* (pp. 113–128). Oxford, UK: Elsevier. doi:10.1016/B978-0-12-804412-4.00007-3

Feinerer, I., Hornik, K., & Meyer, D. (2008). Text Mining Infrastructure in R. *Journal of Statistical Software, 25*(5), 1–54. doi:10.18637/jss.v025.i05

Feldman, R. (2013). Techniques and applications for sentiment analysis. *Communications of the ACM, 56*(4), 82–89. doi:10.1145/2436256.2436274

Fellbaum, C. (2005). WordNet and wordnets. In K. Brown & ... (Eds.), *Encyclopedia of Language and Linguistics* (2nd ed.; pp. 665–670). Oxford, UK: Elsevier.

Griffiths, T., & Steyvers, M. (2007). Probabilistic topic models. In T. Landauer, D. S. McNamara, S. Dennis, & W. Kintsch (Eds.), *Handbook of Latent Semantic Analysis*. Hillsdale, NJ: Erlbaum.

Grün, B., & Hornik, K. (2011). topicmodels : An R Package for Fitting Topic Models. *Journal of Statistical Software, 40*(13), 1–30. doi:10.18637/jss.v040.i13

Hamilton, W. L., Clark, K., Leskovec, J., & Jurafsky, D. (2016). Inducing domain-specific sentiment lexicons from unlabeled corpora. In *Proceedings of the Conference on Empirical Methods in Natural Language Processing. Conference on Empirical Methods in Natural Language Processing* (pp. 595). NIH Public Access. 10.18653/v1/D16-1057

Hassler, M., & Fliedl, G. (2006). Text preparation through extended tokenization. *Data Mining VII: Data, Text and Web Mining and their Business Applications, 37*, 13–21.

Hearst, M. (1999). Untangling text data mining. In *Proceedings of the 37th annual meeting of the Association for Computational Linguistics on Computational Linguistics* (pp. 3–10). College Park, MD: Academic Press. 10.3115/1034678.1034679

Hennig-Thurau, T., Gwinner, K. P., Walsh, G., & Gremler, D. D. (2004). Electronic word-of-mouth via consumer-opinion platforms: What motivates consumers to articulate themselves on the internet? *Journal of Interactive Marketing*, *18*(1), 38–52. doi:10.1002/dir.10073

Hofmann, T. (1999). Probabilistic latent semantic indexing. In *Proceedings of the 22nd annual international ACM SIGIR conference on Research and development in information retrieval* (pp. 50–57). Berkeley, CA: Academic Press.

Hristovski, D., Peterlin, B., Mitchell, J. A., & Humphrey, S. M. (2005). Using literature-based discovery to identify disease candidate genes. *International Journal of Medical Informatics*, *74*(2), 289–298. doi:10.1016/j.ijmedinf.2004.04.024 PMID:15694635

Katyayan, P., & Joshi, N. (2019). Sarcasm Detection Approaches for English Language. In *Smart Techniques for a Smarter Planet* (pp. 167–183). Cham: Springer. doi:10.1007/978-3-030-03131-2_9

Kincl, T., Novák, M., & Přibil, J. (2019). Improving sentiment analysis performance on morphologically rich languages: Language and domain independent approach. *Computer Speech & Language*, *56*, 36–51. doi:10.1016/j.csl.2019.01.001

Litvin, S. W., Goldsmith, R. E., & Pan, B. (2008). Electronic word-of-mouth in hospitality and tourism management. *Tourism Management*, *29*(3), 458–468. doi:10.1016/j.tourman.2007.05.011

Liu, B., & Zhang, L. (2012). *A survey of opinion mining and sentiment analysis. In Mining Text Data* (pp. 415–460). Oxford, UK: Springer.

Medhat, W., Hassan, A., & Korashy, H. (2014). Sentiment analysis algorithms and applications: A survey. *Ain Shams Engineering Journal*, *5*(4), 1093–1113. doi:10.1016/j.asej.2014.04.011

Minka, T., & Lafferty, J. (2002). Expectation-propagation for the generative aspect model. In *Proceedings of the Eighteenth conference on Uncertainty in artificial intelligence* (pp. 352–359). Berkeley, CA: Academic Press.

Mohammad, S. (2019). *NRC Emotion Lexicon*. Retrieved from http://saifmohammad.com/WebPages/NRC-Emotion-Lexicon.htm

Mukherjee, S., & Bala, P. K. (2017). Detecting sarcasm in customer tweets: An NLP based approach. *Industrial Management & Data Systems*, *117*(6), 1109–1126. doi:10.1108/IMDS-06-2016-0207

Nave, M., Rita, P., & Guerreiro, J. (2018). A decision support system framework to track consumer sentiments in social media. *Journal of Hospitality Marketing & Management*, *27*(6), 693–710. doi:10.1080/19368623.2018.1435327

Nielsen, F. A. (2019). *AFFIN Sentiment Lexicon*. Retrieved from http://corpustext.com/reference/sentiment_afinn.html

Porter, M. (1980). An algorithm for suffix stripping. *Program: Electronic Library and Information Systems, 14*(3), 130–137.

Sánchez, D., Martín-Bautista, M. J., Blanco, I., & La Torre, C. J. D. (2008). Text Knowledge Mining: An Alternative to Text Data Mining. In *2008 IEEE International Conference on Data Mining Workshops* (pp. 664–672). IEEE. 10.1109/ICDMW.2008.57

Strahilevitz, M., & Myers, J. (1998). Donations to charity as purchase incentives: How well they work may depend on what you are trying to sell. *The Journal of Consumer Research, 24*(4), 434–446. doi:10.1086/209519

Teh, Y. W., Newman, D., & Welling, M. (2007). A collapsed variational Bayesian inference algorithm for latent Dirichlet allocation. In *Advances in Neural Information Processing Systems* (pp. 1353–1360). Cambridge, MA: MIT Press. doi:10.21236/ADA629956

Vechtomova, O. (2017). Disambiguating context-dependent polarity of words: An information retrieval approach. *Information Processing & Management, 53*(5), 1062–1079. doi:10.1016/j.ipm.2017.03.007

ADDITIONAL READING

Costa, A., Guerreiro, J., Moro, S., & Henriques, R. (2019). Unfolding the characteristics of incentivized online reviews. *Journal of Retailing and Consumer Services, 47*, 272–281. doi:10.1016/j.jretconser.2018.12.006

Guerreiro, J., & Moro, S. (2017). Are Yelp's tips helpful in building influential consumers? *Tourism Management Perspectives, 24*, 151–154. doi:10.1016/j.tmp.2017.08.006

Santos, C. L., Rita, P., & Guerreiro, J. (2018). Improving international attractiveness of higher education institutions based on text mining and sentiment analysis. *International Journal of Educational Management, 32*(3), 431–447. doi:10.1108/IJEM-01-2017-0027

KEY TERMS AND DEFINITIONS

e-WOM: All communication that is shared with peers through Internet-based technologies about the users opinion of goods, services, brands, or experiences.

Graph Mining: A set of techniques to extract and discover non-trivial, previously unknown and useful patterns from graph structures such as online social networks.

Natural Language Processing: A set of techniques based on many different disciplines such as computer science, artificial intelligence and linguistics, that allows computers to understand the human language.

Sentiment Analysis: The use of semi-automated techniques such as text mining, natural language processing and semantic rules to classify text according to its sentiment polarities or according to a sentiment scale.

Text Mining: The discovery of non-trivial, previously unknown and potentially useful information from text.

Topic Models: Topic models are a set of algorithms that uncover the semantic structure of a collection of documents based on a Bayesian analysis.

This research was previously published in Exploring the Power of Electronic Word-of-Mouth in the Services Industry; pages 88-100, copyright year 2020 by Business Science Reference (an imprint of IGI Global).

Chapter 25
DE-ForABSA:
A Novel Approach to Forecast Automobiles Sales Using Aspect Based Sentiment Analysis and Differential Evolution

Charu Gupta
Department of Computer Science and Engineering, Bhagwan Parshuram Institute of Technology, Delhi, India

Amita Jain
Department of Computer Science and Engineering, Ambedkar Institute of Advanced Communication Technology and Research, New Delhi, India

Nisheeth Joshi
Department of Computer Science, Banasthali Vidyapith, Vanasthali, India

ABSTRACT

Today, amongst the various forms of online data, user reviews are very useful in understanding the user's attitude, emotion and sentiment towards a product. In this article, a novel method, named as DE-ForABSA is proposed to forecast automobiles sales based on aspect based sentiment analysis (ABSA) and ClusFuDE [8] (a hybrid forecasting model). DE-ForABSA consists of two phases – first, extracted user reviews of an automobile are analysed using ABSA. In ABSA, the reviews are pre-processed; aspects are extracted & aggregated to determine the polarity score of reviews. Second, uses of ClusFuDE consisting of clustering, fuzzy logical relationships and Differential Evolution (DE) to predict the sales of the automobile. DE is a population-based search method to optimize real values under the control of two operators: mutation & crossover. Score from phase 1 is a parameter in differential mutation in phase 2. The proposed method is tested on reviews & sales data of automobile. The empirical results show a Mean Square Error of 142.90 which indicates an effective consistency of the model

DOI: 10.4018/978-1-6684-6303-1.ch025

1. INTRODUCTION

Sentiment Analysis analyses the emotional tone behind a series of words which can be used to understand the attitudes, opinions and emotions of a holder. The sentiment is expressed as a quadruple *(s, g, h, t)* where, 's' is the sentiment, 'g' is the target, 'h' is the holder and 't' is the time of expression (Liu, 2012; Pang & Lee, 2008). It evaluates written or spoken language to determine if an expression is favourable, unfavourable, or neutral, and to what degree. It also helps to analyse what customers like and dislike about a brand/product/design. Customer reviews from social media, website, call centre agents, or any other source, contains a treasure trove of useful business information. In today's time, it is not enough to know what customers are talking about. One must also know how they feel about the product. Sentiment analysis is one way to uncover those feelings.

Amongst the various products, automobiles are those favourite possessions that someone would cherish throughout their lives. Automobiles are not only today's necessity but to some people it is a mark of status, grandeur and passion. The tangible value of automobiles can be observed from the statistics from year 1990 -2018 (in million units). These statistics indicate a continuous rise of international sale and purchase of automobiles from year 1990-2018. According to the reports, the purchase of automobiles had almost doubled in the last ten years. This is just one aspect of automobile industry, where it can be observed that people love to buy automobiles of their choice.

In view of this scenario, another objective outlook in the automotive industry is the management of the supply and demand. As the market is moving at a fast pace, the manufacturers, investors and managers are constantly trying to make unprecedented investments to grow their businesses worldwide. The survey conducted by OICA (Organisation Internationale des Constructeurs d'Automobiles), the International organization of motor vehicle manufacturers reported the yearly production of automobiles (passenger cars) from year 1999-2016. Figure 1 shows these statistics of the automobiles produced/year internationally.

Figure 1. Yearly production of automobiles (passenger cars) from year 1999-2016

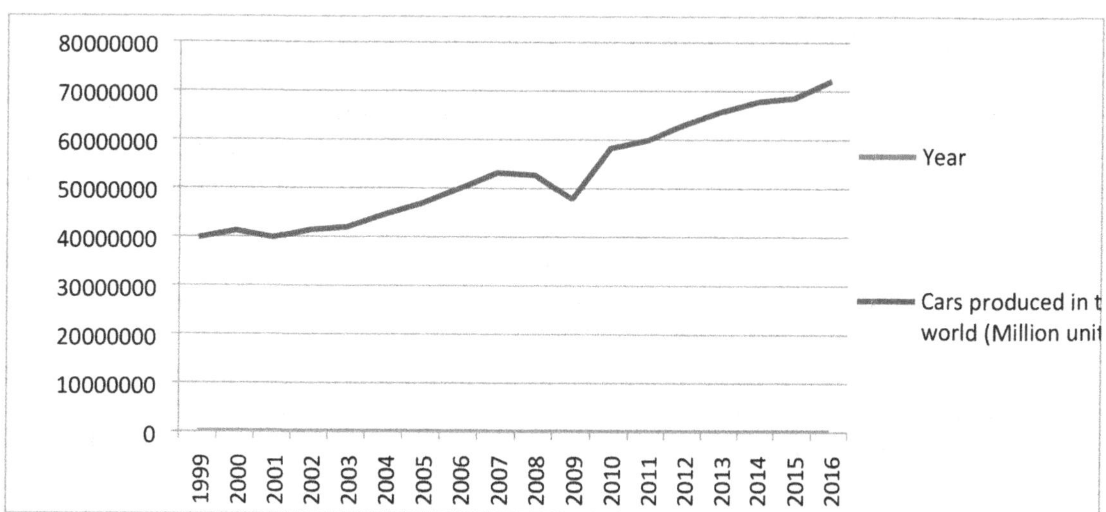

According to the market tread analysis, automobile manufacturing company decides for automobile production based on some factors. These are the monthly data of domestic sales & export report, sub-segment & company wise domestic and export report, cumulative domestic sales & exports and analysis of market & shares. These mentioned factors are tangible but in order to meet today's demand, there is a dire need to examine and analyse the intangible attribute of the market also. One of them is the user opinion/view of the automobile. User reviews carry important information (user perception) which can be put to use to understand the flow and slope of market. As the internet is growing, more and more online users/consumers/buyers are becoming vocal and active about their opinion on the automobile irrespective of the brand/make/region.

Careful examination of the user reviews helps in understanding what the users want. According to a report by Megan Wenzl, 59% of the people use rating filters when searching for an automobile. Now-a-days "word of mouth" opinion is a major market force running the e-commerce. This fine-grain analysis not only benefits the supply-demand chain, but is fruitful for the investors, manufacturers, managers. In (Tseng, Lin, Zhou, Kumiajaya & Li, 2018), it is observed that the online review/opinion directly influences the user's sale and purchase. It affects the management of manufacturing sector and enables investors, managers to make informed choices and decisions regarding resource management, logistics management, planning management, financial management and overall project management. This, in turn, will reduce overheads and increase efficiency of the entire automobile sector.

In this paper, the authors have focused on capturing the intangible factors which affect the production of automobiles in the manufacturing domain. The proposed approach, named as, DE-ForABSA is a first of its kind, which uses a robust method of forecasting numerical data with Aspect Based Sentiment Analysis (ABSA). The approach captures the historical statistics of sales of the automobile (passenger car) in any given period of not less than twelve months. The approach involves two phases:

- In Phase 1, the intangible user reviews are gathered and analysed using machine learning algorithms to understand the polarity of a particular automobile/brand (Polarity refers to the analysis of opinions as either negative or positive which help in foreseeing the future demands and other prospects).
- Phase 2 deals with the forecasting of the sales value in the coming year using historical sales data.

ClusFuDE, a method of forecasting numerical data is adapted from (Gupta, Jain, Tayal & Castillo, 2018), where the authors have used automatic clustering, fuzzy logical relationships and Differential Evolution to forecast and optimize the results. The broad steps of phase 2 can be summarized as follows:

- Automatic clustering helps in aggregating similar features together. Fuzzy logical relationships map the crisp value of the sales data to a fuzzy interval. These fuzzy intervals are then used to establish strong relationships in the sales data.
- These relationships give a useful insight in understanding the dependencies amongst the numerical data. Further the forecasted values are optimized using Differential Evolution, a population-based search method (Das, Abraham & Konar, 2008a; Das, Abraham & Konar, 2008b; Paterlini & Krink, 2006).
- The proposed methodology improves the mutation operator, F also called as scale factor. The polarity/score of the user reviews help in understanding the diversification of the opinion about an automobile.

- This score is then used to dictate the mutation operation in Differential Evolution. A conceptual diagram in Figure 2 presents the details of the two phases.

Figure 2. Conceptual Diagaram

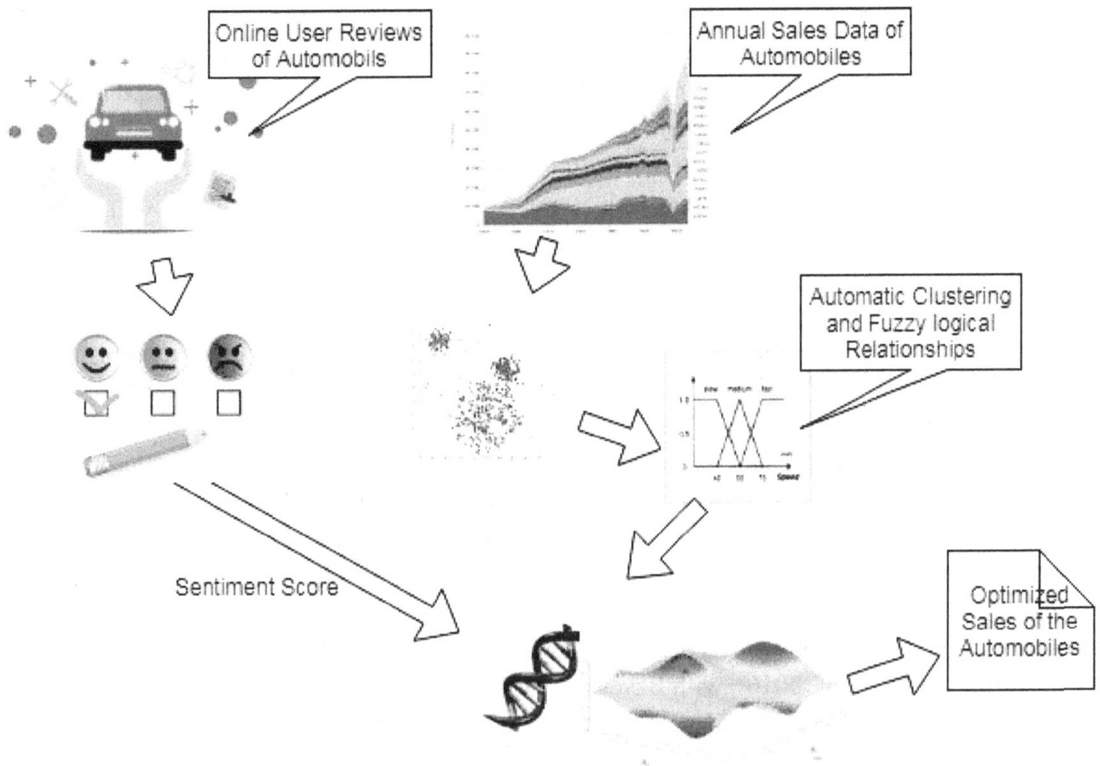

The rest of this article is organised as follows: section 2 discusses the motivation behind the proposed methodology. Section 3 presents the literature review. Section 4 and 5 explains the research framework and empirical analysis & results respectively. Section 6 and 7 presents the conclusion and future work.

2. MOTIVATION

There is a huge volume of information available on the internet about various automobiles. A number of websites provide plethora of information about these automobiles. The online textual information in the form of reviews is available over the internet. This information not only benefits the consumer/user but is also very useful for the investors and managers. The investors are searching for approaches that can be used for compounding. They need models that aid in the ability to grow money. On the other hand, managers, for a successful organization require making informed decisions. These decisions eventually help them take effective "do-first" sense-making actions. This paper, tries to understand the underlying requirements of both and thus, presents a model which is beneficial to both. The idea proposed is simple yet effective, has robust implementation and follows a heuristic approach.

3. LITERATURE REVIEW

E-commerce is in its prospering years. So many researchers are focusing on topics which are closely related to e- commerce industry. Forecasting has also become an indispensable part of this industry. It is because investors and managers are putting their heart and soul in providing and arranging the resources required for the product and also for inventory management. So, they want to know the correct value of their product in the market. Now there are two ways in which this can be accomplished: first, through technical analysis, where the past purchase/price of the product is reviewed and second, through fundamental analysis, where the intangible attributes like velocity of user reviews and its polarity. Researchers have worked on these aspects. For example, the forecasting of sales of physical stores (Daskin, Coullard & Shen, 2002), energy forecasting (Lagarto, deSousa, Martins & Ferrao, 2012), crude oil prices prediction (Yousefi, Weinreich & Reinarz, 2005), forecast stock prices (Kimoto, Asakawa, Yoda & Takeoka, 1990). The forecasting methodologies explored so far are based on factors specific to the application. Along with the techniques that fully explore the potentiality of the method, researchers have proposed various optimization methods like swarm intelligence (Ünler, 2008; Wu, 2010), genetic algorithms (Kuo, 2001; Grichnik, 2007), evolutionary computing (Doganis, Alexandridis, Patrinos & Sarimveis, 2006; Hu, Liu, Zhang, Su, Ngai & Liu, 2015) and so on. In the field of evolutionary computation, Differential Evolution is a promising population-based search heuristic (Brest, Greiner, Boskovic, Mernik & Zumer, 2006; Vesterstrom & Thomsen, 2004; Price, Storn & Lampinen, 2006). The potentiality of the method is derived from its two operators- mutation and crossover. Researchers have experimented with various self-adaptive methods to dynamic mutation and crossover (Qin & Suganthan, 2005; Tayal, Gupta & Jain, 2012; Tayal & Gupta, 2012). Sentiment analysis with evolutionary algorithms has always attracted researchers. Studies focus on using Differential Evolution with a multi-objective ensemble classifier (Onan, Korukoğlu & Bulut, 2016), with Bayesian classifier (Diab & ElHindi, 2017), for improving the distance measures in various classification algorithms (Diab & ElHindi, 2018). The limitation with this method is the lack of robust usage of differential operators – mutation and crossover. These operators provide a robust compute and flexible search space (in self-adaptive variations of Differential Evolution).

In this paper, the focus is on the explorations with Differential Evolution to predict the annual/monthly sale of the automobiles which can help the manufacturers and managers to manage the inventory and other liabilities efficiently. This is the first approach to predicting the sales of the automobiles using sentiment analysis and differential mutation operator as a sentiment score. The details of the proposed method are explained in subsequent sections.

4. THE RESEARCH FRAMEWORK

In this paper, a hybrid forecasting model is presented which will enable the decision maker to predict the sales of the automobile based on sentiment analysis of user reviews. The proposed methodology presents a model to predict the sales of an automobile based on the information measured through ABSA of user reviews. Inherently, the nature of reviews is complex. The complexity arises due to a vast and varied feature set. So, to understand the complex nature of the feature set, Table 1 presents the data collected from an automobile website. From Table 1, for example, the basic variants of Maruti Suzuki are listed. If the system explores one particular automobile, say, Alto, then from Table 1, it can be validated that feature details along with Alto variants is quite complex.

Table 1. ALTO Feature set and Variants (Sample Table)

Variants	STD	STD(O)	LX	LX(O)	LXI	LXI(O)	VXI	VXI(O)	LXI (CNG)	LXI CNG(O)
Price (In Rupees)	2.66	2.72	2.98	3.04	3.24	3.3	3.44	3.5	3.86	3.92
Length	3430mm	3430mm	3430mm	3430mm	3430mm	3430mm	3430mm	3430mm	3430mm	3430mm
Width	1490mm	1490mm	1490mm	1490mm	1490mm	1490mm	1490mm	1490mm	1490mm	1490mm
Height	1475mm	1475mm	1475mm	1475mm	1475mm	1475mm	1475mm	1475mm	1475mm	1475mm
Seating Capacity	5Person	5Person	5Person	5Person	5Person	5Person	5Person	5Person	4Person	4Person
Displacement	796cc	796cc	796cc	796cc	796cc	796cc	796cc	796cc	796cc	796cc
Fuel Type	Petrol	Petrol	Petrol	Petrol	Petrol	Petrol	Petrol	Petrol	CNG	CNG
Max Power	48 bhp @ 6000 RPM	48 bhp @ 6000 RPM	48 bhp @ 6000 RPM	48 bhp @ 6000 RPM	48 bhp @ 6000 RPM	48 bhp @ 6000 RPM	48 bhp @ 6000 RPM	48 bhp @ 6000 RPM	40 bhp @ 6000 RPM	40 bhp @ 6000 RPM
Max Torque	69 Nm @ 3500 RPM	69 Nm @ 3500 RPM	69 Nm @ 3500 RPM	69 Nm @ 3500 RPM	69 Nm @ 3500 RPM	69 Nm @ 3500 RPM	69 Nm @ 3500 RPM	69 Nm @ 3500 RPM	60 Nm @ 3500 RPM	60 Nm @ 3500 RPM
Mileage (ARAI)	24.7kmpl	24.7kmpl	24.7kmpl	24.7kmpl	24.7kmpl	24.7kmpl	24.7kmpl	24.7kmpl	33.44kmpl	33.44kmpl
Alternate Fuel	Not Applicable	Not Applicable	Not Applicable	Not Applicable	Not Applicable	Not Applicable	Not Applicable	Not Applicable	Petrol	Petrol
Transmission Type	Manual	Manual	Manual	Manual	Manual	Manual	Manual	Manual	Manual	Manual
No of gears	5Gears	5Gears	5Gears	5Gears	5Gears	5Gears	5Gears	5Gears	5Gears	5Gears
Drivetrain	Front Wheel Drive	Front Wheel Drive	Front Wheel Drive	Front Wheel Drive	Front Wheel Drive	Front Wheel Drive	Front Wheel Drive	Front Wheel Drive	Front Wheel Drive	Front Wheel Drive
Air Conditioner	No	No	Manual	Manual	Manual	Manual	Manual	Manual	Manual	Manual
Power Windows	No	No	No	No	Front Only	Front Only	Front Only	Front Only	Front Only	Front Only
Central Locking	No	No	No	No	No	No	Yes	Yes	No	No
Anti-Lock Braking System (ABS)	No	No	No	No	No	No	No	No	No	No
Airbags	No	1 (Driver Only)	No	1 (Driver Only)	No	1 (Driver Only)	No	1 (Driver Only)	No	1 (Driver Only)
Seat Upholstery	Vinyl	Vinyl	Fabric	Fabric	Fabric	Fabric	Fabric	Fabric	Fabric	Fabric
Front Tyres	145 / 80 R12	145 / 80 R12	145 / 80 R12	145 / 80 R12	145 / 80 R12	145 / 80 R12	145 / 80 R12	145 / 80 R12	145 / 80 R12	145 / 80 R12
Rear Tyres	145 / 80 R12	145 / 80 R12	145 / 80 R12	145 / 80 R12	145 / 80 R12	145 / 80 R12	145 / 80 R12	145 / 80 R12	145 / 80 R12	145 / 80 R12

The proposed model is experimented on a test bed of online user reviews and sales chart of the last twelve months of Maruti Suzuki automobiles. The proposed method can be extended to other automobile makes also. Another important concern is the type of reviews gathered for the automobile to correctly classify them as positive or negative. In this paper, we consider binary classification of reviews. In order to construct a more reliable system, few assumptions are taken into consideration:

- To construct a feature vector from feature list of the automobiles, one of the feature is selected for defining the level boundaries
- For a particular level, the features are arranged in increasing weight order.
- The textual reviews extracted are treated as authentic reviews

There are two phases of the proposed approach:

Phase 1: Compute and analyse impact of online user reviews on the automobile sale using ABSA. The sentiment (polarity) score is taken as differential mutation operator in Phase 2.

Phase 2: Forecast the monthly/annual demand of automobiles using Clustering, Fuzzy logical relationships and Differential Evolution. The mutation operator in Differential Evolution is the analyzed sentiment score from phase 1.

In this section, the technical details of these phases are explained with the help of a flowchart and algorithm. In Table 2 the data obtained from the sales statistics of the automobiles is considered as the historical data from March 2017 to February 2018. The model is trained for the reviews obtained for five automobiles of Maruti Suzuki make.

Table 2. Historical sales data for automobiles of maruti suzuki make

Time -->	Mar	Apr	May	Jun	Jul	Aug	Sep	Oct	Nov	Dec	Jan	Feb
Automobile	2017	2017	2017	2017	2017	2017	2017	2017	2017	2017	2018	2018
Maruti Suzuki Alto K10	18868	11275	11809	14856	26009	21520	23830	19447	24166	20346	0	0
Maruti Suzuki Wagon R	12015	16348	15471	10668	16301	13907	14649	13043	14038	11800	14182	14029
Hyundai Eon	5747	5379	5330	4231	4032	4058	5144	6350	5137	5672	6111	4551
Datsun GO	707	607	430	594	404	482	532	579	351	442	411	426
Renault Kwid	10296	7956	6990	5439	7471	7802	9099	8136	5726	6953	5590	6074

As stated earlier, the impact of online reviews on the sales is studied in Phase 1. The stepwise procedure of Phase 1 is as follows:

Step 1: Input textual reviews of the automobile

Step 2: Extract aspects, classify them as positive or negative and aggregate them to get the total positive and negative reviews of the item.

Step 3: Arrange the aspects in descending order of their importance. Calculate the score of each aspect.
Step 4: Calculate the weighted average of all the positive and negative aspects
Step 5: Output the best item (from the range and segment) based on the polarity score. Save the weighted aspect vector of the item.

The proposed phase 1 consists of three major steps – first, pre-processing; second, sentiment extraction and third, sentiment aggregation (please refer to Figure 3). The features of the automobiles are analysed in a hierarchy (feature hierarchy) as in (Gupta, Jain & Joshi, 2018) which forms a feature hierarchy for the automobile domain to understand the overlapping of features in various segments.

Figure 3. Steps depicting the steps of Phase 1

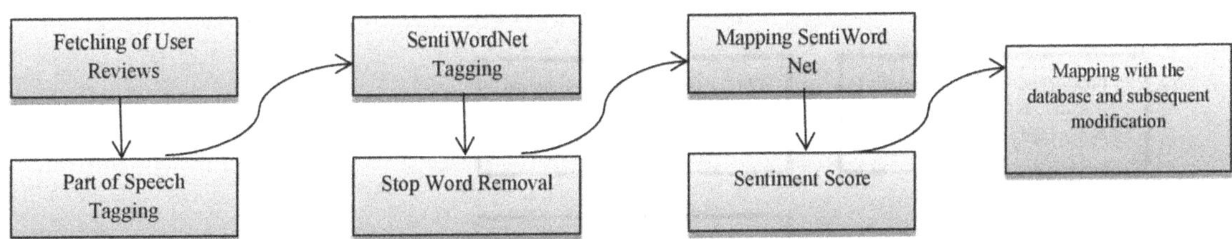

Pre-processing phase- It includes assigning POS tags, converting it to SentiWordNet (SWN) understandable tag and then, finally removal of stop words.

Sentiment Extraction- It includes mapping of non- stop words with their respective SWN understandable tags. SWN vocab contains a unique identifier for each word which further map words with their respective sentiment score.

Sentiment Aggregation- In this step, sentiment scores computed in previous step are then mapped with the feature hierarchy present in the database. Scores are then modified based on the database entry.

Phase 2: A new parameter in mutation in Differential Evolution

The *sentiment score* computed from analysing the user reviews of the automobile is the mutation operator in Differential Evolution. The scale factor (mutation operator) F, is a positive control parameter for scaling the difference of the vectors as given in Equation 1:

$$F = s_{t(a_i)} * rand(0,1) \tag{1}$$

where, $s_t(a_i)$ is the new mutation parameter based on the user reviews for the automobile computed with aspect-based sentiment analysis.

The new parameter in mutation gives an extra exploratory strength to the Differential Evolution procedure. As discussed in section –I, it is very necessary to compute the intensity of user perception. This user perception, in DE-ForABSA is modelled as a very effective mutation operator of Differential Evolution. It has thus, helped in a unique way to identify the weightage of user perception in the purchase of automobile. This on the other hand encourages the investors and managers to effectively look at the ongoing and upcoming sales of the automobile. Thus, satisfying the motivation for DE-ForABSA. The design methodology is explained with the help of a flowchart in Figure 4. It describes the procedure used in Phase 2 clearly.

Figure 4. Flowchart for the proposed Phase 2 in DE-ForABSA

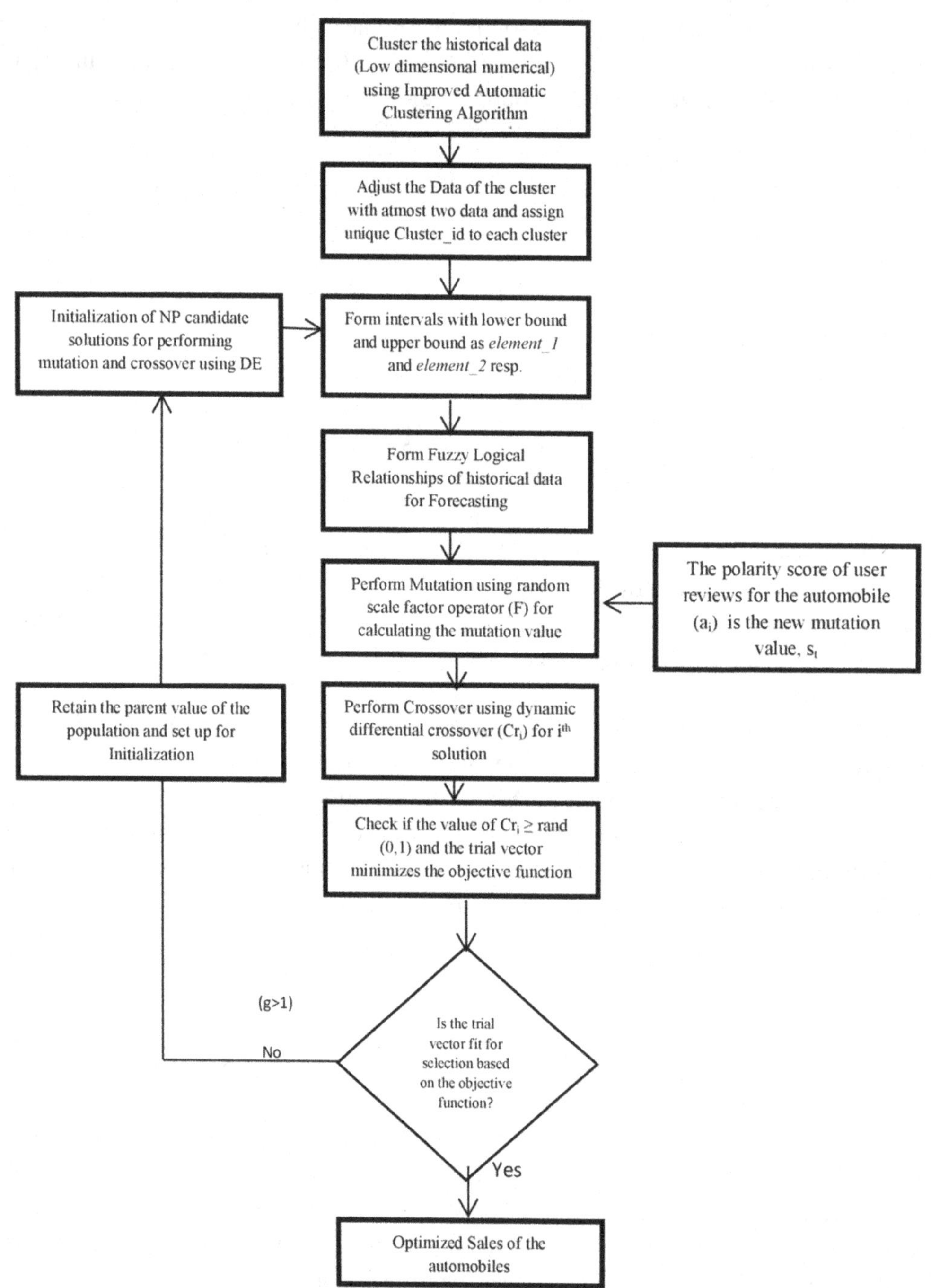

The methodology explained in Figure 4 takes as input the historical sales data and clusters it is using improved automatic clustering technique. The clustering technique clusters homogenous elements together which helps in better understanding the data pattern. Then, the clustered data is transformed into intervals which then fuzzify the historical data into a regular time series pattern to obtain an "*antecedent -> consequent*" relationship in the data (Tayal, Sonawani, Ansari & Gupta, 2011). Once the clustered data are transformed into intervals and fuzzified into fuzzy sets, then it can be used to predict the value as explained in ClusFuDE (Gupta, Jain, Tayal & Castillo, 2018) with the said principals. For the sake of brevity, the details of the existing method are omitted here. For detailed reading of the methods of automatic clustering, fuzzy logical relationships and Differential Evolution the readers are advised to read (Gupta, Jain, Tayal & Castillo, 2018).

5. EMPIRICAL ANALYSIS AND RESULTS

In this section, the proposed model is tested with the user reviews extracted from an automobile site. Manual pre-processing of the user reviews is done by removing redundant, irrelevant, non-contextual reviews.

As stated earlier, the proposed methodology consists of two phases. In phase 1, all the extracted user reviews are transformed into vectors using CountVectorizer. It turns the text into numerical feature vectors. It is also known as a bag-of n gram approach. Then, the dataset is split into two sets, one for training and other for testing. The testing is done using K- fold cross validation with k=4. DE-ForABSA is trained and tested using 3 different models viz SVM, Logistic Regression and Naive Bayes. Their accuracy is computed. Out of these three algorithms, the prerequisite of a learning function in SVM is determined and the learning rate is taken as 0.054469.

Finally, the dataset is tested using the best-of-all approach, in which the results of all the models are compared to increase the accuracy. DE-ForABSA is applied on extracted reviews to obtain useful insights. Phase 2 forecasts the optimized sales of the automobile in a year/month. It analyses impact of user reviews on the sales of the automobile using modified mutation operator.

For phase 1, the proposed model is built with Python 3.5 with MySQL Database on Windows XP with Intel Core i5, minimum 32 GB RAM and minimum 2 GB hard disk capacity. For phase 2 the system is built with the same hardware configuration with MySQL (stored procedures) and C#. The sample review is given in Figure 5.

Settings: Training and Testing Data Set

The testing and training datasets are formed to understand the effectiveness of the proposed method. In phase 1, 70% of the reviews are used to train the model and 30% are used to test the accuracy of the classification performance. The train set for phase 1, has train_test_split with train_size=0.70, random_state = 1234. In SVM, following are the parameter setting random_state is 0, gamma=0.054469. The input text (user review) is classified using three popular techniques – SVM, Logistic Regression and Naïve Bayes. The proposed methodology uses the best approach to classify the text into positive and negative. For example, if SVM and Naïve Bayes predict a polarity score of 1 towards a user review and logistic regression predicts a 0, then the Best-of-all approach will take the polarity of the user review as 1. The accuracy can be related from Table 3, where the Best-of-all approach achieves better classification accuracy.

Figure 5. Sample text is fed as an input

```
import nltk
from nltk.corpus import stopwords
from nltk.corpus import state_union
from nltk.tokenize import PunktSentenceTokenizer    #unsupervised machine learning sentence tok
train_text= state_union.raw("2006-GWBush.txt")
sample_text="this has been liked by many people but I do not like this at all"
custom_sent_tokenizer= PunktSentenceTokenizer(train_text)
tokenized=custom_sent_tokenizer.tokenize(sample_text)

def process_content():
    try:
        for i in tokenized:
            words=nltk.word_tokenize(i)
            tagged=nltk.pos_tag(words)
        return tagged
    except Exception as e:
        print(e)

tagged=process_content()
print(tagged)
```

Table 3. Performance Analysis

Model	Best-of-all approach	SVM	Logistic Regression	Naïve Bayes
Accuracy	0.774444444444444	0.7666666666666	0.763333333333333	0.752222222222222

The polarity score so obtained in then used as a parameter in mutation operator in Phase 2 as explained in section IV. The historical data of annual sales of WagonR are taken as sample data (please refer to Table 4). The objective function is the minimization error function computed with Mean Square Error (MSE) and Mean Absolute Percentage Error (MAPE) using Equation 2 and 3.

$$MSE = \frac{\sum_{i=1}^{n}(O_i - A_i)^2}{N} \quad (2)$$

$$MAPE = \frac{I}{N}\sum\left\|(O_i - A_i)\right\| / A_i * 100\% \quad (3)$$

Where, O_i is the optimized value, A_i is the actual value and 'n' is the total number of sales data available.

The historical data is then clustered and fuzzified using principals from (Gupta, Jain, Tayal & Castillo, 2018).

The forecasted value is then optimized using aspect-based sentiment analysis and Differential Evolution with G=100. The experiment is run with the forecasted candidate values obtained from Table 8.

Table 4. Historical Sales Data for the Automobile (sample)

Month/Year	Sales of Automobile
Mar-17	10296
Apr-17	7956
May-17	6990
Jun-17	5439
Jul-17	7471
Aug-17	7802
Sep-17	9099
Oct-17	8136
Nov-17	5726
Dec-17	6953
Jan-18	5590
Feb-18	6074

Table 6. Formation of intervals with cluster_id

min_value	max_value	cluster id
7471	8136	4
5439	5726	1
6953	6990	3
5633	6515	2
8658	9540	5
9855	10296	6
7471	8136	4
5439	5726	1
6953	6990	3
5633	6515	2
8658	9540	5
9855	10296	6

Table 5. Fuzzified Sales Data

Year	Value	Cluster id	Fuzzified Data
Mar-17	10296	6	A20
Apr-17	7956	4	A16
May-17	6990	3	A15
Jun-17	5439	1	A1
Jul-17	7471	4	A16
Aug-17	7802	4	A16
Sep-17	9099	5	A18
Oct-17	8136	4	A17
Nov-17	5726	1	A12
Dec-17	6953	3	A14
Jan-18	5590	1	A1
Feb-18	6074	2	A12

The results obtained from Tables 5 to 9 depict the consistency of the proposed method with the existing model as in ClusFuDE (Gupta, Jain, Tayal & Castillo, 2018) and proves to be efficient. This section has summarized the complete methodology used in experimenting with the historical sales data as well as the online user review dataset.

Table 7. Interval id with Interval Midpoint

Lower Bound	Upper Bound	Interval Midpoint	Interval_id	Lower Bound	Upper Bound	Interval Midpoint	Interval_id
5439	5726	5583	1	5439	5726	5583	1
5726	6515	6121	2	10296	5726	8011	11
6515	6953	6734	3	5726	6515	6121	12
6953	6990	6972	4	6515	6953	6734	13
6990	7471	7231	5	6953	6990	6972	14
7471	8136	7804	6	6990	7471	7231	15
8136	8658	8397	7	7471	8136	7804	16
8658	9540	9099	8	8136	8658	8397	17
9540	9855	9698	9	8658	9540	9099	18
9855	10296	10076	10	9540	9855	9698	19
				9855	10296	10076	20

Table 8. Final Forecasted Value of the Sales of Automobile

Month_id	Month	Fuzzified _Sales	Forecasted Sales value
1	Mar-17	A10	5583
2	Apr-17	A6	7052
3	May-17	A5	6734
4	Jun-17	A1	7491
5	Jul-17	A6	7052
6	Aug-17	A6	7052
7	Sep-17	A8	8397
8	Oct-17	A7	9099
9	Nov-17	A2	7909
10	Dec-17	A4	10076
11	Jan-18	A1	7491
12	Feb-18	A2	7909

Threats to Validity

The estimated parameter in MSE is either scalar or vector. It helps in assessing the risk of the estimated parameter. In either of the two cases, the difference between the estimator and parameter or Euclidean distance is computed. The loss function is computed from Equation 4 as follows:

$$MSE = e\left[\left\|\delta - \delta_0\right\|^2\right] \tag{4}$$

Where, e is the expected error bias, δ and δ_0 are the estimator and the parameter. The validity of the method is assured with the use of MSE for binary outcomes.

Table 9. Final Optimized Results obtained by DE-ForABSA for Month wise Sales Data of Automobiles (G=100)

Year	Forecasted Sales (candidate solution)	Optimized Enrollments (Using DE-ForABSA) (G=100)	Year	Forecasted Sales (candidate solution)	Optimized Enrollments (Using DE-ForABSA) (G=100)
Mar-17	-		**Sep-17**	8397	8398
Apr-17	7052	7050	**Oct-17**	9099	9098
May-17	6734	6700	**Nov-17**	7909	7900
Jun-17	7491	7491	**Dec-17**	10076	10059
Jul-17	7052	7052	**Jan-18**	7491	7491
Aug-17	7052	7050	**Feb-18**	7909	7903
				MSE	142.9091
				MAPE	0.085718

6. CONCLUSION

The reviews provide fruitful qualitative information which can be utilised to analyse the mood, attitude, culture and recommendations of a user. The proposed approach emphasizes that the reviews posted by a user (authentic user) for an automobile greatly reflect the change in trend towards the sale of the automobile. The importance of a user's voice can be understood with the e-commerce architecture where a user is the primary stakeholder.

In view of this user- specific framework, the proposed system designs a novel method to predict the future sales of an automobile using the "voice of the user". The proposed approach DE-ForABSA, involves two phases where in Phase 1 the user reviews are extracted and analysed to understand the emotional inclination of the people for a particular automobile. The automotive domain, specifically, passenger car reviews are analysed to understand the sentiment of the user using aspect-based sentiment analysis. In Phase 2, the polarity score from phase 1 is used as an indicator of potential diversification of user reviews into positive and negative class. In this phase, a hybrid method comprising of automatic clustering, fuzzy relationship and Differential Evolution is used. DE-ForABSA is a novel approach to predict the sales data of an automobile which has not been attempted earlier.

Differential Evolution comprises of the use of two major operators- mutation and crossover. The mutation operation has the potential to randomize the population vector by inducing a random deviation to the component. The objective function is a minimization function which is sensitive to the parameter setting.

It is observed that crossover determines how many expected parameters should change in the population. In the proposed framework, a dynamic crossover (adapted from ClusFuDE), and a sentiment aided mutation operator is used for optimized forecasting (as explained in section IV). This helps in favourable perturbation in the population aiming for a better derived vector. The results so obtained are consistent with the methodology. The learning rate in SVM is taken as 0.054469 through empirical calculations. The accuracy of the proposed model in phase 1 is 0.77 and in phase 2 the MSE, MAPE values are 142.90, 0.085717849 respectively. This indicates a higher adaptability of the model to the forecasting of the sales of automobile using aspect-based sentiment analysis with differential mutation.

7. FUTURE WORK

DE-ForABSA is a novel forecasting model. The potentiality of proposed approach can be further experimented and analysed with other soft computing paradigms such as neural network, other genetic algorithms. In future, the model can be extended with high order fuzzy logical relationships, type-2-fuzzy sets, and hesitant sets. The performance of Differential Evolution can be investigated more deeply with other evolutionary techniques for a multi-dimensional model.

REFERENCES

Brest, J., Greiner, S., Boskovic, B., Mernik, M., & Zumer, V. (2006). Self-adapting control parameters in differential evolution: A comparative study on numerical benchmark problems. *IEEE Transactions on Evolutionary Computation*, *10*(6), 646–657. doi:10.1109/TEVC.2006.872133

Das, S., Abraham, A., & Konar, A. (2008a). Automatic clustering using an improved differential evolution algorithm. *IEEE Transactions on Systems, Man, and Cybernetics. Part A, Systems and Humans*, *38*(1), 218–237. doi:10.1109/TSMCA.2007.909595

Das, S., Abraham, A., & Konar, A. (2008b). Particle swarm optimization and differential evolution algorithms: technical analysis, applications and hybridization perspectives. In *Advances of computational intelligence in industrial systems* (pp. 1–38). Springer. doi:10.1007/978-3-540-78297-1_1

Daskin, M. S., Coullard, C. R., & Shen, Z. J. M. (2002). An inventory-location model: Formulation, solution algorithm and computational results. *Annals of Operations Research*, *110*(1-4), 83–106. doi:10.1023/A:1020763400324

Diab, D. M., & El Hindi, K. (2018). Using differential evolution for improving distance measures of nominal values. *Applied Soft Computing*, *64*, 14–34. doi:10.1016/j.asoc.2017.12.007

Diab, D. M., & El Hindi, K. M. (2017). Using differential evolution for fine tuning naïve Bayesian classifiers and its application for text classification. *Applied Soft Computing*, *54*, 183–199. doi:10.1016/j.asoc.2016.12.043

Doganis, P., Alexandridis, A., Patrinos, P., & Sarimveis, H. (2006). Time series sales forecasting for short shelf-life food products based on artificial neural networks and evolutionary computing. *Journal of Food Engineering*, *75*(2), 196–204. doi:10.1016/j.jfoodeng.2005.03.056

Grichnik, A. J. (2007). U.S. Patent No. 7,213,007. Washington, DC: U.S. Patent and Trademark Office.

Gupta, C., Jain, A., & Joshi, N. (in press). A Novel Approach to feature hierarchy in Aspect Based Sentiment Analysis using OWA operator. In *2nd International Conference on Communication, Computing and Networking*. Springer.

Gupta, C., Jain, A., Tayal, D. K., & Castillo, O. (2018). ClusFuDE: Forecasting low dimensional numerical data using an improved method based on automatic clustering, fuzzy relationships and differential evolution. *Engineering Applications of Artificial Intelligence, 71*, 175-189.9.

Hu, Y., Liu, K., Zhang, X., Su, L., Ngai, E. W. T., & Liu, M. (2015). Application of evolutionary computation for rule discovery in stock algorithmic trading: A literature review. *Applied Soft Computing, 36*, 534–551. doi:10.1016/j.asoc.2015.07.008

Kimoto, T., Asakawa, K., Yoda, M., & Takeoka, M. (1990, June). Stock market prediction system with modular neural networks. In *1990 International Joint Conference on Neural Networks IJCNN* (pp. 1-6). IEEE. 10.1109/IJCNN.1990.137535

Kuo, R. J. (2001). A sales forecasting system based on fuzzy neural network with initial weights generated by genetic algorithm. *European Journal of Operational Research, 129*(3), 496–517. doi:10.1016/S0377-2217(99)00463-4

Lagarto, J., de Sousa, J., Martins, A., & Ferrao, P. (2012, May). Price forecasting in the day-ahead Iberian electricity market using a conjectural variations ARIMA model. In *2012 9th International Conference on the European Energy Market (EEM)* (pp. 1-7). IEEE. 10.1109/EEM.2012.6254734

Liu, B. (2012). Sentiment analysis and opinion mining. *Synthesis lectures on human language technologies, 5*(1), 1-167.

Onan, A., Korukoğlu, S., & Bulut, H. (2016). A multiobjective weighted voting ensemble classifier based on differential evolution algorithm for text sentiment classification. *Expert Systems with Applications, 62*, 1–16. doi:10.1016/j.eswa.2016.06.005

Pang, B., & Lee, L. (2008). Opinion mining and sentiment analysis. *Foundations and Trends in Information Retrieval, 2*(1–2), 1-135.

Paterlini, S., & Krink, T. (2006). Differential evolution and particle swarm optimisation in partitional clustering. *Computational Statistics & Data Analysis, 50*(5), 1220–1247. doi:10.1016/j.csda.2004.12.004

Price, K., Storn, R. M., & Lampinen, J. A. (2006). *Differential evolution: a practical approach to global optimization*. Springer Science & Business Media.

Qin, A. K., & Suganthan, P. N. (2005, September). Self-adaptive differential evolution algorithm for numerical optimization. In *The 2005 IEEE Congress on Evolutionary Computation* (Vol. 2, pp. 1785-1791). IEEE. 10.1109/CEC.2005.1554904

Society of Indian automotive manufacturers. (n.d.). SIAM Monthly Flash Report on production & Sales Retrieved April 26, 2018 from http://www.siamindia.com/publications.aspx?mpgid=42&pgidtrail=45

Statista. (n.d.). How do online customer reviews affect your opinion of a local business? Retrieved April 26, 2017 from https://www.statista.com/statistics/315751/online-review-customer-opinion/

Statista. (n.d.). Number of cars sold worldwide from 1990 to 2018. Retrieved April 7, 2018 from https://www.statista.com/statistics/200002/international-car-sales-since-1990/

Tayal, D., & Gupta, C. (2012) A New Scale Factor for Differential Evolution Optimization. In *7th National Conference Communication Technologies & its impact on Next Generation Computing (CSI)* (pp. 78-83). Computer Society of India.

Tayal, D., Gupta, C., & Jain, A. (2012, October). A new crossover operator in Differential Evolution for numerical optimization. In *2012 International Conference on Communication, Information & Computing Technology (ICCICT)* (pp. 1-5). IEEE. 10.1109/ICCICT.2012.6398178

Tayal, D., Sonawani, S., Ansari, G., & Gupta, C. (2011). Fuzzy time series forecasting of low dimensional numerical data. *Proceedings of International Journal of Engineering Research and Applications*, *2*(1), 132–135.

Tseng, K. K., Lin, R. F. Y., Zhou, H., Kurniajaya, K. J., & Li, Q. (2018). Price prediction of e-commerce products through Internet sentiment analysis. *Electronic Commerce Research*, *18*(1), 65–88. doi:10.100710660-017-9272-9

Ünler, A. (2008). Improvement of energy demand forecasts using swarm intelligence: The case of Turkey with projections to 2025. *Energy Policy*, *36*(6), 1937–1944. doi:10.1016/j.enpol.2008.02.018

Vesterstrom, J., & Thomsen, R. (2004, June). A comparative study of differential evolution, particle swarm optimization, and evolutionary algorithms on numerical benchmark problems. In Congress on Evolutionary Computation CEC2004 (Vol. 2, pp. 1980-1987). IEEE. doi:10.1109/CEC.2004.1331139

Wenzi, M. (2017). Analysis of online reviews reveals what automotive buyers really want. ReviewTrackers. Retrieved April 26, 2018 from https://www.reviewtrackers.com/automotive-insights-2016/

Wu, Q. (2010). Product demand forecasts using wavelet kernel support vector machine and particle swarm optimization in manufacture system. *Journal of Computational and Applied Mathematics*, *233*(10), 2481–2491. doi:10.1016/j.cam.2009.10.030

Yousefi, S., Weinreich, I., & Reinarz, D. (2005). Wavelet-based prediction of oil prices. *Chaos, Solitons, and Fractals*, *25*(2), 265–275. doi:10.1016/j.chaos.2004.11.015

This research was previously published in the International Journal of Information Retrieval Research (IJIRR), 9(1); pages 33-49, copyright year 2019 by IGI Publishing (an imprint of IGI Global).

Index

A

B

C

D

E

F

G

H

I

K

L

M

N

O

P

Q

R

S

T

U

V

W

Y

Printed in the United States
by Baker & Taylor Publisher Services